Sourcebook on Aging

Reference books published by
Marquis Academic Media

Annual Register of Grant Support
Consumer Protection Directory
Current Audiovisuals for Mental Health Education
Directory of Certified Psychiatrists and Neurologists
Directory of Publishing Opportunities
Directory of Registered Lobbyists and Lobbyist Legislation
Environmental Protection Directory
Family Factbook
Grantsmanship: Money and How To Get It
Mental Health in America: The Years of Crisis
NASA Factbook
NIH Factbook
NSF Factbook
The Selective Guide to Audiovisuals for Mental Health and Family Life Education
The Selective Guide to Publications for Mental Health and Family Life Education
Sourcebook of Equal Educational Opportunity
Sourcebook on Aging
Sourcebook on Food and Nutrition
Sourcebook on Mental Health
Standard Education Almanac
Standard Medical Almanac
Yearbook of Adult and Continuing Education
Yearbook of Higher Education
Yearbook of Special Education
Worldwide Directory of Computer Companies
Worldwide Directory of Federal Libraries

Sourcebook on Aging

Second edition

Marquis Academic Media
Marquis Who's Who, Inc.
200 East Ohio Street
Chicago, Illinois 60611

Library of Congress Card Number 79-89697
International Standard Book Number 0-8379-4402-3
Product Code Number 031072

Manufactured in the United States of America.

Contents

Preface

Sourcebook on Aging, second edition, provides older Americans, those who serve them, and those who want to learn about them with articles, tables, and lists. Materials from government and private sources comprise four sections, accessible through subject, organization, and geographic indexes. A source citation appears on the first page of each new item.

The first two articles in the "Selected Readings" section discuss physical and mental health problems related to age. "Our Future Selves" also deals primarily with health, but toward the end touches on other aspects of the aged person's life such as his need for transportation, legal services, and economic support. Four articles in the "Retirement" subsection deal with developments that influence retirement decisions and current patterns of retirement, mandatory retirement, and pre-retirement counseling. "The Proposed Fiscal 1980 Budget" is the first item in the "Other Topics" subsection, and shows what the impact of the proposed budget will be on programs serving older Americans. "Two Generations of Elderly in the Changing American Family" points out that first generation elderly individuals aged 75 and over often have needs that conflict with those of their children in the 55-65 age range. Articles on congregate housing for older people, the special needs of Hispanic elderly, and library services for senior citizens complete "Part one."

The Age Discrimination Act of 1975 is the topic of the first two articles in the "Legislation" section. They are followed by a summary of the Older Americans Act, and Amendments to the Act passed in 1978 by the 95th Congress.

The "Statistics" section, the most lengthy in this second edition of *Sourcebook on Aging,* is filled with graphs and tables on the numbers of older persons in the United States, their health, pension and retirement programs. Two articles focus specifically on the black elderly. If there are figures you are *not* able to find in this section, "Guide to Census Data on the Elderly" may point you to a source.

"Part four: Resources" includes a bibliography from 1940 to 1977 on transitions in middle-age and aging families, a directory of state and area agencies on aging, a list of organizations about and for the aging, and a list of periodicals.

In an effort to provide a reference tool that will be of optimum value to its audience, Marquis Academic Media, a division of Marquis Who's Who, Inc., invites reactions to the contents, organization, and scope of *Sourcebook on Aging.*

Part one:
Selected readings

Health

Special Report on Aging: 1979

U.S. Department of H.E.W., Public Help Service, National Institutes of Health, September 1979.

One of the most important contributions that aging research has had to make to society is the demonstration that aging and disease are not one and the same. The acceptance of this distinction marks the dissolution of the stereotyped view of old people as diseased and decrepit, a view that once pervaded not only the health care system, but the social fabric of our country as well. Geriatric clinicians know the dire consequences of such prejudicial attitudes toward elderly patients: treatable illnesses are ascribed to the supposedly "untreatable" process of aging. Often, apparently disoriented patients are labeled "senile" and sent home, when the disorientation may be a symptom of infection or some other condition that has stressed the individual's cerebral circulation. Conditions such as these can often be managed or even cured, at substantial cost savings when compared to lengthy commitments to long-term or home care. The mistaken belief that the diseases afflicting many elderly persons are unavoidable extensions of the aging process can be a self-fulfilling prophecy—a person who has been labeled "senile" may begin to think of himself or herself in those terms, and act accordingly.

Research on both the medical and social problems of the elderly can reduce the costs of serving them. For example, if we discover means of lessening the physical and mental deficits that can be caused by disease, we will have changed the needs of the patient for medical, social, and other services. By the same token, if we change the socioeconomic circumstances of the elderly, we may also change their needs for certain services.

Research on aging is multidisciplinary, for the demographics of our aging population have an impact on all aspects of the quality of life and on the costs for health care and social services. The over 65-year-old group is expected to increase in size from 23 million in 1976 to 32 million in 2000, and then to 45 million by 2020. All age segments of the elderly population are expected to grow rapidly, but particularly the extremely aged, so that in the year 2000 there will be about 17 million persons 75 and over, and about 5 million who are 85 and over. Since the very old are the most frequent users of the health care system, we must prepare now so that we will be able to meet their needs as their numbers grow.

The broad mandate of the National Institute on Aging (NIA) reflects this need for a multidisciplinary approach to the study of aging. Among the NIA's many areas of interest are the following, which received special emphasis during 1978:

Treatable Brain Diseases. "Senility"—the most frightening spectre of old age—is not an inevitable consequence of growing old; in fact, it is not even a disease. Rather, "senility" is the word commonly used to describe a large number of conditions with an equally large number of causes, many of which respond to prompt and effective treatment. The symptoms characteristic of what is popularly called "senility" include serious forgetfulness, disorientation, intellectual confusion, and certain other medical and emotional disturbances. Although doctors and patients alike have traditionally dismissed these symptoms as incurable consequences of old age, they are not. Thus, it is imperative that a complete, careful investigation of the source of these symptoms be made so that proper treatment can be initiated. Some 100 reversible conditions may mimic a few irreversible brain disorders (such as cerebral arteriosclerosis, senile dementia, and Alzheimer's disease). A minor head injury, a high fever, improper nutrition, or adverse drug reactions, for example, can temporarily interfere with the supply of blood and oxygen to the brain and thus inhibit the normal functioning of extremely sensitive brain cells. If left untreated, such medical emergencies can result in irreparable damage to the brain, and possibly even death.

To draw physicians' attention to the danger of accepting the stereotype of the old as "senile" and of the need for providing effective treatment to the aged, the NIA and the Fogarty International Center (FIC) brought together experts in the fields of internal medicine, neurology, psychiatry, epidemiology, radiology, psychology, geriatric medicine, and general medicine for a consensus development conference on treatable brain diseases in the elderly. Throughout the course of the two-day conference, discussion focused on several basic questions, including: 1) What is dementia? 2) How common are treatable brain diseases which cause cognitive impairment? 3) What information should physicians have to obtain the most comprehensive and useful history of impaired patients? 4) What is the best kind of physical examination to carry out in impaired patients? 5) Given a diagnosis of irreversible brain disease, what is the physician's responsibility to both the patient and the family?

Having examined these issues at the meeting, the NIA is now preparing a summary document to be circulated throughout the medical community to achieve final consensus. When this phase of the consensus process is completed, the Institute will begin the task of disseminating the consensus position to all health care practitioners.

The Last Days of Life. Because mortality is now associated primarily with old age, the NIA is especially concerned about the quality of the last days of life. When our nation was founded—just a little over 200 years ago—only 20 percent of newborns survived into old age. Today, the reverse is true: 80 percent of newborns survive into old age, while only 20 percent do not. This shift in life expectancy is largely the result of triumphs over maternal, childhood, and infant mortality, although advances in cardiology and other aspects of health care have led to decreased mortality in later life as well.

The gathering force of what is referred to as the "hospice movement" has served to focus long-overdue attention on how we as individuals and as a society deal with death. The result has been a more humanistic approach to the care of the terminally ill. There are at least four elements which are crucial to hospice care:

- Educating and training medical, nursing, and allied health personnel to be sensitive to the rights, needs, and problems of those in the last days of life;

- Discovering new therapies for managing pain and other discomforts of the terminally ill;

- Providing home care, so that people can remain at home for as long as they desire, and be able to die at home if they wish and if it is possible; and,

- Attending to both the immediate and long-term needs of grieving survivors.

Training programs must not neglect the many volunteers whose dedicated efforts have played an essential role in hospice development and home care. The services of these volunteers add immeasurably to the all-important humanity of a hospice. Therefore, volunteer training and orientation programs must be carefully designed to properly sensitize volunteers to the extraordinarily demanding, albeit rewarding, nature of hospice work.

The issue of the palliative management of pain is now being studied by an Interagency Committee on New Therapies for Pain and Discomfort. Representatives from the National Institutes of Health; Alcohol, Drug Abuse, and Mental Health Administration; Health Care Financing Administration; Food and Drug Administration; Health Resources Administration; Veterans Administration; Department of Defense; Department of Justice; Drug Enforcement Agency; Office of the Assistant Secretary for Health, DHEW; and the White House will consider ways to evaluate drug administration practices and patterns, examine the psychosocial aspects of death and dying, and alter practitioners' approaches to health care so that they deal with dying patients in terms other than the curing of disease.

In the area of pain control, the NIA's interest is focused on how analgesics act differently in older people and on less traditional, non-pharmacological approaches to pain control, such as acupuncture. As a part of its research program, the NIA has identified the pharmacology of aging as a priority area. We know that the body handles drugs very differently at different periods of life. The NIA has already co-sponsored a workshop on the state of knowledge on age-related changes in response to drugs, and more recently issued a request for grant applications on the pharmacology of aging.

In an effort to understand the immediate and long-term needs of grieving survivors, the Institute recently commissioned a paper on bereavement as a risk factor in mortality. This study, done by Dr. Adrian Ostfeld, Professor of Epidemiology at Yale University, shows the possibility of an increased death rate of some 25,000 Americans annually as a consequence of significant personal losses they experience. Bereavement is associated with a higher incidence of illness, death, and psychosocial stress. It is clear that we need imaginative, but systematic, studies to understand better the impact of bereavement. In order to encourage scientific work in this area, the NIA has recently announced its desire to support additional studies on the nature of bereavement, widowhood, dying, and death, and methods of coping with them effectively. Bereavement requires a variety of adjustments, such as realignments within the family, the development of new intimacies, and changes in relationships with children. Yet few social supports have been developed to assist people at this critical time.

Since we cannot determine where a person will die, nor can the dying person always choose the location of his or her death, the NIA is currently in the process of developing a special epidemiological study of where people do die, under what circumstances (awake or asleep), and to what degree they experience pain. People should not have to live with fears that may be based on an inadequate supply of accurate information regarding the last days of life.

Nutrition and Aging. Proper nutrition may spell the difference between active, productive old people and those who are physically and emotionally disabled and in need of frequent medical attention, hospitalization, and even institutionalization. The NIA subscribes to the

NIH-wide position that good nutrition is the cornerstone of preventive medicine. Adequate diet throughout life, including the later years, is an effective means to maintain good health and minimize degenerative changes in old age.

This year, the NIA held a conference that brought some of the nation's most outstanding clinical nutrition experts together to discuss "Nutritional Needs and Health of the Aging Adult." The goal of this conference was to provide the Institute with recommended directions for its research program.

It is generally believed (although some argument has arisen in recent months) that as a person ages, he or she experiences a loss in lean body mass (LBM). This decrease in LBM is usually accompanied by an increase in fat (adipose) tissue. Scientists also agree that the older individual is less active physically than in the early and middle adult years. Because fewer calories are used via physical exertion, it is assumed that the older person requires less caloric intake. In order to preserve lean body mass and optimal health, these calories must be of the highest nutritional quality. The question remains—what is the best combination of required daily allowances for the aged adult?

Age-related degenerative changes in body composition also include a loss of muscle mass (with concomitant loss in motor function) and a loss in bone tissue (resulting in fragile, easily fractured bones). Thus, we also need to know if this age-related decrease in muscle fiber can be prevented or stabilized by eating more foods with protein and amino acids and, if so, how much and how soon? Can osteoporosis, a brittleness of the bones especially problematic in older women, be avoided with calcium-rich diets and, if so, how much calcium is required?

As individuals grow old, the efficiency of their kidneys decreases. This raises several questions, such as: Can ingestion of high-quality protein and amino acid-containing foods moderate this change? Should we be looking at the role of fluid and sodium intake on a weakened renal (kidney) system?

It is well known that the elderly suffer from a number of gastrointestinal maladies, the most common one being constipation. In addition to studying the effects of high-fiber foods, we need further investigation to determine if there are other dietary adjustments which will alleviate these knds of gastrointestinal disorders.

We know that the elderly person has experienced a lifetime of diseases and environmental assaults on his or her body, but we do not know how to plan a good diet during or in the aftermath of the acute and chronic illnesses common among the elderly.

Old age often necessitates major changes in lifestyle that adversely affect eating habits. The aged person often finds himself or herself poorer than he or she had been during the early and middle years. In addition, an elderly person is more apt to experience the death of a spouse or close friends than any other age group. The old frequently are less able to take care of themselves, largely due to degenerative physical changes. An aged individual may suddenly find that the neighborhood where he or she has enjoyed security for many years has become a high crime area. Finally, old people may suddenly find themselves the victims of age prejudice, or "ageism." Any of the above situations can cause sufficient emotional trauma (grief, loneliness, depression) so great that one loses the desire to eat. This loss of appetite, known as anorexia, combined with financial restrictions on food purchase and fear of going out to the store, makes it easy to understand why many old people are seriously undernourished.

As a first step towards implementing the recommendations made at the conference, the NIA recently issued a revised, expanded request for research grant applications, with emphasis on the following areas:

- Epidemiologic and clinical research on the relationship between aging, nutritional status, dietary intake, and health status;

- The effects of specific diseases on nutritional status and inter-actions of nutrients with therapeutic agents, surgical procedures, or preventive regimens;

- The effects of aging on nutrient requirements and utilization, digestion, absorption, and metabolism;

- Basic and clinical nutrition studies on the interrelationships between aging and: 1) factors which may regulate changes in lean body mass, body composition, energy balance, regulation of metabolic processes, and disease susceptibility; 2) the effects of nutritional deficiencies on long-term health and longevity; and, 3) the effects of nutrition on age-related mental changes.

The Older Woman. Are women really the weaker sex? If there is strength in numbers, they are not. Women in the 65-and-older age group are the fastest growing segment of the U.S. population, with 13.9 million older women (versus 9.5 million older men) in 1977, expected to increase to 33.4 million women (versus 22.4 million men) by the year 2035. Women are also living much longer than men, a gap in life expectancy which will continue to widen into the next century. This growth in the number of older women is having an enormous impact on society. Yet the needs and achievements of older women have largely been overlooked.

To explore a wide range of issues concerning the older woman and to identify areas in which research is needed, the NIA and the National Institute of Mental Health (NIMH) co-sponsored a workshop on the older woman. From these discussions—and a diversity of research studies, backed by statistical and case material—emerged a portrait of the typical woman in her seventies and beyond. Her life is marked by the continuities of working in the home and of maintaining emotional connections with family, children, and peers. But her life is also marked by the discontinuities of an interrupted career and large numbers of losses—including the departure of children from the home, and the likelihood of outliving her husband. She is assailed by unflattering stereotypes and by poverty, poor access to transportation, loneliness, and isolation. She is three times as likely as her male peer to live in a nursing home. Her life seems precarious at times: there is the real possibility that she may become a patient and/or a pauper. Despite the litany of problems the older woman faces, she also possesses great strength and potential, as witnessed by her ability to survive.

Of considerable interest to this country's 31 million postmenopausal women and their doctors are the risks and benefits of estrogen administration. In a preliminary effort to organize the study of these risks and benefits, the NIA convened a group of experts to assess the suitability of holding a consensus meeting on estrogen use. Although some participants felt that the issues require so much more research that it is premature to attempt to reach consensus at this time, the prevailing view was to proceed in order to compile, evaluate, and effectively disseminate the information already available. Therefore, the NIA will sponsor a consensus exercise in the near future, with emphasis on the following topics: the benefits of estrogen use for the treatment of menopausal symptoms and for the prevention of osteoporosis and possibly heart disease; the hazards of estrogen use, particularly cancer; the relative risks and benefits of various forms, routes, doses, and schedules of estrogen therapy and acceptable indications for and patterns of estrogen use.

In addition to NIA efforts to stimulate interest in the problems of older women among the scientific and academic communities, the recent inclusion of women in the Baltimore Longitudinal Study of Aging will provide Institute scientists with an opportunity to study the aging process in women firsthand, and perhaps shed some light on the differential life expectancy between the sexes and among various racial and ethnic groups. As of the fall of 1978, some 150 women have been introduced into the study.

Geriatric Medicine. The NIA's continuing interest in facilitating the teaching of geriatric medicine as a part of basic medical training gained momentum during 1978 with several key developments. The NIA contracted with the Institute of Medicine (IoM) of the National Academy of Sciences to examine how best to incorporate geriatric medicine into medical school curricula. The IoM report noted that current medical training in the care of the elderly is deficient, but the committee recommended against establishing a separate specialty or subspecialty of geriatrics, instead suggesting the creation of sections on geriatric medicine within departments of internal medicine. By encouraging the inclusion of geriatric medicine in the mainstream of medical practice, the report avoids possible arguments on the necessity of still another specialty and prevents the further isolation of the elderly from the mainstream of American medicine.

The American Medical Student Association has shown a great deal of interest in geriatric medicine, most recently devoting an entire morning session to the subject at its annual meeting in March 1978. Two months later, the Association of Professors of Medicine considered geriatrics at its annual meeting. The Director of the NIA participated in both discussions. In September 1978, the Board of Governors of the American College of Physicians also heard a presentation by the NIA Director on geriatric medicine.

In the spring of 1978, Dr. Milo D. Leavitt, then Director of the Fogarty International Center (FIC), spent 6 weeks in the United Kingdom visiting eight out of ten British medical schools with chairs in geriatric medicine and studying the educational, research, and service aspects of geriatric medicine in that country. Upon his return, Dr. Leavitt became the NIA Director's Special Assistant for Medical Program Development and Evaluation. In this role, he prepared a report which detailed the strengths and weaknesses of the British system, concluding that although the United Kingdom is ahead of the United States in its understanding of aging, a direct transplantation of their practice of geriatric medicine to this country would probably not be appropriate.

The NIA's nomination of Sir Ferguson Anderson, one of the world's foremost geriatricians, to be a Fogarty International Scholar was accepted. He plans to begin his year here in September 1979, participating in a variety of activities designed to speed the transmission of knowledge regarding geriatric medicine to American medical school students and faculty, as well as policymakers and scientists in the field of aging.

Funds for training in geriatric medicine have been provided to the FIC Senior International Fellowship Program (also known as the Magnuson fellowship) and the Bureau of Health Manpower of the Health Resources Administration. The NIA will coordinate with these agencies on both efforts.

Finally, the NIA recently initiated a Geriatric Medicine Academic Award to provide a stimulus for the development of a curriculum in geriatric medicine in those schools that do not have one and to strengthen and improve the curricula in those schools that do. At the same time, a Clinical Investigator Award was announced, which would provide an opportunity for promising clinically trained individuals to develop research ability in preparation for independent research careers. Post doctoral training opportunities in both clinical and basic research continue to be available at the NIA Gerontology Research Center.

Longevous Populations. Since the beginning of time, man has searched for the key to perpetual life. Reports of groups of people living past 100 in certain parts of the world have sparked the imagination and conjured up dreams of Shangri-la. At a meeting sponsored by the NIA and the FIC, Dr. Richard Mazess of the University of Wisconsin at Madison and Dr. Sylvia H. Forman of the University of California at Berkeley disclosed that those persons thought to be centenarians in Vilcabamba, Ecuador, are not. In cooperation with Ecuadorian scientists, Drs. Mazess and Forman investigated civil and church records and found that the oldest living villager was 96. Much of the confusion stems from the custom of passing a family name from one generation to the next. Because of this tradition, the actual recorded birth dates of those persons living in Vilcabamba are frequently confused with those of their parents and grandparents. Another common practice is to give a surviving child the same name as that of a sibling who has died. Consequently, a person's "age" is often the sum total of more than one family member. The scientists also found that after the age of 60, many villagers begin to exaggerate their ages. Increased worldwide attention only exacerbated this phenomenon.

However, there is still much that can be learned by studying the people of Vilcabamba and other long-living populations. For one thing, the incidence of arteriosclerosis in Vilcabambans 80 and over is particularly low, whereas in the United States the number of deaths caused by this hardening of the arteries peaks at age 80. In addition, Dr. Mazess' work shows that there are fewer bone fractures in elderly Vilcabambans despite the loss of bone density that is common in old age in the United States.

Cellular and Animal Resources. Many aging research advances would not have been possible without the NIA's development of special resources for gerontology researchers. Currently, the NIA's Basic Aging Program contracts with the Institute for Medical Research (IMR) in Camden, New Jersey, for two cell resource/services. The first is a cultured cell bank. Via this effort, NIA establishes, characterizes, stores, and distributes standard and genetically-marked human cell lines for aging research. The second, more recent NIA-IMR resource is a mycoplasma contamination testing service which performs a vital function for researchers who use cells to study aging processes. Mycoplasma are tiny, evasive organisms, smaller than bacteria but larger than viruses, which frequently infect cell cultures. Mycoplasma can alter the characteristics and behavior of cultured cells so dramatically that their mere presence compromises research results. The mycoplasma testing facility enables researchers to spot-check their cell cultures by periodically sending in samples for analysis. The testing facility focuses not only on mycoplasma detection but also on mycoplasma prevention and control.

Because practically every field of biomedical aging research depends heavily on the development and availability of appropriate laboratory animals as research models, several animal resources have been established by the Biophysiology and Pathobiology Aging Program of the NIA. Disease-free aged rodents are available to NIA scientists today because the selection processes and logistics necessary to establish these colonies began several years ago. In addition to providing the animals themselves, the NIA keeps scientific data on the animals' life spans, growth patterns, organ weights, age-associated diseases, and blood chemistries.

The NIA is working with the National Academy of Sciences (NAS) to determine which animals will prove to be the most relevant to future aging research investigations. The NAS is at work on a report which will assess selected vertebrate species for aging research. The NIA is also working with the Division of Research Resources, NIH, to survey existing colonies of aged laboratory animals for use by gerontology researchers.

Geriatric Dentistry. Currently, all three major programs of the NIA are involved in the conduct or initiation of work in geriatric dentistry. Approximately 6 months ago, NIA intramural scientists added a dental evaluation component to the already extensive physical and mental examination protocol used in the Baltimore Longitudinal Study of Aging. Dr. Bruce Baum at the Gerontology Research Center (GRC) developed the dental protocol, which includes clinical evaluation of gum diseases, cavities, changes in the senses of taste and smell, oral hygiene, salivary and related oral gland function, and alterations in denture-retaining ridges. Biochemical tests are also performed on saliva samples.

The NIA Extramural and Collaborative Research Program (ECRP) is coordinating with the National Institute of Dental Research to identify areas of overlapping interest and high priority with the eventual goal of funding meritorious research to explore the many aspects of geriatric dentistry. Topics of interest to both Institutes include: root cavities, gum disease, oral tissue changes, wound healing, immune capacity, elderly cleft palate, removable dental appliances, loss of teeth, oral bone loss, nutrition, oral cancer, denture sores, salivary function, therapy compliance, oral hygiene, and taste and smell changes which accompany aging.

The Epidemiology, Demography, and Biometry Program (EDBP) of the NIA has taken steps to initiate the compilation of dental information from already existing surveys. With guidance and funding from the NIA, data from the Health and Nutrition Examination Survey (HANES) will be reexamined closely to collect important information on the older population. During the first planning year of this effort, the EDBP will recommend a special examination of the dental information originally collected by the HANES researchers. The EDBP also hopes to support a team of nutritionists, dental researchers, and epidemiologists to look at the relationship between dental problems and nutrition in the old.

Accidental Hypothermia. NIA information activities continue to alert the public, and particularly the elderly, to the danger of accidental hypothermia, a potentially fatal drop in deep body temperature that can result from prolonged exposure to even mildly cool temperatures. A press conference was held in December 1977 on this topic and a lay-oriented brochure was prepared which describes the condition, explains who is at risk, and tells the elderly how to protect against accidental hypothermia. The story received wide coverage in both national and local media, and led to the addition of a warning to the elderly in the Department of Energy's "Tips for Energy Savers" booklet. The brochure was widely distributed during the winter in supermarket information racks in states with cold winter climates. A similar broad distribution is underway this winter, supplemented by a national public service announcement warning the elderly and their families about accidental hypothermia and directing them to their supermarket information rack or to the NIA for further information. Requests for additional information have come in from state health departments and energy offices, and also from a variety of organizations concerned with the elderly.

Research Advances

Osteoporosis and Vitamin K. The effects of osteoporosis, a degenerative weakening of the bone that leads to hip fractures in many elderly women, may be arrested with adequate vitamin K intake. Osteoporosis is believed to precipitate about 195,000 hip fractures annually, primarily among elderly women, and is a major cause of physical disability in old age.

Institute grantees have discovered that when an individual experiences vitamin K deficiency, the resulting decrease in the protein osteocalcin causes calcium loss in bone. This calcium loss, in turn, causes a decrease in the amount and strength of bone tissue in old people, making affected bones weak, porous and highly susceptible to fracture.

Vitamin K, long recognized for its role in blood coagulation, is now believed to be vital to calcium "turnover" in bone. Among the evidence for this relationship is the fact that fetal bone deficits have been common in children whose mothers received drugs during their pregnancies that interrupted the metabolism of vitamin K.

By selecting foods which are "easy to digest," the elderly often exclude vitamin K-containing foods such as green vegetables, cauliflower, potatoes and liver. Older people frequently use mineral oil laxatives which coincidentally interfere with vitamin K absorption. They may also take drugs which cause metabolic inactivation of vitamin K. Finally, estrogen deficiency experienced by postmenopausal women often contributes to impaired vitamin K metabolism.

Continued research is expected to delineate further the relationship between vitamin K, calcium metabolism, and osteoporosis.

Calorie Counting Can Change Number of Fat Cells. The number of fat cells (adipocytes) in the body has long been believed to remain constant throughout adult life. An overabundance of food during the first year or so of a human's life, according to this theory, was likely to lead to a large number of fat cells in adulthood but the number, once established, has been thought to remain unchanged.

Now Institute-supported studies of rats show that the number of fat cells, rather than remaining constant throughout adult life, increases in the fatty tissue around the kidneys of these animals. Related studies show that restriction of food intake lowers the size and number of adipocytes formed in the same tissues. This effect occurs not only during the early life of rats, but at any point during adult and later life, a finding which may enhance the medical evaluation and management of obesity, a serious problem in old age.

Further work by the same grantees indicates that the adipocytes of animals whose caloric intake is restricted are significantly more responsive to certain hormones which release fat from fat cells and carry it to the blood, so that the body's tissues can convert it into energy. Food restriction appears to delay decline in this function which ordinarily accompanies aging.

The investigators also found that food restriction enhances an animal's ability to maintain muscle functioning and keep blood fat levels from increasing. Rats whose food was restricted maintained a more youthful appearance and behavior than was "normal" for their age group. These findings have important implications for the prevention and treatment of diabetes and coronary heart disease.

Enhancing Wound Healing in the Aged. Serious physical injury in both humans and rats is associated with increased excretion of nitrogen in urine, which indicates an increase in protein loss from the body. In humans, the quantity of nitrogen lost may cause a negative nitrogen balance in the body that is believed to adversely affect wound healing. The extent of this nitrogen/protein loss is usually related to the severity of the trauma suffered, previous protein nutrition, cold or heat stress, sex, and age.

Thus a major clinical problem for the aged is maintaining a positive protein (nitrogen) balance in order to enhance wound healing and reduce surgical and post-surgical risks. Conventional diet therapy programs following severe injury have been aimed at providing liberal amounts of protein and energy to the patient. Another approach is to minimize the excretion of nitrogen.

Institute grantees studying protein metabolism and stress in aged rats have reported that rats traumatized under ether anesthesia showed an increase in nitrogen excretion that was accompanied—and perhaps caused—by a trauma-associated decrease in the liver content of copper, manganese and zinc. By increasing the intake of these minerals above the usually recommended dietary levels, the investigators were able to reduce nitrogen excretion. They also discovered that nitrogen loss could be reduced in traumatized animals by adding two amino acids, arginine and glycine, to their diets.

In addition, the grantees demonstrated that about 50 percent of the total nitrogen loss may be caused by ether anesthesia alone. This suggests that in surgical procedures, the use of anesthesia should be considered sufficiently traumatic to be accounted for in planning the nutrition of the patient.

Important Developments in Cell Biology. For years, human cell culture science has profoundly affected many areas of biological research, including immunology and genetics. Observations of human cells are vital to the study of human aging as well, especially since hundreds of experiments, otherwise impossible to perform on man, can be carried out on live cells grown in the laboratory from small slivers of human skin and other tissues.

Cell biologists have long known that human cells grown in laboratory culture medium (*in vitro*) lose their ability to reproduce at a certain point, and that the younger the age of the cell donor, the greater the number of cell divisions in culture.

Recently Institute-supported researchers have made several important discoveries about the structure and function of live human cells grown *in vitro*. One discovery concerns the structure of WI-38 cells, a strain derived from female fetal lung tissue. For many years, this normal human cell line was the "line of choice" in cellular aging research because of its limited "life span" or ability to proliferate in culture.

Using a high voltage electron microscope, grantees at the University of Colorado have been able to observe three-dimensional detail of subcellular structure and have discovered that the WI-38 cell has a three-dimensional lattice structure. As part of the skeletal system of the cell, this structure helps determine the cell's shape, and may also be part of the mechanism whereby other structures move around within the cell. Having described this aspect of subcellular structure, researchers are now looking for age-associated changes in this structure.

In another significant development, grantees at the Massachusetts Institute of Technology have recently suggested that when normal skin cells lose their ability to proliferate in a culture medium, this may be a sign not of cell aging, but of cell differentiation. Thus, instead of continuously proliferating, these cells lose the capacity to divide as they perform new functions. This change, or differentiation, may be similar to a change this cell type undergoes in the body.

This work suggests that investigators should consider that "differentiation" as well as "aging" may be the reason normal cells lose their capacity to divide in culture. It emphasizes the need to extend cellular aging research to other cell types, and to determine how cells in the normal body compare to cells grown in culture.

Old Animals Can Compensate for Nerve Cell Loss. The biological basis for learning and memory stems from the unique ability of brain cells to change their functioning according to repeated experiences. No other group of cells in the body other than nerve cells has this capability, known as functional plasticity.

Decline in memory and ability to learn in old age is a critical problem because the aged brain is highly susceptible to loss of nerve cells. Such losses are part of the normal aging process as well as a side effect of stroke, tumors, senile dementia and similar disorders.

In recent studies comparing aged and young animals, Institute grantees have shown that old as well as young animals are able to compensate for nerve cell loss. As part of a system similar to a complex communications network, each nerve cell in the brain receives inputs from thousands of other nerve cells and each of these, in turn, forms connections with hundreds of other nerve cells. When one or more inputs to a nerve cell are destroyed, in some instances the remaining cells which still maintain "terminals" to a target cell form new connections compensating for those that were lost. This process, known as reactive synaptogenesis, has been well documented in the developing nervous system, but was not known to take place in the aged brain.

Now grantees have demonstrated that aged rats the equivalent of about 80 human years exhibit similar reactive synaptogenesis, or the ability to regrow new brain circuits. But the regrowth is much weaker than in younger animals and sometimes forms improper connections to existing brain cells, causing the animal to behave abnormally.

Why connections are made properly or improperly is still not known, although further studies will explore these mechanisms. The discovery that older nerve cells can compensate for cell loss could—if ways are found to enhance the proper type of regrowth—reduce the damage caused by senility, stroke, memory loss and other degenerative changes that may accompany old age.

How Smell and Taste Change with Age. To meet the often neglected nutritional needs of the elderly, it is necessary to learn how foods taste and smell to them, and how foods can be modified to enhance flavor. NIA-supported studies of young and elderly subjects revealed that the older group was considerably less able than the younger to identify, by taste and smell, a variety of foods and flavors including chocolate, grape, orange, lemon, cherry, tomato, cheddar cheese, bacon and mushroom. Reduced sensitivity to food odors, rather than lack of taste, appeared to be the main reason elderly subjects incorrectly identified these foods.

Other studies by the same investigator indicated that the continued use of smell—for example, by professional perfumers—over a person's life span may retard the decline of smell sensitivity and that stronger odor made food more flavorful to the elderly.

The investigator also suggested that one way to enhance food flavor might be to add certain amino acids with sweet or salty components to the diets of the elderly. This would make it possible to lower the undesirably high salt and sugar content of many elderly persons' diets, and perhaps improve the protein intake without increasing saturated fats.

The diets of the elderly may improve with better understanding of how taste and smell of foods and nutrients are affected by normal aging and by age-related diseases, and of how food palatability can improve with salt and sugar substitutes and other taste- and flavor-enhancing substances.

New Method Allows Study of Permeability of Blood-Brain Barrier. Age-related changes in the central nervous systems of man and animals may be caused by breakdown of the blood-brain barrier, which restricts exchange of water soluble drugs and proteins between the blood and brain.

Institute scientists at the GRC have developed a new way to measure permeability of the blood-brain barrier in rats. This method, which is 1,000 times more sensitive than other tests currently available, allowed the researchers to demonstrate that blood vessels in the brain remain intact despite age-related brain changes in senescent rats.

This method also measures the rates at which certain drugs enter the brain, until now a problem because the blood-brain barrier made it impossible to measure the actual concentration of a given drug in the brain. Old people tend increasingly to react adversely to drugs that affect the central nervous system, although the same drugs normally are not toxic in younger individuals. It is not known, in some cases, whether changes in response to a drug are caused by increased entry and retention of the drug within the brain, or to altered brain sensitivity to a given concentration of a drug. It should now be possible to distinguish between these effects and to predict, based on the measured concentration of a drug in the blood, the actual concentration in the brain.

These investigators also developed a way to temporarily increase the permeability of the blood-brain barrier to drugs that normally cannot enter the brain. It is now possible to allow certain drugs and other substances that affect the central nervous system into the brain to study how they interact with brain cells in relation to central nervous system function, disease and aging.

Cardiovascular Disease and Intellectual Decline with Aging. While the debate continues over whether cognitive behavior and intelligence normally decline with advancing age, one Institute-supported longitudinal study has related cardiovascular disease to intellectual decline in middle-aged and older people. Cardiovascular disease has long been suspected of undermining cognitive function to the extent that it disrupts blood flow to the brain. Grantees followed a sample of subjects—an original 500 narrowed to 156 over time—and divided them into groups with or without cardiovascular disease based upon their health histories. Results showed that subjects with stroke or arteriosclerosis (hardening of the arteries) were the most likely to drop out of the study, and that members of the groups that remained were more likely than those who left to show a greater drop over time in scores on tests measuring mental ability and speed of performance.

However, individuals with high blood pressure were not as likely to drop out of the study or to show a decline in intellectual performance on the various tests administered. This result confirms earlier work suggesting that mildly elevated blood pressure may help maintain intellectual functioning in old age.

The study does not explain how intellectual decline takes place, although reduced oxygen supply caused by decreased blood flow in the cerebrovascular system may impair the function of the nervous system, and the lifestyle changes and social isolation that cardiovascular disease often enforces may adversely affect intellectual functioning.

By showing that changes in cognitive behavior vary according to the subgroup involved, this study alerts investigators to consider such individual differences in future attempts to predict how cognitive development changes with advancing age.

Relationship of Aluminum to Alzheimer's Disease. Alzheimer's disease is a poorly understood disorder of the brain cells in which groups of nerve endings in the outer layer of the brain degenerate and disrupt the passage of electrochemical signals between the cells. These areas of degeneration have a characteristic appearance under the microscope, and are called plaques. The larger the number of areas of degeneration, the greater the disturbance in intellectual function and memory.

Until recently, Alzheimer's disease was believed to be rare, but new evidence demonstrates a high frequency: it is estimated to affect from 500,000 to 1.5 million Americans of all ages. The cause or causes of Alzheimer's disease remain unknown, although recent evidence points to several possibilities. Research by grantees at the University of Toronto shows that the brains of people dying of Alzheimer's disease contain high accumulations of aluminum. Other studies by these grantees in collaboration with scientists at the GRC suggest that the aluminum may interact with DNA, a substance found in all living cells that carries primary genetic information.

Early results indicate that this binding has dramatic effects on the structure of DNA molecules. Specifically, aluminum forms crosslinks between the DNA strands and could be responsible for the lesions that characterize Alzheimer's disease. Further research is needed to verify this possibility and to explore the mechanisms by which aluminum affects DNA.

Baltimore Longitudinal Study of Aging Results. Two of the most life-threatening conditions in old age are cancer and infectious diseases. The NIA's Baltimore Longitudinal Study of Aging has recently provided information about age-related changes in human immune function that may influence susceptibility to these conditions. Studies of participants in the Longitudinal Study have shown that the ability of certain immune cells (lymphocytes) to kill human tumor cells decreases markedly beginning in the fifth decade of life. Furthermore, those immune cells which fight acute infection (neutrophils) now appear to become less efficient with advancing age. These and other research results permit a better understanding of immune function in both young and old persons, and may form the basis of improved diagnostic procedures for detecting immunodeficiencies.

Another study at GRC involves the effects of aging on motor behavior such as turning or walking. It is well known that some disorders associated with senescence may result from age-related changes in the activity of specialized receptors which control the body's ability to respond to specific hormones and other body chemicals. GRC investigators have recently characterized these changes more specifically in studies of the rodent showing that aberrations in motor behavior may result from a failure of certain neurotransmitters, which carry nerve signals to receptors, to be released as effectively in the senescent animal as they are in the young. Motor behavior changes may also result from a loss of receptors upon which these neurohormones act during the transmission of nerve impulses within the motor areas of the rat's brain. These studies characterize, for the first time, a possible hormonal change in the central nervous system in relation to a very simple motor behavior in the aged rat.

Personality Characteristics of Men with Good Visual Memory. A study of 857 men between the ages of 30 and 80 in the Baltimore Longitudinal Study of Aging revealed that while visual memory of designs declines with age, particularly after age 70, it does not decline for everybody. In a sample of men measured for the first time when they were 70 and over, one in four showed no decline in visual memory performance when tested 6 years later. Another analysis of men measured initially during their sixties showed no decline 6 years later, but at 12 years showed a decline similar to that of the 70-year group. The performance test consisted of reproducing geometric designs from memory after each design was displayed for 10 seconds and then withdrawn.

These researchers are also exploring why some individuals decline in memory performance and others do not. They are attempting to identify personality characteristics associated with changes in memory performance among men 70 and over. Initial results show that men who maintain memory performance have good emotional control, are energetic, and are oriented toward impersonal, analytic tasks. Individuals who decline in memory performance over time exhibit emotional instability, low energy levels, and less orientation toward tasks.

Calorie, Cholesterol and Fat Intake Decrease with Age in Longitudinal Study. Longitudinal research at the Institute's Gerontology Research Center has revealed that as a sample of 180 men in the study grew older, there was a decrease in their intake of fat and saturated fatty acid. Relative caloric intake also changed with age. For example, as age increased, fats contributed less to caloric intake and carbohydrates contributed more.

The study covered the period from 1961 to 1975, and included men ranging from 35 to 74 years of age at the beginning of the study. Analysis of their 7-day dietary diaries revealed that the ratio of polyunsaturated to saturated fatty acids increased an average of 26 percent during this time period when age was held constant, thus representing a change over time and not an effect of aging. Cholesterol intake decreased by 19 percent, from an average of 587 milligrams per day during the period 1961-65, to 478 milligrams per day in the period 1971-75. It is not yet clear how these diet changes will affect the health or life spans of these men.

A related study covering the period 1963-1976 showed a recent drop in the serum cholesterol levels among men aged 17 to 102 years who are subjects in the Longitudinal Study. This finding confirmed evidence that cholesterol levels increase in young adults, level off in the middle years, and decrease in late adulthood. However, a striking drop of about 7 percent that was observed in all age groups in early 1970 cannot be explained either by changes in obesity or by men with high cholesterol dropping out because of death.

Although the diets of the subjects as a group did change over this time period (cholesterol intake decreased as noted above), the individual changes in cholesterol intake did not correlate with the individual serum cholesterol changes.

Exercise or other factors may have contributed to the change in cholesterol levels, and these variables will receive further study.

The Use of Psychological Tests in Predicting Death. Institute grantees have identified a number of behavioral measurements which are an important step toward being able to predict the deaths of a significant number of older adults within 5 years following testing.

Since the early 1960's, a growing body of research has shown that the psychological test performance of elderly people may be used to predict ensuing death. But tests thus far have often discounted the age of the subjects, have looked backward over a span of years rather than forward, and in most cases, have included institutionalized or ailing subjects.

The present study included 380 men and women who were healthy and capable of independent living, and took into account their age, which ranged from 60 to 89 years.

A wide variety of variables were assessed including demographic, cognitive, perceptual, psychomotor, personality, health and social factors. Used in combination, 13 predictors seemed indicative of ensuing death. These included a rating of how much vitality the subject displayed during a brief interview, three psychomotor tasks believed to measure brain and neural function, and two personality tests measuring depression and whether the subjects felt in control of themselves and their lives.

Such tests—which are brief, easy to administer by untrained personnel, and easy for subjects to take—are currently undergoing further validation. Once validated, they might prove a useful part of routine health assessments of elderly patients. They might also alert physicians—just as a high blood pressure measurement signals circulatory problems—to begin preventive and remedial efforts and to advise patients to adjust their lifestyles. These tests are not intended to be used as the sole index of impending death or medical status, but are a supplement to existing biomedical assessment techniques.

Antecedents of Health in Middle Age. In an NIA-supported longitudinal study designed to assess various manifestations of health throughout the life span, a sample of about 350 men and women who entered the study as infants or children were followed up at ages 30 to 50. Results showed that:

- Health deteriorated slightly between the third and fourth decades and continued deteriorating into the fifth decade for the men, but not for the women.

- Participants tended to assess their health as "good" despite their own reported complaints, experience with illness, and objective findings. Sixteen percent of the women, but none of the men, reported poor health at age 50.

- The most consistent complaint about ill health among women throughout the middle years involved the reproductive system. In men, it involved the digestive system. In both sexes, complaints of acute illness diminished with age, while complaints of chronic conditions increased. Women complained about physical problems more often than men.

- Paralleling these complaints, pathology in women was most frequently found in the reproductive system. In men—despite their complaints about digestion—the most common actual problem was hypertension. There was a gradual elevation of blood pressure in both sexes throughout life.

- The health of men appeared to be related to their education and to that of their fathers. Women's health reflected the education of their fathers and their husbands. Overall, a calm, self-controlled, and responsible personality, manifesting itself as early as 11 to 13 years, was found to be conducive to good health in adulthood.

Institutional Adaptation of the Aged. At every phase of life, people strive to control their environments. Old age, illness, and insufficient finances may cause a decline in control. This decline becomes even more pronounced in old people who must enter nursing homes and succumb to an institutional environment that exerts almost total control over the individual. The degree to which a person adapts successfully to institutionalization, one Institute grantee reports, depends upon his or her feelings about predictability and control. The greater the choice the individual feels he or she has and the more predictable the new environment, the less negative the effects of relocation tend to be. And, once there, individuals who view themselves as controlling their own fate adapt less well to a controlling institutional environment than people who perceive themselves as ruled by the world around them.

Personal control, or the ability to manipulate some aspect of the environment, can be exercised by involving the individuals in arranging for admission to the nursing home.

Feelings of predictability depend upon the amount of preparation individuals receive before the move to a nursing home. They can be prepared for a new environment through educational programs, visits to the facility, or personal counseling.

Those patients who felt more in control over the move to a nursing home showed increased activity levels afterward, and reported they felt better emotionally and physically. Nurses' ratings of the group exerting more control showed these individuals to be healthier and to have a greater "zest" for life.

Although only 5 percent of the population over the age of 65 is in nursing homes, this still represents about one million older people, each of whom might be aided by such tools for adapting to the stressful experience of institutionalization.

Other Findings from Aging Research. Aging research spans a wide range of disciplines, from cellular biology to the social sciences. From some of these areas, Institute-supported researchers reported that:

- A system has recently been devised that measures the quantity of insulin-like hormones (somatomedins) in the blood serum of animals of various ages. This makes it possible to study how somatomedins and insulin interrelate in maturity-onset diabetes, and how the levels of other hormones change during aging.

- Loss of the heart's ability to contract is a major cardiovascular problem for the aging person. Grantees have discovered that increased levels of calcium between the cells can compensate for this loss of ability to contract. Their findings suggest that drugs which help calcium to enter the heart may alleviate this condition in the elderly.

- In a study of kidney function in aging rats, grantees found that the activity of certain enzymes decreases with age. This resulted in decreased efficiency of the metabolic machinery in the kidneys of aged rats. Under stressful conditions like starvation or acidosis, kidney failure occurred.

- Recent studies provide further evidence that a decline in thymus hormone secretion may play an important role in the age-related impairment of the body's immune system. This system enables the body to protect itself against foreign substances such as viruses, and against various diseases. Institute grantees have discovered that removal of the thymus—a gland at the base of the neck that is key in the immune system—accelerates age-associated changes in immune function. The grantees also reported that when spleen cells from old animals are transferred to young mice with intact thymus glands, the spleen cells regain their former immune function. This suggests that the thymus gland or its products may reverse or improve the immune deficiencies that accompany aging.

- Regular exercise results in an increase in lean body mass, improved heart and lung function, better oxygen uptake from the blood into the heart and skeletal muscle, and increased glucose tolerance. Studies of exercised animals have clarified the biochemical changes responsible for these physiological improvements, and have provided a scientific basis for intelligent use of exercise as a tool in preventive and curative medicine.

- A behavioral study of migration patterns of the elderly population, compared to the general population, reveals that the elderly are more likely than the general population to move between, rather than within, states. Elderly movers are also more likely to live in the same household with one of their children, and to rent rather than own their dwellings.

- A project which compares contemporary families with a large nationwide sample for 1880 and 1900 shows that older southern whites at the turn of the century were more likely to live in extended families, while southern blacks were much more likely to live apart from kin. At present, the tendency appears to be for older whites to live near, rather than with, their children, while older blacks are more likely to live with their children.

- A model has been developed that relates age, race and sex to deaths from five chronic diseases which account for 64 percent of all deaths: heart disease, stroke, arteriosclerosis, hypertension, and cancer. Already the model has demonstrated consistent race differences in circulatory diseases. An early increase in black mortality appears, for example, to be related to a lower resistance of blacks to circulatory problems and risks. In addition, the model has delineated for each of these individual causes of death the "crossover" phenomenon in which blacks shift, at about age 75, from a disadvantage to an advantage over whites in terms of life expectancy.

Such modelling is a fast, cost-effective way to look at age-related diseases in a population, and to relate mortality data to other epidemiological studies. The model may also help researchers predict the physiological makeup of the older population, assess the impact of health programs over time, and understand how social, economic, medical and other factors affect aging and mortality.

National Institute on Aging
Obligations for Programs in Aging
(thousands of dollars)

	1976	1977	1978	1979 Estimate	1980 Estimate
Public Health Service:					
National Institutes of Health:					
National Institute on Aging	$19,221	$29,879	$37,057	$56,911	$56,510

Research on Organic Brain Diseases

Excerpted from the Report of the Task Panel on Mental Health of the Elderly

Volume III of the *Task Panel Reports Submitted to The President's Commission on Mental Health,* 1978. U.S. Goverment Printing Office, Stock No. 040-000-00392-4.

Few would argue with the assertion that the most feared aspect of growing old is losing one's capability to relate, physically and emotionally, to one's friends, family, and environment. Clearly, however, that is the fate of an all too significant proportion of our older citizens. In a distressingly large number of older people, age-related degenerative changes in both the central and peripheral nervous systems lead to a loss of bodily and cognitive functions, which often makes expensive institutional care necessary.

Although it is true that considerable Federal presence already exists in support of studies of both normal and disordered nervous function, altogether too little attention is presently being given to the problems of the aging and the aged, even in light of the fact that various forms of nervous system impairment account for a great majority of admissions of older people to hospitals and nursing homes. Perhaps the most stark example that can be offered regarding the catastrophic nature of this process of mental decline in the elderly is that of senile dementia, the end point in which is a complete lack of awareness of the environment surrounding the individual, frequently accompanied by a loss of both voluntary and involuntary motor functions, leading to muscular uncoordination, disorientation with respect to the time and place, and failure of sphincteric function (i.e., incontinence).

Systematic research on the function of the nervous system is an extremely difficult task, requiring highly sophisticated technology and substantially more manpower than is currently devoted to it. Even more difficult, therefore, is the study of changes in nervous function as a consequence of the aging process, since the age dimension requires observation over a substantial period of time for research analysis and definition.

Despite these difficulties, the Task Panel on the Elderly unanimously agrees that the National Institutes of Health would be derelict if they did not attempt to approach the specific issues of aging as they relate to the nervous system. One requirement of the Research on Aging Act of 1974 that created the National Institute of Aging (P.L. 93-296) was the development of an HEW-wide research plan for aging. NIA as the lead agency in aging research has developed plans for descriptive and analytic research on the alterations which occur in neural function as a consequence of age.

This planned program will focus on clinical intervention in brain aging problems to minimize and ultimately prevent these disorders and their consequences. It will have the following components:

(1) A considerably greater degree of understanding must be obtained concerning the morphological changes in both central and peripheral nervous systems with age, requiring a competence in the neuroanatomical and neuropathological sciences. The techniques to be employed would include electron microscopy, autoradiography, and histochemistry and cytochemistry.

(2) Structural information is valuable only to the extent that it can be correlated with functional change. Accordingly, a second capacity would be developed simultaneously in the area of neurophysiology, requiring both basic and clinical neurological competence to interpret alterations in electrical and neuromotor activity as a consequence of aging, in both animal and human populations (including the Baltimore Longitudinal Study on Aging Population by NIA).

(3) While it is asserted that most if not all of the detrimental changes in nervous function with age are intrinsic to the nervous system itself, it also seems possible that some proportion of these changes relates to alterations in the nutritional status of the nervous system, i.e., the supply of oxygen and other nutrients provided by the vascular system. Accordingly, a competence in the area of cerebrovascular and blood-brain barrier physiology would seem clearly appropriate to develop a knowledge base complementary to that achieved by the morphological and physiological units described previously.

(4) It is most apparent that an increased understanding of the mechanisms whereby nerve impulses are transmitted or impeded in the elderly would demand an increased competence in the areas of neurochemistry and neuropharmacology. Little significant information exists today as to the systematic changes which may occur in the aging nervous system with respect to its responsiveness to so-called neurotransmitter substances. Selected changes in responsiveness to, or synthesis of, neurotransmitter materials could account for a number of alterations in normal nerve function observed as a result of the passage of years, not from pathological degeneration.

(5) Of all brain aging problems, senile dementia of the Alzheimer's disease type stands as the most formidable to individuals and society. Research will be encouraged in the clinical, behavioral, biomedical, and social aspects of this disease. Related dementias will be studied concurrently, with the intent of improving diagnosis and treatment of reversible syndromes.

(6) Many aged commonly suffer from sleep problems which detract markedly from the quality of their lives and their capacity to function normally. These problems require--and are amenable to--clinical, biomedical, behavioral, and social investigation.

The scope of the program outlined would require close collaboration among the National Institute on Aging, the National Institute of Neurological and Communicative Disorders and Stroke, and the National Institute of Mental Health. These institutions have already begun this process of active cooperation with the joint sponsorship of a conference on senile dementia/Alzheimer's disease and related disorders. Future efforts in the neurosciences, both in intramural research conducted by government scientists and extramurally supported grant research, would require continued cooperation to maximize the use of scarce resources and to ensure a comprehensive approach to the research problems addressed.

The new knowledge obtained through research is the ultimate service and the ultimate cost container. Without new knowledge, we will just keep on doing the same things in the same ways, at ever-increasing costs. We will continue to warehouse older people in nursing homes instead of preventing the conditions that brought them there.

Some people, in search of quick payoffs and instant cures, have come
to mistrust the scientists' long years of step-by-step basic research. Some
may consider this "test tube" research impractical, without directed goals
and not tied closely enough to human health needs. In reality, research can
be people-oriented and practical.

Breakthroughs in discovering the causes of the devastating brain diseases
which are responsible for the majority of institutionalizations in later years,
followed by effective diagnosis and prompt treatment, could reduce the nursing
home population. If we released even 10 percent of admissions, we could cut
institutional costs by $1 billion annually (Butler 1977a).

American industry spends 3.2 percent of its net sales on research and
development (Butler 1977a). In 1977, the Federal government spent an estimated $24 billion on health services to the elderly, but only invested two-
tenths of 1 percent of this amount on aging research (Butler 1977a). Therefore, the Task Panel on the Elderly concludes:

> There must be a major national effort to promote and
> support accelerated research on the single most ter-
> rifying mental health problem of the elderly--organic
> brain diseases. Additional funds must be earmarked
> to intensify research in medical schools, hospitals,
> and research institutes on these dread diseases which
> are so costly in terms of human anguish and health
> care expenses. Further, the National Institute on
> Aging, the National Institute of Neurological and Com-
> municative Disorders and Stroke, and the National In-
> stitute of Mental Health should be directed to con-
> tinue to conduct and support such research. This ef-
> fort should be coordinated by the National Institute
> on Aging.

Implementing Agency

DHEW - National Institutes of Health with the National Institute on
Aging as the lead agency.

Estimated Costs:

First year - $5 million and 3 positions
Fifth year - $50 million and 25 positions

A well thought-out program, phased in over a 5-year period, would make
the most efficient use of available resources. The panel believes that every
tax dollar spent on aging research will return to us--and to our children--a
thousandfold.

ALLOCATION OF RESEARCH RESOURCES

The study of aging is not just the study of decline, loss and decre-
ment--which do indeed accompany aging--and it is not just the study of disabilities which may in part be due to social adversities. Rather, it is the
study of the normal processes of development which are fundamental to life
and about which we know precious little. Research leading to a greater
understanding of the normal aging process and the diseases which afflict
the elderly must be included in the scope of existing research programs.
Some research priorities are listed below:

> Systematic research on the normal mental and emotional
> development of the elderly is needed. The later stages

of adult personality development and life cycle have
been neglected in past investigations. Valid and reliable normative data on behavioral, mental, and emotional
functioning are needed to dispel many of the myths about
the elderly. Such data will increase the quality of research on dysfunctional behavior and pathological mental
processes. Psychological and behavioral problems such
as alcoholism, drug abuse, suicide, sexual difficulties,
and depression also need to be researched in relation to
their special significance for the elderly. Specialized
treatment techniques can then be developed and assessed.

In this country there has been a general upward trend
of suicides over the years. In 1975, there were approximately 27,000 recorded suicide completions and an estimated 216,000 suicide attempts (Frederick 1977a). The
elderly consistently account for about 25 percent of all
reported suicides (primarily because of the very high incidence rates among elderly men) (Cohen 1977; Frederick
1977a). Research, prevention, and treatment studies and
personnel training must be included in the Forward Plans
of the National Institute of Mental Health and other
health agencies. In this instance, it may not be the
elderly alone who will benefit from such studies in spite
of their high suicide rate. The younger age groups have
shown marked increases in both committed and attempted
suicides over the past two decades (as high as 200 percent increase since 1955) (Frederick 1977b).

Nutritional research should be increased. At present,
scientists, physicians, and lay persons have no adequate
nutritional guidelines for the elderly. This is especially disturbing since poor nutrition has been shown
to cause a reversible brain syndrome that may be misdiag-
nosed as senile dementia. Research also needs to be done
on the economic, social, and psychological factors which
influence the eating habits of the elderly.

Existing evidence on the effects of age suggests that the
body's capacity to defend itself against challenge declines
in almost direct proportion to the age of the experimental
animals. It is now necessary to undertake detailed exploration of the immune system in elderly human beings
to determine whether their loss of immune competence
follows the pattern observed in rodents. Investigations
will also focus on whether this decline in resistance to
disease can be slowed.

It is a common clinical observation that sensitivity to
drugs and the degree of adverse reaction to even small
doeses of therapeutic drugs tend to increase with age
for reasons which thus far remain unexplained. Given the
fact that Americans over age 65--who comprise 11 percent
of the U.S. population--use 25 percent of all medications
prescribed (Besdine 1977), the need for attaining
a better understanding of the reactions of older individuals to pharmacological agents is among the foremost
priorities in research on aging.

The elderly use prosthetic aids to compensate for sensory
and motor losses and to maintain vital processes such as
cardiovascular function. The use of advanced technology

that has been developed in recent years for military, astronautical, and industrial purposes should be explored for applications which will compensate for the physical losses suffered by the elderly. The National Institute on Aging should coordinate with the National Aeronautics and Space Administration to conduct animal studies and clinical trials to further explore the possible development of prosthetic aids for the aged which will reduce the need for institutional care.

Various forms of nervous system impairment account for the majority of admissions of older people to hospitals and nursing homes. Some mental disorders are actually due to other causes such as poor nutrition, pneumonia, excessive medication, and anemia, and are therefore reversible. Other disorders involve irreversible damage to the nervous system. Research on the causes, prevention, and treatment of these disorders could result in significant economic benefits to society and prevent much suffering on the part of afflicted individuals and their families.

Demographic and epidemiologic studies must be conducted routinely to improve our identification of populations in need and to enhance our ability to allocate limited resources according to need and potential benefits.

Despite demonstrated gaps in ongoing research and documented need for research training and services designed to maintain--and if necessary, improve--the mental health of the aged population, relatively little is being done. Approximately 3 percent of the total NIMH budget is set aside for research, training, and services designed for the elderly (Butler 1975). The panel believes that this country cannot continue to pour out money for treatment of an ever-increasing number of elderly and not attempt to plan its research and prevention spending so the needs of the elderly are taken into account. Therefore, the Task Panel on the Elderly concludes that:

The Secretary of Health, Education, and Welfare and the Office of Management and Budget should independently reexamine how existing Federal resources are being spent-- with special attention to NIMH and NIA--and to increase or reallocate such resources available in research, training, and mental health services for the elderly proportionate with their current needs and the needs of the larger future populations of elderly.

Our Future Selves: A Research Plan Toward Understanding Aging

Our Future Selves, Summary Reports: Panels on Biomedical Research, Behavioral and Social Sciences Research, Research on Human Services and Delivery Systems of the National Advisory Council on Aging 1978, Department of Health, Education and Welfare, Washington, D.C.

Biomedical Research

The goal of biomedical research on aging is to prolong the useful and active lives of the elderly and to raise the quality of their lives. That can be accomplished if we understand the normal process of aging, the nature of diseases common to the aged, and the sources and remedies for many of the painful disabilities suffered by the aged.

The major systems within the body may lose their functions at different rates, depending upon the genetic blueprint and environmental experiences of the individual, although evolution has insured that, for most individuals, these rates of failure are not so out of synchrony as to interfere with reproduction. One goal of biomedical research, then, is to characterize, for the various systems, the progressive loss of function that occurs as the human being grows older. We must discover how the basic biologic processes of aging predispose people to a great variety of disabilities. In addition to more subtle and insidious infirmities, such as progressive loss of muscle strength, these disabilities include a striking array of major disease processes: arteriosclerosis (hardening of the arteries), the most common forms of cancer (skin, lung, and gastrointestinal tract), diabetes (the most common form), obesity, osteoporosis (loss of bone mass), osteoarthritis (chronic degenerative joint disease), benign prostatic hypertrophy (enlargement of the prostate gland), pulmonary emphysema, cataracts, depression, and senile dementia (mental deterioration).

Research on the biology of aging involves virtually all of the major ailments of modern man. However, the approach of investigators in aging research is unique: The emphasis is not so much on the specific disease process, but on the genetically controlled, time-dependent mechanisms that result in progressive changes in structure and function of the body, changes that are likely to set the stage for disease. Investigations must be carried out on many levels -- molecular cell, tissue, organ, organ system, individual, and population. Eventually, a detailed understanding should emerge of how some interactions between an individual's nature (his genetic endowment) and nurture (the environment to which he is exposed) result in premature senescence of the brain, while others result in premature death from the complications of severe arteriosclerosis or in disability from osteoporosis. It is hoped that means of retarding or preventing these processes in susceptible individuals can be developed.

In this report, the state of the art and priority areas of research in biological and medical aspects of aging are highlighted.

Biomedical research in aging may be usefully categorized into three major areas: basic biological aspects of aging (intrinsic aging), interaction of aging and disease, and interaction of aging and external influences.

Chair: Edwin L. Bierman, M.D., School of Medicine, The University of Washington, Seattle, Washington.
Co-chair: Harold Brody, Ph.D., M.D., Faculty of Health Sciences, The State University of New York at Buffalo, Buffalo, New York.

Basic aspects of aging that may influence investigations at various levels of biological organization include:

1) Genetics of aging.

2) Mutation and repair of genetic material.

3) Ability of cells to synthesize and maintain key molecular components.

4) Maintenance and integrity of cellular organelles.

5) Cell function and loss.

6) Physiological function and decline.

Studies on the interaction of aging and disease should, while focusing on specific diseases common to the elderly, attempt to resolve the classical dilemmas of "aging versus disease" and "aging plus disease," -- that is, distinguish changes due to normal aging from those due to disease and clarify the relationship of aging to the etiology, course, nature, and treatability of different diseases.

External (environmental) influences that interact with aging include:

1) Nutrition.

2) Drug metabolism.

3) Physical and chemical factors.

Because of their importance to biomedical research, special attention must also be given to:

1) Experimental model systems for study of aging.

2) Study of human populations.

3) Resources and training needs.

Although research in each of these areas is important, we emphasize a few in order to indicate areas of particular need and significance. Further details are available in the full report on biomedical research that has been prepared by the National Advisory Council on Aging and published by the National Institute on Aging (NIA).

Mechanisms of Aging

In general, physiological functions of an organism tend to decrease and deteriorate with age. Ultimately, this must reflect cellular involvement either within the organism's molecular or biochemical structures or its cellular organelles. Among these may be included DNA (deoxyribonucleic acid), RNA (ribonucleic acid), cell membranes, mitochondria, lysosomes, ribosomes, nucleus, and nuclear and cytoplasmic interactions. A clear understanding of the changes that occur with age in these cellular structures and processes -- an understanding that we do not have -- is essential to elucidating basic biological phenomena of aging.

The cell remains the foundation of biomedical research, and any investigation into its structure, genetics, biochemistry, and physiology must be given priority. Attention should be directed toward those factors which relate to the cell, its genetics, and the effects of experimental or natural alteration in any of its components on the life span of the cell. Studies of cell function and death are critical in providing a framework to answer the question of whether a loss of cells with age leads to a decline in physiological function, or, conversely, decreases in physiological functions result in cell losses. These questions are of great concern in considering the viability of several systems, such as musculoskeletal and connective tissue systems, central nervous system, gastrointestinal system, and endocrine system.

The concept of relating decline in physiological function with advancing years has received little attention, particularly at the systems level. What information is available is of questionable value due to deficiencies in experimental design and failure to engage in effective longitudinal studies. However, the natural next step beyond investigations at the cellular level is an appreciation of normal phenomena occurring within organ systems. Among the systems that have specific relevancy to aging are the cardiovascular, pulmonary, endocrine, and nervous systems. These account for a large proportion of death and morbidity within the aging population. The NIA must support research leading to an elaboration of normal aspects of aging in these and other systems so that a reasonable base line may be determined, against which disease processes may be measured under the auspices of disease-oriented institutes within the National Institutes of Health (NIH).

Since a basic objective of aging research in general, and gerontological biomedical research in particular, is to effect a significant increase in useful life span, the understanding of normal components of systems aging should be given high priority. In relation to this, basic research in exercise physiology should be supported to determine whether normally aging systems may be influenced positively to withstand the stresses of aging. If they can, the application of knowledge gained from research in this area could have major results in public health and social terms.

It appears that the immune system may be most promising, from both biological and clinical points of view, for the study of the process of aging. The immune system is intimately involved with the body's adaptation to environmental stress and change. Recent studies have established that certain normal functions decline with increasing age and that, associated with the decline, is the rise in immunologically related diseases, including autoimmune diseases, cancer, and antigen-antibody complex diseases. Considering the impact that immunology has had on recent concepts in medicine, it is essential that the normal range of immune activity be determined in relation to age and that studies in the restoration of declining normal immune functions be supported.

Interaction of Aging and Disease

The exponential increase in the death rate with age is necessarily associated with increases in the rate of development of a large number and variety of specific diseases. Indeed, some important diseases occur almost exclusively in the aged. Nevertheless, clinical research on many of these diseases has failed to consider the pathophysiologic changes that take place with aging, changes which so alter the organism that susceptibility to disease is remarkably increased.

Studies on physiological processes of aging and on the diseases of the aged have often been conducted by two distinct groups of investigators -- physiologists and clinicians. The physiologic studies are commonly surrounded by an aura of inevitability -- that irreversible, nonpreventable processes are being investigated, that differences found in different age groups or changes found in individuals as they age represent "normal aging." However, indistinguishable changes occurring earlier in life may well be classified as diseases. There has thus arisen an "aging versus disease" dilemma, which is commonly discussed but rarely investigated in depth. Some of the more obvious examples of this problem are the deterioration of glucose tolerance with age versus diabetes mellitus, the increase in blood pressure with age versus hypertension, and decreases in pulmonary function versus chronic obstructive pulmonary disease.

An integral aspect of this problem of aging versus disease is the definition of "normal" used in specific diagnostic tests. Despite the documented decline in function in many organ systems with age, standards of normality rarely take this age factor into account. In addition to the examples cited above, creatinine clearance (a test of kidney function) has had no clear-cut standards established for age. Even where some efforts have been made to take aging into account, studies have been carried out mainly on man, despite well-recognized, major sex differences in many physiological functions.

An equally important research problem might be categorized as "age plus disease." The expression of diseases (the symptomatology, physical signs, drug effectiveness and toxicity, prognosis) may differ substantially by age group. The characteristic expression of such diseases as hyperthyroidism and diabetes in youth and in old age may be so different that they appear to be totally different diseases. Investigation of the mechanisms of this type of age effect is also a major need.

Differences between the very old and the young adult are so spectacular that research comparing these age groups is almost guaranteed to produce large and statistically significant differences. The middle-aged are often neglected in clinical investigations; the tacit assumption seems to be that an adult "plateau period" exists. But there is evidence from physiologic studies of many organ systems that decreases in organ function begin in early adult life and are progressive throughout the life span, sometimes (but by no means always) accelerating in very old age. An example of this failure to appreciate the progressive nature of age changes is the recommendation in some textbooks of medicine that diagnostic standards for glucose tolerance tests are valid to age 50 but need to be adjusted after that age. Research on the middle-aged must be included if the aged person is to be fully understood. Furthermore, the middle-aged person is biologically different from the young adult and needs to be studied for his own sake.

Among the diseases associated with aging, a number should receive high priority, and research on several diseases that are already the focus of programmatic commitments by specialized institutes should be expanded. The NIA is in a unique position to support research emphasizing the role of intrinsic aging in the interaction of aging and disease. While all such processes cannot be named, those of particular clinical significance include senile dementia, cerebrovascular disease, cardiovascular disease, prostatic disease, menopause, renal diseases, endocrinopathies, osteoporosis, osteoarthritis, chronic lymphatic leukemia, breast cancer, hematologic disease, and response to infection.

External Influences and Aging

Nutrition appears to affect aging, as well as exerting profound effects upon growth and development. While early dietary practices may affect longevity, the adult diet emerges as a factor in such age-related diseases as artherosclerosis, diabetes, and biliary tract disease. Until more basic information regarding nutrient metabolism with age is obtained, there will be no rational basis for nutritional recommendations for the elderly. This is a critical area since so many government-supported programs relate to nutrition in the older age group.

Resources and Training Needs

Among other areas that require special attention because of a critical relationship to biomedical research, development of programs to support resources and training needs should be given immediate and high priority.

Centers. Because of the complex subject matter of gerontology the individual gerontologist working independently in his laboratory is at a disadvantage. Gerontology is of only peripheral interest to his parent institution, the enormous expense of maintaining appropriate resources and of providing proper training for pre- and postdoctoral personnel is, at best, extremely difficult to overcome, and the opportunities for collaboration between laboratories are minimal. Furthermore, the opportunity for researchers in aging to be inspired by the work of highly regarded investigators in related fields is also held to a minimum. Regional centers for biomedical research on aging should be organized so that the multidisciplinary talent needed to investigate this problem can be utilized most effectively. The objectives of such centers should be to centralize talent, to provide the accessibility to unique resources, and to offer the mechanism for relevant training.

Resources. There are three general categories of resources, any one or more of which could exist in its own right or provide the basis for appropriate research programs as part of a center. One such resource consists of geriatric human populations. Mechanisms should be developed so that such populations can be encouraged to participate in programs of gerontologic research. For example, many public and private hospitals, nursing homes, and homes for the aged would undoubtedly be interested in and available for collaborative studies with researchers in the field of aging.

In addition, a patient population with specific age-associated diseases is needed for medical-school or hospital-based research. Cohorts of normal subjects are needed for long-term, multidisciplinary studies of aging. Cross-sectional studies, although faster and easier to conduct, may provide misleading information. Differences among age groups may not be attributable to aging per se, but to cohort differences, environmental changes, or survivor artefacts, whereby a select group of subjects survive. The availability of corps of healthy volunteers covering the entire adult span of life would provide a valuable and continuing resource. Just as the unavailability of aging experimental animals has hindered progress in biological gerontology, difficulties in recruiting human volunteers has inhibited clinical gerontology.

The multidisciplinary approach, especially in the study of human aging, is essential to answer certain types of questions. For example, recent studies on alcohol and aging required the collaboration of clinical gerontologists, physiologists, pharmacologists, biomathematicians, and experimental psychologists in order to design a study on the distribution kinetics, metabolism, and effects of alcohol in man. Another example of the need for a multidisciplinary study team and of the longitudinal research strategy is the need to understand the mechanism underlying the rise and fall of serum cholesterol from the early to middle to late adult years. The interactions of such factors as obesity, inactivity, dietary habits, and decline in glucose tolerance and attendant endocrine alterations in these age changes need clarification.

In addition to population studies, studies in depth using representative research subjects can best be carried out in specialized facilities, such as the existing Clinical Research Centers. For purposes of aging research using human subjects, support for the maintenance of a viable Clinical Research Center program should be encouraged.

A second general category of resources needed for aging research is colonies of experimental animals, the most popular of which are rats and mice. Largely through NIA efforts, it was established that colonies of aging rodents can be maintained reliably and reproducibly into healthy old age in an appropriate commercial facility; they can then be shipped to various investigators. However, the enormous cost cannot be met by most researchers. For example, there currenty are only two NIH-supported, commercially maintained colonies in the extramural program. These animals, plus the intramural colonies, are not sufficient to meet the demands either of investigators already committed to aging research or of those who have proposed relevant pilot experiments. Clearly, there is an urgent need to establish regional animal distribution centers if federal agencies hope to catch up with the interest in aging research generated in the last five years. In addition, support for the existing specialized nonhuman primate centers needs to be encouraged and developed, since aging monkeys bred in these colonies provide a valuable resource.

Distribution and availability of cellular models (such as standard fibroblast cells), although as expensive as animal models, have progressed further. However, two new directions of aging research based on cellular models must be recognized. One of these is the establishment of biochemical features that are intrinsic to cells derived from species of different life spans. The other concerns establishing banks of cells from individuals afflicted with genetic diseases related to premature aging, such as Werner's syndrome and progeria. These two new areas of work should inspire a further burst of interest in gerontological research. Resources must be available to meet the demand.

Training in biological aspects of aging. There are but a handful of highly regarded courses or lecture series on the biology of aging in the United States. These programs neither meet the current degree of national interest in the biology of aging nor provide adequate, well-rounded training for pre- and postdoctoral students who desire to enter the field. There is almost no mechanism for the established investigator outside of gerontology to focus his research on problems of aging and to consult with investigators in gerontology, except for sabbatical leave or a fortuitous relationship with someone currently involved in aging research. The rapidly growing interest in aging research outside of gerontological circles is evidenced by two symposia held by the American Association for the Advancement of Science on biological aspects of aging during the past three years, a feature conference in the biology of development and aging at the annual meeting of the Federation of American Societies for Experimental Biology two years ago, and the fact that the 1976 Gordon Research Conference on the biology of aging received applications from more than twice the number of people that could be accepted, many of them from people new to the field.

In order to meet this increasing demand, the following recommendations should be considered: (i) the availability of training grants related to basic research on the biology of aging, including laboratory work, formal courses, and lecture series or symposia; (ii) availability of pre- and postdoctoral fellowships specifically designated for study of the biology of aging; (iii) availability of career-development awards and special fellowships designated specifically for study of the biology of aging; and (iv) continuation of the NIA intramurally sponsored summer courses on the biology of aging and the pathobiology of aging.

Training in clinical aspects of aging. The research needs in clinical gerontology can be met only by developing new training programs. Biomedical research efforts on man must, of course, involve physician-scientists. The physician half of this dual personality may be a practitioner in any of the recognized specialty and subspecialty areas, but there is a need for internists who are specifically interested and trained in the problems of the aged -- that, the geriatrician or the clinical gerontologist. The one million long-term care beds in the United States, occupied almost completely by the elderly, are matched by only two formalized training programs in geriatric medicine.

There are very few centers that offer training for research in clinical gerontology. This discrepancy between need and supply is especially critical now, since an increasing number of medical schools, veterans' hospitals, and research centers are searching for persons to establish new, coordinated programs of aging research. The innovative training efforts needed might involve, for example, a five-year postgraduate program of internal medicine emphasizing geriatrics, clinical gerontologic research, and didactic work in a school of public health.

In addition to these postgraduate (or post-M.D.) programs, clinical gerontology should be introduced into the curricula of the health schools -- medicine, dentistry, nursing, and allied health programs. There is evidence that, as students progress through school, their interest in the aged declines. The reasons for this are in themselves subject to research so that corrective steps may be taken.

The training of basic investigators and clinicians has been discussed separately to emphasize the special needs of each group; however, there must be constant and ready dialogue between the two groups for truly significant advances in aging research to occur. The researcher gains an understanding of real, as distinct from theoretical, problems encountered in clinical medicine; the clinician, beset by day-to-day concerns in treating patients, is made aware of new advances of possible significance to him. It is through this mutual reinforcement by highly skilled professionals interested in the same goal but taking different routes that we will begin to understand and effectively treat many of the problems that plague the aged.

Behavioral and Social Sciences Research

Long life expectancy is a decidedly modern achievement. While the total population of the United States increased 2.5 times from 1900 to 1970, the number of persons ages 65 and above increased 7 times.

This trend is expected to continue. Persons age 65 and over now constitute about ten percent of the total population (about 22 million). Over the next 50 years, the proportion is expected to be between 12 and 16 percent. If zero population growth is reached within the next 50 or 60 years, there would be one person over 65 for every 1.5 persons under 20; the ratio is now one to four.

About one-third of the older population is very old, 75 years or above. This proportion will stay about the same for the foreseeable future if mortality rates remain constant. If they do, there will be about 12 million very old persons by the year 2000. If mortality rates decline, however, the number of very old persons may be as high as 16 or 18 million.

A 65-year-old man can now expect, on the average, to live to 78; a woman of 65, to the age of 82. By the year 2000, life expectancies for 65-year-olds may increase by another two to five years.

The gain in life expectancy during the twentieth century represents an achievement for modern industrialized societies, but it brings with it substantial changes in the society as a whole and enormous challenges for policy-makers. In oversimplified terms, policy-makers must consider two different sets of issues. One set arises from the fact that there are increasing numbers of the "young-old" persons in the late 50's, the 60's, and the early 70's who are retired, who are relatively healthy and vigorous, who seek for meaningful ways to use their time (either in self-fulfillment or in community participation), and who represent a great resource of talent for society.

The second set of issues stems from the fact that there are even more dramatic increases in numbers of the "old-old" persons in the mid-70's, the 80's, and the 90's. In this category, an increasing minority remain vigorous and active, but a majority need a range of supportive and restorative health and social services. The old-old of the 1970's also represent a disproportionately disadvantaged group. The reasons are several, including the fact that this population group contains immigrants who came in the early twentieth century, who were largely uneducated and unskilled, and who survived by taking jobs that established persons in American society did not want. Large numbers of adults suffered traumas during the depression from which many never fully recovered; and many did not build up sufficient equity in the social security system during their earning lifetime to adequately sustain them through decades of retirement.

Future cohorts of the young-old and old-old will have different characteristics. They will have been better educated, will have received better medical care, and will have been provided the now common benefits of the social security system. Their life experiences will have been markedly different from earlier cohorts of elderly persons; consequently, their expectations of life, including old age, will be different.

Chair: Bernice L. Neugarten, Ph.D., The University of Chicago, Chicago, Illinois.
Co-chair: George L. Maddox, Ph.D., The Duke University Medical Center, Durham, North Carolina.

The point is that programs suited to the young-old and old-old populations of today may not -- and probably will not -- apply to future cohorts. Our planning must take this into account.

We need, moreover, to understand the effects of the aging society on all our social institutions: family, community, labor force, educational, political, and economic. The needs for both basic and applied research in the behavioral and social sciences will become ever more pressing if we are to formulate enlightened social policies for both the old and the young, policies that are adequate both for the present and for the future.

The State of Knowledge

Some observers as early as the 1930's studied demographic projections and foresaw that the growth of the aged population would bring with it widespread changes in family structures, in housing, in patterns of work and retirement, and in needs for health and social services. But it was not until the 1950's that a significant number of scientists began systematic studies of behavioral and social aspects of aging as a set of complex scientific problems.

We do not yet have powerful theories in psychology, sociology, anthropology, economics, or political science to explain the behavior of the aging individual or changes in the aging society. Nevertheless, a number of generalizations based on research findings over the past two decades now seem warranted. Some of these generalizations have important theoretical implications for future research, as well as important practical implications for policy decisions. For example:

1) Chronological age in the second half of life is demonstrably related to increasing risk of decrement, morbidity, and mortality. Cross-sectional studies (those in which persons of different ages are compared) appear to exaggerate the decrements with age; but longitudinal studies (those in which the same persons are followed over time) may underestimate them. Selective attrition in samples used in longitudinal studies complicates the interpretation of findings. The best available data show, however, that the large majority of older persons followed over time do not decline markedly in intellectual and social competence until very advanced old age. Many social and psychological functions hold up well beyond the age of 70, although some functions may decline as early as middle age. Intellectual functioning is a case in point. Some of the observed declines in old age are probably more attributable to poor health, social isolation, poverty, limited education, and lowered motivation than to processes intrinsically related to aging. Where declines do appear, they occur primarily in tasks in which speed of response and integrative processes such as reasoning are critical. At least some of these declines can be compensated for by appropriate teaching methods.

2) The social integration of the great majority of older persons has been demonstrated in every society that has been systematically studied: That is, most young-old persons are engaged in a wide range of social roles and are active participants in the community, and most old-old persons are not isolated from family, from friends, or from neighborhood networks. At the same time, social isolation, age segregation, and inadequate social participation characterize substantial numbers of older persons, particularly the very old, in our own and other societies.

3) Neither the experience of crisis nor the response to it is uniform among older persons. This has been repeatedly demonstrated by research on life transitions and on crises of late life often associated with physical and psychological deficits or with the loss or modification of central life roles. Deleterious effects that do occur seem to be significantly modified by the timing of the event in the life cycle, by earlier styles of coping behavior, and by the social resources available to the individual. It has become clear that chronological age per se is a relatively weak predictor of adaptation patterns.

4) Illness and disease often occur in individuals who have experienced a series of psychologically stressful events, a fact particularly pertinent to an understanding of illness in old age. It appears to be the stressful events, not age per se, that are the critical factors. To the extent that the effects of such events can be ameliorated by education, counseling, and the provision of various intervention programs that provide social supports, patterns of aging can be altered and improved.

5) Studies of development in late life, and studies of development generally, have shown the importance of environmental variables and personality characteristics in understanding behavior. In many instances, it appears that environmental variables that have influenced the individual early in the life cycle are of major importance in later life; for example, level of formal education is related to social and psychological competence in old age. We need to know a great deal more, therefore, about the significance of both environmental and personality factors as they affect physical and mental health in old age, and we need to know more about how to measure such factors. In particular we need to distinguish age <u>changes</u> from age <u>differences</u>. With improved methods and data sources, investigators can now begin to pinpoint which of the differences between younger and older persons are attributable to the effects of aging (maturation) and which are attributable to differences between cohorts (groups of persons who were born at different points in history and who therefore have had different life experiences).

6) Among members of a birth cohort, variability in biological, psychological, and social characteristics does not decrease with chronological age, at least not until the very end of life. Related to this fact, there are multiple life-styles and multiple patterns of successful aging. One important implication is that, if we are to improve the quality of life for older persons, public policies should provide a wide range of options with regard to housing and living arrangements; opportunities for work, education, and leisure; and health services and social services.

7) There is a positive, but not exact, relationship between the physiological state and the social competence of the individual. The extent and nature of this relationship is not yet clear, nor is the possibility that changes in both physiological state and behavior stem from some underlying set of processes (for example, genetic factors or social factors).

8) Modern industrial society has the resources to maintain adequate income for older persons and to finance essential services for those who need them. The willingness to allocate resources in behalf of older persons is primarily a sociopolitical issue involving cultural values, national priorities, and principles of equity. While competing claims of different age groups for scarce social resources have not yet led to conflict, they might do so in the future.

9) Social and professional concerns with death and dying have increased in recent years, partly because the process of dying can be partially controlled by modern technology. These concerns have been based upon personal and humanistic insights and have prompted various clinical, educational, and research programs designed to assist seriously impaired and dying individuals and their families. Associated with these concerns are the emerging medical, legal, and ethical issues regarding the definition of life and the prolongation of life by technological means.

Research Support

Except for minimal investments by private foundations in past years, research in adult development and aging has been largely dependent on federal support. In recent years, NIH has been the most important single source, including the Adult Development and Aging Branch, which was formerly part of the National Institute of Child Health and Human Development and which in 1975 was incorporated into the NIA. In large part, NIH support generally, and NIA resources specifically, have been directed toward biomedical research. Agencies such as the National Institute of Mental Health, the Social Security Administration, the Department of Housing and Urban Development, the Veterans

Administration, and the Administration on Aging have contributed to behavioral and social research on aging, but the contributions of these agencies have tended to emphasize primarily applied and policy-related research and evaluation. As the problems of our aging society become more apparent, both basic and applied research need to be expanded; and both biomedical and social-behavioral scientists need to be encouraged to turn their attention to this field.

Research Areas of Greatest Promise and Need

1) Dependency -- social, economic, and physical -- is a major problem for the very old and for the young who care for them. Research is needed on how such dependency can be reduced and prevented. The problem is complex, and should be approached from several perspectives.

Increasing numbers of older people are retiring from productive roles in the work force, in spite of demonstrated competence to remain productive. If the numbers of older people continue to increase, and if the growth rate of the total population continues to decrease (as a result of declining birthrates), the cost of public income-maintenance programs for retired persons will probably rise, particularly in the decades after the year 2000. Research should be directed, therefore, to the development of accurate demographic projections of the population and of the work force. A related need is research on the development of forecasts of the costs of income-maintenance programs; health, housing, and welfare services; and tax rates on individual and corporate income. One research priority is to develop appropriate models for simulating the economic and social outcomes of alternative arrangements for the provision of income and services. Such studies will help clarify alternative social policy options with regard to the social and economic welfare of older people.

Societal concern is growing about age discrimination in employment and in other social opportunities. Functional criteria of competence, particularly work competence, need to be developed, as do programs aimed at demonstrating how those individuals who wish to remain economically productive can do so. Moreover, research is needed on how the conditions of work may be reorganized toward the same goal. Particularly important are studies of values and attitudes of both young and old persons with regard to work and leisure.

Research is needed on the factors involved in an individual's decision to retire, on the retirement process, and on the effects of retirement patterns on the wide society. Studies should be focused on such factors as health, economic status, personal preference for work and leisure, and social and economic constraints on labor force participation. Studies are also needed on the social, economic, and political effects of retirement on society.

There is insufficient understanding of the cumulative impact of earlier life experience on the situation of the aged. Many problems that today are regarded as inherent problems of aging may actually be problems of the particular cohorts who constitute the present aged population. Thus, studies are needed that encompass the whole period of adulthood and late life. An obvious example is the impact of lifetime earnings on the economic status of the aged; another is the changing pattern of work and leisure over the adult life span. There are also more subtle influences of earlier adult experience: life crises and their management, the intermeshing of different social roles (in family, occupation, and community), the changing value patterns among the young and the old, their changing expectations with regard to the effects of aging, and the effect of negative stereotypes of aging on both young and old.

2) An individual's social competence is related to the degree to which he or she is integrated into the social life of the family and the community. What needs further exploration are those specific personality, social, cultural, and environmental factors that produce social competence and personal satisfaction in late life. Attention should be directed toward differences in attitudes and behavior between men and women, and toward subcultural variations, such as those based on race, ethnicity, and social class.

Anthropological research on patterns of aging in other cultures should also be encouraged, particularly in traditional societies, which are fast disappearing. Such studies will help clarify the significance of cultural values in influencing processes and patterns of aging; they will help to distinguish those psychological and social changes of aging that are common across cultures from those changes specific to our own culture.

3) Special attention should be given to research on family and kinship networks. Specifically, research is needed on intergenerational relationships, on the changing roles of women, on how family networks may be changing as social resources for the older person, and on the role of the family in maintaining the old-old person as a member of the communtiy. Such knowledge is critical in developing policies aimed at reducing the unnecessary institutionalization of older persons.

4) Research is needed on the relationships among psychological, social, and physical aspects of health in middle and late life and on how health is related to socioeconomic status, ethnicity, rural-urban residence, and other social factors. Investigators are giving increased attention to stress, its correlates and its consequences, and to factors that ameliorate negative consequences. The relationships among life satisfaction, illness status, perception of illness, and self-concepts should be studied.

Reactions to bereavement also need further study. Although most persons adapt reasonably well to such life events as retirement and widowhood, many do not. For example, there is evidence that widowhood is associated with high rates of morbidity. Little is known about the causal relationship between physical and psychological changes in widowhood or about the effectiveness of intervention programs.

Research should also be addressed to the effectiveness with which older persons utilize health services and related social services, and to how such utilization can be improved.

5) The life expectancy of women is considerably greater than that of men. Basic research is required in the behavioral and social, as well as in the biomedical, sciences to understand the observed differences and to improve the life expectancy of men. The different life-styles of men and women, the different stresses to which they are exposed, and other social factors that contribute to the greater morbidity and mortality of men must be investigated.

6) Careful studies should be made of what has been learned from "natural" social experiments, such as the Medicare and Medicaid programs, and their effects upon older persons, upon families, and upon the health care system. Parallel with such surveys, there should be limited social experiments with regard to the effects of (i) flexible or phased retirement; (ii) the creation of community-wide service corps of older persons; (iii) new educational opportunities for older persons, including not only the role of education in second careers and in meaningful leisure pursuits, but also the role of health education for self-care in old age; (iv) alternate forms of social and health services systems; and (v) effects of alternative physical and social environments on the well-being of older persons, including housing arrangements and the environments of long-term care institutions.

7) With regard to the problems of dependency in old age, we need particularly to understand how impairment is translated into functional disability, what social and biomedical factors are involved, and how the intellectual competence that is characteristic of middle age can be maintained.

Many aged persons show deterioration in their abilities to perceive and respond appropriately to environmental stimuli, abilities that are crucial to maintaining personal competence. Thus, studies are needed of stability and change in cognitive functioning, including memory, learning, intelligence, and perception, and of the physiological and psychosocial variables involved. Decrements associated with aging processes must be distinguished from decrements associated with environmental or disease factors; and factors that are subject to direct intervention should be identified.

Experimental studies are needed, not only to clarify age-related changes in performance, but also to assess procedures designed to compensate for observed deficits. Animal models may be particularly useful in developing hypotheses to be confirmed in studies of human behavior.

Research is needed on the psychopathologies of advanced old age and on the behavioral and psychophysiologic, as well as neuropathologic, factors involved. Such studies are now in the forefront of scientific activity and are likely to produce important findings soon.

Behavioral and medical interventions directed at the maintenance of intellectual functioning and at the prevention of the organic brain syndromes, or senile dementias, should receive high priority. Research of these types may be expected to stimulate the development of a clinical psychology and psychiatry of late life.

8) Studies should be carried out on the effects of various governmental and nongovernmental policies upon aging and the aged: For example, how do policies directed toward other age groups affect the aged, and vice versa? What is the effect of manpower and training programs on the employment of older persons? How do macroeconomic policies designed to stimulate the economy or to restrain inflation affect retirees? What are the effects on older persons, their families, and their communities of governmental policies related to housing, transportation, health care, and retirement? As the numbers of older persons increase, and as successive cohorts show different characteristics, research of this kind will be particularly important with regard to city, regional, and national planning in the next two decades.

Research Training

Research training in the field of aging is a critical need. The number of trained personnel with career commitments to research in aging is very small. Individuals should be attracted from adjacent fields, through such mechanisms as postdoctoral and other special training opportunities; and greatly increased numbers of students should be trained at predoctoral levels, both in single disciplines, where aging can form an area of specialization, and in interdisciplinary graduate programs focused directly upon aging. Perhaps an overly modest goal would be to increase the number of competent researchers in the next ten years by at least the same proportion as the increase in numbers of persons age 85 and over in the population -- that is, by nearly 50 percent.

Research on Human Services and Delivery Systems

The primary focus in this area of research is on methods for organizing and delivering services to people to assure availability and quality of care. Research on human services and delivery systems overlaps the biomedical and behavioral-social fields, which produce the knowledge directly or indirectly applicable to the provision of services to the aging and aged. This third sector of research is needed as a bridge between the biomedical-behavioral-social findings and the actual provision of services. It concerns itself primarily with measuring the magnitude of service needs in populations, the corresponding needs for and availability of the manpower and facility resources to meet those needs, the manner and extent of use of those resources, the ways in which service systems are organized and function, the kinds and content of services received, their quality and cost, and their outcomes in terms of people's well-being.

Research on human services and delivery systems is naturally oriented to practice settings and applications. Within this orientation, however, it encompasses both basic and applied research. It deals with all aspects of living: health, nutrition and food service, physical living environments, employment and other economic supports, the commercial marketplace, transportation, communication, social services, legal and physical protection, education, participation in the community, and spiritual well-being.

Pioneering research work has been done or is underway in the various content areas of human services. Study of options for providing continuity and coordination of services, including preventive and rehabilitative care and methods for organizing and financing services and service delivery systems, is needed to bring practical benefits to older Americans.

Current State-of-the-Art

An examination of public and private programs aimed at human betterment has shown that some of these programs fail because historical factors and culturally determined attitudes, beliefs, and values are not adequately studied or understood. Research has not yet given us adequate knowledge to design appropriate service organization and delivery.

Health

The organization of health resources tends to be mismatched with the patterns of illness and disability among older persons. Health care tends to concentrate on the specialized management of acute, episodic disease in hospital settings, which, in turn, are not linked with community-based primary, preventive, or rehabilitative care. This mismatch has become increasingly obvious, as in Medicare. The escalating cost of health care for older persons underlies a general, widespread sense of urgency in devising more efficient and effective health care systems. However, little is known beyond survey data regarding how well Medicare and Medicaid programs serve the needs of older persons (particularly subgroups within the aged population). It is not known what impact these programs might have on financing should they be expanded to include those related services necessary to sustain people in their homes or communities. Assuming that some sort of national health insurance plan will be enacted, research is needed to help design it.

Chair: Paul A. L. Haber, M.D., Veterans Administration, Washington, D.C.

Although only a minority of older people are free from chronic disease, the great majority continue to function in the community. The emphasis on avoiding institutionalization and on keeping frail and sick people in the community assumes, inappropriately in many instances, the availability of a family and community service that can be mobilized to care for the older person.

The aging require a variety of preventive health and social measures. The enhancement of their functional capacities must be one of the main goals of health care. Research and development in prosthetic devices, for example, must be matched with dissemination, in which research also plays a role. Paramount in research on health services delivery for the aging is the need for breaking new ground in both disease prevention and rehabilitation. Cost-benefit studies in both areas must be mounted, to be sure, but of even greater importance is the realization that prevention of after effects of disease may be of prime value. With respect to rehabilitation, again cost-benefit studies are important, but there is also great need for studies relating to motivation and dependency-creating programs. Some persons living outside of institutions require home care, which, to a substantial degree, is provided by relatives. Such care has been treated as though it has no economic cost, even though the cost of publicly financed home health care programs is demonstrably high.

Inappropriate placement of older persons in institutions reflects medical custom and the unavailability of other services and facilities, rather than a careful decision on the part of the older person or his family. Where home care programs are limited, institutionalization of an older person is often the only option available. Resurgent interest in family care of the aged is in part an emotional reaction to long-term care institutions and their negative connotations and in part a search for cheaper alternatives to the cost of institutional care.

Approximately five percent of the persons age 65 and older in the United States are in long-term care institutions, and another ten percent are considered very likely candidates for institutional care. Though excellent care is provided in many institutions, the long-term care industry has been seriously criticized. Long-term care facilities are all too often isolated from the more extensive backup services of hospitals, from community-based programs, and from major professional schools. Studies of utilization patterns of long-term care facilities have indicated that availability and utilization of services tend to follow changes in reimbursement mechanisms.

Mental Health. Available data reveal that mental health care resources are insufficient to meet the needs of the rapidly expanding older population. At least 15 percent of the population age 65 and older are in need of mental health treatment and are responsive to appropriate treatment techniques. Communtiy-based treatment centers, where they do exist, treat approximately two to three percent of those in need of care. Research is needed on whether mental health problems among the aged would be treated more or less efficiently if such programs were integrated into a comprehensive health service system.

Studies have shown that the provision of comprehensive community mental health services can substantially reduce the number of older people admitted to state mental hospitals; when institutionalized elderly patients are offered modern treatment programs, a significant proportion of them can be rehabilitated and discharged from the institution; and the provision of individualized treatment and activity programs can substantially increase the well-being of old people who remain in institutions.

Nutrition and Food Service. Studies of food consumption and nutritional status have indicated that the elderly eat less as they grow older and that their diets are frequently low in minerals and vitamins. The reasons have been cited as economic, lack of motivation, loss of mobility, changing health status, lack of information, food fads and quackery, and long-standing food habits. Further studies of services to improve the diet of older people are needed and might best be pursued as a component of broader investigations of delivery systems for health and social services.

Research in nutrition services has generally taken two forms: (i) efforts to describe and define nutrition problems of a specific population; and (ii) demonstration models for delivering nutrition services or testing new approaches. Anthropometric, biochemical, and clinical measures have been found to be effective and acceptable accompaniments of survey techniques; they may even enhance the acceptability of follow-up evaluation (a question that bears investigation since policy-makers are increasingly weighing costs of services against benefits).

Demonstration models in nutrition services for the elderly have been largely descriptive in nature, testing feasibility and determining costs. The major effort has been in relation to individual, home-delivered and group meals programs. As these programs move from the demonstration phase into established community services, research needs shift to questions of their appropriate utilization, manpower and training needs, quality controls, and impact on the client and the community. Other research is testing the effectiveness of various techniques to change the food habits of the elderly.

As part of preventive health services, models should be developed to test ways of incorporating more extensive nutritional counseling into health maintenance services. Nutritional assessments could be built into preretirement counseling, health screening programs, and industrial health services. Assessment methodologies, training needs, reimbursement mechanisms, utilization and referral patterns, and impact on client use of other health services should be explored.

Policy questions regarding public funding of home support services as alternatives to institutional care demand early answers. Research should focus on packages of services based on the needs of clients, considering shopping assistance, home-delivered meals, homemaker services, and nutritional counseling.

Finally, there is a need to evaluate nutrition services in institutions that care for the elderly. New techniques for monitoring the nutritional status of patients in hospitals, as well as in skilled nursing facilities, should be applied, along with well- d designed studies to establish standards applicable to the aged and to evaluate the costs of routine monitoring in long-term care settings. Models are needed to demonstrate nutritional rehabilitation programs, to measure their impact on patients' mental and physical functioning, and to identify appropriate staffing patterns and training needs.

Dental Health. Related to nutrition, with additional implications for general health and social well-being, are the twin problems of loss of natural teeth and greater need for dental care with advancing age. Further complications arise out of the importance of bringing dental health care to the patient who is homebound, institutionalized, or otherwise lacking in mobility. Even existing health care systems and reimbursement procedures rarely provide for dental coverage. Part of the problem of using mobile equipment to deliver dental care seems to be resistance by the dental profession.

The major strengths of the health care system in the United States are its diversity and high degree of specialization. In terms of the needs of older persons, however, the diversity and specialization entail some loss in treating the individual holistically. Consequently, emphasis has been placed on comprehensive, integrated service delivery systems. But research is needed to determine the actual effectiveness of integration: What degree of integration is desirable? In what forms? What impact will different forms of integration have on the dependence or independence of older persons? What resources will be needed? What cost mechanisms (cost sharing, third-party payment, and so on) would be most effective?

Physical Environment

Physical environments may either enhance and complement the quality of life for older people or restrict their opportunities for maximum independence and satisfaction. There is evidence that, for most Americans, old age is a time when choice becomes constricted, the environment narrows, and functional decrements press more and more with each passing year. Reduced morbidity and mortality are associated with housing built, especially for the elderly. The needs and conditions of older persons are multifaceted -- housing needs are linked to health status and conditions, and both, in turn, may be directly related to income. Service interventions, therefore, require linkage between medical, health, social, environmental, and other services. However, research and social experiments are needed to determine what services should be part of the housing environment or of accessible, "one-stop" centers.

Transportation

Transportation is often the factor in the physical environment that links the elderly person to the services, facilities, resources, and opportunities necessary for his existence. Studies of transportation systems indicate that the elderly depend on walking, which is limited by inadequate pedestrian accommodations and security. Studies also indicate that transportation is least adequate for the groups who need it most -- the physically frail, persons without relatives, minorities, inner-city dwellers, and the poor. Older persons have been shown to prefer adequate transportation to the clinic or hospital of their choice over moving to be near a facility.

The decline in ownership of automobiles in the older age groups is mostly a reflection of their income situation, but it is also influenced by decline in physical, psychological, and motor skills. This problem will become even more serious as automobile-oriented suburban populations age.

The need for improved transportation has been documented. So has the need for living environments that include services, facilities, and so forth. Still needed are research and social experiments to formulate and test other means of linking people and services (that is, home-delivered services of all types and new technologies).

Communication

Just as transportation links people to services and facilities, communication and information are essential to older persons in need of services. Research has shown that over half the services provided to clients by public social services are information exchanges of one sort or another; hence, some may be directly amenable to enhancement by telecommunication.

For the present aged, traditional face-to-face communication is very important, but this does not mean that other media are necessarily inferior. Symbolic transaction is not the sole component of human communication -- hosts of nonverbal or nonsymbolic signs and signals round out human communication. Research is needed to determine what mix of media can meet the communication needs of the elderly.

Social Services

A limited range of social services was made available with the passage of social security legislation. However, implementation of social services for the aged has received low priority. This is reflected in the limited interest of research, education, and training to develop and apply the knowledge required for service intervention and in the inadequate funding of both research and services.

Legislative attempts to increase the development of social services through revenue sharing and the new Title XX have not yet produced much. Research is needed to determine what social services are already available at the state and local levels, what additional services are needed, why states have not utilized revenue-sharing funds on behalf of the elderly, and whether revenue sharing or other alternatives are needed to increase or improve social services for the elderly.

Legal Services

Older persons are frequently unable to negotiate the bureaucratic maze of eligibility and entitlements; their personal freedom and control of property are subject to vagaries of the laws of guardianship, conservatorship, and involuntary commitment; and they are frequently the victims of crimes. Congressional investigations of fraud and quackery, credit problems, and the like illustrate the negative approach to the older person as consumer.

In the quest for adequate and effective legal assistance to the elderly, two types of research are needed: (i) basic research into existing statutes and laws relating to guardianship, conservatorship, and so on and (ii) demonstrations that address problems of entitlements.

Commerce

Among the many issues affecting the availability, adequacy, and utilization of services are those related to the mix of income and service strategies and to the development of service standards and licensure. It has been suggested that, if older persons were to receive sufficient incomes, the marketplace would respond to their needs by providing services. The marketplace shows comparatively little recognition of the older population, and, where it does, it is concentrated in a few fields such as health insurance, life and annuity insurance, banking services, travel, and housing. But most of these efforts have been directed at the more affluent aged. Recent and more rapid growth has been in the health care fields (health services, drugs, nursing homes), where there is major subsidization from the public sector.

The remainder of the commercial marketplace has failed to recognize the possibilities of the older market in terms of the design of consumer products (clothing, furniture, and so on) in which research can play an important guiding role.

Education

There are two issues in the area of education: (i) education for improving the delivery of human services to the aged and (ii) education throughout life as a human service to society. The first addresses the education of professionals and practitioners working for or with the aged. The second focuses on the ideal of continuing human development through the process of lifelong learning.

There is widespread documentation of the failure of the professions and the services to respond to the health, environmental, and psychosocial needs of the aging. The trend toward narrow technical and professional expertise and research needs to be halted. Greater emphasis needs to be placed on the whole person, on quality and continuity of care, and less on fragmented services.

There are a variety of questions that research should address. For example: Should gerontologic subject matter be introduced as a specialized subject area or be integrated into more generic subject matter? Should exposure be early or late in the education sequence, or in what combination? What mix of practical and didactic training is most effective? These kinds of questions apply across the board to all professions and disciplines -- nursing, medicine, social work, aides. There is a need to develop and test models for educating a variety of professionals and allied service personnel.

The main characteristic of research on adult education seems to be that there is so little of it. Review of literature and research articles reveal three general types of information: (i) "think" pieces reflecting policy and program development issues, as well as broad overviews of adult, lifelong, and continuing education needs and accomplishments; (ii) reports of successful -- although typically idiosyncratic -- case histories and individual programs; and (iii) demographic survey reports of people, programs, needs, accomplishments, and so forth. The Future Shock syndrome of rapid obsolescence combined with increasing amounts of leisure time has been reflected in the quantity and availability of continuing, avocational, and activity courses and programs.

In addition to continuing and avocational education, more attention must be focused on health education and consumer education. Lacking in all these areas are research efforts to develop appropriate training materials and social experiments to test the impact of training.

Social-Emotional Services

Maintenance of health in old age requires, in addition to essential economic and social services, sufficient recreational, educational, spiritual, vocational, and community service opportunities to assure a satisfying life. Retirement has become an accepted pattern in present-day society. This stage of life, with its extended nonwork use of time, has created new organizational arrangements -- that is, senior centers, special residential living arrangements, new components of social services, adult education for lifelong learning, and recreational, voluntary, and civic activities. The premise underlying attention to recreational, cultural, spiritual, and leisure activities is that they have important effects on a persons's well-being, sense of self-esteem, and mental and physical alertness.

Published materials are of uneven quality, although there is a miscellany of studies that are suggestive and useful. The individual's valuation of work and leisure relative to each other is more attributable to his personality and sense of accomplishment than to economic need and hardship. Thus, some people view leisure and recreational activities negatively, regarding them as frivolous. Accessibility to or convenience to public parks, movies, and sports events has been judged to be far lower for the old than for the young because of such factors as lower income, health problems, fear of crime, and transportation problems.

While some service programs have been developed and some demonstrations funded, relatively little research has been conducted in these areas, either because of low priority or because of limited resources. Yet the significance of these services increases, particularly with the growing number of older persons spending more years in nonwork. Research needs to identify ways to ease the transition from work years into retirement, emphasizing (i) continuity rather than crisis-oriented provision of services and (ii) the special problems of women.

Economic Support

While we search for the most appropriate combination of programs to provide quality care at the lowest cost, we must decide how these costs -- whatever they turn out to be -- will be financed. The social security system remains the major source of retirement income, replacing an estimated one-third to one-half of preretirement earnings. Private pension plans cover a minority of employees and fewer still retirees. Supplemental Security Income seems to be an improvement over Old Age Assistance, but little is known about why the projected increases in beneficiaries did not materialize, in view of the number of older persons living below the poverty threshold. Medicare, providing third-party payment of certain health costs, has obviously helped but is playing a decreasing role and seems to be most inadequate in the most serious area -- long-term care. Supplemental private health insurance still plays a minor role.

Except for economists in a few federal agencies (Social Security Administration and Census Bureau), there is little activity in the study of the economics of aging. Much can be learned by studying foreign social security systems and experiences. Study of the impact of growing early retirement, retirement income as a proportion of income just prior to retirement, and projections of future retirement income levels and adequacy are among priority research questions.

These issues in the economic sphere cry out for policy research that would take into account the significant demographic changes taking place, inflationary pressures, economic growth patterns, trends in benefit levels, equity, and national priorities.

Systematic Data Needs

The major difficulty in the study of human services and delivery systems is the lack of an adequate data base, both within and surrounding the service systems. While we know that services exist in most communities, we have inadequate information concerning the extent of such services, particularly in rural areas. Basic knowledge is needed -- what services exist, their adequacy, the gaps in services, the population groups and subgroups utilizing the services, and the extent to which services are utilized or not utilized.

Corresponding demographic and epidemiologic information about population subgroups is needed, along with the implications of such data for the upcoming aged, so that service needs can be anticipated and planned for.

Such information on an ongoing, systematic basis is essential for informed policy decisions and for underpinning much important research.

Suggested Areas of Research

In a summary report it is not possible to cover all the specific areas of human services delivery that need research. Priority areas of current and potential research include the following.

Delivery Process

1) What types of facilities, programs, and services are needed for the care of frail elderly in the community?

2) When is it desirable to integrate services? That is, what are viable mixes of general health, mental health, preventive, and rehabilitative, social, and legal services? What impact does integration of services have on patients? How does integration affect cost and efficiency?

3) What are the means for ensuring high quality of care and improved standard-setting procedures? How do we define and measure quality and outcome of care? How do we determine cost-effectiveness of alternative means of service delivery? How do we determine the relationship between type and quality of care and the impact on the people being served?

4) What are the appropriate roles of the various formal service sectors and of other social institutions such as kin, ethnic, and neighborhood groups and voluntary groups and agencies? How do these best interrelate to serve effectively?

Utilization of Services

5) To what extent do people use services? How has the extent of use been changing? What is the extent of use likely to be in the near future, given the current trends?

6) How would national health insurance coverage for health care and related services affect utilization? How are services to be financed? What types and numbers of manpower and facility resources will be needed?

7) What is the impact of attitudes of professionals and other service providers on services to the elderly and on the utilization of the services? What are the cultural, social, and ethnic barriers to access to and effective use of available services?

8) What are the means for ensuring equity of access to services and equity of services for all those needing them?

9) How and in what way do physical environmental factors benefit or hinder individuals in maintaining their maximum level of functioning?

Research Methods

10) What techniques and methodologies should be developed for evaluating the efficiency, effectiveness, and social benefits of services?

To overcome gaps in knowledge, we need reliable data, more accurate ways of measuring needs for an effectiveness of services, and ways of financing services. To successfully deliver services, imaginative solutions and social experiments must be applied to problems related to the institutions and individuals that provide and receive services.

Retirement

The Increasing Complexity of Retirement Decisions

Frank H. Cassell

MSU Business Topics, Vol. 27, No. 1, Winter 1979. © 1979 Board of Trustees of Michigan State University, Ann Arbor, Michigan. Reprinted with permission.

A tradition of long standing is undergoing change as workers opt out early or extend the usual worklife.

Two seemingly contradictory developments are influencing retirement decisions. The first is reflected in the amendments (effective January 1, 1979) to the Age Discrimination in Employment Act of 1967. The second is the growth of early retirement provisions in private industry, sometimes known as *Thirty and Out*, which were negotiated in the mid-1960s. Although private pension plan improvements appear to have led to lower retirement ages, the age 70 amendment, among other factors, may raise the average retirement age to 65–70, reversing the trend to early retirement.[1]

These developments are occurring in the larger context of a drop in male labor force participation of nearly ten percentage points in the years 1957–1977. Accompanying this general trend has been a drop of nearly twenty percentage points in labor force participation of males aged 60–64 — from 82.5 percent to 63 percent. Of possibly greater significance has been labor force participation slippage beginning as early as the 40–50 age bracket, declining to 75 percent in the 50–60 age group. In ten years the 60–61 age cohort slid ten percentage points, to 74.5 percent; 61–62 from 70 to 56 percent, and 64–65 from 48 to 33 percent.

More generous and expanded private pension coverage, Social Security retirement income, and more liberal application of disability payments explain much of the decline in male labor force participation, but there are other contributing causes. Among these are a rise in female labor force participation rates and the growth in multiple-earner families, an arrangement which provides the continuity of income needed to finance the cost to withdraw from employment and the time to search for more advantageous work or return to school and change careers.

The Age Discrimination in Employment Act prohibits employers from refusing to hire older rather than younger workers. Furthermore, pension plans and seniority may not be used to force retirement because of age. The new law prohibits mandatory retirement below age 70 for workers in private employment as well as in state and local government employment. There are some exceptions, such as executives or persons in policy level positions, and college professors.[2]

There are several reasons this matter comes up at this time. First, earlier retirement can be afforded by more people because more people are covered by private pension plans which are more generous and more fully vested than ever before. This is despite the inroads of inflation upon benefits. Second, there is increasing demand on the part of potential retirees to have greater choice in how they live their lives — whether to retire early or later; before age 65 or between 65 and 70; or to retire only part time. This may quite possibly be a spillover from resurgent individualism in the society and rising educational levels. Third, increasing numbers of older persons now have the political power to share in writing the rules which govern their lives. This is a sharp reversal from the past. Fourth, the public is concerned about rapidly rising costs of both public and private pensions. This is compounded by a sharp rise in

Frank H. Cassell is in industrial relations in the Graduate School of Management at Northwestern University.

benefits and eligible persons and by a desire to control such costs by retaining people in the work force.

This last expectation is realistic because many occupations which could be filled by older workers with high skills and extensive experience are going unfilled. Furthermore, 70 percent of employment is now concentrated in the service sector, and a substantial part of it is located in suburbs and small towns, close to workers' homes, and often is accompanied by flexible working arrangements such as part-time work, part-year work, and flexible hours and weeks. Such employment is peculiarly responsive to older workers' health and income needs and to employers' skill and flexible labor supply needs.[3]

Future conditions are likely to be no less favorable for older persons who wish to work. Young persons (16–24) in the labor force are expected to decrease sharply, by 3.4 million, between 1980 and 1990. The number of older workers should decline somewhat during that period. The shortage probably will be filled mostly from the anticipated bulge in the prime age group of persons born after World War II and by older persons who elect to continue work or reenter the labor force after 65.[4] This suggests that current projections of labor force participation for this group, which now show a decline, may have to be reevaluated in light of the new dynamics created by the age 70 retirement provision and the realities of demand for skills.

To retire or not to retire

The decision to retire early or late, to take advantage of a generous pension plan or of the new age 70 retirement law, is a product of a complex assessment of net advantage. This assessment involves a number of critically important issues. These include (1) comparative economic incentive to retire or to continue work; (2) health needs and benefits available and affordable both currently and after retirement; (3) financial resources to supplement private pensions and Social Security; (4) general level of unemployment or number of jobs, full or parttime, open to older persons; (5) quality of life desired or possible now or in retirement, including psychological and social needs; and (6) assessment of likely life-span.

Society has its set of issues, too: (1) What is a supportable beneficiary-worker ratio? Over the past 20 years this ratio has increased from 4.6 percent to 21.5 percent, that is, from one beneficiary per twenty workers to one per five workers. (2) Is too

much of the gross national product being allocated to the cost of benefits? In 1929, wage supplements, including pensions for time worked in private industry, amounted to 1.4 percent of total compensation. By 1972, such fringe benefits constituted as much as 40.3 percent of payrolls for large firms. Private pension plans now include almost 50 percent of workers. In 1975, companies contributed $20 billion to pension funds; employees contributed $1.6 billion. These amounts were up 157 percent and 79 percent, respectively, over the past eight years.[5] (3) Is retirement income adequate for retirees? Available evidence suggests that the higher the income before retirement, the more adequate will be the income during retirement. A recent Conference Board study showed that the median family incomes of retired managers surveyed was $20,600 annually after taxes, as compared to $7,298 (after taxes) for retirees from the general population.[6] To maintain income in retirement requires a replacement rate of about 80 percent of untaxed gross of a $4,000 annual salary and about 67 percent of a $15,000 salary. Most retired managers fall into the latter replacement rate catgory, although a surprising number receive less replacement income. A substantial percentage of retirees live close to the poverty level despite government supplements. Nevertheless, the number of aged in poverty was reduced from 38 percent to 16 percent in the period 1959–1974 as a result of high levels of employment and liberalization of Social Security benefits to bring replacement income up to tolerable levels. (4) Can we prevent loss of skills and productivity needed by society? As suggested earlier, lower labor force participation rates at both ends of the age scale and declining birth rates beginning in the 1960s deprive the economy of needed skills and talents.[7]

Companies, too, have interests in the retirement issue: (1) cost, which must be included in the price of the product; and (2) staffing policies, which may include early retirement to make way for younger middle-level executives or continuation of older workers in employment to supply needed skills and quality of performance which is often said to be missing in new entrants into the labor force.[8]

Private retirement plans

Before discussing the key issue of choice, it may be useful to review some general information. Between 1940 and 1974, workers covered by private retirement plans increased from 4.1 million to 29.8 million. Of these, 23 million are full-time workers,

16 million are covered by mandatory retirement plans, and 7.5 million are covered by multiemployer plans. The 29.8 million figure includes 44 percent of the privately employed wage and salary workers.

As to vesting, a recent Bankers Trust study reports that, between 1955 and 1969, vesting in conventional plans had increased from 74 percent to 99 percent. The higher the income level, the more liberal the vesting, and the more people covered. Among workers earning more than $25,000, 59 percent have vesting provisions, as compared with only 37 percent in the $10,000 to $15,000 salary bracket. The shorter the service, the less the vesting, as one would expect. Only 20 percent of workers employed five years or less by a particular employer are covered by vesting provisions, whereas 50 percent of workers with 20 or more years' service are covered.[9]

These data will change, however, with the effects of ERISA, which requires (1) full vesting for all accrued benefits after ten years of service; (2) 25 percent vesting after five years of service plus a 5 percent increase annually over the next five years, plus 10 percent annually for the following five years, or 100 percent in fifteen years; (3) the rule of forty-five — five years service granted 50 percent vesting at the point at which age and years of service combine to total 45; thereafter 10 percent of accrued benefits vested annually. This should enable a higher proportion of workers covered by pension plans to achieve a retirement income based on pension benefits.

Some groups and some people are covered less than others. For example, the highest retirement coverage is in communications and public utilities. The lowest is in retail trade and services. More male workers (52 percent) than female workers (36 percent) are covered by pension plans. The higher the skill and status in an organization, the more likely the person is to be covered. Tenure on the job is critical. Only 45 percent with ten years or less of service on the present job are covered by pension plans, while 70 percent with more than ten years on the present job are covered. The Conference Board study is instructive in this regard: 68 percent of the managerial retirees had thirty-one or more years service with the company from which they retired. One-half had worked for only two firms.[10] Continuity of employment with one or very few employers was the key to pension adequacy in the absence of portability.

Social Security

Today, 98 million persons are covered by So-

cial Security, up from 32.4 million in 1940. Beneficiaries in 1940 numbered 200,000 persons. Today, they number more than 31 million. Benefits for a couple have risen from $36.40 in 1940 to $312 in 1975. The replacement rate is about 43 percent. The tax increased from $30 annually in 1940 to $824.85 in 1975. (That figure is doubled when both employer and employee contributions are included.) An early retirement decision must take account of the fact that there is a reduction factor of .0056 per month in benefits each year prior to age 65, or a reduction of 20 percent at age 62. However, each year worked beyond age 65 increases benefits by 3 percent, or a total of 15 percent between the ages of 65 and 69. Furthermore, recent amendments to the Social Security Act are designed to keep benefits from losing value during inflationary periods. Benefit protection will be kept up to date with rising prices or in line with the standard of living of current workers.[11]

The retirement decision also is affected by earnings limitations on retirees who decide to work during retirement. An individual can earn $4,000 without a decrease in Social Security. This is scheduled to rise to $4,500 in 1979, $5,000 in 1980, $5,500 in 1981, and $6,000 in 1982. This determines how much labor the retiree can sell and at what price. (The specific problems of female retirees will not be dealt with here.)

Demographic trends

In 1900, those 65 years of age or older made up 4 percent of both the labor force and the population. Sixty-three percent of men over 65 worked. Since then, life expectancy has soared; by 1977, the same age group composed nearly 10 percent of the population. Because of public and private pensions and shifts from farm to city they still constitute only 4 percent of the labor force. The 63 percent of men over 65 in the labor force had plummeted to 25 percent by 1977. The implications of these data are that people have better health, live longer, and retire earlier, which suggests potential for growth in labor force participation by people above age 65.

Life expectancy in 1900 was 46.3 years; by 1970 it had risen to 70.9 years and is now well above that figure — an increase of nearly 25 years. Something new, however, has been added — several years of retirement which did not exist in 1900. More recent data suggest that persons retiring at age 65 have a likelihood of living 13 years or more (as of 1977, TIAA-CREF annuitants have a life expectancy at age 65 of 21 years for women, 17 years for men). Thus, a net advantage calculation requires planning around the uncertainties of economic conditions, political climate, and life itself over longer periods. Each additional year of expected life-span increases planning uncertainty.[12]

In this connection it is useful to keep in mind the educational aspect of demographic changes. First, the withdrawal of older workers from the work force will increase the educational attainment of the work force. Second, the rapid increase in educational achievement of the younger part of the work force will begin to affect their choices regarding continuing education, work, and leisure in the 1980s as well as their quality-of-life expectations both before and after retirement. Third, the inverse relationship between unemployment rates and education suggests a further connection between education, income or employment continuity, and health, which interact and affect the work or retirement decision in ways not fully measurable, but noticeable. That is, those who can afford education and health care, compared to those who cannot, seem to have a better chance for (1) continuous employment, (2) high income, (3) wide experience, (4) adequate pensions, and (5) skill acquisition, all of which afford such individuals a substantial range of choice, including a longer period over which to exercise such choice.

Two pieces of evidence support this generalization. First, male labor force participation of the 55–64 age group increases with years of school completed. Second, recent declines in male labor force participation affected most heavily those men with eight years of elementary school or less, and affected least those with four years of high school or more (see Table 1). One could expect that as the 55 and older age groups receive more highly educated persons and lose the less educated, these groups will become more competitive and increase their labor force participation — unless, of course, incentives to leave the work force are increased.

Net advantage

From an employee's standpoint, a starting point in calculation of net advantage is replacement of income and maintenance of personal living standard in retirement. A key consideration is the ability to compensate for the rise in cost of living. Although the Social Security Act provides certain protections against inflation, private pension plans generally do not include cost-of-living escalator clauses.

Inflation takes a severe toll of real income. A 5

percent rate of inflation over five years decreases real pension income from 100 percent to 78 percent; a 10 percent rate over ten years decreases the purchasing power of the pension to 39 percent. Thus, most retirees achieve protection against deteriorating real value of their pension mainly through Social Security. High income persons, whose chief retirement income is a mixture of company pension and investment and savings income, also find themselves lagging behind inflation, in part because Social Security, which provides protection against inflation, is so small a part of their income, and in part because investments, stocks, and savings income have generally not kept pace. An exception to this may be investments in housing and land.[13]

If a person decides to retire early, that is, before the normal retirement age of 65, which is permissible in many pension plans, there are two deflators. The first is a reduction of 20 percent in Social Security benefits if the individual retires at age 62. The second is an actuarial or negotiated reduction of the private pension plan for each year of early retirement. If one then projects a 15-year life expectancy at an annual inflation rate of 10 percent, the deflated pension would be worth only 24 percent of its initial value. The influence of continuing inflation on retirement decisions may already be in evidence. Information is beginning to accumulate which suggests that the retirement age in the steel and other industries may be rising again, after a long decline.

TABLE 1

LABOR FORCE PARTICIPATION RATES FOR MALES AGED 55–64

Years of school completed	March 1962	March 1973	Decrease
Elementary: eight years or less	83.9	70.9	13.0
High School: four years	90.6	84.9	5.7
College: four years or more	93.8	87.0	6.8

SOURCE: Howard Hayghe, "Marital and Family Characteristics of the Labor Force in March 1973," *Monthly Labor Review* 97 (April 1974): 22.

Obviously, all individuals attempt to estimate their own longevity and assure themselves that they will not outlive their resources — thus the concern over loss of pension value. At the same time, they also try to maximize their satisfactions in work and leisure after retirement.

Such individuals have several options.

1. They can continue to work to age 70, maximize their income, and invest savings at from 5.5 percent to 8 percent, perhaps higher. In many large firms their pay might also be linked to cost of living adjustments. The delay time to retirement will increase their Social Security benefits. Their firms may hike pension benefits to match the rise in the cost of living, but this is not a high probability. Had they retired at 62, 63, or even 65, their pension payout level would have been frozen as of the date of retirement. Working to age 69 is thus some protection against a high rate of inflation and an opportunity to increase income from savings and Social Security.

2. Workers can, of course, retire early at age 65 and use their savings, if they have any, to supplement retirement income from parttime work. However, few middle or low income families achieve a savings rate needed to replace even as much as 50 percent of retirement income. This is especially true of the 50 percent or more workers in private industry who are not covered by pension plans, have little or no savings, and depend primarily upon Social Security. Most people do not have sufficient capital to draw on during retirement. Average net worth of retirees is about $2,400, exclusive of nonfarm home equity.

3. A third option is to retire at 65 or earlier and supplement pension and Social Security income by using skills and experiences acquired during employment. Early retirees (before 65) often are willing to risk reduced Social Security and pension benefits to capitalize on their skills, health, and vigor to establish a small business or to engage in parttime work. In other instances, however, they wish to escape work-a-day frustrations, tensions, and unfulfilled aspirations and seek a better life, autonomy, and even new job and career opportunities. The Conference Board study of retirement of middle and high income executives found, not surprisingly, that many retirees do indeed have transferable and needed skills plus the resourcefulness to make use of them. Their retirement occupations ranged from engineering consultant to tree farmer, real estate broker, nursing home operator, and so on. In contrast, at the bottom end of the occupational and income scale, retirees who lack skills become merely a part of the labor pool which includes young workers, for whom there is also too little work and too much unemployment.[14]

Quality of life

For many high income persons, retirement is the means for giving greater or more varied meaning to their lives. For them, options for what one can do with one's life seem to enlarge.[15] In contrast, at the low income end of the scale, income from work often is necessary to supplement income such as Social Security. For such persons, employment opportunity has lessened, and options for allocating one's time have shrunk.

One is bound to be concerned about maintaining living standards in retirement. As suggested earlier, current income is compared with future income, both of which are affected by inflation and deflators in different ways: individuals' present jobs, the work they are doing, the satisfactions they get out of it; whether they are in dead-end or "shelf" type jobs or ones in which individuals feel they are genuinely needed and are making a contribution as compared with other possibilities.

Additional considerations include shifts in interests and values, and a desire to change one's life-style. This could include greater autonomy in deciding how to live one's own life, the kind of work one does, the hours one works, and even the kinds of compromises one makes. Often these factors are decisive in terms of allocating time, whether the choice be full or parttime retirement, becoming self-employed, or engaging in leisure activity.

Adaptations in retirement

There is the matter of anticipating the length of retirement. Each additional year of life increases costs in retirement, which arise mainly out of increases in health and medical costs, despite the availability of Medicare and Medicaid. In addition, the fixed nature of pensions (except Social Security benefits), especially in inflationary periods, means the pension loses value at the very time of increased need. Furthermore, the amount of supplemental income which can be generated by employment is subject to changes in the health of the individual.

On the one hand, the decision to continue working or to retire may be related to the demand for one's skills and one's physical capacity to supply them. The price (wage) may be so attractive that the worker may feel it is worth more to sell those services than it is to retire. On the other hand, the decision to continue working full or part time may be based simply on income need. This is especially true for persons who have earned low incomes, who may not have accumulated rights to a pension, and who receive a minimum Social Security retirement payment. For individuals who have health problems, part-time retirement (Social Security plus part-time employment) may be the only way to maintain an income without overtaxing their health.[16] In short, people attempt to maintain both the economic and qualitative aspects of life as nearly as possible in the transition from work to retirement and during the retirement years. But both income and health are crucial to the availability of choice, that is, how individuals divide their time between work and leisure, among various kinds of employment (paid or unpaid) and varieties of leisure activities, and where these activities take place.

A further consideration concerns the person's own adaptation to retirement. This, of course, may be a matter of definition. One can be retired from a firm or government agency and work for someone else or be self-employed. Some persons never regard themselves as retired, even though they collect a pension. They see themselves as being as busy as ever. If not paid work, they may undertake volunteer work, which occupies a substantial amount of time of upper income persons and much less of lower income persons. Experience suggests that people who have acquired substantial skills during their working life and who have continued to keep their minds active are likely to be adaptable, capable of switching careers, using their skills in new ways, transfering them when necessary, and applying experience in effective competition with younger persons.

The higher people are in the occupational hierarchy, the greater the chance they have to use their skills to continue working or to engage in volunteer work. Associated with this is the reality of health. Higher income people are generally able to afford better health care over a lifetime and have greater ability to sustain vigor into retirement. Thus the outlook in retirement for persons at the upper end of the income scale tends to be more optimistic than for persons at the bottom. This is true despite government efforts to provide a floor below which public pension payments cannot fall.

From age 65 to age 70

Raising the normal retirement age to 70 introduces a new set of dynamics. Will the private employer encourage or discourage work beyond 65? There are a number of possibilities. (1) Employers could encourage workers to continue beyond age 65. This would depend on management's percep-

tions of the value, productivity, training costs, and scarcity of the skill possessed by the individual in comparison with others and flexibility of the firm's internal retirement rules. There is some evidence that urban service employers will substitute older, trained, and high productivity workers for young entrants into the labor force because of expected lower productivity of the young people. This may occur especially in clerical occupations.[17] (2) The employer, depending on the firm's rate of growth, could encourage retirement or job change before 70 or 65 among executives in order to make way for younger talent and improve college recruiting. In such cases, it is likely employers would develop more rigorous evaluation mechanisms to supply the rationalization for dismissal well before the normal retirement age and protect the firm from charges of age discrimination. (3) Employers who wanted to accommodate both needs — greater mobility for highly talented employees and high productivity at all levels — could devise means to use the abilities of retirees in productive and innovative ways, providing pay were properly geared to alterations in the difficulty of the work. This could provide the means for accommodating both the interests of the organization and the needs of the potential retiree.

The costs of continuing individuals on the payroll or of retiring them must be balanced. This involves factors such as the productivity of individuals, the cost of continued payments into pension funds, and the maintenance of health insurance coverage between the ages of 65 and 70.[18] People who work to age 70 will probably have fewer years of retirement and pension payments than will those who retire at 65 or earlier who receive more and smaller payments. There are, thus, offsetting elements of cost.

Retention or retirement also may depend on the state of the firm's development: growth, no growth, or retrenchment. In a growth situation it may be necessary to retain or recruit older persons with scarce talents and skills in order to maintain important operations of the firm while it is growing in other directions. Training costs would be low or nil. In a condition of stability, the need for increased productivity becomes critical, and the productivity of older persons needs to be balanced against that of younger persons. Retrenchment suggests the encouragement of retirement — and perhaps early retirement. Some firms cope with skill shortages by rehiring their retirees as independent consultants or contractors to perform tasks that cannot be filled internally or from the external market without a substantial training investment.

Given substantial uncertainty about what is likely to happen to them over the next ten or fifteen years of their lives, retirees are confronted with extraordinarily difficult planning decisions and the need to provide for the contingencies of retirement. This is true of companies, too, as they decide whether to retain people on the payroll or encourage them to retire.

Research needs

From a research standpoint, we know too little to enable us to make retirement decisions with equanimity. As a nation, we do not have the experience or family structures of older societies which have evolved means for their older workers to adapt gracefully and usefully to retirement. Our policies have been heavily influenced by the desire to achieve administrative efficiency and maintain a competitive business edge, and to an extent by negative stereotypes of older workers held by young administrators and, for that matter, much of society. The United States is unlike Japan, where skills have been developed to ease the transition from work to retirement so that people can maintain their sense of self-worth, perform useful tasks, and be respected. We are frozen at the cost-effective stage at which economic trade-offs are the mode of analysis, and we are just beginning to examine the possibility of increasing the quality of choice in these areas.

Expanding the range of choice increases the number of considerations which enter into making a choice. It also increases the need for research to understand better what is involved.

Choice for the individual is widened by improved health, prolonged life, increased adequacy and variety of income sources, continuous learning, a widened range of leisure activities, and the presence of second earners in families. At the same time, family instability, separation, divorce, death of a partner, mobility of the offspring, tenuous intergenerational connections, and persistent high unemployment for the lesser skilled, minorities, and women all seem to limit the choice for many people in the matter of work, leisure, and retirement. What are the elements which establish the range of choice? What combination of elements operates as a tipping point — to retire or stay at work?[19]

In particular, how do the tendencies on the part of women to become more established in the work force affect family decisions about retirement, as against maintenance of income in light of infla-

tionary conditions? Does this increase the flexibility of men's labor market experience? Women's?

Other questions deserve attention. For example, to what extent is choice about work or retirement affected by the sectoral shift from production of goods to provision of services (which is associated with suburbanization of industry, greater opportunity for flexible hours of work, and less physically demanding tasks)? To what extent are individuals aware that their range of choice is affected by decisions made by or for them at an early age? For example, this would involve acquiring a specialized skill which would enhance early employability but also early skill obsolescence. There also is the matter of leaving school for the sake of immediate income. Furthermore, frequent job changes may or may not enhance the individual's long-range job viability, depending upon the transferability of the skills acquired and the pattern of the experience acquired.

Choice among opportunities involves deciding in some manner — through cosmic consultation, or careful assembly and analysis of data — net advantage among alternatives. To what extent is information available to make this determination? What kind of framework is needed — the reality of internal organizational opportunities and constraints; perception of external possibilities; a forecast of things to come with respect to income flow, health, and employment expectations, and personal resources which influence opportunities, realities, and health?

Use of older workers' skills, as mentioned earlier, may be advantageous to the firm. Some research studies suggest, however, that young managers have negative perceptions of older workers. What are the realities of their performance? What are the source and validity of managers' stereotypes of ability, personality, and performance? How prevalent are they? To what degree is holding such a stereotype disadvantageous to the firm? Do such perceptions change with the law, such as extension of the retirement age to 70, or with shortage of labor? If so, in what manner do perceptions change?

What, for example, do we know about continuing to work and mental health or longevity? Would the effects vary, in part, according to the kind of work performed, or the balance of work and leisure?

Finally, and by no means exhausting the research needs in this field, there is the question of whether wiping out the certainty of an arbitrary tirement range, perhaps 60–70 or 55–70, would encourage better and earlier anticipation and planning by both the employer and the worker to take advantage of options inherent in this flexibility. What would change? Or will the exit rules vary from time to time according to the social cost society is willing to bear, or its willingness to enlarge the number of taxable units by increasing births and keeping older persons in the work force and spreading the costs accordingly?

1. In the auto industry, average retirement age is 59, with 30 percent of workers retiring after 30 years of service. The age in steel is somewhat higher — about 61–62 years. The steelworkers have concentrated on higher pensions for those retiring later (age 62 and over).

2. The act does not prohibit age-mandated retirement between ages 65 and 70 for tenured employees of colleges and universities until 1 July 1982. Application of the new retirement age provision (under certain conditions) also is not required for employees covered by collective bargaining agreements in effect on 1 September 1977, until that agreement terminates or until 1 January 1980, whichever occurs first. Finally, it does not apply to persons employed in executive or policy-making positions who are entitled to an employer-purchased pension, exclusive of Social Security, of at least $27,000 per year.

3. Part-time work of employed men increases rapidly after age 59 (2 percent), to 4 percent at age 60, 28 percent at age 65, and 53 percent at age 70. See Philip L. Rones, "Older Men — The Choice between Work and Retirement," *Monthly Labor Review* 101 (November 1978): 5.

4. Howard N. Fullerton, Jr., and Paul O. Flaim, "New Labor Force Projections to 1990," *Monthly Labor Review* 99 (December 1976): 3–13.

5. These data should not obscure the fact that the capacity of the work force to support these social responsibilities is likely to be greater rather than less in the future. The average number of nonworkers for every 100 people in the labor force is expected to drop from about 125 in 1975 to 111 in 1990. Ibid., p. 7.

6. "The Productive Retirement Years of Former Managers," Conference Board Report, Table 1, p. 3, 1978.

7. An underlying logic is contained in the fact that the 8.1 million growth in the labor force in the 1980s will be concentrated among the 35–44 age group and will result in crowding and intense individual competition for jobs which could lead to shoving older workers into lesser jobs or into encouraged early retirement. This growth may also result in the downgrading of some in the 35–44 age group, who would then compete with younger workers for lesser jobs. The rapid rise in cost of fringe benefits, to nearly 40 percent of payrolls of large firms, together with minimum wage requirements raise a broad societal issue, namely, the employment of untrained youth. Such costs often lead to a shift of employer hiring preferences to segments of the work force — women and older workers who are trained — who are expected to be more productive.

8. Employers frequently make the point that the generation that lived through the depression has a better work ethic than do younger workers. This may or may not be true; it may be nostalgia or a yearning for a work force that does what it is told to do.

9. Robert Clark, *The Role of Private Pensions in Maintaining Living Standards in Retirement*, National Planning Association, 1977, p. 24.

10. Conference Board Report, p. 42, Chart 4.

11. Projections show that benefit payments as a percentage of payroll will not exceed 11 percent until after the year 2000. The matching amount from employers would be 5.5 percent, less than .5 percent more than the present contribution rate.

12. Neil W. Chamberlain and Donald E. Cullen, *The Labor Sector* (New York: McGraw-Hill, 1965), p. 27. The figures were brought up to date using the TIAA-CREF 1977 Annual Report, p. 5.

13. The most important income for about half of the managerial retirees is a company pension; 95 percent list this as among the first three sources in importance. Investment income is the next most important source. Conference Board Report. For the lowest income families, however, asset income accounted for only 4 percent of their total income, whereas Social Security furnished more than 80 percent. Clark, "Role of Private Pensions," pp. 16–17.

14. These comments omit reference to workers in skilled crafts, and the like, who may have the best chances of adapting and finding work because of demand for their services.

15. Conference Board Report, pp. 36 and 37. The report contains a remarkable series of insights into quality of life in retirement as defined by high income retired managers. A comfortable retirement income finances this quality.

16. The new beneficiaries data indicate that those older persons who have had poor career earnings (and thus low levels of retirement benefits) are most likely to find it necessary to continue working. Persons who were partly retired had considerably lower levels of primary insurance amount from Social Security than did those either retired or not retired. Rones, "Older Men," p. 6.

17. A study by the Chicago Urban League of Chicago public school graduates entering employment in 1973 showed that employers had to supply both formal and informal training of a substantial and extended nature to prepare them for beginning clerical jobs. Employers often assign such work to their own retirees on a contract basis, thus avoiding search, training, and benefits costs. The volume of such activity may increase in 1982 when Social Security recipients can collect full benefits, regardless of earnings, at age 70 (instead of 72).

18. Proposed Department of Labor guidelines, in requiring that older employees have the same total benefit protection as younger workers, recognize that most medical expenses for persons over 65 normally will be paid by Medicare. (Washington, D.C.: U.S. Department of Labor, 1978). A report to employers with pension plans on the effects of the Age Discrimination in Employment Act concluded that upward adjustments in funding were not likely to be needed for pension funds to account for additional older workers retained beyond age 65; cost effects on death benefits should be minimal; medical expense plans coordinated with Medicare coverage might be less severe than originally anticipated; but long-term disability plans extended beyond age 65 might have cost implications and, thus, require redesign. *Mandatory Retirement in Perspective*, (Chicago: Alexander and Alexander Services, Inc., 1978).

19. Research on retirement decisions seems often to have been based on a ranking of factors which may elicit a socially acceptable response rather than one which reflects what the potential retiree really prefers. Recent research on

worker job preferences focuses on the job (and the situation as a whole) as the means for reducing the influence of social desirability. In one such study it was shown that a very few cues (factors) really entered into judgment or rating even when a much larger array of cues was available to the rater (worker or potential retiree). Moshe Krausz, "A New Approach to Studying Worker Job Preferences," *Industrial Relations* 17 (February 1978): 91–95. Such research would, of course, need to relate the realities surrounding individuals' lives at the age they are responding to the inquiry in comparison to a range of scenarios which portray life at a later age, after an initial retirement action. These realities include options such as retirement, full or parttime work, leisure, or some combination including income and living conditions.

The Patterns of Retirement

Larry Smedley

AFL-CIO American Federationist, Vol. 86, No. 5, May 1979. © AFL-CIO,
Washington, D.C. Reprinted with permission.

The Age Discrimination in Employment Act (ADEA) amendments of 1978, signed into law in April 1978, prohibit mandatory retirement prior to age 70 for most private employees. Collective bargaining agreements are exempt for the duration of a current contract or until Jan. 1, 1980, whichever comes first.

Estimates of the impact of the law vary—from claims that the resulting retention of older workers will be a major factor in solving the economic burden of a growing retiree population to assertions that the legislation will have a minimum impact. The law also will affect hiring, promotion, personnel policies and fringe benefits—traditional concerns of collective bargaining. Sufficient information is available to attempt some general observations as to the impact in a number of them.

Employment is the key issue and the major test of the law's impact is how many workers will now stay on the job after age 65. One of the main arguments in support of abolishing mandatory retirement before age 70 was that it would retain large numbers of productive workers in the labor force, thus substantially reducing public and private expenditures for retirement benefits. The data indicate the potential for achieving this objective is small.

There are approximately 8.3 million Americans between the ages of 65 and 70 and only 1.6 million of them hold jobs. Most of those not in the labor force retired voluntarily long before the age of 65 and, in the absence of vastly improved economic conditions, are not going to re-enter the labor force. In any event, bad health prevents many of them from working.

Social security first began paying actuarially reduced benefits in 1961, permitting men to collect benefits at age 62 instead of age 65 if they were willing to accept permanently reduced monthly benefits. More men retired on reduced benefits than on regular benefits during the first year. The proportion of early retirees has constantly increased so that now roughly two-thirds are retiring on social security before age 65. Social security surveys show that more than two-thirds of them do so for two reasons—poor health and layoffs or discontinuance of jobs — and only a very small number because of compulsory retirement prior to age 65. Social security research has tended to center on men rather than on all social security retirees because the retirement patterns of married women are influenced by factors not common to most retirees.

One of the best sources of data, the Social Security Administration's survey of newly entitled beneficiaries, was most recently made between 1968 and 1970. Of the total retirees in the survey, 30 percent said their most recent employer had a compulsory retirement policy. Two percent of them reported a compulsory age below 65 and 6 percent stated age 70 was the age for mandatory retirement.

Of the total group subject to mandatory retirement, or 30 percent of the sample, roughly 13 percent voluntarily retired before the required age. Of the remaining 17 percent, 7 percent retired at the required age and 10 percent were still at work—many of whom would retire in the future prior to the age of mandatory retirement. About one half of the 7 percent said they had wanted to retire at the age of compulsory retirement. Thus, only about 4 percent of the total were forced to retire against their wishes. If half of the 10 percent at work were similarly affected, then only 9 percent of the total group was involuntarily forced out of the labor force. This survey provides a good basis for gauging the impact of the prohibition against mandatory retirement prior to age 70.

*LARRY SMEDLEY is the associate director of the AFL-CIO
Department of Social Security. This article is taken from a paper
he presented to an April 1979 industrial relations seminar.*

These results have been confirmed by two other surveys—the Parnes or National Longitudinal Survey and a 1968 survey of social security beneficiaries by James H. Schultz, a Brandeis University professor. The Parnes survey was based on an eight-year study of a sample of males 45 to 59 first interviewed in 1966, then in 1967, 1969 and 1971. The final interview took place before any of them reached age 65. But even though they were then aged 50 to 64, 14 percent had already retired by 1971.

Thirty-two percent of the total sample reported employment covered by a compulsory retirement policy. Only 8 percent of them stated they wanted to continue working at their current job. Thus, this study indicates that about 8 percent of workers would continue to work and be affected by a prohibition against mandatory retirement prior to age 70.

Schultz's study indicated that 46 percent of his sample of social security beneficiaries were in jobs subject to compulsory retirement and about 25 percent of them voluntarily retired prior to age 65. Of the remaining 20 percent, 7 percent willingly retired and 10 percent were forced to do so. Of the 10 percent forced to retire, health conditions would have prevented 3 percent of them from working even if they had not been forced to retire. Thus, only 7 percent of the group subject to compulsory retirement would have been affected by its prohibition prior to age 70.

Johnson & Higgins, an employee benefit consultant firm, has just released a nationwide survey on attitudes toward pension and retirement conducted for them by Lou Harris and Associates. The survey was based on interviews with two separate samples—a national cross-section of 1,699 current and retired employees and a representative cross-section of 212 employers. Included in the survey were questions relating to preference for employment among retired employees. Twenty-two percent of the sample indicated they "would have preferred to continue to work full-time at the same job for the same pay as long as possible, instead of retiring." This percentage is considerably higher than from other studies.

The large percentage of the total retirees (22 percent) who were presumably forced to retire prior to age 65 seems unusually large, but there are several possible explanations for this difference. The survey indicated that the median age of retirement for retirees surveyed was 60.6. The social security, Schultz, and Parnes studies were made on the basis of retirement prior to age 65. Thus, it is likely that many individuals in the Johnson & Higgins survey group would have retired by age 65 and another significant number would have developed health conditions and retired by that age. Studies have indicated that compulsory retirement prior to age 65 was rare and only an extremely small percentage of retirees were forced to do so prior to that age. The small sample of 391

retirees on which the Johnson & Higgins survey is based may not accurately represent all retirees.

The Johnson & Higgins study also indicated that large numbers of workers would like to continue working at jobs other than the full-time job from which they retired. It's not likely this group—largely seeking part-time work—will secure work when the job market is tight for all. Such efforts will work only in a favorable economic framework. The most important factor in increasing labor force participation of older workers is a full employment economy, not abolition of mandatory retirement.

The U.S. Department of Labor did a "quick" study of the effect of the elimination of mandatory retirement prior to age 70 on the size of the labor market at the time the legislation was under consideration by Congress. This study estimated the total labor force would increase by approximately 200,000 older workers over the next five years. Marc Rosenblum of the National Commission on Employment and Unemployment Statistics used a labor force participation trend model to ascertain the law's impact. His estimate was essentially the same as that of the Department of Labor. Thus, two studies, totally independent and using different analytical approaches, reached essentially the same conclusions.

An increase of 200,000 older workers during the next five years is very small considering a civilian labor force of approximately 100 million—an increase of about two-tenths of 1 percent in labor force participation. The maximum possible impact—assuming that total unemployment among all workers would rise by an equal amount—would be a 0.2 percent increase in the unemployment rate. This is highly unlikely since other vulnerable groups—youth, women, minorities—are not likely to be qualified to replace many or most of the older workers. In any event, the probable impact on the size of the labor force and employment is extremely small.

The best available evidence indicates a very small impact on labor force participation by workers age 65 and over as a result of the passage of the new law. And, the social security, Parnes and Schultz studies, all based on data about 10 years old, may even overstate the impact since the early retirement trend has accelerated in the past 10 years. In any event, if roughly accurate, the results do provide a basis for judging the impact of the legislation not only on labor force participation and employment but also for judging its impact in other areas as well.

Social security funding will not feel a major impact from the new law because the number of workers who will remain at work is much too small. Social security actuaries estimate that the savings resulting from the reduction in benefit payments and increased contributions (excluding Medicare) will total about $1 billion for calendar year 1984. Benefit payments (excluding Medicare) are projected in the 1978 trustee's report to total about $165 billion for the 1984 calendar year. Thus, the expected increase in the labor force resulting from the new law will not reduce program costs sufficiently to permit any significant reduction in social security cost estimates and scheduled tax rates.

A major concern has been the impact of the new law on pension and fringe benefit costs. The law does not require employers to continue accruing pension benefits for workers in defined benefit plans after the normal retirement age. Even if benefits accrue after normal retirement age, the savings realized by the period of nonpayment of benefits will operate to offset the increased costs resulting from continued benefit accruals. Whether this will represent a cost increase or decrease depends on the individual plan but, in any event, there is not likely to be either a significant cost or saving. Similarly, a defined contribution plan, which is not a supplemental plan, can discontinue contributions to the worker's retirement account after the normal retirement age. Defined benefit plans, which cover about three-fourths of all pension participants, specify that a certain number of dollars or percent of salaries will be paid in benefits. Defined contribution plans provide whatever level of benefits the contributions can "buy" for the worker at the time of retirement.

The law recognizes that certain fringe benefits costs are more for older workers and allows benefit reductions for "actuarially significant cost considerations." The Department of Labor issued proposed regulations on the new law in September 1978, but the Jan. 1, 1979, effective date has come and gone without final regulations being issued. But while awaiting final action, we can assume the proposed regulations will be very close to the final ones adopted.

The cost of these regulations will affect employers in different ways depending on their employee fringe benefit package. However, the regulations are clearly designed to minimize the cost impact of the law by allowing benefit reductions for workers over 65 to roughly equalize benefit costs so that the actual cost incurred for older workers is equal to that for a younger worker. In short, the law is not likely to result in significant increases in employer fringe benefit costs.

Collective bargaining agreements can be expected to experience a similarly small impact. As pointed out earlier, the data indicate relatively few employees will want to continue working. The early retirement trend is less subject to change than the normal retirement experience because so many who retire early do so because of health reasons, layoff or discontinuance of jobs.

Among employees who have greater options in their retirement decisions, the pension is widely considered to be a primary factor in the decision to retire. The surveys indicate a strong correlation between re-

tirees who want to retire and higher levels of retirement income. The social security study found that workers with a second pension in the age 62 group were 2.5 times more likely to want to retire than those with only a social security benefit. Workers covered by collective bargaining tend to have the better pensions and thus the number who want to work beyond 65 will probably be even less than shown by the surveys mentioned earlier.

This assessment is supported by surveys of top employers and personnel officers responsible for achieving the objectives of the law. A Conference Board survey of 41 personnel officers, all representing major U.S. firms, found the law would have only a slight impact on most company operations. The Bureau of National Affairs, Inc., in a similar survey of a majority of members of the American Society of Personnel Administrators, concluded "most employers appear to have little concern about the prohibition against mandatory retirement before age 70 and anticipate that the effect of the 1978 amendments will be relatively minor."

However, though not having a major impact, the law will probably influence collective bargaining situations in a number of ways. For example:

● Unions will object to any attempts by employers to stop accruals of pension benefits for employees after age 65, or efforts to reduce fringe benefit protections.

● Employers will resort to greater use of medical examinations or performance evaluation procedures for older workers. They will also tend to place greater emphasis on job descriptions specifying in greater detail the skills and requirements for satisfactory performance. These are not new collective bargaining issues but the number of grievances involving them will probably increase.

● Unions and employers will negotiate "sweeteners" to a greater degree than in the past to encourage workers to retire before age 70.

All the previous assumptions are for the short run and the factors on which they are based could change over the long run. Some experts are predicting the growth of the American labor force will peak around 1980 and slow dramatically after that. Beginning early in the next century, the baby boom group born after World War II will be reaching retirement age. As a result of the low birth rates of recent years, there will probably not be enough younger workers to replace them. Thus, some experts are predicting a chronic labor shortage in the future which will result in more hiring and retention of older workers.

Inflation may cause more older workers to remain in their jobs. Only a very small number of private pension plans automatically adjust benefits in accordance with increases in the cost of living. Thus inflation should be a deterrent to early retirement since there must be great concern among potential retirees about erosion in the value of their pension benefits. Yet, nothing like this seems to be happening. Social security actuaries have not observed any recent significant change in the patterns of early retirement within the social security program. But, if high inflation rates continue and potential retirees come to believe that inflation is a permanent and not a temporary feature of the economy, many more of them will likely work beyond age 65. Similarly, any increase in the age of eligibility for social security benefits would have a significant impact on the labor force participation of older workers.

So since the prohibition of mandatory retirement before age 70 will have little effect on the labor force participation of older workers, adaptation to the new law should not be difficult. But there may be some specialized problems. And the longer run impact may be more significant.

An Evaluation of Mandatory Retirement

Harrison Givens, Jr.*

Reprinted from An Evaluation of Mandatory Retirement by Harrison Givens, Jr. in volume no. 438 of THE ANNALS of The American Academy of Political and Social Science. © 1978, by The American Academy of Political and Social Science. All rights reserved. Reprinted with permission.

ABSTRACT: This paper discusses the issues raised by mandatory retirement, the meaning of the new law, the law's specifics, and the uncertainties still ahead. The new law, prohibiting mandatory retirement before age 70 in the private sector, and altogether for most federal employment, is in form an amendment to the Age Discrimination in Employment Act of 1967, or ADEA.

The pros and cons of mandatory retirement at any fixed age are reviewed, including the changing financial and demographic considerations affecting the retirement decision. The paper then discusses the likely effects of mandatory retirement on employees and employers and on the composition of the work force. About 90 percent of both men and women have in recent years retired before age 65, and those few working to age 65 have generally stopped well before 70. Nevertheless, the sure opportunity to work to 70, and a developing perception of the great erosion of financial security caused by continuing substantial inflation, may well lead to significant shifts in retirement decisions. Uncertainties arise from the independent operation of state laws and the likelihood of extensive dispute requiring judicial resolution.

*Harrison Givens, Jr., Vice President and Actuary of the Equitable Life Assurance Society of the United States, heads the Group Pension Marketing Services Department. A Fellow of the Society of Actuaries, he is also a charter member of the American Academy of Actuaries and an Enrolled Actuary. Mr. Givens is a Director of the ERISA Industry Committee and a member of the pension Committees of the American Academy of Actuaries, the American Council of Life Insurance, and the National Association of Manufacturers.

THIS PAPER will consider the issues raised by mandatory retirement, the meaning of the new law, the law's specifics, and the uncertainties still ahead of us, in as objective and as nontechnical a way as possible.

President Carter signed the new law on April 6, 1978. It came into being rapidly— astonishingly so, to many people. Its prospects were generally considered minimal as late as last August, and then in September, the House passed it. With a little delay the Senate passed it; there were then some months of agonizing, difficult reconciliation on two obscure points, and finally the compromise bill. It is in form an amendment to another law ten years old—the Age Discrimination in Employment Act of 1967, or ADEA. That law said, briefly, that you must not pay attention to age in employment for those who are between the ages of 40 and 65.

WHAT ARE THE ISSUES?

Now, what are the issues? In favor of mandatory retirement, there are these points: First, that it is really humane. The premise here is that a large percentage of people really do run out of steam noticeably some time in their 60s but that it is much nicer not to say so. With mandatory retirement, you can say: "How are we going to get along without you? But you are 65, and you know the rules, and it is a shame." This is much better than telling Joe he can no longer hold down his job and has to leave, and having everyone know why he has to leave.

Second, under mandatory retirement, employees can plan ahead. The older employee is on notice that his working career will be over on a fixed date, and that there is no escaping it. And the younger employee can see more clearly when the path ahead will be opening up for him. Third, the employer can plan ahead: he can arrange for an orderly succession and avoid inadequate staffing or overstaffing. Fourth, unemployment is high enough now. Leaving older people in jobs will prevent or delay opening up those jobs to younger people already employed and, in turn, by a multiplier effect, open up many more jobs at the starting level for new entrants to the labor force.

Finally, the affirmative action implications: the people you are trying to bring into the labor force in special numbers—the women, the minorities—will be the ones that have to wait. The type and distribution of people who are in their 60s will be staying on, rather than being replaced by different distributions of people you are trying to bring in now at the commencement of their careers.

There are, of course, arguments against mandatory retirement, either at any time, or at least at age 65. First, some people say mandatory retirement is unconstitutional. It would be hard to argue that the people who wrote the Constitution thought that there should be no mandatory retirement. But perhaps, with our greater sophistication and insight, we know better than they did what they meant to say—or, at least, what they would have said if they had been as enlightened as we are.

Second, it may at least be immoral or, what passes for immoral these days, unpopular. We can agree that in the last decade or two there has been an increasing sensitivity to distinctions. It's been said that we have eliminated racism and sexism, and that we are now eliminating ageism. We have unisex clothes and unisex haircuts. Is it equal opportunity we want, or sameness of result? How far shall we go, without becoming neo-Procrusteans? In the case of mandatory retirement, as Harold Sheppard notes in his article, half the general public favors the right to work after age 65—the right to work, the choice. Indeed, half of those who retire early favor the right to work. Is the glass half full or half empty? It could also be said that half the general public does not favor the right to work; that half of those retiring early do not favor the right to work.

Third, there is surely a problem in forcing someone into retirement with an inadequate income. Half the population now is covered by pension plans, but half is not. The people who are forced out with only Social Security and with inadequate private savings are in a financial bind. One would expect that they would prefer the opportunity to keep on working, particularly with the frightening experience in the last few years of substantial, prolonged inflation. Even those with adequate pensions at the point of retirement have suffered a vicious depreciation of purchasing power with inflation. As people increasingly perceive that situation, they will be more reluctant to retire.

Fourth, why 65? Why not 70? Why not some older age? The Social Security law started the 65 custom in this country and that, in turn, came from the social insurance scheme in Germany set up by Bismarck 100 years ago. To be fair to Bismarck, however, and to show his prescience, he set retirement at age 70, and it did not go down to 65 until 1916. But age 65 is arbitrary. Even if it was right in 1935, maybe today, because there has been some improvement in mortality, it is not right. In 1935, people had roughly the same life expectancy at age 65 that they now have at about age 68.

Fifth, compulsory retirement may adversely affect health. It is common to see obituaries of people who died a year, or two, or three after retirement. People notice this; they rarely notice the people who died before retirement or many years after retirement.

Sixth, the act of retirement, voluntary or involuntary, may hurt one's health. This is very likely true; any major change affects health. One interesting study assigned point counts to various traumatic events in an individual's life—the death of a spouse, the marriage of a daughter, promotion, change in location, change in job—all of those events, good or bad, that significantly affect an individual's life produce stress. The study suggested watching stress points: if a person changes jobs and cities and his wife has just died, it is not the time for retirement.

Of course, to retire does not neces-sarily mean becoming a vegetable. One can work elsewhere, either on a compensated basis or on a voluntary basis. The voluntary basis would be feasible if an adequate pension income were available.

THE DEEPER ISSUES

Those are the arguments typically heard for and against mandatory retirement. There are deeper issues. First, private pension plans, which help make the transition to nonearning status more attractive, are not growing. Indeed, about 20 percent of the defined benefit plans that existed in 1974 have since been terminated. The enormous federal regulation introduced in 1974 as ERISA—with the best of intentions —has clearly been the dominant cause. More attention must be paid to encouraging private accumulation for retirement, which provides security for the future retiree and capital for business investment today.

Second, if people can and do retire later, the faltering Social Security system would be helped. It will mean benefits starting at a later date, resulting in paying fewer benefits. It will also mean more revenue for Social Security from those employees who retire later as they continue to pay taxes on their salaries.

Third, age affects the body sooner than the mind. We seem to be increasingly what Peter Drucker calls a class of knowledge workers: We are really not on the farm any more; we are really not doing much physical work—machines have taken over a great deal of that; we are using our minds more. Nevertheless, some fear that, although the older worker may be as capable, he has a higher mortality, a higher disability: the worker who is 80 may be just as capable, but he may die tomorrow. The mortality rate for age 70 is 2½ times as high as that for age 60. The permanent disability rate for age 70 is four times as high as that for age 60. Still, these are multiples of a very small number. The probability that a person age 75 will die the next year is only ½ of 1 percent.

Fourth, there are demographic considerations. The proportion of the population at the younger ages—under 18 or 20—is decreasing with the lower birth rate. The proportion of the population over age 65 is increasing, but not so rapidly: in the year 2030, the population over 65 may be 20 percent of the total, but at present it is 10 percent, and in the year 2000, according to the middle population projection from Social Security, it will be only 12 percent. The proportion in the middle, the working force, from age 18 or 20 to 65, is increasing slowly: about 56 percent in 1970 to 62 percent in the year 2010. So the biggest increase proportionately in the total, the most rapid increase in market share, is in the over 65 age group. Next is the work force, which is also increasing its proportion, but more slowly; and the people who make up the balance, the young, are a slowly decreasing proportion of the population.

What are the implications of these other, less frequently mentioned issues? Well, it might have been better to delay action on mandatory retirement until unemployment was contained. It might have been better not to move it back five years at once, but to phase it in one year at a time. It might have been better to move the normal retirement age for Social Security back concurrently. It might have been better to say that mandatory retirement can be enforced if you have an adequate pension, and cannot if you do not, although this would seem to give too much importance to the form of compensation, rewarding pensions and ignoring cash or other forms of compensation. It would surely be better to encourage the spread of private pensions, so that more people can and will choose to retire earlier.

WHAT DOES THE LAW MEAN?

What will the mandatory retirement law mean to the employee? There is no one single meaning for all employees because there are too many categories of employee. There is, for example, the knowledge worker and the laborer. There is the person who is union and the person who is nonunion. (An interesting aspect of this legislation, is that as of April 6 collective bargaining agreements can no longer require mandatory retirement.) There is the salaried employee and the wage earner; line people and staff; high income and low income. The achiever, the type A personality and the more dispassionate, the less committed person.

What does it mean to the employer? Surely a great deal of employee uncertainty, and so perhaps a great deal more need for preretirement counseling, or at least a great deal more demand for it. Preretirement counseling is an activity much talked about, but difficult to assess.

The employer may want to help people to prepare for second careers. IBM, often innovative, has a program that provides up to $500 a year for tuition or other training expenses to phase their employees into other activities as they leave IBM—$500 a year for the three years preceding departure and the two years following departure. If an individual retires at 55 from IBM, the money is available from age 52.

The most significant implication for the employer is surely the need for more thoroughgoing performance evaluation, and at all ages. In the past he could and did rely on a mandatory retirement age to move people out that he felt really needed to go. That is no longer permissible. He will now have to decide whether each employee is pulling his weight, irrespective of age. The alternative is to accept inefficiency and inadequacy—at all ages—and the attendant competitive drag. Note particularly that people are not going to agree on the assessment of performance. Employers and employees are bound to look at performance differently. There will inevitably be controversy and dissatisfaction.

The employer may wish to create opportunities for part-time employment. There will be people who wish to continue in employment but at the same time cut back their work load—fewer days, or fewer hours per day. Implications for benefit plans are not too formidable. The essential approach is for the employer to decide what he wants his employees to do and to see that the benefit plans support that objective, whether by encouraging early retirement or late retirement, or by being neutral. Different effects can be arranged for long-service versus short-service employees, or high-salaried versus low-salaried ones, or able workers versus mediocre ones. Correspondingly, the mistake to avoid is asking what our present benefit plans tell us to do.

Later retirement surely implies higher wage costs—a person who leaves at age 65 is replaced by someone younger, at a lower salary.

What does it mean to the composition of the work force? Here, some reassurance: perhaps not too much. Government data from mid-1977 show that the civilian work force over 16 now numbers about 97.7 million. Of these, 6.4 million are unemployed. Of the 91.3 million who are employed, there are only 1.5 million over 65. About 350,000 employees reach age 65 each year.

The principal fact needed to appraise the impact of delaying mandatory retirement is this: now, and last year, and the year before that, and actually all through the 1970s, 85 percent or more of the people who stopped working did so before they reached 65. Only 15 percent or less of the people who stopped working did so at 65 or later.

The second fact needed for this appraisal is that of those who do work until they are 65, two-thirds of the men and not quite half of the women continue to work, but not too much longer: three years after age 65, only 30 percent of those who did continue are still working. The Senate Committee on Human Resources started with the fact that 350,000 people reaching 65 this year are still employed, took one-half that number, or 175,000, and rounded to 200,000, to estimate the number per year who will continue to work after age 65. This is the number that Harold Sheppard mentions in his

paper; it is a reasonable estimate today. It may not be for the future, as I will suggest later. In any case, after five years, entrants to and exits from the labor force will stabilize again as people once more resume retiring.

THE LAW'S SPECIFICS

Now that the issues of mandatory retirement and what they mean to people have been considered, let us turn to the specifics of the law—Public Law 95–256—the Age Discrimination in Employment Act Amendments of 1978. They apply, as does the ADEA law itself, to employers in the private sector except those with fewer than 20 employees, which excludes about 30 percent of the labor force. There is an exclusion for those in bona fide executive or high policymaking positions if the employer provides a private pension of at least $27,000 per year. The $27,000 pension is the minor part: the conference report makes it quite clear that "bona fide executive or high policymaking position" is to be construed quite narrowly. Peter Drucker suggested in a recent issue of the *Wall Street Journal* that high potential people might refuse promotion to the elegant circle of the bona fide executive or the high policymaking position because they already enjoy greatly what they are doing and have no desire to be pushed out at 65. He suggests avoiding that problem, wihout losing the opportunity to prune these senior people at age 65, by establishing the practice of moving the 65-year-old bona fide executive or high policymaker out of his line position into staff work that does not qualify for mandatory retirement. The 65-year-old employee can remain working if he so wishes and the widest choice remains for the top jobs among those under 65. Another interesting exception is for those with contracts of unlimited tenure at institutions of higher learning: these people can still be retired mandatorily at 65.

As of April 6, 1978, the law was amended—quite clearly in direct response to a recent Supreme Court decision—to "clarify" that from now on no seniority system and no benefit plan can require retirement before 65. The Supreme Court dealt with a retirement plan with mandatory retirement at 60. The original ADEA protected people between ages 40 and 65 from discrimination by an employer on account of age, but it specifically permitted retirement plans to operate if they were bona fide and not a subterfuge to evade the law. The plan at issue was put into effect in the 1930s and so obviously not set up to evade ADEA, which was passed in 1967. The new, "clarifying" amendment makes it clear that a benefit plan cannot have a mandatory retirement age below 65 (not 70—that comes later). It also makes clear that there cannot be mandatory retirement before age 65 (again, age 70 will come later) pursuant to a collective bargaining agreement: the union is not allowed to bargain away an individual's right to continue working. As a temporary exception, mandatory retirement pursuant to present bargaining agreements—those in effect September 1, 1977—can continue to the termination of the agreement, but no later than January 1, 1980.

It is on January 1, 1979 that mandatory retirement is prohibited before age 70, rather than 65. That is also the date for the bona fide executive exclusion and for the tenure exclusion. The tenure exclusion, however, is not with us for long: it is automatically repealed on July 1, 1982, after which even teachers cannot be retired before age 70. Those are the rules for the private sector.

In the case of federal employment, mandatory retirement has not been allowed before age 70, and that limit is removed altogether, effective September 1, 1978. This applies to about 95 percent of the federal employees, but mandatory retirement continues to be available for certain specialties: federal fire fighters, law enforcement personnel (the FBI, for example), air traffic controllers, foreign service officers, foreign intelligence personnel, and —note the fine tuning of Congress

—employees of the Alaska railroad and the Isthmus of Panama. The Civil Service Commission is required to study and report finally by January 1, 1980 on the effects of these amendments on federal employees (in the brave spirit of legislate first and find out afterwards). It is also to study the exclusion of those under 40.

The Secretary of Labor, also, is required to study and report, but not until January 1, 1982. His topics are, what did we do when we changed age 65 to 70? Is it feasible to have no limit? Or is it feasible to have a higher limit? What did we do by having an executive exemption? What did we do by having a tenure exemption? We will all look forward with great interest to finding out what it is that Congress did.

As a result of the new law, jury trial of facts is available now not only for wages but for liquidated damages. There is no provision for punitive damages.

UNCERTAINTIES

There are uncertainties with this law, as with any legislation, although it is remarkably brief, only three pages. The states are not pre-empted by this law: they are free to add further prohibitions, rules, penalties, and so forth. California has a new law on mandatory retirement, but it is not quite clear when it is effective. The state legislative counsel issued an opinion that mandatory retirement can continue under existing plans for two years or until collective bargaining agreements expire, whichever comes first. The California Fair Employment Practice Commission issued a staff proposal with the same conclusion. Neither opinion is binding, however. The only one opposing these views is the assemblyman who was the author of the law, and he says the ban is in effect now.

Florida, too, has a law prohibiting mandatory retirement because of age. Alaska, Montana, and North Carolina have laws that may prohibit mandatory retirement at age 65. Some 38 jurisdictions, in fact, have laws prohibiting discrimination on account of age.

Uncertainties will, of course, arise from the words of the federal law itself. There will be dispute, and in time court decisions will trace out a pattern of interpretation. (We are an increasingly litigious society: Some say that now everyone is in court except the criminal.) Disputes are bound to arise from differences in perception of performance. And to what extent can an employer re-assign someone to lighter responsibilities? At a lower salary? How finely can that be tuned?

I find the estimates of continued employment beyond 65 to be plausible, but I wonder if they are reliable. Will the new law change people's perceptions? Until now almost everybody has retired before 65, but someone leaving employment at 64 was giving up only one year of further employment; now it will be six. Will that kind of comparison shift people's thinking? Will people come more and more to perceive the prospects of continued substantial inflation and be more fearful of retiring early, thus exposing themselves to the cruel erosion of income? It used to be that everyone retired at 65; then more and more people retired early, until, now, 90 percent retire before 65, and the few who work beyond 65 stop after a few years more. I wonder if we will see a drift to a broader, more even dispersion of retirement over the range 55 and 70, depending very sensitively upon financial resources and the satisfaction of the work. And while we peer ahead to see as best we can what this new law will bring, let me point out that Claude Pepper, the sponsor of the new law, says that the next thing he plans to do is introduce a bill to prohibit mandatory retirement at any age.

Conclusions?

It is true that the theme of the 1978 annual meeting is Planning for the Elderly, but the concept behind the ADEA legislation is not planning for others. Rather, it is the freedom of each individual to plan for himself or, more simply, to broaden his choices. So in keeping with that concept, I offer no plans for the elderly, and I leave the conclusions to you.

Yet perhaps you will accept an observation without judgment. The greater freedom of choice for employees is not a pure addition to free action: it is gained at the expense of the employer's freedom to choose his staff. Few among you have much experience as an employer; fewer still, in risking all to begin a new business venture. Recall for a moment that almost all new businesses fail. They are heavily taxed; they are heavily regulated. The employer is not allowed to hire the people he wants to; he is not allowed to fire the people he wants to. Sir Walter Scott wrote:

Oh, what a tangled web we weave,
When first we practice to deceive.

Perhaps we should say here, instead:

Oh, what a tangled web we enter,
When first we start a private venture.

Q: Most of us would agree that there are not enough meaningful jobs for many parts of the population. But where is the evidence that providing greater opportunity for any one segment necessarily disadvantages another?

A (Givens): There is apparently no universal one-to-one substitution of a retiree with a replacement, young or old. There is no mechanistic domino effect produced by retirement, whereby first a slightly younger coworker or new hiree, takes the place of a higher level retiree. Or that that replacement is succeeded by a slightly younger person, and then downward through the ranks, thus solving the youth unemployment program. This is too mechanistic a doctrine, and it assumes that every man and woman is a smoothly interchangeable part in a simple and homogeneous work structure for the total society. The crux of the teenage unemployment problem has nothing to do with keeping a 65-year-old in an organization.

Q: You mentioned that there are 200,000 more older workers likely to stay on in the work force, and I wonder if we are not setting in motion here a change in values that might place an increasingly high value on continuing to work. I foresee the possibility of many millions of older workers choosing to stay on because of this whole change in the value system.

A (Givens): I think you are reading too much into this Amendment. It is not stating that you are more valuable if you keep on working; it states that you have a broader choice. But let's say, mechanistically and simplistically, that 200,000 people do not join the labor force—what you are then doing is counting those 200,000 whom you would not have counted otherwise. 200,000 related to about 7 million unemployed means two tenths of a percent. If your unemployment rate is 6.9, that would push it to 7.1. But what you're doing is artificial. You are now recognizing the young people who are unemployed. You are not recognizing that the retiree is unemployed, so you have simply moved people into an area where they are not counted and started counting people that you have not counted before.

Q: You mentioned that one of the implications of the ADEA amendments might be the need for more preretirement counselling. How much preretirement counselling is actually going on and who is doing it?

A (Givens): The larger corporations are the ones doing it. Almost all of them will have a program where, at the very least, a person is brought in either three or five years before normal retirement age and told that if he or she wants his pension to be paid with a continuation in some part to a spouse, that election should occur before normal retirement.

Q: Particularly in the federal government, where there is no age limit, we are going to have people around who will barely be able to shuffle around while drawing salaries at the top of the scale. With this increased cost and what we are going to receive for it, what will be the impact upon costs of government and the delivery of services?

A (Givens): I can't agree that the managers in the public system are going to be forced to keep shuffling Sam around, and I think there will be greater pressure to demand better job performance assessment measures to start winnowing out incompetents. I also believe that people will self-select themselves out of the system. Most people do not wait forever and die on the job. They choose to retire, and I think this will continue to happen in the federal sector unless pensions become less and less attractive.

Pre-Retirement Counseling

Nancy Diekelmann*

Retirement may be viewed as an event, a process, or a social adjustment. Many gerontologists believe that retirement is the most crucial life change to which the older adult is subjected(1). Nurses, unfortunately, often see in clients the results of poor retirement planning. Some retirees have limited financial resources; some have made sudden decisions about living arrangements, selling their houses precipitously, moving away, and later deeply regretting their decisions.

Many middle adults are reluctant to discuss retirement plans. Their view is, "There's plenty of time for that." Yet, often there is not. Unwise decisions are made that might have been avoided by looking ahead. What, then, is the primary care nurse's role in helping older adults prepare for retirement? What areas of assessment should the nurse consider as clients approach retirement age? How can the nurse use these assessments and provide anticipatory guidance?

There is a strong correlation between successful retirement and good health. There is also strong correlation between successful retirement and retirement planning. Accordingly, the nurse can assess

*Nancy Diekelmann, R.N., M.S., is a lecturer at the University of Wisconsin School of Nursing, Madison and a doctoral student in the department of curriculum and instruction at the University of Wisconsin.

the following six areas.

The first should be *retirement income*. Usually, retirement means a decrease in income. The primary health care nurse should not be shy in discussing finances. Income affects diet and living arrangements and, thus, the level of health.

All adults in their mid-fifties or younger should inquire about their future social security benefits. But certainly older adults should know how much retirement income they will receive from social security and from their employers.

Some older adults will need to be encouraged to supplement their income. Possibilities vary from part-time employment that may or may not be related to their previous work to a new career. Clients, however, will need to inquire at the local social security office about how additional income will affect their social security benefits.

The second area of assessment is *activities*. What preretirement abilities, skills, and interests does the client have that can be drawn upon? Nothing will contribute more to the mental as well as the physical health of clients than stimulating retirement activities. Many have money-making potentials. Self-employment possibilities include sewing and doing alterations, staging parties and puppet shows for children, serving as a companion, and typing manuscripts.

Hobbies also sometimes have

money-making possibilities, for example, making doll houses, breeding pets, and doing genealogy and local history research. In indicating job possibilities to clients, the nurse should emphasize that the income earned should be second in importance to the enjoyment of the work.

Retirement affords time for travel; how much of course depends on one's finances. Retirement is also a time to volunteer services within the community. Middle adults are generally busy and pressed for time; but the middle adult years are an excellent time to give a few hours a month at a community agency to see if it is work that could be enjoyed in retirement.

A third area involves *living arrangements*. Among the many considerations are the following:

• Is the current house too large, now that the children are gone?

• Are the taxes too high for a retirement income?

• Are there too many stairs to climb?

• Would an apartment be better?

• Would a milder climate be more pleasant? When counseling about a change in climate, the nurse must include a discussion of benefits, like a warm, dry climate for some, and such disadvantages as high altitudes for others.

It is wise for clients not to sell their homes until they are sure of where they want to move, have considered the advantages and disadvantages of several locations before deciding which is best for them, and—ideally—have had some firsthand knowledge of the new community. If possible, those considering a move ought to rent an apartment in the new town for a year before buying or building.

A move may be to a retirement facility rather than to a new community. Clients making this change need to ask if the facility has lifelong medical care, nursing care when necessary, and personal care to the end of life. They must ask such questions as what does it cost? What type of contract is involved?

Any move that involves disposing of most of a client's accumulated possessions will be at best hard and at worst traumatic. Disposing of belongings will be easier if the decision is made as a result of prolonged deliberation rather than in the shock of emergency.

A question often posed is, Should retired persons move in with their children? This, of course, is a family decision. But the nurse can suggest that clients discuss such a decision before an emergency arises requiring instant action, sometimes deeply regretted later.

Although circumstances differ, generally it seems preferable for older adults to maintain their independence and to live apart from family as long as possible.

Role change is the fourth area of assessment. Once retired, spouses spend more time together. Their success in enjoying this time is generally in proportion to their common interests in the middle years after the children have left home.

Parents who have been successful in adapting to their children's growth to adulthood and independence will probably continue to have a good and satisfying relationship. If they have not, they may face a lonely old age. Women generally have a closer relationship with children than men, but that closeness may be a source of friction. If the parent-child relationship is satisfactory until the parent is 50

to 55, it is unlikely that new alienation will develop(2).

Some elderly persons, however, depend on their children for companionship, continue to think of them as children, and want to exert parental authority. Grown children resent this. These clients will need to develop a variety of new interests.

Grandparenting can also involve role changes. When men and women reach old age, their grandchildren are teenagers or young adults. A generation gap can develop. When members of different generations live together closely, friction is likely to result.

The loss of a spouse by divorce or death is a common change faced by retirees. Since men tend to die earlier than women, widowhood is more common that widowerhood. About half of American women over 60 are widows; by age 85, 85 percent of them are widowed(3).

As one grows older, adjustments are more difficult to make. Adjusting to the loss of a spouse is difficult indeed. Many elderly people assuage their loneliness by having a pet; others remarry.

We have no evidence for the popular belief that an elderly person who has never married will face an unhappy and lonely old age. Actually, these persons often have learned to develop interests and take part in activities that compensate for the lack of a spouse. In old age, these interests are continued.

The fifth area of assessment involves *health-related issues*. Medical and dental insurance needs to be discussed with the client. In addition, exercise, diet, mental health, sexuality, and other aspects of life-style ought to be discussed in terms of how retirement may affect these areas of health.

Sixth, clients' knowledge of *legal matters* ought to be assessed. Have they made out their wills? Do they have questions about inheritance laws? For preretirement counseling, the nurse must be familiar with community resources to which clients can be referred. Many senior citizens groups, YMCA or

YWCA organizations, and sometimes junior colleges have courses that provide older adults with this information. Where preretirement programs do not exist, nurses can stimulate interest in the subject and help to organize some through the health department, churches, or community organizations.

Another resource sometimes available to a client is a retirement program at his or her place of employment. Many clients know that their companies have such programs, but are reluctant to attend.

Of course a basic quesion the client must consider about retirement is *when*. The time for retirement may or may not be the choice of the person involved. Mandatory retirement is universal in government employment, and many firms follow this policy. In mandatory retirement, the cutoff age can range from 55 to 70, but retirement before 65 generally means reduced postretirement benefits. Presently, only one person in 10 must retire because of reaching a mandatory age. This proportion, however, is changing and will probably increase even more in the future, particularly since present retirement ages for some groups may be lowered. On the other hand, more attacks are being made against mandatory retirement. It is considered a waste of social resources and a heavily increasing economic burden on the young. In some fields, experiments have begun in the continuation of work.

Poor health may be a cause for retirement, but other evidence indicates that retired persons are in as good health after retirement as before, or sometimes better(4). A recent study revealed that poor health was given as the reason in only a quarter of the cases. Nearly 70 percent of these early retirees thought they could afford to quit or wanted more free time(5). The desire for leisure is now becoming a more popular reason to retire.

While the ideal age for retirement is largely an individual matter, finances are often an important factor in the decision. The need and enjoyment of work are other determinants that vary. Tapering off a work pattern is preferable to a sudden break. One way to do this is to increase gradually the length of the annual vacation or reduce the length of the working day.

At present, most persons who retire suddenly do so because of unexpected illness or an unexpected economic emergency. Some individuals not regularly employed may find it hard to secure jobs as they grow older and may choose to retire. Employers sometimes discriminate against the elderly, alleging they cannot meet job requirements, though often there is no foundation for these allegations.

Whether the retirement date is a free choice or not, retirement planning needs to be discussed.

References

1. Miller, S. J. The social dilemma of the aging leisure participant. IN *Older People and Their Social World*, ed. by A. M. Rose and W. A. Peterson. Philadelphia, F. A. Davis Co., 1965.
2. Burr, W. R. Satisfaction with various aspects of marriage over the life cycle: a random middle class sample. *J.Marriage Fam.* 32:29-37, Feb., 1970.
3. Hurlock, E. B. *Developmental Psychology*. rev. 4th ed. New York, McGraw-Hill Book Co., 1974.
4. Atchley, R. C. *Social Forces in Later Life*. 2d ed. Belmont, Calif., Wadsworth Publishing Co., 1977.
5. Pollman, A. W. Early retirement: A comparison of poor health and other retirement factors. *J.Gerontol.* 26:41-45, Jan. 1971.

Other topics

The Proposed Fiscal 1980 Budget: What It Means for Older Americans

Staff of the Special Committee on Aging of the United States Senate, 1979.

President Carter submitted his fiscal 1980 budget to the Congress on January 22. The new budget proposes $532 billion in outlays for fiscal 1980, and projects a deficit of $29 billion.

The committee staff has prepared the following analysis to summarize the impact of the fiscal 1980 budget on programs serving older Americans, including trust fund outlays and discretionary spending.

ADMINISTRATION PROPOSES CUTBACKS IN SOCIAL SECURITY PROTECTION

The administration's fiscal 1980 budget includes several legislative recommendations affecting social security. Most proposals are designed to reduce social security outlays in fiscal 1980 and subsequent years.

(1) *Limit disability benefits.*—The maximum family benefit for a disabled person would be limited to 80 percent of the worker's average indexed monthly earnings (1980 savings: $21 million). This proposal is designed to preclude a disabled worker and his or her family from receiving more in benefits than the employee made while working prior to becoming disabled. Recent data indicate that as many as 6 percent of all disability awards exceed predisability earnings levels.

(2) *Reduction in dropout years.*—In general, five low earnings years may be dropped out now in computing social security benefits for most eligible workers. The administration proposes to reduce the number of dropout years for younger disabled or deceased workers according to the following formula:

Age:	Number of dropout years
Under 27	0
27 to 31	1
32 to 36	2
37 to 41	3
42 to 46	4
47 and over	5

This proposal would reduce benefits (1980 savings: $14 million) for some younger disabled or deceased workers (and/or their families).

(3) *Proposals to increase work incentives.*—Four proposals are recommended to increase work incentives (1980 cost: $39 million) for disabled beneficiaries:

—An extension of the current 12-month trial work period to 24 months. Benefits would not be paid during this second 12-month period, but the disabled worker could be automatically reenrolled in the program if his or her attempt to return to work failed (thus avoiding a lengthy reapplication process).

—Continuation of medicare and medicaid coverage for 2 years after a disabled worker leaves the benefit roll.

—Require that only one waiting period for medicare protection (presently 24 consecutive months) must be met if a disabled worker fails at an attempt to return to work.

—Allow a deduction for impairment-related work and attendant care expenses in computing eligibility for disability benefits.

(4) *Phase out postsecondary student benefits.*—Benefits paid to dependent children (18 to 22 years old) who are attending postsecondary schools would be phased out over a 4-year period (1980 savings: $155 million).

(5) *End mother's or father's benefit when youngest child is 16.*— Benefits paid to an adult caring for children would end when the youngest child reaches age 16, instead of 18 as under present law (1980 savings: $23 million). The provision would be phased in over a 2-year period. Benefits for dependent children would still be payable until age 18.

(6) *Eliminate minimum for new beneficiaries.*—The regular minimum monthly benefit (now frozen at $121.80) would be eliminated for workers (and their survivors) who become entitled after May 1979 (1980 savings: $53 million).

(7) *Eliminate lump-sum death benefit.*—The $255 lump-sum social security death benefit would be eliminated (1980 savings: $221 million). The administration would replace it with a new SSI (supplemental security income) lump-sum death benefit (equal to 1 month's benefit or about $220 in 1980 and increasing each year thereafter according to cost-of-living increases). This would have the effect of limiting the lump-sum death benefit to low-income aged, blind, and disabled persons.

(8) *Federal pension offset.*—Social security benefits would be reduced by $1 for each $3 of pension income received from Federal employment which is not covered by social security (1980 savings: $14 million). The offset would not apply if the Federal annuity is less than the average social security benefit (estimated at $285 per month in 1980 for a retired worker without dependents). If the Federal pension exceeds the average social security benefit, only the portion above the average would be subject to the $1-for-$3 offset. The social security benefit, though, would never be less than 32 percent of the average indexed monthly earnings.

9.1 PERCENT COST-OF-LIVING INCREASE PROJECTED FOR SOCIAL SECURITY

The administration projects a 9.1 percent social security cost-of-living increase in July 1979. The adjustment will be based upon the rise in prices from the first quarter (January, February, and March) in 1978 to the first quarter in 1979. A 7.1 percent cost-of-living adjustment is forecast for July 1980.

Social security beneficiaries and benefits.—Nearly 30.7 million persons are expected to receive $98.9 billion in retirement and survivor benefits in fiscal 1980, compared with $87.1 billion in benefits for 30 million persons in fiscal 1979. The number of disabled social security beneficiaries is expected to increase from 4.9 million in fiscal 1979 to 5 million in fiscal 1980. Benefit payments are projected to rise from $13.6 billion to $15.3 billion.

$558.766 MILLION PROPOSED FOR AoA ACTIVITIES

A $558.766 million funding level is recommended for AoA activities in the administration's fiscal 1980 budget, or $38 million above the comparable 1979 amount. AoA is now operating under a continuing resolution which, in effect, provides $508.75 million. In addition, the administration will seek $12.016 million in the fiscal 1979 supplemental appropriations bill:

—$4.546 million for congregate meals because of the "hold harm-

RETIREMENT AND SURVIVOR BENEFITS

	1978 actual	1979 estimate	1980 estimate
Beneficiaries (millions):			
Retired workers	18.1	18.7	19.4
Dependents of retired workers	3.6	3.7	3.7
Survivors	7.6	7.6	7.6
Total beneficiaries	29.3	30.0	30.7
Benefit payments (billions):			
Retired workers	52.1	58.6	67.0
Dependents of retired workers	5.8	6.3	7.1
Survivors	20.6	22.2	24.7
Total benefit payments	78.5	87.1	98.9

DISABILITY BENEFITS

	1978 actual	1979 estimate	1980 estimate
Beneficiaries (millions):			
Disabled workers	2.8	2.9	3.0
Dependents of disabled workers	2.1	2.0	2.0
Total beneficiaries	4.9	4.9	5.0
Benefit payments (billions):			
Disabled workers	10.1	11.2	12.7
Dependents of disabled workers	2.2	2.4	2.6
Total benefit payments	12.2	13.6	15.3

less" provision in the 1978 Older Americans Act and to compensate for population shifts in determining State funding.
—$3.97 million for social services because of the "hold harmless" provision and to compensate for population shifts in determining State funding.
—$3.5 million because of the increase in the floor (from $200,000 to $300,000) for State administration.
The administration will also request $3 million in the 1979 supplemental appropriations bill for the White House Conference on Aging to be used over a 3-year period to pay for support staff, a statutorily mandated advisory committee, preconference activities, and the actual cost of the conference (including travel expenses of delegates).

FUNDING FOR OLDER AMERICANS ACT

[AoA activities; in millions of dollars]

	Fiscal 1979 estimate	Fiscal 1980 request	Fiscal 1980 authorization
Title II:			
National Clearing House	2.0	2.0	(1)
Federal Council on Aging	.45	.45	(1)
Title III:			
Administration	22.5	22.5	(1)
Social services and senior centers [2]	196.97	196.97	360
Congregate meals [3]			375
Home-delivered meals [3]	254.546	277.546	100
Title IV:			
Training	17.0	17.0	(1)
Research	8.5	8.5	(1)
Gerontology centers	3.8	3.8	(1)
Special projects, including long-term care and legal services	15.0	30.0	(1)
Title VI:			
Direct Indian grants	0	0	(1)
Surplus Indian facilities	0	0	(1)
Total	[4] 520.766	558.766	[5] 835

[1] Such sums as may be necessary.
[2] At least 1 percent or $20,000, whichever is greater, of a State's title III social services allotment must support a statewide nursing home ombudsman program.
[3] The budget request does not break down the amount allocated for congregate meals and home-delivered meals.
[4] The total funding includes $12,016,000 in the administration's fiscal 1979 supplemental appropriations request.
[5] Plus such sums as may be necessary.

The 1980 budget request for title III–B ($196.97 million) social services would support 560 area agencies on aging and more than 2,000 multipurpose senior centers. AoA estimates that 3,283,200 persons will receive community and neighborhood services in fiscal 1979, including information and referral, transportation, residential repairs, legal services, and outreach. AoA projects that 19,640 older Americans will receive in-home services: homemaker, home health, escort, and others.

A $277.546 million request for the nutrition program would permit a modest increase in the number of meals served, from 563,370 in 1979 to 575,795 in 1980.

ESTIMATED DAILY MEALS SERVED (5 DAYS PER WEEK)

	Fiscal 1979	Fiscal 1980	Change
Congregate	478,864	451,603	−27,261
Home delivered	84,506	124,172	+39,666
Total	563,370	575,775	+12,405

States will be encouraged to maintain the current level of home-delivered meal services, which nationally is about 15 percent of the total nutrition program. Additionally, $23 million has been requested for home-delivered meal activities.

Funding for training will focus on gerontological programs at higher educational institutions, State level training programs, continuing education for service providers, technical assistance projects, and other activities. Research activities will be concentrated primarily in three areas: (1) Demographic characteristics and social conditions affecting older persons, (2) advocacy-related activities (e.g., the impact of current policies on older persons and recommendations for change), and (3) the development of community operated services, with special attention to assisting the vulnerable elderly. A substantial portion of the request for multidisciplinary centers of gerontology will probably be used to fund qualified centers of special emphasis (e.g., health, income maintenance, and housing), as provided in the 1978 amendments. A $15 million increase is provided for special projects. Funding will be targeted primarily in five areas:

—Identifying and assisting elderly blind persons who need social services.
—Problems of nationwide concern, including long-term care services, in-home services, and minorities.
—Legal services.
—Disaster assistance; and
—Community services, especially for the vulnerable aged.

Funding for the National Information and Resource Clearing House will cover the annualized costs of the central control facility and the three resource centers for the Service Center for Aging Information (SCAN). The three resource centers (biomedical, social practice, and behavioral/social science) will probably be operational by September 1979.

MEDICARE BUDGET PROPOSES EXPANDED MENTAL HEALTH BENEFITS—RESTRUCTURING OF PART A BENEFITS FOR WORKING AGED

The fiscal year 1980 medicare budget proposed additional taxes to cover the cost of hospital insurance from employers of individuals who are 65 or older and from self-employed individuals age 65 or older. The proposal would produce estimated savings of $200 million in fiscal year 1980. This, along with hospital cost containment and four other legislative proposals (see below) for medicare's hospital insurance (part A) program would result in total savings of about $1.7 billion during 1980.

The budget also proposes legislation to expand medicare part B supplementary medical insurance benefits for outpatient mental health services by increasing the rate of payment for outpatient psychiatric services from 50 percent to 80 percent of reasonable charges, and increasing the maximum amount payable in a calendar year from $250 to $750. The cost of this expanded benefit is an estimated $22 million in fiscal year 1980.

PROPOSED LEGISLATION—HOSPITAL INSURANCE

The 1980 budget proposes new legislation for hospital cost containment which could save medicare part A (hospital insurance) $350 million in fiscal year 1979 and $1.5 billion in fiscal year 1980. The budget estimates an additional cost of $115,000 during 1980 for Federal administrative expenses to implement the proposed hospital cost containment program.

A proposal for medicare/medicaid common audits is estimated to save $6 million in fiscal year 1980.

Another proposal would require employers of individuals who are 65 or older to contribute to the cost of hospital insurance for these individuals. The specifics of this proposal are under development and could involve changes in an employer's support of either private group health insurance or medicare. Self-employed individuals who are over 65 will be required to pay a small tax toward the costs of their medicare protection, depending upon income level.

Legislation is also proposed to eliminate the additional 24-month waiting period for medicare coverage for re-entitled disabled individuals, resulting in an additional cost of $20 million during fiscal year 1980. Proposed legislation to extend medicare coverage to disabled workers who return to work but are not medically covered would cost an estimated $5 million in fiscal year 1980.

MEDICARE HOSPITAL INSURANCE: PROPOSED LEGISLATION

[In millions of dollars]

	1979 estimate	1980 estimate
Hospital cost containment (savings)	$350	$1,500
Administration (cost)		.115
Common audit (savings)		6
Restructured coverage for working aged (savings)		200
Disability/waiting period (expanded benefits)		20
Disability benefit expansion (expanded benefits)		5

PROPOSED LEGISLATION—SUPPLEMENTARY MEDICAL INSURANCE

The fiscal year 1980 budget proposes to increase the rate of payment for outpatient psychiatric services from 50 percent to 80 percent of reasonable charges and raise the maximum amount payable in a calendar year from $250 to $750. This benefit expansion is estimated to increase costs by $22 million during fiscal year 1980.

The budget also proposes only one waiting period for medicare protection (now 24 consecutive months) for reentitled disabled individuals (additional cost: $7 million during fiscal year 1980). Extending part B coverage to disabled workers who return to work will result in an additional cost of $2 million.

Part B reimbursements which would be eliminated or changed include (1) elimination of reimbursement for chiropractic services (savings: $34 million); (2) changing reimbursement practices to "eliminate excessive reimbursement" to hospital-based radiologists, anesthesiologists, and pathologists (savings: $48 million); and (3) a change in reimbursement for physician services (savings: $3 million) in hospital outpatient departments and clinics (e.g., to insure that total reimbursement is made on the basis of costs, rather than charges).

Also proposed is legislation to authorize the Secretary of HEW to assess a fine, up to a maximum of $2,000, against any person (after notice and opportunity for a hearing) filing a fraudulent claim. The budget estimates a savings of $9.3 million, offset by $1 million in new administrative costs for implementation. Under existing law, the Secretary must prove criminal fraud through the Justice Department and the courts.

MEDICARE SUPPLEMENTARY MEDICAL INSURANCE: PROPOSED LEGISLATION

[In millions of dollars]

	1980 estimate
Outpatient psychiatric services (expanded benefits)	22.0
Disability/waiting period (expanded benefits)	7.0
Disability benefit expansion (expanded benefits)	2.0
Chiropractic services (savings)	34.0
Hospital-based physicians (savings)	48.0
Reasonable cost reimbursement (savings)	3.0
Civil penalties (savings)	9.3
Administration of civil penalties (additional cost)	1.0

CURRENT SERVICES

Total outlays for medicare hospital insurance (part A) are expected to increase by about 14.5 percent from fiscal year 1979 to fiscal year 1980. Estimated total payments for fiscal year 1980 are $23.2 billion, compared to $20.2 billion during fiscal year 1979. This increase results primarily from rising medical costs and the size of the covered population.

Approximately 600,000 additional elderly and disabled beneficiaries will become eligible for hospital insurance during 1980, and an estimated 180,000 additional beneficiaries will receive reimbursed services during the year.

Payments for inpatient hospital services are expected to increase by 15 percent from fiscal year 1979 to fiscal year 1980; payments for skilled nursing facility services are expected to increase by 8 percent; and home health benefit payments will increase by 20 percent.

MEDICARE HOSPITAL INSURANCE

[In millions]

	1978 actual	1979 estimate	1980 estimate
Beneficiaries:			
Persons with hospital insurance protection (average):			
Aged	23.5	23.9	24.3
Disabled	2.8	3.0	3.1
Beneficiaries receiving reimbursed services:			
Aged	5.3	5.5	5.6
Disabled	.7	.75	.8
Benefit payments:			
For inpatient hospital services:			
Aged	$14,696	$16,965	$19,344
Disabled	1,935	2,325	2,744
For skilled nursing facility services:			
Aged	380	434	468
Disabled	15	18	20
For home health services:			
Aged	361	460	548
Disabled	28	37	47
Total benefit payments:			
Aged	15,437	17,859	20,360
Disabled	1,978	2,380	2,811
Total	17,415	20,239	23,171

40-638—79——2

Total outlays for medicare supplementary medical insurance (part B) will increase by about $1.4 billion, or 17 percent, from fiscal year 1979 to fiscal year 1980. Rising medical costs and an increase in the number of covered beneficiaries are the two major reasons for the projected additional outlays.

The budget estimates that approximately 700,000 elderly and disabled beneficiaries will be added to the SMI rolls during 1980, and 900,000 additional beneficiaries will receive benefit payments.

Payments for physician services are expected to increase by 15 percent; home health services by 19 percent; outpatient services by 20 percent; and payments for other medical and health services by 19 percent.

MEDICARE SUPPLEMENTARY MEDICAL INSURANCE

[In millions]

	1978 actual	1979 estimate	1980 estimate
Beneficiaries:			
Persons enrolled (average):			
Aged	23.3	23.9	24.4
Disabled	2.5	2.7	2.8
Beneficiaries receiving reimbursed services:			
Aged	14.1	14.9	15.6
Disabled	1.5	1.7	1.8
Benefit payments:			
For physician services:			
Aged	$4,479	$5,142	$5,909
Disabled	546	656	779
For home health services:			
Aged	147	198	235
Disabled	12	16	19
For outpatient services:			
Aged	665	916	1,105
Disabled	456	637	756
For other medical and health services:			
Aged	498	604	711
Disabled	49	59	75
Total benefit payments:			
Aged	$5,789	$6,860	$7,960
Disabled	1,063	1,368	1,629
Total	6,852	8,228	9,589

SENIOR COMMUNITY SERVICE EMPLOYMENT PROGRAM TO REMAIN UNCHANGED

President Carter's fiscal 1980 budget would maintain the operating level of the title V (formerly title IX of the Older Americans Act) senior community service employment program at about 47,500 during the 1980–81 program year (July 1, 1980, to June 30, 1981). Title V is now operating at $200.9 million.

Sponsor	Funds	Positions
Green Thumb	$65,733,500	15,405
National Retired Teachers Association/American Association of Retired Persons	27,243,000	6,383
Forest Service	13,209,000	3,095
National Council of Senior Citizens	36,157,000	8,920
National Council on Aging	18,208,000	4,264
National Center on Black Aged	1,305,000	366
National Association for Spanish-Speaking Elderly	1,305,000	300
Urban League	2,871,000	715
States	34,868,500	8,028
Total	200,900,000	47,476

A funding level of $211.7 million is projected for the national senior services corps for program year 1979–80 (July 1, 1979, to June 30, 1980). However, the administration will propose an additional $8.9 million in a fiscal 1979 supplemental appropriations bill to cover additional costs from increases in the minimum wage (from $2.65 per hour to $2.90 in January 1979 and then to $3.10 in January 1980), bringing the total amount from $211.7 million to $220.6 million. A $234.8 million funding level is requested for program year 1980–81.

TITLE V SENIOR COMMUNITY SERVICE EMPLOYMENT PROGRAM

[In millions of dollars]

	Fiscal year—		
	1979	1980	1981
Authorization [1]	$350.0	$400.0	$450.0
Appropriation or budget request [1]	200.9	[2] 220.6	234.8

[1] The authorization figures are based upon fiscal years 1979 (Oct. 1, 1978, to Sept. 30, 1979), 1980 (Oct. 1, 1979, to Sept. 30, 1980), and 1981 (Oct. 1, 1980, to Sept. 30, 1981). The appropriation or budget request figures are based upon program years 1978–79 (July 1, 1978, to June 30, 1979), 1979–80 (July 1, 1979, to June 30, 1980), and 1980–81 (July 1, 1980, to June 30, 1981).

[2] Figure includes $8,900,000 in the supplemental request for fiscal year 1979 to cover the additional costs attributable to the minimum wage.

Section 202 Loan Authority to Remain at $800 Million

Section 202.—The fiscal 1980 budget includes $800 million in loan authority for the section 202 program, which provides loans to non-profit sponsors of housing for the elderly and handicapped. This level is the same as for fiscal 1979. At least $50 million must be used to finance an estimated 1,300 units for nonelderly handicapped persons; units constructed for the elderly from fiscal 1980 funds should total approximately 18,400.

This fiscal 1980 total of 19,700 units represents a decrease of 1,500 units from the estimated 21,200 units which will be reserved under fiscal 1979 loan authority.

Section 8 (housing assistance payments program).—The fiscal 1980 budget proposes budget authority of $20 billion in the section 8 rental assistance program, which will support reservations for 250,000 units. The proposed distribution calls for 102,000 existing units and 147,000 substantially rehabilitated or newly constructed units. About 300,000 reservations will be made with fiscal 1979 budget authority.

Community development block grants.—A $3.9 billion funding level for community development block grants is requested in the new budget. This represents a slight increase above the $3.75 billion in budget authority for fiscal 1979, and $3.6 billion for fiscal 1978.

Public housing operating subsidies.—The administration recommends increasing public housing operating subsidies from $727 million in fiscal 1979 to $741.5 million in fiscal 1980.

Congregate services program.—No additional resources are requested for this new program which provides meals, housekeeping assistance, and personal care to frail elderly residents of public and section 202 housing. The Congress appropriated $10 million for congregate services in fiscal 1979.

FmHA repair grants.—Section 504 of the 1949 housing act authorizes grants and low-interest loans to very low-income elderly homeowners in rural areas. This assistance may be used for essential repairs and the correction of health and safety hazards. The program is administered by the Department of Agriculture's Farmers Home Administration. President Carter has requested $24 million for fiscal 1980, a $5 million increase above the $19 million fiscal 1979 appropriation. It is estimated that this new funding level will permit 7,650 housing units to be assisted in fiscal 1980, compared to an estimated 6,300 units in 1979 and 3,183 units actually repaired in 1978.

Supplemental Security Income

The number of aged, blind, and disabled persons projected to receive supplemental security income during fiscal year 1980 is 4.245 million (including 480,000 who receive only a State supplement). Nearly 1.9 million older Americans will receive Federal SSI payments and/or State supplemental payments in fiscal year 1980. The budget projects $5.635 billion in Federal benefit payments in fiscal 1980 and $1.638 billion in State supplemental payments.

Several legislative recommendations are incorporated in the budget, including:

(1) Restrict SSI eligibility for persons who dispose of assets in order to qualify for benefits (outlay reduction: $6 million in 1980).

(2) Offset windfall SSI benefit payments when there is a retroactive social security payment in certain dual entitlement situations (outlay reduction: $19 million in 1980).

(3) Phase in a system to determine SSI eligibility and payment amount based on a retrospective monthly accounting period.

(4) Provide that "affidavits of support" for legal aliens are enforceable contracts, with sponsors responsible for the support of legal aliens during the first 5 years of residence.

Nursing Homes

Nursing home costs continue to rise. Medicaid will account for approximately 50 percent of the total industry revenues. Medicaid funding for nursing home care (Federal and State) is projected at $6.3 billion in 1979, and is expected to rise to $6.7 billion by 1980. The Federal share for the above figures is about 55 percent, and the States contribute the remaining 45 percent. Payments for nursing home care continue to comprise the largest portion of Federal medicaid outlays, almost 38 percent of total payments.

Medicare's contributions to nursing home care are small by comparison. In fiscal 1979, medicare paid $452 million to nursing homes on behalf of beneficiaries. In 1980 the President's budget projects $488 million. The percentage of medicare funds to pay for nursing home care has decreased slightly over the last several years—from 5 percent in the late 1960's to around 2.3 percent.

The Veteran's Administration also pays for nursing home services, estimated at $329 million for fiscal year 1979 and $359 million for fiscal year 1980.

Private contributions continue to be an important source of nursing home payments, accounting for slightly more than 45 percent of total nursing home revenues.

Small Funding Increases Requested for ACTION's Older American Volunteer Programs

The budget requests an increase of $3.1 million for the retired senior volunteer program (RSVP); an increase of $1.1 million for senior companions; and an increase of $5.8 million for the foster grandparents for fiscal year 1980.

No new programs are anticipated. Increases are to be used primarily to raise (1) volunteer allowances and stipends, and (2) increase administrative support. Stipends for foster grandparents and senior companions will be raised from $1.60 an hour to $1.80 an hour on October 1, 1979. RSVP program increases will be used for additional support in volunteer insurance and transportation expense reimbursement.

OLDER AMERICAN VOLUNTEER PROGRAMS
[In millions of dollars]

	1978 actual	1979 estimate	1980 estimate	1980 authorization
RSVP	$20.1	$20.1	$23.214	$30
Senior companions	7.0	7.0	8.135 }	¹ 62.5
Foster grandparents	34.9	34.9	40.651 }	

¹ Senior companions and foster grandparents have a combined authorization of $62,500,000 for fiscal year 1980.

Approximately 250,000 older Americans participated in RSVP during fiscal year 1979. The same number will participate during 1980, but emphasis will be placed on increasing the proportion of male and minority participants.

During 1979, the foster grandparent program provided service opportunities for about 16,600 low-income older Americans. Approximately 41,600 children with special needs would be served during 1980.

Moreover, the senior companion program would provide volunteer opportunities to 3,300 low-income older Americans. Senior companions provide help, support, and companionship to other elderly with special needs.

National Institute on Aging

The National Institute on Aging's 1980 budget request of $56.51 million is slightly below the 1979 level of $56.91 million. In addition, NIA staff positions would decline from a ceiling of 258 positions to 233 positions in 1980.

The new NIA budget is projected to support 462 awards during 1980—385 for research, 50 for training, and 27 for research and development contracts. This is approximately 100 below the number supported in fiscal year 1979.

MEDICAID BUDGET PROPOSES LEGISLATION TO SAVE $19.3 MILLION

The fiscal year 1980 medicaid budget makes 13 separate legislative proposals estimated to reduce Federal costs by $19.3 million.

Proposed hospital cost containment legislation could save $225 million in 1980 and an additional $53 million in 1979. A proposal for a medicare/medicaid common audit is projected to save $28 million in fiscal year 1980.

Other major cost saving proposals include (1) requiring individuals who have resources to pay for some portion of their long-term care (estimated savings: $5 million); (2) permitting the Secretary of HEW to release social security wage information to States in determining medicaid eligibility, and permitting State unemployment agencies to release wage information to State medicaid agencies (estimated savings: $13 million); (3) eliminating reimbursement for chiropractic services (estimated savings: $1 million); (4) eliminating "excessive reimbursement" to hospital-based radiologists, anesthesiologists, and pathologists (estimated savings: $7 million); (5) authorizing the HEW Secretary to assess civil penalties for fraudulent claims (estimated savings: $14.3 million); and (6) considering stepparent income for AFDC/medicaid eligibility determination and standardizing the work expense disregard for AFDC/medicaid recipients (estimated savings: $27 million).

Legislation is also proposed to expand medicaid benefits for the disabled by eliminating the "abrupt and complete" cutoff of medicaid when earnings of employed disabled persons exceed the current allowed level of $240 per month. This proposal is estimated to cost $4 million during fiscal year 1980.

Expanded benefits are also proposed for an additional 2 million low-income children and 100,000 low-income pregnant women, at a cost of $288 million. In addition, the Secretary of HEW would be given authority to insure medicaid payments to eligible migrant workers, at an estimated cost of $9 million during fiscal year 1980.

MEDICAID: PROPOSED LEGISLATION

[In millions of dollars]

	1979 estimate	1980 estimate
Hospital cost containment (savings)	$53	$225.0
Common audit (savings)		28.0
Transfer of assets (savings)		5.0
Social security wage information (savings)		13.0
Eliminate chiropractic benefits (savings)		1.0
Hospital-based physician reimbursement (savings)		7.0
Civil penalties (savings)		14.3
AFDC stepparent income (savings)		16.0
AFDC income disregard (savings)		11.0
Disability benefit expansion (cost)		4.0
Child health assurance program (cost)		220.0
Low-income pregnant women (cost)		68.0
Migrant workers (cost)		9.0
Total savings		19.3

CURRENT SERVICES

Total Federal and State medicaid expenditures are expected to be about $22.3 billion during fiscal year 1980. This is an increase of approximately 7 percent from total fiscal year 1979 Federal and State expenditures of $20.9 billion. The Federal share is expected to increase by about 12 percent, from $11.3 billion during fiscal year 1979 to $12.6 billion during fiscal year 1980.

Nearly 3.7 million elderly persons are expected to receive medicaid-reimbursed services in fiscal years 1979 and 1980. The budget estimates a slight increase in medicaid reimbursements for health services for the permanently and totally disabled, from 3.1 million in fiscal year 1979 to 3.2 million in fiscal year 1980.

Fiscal year 1980 Federal medicaid expenditures for nursing home care are estimated to increase by about $276 million from fiscal year 1979 levels. Nursing home care will account for about 38 percent of total Federal medicaid payments. Payments for skilled nursing facilities will constitute 16 percent of total Federal medicaid payments.

Federal medicaid payments for home health care are estimated to increase $12 million, from $142 million during fiscal year 1979 to $154 million during fiscal year 1980. Home health payments continue to represent about 1 percent of total Federal medicaid payments.

RAILROAD RETIREMENT ANNUITIES

Payments for retirement, disability, and survivor benefits are projected at $4.590 billion in fiscal 1980, nearly $350 million above the fiscal 1979 estimate of $4.255 billion. Actual payments during fiscal 1978 totaled $3.984 billion. The number of persons receiving benefits is expected to decrease slightly from 1,024,000 at the end of 1978 to an estimated 1,016,000 at the end of 1979, with another decrease to 1,011,000 at the end of 1980. The number of persons receiving supplemental annuities is projected to increase from 176,000 at the end of 1978 to 178,000 at the end of 1979 and 184,000 at the end of 1980.

The administration plans to recommend legislation to strengthen the railroad retirement trust fund during 1979 through an altered payroll financing mechanism, changes in the computation of benefits, and the prospective application of social security rules to disability benefits.

4 PERCENT APRIL ANNUITY INCREASE FORECAST FOR FEDERAL RETIREES

The administration forecasts a 4-percent cost-of-living increase for Federal civil service annuitants in April 1979, followed by adjustments of 3.9 percent in October 1979 and 3.3 percent in April 1980. Cash outgo from the civil service retirement and disability fund is projected to increase from $12.4 billion in fiscal year 1979 to $14 billion in fiscal year 1980.

	1978 actual	1979 estimate	1980 estimate
Cash outgo during year:			
Payment of claims to retired employees	$9,186,683	$10,446,041	$11,898,056
Payment to employees engaged in construction of Panama Canal	176	168	127
Payment to widows of former employees of the Lighthouse Service	851	852	866
Payment of claims to survivor annuitants	1,382,204	1,569,967	1,782,595
Lump sum payments to estates or beneficiaries of deceased annuitants and employees	28,168	28,000	28,000
Refunds to living separated employees	287,084	300,000	300,000
Administration	22,044	25,561	25,414
Gain from premium or discount on investments	417		
Total outgo	10,907,627	12,370,589	14,035,058

The number of annuitants is expected to rise from 1,638,600 in 1979 to 1,689,600 in 1980.

VETERANS' BENEFITS FOR OLDER AMERICANS

More than $11.2 billion is projected to be expended in fiscal 1980 for Veterans Administration non-service-connected disability pensions ($4.2 billion), service-connected disability compensation benefits ($6.8 billion), and burial and other benefits ($.2 billion). Of this total, veterans and survivors from World War I and prior conflicts are expected to receive $989 million in pension payments and $214 million in compensation payments for fiscal 1980. The projection for compensation payments will increase if the Congress enacts President Carter's proposed cost-of-living adjustment, expected to be 7.8 percent for veterans and their dependents, effective October 1, 1979.

The VA also operates the largest medical care delivery system in the Nation, with 172 hospitals, 16 domiciliary care units, 95 nursing homes, and 228 outpatient clinics. This system will treat over 1.3 million patients in 1980, and more than 18.1 million outpatient medical and dental visits will be funded by the VA. Approximately $5.6 billion is expected to be expended.

Type of care	1978 actual	1979 estimate	1980 estimate
Nursing home care:			
Patients treated	11, 671	12, 308	12, 662
Average daily nursing patient census	7, 480	8, 119	8, 351
Domiciliary care:			
Members treated	17, 275	17, 197	14, 936
Average daily member census	8, 721	8, 668	7, 668
State nursing home care:			
Average daily nursing census	4, 945	5, 184	5, 698
Patients treated	9, 074	9, 539	10, 484
State home care (domiciliary):			
Average daily member census	5, 236	5, 628	5, 746
Members treated	10, 497	11, 706	11, 952
Community nursing home (contract care):			
Average daily nursing census	7, 997	8, 500	8, 500
Patients treated	26, 996	28, 261	28, 261
State hospital care:			
Average daily patient census	1, 004	1, 050	1, 050
Patients treated	6, 478	6, 778	6, 778

Military Retirement Pay Expected to Reach $11.5 Billion

The budget projects a $1.31 billion increase in military retirement pay, from $10.14 billion in fiscal 1979 to $11.45 billion in fiscal 1980.

PROGRAM AND FINANCING

[In thousands of dollars]

Program by activities	1978 actual	1979 estimate	1980 estimate
Nondisability	7, 362, 993	8, 199, 011	9, 311, 081
Temporary disability	61, 861	63, 021	68, 851
Permanent disability	963, 342	1, 022, 485	1, 107, 572
Fleet reserve	637, 166	660, 396	731, 885
Survivors' benefits	147, 802	194, 925	232, 111
Total	9, 173, 164	10, 139, 838	11, 451, 500

The average number of individuals on the retired rolls is expected to rise by about 38,000, from 1.26 million in 1979 to 1.3 million in 1980.

AVERAGE NUMBER

	1978 actual	1979 estimate	1980 estimate
Nondisability	921, 385	959, 795	991, 269
Temporary disability	12, 426	12, 306	12, 167
Permanent disability	140, 354	140, 834	140, 229
Fleet reserve	98, 165	94, 947	96, 115
Survivors' benefits	47, 514	54, 031	60, 230
Total	1, 219, 844	1, 261, 913	1, 300, 010

ADEA Enforcement Transferred to Equal Employment Opportunities Commission

Effective July 1, 1979, responsibility for the enforcement of the Age Discrimination in Employment Act will be transferred from the Department of Labor's Employment Standards Administration to the Equal Employment Opportunities Commission.

The administration requests $125 million for EEOC's antidiscrimination activities, as well as full-year funding to support functions transferred from the Department of Labor's Employment Standards Administration and the Office of Personnel Management and the Merit System Protection Board (formerly the Civil Service Commission). Also, $8,230,400 is allocated for ADEA enforcement activities. This amount will support 287 staff positions.

To improve its operations, EEOC has abolished its regional administrative and litigation office and will provide direct service through 22 full-service district offices and 37 area offices to persons who believe they have been victims of discrimination.

CETA FUNDING DOWN, NEW PROGRAM DIRECTIONS SPELLED OUT IN REAUTHORIZATION

The fiscal 1980 budget recommends $9.4 billion for the Comprehensive Employment and Training Act, down $2.1 billion from the $11.5 billion recommended budget authority for fiscal 1979. Public service employment (PSE) will experience the sharpest cutbacks. CETA-financed jobs would be trimmed from 625,000 to 467,000, producing an estimated savings of $1.5 billion.

The 1978 amendments to CETA restructured public service employment (PSE) into two new major programs. Title II–D authorizes PSE for low-income, long-term unemployed persons to help them obtain skills, experience, and placement aid. Title VI authorizes public service employment for individuals who are out of work primarily because of cyclical changes in the economy.

In addition, the CETA reauthorization and the Revenue Act of 1978 place increased emphasis on securing unsubsidized private sector jobs. A supplemental appropriation of $400 million is requested to carry out this goal.

The 1980 budget continues the 1979 level of 267,000 public service jobs for the structurally unemployed with outlays of $2.4 billion. However, the 1980 budget request would reduce the title VI countercyclical public service employment program from a 1977 high of 415,000 jobs to 200,000 jobs by the end of 1980.

COMMUNITY SERVICES ADMINISTRATION

Senior opportunities and services (SOS).—The 1980 budget requests $10.5 million for SOS, the same spending level as for fiscal year 1979. Approximately 1 million low-income elderly are served by the program.

Community food and nutrition.—The 1980 budget requests $8 million for the community food and nutrition program, a decrease of $22 million from the fiscal year 1979 funding level of $30 million. The reduction would occur primarily in food stamp outreach activities, as the Department of Agriculture improves and expands its outreach efforts. The $8 million requested in the budget would be used for crisis relief, advocacy, and self-help activities.

Energy conservation services.—The fiscal year 1980 budget requests no funding for energy conservation services, since funding for weatherization activities is provided in an energy conservation program, now administered by the Department of Energy (see below).

Energy crisis intervention.—A $40 million contingency fund is requested for fiscal year 1980 to enable CSA to meet emergency situation needs for purchase of home-heating fuels and other energy-related crisis intervention. A portion of CSA's energy conservation program, primarily weatherization activities, had been allocated for crisis intervention in prior years, but this is the first administration request specifically for this purpose. Congress appropriated $200 million for this activity for fiscal years 1977 and 1978. Moreover, $200 million is available for fiscal year 1979 through a continuing appropriations resolution.

Community action agencies.—$381 million is requested for community action agencies for 1980. This is an increase of $12 million from the fiscal 1979 spending level of $369 million. The increase would be used to strengthen the administrative capacity of existing community action agencies, particularly small, rural agencies.

DEPARTMENT OF ENERGY ACTIVITIES

Weatherization grants for low-income persons.—The fiscal 1980 budget for the Department of Energy includes $200 million in budget authority for weatherizing the homes of low-income persons, with particular attention devoted to the elderly and handicapped. This is the same amount that was appropriated for the program's first year of operation in fiscal 1979.

Utility programs and regulatory intervention.—The Economic Regulatory Commission is authorized by the Public Utilities Regulatory Policies Act of 1978 to encourage the adoption of utility rate reforms which promote conservation and equity. The administration has requested $28.1 million for these activities in fiscal 1980.

CONTROL OF FRAUD AND ABUSE IN HEALTH CARE DELIVERY TO THE ELDERLY

Office of the Inspector General, Department of Health, Education, and Welfare.—The fiscal 1980 budget proposes a funding level of $39,868,-000 for antifraud activities, which include operations of the Immediate Office of the Inspector General, the Office of Health Care and Systems Review, the Audit Agency, and the Office of Investigations. This funding would continue staff at approximately the same level as in fiscal 1979.

The Health Care Financing Administration, the Office of Program Integrity (HCFA).—Major initiatives in the control of fraud and abuse are managed by the Health Care Financing Administration and the Office of Program Integrity within HCFA. The 1980 budget recommends $156 million for overall HFCA administrative management of these programs. Of this total, the Office of Program Integrity is projected to receive about $15 million.

State fraud control units.—Public Law 95–142 (medicare-medicaid anti-fraud and abuse amendments) provide 90 percent Federal funding for a 3-year period for States to establish antifraud units. Federal funding for 21 units currently authorized is $55 million.

MENTAL HEALTH

The administration's budget requests $916 million for the National Institute of Mental Health, which includes the Center for Mental Health and Aging, to continue research, training, and service activities. This is $100 million below the 1979 estimated expenditure but slightly more than the 1978 figure.

LEGISLATION

The administration plans to propose legislation to restructure Federal support to States and communities for the development and delivery of comprehensive mental health services, reflecting the recommendations of the President's Commission on Mental Health. An additional $198 million has been requested by President Carter to make appropriate mental health treatment and preventive services available to the unserved and underserved. The new services will focus on elderly, minorities, children, and persons with chronic mental illness.

The administration has also recommended legislation to improve outpatient psychiatric services under medicare.

HOME HEALTH DEMONSTRATION PROGRAM TO BE PHASED OUT

The 1980 budget proposes to phase out the home health demonstration program in 1980, requesting only $804,000. The fiscal year 1979 funding level was $6 million. The $804,000 would be used during 1980 to fund approximately 15 new projects. The program has assisted more than 200 agencies to develop new home health services or expand existing services.

$2 Million Increase Proposed for Hypertension Screening

The budget requested $13,261,000 for hypertension screening programs, an increase of over $2 million from the 1979 funding level of $11 million. Approximately one-third of all older Americans suffer from some form of hypertension.

Administration Requests Increase in Title XX Ceiling

The Congress increased the title XX social services ceiling from $2.5 billion to $2.9 billion for fiscal year 1979. The administration is requesting a $2.9 billion ceiling for fiscal year 1980 to "accommodate the amounts which have previously been made available for child day care and also to focus on assistance to areas of special need as emphasized in the President's urban initiative." Of the $2.9 billion, the administration estimates that approximately $332 million would be spent on homemaker and chore services and approximately $140 million for health related services.

New Initiatives in Community Care Research and Demonstration

Increased budget authority for research and demonstration programs in community long-term care and community services is requested for the Administration on Aging, the Health Care Financing Administration, and the Administration for Public Services.

Administration on Aging.—The 1980 budget request includes $15 million for special demonstration programs in community long-term care services.

Health Care Financing Administration.—An increase of almost $19 million is requested for research, demonstration, and evaluation projects (from $32.5 million in fiscal 1979 to $51.3 million in fiscal 1980). Of this amount, $15 million is to be used for special projects in community long-term care and nursing home improvement projects.

Administration for Public Services.—The 1980 budget requests an increase of about $3 million for research and demonstration projects (from $2,955,000 in fiscal year 1979 to $5,975,000 in fiscal year 1980). A portion of the increase is to be applied to demonstration and evaluation of social/health maintenance organizations and coordination of systems for delivery of health and social services.

Small Increase in Legal Services

The administration is requesting a $13 million increase in funding for direct legal services grants under the Legal Services Corporation, from $235 million in fiscal year 1979 to $248 million for fiscal year 1980. In addition, the Corporation would receive funding for administrative functions and research, bringing its total fiscal year 1980 budget request to approximately $282 million. This budget is expected to support about 7,000 attorneys and 3,000 paralegals in 360 local legal services programs.

Transportation

Urban Mass Transportation Administration.—Section 16(b)(2) of the Urban Mass Transportation Act, as amended in 1978, reserves up to 2 percent of the annual allotment of urban discretionary funds for capital assistance grants to private nonprofit groups for transit services to elderly and handicapped individuals.

Urban discretionary grants under the proposed 1980 budget would be $1.279 billion, compared to an estimated $1.250 billion in fiscal 1979 and an actual $1.399 billion in 1978. Thus, up to $25.6 million would be available in fiscal 1980 for 16(b)(2) capital assistance.

Revisions of transit legislation in 1978 also created a new nonurban formula grant program to provide both capital and operating assistance for small cities and rural areas. For fiscal 1980, $75 million is planned for this new activity. This would support about 50 grants.

Federal Employees Part-Time Career Employment Act of 1978

No new spending authority is provided for the Federal Employees Part-Time Career Employment Act. However, the law requires Federal agencies to express schedules of permanent positions in terms of full-time equivalence in the work year ceilings (by the end of 1980). This would be achieved by counting the number of hours worked rather than the number of staff positions.

Controls imposed by rigid personnel ceilings, rather than the more flexible full-time equivalence approach were cited by the GAO as a significant barrier to the employment of workers unwilling or unable to work the standard workweek.

The Congressional Budget Office estimates that some 3,000 new employees will fill part-time positions which, under the full-time equivalence standards, will be counted as part of the current employment ceiling.

Beginning October 1, 1978, selected test agencies (Veterans Administration, General Services Administration, Environmental Protection Agency, Federal Trade Commission, and the Export-Import Bank) began to measure and report on their employment by counting the number of hours worked rather than staffing levels.

The experiment is designed to accomplish two objectives: (1) To break down artificial barriers that may have inhibited the employment of permanent part-time workers; and (2) to determine whether full-time equivalent controls can improve personnel management, overcome some of the criticisms directed at the existing year end control systems, and not significantly increase the Federal work force.

Food Stamp Program

The administration estimates that food stamp participation will increase from 16.5 million recipients in 1974 to 17.4 million in 1980. Approximately $6.5 billion will be paid out in food stamps. Regulations became effective on January 1, 1979, to eliminate the purchase requirement for food stamp recipients.

$2.2 Million Cutback Proposed for Community Schools

Funding for community schools would be cut back by $2.238 million under the new budget, from $5.376 million in fiscal 1979 to $3.138 million in fiscal 1980. The community schools program provides Federal funds to State and local educational agencies to assist in the delivery of coordinated social, recreational, and cultural services.

SCORE and ACE

The fiscal 1980 budget requests $2.27 million for the Service Corps of Retired Executives (SCORE) and the Active Corps of Executives (ACE). The fiscal year 1979 funding level was $2.25 million. The 1980 request would enable approximately 12,500 retired executives to continue to provide volunteer services. The Small Business Administration administers SCORE and ACE.

Two Generations of Elderly in the Changing American Family: Implications for Family Services

Donald E. Gelfand, Jody K. Olsen, Marilyn R. Block*

The Family Coordinator, Vol. 27, No. 4, October, 1978.
Special Issue: Aging in a Family Context, Timothy H.
Brubaker and Lawrence E. Sneden, II, Guest Editors.
Copyright © 1978 by the National Council on Family
Relations, Minneapolis. Reprinted with permission.

Coping with the problems of growing old may be complicated by demands for economic, psychological, and social support for aging parents. Second generation children facing major age-related role shifts may not be equipped to provide such supports. Both generations are coping with their own aging process as well as with the changing family relationships caused by the process. Where such intergenerational family compositions exist, service providers must be able to understand the accompanying unique interaction patterns and maximize opportunities that can strengthen these relationships.

A well-known maxim asserts that major demographic policy decisions are not made in Congress, but in the privacy of couples' bedrooms. The results of these decisions are seen by service providers long after their inception. They cause scratching of heads and discussions of "social problems" as clients with new service needs begin to appear.

Individual attitudes toward marriage and children among the birth cohort of 1895 are still having their effect on family relationships today, producing increasingly complex patterns of interaction as well as new problems and issues of mutual support for individuals in families with three, four, or even five generations.

This paper will explore the changes in mutual support among family generations resulting from increased life expectancy and the consequent increase in numbers of elderly in the family. Specifically, it will focus on two

generational strata: first generation elderly individuals aged 75 and over and second generation individuals aged 55 to 65. Both of these are "aging" groups facing problems common to the aging process but also contending with problems unique to their different age, family, and work roles.

Coping with the problems of growing old may be complicated by the demands for support from the individual's family. In contemporary American families, support demands placed on adult children in their late 50's by 75 + -year-old parents may be exacerbated by the additional demands of a third generation of adult children developing their own nuclear families and having small children of their own. To clarify the threads of this complex situation we will examine available data and indicate what additional inputs are needed to fill the gaps in our knowledge. Similarly, we will then turn our attention to the literature on intergenerational family relationships to ascertain what guidance it can provide and what deficiencies still exist in the area of families with two generations of aging. Finally, we will conclude with an attempt to explicate the implications of these changes for professionals in the field of aging and family services.

*Donald E. Gelfand is Associate Professor, School of Social Work and Community Planning, University of Maryland at Baltimore; Jody K. Olsen is Director, Center on Aging, University of Maryland at College Park; Marilyn R. Block is Research Associate, University of Maryland at College Park, Maryland 20742.

The Future and the Four Generation Family

Aging and Family Composition

Two major demographic changes are affecting the structure of the family today: the increase in absolute life expectancy among Americans to age 72 and the average increase in life expectancy of another 15 years for those individuals who survive to 65 (National Clearinghouse on Aging, 1977). Both of these figures clearly relate to what has been popularly termed the "graying" of the American population. Within these statistics it can be noted that the growth of the conventionally defined aged population has not been occurring evenly among those 65 and over, but is concentrated in the 75 and over age group. Projections of the census bureau (1974) indicate that the population 75+ which now accounts for 38% of those 65 and over in the United States will grow to 41% of this same population group by the year 2000.

"As of mid-1975 most older Americans (65+) were under 75 (62%), half were under age 73 and more than a third (36%) were under 70. Between 1960 and 1975 the population aged 75+ increased 52%. Close to 1.9 million Americans are 85 years of age or over" (U.S.Senate, 1976).

Practitioners in the field of aging have become aware of these changes by observing their own case loads. Family problems resulting from the presence of an older family member with chronic physical limitations have become more pronounced. Many families are making plans for caring for an elderly parent for an extended period of time. This latter situation is complicated by the fact that the second generation children most relied on to provide this "parent caring" are themselves approaching "old age." These family members are beginning to face the personal, economic, social, and psychological issues of aging that are common to industrialized societies.

Compounding further the changes taking place between the first and the second generation family members are the dynamics between the second and third and second and fourth generation members of the same family. As noted a decade ago:

"The nature of the problems of old age is therefore changing. A common instance in the past has been the middle-aged woman faced with the problem of caring for an infirm mother as well as her young children. A common instance of the future will be the woman of 60 faced with the problem of caring for an infirm mother in her eighties. Her children will be adult but it is her grandchildren who will compete with the mother for her attentions. The four generations of surviving relatives may tend to separate into two semi-independent groupings—each of two generations" (Townsend, 1968, pp. 256-257).

Demographic Projections

To understand the extent of this demographic configuration already seen by service providers, we can carry through complex projections of current census data. Projections are necessary because the census does not provide information on the presence of family relationships when the first generation is maintaining independent residences or living in institutional settings, situations that account for the vast majority of the elderly. Using two valuable pieces of data—age of first marriage for white women and the fact that "American women on the average have at least half of their children by the time they are married five years" (U.S. Bureau of Census, 1974, p. 23)—we can project age structure of the generations making up these four generation families over the next fifty years.

Although demographic projections have never been noted for their long term reliability, a conservative projection of future demographic patterns indicates the continued growth of two generations of elderly within the family through at least the middle of the next century. As discussed below, the three generation family may again become dominant after that period, but the presence of two generations of individuals aged 55 and over in the family structure should continue to be a factor in familial relationships throughout the 21st century. This analysis is detailed in Tables 1-3.

White women born in 1864 had a median age at first marriage of 23 and bore their first child by the time they were 28 (Table 1). If still alive, these women would be 113 in 1977 and have an 85-year-old child (and perhaps another child a few years younger). The median age of first marriage for women declined through the 1950's to approximately 20 years. The period from the 1950's to the 1970's however, produced a reversal in this trend with median age at first marriage increasing to 21.3 in 1973. As can be seen in column "e" of Table 1, there is likely to be a substantial number of four generation families in 1977 with first generation members in their 80's and second generation children at least 55 years old. The increased life expectancy for both men and women will influence the prevalence of both the two elderly generations and the four-generation configuration.

The figures contained in Table 2 indicate a continuation of this pattern 25 years later with the significant change that first generation elderly will only have to reach 83 to have the

Table 1.
Configuration of White American Family by Age and Generation in 1977

(a) Year of birth of women	(b) Median age of women at 1st marriage[1]	(c) Age of women at birth of ½ of children	(d) Age of women in 1977	(e) Age of child 1977
1864	23	28	113	85
1892	22	27	85	58
1919	21	26	58	32
1945	20	25	32	7

[1] Figures have been rounded off to the nearest integer.

Table 2.
Configuration of White American Family by Age and Generation in 2002

(a) Year of birth of women	(b) Median age of women at 1st marriage[1]	(c) Age of women at birth of ½ of children	(d) Age of women in 2002	(e) Age of child 2002
1892	22	27	110	83
1919	21	26	83	57
1945	20	25	57	32
1970	23	28	32	4

[1] Figures have been rounded off to the nearest integer.

Table 3.
Configuration of White American Family by Age and Generation in 2027

(a) Year of birth of women	(b) Median age of women at 1st marriage[1]	(c) Age of women at birth of ½ of children	(d) Age of women in 2027	(e) Age of child 2027
1919	21	26	108	82
1945	20	25	82	57
1970	23	28	57	29
1998	24	29	29	—

[1] Figures have been rounded off to the nearest integer.

four generation family established. The age differential between first and second generation individuals in 2002 is thus 26 years as compared to 27 years in 1977. It can be expected that there will be a significant increase in the presence of elderly in the family and an expanding number of four generation families. This expectation is buttressed by the fact that the 1950-54 marriage cohort (individuals born in the 1930's) will probably be the most fertile cohort of the 20th century (U.S. Bureau of the Census, 1971). Table 2 also represents a projection of the continuation of the demographic trends witnessed in the last 20 years. This includes primarily an increase in the median age of women at first marriage. While this figure increased from 20.3 in 1950 to 21.3 in 1973, from the information in Table 2, one might postulate a sharp increase to 23 in 1993 to provide a conservative estimate of family structure into the next century.

In Table 3, age 24 is the projected age at first marriage for the generation born in 1998. As a result of these estimates an 82-year-old individual is likely to have a 57-year-old child and a 29-year-old grandchild. Upon reaching 85, the aging first generation individual would be likely to find him/herself part of a four generation family structure. The age differ-

ential in 2027 between first and second generations has continued to decline to 25 years.

A median age at first marriage that did not reach 23 or 24 would accelerate the number of families with two generations of elderly and the growth of four generation families. A decline in the median age at first marriage from the 1973 figure (age 21) would heighten the trend even further.

Changes in Intergenerational Family Relationships

Both the first and second generations of the four generation family as outlined by the data projection will be undergoing major changes unless age norms in American society change drastically during the next fifty years. These changes seriously affect the three major areas of mutual family support: economic support, psychological support, and social support.

Economic Support

First generation members of the family (75+) have already experienced major economic changes. Reduced discretionary income, and increased reliance on fixed income and savings are all part of a well-known and widely discussed aspect of the American aging process. Second generation individuals (55+) will be beginning to experience and cope with these economic changes as they approach retirement.

Therefore, this period may, for the second generation, involve both a reorganizing of life styles and major attempts to marshall resources for future non-work years. Demands for major financial support from elderly parents facing major economic problems relating to extensive physical illness may increase the strain on the intergenerational relationship and decrease the ability of these individuals to cope with their own aging. While Social Security, SSI, Medicare and Medicaid programs have helped to alleviate this potential economic burden, the level of governmental support will probably remain far from adequate for most individuals or elderly couples. In addition, the perceptions of economic need can at times have as much effect on the relationship as the actual need itself.

Psychological Support

Individuals in their late 50's and early 60's are dealing with important developmental issues related to approaching old age and role changes. As Neugarten (1968, p. 140) notes, "the middle years of life—probably the decade of the fifties for most persons—represent an important turning point with the restructuring of time and the formulation of new perceptions of self, time, and death. . . . The reflection of middle age is not the same as the reminiscences of old age; but perhaps it is its forerunner."

The aging process may thus require a major change in the life styles which will seem threatening to many individuals. First generation elderly may already have undertaken a reassessment and established a reintegration of their lives which they attempt to maintain barring physical incapacities. However, increased physical changes, particularly prevalent after 75, can affect this often times fragile reintegration. Second generation children may still be in the process of this initial readjustment and find it difficult to provide the psychological support that may be needed by elderly parents.

Social Changes

Individuals in their eighties may suffer a number of role losses resulting from physical incapacitation and loss of ambulation. The ability to maintain social relationships, interact in community settings or attend a variety of cultural or leisure time activities may be severely diminished. Second generation individuals in their 50's and early 60's are less likely to suffer from chronic physical condi-

tions. Instead they face the social adjustments that are intertwined with shifting their schedule from one oriented to daily work routines to one revolving around extended free time. The problems of developing a satisfying stance towards retirement can be intense, especially for those individuals whose work patterns have emphasized physical labor. These readjustments may be compounded by increasing mortality among friends and relatives.

Second generation children may be facing major role shifts and seeking new definitions of their role. They may not be ready to provide the social support necessary to enable first generation elderly to maintain contact with surviving friends or relatives or engage in recreational activities.

Studies in Intergenerational Family Relationships

Although there has been almost no research on family interaction in which both generations are 55 and over, the work related to intergenerational family relationships gives a background to the observed behavior being discussed.

This research can easily be broken into two distinct phases or trends. Early work in the area of family studies, undertaken during the 1940's and 1950's, was based on the assumption that nuclear families lived in isolation from extended family members and thus the aged were largely ignored (Parsons, 1955). When the aged were an issue, the focus was on role reversal as the inevitable developmental task to be faced by both the aging parent and the adult child. The underlying assumption was that the aging parent was competent only up to a certain point in the life span, at which time there was a reverting to childlike behaviors and the adult child took over the role of parent to his or her own parents. That this theme was the core around which much early work revolved is testimony to the negative stereotype assigned to the aged.

During the 1960's there was a shift away from the notion of role reversal as the sole pattern of aging (Blenkner, 1965). There was acknowledgement that, while middle-aged adult children maintained close ties with their aging parents, those links were not forged out of growing parental dependence. Rather, middle-aged adult children were concerned with their parents' changing needs and attempted to help them meet these needs on a mutual level. The realization that aging parents cannot always offer emotional and economic supports to their children, that they may in fact require such *from* their children, has been termed "filial maturity" (Blenkner, 1965). It is the shift from middle age to old age that can then jeopardize the "filial maturity."

The body of literature shows that it is difficult to sort through the many factors tied to the interaction between adult children and their aging parents. While emotional ties are influential in the process, guilt may be a stronger force (Sussman, 1965). Regardless of the reasons, adult children tend to internalize the social and moral belief that they are responsible for their parents, and behave very responsibly with regard to their parents' well-being (Brody, 1970).

Living Arrangements

One of the many family issues tied to familial interaction is living arrangements. Most surveys (Adams, 1968; Gibson, 1972; Kerckhoff, 1966; Shanas, Townsend, Wedderburn, Friis, Milhhoj, & Stehouwer, 1968; Sussman, 1965) indicate that older people do not desire to reside with their children; rather, they wish to maintain their own households for as long as possible. Troll (1971) finds that the aged move in with their children only in cases of inadequate economic support or poor health. Although joint households are not typical, related nuclear families tend to maintain households near each other. One study (Shanas et al., 1968) states that approximately 84% of those over the age of 65 live within an hour's distance of one child.

Institutionalization offers an alternative living arrangement for the elderly. The proportionately small number of aged who reside in such institutions (5% of the population over 65) seems to indicate that this form of housing alternative is used only as a last resort. It is important to note that these last resort alternatives relate to poor health among the first generation, a factor of growing importance when both generations are 55 and over.

Economic and Social Interdependence

A second family issue concerns economic interdependence (Brody, 1970; Troll, 1971). Mutual aid, particularly in the form of services and favors, or money, has been employed as a measure of extended family status. It is interesting to note that sons tend to give aid in the form of money while daughters tend to offer aid in the form of services. This may be a reflection of the form of aid received from parents at an earlier stage; it could also reflect a son-in-law's unwillingness financially to support his in-laws, or a daughter-in-law's unwillingness to take the time to provide services for her in-laws; or it might reflect a son's involvement in the role of breadwinner to the exclusion of family orientation, while reflecting the more nurturant role of the daughter.

Perhaps the most important issue as far as the elderly are concerned is their own interaction with their children, where interaction is measured by how often relatives visit, telephone, or write to each other (Brody, 1970; Shanas et al., 1968; Troll, 1971). Parents and children tend to see each other often, although age, stage, and generational variations exist in the visiting patterns. Shanas et al. (1968) indicate that 85% of middle-aged children find time to visit their aging parents weekly. Troll (1971) presents more conservative estimates—40% of the middle aged see their parents weekly, while only 10% of the young adults see their grandparents weekly. The middle aged tend to bridge the chasm between grandparents and grandchildren, interacting with both groups (Lowenthal & Robinson, 1976). However, one component affecting the interaction process is what is called "parent caring."

Reactions to Family Demands

The need for "parent caring," a predominant phenomenon when both generations are 55 and over may place second generation individuals in a quandary. It is indicated in the literature (Clark & Anderson, 1967) that the needs of the 75+ parent may be increasingly extensive, and require the reversal of the assistance that has previously flowed from parent to children. For the second generation child approaching old age with its own role changes, these needs as well as the needs of his/her own children may approximate an approach-avoidance situation. The second generation individual may strive to deal with his/her own problems as well as provide support for the elderly parent and children and grandchildren. On the other hand, the second generation child may move towards favoring either the elderly parent or the children (Lowenthal & Robinson, 1976). Elderly parents may be seen as more needy because of their diminishing resources and a second generation child may attempt to provide maximal support. Taking the opposite position, second generation individuals may view their children as having the greatest call on available resources, one reason being the "buying of kinship insurance" (Sussman, 1965). Finally, second generation children, feeling trapped between competing demands on resources that may be dwindling because of impending retirement, may decide to withdraw completely from relationships with parents, children or grandchildren and focus exclusively on their own needs.

While research during the 1960's focused on a shift in thinking toward interdependence, away from the role reversal orientation of the 1940's and 1950's, it emphasized families where the adult children were *middle-aged*. The 1970's has brought about demographic shifts that indicate an increase in the number of four generation families where both the first and the second generations are dealing with issues related to aging. It is with these families that special consideration should be given as the relationship to the aging process affects the previously identified interaction patterns.

Implications for Family Services

Professionals working with families have always been aware of the interdynamics that play upon each family member in relation with others. This discussion has focused on the unique inter-relationships that can be present when both parent and child are coping with changes relating to the aging process. Coping with these changes cannot only put stress on the individual, but on the relationship between parent and child, bringing changes difficult to adjust to and in some cases even understand by each participant. Because of the stresses endemic to these ages, it is important for any person or group working with those identified in the discussion to be sensitive to these issues in addition to the ones normally associated with adult parent-child relationships.

Problem Identification

First, it is important to get information helpful to identifying the potential problem. When working with the old-old, (75+), one usually identifies their children, their physical and emotional proximity and their history of interaction dynamics. However, when beginning work with the young-old (55-75), information about living parents is not always elicited (Leichter & Mitchell, 1967). One of the authors had the experience of developing a nursing home placement for a hospital patient before knowing that the patient's mother was at the same home. This knowledge explained much of the observed pre-hospital discharge behavior.

The identification, not only of the existence of parents and/or children, but of the perceived current relationship, can affect the developing treatment plan, even if the treatment plan focuses on the third and fourth generations. This is particularly true if there have been recent changes in the relationship.

Involving Secondary Family Members

Next, it is important that special individual or group counseling services be made available to the family member secondarily involved in treatment—services that relate specifically to the aging process and how each person fits into it. The young-old are caught trying to cope with retirement income change and changing use of time, while seeing in a parent major health changes and a growing emotional and/or physical dependency. If the children of the young-old have only recently left the house, this dependency can cause particular resentment and guilt for having to give up planned-for freedom to an aged parent.

Ascertaining Resources

Finally, help is often needed in locating community and institutional resources for the parent and in understanding what the use of the resources will mean in familial relationships. As pointed out, because of increasing longevity, there is a greater chance that the first generation will live to an age that requires extensive supportive services. These services can follow a pattern of support for a parent in his own living environment such as recreation programs and transportation programs. Alternatively, support such as visiting nurse services can be provided for a parent or child in a joint living situation. Parents can also be supported within an institutional setting such as a nursing home. Many children, while developing behavior patterns related to their own aging process, try to reach out to the increasingly dependent parent, but feel that they will soon be overwhelmed by the demands made on them. Being able to identify and locate appropriate support services gives a sense to the second generation that they are not alone in their efforts to provide support, a feeling not as uncommon as might be imagined. The pressure for having to give all the support is relieved, bringing an opportunity for selective involvement. For example, a five-day-a-week Meals on Wheels program gives the opportunity for family members to provide meals and companionship on the remaining two days a week. Geriatric day care affords these same opportunities. With outside support services being drawn in as needed, family members can concentrate on sharing emotional relationships, those that community services cannot give.

Needing and Accepting Support

It is important to understand that needing outside support is not a sign of failure or rejection. Increased longevity itself brings changes in mental and physical conditions not readily seen in earlier generations, changes that complicate care giving situations. Families in which two generations are over 55 are particularly susceptible to these complications and are most in need of community support in order to preserve their familial relationships. Although true, this phenomenon is initially difficult to accept, particularly by the old-old.

For them, acceptance of services is a three-part threat. First, it is an admission of growing dependency and age, an admission postponed if possible. As Butler (1975) points out, one can fight hard to sustain continued functioning, refusing services others consider essential. Once a service is received, however, the admission is made, and increased dependency can grow rapidly.

Second, many have developed pride in being self sustaining. Any type of service is considered welfare, something that is abhorred. Even programs with reimbursement mechanisms such as congregate and home delivered meal programs can be initially resisted for this reason. Helping children understand the reasons for the resistance is an important service-provider function.

Third, the acceptance of services can be seen as an opportunity for the family to become less involved. A fear that children will use services as an excuse to cease any involvement will manifest itself in service rejection. Many on a five-day home-delivered meal program did not want a seven-day program when asked because, as they emphatically indicated, their children might stop making contact with them.

Program Components and the Elderly

Many programs set up for the elderly, either those primarily for the old-old or the young-old, do not focus on the family dynamics affecting the attempted service delivery. Only those that are designed to serve primarily the extended family living together have identifiable family relation components. Geriatric day care is an excellent example of this situation. A program designed for those people who cannot function independently, the participants are primarily first generation living in homes of young-old second generation family members. In Baltimore, many program directors, under the auspices of the Baltimore City Commission on Aging, sponsored a series of sessions for family members to discuss the aging process and its effect on family relationships. The success of these sessions is related to the fact that daily contact keeps the potential problems in sharp focus, and also to the fact that the family relationships are most likely to be changing because the first generation members are experiencing health and physical changes. Sessions for families of elderly receiving services where the elderly are stabilized either in the community or an institution and not living with the family, have been less successful.

Thus, if resources for family counseling are limited, they can be most effective when linked to programs that involve single household extended families and/or, more importantly, when either the parent or child or both are experiencing health changes. The pressures involved in these situations (in addition to pressures already discussed as components of the aging process for both the young-old and old-old) provide the motivation needed for participation.

However, in all aging service situations, whether they are recreational, social, functional, health, or institutional it is important to identify the two generation geriatric family unit where it does exist. Understanding the changes that affect inter-relationships is vital. Additional support services as needed for physical and psychological adaptation must be generated, while counseling to help the family maintain intact appropriate emotional linkages is provided. Further, special attention needs to be focused on the family members not directly involved in the agency contact to assure that they are not continuing possible dysfunctioning forces on the family member when outside the agency setting. Giving special attention through individual counseling will help sensitize family members to their own actions, and the relationship of these actions to their own and their parents' aging process.

Conclusion

With the increased longevity superimposed on current role changes and attitudes towards the elderly, there are changes in the concept of mutual support among family generations. For the first time, we are seeing the phenomenon of the two generation geriatric family, a parent in his or her late 70's or early 80's with children in their late 50's or early 60's. Thus two generations are coping with their own aging processes as well as with the changing family relationships caused by the process.

The second generation is planning for retirement and anticipating a fixed and probably reduced income while their parents, having lived on such an income for fifteen to twenty years are now coping with new economic limitations related to increased illnesses. The second generation family members are coping with impending role changes, the restructuring of time, and the formulation of new perceptions of self. The old-old, having completed this developmental stage are trying to cling to the already existent communication patterns despite their changing physical condition. Thus the second generation is looking for changes while the first generation attempts to prevent these very changes.

In addition, physical difficulties limit the ability to establish social relationships among peers within the oldest group, forcing increased dependence on the children for social interaction. This comes at a time when new friendship interaction patterns are being established among young-old groups as retirement triggers related changes.

All this points up the need for service providers to identify the existence of such an intergenerational family composition, understand clearly the unique interaction patterns likely to be seen and provide information and support that can maximize the opportunity for the relationships to remain as strong as possible. The single most important potential crisis point is at the time the old-old suffer possible dependency-producing health changes. Special counseling in anticipation of this time has the greatest potential of being well received.

As our literature review indicates, there are few hard data (other than census projections) on the prevalence of the discussed phenomenon. The research to date deals with the elderly and their children, but does not factor out the age of the children in order to identify those who are themselves approaching old age. Moving in this direction is vital if we are to be able to identify techniques useful for clinical support. The entire subject demands intensive attention in order for appropriate service solutions to emerge.

References

Adams, B. N. Kinship in an urban setting. Chicago: Markham, 1968.

Blenkner, M. Social work and family relationships in later life with some thoughts on filial maturity. In E. Shanas & G. F. Streib (Eds.), Social structure and the family: Generational relations. Englewood Cliffs: Prentice-Hall, 1965.

Brody, E. M. The etiquette of filial behavior. Aging and Human Development, 1970, 1, 87-94.

Butler, R. N. Why survive? Being old in America. New York: Harper & Row, 1975.

Clark, M., & Anderson, B. G. Culture and aging: An anthropological study of older Americans. Springfield, Ill.: Thomas, 1967.

Gibson, G. Kin family network: Overheralded structure in past conceptualizations of family functioning. Journal of Marriage and the Family, 1972, 34, 13-23.

Kerckhoff, A. C. Family patterns and morale in retirement. In I. H. Simpson & J. C. McKinney (Eds.), Social aspects of aging. Durham: Duke University Press, 1966.

Leichter, H., & Mitchell, W. Kinship and casework. New York: Russell Sage, 1967.

Lowenthal, M. F., & Robinson, B. Social networks and isolation. Handbook of aging and the social sciences. New York: Van Nostrand Reinhold, 1976.

National Clearinghouse on Aging. Facts about older Americans 1976. Washington, D.C.: Department of Health, Education and Welfare, 1977.

Neugarten, B. Adult personality: Toward a psychology of the life cycle. In B. Neugarten (Ed.), Middle-age and aging. Chicago: University of Chicago Press, 1968.

Parsons, T. The American family: Its relations to personality and to the social structure. In T. Parsons & R. Bales (Eds.), Family, socialization and interaction process. New York: Macmillan, 1955.

Shanas, E., Townsend, P., Wedderburn, D., Friis, H., Milhhoj, P., & Stehouwer, J., Older people in three industrial societies. New York: Atherton, 1968.

Sussman, M. B. Relationships of adult children with their parents in the U.S. In E. Shanas & G. F. Streib (Eds.), Social structure and the family: Generational relations. Englewood Cliffs: Prentice-Hall, 1965.

Townsend, P. The emergence of the four-generation family in industrial society. In B. Neugarten (Ed.), Middle-age and aging. Chicago: University of Chicago Press, 1968.

Troll, L. E. The family of later life: A decade review. Journal of Marriage and the Family, 1971, 33, 263-290.

U.S. Bureau of the Census. Fertility indicators, 1970. Current Population Reports: Special Studies. (Series P-23, No. 32). Washington, D.C.: U.S. Government Printing Office, 1971.

U.S. Bureau of the Census. Population of the United States: Trends and prospects, 1950-1990. Current Population Reports: Special Studies. (Series P-23, No. 49). Washington, D.C.: U.S. Government Printing Office, 1974.

U.S. Senate. Special Committee on Aging. Developments in Aging: 1975 and January-May 1976. Washington, D.C.: U.S. Government Printing Office, 1976.

The Concept and Role of Congregate Housing for Older People

Frances M. Carp

A paper from the First National Conference on Congregate Housing for Older People conducted by the International Center for Social Gerontology Administration on Aging, U.S. Department of H.E.W., Washington, D.C., 1977.

Congregate housing is "officially" defined in the 1970 Housing and Urban Development Act and in the 1974 Housing and Community Development Act as low-cost housing in which some or all dwelling units have no kitchens and in which there is a central dining facility. In implementing the program, the U.S. Department of Housing and Urban Development (HUD) has tended to interpret the legislative language as restrictive to food service. Other definitions and different names for the basic concept have been suggested, all deriving from some dissatisfaction with the legislative language and/or HUD's interpretation of it.

What is the source of this unease? Generally, dissatisfaction arises either from some discontinuity between expectation and reality—some gap between problem and proffered solution—or from some ambiguity. Both may be involved in the present instance. Some ambiguities in the terminology will be considered later in this paper, but first let us examine the malaise that seems to stem from the definition. The question then becomes: What is the problem that congregate housing is intended to alleviate?

Housing's Role in Attaining Societal Goals for the Elderly

With regard to older citizens, society has established certain goals which may be summarized as "good quality of life." Dignity, independence, and the exercise of options are among the common descriptors of life quality; to achieve them, programs have been devised to help provide the elderly with adequate income, good living environments, nutritious food, and access to other people and to needed services (health, recreational, cultural, religious, and social).

Housing has been a major focus of efforts to achieve these goals. A large number and some variety of housing facilities for the elderly have been erected, and other types of housing have been made available to them through various programs. Many national and international meetings have been organized around the subject of housing the elderly. There also has been clear documentation in several research studies that the living environments of older people have decisive impact upon aspects of their life styles and well-being which are reasonably subsumed under "quality of life."

One of the most impressive occurrences in this country in the past 15 years has been the construction of housing which benefits the elderly. These programs were initiated more on faith than on anything else, on the conviction that good housing would be beneficial. There were those who thought that older people would be unable to adapt and that relocating them would be hazardous. And there were those who thought it would make no difference.

Many Federally-funded housing programs affect the elderly, directly or indirectly. Those that have had the most impact upon poor and moderate income elderly are public housing, Section 202, Section 236, and rent supplement programs.[1] Section 231 housing has touched those who are relatively affluent. Currently, attention is turning to the need to more actively involve the private as well as the public sector in improving housing for the elderly. This urgent need was stressed at the 1973 International Symposium on Housing and Environmental Design for Older Adults:

> One of the principal objectives of the Symposium was to encourage increased investment of untapped private capital in housing for older people with an economic return satisfying to investors.[2]

Under its various programs HUD has re-housed approximately 750,000 older people, and today about 600,000 of them live in special housing for the elderly. On the basis of this rather impressive amount of re-housing, what can be said about the impact of living environments upon the well-being of older people and, in particular, what are the implications of this experience for congregate housing? Despite the impressive number of older people re-housed, the larger figure (750,000) represents only about three percent of the total elderly population. Those persons re-housed probably are a select segment of this population, rather than representative of their age peers in general. Therefore, our knowledge is of limited generalizability with regard to "older people." However, for those who have been re-housed and for others like them, it is instructive to ask: What have we learned about the importance of housing, and how can this information enlighten our work with congregate housing?

Is Housing Important to Older People?

Does improving the housing of older people really help? Benefits following a move to an apartment house which was built under the Section 202 program (and included some respondents who received rent supplements) were reported by Donahue.[3] Similarly, beneficial effects following a move to a retirement community for the relatively well-to-do were reported by Hamovitch.[4] Since neither study included non-movers for comparison purposes, the capacity to generalize their findings is limited.

Studies using comparison groups found associations between moving to a better housing situation and various indexes of well-being.[5,6,7] Even these studies are not conclusive. They compared movers with non-movers, but not across time, and, therefore, do not speak definitely about change due to re-housing.

A longitudinal study that compared movers and non-movers in relation to public housing for the elderly reported a similarly favorable impact of improved housing over the first year of tenancy.[8] This finding has been cross-validated in five different housing environments over a similar one-year interval.[9] With the exception of functional health, the results are consistent with earlier findings, confirming the beneficial effects of good housing, at least over the short run.

Obviously, reactions at the end of one year may represent a "honeymoon" response. Unless benefits are lasting, the investment is questionable. The longitudinal study cited previously has been "validated across time."[10] Data from this eight-year follow-up study support the early favorable conclusions. In addition to the "softer" indexes of life satisfaction, well-being, and desired life style, it is now apparent that death and institutionalization rates are lower. Not only has better housing increased the length of life, but also it has increased the quality of the added years. The feasibility of attaining societal goals for older citizens through the medium of housing seems now to be well documented.

Implications of Research Studies for Congregate Housing

Studies to date justify concluding that: (1) low-cost housing for the elderly is beneficial to competent older people who select it; (2) retirement communities can be beneficial, at least over the short run, to those financially and otherwise privileged persons who choose them; and (3) the elderly who have been studied have not included those most in need of services as well as shelter. Because of the eligibility requirement of "wellness," these elderly have been explicitly or implicitly excluded from re-housing projects (and consequently from the research), either by not being admitted or by having to move out when it became impossible to sustain independent living because the requisite supporting services were not available.

It is clear that improved housing with limited services has positive effects on the physical and socio-psychological health of the elderly. There exists, however, a large but relatively unknown group of older persons whose ability to function independently and to enjoy life is dependent upon the receipt of one or more services. These individuals may be physically impaired or socially deprived, or both, but their needs would not be well met in a nursing home or a "bed care" environment. On the basis of need estimates made nationally by the Urban Institute, Washington, D.C., there are 2.4 million persons age 65 and older who do not need institutionalization but do need appropriate shelter and services in order to remain outside of institutions. The estimates suggest that 1.1 million of them need congregate housing.[11]

In applying to congregate housing any wisdom acquired through experience with earlier housing concepts, it is important to keep in mind that the "independent living" environments which have been created and studied are, for the most part, far more than simply shelter. Lurie Terrace, the project studied by Donahue, had a dining room in which one meal a day was served as well as a number of recreation areas in which community groups provided various services and activities. The retirement community studied by Hamovitch advertised its "country club" life style with all manner of services and amenities. Victoria Plaza in San Antonio, Texas (a study of whose residents is referenced in footnotes 6 and 8) included, on the ground floor, the first senior center in the country to be located in a public housing project. Housing for the elderly is not now and never has been viewed as shelter in isolation from other aspects of the surrounding environment. The concept of congregate housing is the newest development in the respected tradition of viewing housing for the elderly within the context of the broader environment and of interpreting housing for independent living to include shelter plus other service elements necessary to support dignified lives of good quality.[12]

What is *new* is the recognition that the service components in earlier housing programs are still insufficient to enable an important segment of the older population to maintain or return to highly valued independent living and to relieve society of the financial burden of their unnecessary institutionalization. The success of the more limited early models of congregate housing justifies the expectation that provision of appropriate and adequate services will assist in achieving these vital individual and societal goals. The service provision aspect for the congregate housing program is different from previous programs in that it permits services to be *funded together* with shelter, acknowledging the central importance of services, in conjunction with shelter, to prolong independent living and to support life quality.

Questions in Defining Congregate Housing

What is to be congregated—living units? old people? services?

Congregate housing—taken literally, gathering housing units into close proximity—is not novel and is far from unique to the elderly. The decline of free-standing individual family residences and the rise of dwelling units "congregated" into apartment houses, multiplexes, and condominiums are widespread for all age groups, due to population growth, urbanization, land values, and building costs. The overriding advantage is economy in providing living units. In its literal sense, congregate housing is simply descriptive of a national trend for people of all ages.

Another interpretation of the term is that old people are to be gathered together for residential purposes. Such age clustering may have significant advantages for sociability and mutual assistance.[13] It is efficient for service delivery; obviously, it is in many ways easier to provide services to a concentrated and homogeneous population with similar needs and life styles.[14] However, there is evidence that not all older people desire or benefit from age-homogeneous living environments, and that congregating deprived people of any type may impede rather than facilitate societal attention to their needs.[15]

This leads to the third possibility, that the essential "congregating" is that of services rather than either living units or old people. The scattering of services needed by the elderly and the imperfect efforts to coordinate them are continuing problems. Concentration of services within a residential setting is one way of focusing relevant services and making them available to residents. It is not the only viable model for meeting shelter and service needs nor the best one for all situations. It is of central importance and yet cannot solve the entire problem.

Let us consider the working definition of congregate housing prepared for this conference:

> Congregate housing is an assisted independent group living environment that offers the elderly who are functionally impaired or socially deprived, but otherwise in good health, the residential accommodations and supporting services they need to maintain or return to a semi-independent life style and prevent premature or unnecessary institutionalization as they grow older.

I propose that this definition be altered somewhat and be reformulated as a broad societal objective, in the pursuit of which "congregate housing" is one vastly important model for assisting independent living. This subordination is not intended to be demeaning, but rather to further the progress of congregate housing by setting realistic goals. As a background to this proposal, let us examine the major terms in the proposed definition.

What is "Assisted Independent Living"?

Independent living is widely accepted as a central goal among older people and as a major goal for society with regard to the elderly. As people age, their maintenance of independent living becomes more dependent upon environmental supports and upon easy access to more services more frequently. Some portion of the older population seems capable of fending, each for himself, with no special provisions or considerations other than those available to persons of all ages. At the opposite end of the spectrum there is a relatively small proportion of persons who are unable to live independently even with maximal supports, including appropriate services, but who instead need care. The size of this latter group remains indefinite, but evidence suggests that it is not as large as the number of elderly persons now in institutions. Between these two extremes lie the majority of older persons at any one time and the majority of years of "old age" for an individual. The more appropriately the living environment supports the capabilities and meets the needs of this majority of older persons, the longer will be the period during which they can maintain autonomous lives, and the better will be the quality of their living during that span.

Who Are the Elderly Who Are "Impaired" But Otherwise in Good Health?

In this context, illness or the absence of "good health" refers not to a temporary condition, but to chronic incapacitation for the autonomous conduct of the routines of everyday life. We are not charged with designing convalescent centers but with describing living conditions for persons during relatively stable periods of health. But what is the meaning of "impaired"? In some sense, probably every person past any given age in later years is "impaired" in one or more ways, compared to his previous condition. Almost uniformly, the senses become less acute and motor responses slower. Old friends and family members die, and people are increasingly alone. Income is reduced. Drivers' licenses are not renewed. All these things and more occur, in addition to the increasing incidence of various disease processes, some of them entailing cognitive loss. But the vast majority of older people, despite physical and other problems, prefer and manage to carry out normal routines of daily life on their own.[16] The cost of such efforts is not known.

What are the "Residential Accommodations and Supporting Services Needed"?

In implementing programs to enable people to "maintain or return to" independent living, both the characteristics of persons and of environments must be specified. The domain covers a wide range of life styles which lie between a total lack of need for any special assistance and an absolute need for total care in an institutional setting where occupancy is defined in terms of "beds" rather than "living units." The problem is complicated by the fact that the person and his environment interact. An appropriately supportive and stimulating environment can improve competency, while an overly supportive one can lead to deterioration.

Although much lip-service has been paid to the participation of older people in the design of living environments, in actuality they have been given almost no voice. There is now considerable evidence that the user or potential user may have quite a different viewpoint from the expert.[17] Shelter and service programs have traditionally been designed by the experts. Older people should be asked to define what is meant by "residential accommodations and supporting services" for a variety of subgroups and stages of aging.

What are "Assisted Independent Living"
and a "Semi-Independent Life Style"?

Clearly implied in both terms is that each is *not* any form of institutionalization. Surely another implicit descriptor is adequate quality of life. The old person who lived alone, died alone, and whose body was found a week later by a delivery man is hardly our goal model, despite his "independence."

To look at the issue from another perspective, can we identify any other age group that carries on quality living with no societal assistance? School children have hot lunch programs, counselors, nurses, sometimes physicians and social workers. Employers usually provide a meals service, often medical care, and sometimes types of counseling. Our major transportation systems are designed to ensure that the labor force can get to work.

We live in an interdependent society, and many of our major services are delivered through institutions that exclude the elderly. The absolutely independent life style, if it ever existed, rarely does so today for persons of any age. Some of the "impairment" of older people stems from the fact that they do not have access to the societal supports which enable people in other age groups to "live independently." For example, one problem in assessing the impact of retirement upon physical health is that some people see a physician less often after retirement, not because they have fewer symptoms or feel better but because they no longer have access to the "company doctor."[18]

As people age, they tend to need more services, it is true; but they should suffer no unusual onus over an inability to live in total "independence." Some need only the types of societal assistance ordinarily available to younger persons; others need more. "Assisted independent living" in the present instance means a need for something more than is currently available to the old person. That, obviously, will depend not only upon his abilities to cope but also upon what is available in the community *and* upon his access to it.

The general issue with regard to the maintenance of independence among the elderly concerns the degree of "fit" or congruence between people's needs and abilities, on the one hand, and the demands, supports, and opportunities within their environments, on the other. For some persons the "fit" of competence and need in relation to environment is adequate, but evidence suggests that they are the minority. The task is to modify environments for better congruence with human capabilities and needs. This is the basic problem to which congregate housing and other programs for the elderly are addressed. In this light I propose that the conference definition be slightly amended as follows:

> Assisted independent group living is made possible by a residential
> environment which incorporates shelter and services needed by the impaired or

socially deprived (but not ill) elderly to maintain or return to a semi-independent life style and to avoid premature institutionalization as they grow older.

There is not going to be one or even one best solution. A variety of models must be developed to meet the needs created by the diversity of persons and situations. One major "model" for meeting the needs of elderly people for shelter plus other services is to incorporate services within shelter. I propose that this is the appropriate concept and role of congregate housing.

Building for the Future

Because the construction of physical facilities is involved, it is wise to include some consideration of future as well as current needs in any decision making process for the development of congregate housing arrangements.

Aging of Tenants

Facilities designed to meet the needs of applicants are soon "outgrown" as the original occupants age and as the age structure of the tenant group skews upward. This has proved true both in retirement communities for the relatively affluent and in public housing for the elderly.

The aging of the tenant population might be slowed or stabilized by a gradual, rather than an immediate, filling of units in a new facility and by selection of replacements on the basis of age rather than time on the waiting list. Simulation studies could estimate the effects of such strategies. However, even if they were favorable with regard to age structure, serious problems would remain in terms of the equity of public funds involved and in terms of early cash flow and later public image for private developers.

Alternatively, the metamorphosis of the resident group suggests the possibility of "add on" architectural design and program planning, not unlike that for family homes designed for newlyweds who intend to add bedrooms and bathrooms for a growing family as well as recreation spaces and facilities for children, then teenagers, then young adults. In congregate housing for the elderly, "add on" or expansion features might be services related to health, nutrition, housecleaning, and personal hygiene.

1) Extended and Augmented Health Services. After eight years in residence, nearly a quarter of the residents of Victoria Plaza (23 percent) wanted more complete medical and health services, but non-intrusiveness was important They wanted additional health services on-site, but they did not want them to intrude into everyday activities and, particularly, not into the social center. The need for augmenting health services with the passage of time is not unique to public housing but is currently recognized in private retirement communities for the relatively well-to-do.

This suggests that future projects should make provision for later expansion of health services. This "add on" approach would be cost-effective by avoiding the premature provision of unneeded services and space for them. It would also help achieve social and personal goals for the elderly, since over-protective environments lead to loss of function. Innovation in the design of facilities is needed, accompanied by careful long-term study of the resulting "natural experiments," in order to determine the appropriate role and form of health services in congregate housing for the elderly. This highly controversial topic urgently needs factual enlightenment.

2) Food Service. The other striking change over time among Victoria

Plaza residents was a dramatic increase in their desire for a food service, for some place to buy a meal. After eight years, 79 percent of the residents spoke of this need. It has been assumed that cooking for oneself is a major support of self-esteem and a sign of independence, particularly for women, but recent research findings call into question the universality of this assumption. Surveys in some retirement communities point to the importance of dining facilities; others adhere to a policy of no food service. Conclusive evidence is lacking. Here again, we need innovation on the part of designers and developers, coupled with well-conducted evaluations, in order to determine the relative merits of kitchens, a food service, and combinations of the two for various population subgroups.

3) Cleaning Services. As people age, diminution in strength, agility, and visual acuity, as well as the increment of physical ailments such as arthritis, increase the burden involved in housecleaning. Long before any form of institutionalization is appropriate, assistance with heavier housecleaning tasks would be helpful both in maintaining independence and in safeguarding property. Such services need not be automatic for every resident and may not be necessary for any at the project's initiation; however, as tenants age, these services will become increasingly needed to support independent living.

4) Personal Hygiene. Grooming is an important element in self-esteem; even impoverished men and women desire the services of beauty and barber shops, and these are increasingly important on-site as, with age, the "life space" diminishes in size.[19] As people grow older, the routine tasks of caring for hair, skin, and feet, in particular, become difficult. Unfortunately, relevant services tend to be available only to the wealthy and the institutionalized. Again, innovative solutions should be found to provide these basic aids in congregate housing.

Changes in the Older Population

The elderly who will replace the original residents may be different in many respects from those for whom the facilities were planned. A building is relatively static for the 30 or 40 years during which it stands, but the characteristics of the older population will be quite different that many years in the future. "We are not only talking about improving the lot of those who are already in their later years; we are talking about ourselves."[20] And we might add, in connection with buildings, that we are constructing even for our children's old age.

Some projections for the future can be made with relative safety. There will be more old people, both absolutely and relative to the rest of the population, and this will be particularly striking in regard to the "older old." One clear implication is that there will be more people to shelter and serve over longer periods. Other implications are not so clear. Can we project service needs on the basis of the characteristics of today's old people at the same ages? Probably not.

Tomorrow's old will be chronologically older, but will this be true on functional indexes? This will depend partly upon lifelong nutrition and health care and partly upon the nature of anticipated medical research advances. For example, what will be the environmental design implications of "payoffs" from the current large investments in research on cancer and cardiovascular diseases, and from the progress in organ transplantation as it moves from experimental to technique-refinement stages? As the "killers" in later life are eliminated and their usual victims survive, how will shelter and service needs be affected? What if these "killers" are conquered earlier than the "cripplers"? For example, arthritis and related disorders appear to be highly resistant to treatment or prevention. Today, for a small number of people, someone to "do the buttons" and "cut the toenails" provides the single additional service which allows them to maintain independent living in a setting where basic housework and cooking are provided. This small extra service stands between these individuals and institutionalization, which is totally inappropriate. How many more of them will there be in the years ahead?

As the "killers" and "cripplers" of the later years are brought under management, we will recognize more clearly our need for understanding intrinsically age-related changes in order to plan congregate housing appropriately. It appears that we need not prepare for a great increase in the number of cognitively defective persons as a consequence of the changing age distribution. But to what extent are sensory-motor changes essentially a matter of years since birth? Losses in sensory acuity after about age 70 seem to be so regular as to appear inevitable, as do losses in the speed and agility of motor response, and particularly in perceptual-motor speed, even before age 70.[21]

Lifelong experience and ingrained habits will differ also among tomorrow's old. They will have had more formal education and probably better retirement incomes. Both suggest higher levels of expectation regarding living environments, and more aggressiveness and competence in demanding what they consider their due. This tendency will be supported by their relatively greater numbers in the population (probably swelled further by earlier retirement ages).

Moreover, they will increasingly have lived habitually in housing that is "congregate" in the literal sense, that is, in apartments or condominiums. As a consequence, they will also be accustomed to receiving some services and amenities along with shelter. New forms of housing for young adults and families typically include yard care and the maintenance of building exteriors, a variety of recreational facilities and services, and often a place to buy meals. Therefore, what we consider today as a novelty in the way of living environments—and what *is* a novelty to many older people today—will be "old hat" to those who retire in 15 or 20 years. They will be accustomed to the provision of basic services along with shelter; they will no longer belong to the tradition of the "do-it-yourself" householder with his separate yard and individual maintenance problems. Due to these life style changes in younger cohorts, what we plan today as a goal may be quickly outmoded, and a much richer assortment of services may soon be viewed as basic and necessary.

Summary and Conclusion

The need for shelter and a variety of services is admittedly great and probably much more extensive than any estimates to date. All indications are that it will continue to grow and diversify. Estimates based on the characteristics of re-housed elderly persons are unrealistically low because of admission policy requirements that call for the capability of living independently without services. Population projections indicate escalating service and shelter needs. A solution to this gargantuan problem will require the development of a wide spectrum of "models" for meeting these human needs through fiscally sound programs. Congregate housing—the provision of services in conjunction with grouped shelter—is one model, or rather, one set of models in that spectrum.

While local areas must select and devise "best solutions" for their own populations and circumstances, it is essential that "natural experiments" of a potentially wider relevance be studied, using the most sophisticated research designs, and that exemplary solutions be disseminated. Evaluations must be made in terms of supporting human capabilities, meeting human needs, and meeting sound financial considerations, and they must be sufficiently broadgauged and farsighted to provide accurate cost/benefit data.

The financial cost will run high, and it is essential that its payment be made equitably. Voters will not "foot the bill" out of tax dollars unless eligibility is determined by a means test. Perhaps it should be considered that many people need shelter and other services in one package—and are able and willing to pay for them. There is always some inequity at the "edges" of public programs, where people have too much income to be eligible for benefits but too little to purchase them in the market place. Sometimes congregate housing is not available at any price. Experience with the rent supplement program suggests that the "mixing" of clients in programs for the elderly may take place without undue friction. Participation of those who pay "full fare" and those who make partial payment may enable programs to function with fewer tax dollars. At least it seems wise to pursue the possibility of both the humane and the financial advantages of a "pay as you can" approach.

References

1. U.S. Congress. Senate. Special Committee on Aging. *Housing for the elderly: a status report.* Washington, D.C.: Government Printing Office, 1973.

2. International Center for Social Gerontology. Recommendations on the financing of housing. International Symposium on Housing and Environmental Design for Older Adults, Washington, D.C., December 1973. (Mimeographed.)

3. Donahue, Wilma T. Impact of living arrangements on ego development in the elderly. *In* Frances M. Carp and W.M. Burnett (eds.), *Patterns of living and housing of middle-aged and older people.* Washington, D.C.: Government Printing Office, 1966.

4. Hamovitch, M.B. Social and psychological factors in adjustment in a retirement village. *In* Frances M. Carp (ed.), *The retirement process: report of a conference, December 1966, Gaithersburg, Maryland.* Washington, D.C.: Government Printing Office, 1968.

5. Bultena, G.L. and Wood, V. The American retirement community: bane or blessing? *Journal of Gerontology,* 1969, 24, 209-17.

6. Lipman, A. Public housing and attitudinal adjustment in old age: a comparative study. *Journal of Geriatric Psychiatry,* 1968, 2, 88-101.

7. Sherman, S.R. Housing environments for the well elderly: scope and impact. Albany, New York: State Department of Mental Health, 1973. (Mimeographed.)

8. Carp, Frances M. *A future for the aged: the residents of Victoria Plaza.* Austin: University of Texas Press, 1966.

9. Lawton, M.P. and Cohen, J. The generality of housing impact on older people. *Journal of Gerontology,* 1974, 29, 2, 194-204.

10. Carp, Frances M. *Long-term effects of improved living environments on old people.* Final report to the Administration on Aging, AoA Research Grant #93-P-57511, 1975.

11. U.S. Congress. Senate. Special Committee on Aging, Subcommittee on Long-Term Care. *Nursing home care in the United States: failure in public policy: introductory report,* p. 15. Washington, D.C.: Government Printing Office, November 1974.

12. Carp, Frances M. Housing and living environments of older people. *In* R. Binstock and Ethel Shanas (eds.), *Handbook of aging and the social sciences,* in press. New York: Van Nostrand Reinhold Company.

13. Rosow, I. *Social integration of the aged.* New York: the Free Press, 1967.

14. Sherman, S.R.; Mangum, W.P., Jr.; Dodds, S.; Walkley, R.P.; and Wilner, D.M. Psychological effects of retirement housing. *The Gerontologist,* 1968, 8, 1, 170-75.

15. Carp, Frances M. Housing and living environments of older people. *In* R. Binstock and Ethel Shanas (eds.), *Handbook of aging and the social sciences,* in press. New York: Van Nostrand Reinhold Company.

16. Havighurst, R.J. Research and development goals in social gerontology. *The Gerontologist,* 1969, 9, 4, 1-90.

17. Carp, Frances M.; Zawadski, R.T.; and Shokrhon, H. Dimensions of environmental quality. *Environment and behavior,* in press.

18. Carp, Frances M. Retirement and physical health. *Advances in psychosomatic medicine,* in press. New York: S. Karger.

19. Carp, Frances M. *A future for the aged: the residents of Victoria Plaza.* Austin: University of Texas Press, 1966.

20. Burch, G. and Collot, Claudette. *Old people in their towns.* (Translated from French by O. Neaman.) Paris: Centre International de Gerontologie Sociale, 1972.

21. Carp, Frances M. Urban life style and life cycle factors. *In* M.P. Lawton (ed.), *Community planning for the elderly,* in press. New York: John Wiley and Sons.

The Hispanic Elderly: Meeting the Needs of a Special Population

Louise Woerner*

Civil Rights Digest, Volume II, No.3 (Spring 1979). U.S. Commission on Civil Rights, Washington, D.C.

The problems of the minority elderly in America are infrequently documented. They are not only the silent, but the forgotten—alienated from society, often separated from their families. Most are poor but they seldom participate in Federal, State, and local programs designed to assist them.

According to 1976 census figures, the number of elderly Hispanics in the U.S. has tripled in the past two decades and has increased 23 percent since 1970 alone. Their percentage of the total Hispanic population remains small because of the high birthrate among Hispanics in the United States and because of continuing migration by young Hispanics to the U.S. In a country where most citizens are becoming older, it is easy to forget the Hispanic elderly because of the many young Hispanics who are so visible.

Thus, the Hispanic elderly receive little attention, although they have special problems. In a 1977 study for the Community Services Administration to determine the problems of older, rural, poverty-level Hispanics, J. A. Reyes Associates, Inc., a Washington, D.C.-based consulting firm, confirmed that despite their needs the elderly Spanish speaking do not utilize social services that are available to them at the rate that might be expeced.

The Reyes study and other research have shown that elderly Hispanics

- are likely to live with a spouse or alone.
- often have incomes well below the poverty level.
- are often ineligible for social security or are not aware of its availability.
- visit hospitals and physicians far less frequently

than do their Anglo counterparts, particularly in rural areas, although they are often in poor health.
- speak English poorly or not at all.

Explanations for underutilization of available services by minority elderly are often based on the belief that they "take care of their own." But close examination of census data reveals that the stereotypical image of Hispanic families with three generations in the same household is no longer valid. Today about 60 percent of the Hispanic elderly live with a spouse; only about 10 percent live with their children. This shift in living patterns has been accompanied by a concurrent shift in attitudes among young Hispanic Americans. As an example, one witness testified before the U.S. Senate Special Committee on Aging in Los Angeles that "the social distance between generations of Mexican immigrants and Mexican Americans is even greater than the social distance between some Mexican Americans and Anglo Americans."

The number of elderly Spanish speaking with incomes below the poverty level is higher than one in three (37.5 percent). Only the Native American elderly have a lower average income than their Hispanic American counterparts. In rural areas, the numbers are much higher. In South Texas, for example, the proportion of Mexican Americans 60 years and above with incomes below the poverty level is as high as 64.2 percent.

It is clear that income support programs are of primary importance to the Hispanic elderly. The two principal available programs are social security and old age assistance. The Spanish-speaking elderly have often been ineligible for the former because of lack

---

*Louise Woerner is the vice president of J.A. Reyes Associates, Inc., a Washington-based consulting firm.

of citizenship or because the work they did was not covered by social security. Old age assistance is utilized more frequently by Hispanics, but offers lower benefits. Many older Hispanics who qualify for social security payments receive only small benefits owing to a generally low occupational status during their working years. For this reason, many remain in the labor force beyond retirement age—they need the income, small as it usually is.

Why do the poor Hispanic elderly not make better use of available programs that might help them? Social services are generally underutilized by groups with low socioeconomic status regardless of race or ethnicity. But the Spanish speaking are faced with special barriers, foremost of which are language and culture. The traditional system of social service delivery requires that this group of proud working people come for assistance with hat in hand. It is not enough that programs be available—they must attract clients. To date, few programs have been geared to the Spanish-speaking elderly.

The medical problems of the Hispanic elderly are also different from those of other groups. Many have worked at hard jobs all their lives and have never received adequate medical care. It has been shown that Hispanics in general, and migrant and seasonal farmworkers in particular, age more quickly than do Anglos. A 1973 study concluded that "at 48 years a Spanish heritage migrant worker approximates the health of the 65-year-old Anglo." If the definition of "elderly" were adjusted accordingly, and not based solely on age, the number of Hispanic elderly would be much larger.

Therefore, the failure of Hispanics to make use of available health care services is significant because it exacerbates long-neglected health problems. The reasons for this failure are, again, low income, language and cultural differences, and, particularly for the rural Hispanic elderly, a geographic isolation from the source of the services.

Research for CSA by Reyes Associates on the Hispanic elderly was followed by the development and testing of a model program through which poor, elderly, Spanish-speaking Americans could receive the services they needed in order to maintain an acceptable quality of life in their homes.

Reyes designed the model program—called Project EXITO, meaning "success" in English—based on the assumptions that

- to be effective, services must be demand based. This is contrary to most programs, which schedule services and therefore require clients to schedule needs.

- Hispanics would prefer to participate in a program to which they could also contribute, thus maintaining their dignity as elders of their communities.
- an intergenerational model would be most acceptable to Hispanics, as it most nearly replicates a family model.

The demonstration component of the program was conducted in Natalia, Texas, a town of 1,200 located 30 miles west of San Antonio. All members of the community were canvassed to see what their needs were and in what ways they might be able to assist their neighbors. Based on that canvass, an exchange of services was developed where persons with needs were matched with individuals who could assist. That is, a person requiring babysitting services might exchange transportation and assistance with grocery shopping with an older person, who would then provide needed babysitting. Exchanges were not on a one-for-one basis only, and shortly into the demonstration most members of the community were calling the EXITO office to offer assistance and ask for help.

Martin and Roberta Aguinaga

Martin and Roberta Aguinaga participated in more exchanges in the EXITO program than any other residents of Natalia. Mr. Aguinaga was a frequent provider of services, offering transportation between Natalia and Devine, the nearest city of size, to anyone who needed it. All of the Hispanics in Natalia know the Aguinagas. Aged 76 and 72, they have lived there for 70 years and refer to themselves as "los únicos constantes del pueblo" (the only constants of the town). As stalwarts of the Hispanic community, they drew many people into Project EXITO with them.

Mr. Aguinaga came to Natalia from Mexico in 1907, at age 6. He has always earned his living as a farmworker. The Aguinagas live in a one-room house on the edge of town. Their four children are married and live in Texas, three within 30 miles of Natalia. Supplemental security payments are the only income the Aguinagas have; their children are poor as well and are unable to offer their parents financial assistance.

Neither Martin nor Roberta Aguinaga speak English, and they are hampered in speaking Spanish by their lack of teeth. They are functionally illiterate in both languages and need interpreters in contacts with Anglos. Poor health is another major problem. Mrs. Aguinaga is often bedridden with continuing colds and other minor but debilitating ailments. Mr. Aguinaga has periodic back trouble, particularly severe during inclement weather, although he never requested anything for himself.

The Aguinagas were anxious to participate in Project EXITO when the demonstration started in Natalia. They told the project staff that the concept of exchanging services reminded them of life in Natalia when they were much younger. According to the Aguinagas, helping one another was a very common thing years ago, and such actions fostered togetherness. They regarded EXITO as a way to revive an attitude that had long seemed forgotten. The Aguinagas had known the project coordinator, Mrs. Saenz, for many years. Therefore, Mrs. Aguinaga was not the least bit embarrased to call Mrs. Saenz to ask for companionship. Their close relationship had similarities to that of a mother and daughter. In addition to requests for home visits, Mrs. Aguinaga would also ask for assistance in buying medicine and doing household chores.

The involvement of the Aguinagas in Project EXITO was not without problems. There was a period of about 2 weeks during which Mrs. Aguinaga dropped out of the project. About one month into the program, she was upset that Mrs. Saenz had not stopped regularly at her house to pay her a visit and check on her health. Mrs. Saenz explained that it was her responsibility to identify and meet all of the elderly persons in the town; she had assumed that Mrs. Aguinaga would contact her if there were any problems. This answer was unacceptable to Mrs. Aguinaga, who was resentful that she needed to have a problem and was responsible for initiating contact before receiving services through EXITO.

This renewed the awareness of the EXITO staff that the need of older persons for companionship is a continuing one and should not be provided on special request only. Mrs. Aguinaga said that she would feel more comfortable if she could be visited without having to make a special request. As a result the project staff scheduled more group functions as well as regular individual visits.

The Aguinagas were on the EXITO Advisory Committee and cut the ribbon that marked the opening of the Community Center. They remained on the Advisory Board to the Community Center after the demonstration ceased to function.

Pedro and Feliz Martinez

Pedro Martinez, now 77, moved to the United States from Mexico in 1907. He has lived in Natalia since 1939. Mr. Martinez has been a farmworker all of his life and continues to work in the fields surrounding Natalia. He and his 67-year-old wife, Feliz, speak little English. They now receive social security and medicare, but did not become eligible for benefits until about 5 years ago. Both are in poor health. They have seven children, all married, scattered around Texas. Only one of their offspring remains in Natalia. He and his family provide transportation to and from the doctor's office for his parents, as well as other services that they might need. The Martinezes, however, have gotten a great deal of satisfaction from Project EXITO by being able to contribute more to their community.

When visited by an outreach worker early in Project EXITO, Feliz Martinez wanted nothing to do with the project. Her son was nearby; she discussed her needs only with him. Mr. Martinez said he was too tired after a long day of field work to participate in the project.

Nevertheless, the renovation of the American Legion Hall for the Community Center was of great interest to the Martinezes because their three-room house is next to the hall. As soon as the work began Mr. Martinez offered his ladder, which was used during the entire renovation. Mrs. Martinez, who rarely ventures outside her home, delivered refreshments to the young workers on several occasions.

When asked about their sudden involvement, Mrs. Martinez commended the efforts of EXITO in securing the Legion Hall. She said she was happy to have people nearby whom she could visit when she was lonely, or on whom she could rely if her son or husband were not around. This sense of security was heightened by the knowledge that the entire community had supported the endeavor. She still felt, however, that most of her needs could best be met by their son.

Francisco Pedroza

Francisco Pedroza, 93, is one of Natalia's most distinguished and respected citizens. He was the Secretary Commissioner of Political Jurisdiction of Mexico, and he fought in the Mexican Revolution in 1910. In 1911 he left the life of a lawyer in Mexico to become a farmworker in the United States. In 1920 he was appointed to the Department of Protection for Defense of Mexican Citizens by the Mexican government, but he returned to the United States, although he was never able to get a better job than farmwork.

Mr. Pedroza has 15 children, all of whom are married; four daughters remain in Natalia. He receives social security and supplemental security income and relies on his family for added financial support when needed.

Mr. Pedroza was one of the original community organizers for Project EXITO despite the fact that he is going blind and seldom leaves his home. He was one of the first people contacted after Natalia was selected as the Project EXITO site, and it was with his consultation and advice that the project's outreach efforts began.

His support was crucial, since the history of Natalia over the past 40 years is inextricably related to the involvement of Mr. Pedroza. He was the first Mexican American to be elected to either the water or school boards, which distinguished him in the Hispanic community. Moreover, over 30 years ago, he led the successful drive to raise the funds to build the Catholic Church in Natalia. Since that time Mr. Pedroza has been recognized as the leading resource mobilizer in Natalia.

After his initial advisory efforts, however, Mr. Pedroza did not participate. Because his four daughters see to it that his immediate needs are met, he did not request any services. He is so well-known and active that he does not require companionship or need a way to contribute.

He continually praised the project, however, as it reminded him of the way community life used to be in Natalia. The opening of the Community Center proved to be a very heartfelt moment for Mr. Pedroza, so he wrote the following poem, which has been translated into English, to express his feelings:

THE EXITO PROGRAM

It deserves all our consideration, enthusiasm, and cooperation; it is a good deed, from all perspectives.

Let's take a look at the world around us,
and we'll see
that those that have been blessed by fortune
sit down to enjoy life as a banquet
to enjoy all that they desire.
On the other hand
there are the shadows of families that ask
for bread,
stretching out their hands in anguish
demanding help,

energy depleted by hard work, that now demand rest.

But now rises a new fountain of promises and hopes
Program EXITO like a new sun
that brings a new life
that comes to feed our poor.

The eyes of Providence will bestow gifts
on those that work in the vineyards of the Lord.

Francisco Pedroza, 93,
A resident of Natalia

The need for new approaches

The success of the EXITO model is indicative of the desperate need for the development of new and innovative approaches to caring for the poor minority elderly, especially those living in rural areas of the U.S. It is evident from the extremely low socioeconomic status of the older Hispanic population that their needs are considerable. Existing services have failed to meet these needs, and it is therefore essential that special attention be paid to them.

It is, of course, necessary to avoid establishing any policy or instituting any practices that would help perpetuate the rural isolation of or promote urban ghettos for Hispanic Americans as a group. The problems of the elderly of this group, however, need to be addressed in the short term, while the graver social questions raised by segregated living patterns of Hispanics have to be addressed by long-range policy.

Services must be delivered in a setting that recognizes the differences between Anglo and Hispanic culture and language. The resources of the Hispanic community provide the best alternative to institutional care for the aged. New approaches to delivery of services that incorporate these concepts stand the best chance of reaching the Spanish-speaking elderly, where traditional measures have failed. It is with this philosophy that Project EXITO was conceived. It is also with this philosophy that other innovative solutions must be developed. The needs of this population can no longer go unmet.

Serving the Seniors

Pauline Winnick*

American Education, July 1978, Volume 14, Number 6. Office of Education, U.S. Department of Health, Education, and Welfare.

Looking around libraries today, one must be favorably impressed by the attention being given to the older adults of this country, whether as part of the cohort of regular library users or as individuals needing special attention because of some handicap, being homebound or institutionalized, or because of being isolated.

A major funding source being used to start library programs that respond to the requirements of the aging is Title I of the Library Services and Construction Act, which is administered by the U.S. Office of Education through state library agencies. One of its priorities is to support public libraries in providing the educational, informational, and recreational materials and activities described here for senior citizens living both independently and in institutions.

Perhaps the most important thing that public libraries do for older adults is to include them in the family of library users. That is to say that adults over 60 who are active and independent members of their communities may take full advantage of the library's facilities and opportunities, with no differentiation by age when they arrive to register for voting, enter a chess tournament, get help in preparing a tax return, be introduced to creative photography, learn their legal rights or how to write. This may not seem to be a great concession to age, but many oldsters are uplifted to know they have a place where they are welcome and are treated without bias, where they can borrow books about the new and the nostalgic; enjoy concerts, films, the arts; participate in craft demonstrations and forums on consumer and health concerns. Moreover, library-centered independent learning programs offer a broad range of interests and study goals and are attracting an increasing proportion of elderly persons who are pursuing at their own pace a lifelong learning pattern.

*Ms. Winnick is the program coordinator for Title I, LSCA, in OE's State and Public Library Services Branch.

If asked to choose among library services the one that can most dramatically affect the quality of life of the library user, perhaps the older adult would choose the library's information and referral services. I & R is fast becoming a most necessary and vital service in today's complex world. Though it is intended to aid the total population, it has an almost urgent benefaction for society's disadvantaged, undereducated, economically depressed, as well as those with limited English fluency, and, of course, the elderly. Moreover, the fact that I & R exists at all, attests to the librarians' working relationship with fellow professionals in other agencies serving the elderly in their communities.

Aging people, however, do not ask for the services they need. Frequently they do not know about services and support to which they are entitled. And simply learning about them is not enough; they must be convinced that they have a right to them, a proposition difficult to grasp by those brought up in a tradition of self-reliance. Someone has to connect them with the federal, state, and local services intended to ease their most dire problems. For many, the public library is that "someone."

Today, public library-sponsored I & R services are multiplying across the nation as librarians try to help the elderly keep pace with a faster and faster spinning world. One city in Maryland with an extremely active I & R service reports that requests most frequently received from older persons during a typical week in its inner-city central library were concerned with any and all information pertinent to part-time jobs, lists of businesses and restaurants that offer the elderly discounts, advice on tax credits for those over 65, health care information forms for special-rate transit passes, and a list of local recreation opportunities.

In northeastern Iowa, senior citizens have telephone access to an I & R service that gives them information about nutrition, recreation, finances, housing, transportation, health, and other areas of interest. It also links them directly to the services they need. The local libraries supporting this cooperative venture proclaim, "All calls are confidential."

Several Massachusetts libraries have instituted an information exchange for part-time employment of older adults in their communities. And OASIS, a project of the Los Angeles County Public Library System, assures older individuals of doorstep delivery of books, magazines, movies, and cassettes via van service. Or they can dial for prerecorded information on subjects like law, health, safety, and pet care. And if that's not enough, they can thumb through a library mail catalog list of over 800 books and cassettes and receive their choice on loan for a month, postage paid both ways. All this (except postage) in English and Spanish.

Older individuals may also be part of a library senior group that meets regularly for exchange of ideas and companionship, or to work on special interest programs and projects, with, perhaps, a short trip together now and then. This is in addition to rather than a substitution for regular participation in the total span of library activity.

Famous in the history of library service to the aging is the still active "Live Long and Like It Library Club" which the Cleveland Public Library started in 1946 as an informal educational library program for men and women over 60. News of this group stimulated the Boston Public Library to organize in 1950 its "Never Too Late Group," planned "to have special appeal for the mentally alert older persons."

Many older folks are not content to restrict themselves to being users of libraries and attenders. These are the initiators who plan exhibits, teach crafts to children and adults, review books tutor youngsters, help adults who can't read, tell stories to children in either the library or in neighborhood settings, contribute to oral history tapings which become part of the history of their communities. Gulfport, Mississippi, furnished a good example of the latter when some of its older citizens restored a good part of the written history of the town from their memories after a hurricane destroyed Gulfport, records and all. And older persons always have the freedom and choice to be activists and advocates. In Friends of the Library groups they energetically build goodwill and gain support for the library. As members of boards of trustees and advisory councils they exert leadership in representing the community-and the interests of their own age group. In the role of volunteers they help make possible the delivery of individualized library services to isolated, handicapped, institutionalized, or homebound persons.

The visibility of seniors in these active roles can help break down a common misconception of the elderly: that libraries are for the young in years instead of the young at heart. Libraries further destroy common myths about aging by preparing men and women for satisfying retirement through workshops and counsel. Advisors may be retired people who speak from a personnal vantage point. Or they may be experts in money management, psychology, or some other field to help ease persons through the transition from full-time employment to enjoyable leisure or self-directed career change.

The responsibility of the public library extends beyond building a positive attitude in the older folks toward themselves; it also comes to bear on improving the gray image in children and younger adults in the community. Whatever attitudes a person develops toward age as a child remain to influence his or her actions negatively or affirmatively throughout adulthood. The more enjoyable the associations children have with older persons the greater the possibility that they will view the elderly more as "good," "friendly," and "nice" and less as "sick," "ugly," and "sad." Because many children know older people only through books, the selection of these books takes on added importance and demands sensitivity to avoid stereotyped characterizations and exaggerated illustrations of older people.

Intergenerational programs-a need throughout our society-are on the rise in libraries. In one Texas library, the seniors created new puppets for the children to used in puppet shows. In gratitude, they were invited as the children's guests of honor to the first performance of the lively puppets-a proud occasion for all. And a local history project in Vermont drew together senior citizens and teenagers as they worked to locate primary source materials in homes of community residents-letters, diaries, newspapers, photos, maps-to evaluate, photograph, and preserve. In seeking out elderly residents for taping interviews about an earlier era, students came to appreciate their contributions to the community and to the nation.

All these activities reveal the senior citizen gaining and contributing to community life. But what happens to older persons who can no longer live independently without assistance, or who must even find a home in an institution? The psychological impace of aging-failing physical abilities, loss of purposeful daily activities, decay of self-esteem, and disorientation when removed from one's home and family to an institutional setting-is recognized by the public library as an immediate and urgent problem. In this recognition, libraries provide large print books and magnifying aids to keep people reading after they eye-sight beings to fade. When it becomes easier for them to listen than to read, people can turn to talking books on cassettes and discs available from libraries along with the equipment to use them.

When library users are no longer able to come to the building, the library mails materials, or in many cases arranges for staff or volunteers personally to bring the services to the persons' homes. In the face of rising fuel and maintenance costs, bookmobiles are still flourishing, in part because of the smiles and conversation they bring along with the readables and viewables to the homebound and isolated. Some bookmobiles have two-way radios, making them literally on-the-move information centers. And some are even outfitted with hydraulic lifts to set persons in wheelchairs down into the truck to see a film, perhaps, or to choose their own books from the shelves, or at least to feel that they are part of the crowd.

Most grateful to the librarian or library aide who brings a book or tape along with an encouraging word and handshake to their chairs and bedsides are those confined to nursing homes or other extended-care institutions. Merely knowing that someone "out there" cares enough to make such visits is therapy in itself.

This and other work associated with serving the aged requires special training, which is being supported by Title II-B of the Higher Education Act (Library Career Training and Library Research Demonstration). Workshops, institutes, and research programs spon-sored under this Act have already broken ground toward developing leadership and research capability in the field of library service to the elderly.

The Administration on Aging is currently supporting two important training programs: At the University of Wisconsin in Madison, the Library School is in its third year of training leaders in service to the aged; and Rutgers University Graduate School of Library Service is creating a curriculum as part of the new gerontology program.

Thus, in looking at services for the aged today, the view from the library is an optimistic one. By no means does this imply that everything is rosy and the problems are completely under control. Robert N. Butler, director of the National Institute on Aging, makes the counterpoint most poignantly in this Pulitzer Prize-winning book, *Why Survive? Being Old in America:* "The potentials for satisfactions and even triumphs in late life are real and vastly underexplored. For the most part the elderly struggle to exist is an inhospitable world."

But there is increasing evidence that the world is at long last spinning in the right direction. Clearly, public libraries are in the the forefront of a growing movement to explore the potentials for the elderly and to make the world friendlier for those who have traveled farthest through life.   □

Part two:
Legislation

Ending Age Discrimination

Michael D. Batten*

Civil Rights Digest, Volume II, No.2 (Winter 1979). U.S. Commission on Civil Rights, Washington, D.C.

The Age Discrimination Act passed by Congress in 1975 had as its original purpose the prohibition of "unreasonable discrimination" based on age in certain federally administered programs. Its key provision states, "no person in the United States shall, on the basis of age, be excluded from participation in, be denied the benefits of, or be subjected to discrimination under any Federal activity receiving Federal financial assistance."

The effective date of the act was set as January 1, 1979, and a special study—to be conducted by the U.S. Commission on Civil Rights—was mandated in order to determine the existence and document the scope of "unreasonable" age discrimination within federally funded programs. The study was to "identify with particularity" any such programs or activities in which evidence of age discrimination against otherwise qualified individuals is found.

As is the case with most Federal regulatory laws, certain exceptions were written into the statute. Thus, it would not be a violation of the act if a covered agency or a recipient of Federal money from that agency takes an action that takes into account age "as a factor necessary to the normal operation" of a Federal program or the "achievement of any statutory objective of a specific program." Nor would it be wrong for an agency to differentiate by age so long as "such action is based on reasonable factors other than age."

Furthermore, the provisions of the act don't apply to any program or activity *established under authority of any law* (emphasis added) that:

*Michael Batten is a senior staff associate at the National Manpower Institute in Washington, D.C.

1) provides any benefits or assistance to persons based on the age of such persons, or

2) establishes criteria for participation in age-related terms or describes intended beneficiaries or target groups in such terms.

Regarding employment and age, ADA defers to the Age Discrimination in Employment Act of 1968, as amended. The only Federal employment program to be covered by the ADA is the Comprehensive Employment and Training Act of 1974.

The enforcement of the Age Discrimination Act rests with the Federal agencies covered by the law. The agencies are to supervise and monitor all recipients of grants and contracts to assure compliance. The Department of Health, Education, and Welfare is to act as the "lead" agency in the overall compliance effort by taking responsibility for issuing general regulations and guidelines under the act. The covered agencies are then to develop specific regulations pertaining to their own programs and operations. HEW is responsible for coordinating reports and assessing progress under the ADA and making annual reports to the President and Congress.

The study that was to identify age discrimination and the scope of such discrimination within federally funded programs was submitted to the President and Congress in January of 1978. Its key recommendation was to delete the word "unreasonable" from the term "unreasonable discrimination" in the ADA. Thus *all* age discrimination within the Federal agencies, programs, and activities covered would be prohibited. The exceptions noted above, however, would still stand.

The study did not document or illustrate systematic age discrimination in federally funded programs or within any particular program sponsored by a Federal agency. Rather, it found that program administrators "follow policies and practices that effectively deny individuals access to needed services and benefits because of their age." The study identified barriers to participation but not a "pattern and practice" of age discrimination within the programs described.

Unfortunately, in the authors view, the report did not address the complexity of the law itself or possible enforcement procedures. Nor did it report on the extensive enforcement and litigation experience that the government has gained under the Age Discrimination in Employment Act. While the ADA does not relate directly to employment, there are useful lessons to be learned by examining the history and implementation of the ADEA.

(Editor's note: This article was written prior to the release of Volume II of the Commission's study.)

In any case, Congress amended the ADA by deleting the term "unreasonable" from the statement of purpose noted above. However, the major exceptions that would permit age distinctions based on existing laws and distinctions based on reasonable factors other than age were retained. Regarding enforcement, Congress added a provision that would allow individuals access to sue under the ADA when all other administrative remedies fail. A final change in the law deferred the effective date of the ADA from January 1, 1979, to July 1, 1979.

The proposed regulations

In December 1978, HEW issued a proposed set of *general* regulations for the ADA. After appropriate public hearings on these proposals, the Department will issue a final set of general regulations to be published in the *Federal Register*. After a subsequent time period, each Federal agency covered by the act will develop and publish its own set of *specific* regulations.

It should be noted at the outset that the proposed general regulations are broad in scope, fair, and reasonable in every sense of these terms. First, the proposed regulations take into account the complexity of age discrimination. They distinguish clearly between discrimination based on age stereotypes and what might appear to be appropriate age distinctions within the exceptions noted in the ADA. Thus, it is one thing to develop educational programs for young

children, e.g., a Head Start program, and target Federal funds for that group. It is another thing to ignore, discourage, or fail to enroll persons over age 40 in major job training and employment programs sponsored by the Comprehensive Employment and Training Act.

Furthermore, if States and local jurisdictions receive funds under revenue sharing legislation, they may not make arbitrary and discriminatory rules regarding the age of individuals who benefit from these grants.

In sum, the proposed regulations raise the problem of explicitly defining age discrimination and age distinctions and the difficulties involved enforcing the statute on recipients of Federal funds covered by the act. The regulations also note the difficulties in both analyzing and reporting on age factors within such subagencies and the programs they administer.

The proposed regulations then move on to the most difficult and, perhaps, contradictory dilemmas presented by the ADA. What Federal programs are covered by the law, and how does an agency reconcile the controlling purpose of the statute (to eliminate *all* age discrimination) with the exceptions that allow age-based distinctions?

It is somewhat ironic and indicative of the contradictions within the ADA to note that the 1978 amendments to the law were attached to 1978 amendments to the Older Americans Act. The ADA, on its face, protects U.S. citizens aged zero to 100 plus. The Older Americans Act is a categorical program for U.S. citizens over age 55 or 60.

When one totals up the Federal funds allocated to older persons through the Social Security Act, the Older Americans Act, and other mandated age-related programs, the specter of age discrimination and the "pattern and practice" of age discrimination in federally covered programs is considerably diminished. Such overall proportions of the distribution of Federal funds to the upper age groups will not fail to impress Federal judges when younger groups bring suit under the ADA.

Thus, with such big-league programs as social security excluded (since the age of beneficiaries has been clearly established by the authority of other Federal statutes), the number and types of programs covered seems to dwindle.

The proposed regulations then raise several other issues. Consider the following:

1) Nutrition programs under the Older Americans Act provide food for persons over 60 years of age.

2) Certain State laws impose age restrictions on who may qualify for a driver's license.

3) State statutes provide for age differentials in implementation of their respective criminal justice systems.

4) Some local jurisdictions provide certain tax relief and other benefits for the elderly. The age at which one is or is not elderly varies from jurisdiction to jurisdiction.

5) Various transit authorities allow reduced fares for public transportation to various age groups—usually school-age children and the elderly.

Do all these fall within the exception allowing for age distinctions "established under authority of . . . law"? Congress provided little or no guidance on this important issue in the House and Senate committee reports, conferences, or floor debate. The potential for legal controversy is great.

Clearly, programs such as health services for infants or special geriatric services for the elderly contain legislated and functional criteria that appear to meet the age distinction exceptions in the ADA. But age distinctions made over a variety of programs for purposes that are less age-specific can, and most likely will, raise serious problems.

For example, the act and proposed regulations indicate that certain employment programs sponsored under CETA are covered, while others are not. Public employment programs are covered; special apprenticeship programs with age cutoffs as early as age 25 are exempt. But why shouldn't a woman, age 28, be eligible for apprenticeship programs? How valid is the age distinction or the so-called legislative age limit in this instance? One of the major flaws in the design of the ADA and a difficulty that will plague its enforcement is that, with the exception of extreme youth and extreme old age, few rational criteria on which to base age distinctions exist, as we shall see.

Reasonable age distinctions

One difficulty facing enforcement and defining reasonable age distinctions is that particular ages are often selected as a matter of convenience. Thus, we allegedly reach the age of reason at 7. At age 18 a U.S. citizen can vote; he or she theoretically reaches social and political maturity. In programs such as Head Start, 3 is usually the age of eligibility for young participants. But why not 2½—or 4, for that matter? Micro-age distinctions must be confronted as well as the larger age distinctions that may seem reasonable to us.

Under Ttitle VII of the 1964 Civil Rights Act, an employer cannot discriminate against a number of

groups covered. Thus, the employment rights of black persons, as an entire group, are protected. One cannot discriminate against a black person, or make a reasonable distinction on hiring, etc., on the basis of the person being a "little" black. But the ADA proposes to distinguish between participants in programs who are a "little" young—or a "little" old, for that matter. It may be straining a bit to examine the practical and functional needs of programs in light of eliminating age discrimination. But the law and the proposed regulations invite these issues.

Other problems touched on by the proposed regulations include the application of physical fitness tests in public employment programs. Many believe these are mechanisms to exclude older applicants.

Colleges, law schools, and medical schools—supported, in part, by Federal grants—often utilize written tests as a means of selecting and rejecting candidates. Oftentimes these tests serve the practical purpose of discouraging and excluding applicants, say, over age 30. Suits brought under Title VII of the 1964 Civil Rights Act should caution those making age distinctions in these areas.

Pragmatic and other assessments on the overall utility and value to be gained through training an over-30 or over-40 doctor may fly in the face of the ADA mandate. They will, at least, invite challenge when the doctrine of reasonable distinctions is invoked to exclude older participants from entering a recipient program funded, in part, by Federal money.

Enforcing the ADA

Most regulatory laws call for a special agency to enforce their provisions. Thus, the Department of Labor currently administers the Age Discrimination in Employment Act, Equal Pay Act, and minimum wage laws. The Equal Employment Opportunity Commission is mandated to enforce Title VII provisions of the Civil Rights Act of 1964. The proposed enforcement structure of the ADA, however, is different.

Basically, each agency covered is responsible for enforcing, monitoring, and reporting on the ADA as it affects individual agency operations. The programs and activities of these agencies would appear to be extramural. ADA apparently does not apply to internal staffing or management systems of the respective agencies. Thus, HEW would supervise and monitor its "clients"—grantees and contractors—regarding the enforcement of the ADA. All other not-excluded agencies would do the same.

Each Federal agency is required to inform its clients or recipient groups about the ADA, publish an individual set of regulations, and educate the recipient organizations as to compliance, procedures and agency expectations. Each client or recipient group will be expected to evaluate how its programs affect different age groups. When age discrimination appears, the recipient is to make appropriate changes.

Should a recipient invoke exceptions to the ADA and choose to make use of reasonable age distinctions made on operational or other criteria, then it must defend its action. If it disagrees, the Federal agency must try a series of administrative remedies (conciliation, education, and persuasion. If these fail, the Federal agency may withdraw funds from a recipient organization that continues to be in non-compliance.

Actions against a recipient organization can be initiated by the supervising Federal agency or the excluded, would-be beneficiaries of the recipient's services. As is the case with most other civil rights legislation, an individual has the right to initiate a civil action if and when all administrative solutions fail. The proposed regulations set up procedures for such action that are fairly standard.

On its face, the ADA appears to be a logical outgrowth and extension of civil rights activity in the U.S. The Civil Rights Act of 1964 required that a study on age discrimination in employment be made. The Age Discrimination in Employment Act of 1967 and the 1978 amendments to that law protect the employment rights of individuals aged 40 to 70. The Equal Pay Act went a long way toward establishing parity in wages and salary between men and women. The ADA, it seems, is designed to take the next step by trying to eliminate and prevent discrimination based on age—at least in certain federally supported programs. It is the effort to eliminate age discrimination across the total age spectrum that sets up the greatest practical difficulty facing the statute.

The age spectrum

Who gets what when from the Federal government? How does a Federal agency assess equity in distributing public money across the age spectrum when it must take into account the varying needs for specific agency services by different age groups and by the target population of the agency programs? Furthermore, how narrowly should an agency define the age groups to which it renders service? By declaring age discrimination illegal, yet allowing reasonable and therefore legal age discrimination (distinction is discrimination by any other name!), the ADA has charted a course for both administrative and legal conflict. Age may be the only universal variable that applies to beneficiaries and participants in any Federal program—but this fact will not simplify distribution formulas for benefits or services.

The law, the legislative history, and the proposed regulations are uninstructive as to how an agency covered by the statute is to measure and determine what constitutes significant differences or needs between different age groups served, or how, in fact, to define such age groups. Are, for example, young adults generally discounted by public health programs because they are in generally better health than other segments of the population? If so, what age grouping constitutes "young adults"? Cannot this group charge discrimination by claiming that insufficient preventive health strategies and programs were directed to them as a group?

What would health statistics show on the real needs of this cohort as a group? What about the individual young adult who may suffer health problems but encounters programmatic age discrimination—does he or she have a realistic chance to prove a case, given the reasonable age distinction exception?

The same dilemmas face persons over age 65 who wish to participate in a CETA program. Program managers may point out that the diminishing labor force participation rates and the comparatively low unemployment rates for this age group make a focus on youth reasonable.

In fact, these age distinctions are made at present and account, in part, for low participation of older persons in CETA programs. Would this exclusion be justified under the ADA and its exceptions? Will it take litigation to clarify the matter?

Other problems arise from the competitive interests of different age groups for the available Federal resources. Citizens 18 and under may have one set of needs. Those in every subsequent 10-year or 5-year cohort may make different age-related claims. Will these age groups clash if the distribution of funds and services to various groups is more systematic? The proposed general regulations issued by HEW implicitly recognize these and many other difficulties inherent in the ADA. But without much more specific direction to the agencies covered by the act, the ADA can very easily become a non-law.

Age and the Court:

The U. S. Supreme Court has not taken too kindly to age-related issues brought before it. Two major cases bear this out. The Court recently rejected a claim on the part of the U. S. foreign service officers that forced retirement at age 60 was a violation of their rights under the due process and equal protection provisions of the U. S. Constitution. A mandatory retirement age established by the State is reasonable, the Court said, based in part on the needs and aspirations of younger members of the foreign service to advance to the more senior positions vacated by the litigants, who, regrettably, had arrived at age 60.

Given the all-inclusive age protections mandated by the ADA, the permutations of one age group versus another are almost mind-boggling. The precedent the Court relied on in *Vance* was a case upholding the constitutionality of a State law that forced retirement at age 50. In *Massachusetts Board of Retirement v. Murgia*, the Court denied that the State trooper in question had a legitimate age-related complaint under the 14th amendment.

The elderly as a group, the Court said, were in no way similar to minorities and women, who, as a class, had suffered lengthy and systematic discrimination of many kinds. The Nation, the Court went on to state, has provided for older persons in a special way, notably through social security benefits. Finally, the Court agreed with the State's contention that retirement at age 50 was necessary to uphold the morale and promotion aspirations of younger State troopers —an acceptable and rational means to achieve the State's objective of maintaining public safety.

Litigation under the Age Discrimination in Employment Act (ADEA) is also instructive. This statute has matured over the last 10 years. Cases have reached numerous Federal district and appellate courts, and a growing number are coming up before the U. S. Supreme Court. In addition, many cases have been conciliated short of litigation. This is not the place to recount all the lessons that could be learned from the ADEA. One case, however, should be noted.

Mistretta v. Sandia Laboratories Inc. is the only "pattern and practice" case regarding any type of age discrimination. As such it is relevant to ADA enforcement and litigation strategies. The case involved the termination of a large number of employees for economic reasons. The biggest proportion of workers in that group fell between the ages of 40 and 65— then the upper age limit set by the act. These workers, as a group, filed charges under the ADEA and were joined by the U.S. Department of Labor, which had responsibility for enforcement of the act.

The district court judge ruled that Sandia had engaged in a "pattern and practice" of age discrimination. That is, the decision to terminate had been based on age alone and all other factors were incidental. Department of Labor attorneys introduced a massive array of age-related statistics as evidence that covered every major personnel activity in the company over a 3-year period.

What the Labor Department attorneys did, in effect, was to zero-base age factors in the Sandia personnel system. That is, they examined hiring, promotion, and educational policies within the company and then, from stated policies and practices, built up the comparable age patterns over time that were related to these functions. No assumptions were made regarding discrimination.

The statistics told the story. The Court found that no age discrimination occurred in hiring, promotion, or education, but noted that the data were relevant to the charges of discrimination in termination procedures.

The next level of investigation examined salary administration, retirement policies, and termination procedures. The same type of age analysis was applied. Here the Court ruled that systemic age discrimination occurred in the areas of salary administration and in the termination procedures. The statistical evidence presented showed, beyond a reasonable doubt, that the termination of so many older workers could not have happened by chance or by any other means but conscious deselection.

Lessons for compliance

The lessons for ADA compliance procedures are clear. Federal agencies covered by the ADA should:

- Review and clarify major program functions within the agency mandate as these apply or might apply to different age groups served.
- Examine these functions by past and current distribution of services and funds to different age groups. Five-year age intervals are suggested for the initial overview.
- Examine the recipient providers of services under the agency mandate and the major agency functions they administer to different age groups. Use criteria such as size, location, and program variation for the first overview.
- Analyze all age-imbalances that occur within the range of services provided through recipient groups studied. Reconcile the age imbalances with:
  —Overall agency mandate
  —Primary purpose of the ADA
  —Allowable age distinctions under the ADA exceptions
  —Possible/probable violations of the statute.
- Zero in on the above process and data gathered to detect the more serious "pattern and practice" trends of age discrimination that emerge (as distinct from annual variations in the age characteristics of groups served).
- Set up corrective measures to achieve requisite age distributions that will eliminate the serious

age imbalances in the agency service program.

- Record and document the above procedures and utilize as a technical assistance guide to other recipient organizations not within the initial age-study group.

The advantage of a Federal agency taking such steps is that it will obtain firsthand information and experience in dealing with age discrimination problems. Repeating the process several times—with a view towards developing a compliance model—will sharpen agency awareness on age matters and the requirements of the ADA. This, in turn, will help achieve compliance among recipient organizations at a minimal cost and with agency-wide controls over the compliance program.

The inherent dilemmas

The ADA faces the dilemmas inherent in the aspirations of a democratic society. We must strive to achieve justice for all citizens under the laws, but must remain aware that under any one statute, justice for all can become minimal justice—or worse, justice for none. If the purpose of the ADA is to eliminate all age discrimination in a blind and automatic manner—so that all beneficiaries under Federal programs receive an equally rationed amount of services or funds in terms of service—then all age groups will suffer. If solid age-related criteria for different types and amounts of services for different age groups can be developed and tested over the coming year by Federal agencies responsible for enforcing the ADA, then a slavish conformity to the act can be avoided.

The problem seems to be that such criteria do not exist. They must be developed before the general ADA regulations are finalized and the specific sets of regulations are developed by the appropriate Federal agencies. The history of the age cases and the lessons to be learned through the summary age-audit technique described above offer one positive approach for Federal agencies. But like it or not, this or similar methods to achieve compliance to what must be regarded as not the most specific of civil rights law will take time and effort.

It is noble and grand to attempt to abolish discrimination—age or any other kind—by statute. We have learned some hard lessons over the past and we should make every effort to apply them to the ADA. Time, careful work on the part of Federal agencies, some very complicated litigation, and perfecting amendments down the line will tell the story.

The Age Discrimination Act of 1975 and Women on Campus

Project on the Status of Women of the Association of American Colleges, 1818 R Street, N.W., Washington, D.C., March 1978.

INTRODUCTION

Age discrimination affects all people, but older women receive a "double dose" of discrimination—once because of their age and once again because of their sex. If the older woman is a member of a minority group or also handicapped, the problem is intensified.[1]

In education—as in work—women are particularly vulnerable to age discrimination. Many do not follow traditional sequences of study and work. Women often take time out for childbearing and homemaking, a fact which means that many women are often older when they begin or return to study. The phenomenon of "re-entry" is increasingly common to women. Of all students 35 or older in 1976, for example, 59% were women—up from 52% the year before. In 1977, women students accounted for 93 percent of the enrollment growth at colleges and universities in the U.S. Many of these were older women.

The woman who is 25, or 35, or 45 or more, is no longer a rarity on campus. Although fewer women today are interrupting their studies, or are doing so for shorter periods of time, the impact of the traditional patterns of delayed or interrupted training for women will continue for some time to come. Although the diminishing pool of traditional students—those from 18-22—has led many undergraduate programs to try to attract and accommodate the mature student, older women often face special problems when they decide to return to college.

THE ACT

The Age Discrimination Act of 1975—which goes into effect January 1, 1979—will be helpful in eliminating some of the inequities older women (and men) may face in educational institutions. The Act prohibits:

> unreasonable discrimination on the basis of age in programs or activities receiving Federal financial assistance, including programs or activities receiving funds under the State and Local Fiscal Assistance Act of 1972.

A summary of the Act is included.

The Act is unique in that it does not define "age"to limit coverage to any particular group, such as those 65 or older; it simply prohibits discrimination on the basis of age *at any age*, as long as that discrimination is "unreasonable."[2] Thus the Act has significance for persons at all ages and is particularly important for women in education. Employment is not covered by the Act, other than employment funded by the Comprehensive Employment Training Act (CETA). The primary benefits of the Act for women in education are likely to be in areas such as admissions, financial aid, counseling, and health care.

AGE AND EDUCATION

Older women are often better motivated students. Many professors remember the returning veterans of World War

---

*This paper is substantially based upon testimony presented to the U.S. Commission on Civil Rights by Dr. Bernice Sandler, Executive Director of the Project on the Status and Education of Women, September 26, 1977, and by the National Advisory Council on Women's Educational Programs, September 23, 1977.

[1]Black women, for example, earn less money than white women, but women earn less than men regardless of race. In effect, it takes four years of college to pull a woman's earning power up to that of a man with a high school education.

[2]The meaning of the term "unreasonable" is not clear from the Act's legislative history. In addition to allowing statutory programs with age as an eligibility criteria, such as Social Security, to be considered reasonable, the Act may also allow policies or practices to be defined as "reasonable" only when there is no other alternative to the age discriminatory practice to accomplish its objective. For example, a policy prohibiting students over a certain age from intramural sports could be changed to tie eligibility to physical fitness; to use age *per se* in this instance might be considered "unreasonable."

THE PROJECT ON THE STATUS AND EDUCATION OF WOMEN of the Association of American Colleges provides a clearinghouse of information concerning women in education, and works with institutions, government agencies and other associations and programs affecting women in higher education. The Project is funded by Carnegie Corporation of New York and The Ford Foundation. Publication of these materials does not necessarily constitute endorsement by AAC, Carnegie Corporation of New York or The Ford Foundation.

II as among their best students. Similarly, older women returning to school get higher grades than their younger peers and often surpass their own previous school performance. They are in school to learn and they work hard. Whether *all* older people perform as well academically as *all* younger people is difficult to answer because the answer to the question depends on *which older person* and *which younger person* we are talking about. Certainly the spread of intelligence and potential academic achievement is wider *within* any age group than the difference *between* any two age groups. Another way of putting it is that the individual differences are far more important than any group differences. Admission on the basis of *individual* abilities is likely to be far more effective than by uniformly applying characteristics of a group to specific individuals.

But apart from motivation and higher grades, older students also make a valuable contribution to the classroom by adding to its diversity. Young women and young men often have little opportunity to meet and work with adults other than their parents or their teachers. To have older persons as co-students helps younger persons learn about the adult world. Such students are often role models for their younger peers, and it is not uncommon to see friendships develop which cross the age barriers.

In education, age discrimination is not experienced soley by "senior citizens"; depending on the program or activity, the classification "too old" may occur as early as the twenties. There is, for example, a marked falloff in admissions to medical school after age 28, and some programs like the Rhodes Scholarships will not consider applicants over 24. Policies and practices which seem reasonable for students between the ages of 18-22 may deliberately or inadvertently discriminate against older women (and men). Thus requiring half-time student status in determining eligibility for financial aid may deprive the many homemakers and single parents who cannot attend school on a half-time basis of much needed financial aid. While this policy is ostensibly fair to both men and women, there is an overwhelming likelihood that more women than men will be affected because in most instances, the single parent will be a woman—especially if the family is poor.

NEED FOR SELF-ASSESSMENT

Those concerned with the possible impact of the Age Discrimination Act on education must focus on both program and procedure. Age discrimination cannot be eliminated until it is first identified. Too often, age discrimination—especially when its victims are women—is invisible to everyone but the victim.

Much of the discrimination older women and men face in education institutions is not intentional. Personnel are often unaware that a particular policy is unfair or has a disproportionate impact. When the new law goes into effect, there will be a period, as with any new law, when administrators will stumble over the law inadvertently. The process of educating personnel to the law and its regulation could be speeded up if a self-assessment study is required or if institutions voluntarily evaluate their own programs and policies. For example, the Title IX regulation[3] which required such a self-evaluation, gave institutions the opportunity to identify, evaluate and change, where necessary, overtly discriminatory policies as well as those with disproportionate impact. The federal government will not ever have the resources to monitor every in-

stitution; a self-assessment insures that every institution can become aware of the law and self-enforce its provisions.[4]

Data collection can be a powerful tool in institutional self-evaluation. Although data are collected by sex and race for many admissions and other programs, there is little on age and none explicitly tabulated by sex/age or by sex/race/age. Data tabulated in such a fashion for applicants and admittees to a specific program would reveal whether or not older women are indeed experiencing discrimination.

This paper lists areas where overt as well as indirect discrimination may occur. Women's groups are likely to press for coverage of all of these areas by the implementing regulation currently being developed by the Department of Health, Education and Welfare.

ADMISSIONS

Women, even as young as 25 or 30, are sometimes considered "too old" to enroll in postsecondary programs. While this attitude is changing, women who are older than the traditional age of students are somehow seen as deviants. The shortage of 18-22 year olds has, however, created a "buyer's market" for undergraduate students and it has become increasingly easier for "older" women to enter undergraduate programs in many, but not all, institutions.

In contrast, because of their highly competitive nature, some graduate and professional schools have not experienced a shortage of students and there discrimination on the basis of age is likely to be more pronounced.

There seems to be no consistent rationale in the way different institutions (or different departments within the same institution) determine what age is "too old" for admittance. In one school it may be 30, in another 40, in another 45. Others have no set age cut-off but take age into account, nevertheless.[5] Women who have delayed or interrupted their graduate education in order to build their family sometimes find it difficult to gain admittance to such programs.[6] This is also an area in which sex discrimination is clearly compounded by age discrimination.

In many graduate programs, course work done five or ten years earlier is considered invalid. In some disciplines—law and medicine, for example—the time frames are even shorter so that two to three year old credits may have "expired."

Many attitudinal factors also work against admission of older women to education programs at all levels. Faculty may feel

---

[3]Title IX of the Education Amendments of 1972 prohibits sex discrimination in federally assisted education programs.

[4]The Federal government also needs to assess its own programs and policies to ensure that none overtly or inadvertently violate the Act.

[5]If "cost-benefit" is a factor in denying admission to older students, there seems to be little consistency or articulated criteria as to how particular age cutoffs are determined.

[6]At 28 or older, a 1976 applicant had a 1:4.5 chance of acceptance at medical school—at 27 or younger, the ratio was 1:2.5. In a 1971-72 survey, 22% of applicants aged 28-37 were accepted to medical school, but less than 12% of those 38 and over were accepted. In a 1977 study done by the U.S. Civil Rights Commission, of 114 medical schools surveyed, 28 used age as an explicit entrance criterion. One school stated flatly that no applicants over 35 would be considered for admission. These figures apparently reflect the belief that graduate education is an "investment" which yields fewer returns to the discipline and society as the student grows older. However, the longer life span of women in general, as well as individual differences in life span and in career perseverance, may affect the number of years a person devotes to her or his profession as much as their age at the time of admission. For example, older women are less likely to change careers begun later in life; it is quite possible that the "second career" phenomenon is more likely to occur in males who made very early career choices.

uncomfortable relating to students their own age or older. Often, older women are viewed as lacking potential or as having no relevant experience, especially if they have been away from school to raise children. At one institution a few years ago, a special program for attracting retired military personnel was initiated at a time when women in the same age bracket were told they were "too old" to return to school. Additionally, the irregular work and/or school history of women with childrearing and family responsibilities is often viewed negatively, as though it had the same connotation of instability which a similar history might imply for a male or someone without the demands of homemaking.

FINANCIAL AID

Increasingly, receipt of financial aid is key to entry and continuation in post-secondary education at all levels. While women have tended to be the disproportionate users of non-loan federal financial assistance, working and adult women indicate that they rarely use federal aid. Several problems seem to exclude older women from full participation, all of which might be addressed through the Act's regulations.

FEDERAL PROGRAMS

Financial aid is usually limited to at least half-time students. However, two-thirds of adults participating in education attend class for four or fewer hours a week—not enough to qualify for aid. Similarly, employed adults are much more likely to attend school than unemployed adults and are likely to be paying for it by themselves (54.6%), or through employers (25.9%). Many of these students attend part-time. Among many working women, salaries tend to be so far below those of males that little discretionary income is available for education. Extending aid to students with less than half-time enrollments would have the dual advantage of enticing non-participants while encouraging increased participation among others. Women are simply less likely than men to be able to find non-governmental sources of aid. The half-time requirement is a substantial barrier for homemakers and working women who frequently cannot become half-time or full-time students due to other responsibilities.

SCHOLARSHIPS

Some scholarships are restricted to persons under specific ages. At the graduate level, for example, there are many prestigious scholarships which are limited to persons under 35.[7] Thus women who have returned to school after raising a family are frequently too old to be eligible for many of these awards. Additionally, many doctoral and postdoctoral fellowships aimed at the "beginning professional" inadvertently discriminate against older women whose professional achievements may have been postponed or interrupted because of family responsibilities. It is not at all uncommon for women to be ten or more years behind male counterparts in professional achievement.

DEPENDENT v. INDEPENDENT STATUS

The arbitrary definitions of "dependent" and "independent" status used in determining eligibility for financial aid frequently hurt married women, especially those with children. The so-called independent students—including married students—must contribute higher portions of their family's discretionary income to education than those classified as "dependent" students. Therefore, for example, a woman who is entirely dependent upon her husband for financial support may be ineligible for student financial aid because she is classified as an "independent" student while her "dependent" children will qualify for assistance under the same program.

COUNSELING, CAREER PLANNING & PLACEMENT

In many cases, these services are geared to younger, traditional students. Personnel may not be trained to deal with the problems of older students, many of whom may be facing major life crises associated with becoming independent after years of family centered life. (Of particular interest here are the special programs aimed at returning women students. These programs could well serve as models for across-the-board counseling of older students, regardless of gender.)

Although the Age Discrimination Act specifically exempts employment (except under CETA) from coverage, it does not address placement services directly. Placement programs, however, may be covered by the regulations because they are a service provided to students. Placement personnel need to be aware of their obligation not to aid employers in discriminating on the basis of age.

HEALTH FACILITIES AND INSURANCE

While more campuses with health facilities and group insurance plans for students are paying attention to female health problems, many schools still lack gynecological services, and some problems may not be covered by health services. Title IX of the 1972 Education Amendments is having an impact in this area, but personnel in student health services may not be used to dealing with problems affecting older students. Insurance plans may also omit coverage of problems likely to occur among older women.

PHYSICAL EDUCATION

At the undergraduate level, older students may have difficulties in some instances completing physical education requirements. Sometimes, they have been exempted from these requirements. However, it is conceivable that an older student thus exempted might still want to take such a course, and might claim that such discrimination under the Act is "unreasonable." The problem is complex enough to warrant development of standards in physical education based on ability rather than on age *per se*.

RECRUITMENT AND OUTREACH

Recruiting for students is traditionally done in high schools for undergraduate applicants, and in undergraduate schools for graduate applicants. Materials used in recruitment rarely show older persons as students. While not deliberately discriminatory, these practices nevertheless may reduce the number of non-traditional applicants. Recruiting practices and tools need to be age-fair at least, and might involve outreach to settings where non-traditional applicants are concentrated.

SPECIAL PROGRAMS FOR OLDER PERSONS

Some schools and states have developed special programs for older persons, such as free or reduced tuition. Hopefully, such programs would be able to continue; the Act was not intended to abolish programs benefiting the elderly. It is likely that the regulations would define such programs as examples of "reasonable" discrimination.

CONTINUING EDUCATION PROGRAMS

In some schools, special undergraduate programs of continuing education have been developed for non-traditional stu-

[7]Schools also often participate in the selection process for age-restricted scholarships sponsored by outside organizations.

dents, often meaning those over 25 years. Many of these programs began in response to the increasing number of women returning to school and are excellent. These programs cannot be limited by sex any longer; as a result of Title IX, both men and women may attend. In some schools, students have a choice as to whether to enter as a continuing education student or as a regular student; in others, age is a determining factor. Because there are often differences in the requirements and the kinds of courses offered, restrictions such as these, based on age, might end up being violations of the Act. Women's groups are likely to suggest that the differing kinds of programs be optional and based on student needs rather than age.

COORDINATION AMONG AGENCIES

Although HEW is expected to have an integral and lead role in the enforcement of the Age Discrimination Act, it is also important that there be some coordinating mechanism to insure that the various agencies issue regulations consistent with those of HEW [as required by Section 304(a)(4)] and to insure that enforcement throughout the government is also consistent. Title VI of the Civil Rights Act,[8] as coordinated by the Justice Department, might be a useful model to explore for the Age Discrimination Act: currently there is no coordinating mechanism for Title IX. Additionally, it might be helpful to incorporate age discrimination into civil rights compliance reviews.

CONSISTENCY WITH TITLE VI AND TITLE IX

The Age Discrimination Act is patterned after Title VI of the Civil Rights Act of 1964 and Title IX of the Education Amendments of 1972. It will be most helpful to institutions and to beneficiaries insofar as it is possible for the regulation of the Age Discrimination Act to be patterned after Titles VI and IX. Some of the areas to be decided by the regulation which might well be consistent with Titles VI and IX are the following:

- Complaint procedure
- Complainant definition (whether or not organizations can make complaints on their own behalf and/or on behalf of others)
- Time limit for filing complaints
- Whether investigations may be made without complaints
- Whether the entire institution is reviewed or just the program receiving federal funds
- Record keeping requirements
- Prohibition of harassment
- Notification of complaints to institutions

[8]Title VI prohibits discrimination based on race, color and national origin in federally assisted programs.

- Confidentiality of complainants

CONCLUSION

As age increases, the problems women confront are compounded until they become almost insurmountable for women in their 60's. Agism is unique in this regard, and presents special difficulties of language and definition. These difficulties will undoubtedly spill over into enforcement and implementation problems, since the weight of myth about age grows increasingly heavy and difficult to unseat as older and older population groups are considered. What must be central to any understanding of age-based discrimination is that the myths of aging tend to circumscribe opportunities by stereotyping abilities and needs—and that "too old" is a judgement that should be, but rarely is, made on an individual basis, as determined by highly specific circumstances. Few admissions officers at graduate or professional institutions would deny that they are reluctant to enroll students past 50—and most will also say that this is a general bias which takes "exceptions" into account. Yet, the fact that people over 50 are welcome only if they are exceptional is proof only that stereotypes exist—not that judgements based on the age of applicants are grounded in fact. As the National Council on the Aging has pointed out in its booklet, "Facts and Myths About Aging": "In certain societies, where it is not uncommon to find people *living— and working—past the age of 100*, a person of 65 is considered to be middle-age."

Ultimately, even though women today with college educations can expect lower salaries and more limited opportunities than their brothers with high school educations, it is education that affords women the opportunity to achieve self-sufficiency. For women beyond the traditional age for students, education may be the *only* route to that self-sufficiency. For too long, the often unconscious prejudice which bars older women from so much of the educational system has continued unabated. The legislation will not change attitudes directly, but will ensure that all Americans, regardless of barriers born of myth and prejudice, have the same opportunity to exercise their rights to use their talents, and to contribute to the public good. This law affords us the chance to begin to change that by opening up education and training programs. It is a law which affects all of us, for we are each of us, after all, growing older daily.

In summary, the Age Discrimination Act is likely to be welcomed by women in education. Title IX which prohibits discrimination on the basis of sex opened the educational doors to women; the Age Discrimination Act will help insure that they will not be kept out on the pretext of age.

SUMMARY OF AGE DISCRIMINATION ACT OF 1975 AS CONTAINED IN TITLE III OF THE OLDER AMERICANS AMENDMENTS OF 1975 (PUBLIC LAW 94-135, NOVEMBER 28, 1975)[1]

1. **Effective date**	HEW's regulation cannot be effective *before* January 1, 1979. (The U.S. Commission on Civil Rights was to have compiled a report on age discrimination by May, 1977.[2] HEW must publish a *proposed* regulation no later than one year after the report or 2½ years after enactment,[3] (whichever occurs first.) The *final* regulation must be published no later than 90 days thereafter.
2. **Which Institutions are covered?**	All institutions receiving federal financial assistance including funds from the State and Local Fiscal Assistance Act of 1972 [Revenue Sharing Act. (31 U.S.C. 1221 et seq.)].

3. What is prohibited?	Unreasonable discrimination on the basis of age in programs and activities receiving federal financial assistance.[4]
4. Exemptions from coverage	a) It is not a violation for a program or activity to "reasonably" take into account "age as a factor necessary to the normal operation" or "achievement of any statutory objective."
	b) It is not a violation for programs or activities to take into account reasonable factors other than age.[5]
	c) The provisions of this title do not apply to any program or activity where age is the statutory criterion for benefits and assistance.[6]
	d) Employment practices and labor-management joint apprenticeship training programs are exempted [other than public service employment programs or activities receiving funds under the Comprehensive Employment and Training Act of 1974 (29 U.S.C. 801, et seq.)].
5. Who enforces the Act?	Federal departments or agencies which extend financial assistance. HEW will enforce the Act with regard to educational institutions.
6. How is a complaint made?	Procedure not yet determined. A letter will probably be acceptable.
7. Can complaints of a pattern of discrimination be made?	Not yet determined.
8. Who can make a complaint?	Individuals may make complaints. (However, it is not yet clear whether organizations may do so on their own behalf and/or on behalf of others.)
9. Time limit for filing complaints	Not yet determined.
10. Can investigations be made without complaints?	Not yet determined.
11. Can the entire institution be reviewed?	Not yet determined.
12. Record keeping requirements	Not yet determined.
13. Enforcement power and sanctions	If voluntary compliance fails, the head of the federal department or agency granting funds may terminate, or refuse to grant or to continue assistance. Termination or refusal must be limited to the particular program or activity receiving financial assistance. The statute explicitly states that termination of federal funds or refusal to grant such assistance is the exclusive remedy for enforcement of this title. (This may imply that there is no private right of individuals to sue fund recipients directly.)
14. Can back pay be awarded?	The Act does not cover employment except under Comprehensive Employment and Training Act of 1974. It has not yet been determined whether the remedy of back pay will be applicable to such employment.
15. Affirmative action requirements	There are no restrictions against actions which are non-preferential.
16. Coverage of labor organizations	Does not apply.
17. Is harassment prohibited?	Not yet determined, but likely to be prohibited.
18. Notification of complaints	Not yet determined.
19. Confidentiality	Not yet determined.
20. Further information and relevant documents	The U.S. Commission on Civil Rights report on age discrimination in federally funded programs.

[1] The regulation for Title III has not yet been published. The analysis which follows includes information which is explicitly stated in the statute, as well as how the law is likely to be interpreted in light of other precedents and developments.

[2] The Report of the Commission on Civil Rights was published in December 1977.

[3] May 1978.

[4] Nothing in Title III may conflict with the Age Discrimination in Employment Act of 1967 (29 U.S.C. 621-634) as amended.

[5] Such as health or strength.

[6] Such as Social Security.

Prepared by the Project on the Status and Education of Women, Association of American Colleges, 1818 R Street, NW, DC 20009.

SELECTED BIBLIOGRAPHY

Age Is Becoming: An Annotated Bibliography on Women and Aging 1977 revised ed. $3.30 includes postage and handling. Order from:
Older Women's Rights Committee
NOW
3800 Harrison Street
Oakland, CA 94611

Older Women: A Workshop Guide (W-13), Stock No. 052-003-00490-9. National Commission on the Observance of International Women's Year. Order from:
Government Printing Office
Superintendent of Documents
Washington, DC 20402

Past Sixty: The Older Woman, an annotated bibliography edited by Carol Hollenshead, Carol Katz and Berit Ingersoll. The Institute of Gerontology, The University of Michigan, 1977, $3.00.

Older Americans Act: A Summary

Staff Study

Select Committee on Aging

Wm. J. Randall, Missouri, Chairman

Claude Pepper, Florida
Spark M. Matsunaga, Hawaii
Edward R. Roybal, California
Fred B. Rooney, Pennsylvania
Mario Biaggi, New York
Walter Flowers, Alabama
Ike F. Andrews, North Carolina
John L. Burton, California
Edward P. Beard, Rhode Island
Michael T. Blouin, Iowa
Don Bonker, Washington
Thomas J. Downey, New York
James J. Florio, New Jersey
Harold E. Ford, Tennessee
William J. Hughes, New Jersey
Marilyn Lloyd, Tennessee
Jim Santini, Nevada
Ted Risenhoover, Oklahoma

Bob Wilson, California
William C. Wampler, Virginia
John Paul Hammerschmidt, Arkansas
H. John Heinz III, Pennsylvania
William S. Cohen, Maine
Ronald A. Sarasin, Connecticut
William F. Walsh, New York
Charles E. Grassley, Iowa
Gilbert Gude, Maryland

Robert M. Horner, Staff Director
Lyle McClain, Counsel
Albert H. Solomon, Jr., Professional Staff Assistant
Martha Jane Maloney, Professional Staff Assistant
V. Bernice King, Financial Secretary

Editor's Note: The complete "Older Americans Act of 1965," with Amendments made through 1975, can be found in the first edition of *Sourcebook on Aging,* beginning on page 521.

Subcommittee Membership

(Wm. J. Randall, Missouri, Chairman of the full committee, and Bob Wilson, California, Ranking Minority Member, are members of all subcommittees, ex officio.)

Subcommittee No. 1--Retirement Income and Employment

Wm. J. Randall, Missouri, Chairman

Walter Flowers, Alabama
John L. Burton, California
Michael T. Blouin, Iowa
Don Bonker, Washington
Thomas J. Downey, New York

William C. Wampler, Virginia
Charles E. Grassley, Iowa
Gilbert Gude, Maryland

Michael W. Murray, Majority Staff
Nancy E. Hobbs, Minority Staff

Subcommittee No. 2--Health and Long-Term Care

Claude Pepper, Florida, Chairman

Ike F. Andrews, North Carolina
Edward P. Beard, Rhode Island
James J. Florio, New Jersey
Marilyn Lloyd, Tennessee

H. John Heinz III, Pennsylvania
William S. Cohen, Maine

Robert S. Weiner, Majority Staff
Elliot Stern, Minority Staff

Subcommittee No. 3--Housing and Consumer Interests

Edward R. Roybal, California, Chairman

Fred B. Rooney, Pennsylvania
Harold E. Ford, Tennessee
Jim Santini, Nevada

John Paul Hammerschmidt, Arkansas
William F. Walsh, New York

Jose S. Garza, Majority Staff
Patricia Lawrence, Minority Staff

Subcommittee No. 4--Federal, State and Community Services

Spark M. Matsunaga, Hawaii, Chairman

Mario Biaggi, New York
William J. Hughes, New Jersey
Ted Risenhoover, Oklahoma

Bob Wilson, California
Ronald A. Sarasin, Connecticut

Edward F. Howard, Majority Staff
Robetta Bretsch, Minority Staff

Contents

Older Americans Act: A Summary[1]

Title I. Declaration of Objectives

1.1 Legislative Development

Most Federal agencies administer programs that are confined to a single category of activity. For some housing is the exclusive interest. Others devote substantially all of their time to transportation, welfare, education or other statutorily declared and approved objectives. In order to function effectively, it was early recognized that a Federal agency that would be of service to the elderly could not confine its activities to a single concern. Thus when the Administration on Aging was brought into existence, the Agency objectives were broadly stated to make them coextensive with the diverse concerns of the clientele that would be served.

The idea for a special Federal agency to serve the elderly was an outgrowth of the 1961 White House Conference on Aging. After the conference was concluded, the Special Staff on Aging in the Office of the Secretary of Health, Education, and Welfare began drafting legislation that would bring into existence a program that would be devoted to improving the quality of life for older Americans.[2] The legislative vehicle that made both the program and the administering organization a reality is the Older Americans Act of 1965.[2a] Representative John Fogarty of Rhode Island and Senator Pat McNamara of Michigan were the principal sponsors of the legislation.[3] The bill as passed by Congress was signed into law by President Johnson who said that the Older Americans Act "clearly affirms our Nation's high sense of responsibility toward the well-being of older citizens...Under this program, every State and every community can move toward a coordinated program of both services and opportunities for older citizens."[4] On October 26, 1965, President Johnson appointed William D. Bechill as the first Commissioner of the Administration on Aging. Currently Dr. Arthur S. Flemming is Commissioner of the Administration on Aging.

After the Older Americans Act became law in 1965, Congress periodically reexamined the program to see if it was producing the benefits that were intended. In some years Congress thought that a tuneup was all that was needed. In other years, as in 1973, a major overhaul of the program was undertaken. In all the Act has been amended six times, most recently in 1975.[5]

1.2 Objectives

Generally the Older Americans Act is directed to giving older Americans opportunities for full participation in the benefits of our democratic society. A ten-point program to assist older Americans is envisioned by the Act. As stated in the Act, the objectives are to assist older people to secure the full and free enjoyment of:[6]
1. An adequate income
2. The best possible physical and mental health
3. Suitable housing
4. Full restorative services
5. Employment without age discrimination
6. Retirement in health, honor and dignity
7. Participation in civic, cultural, and recreational activity
8. Community service
9. Immediate benefit from research
10. Freedom and independence

Title II. Administration on Aging
2.1 Establishment of Administration on Aging

Congress intended to establish an Agency with high visibility to administer the Older Americans program. But as late as 1973 disappointment was expressed with the organizational arrangements made by the Department of Health, Education, and Welfare, and there was more than a suggestion that Congressional intent had been subverted. The Administration on Aging had been grouped with the Social and Rehabilitation Service with the Commissioner on Aging reporting to the Administrator of the Social and Rehabilitation Service. It was also thought inappropriate that the non-welfare orientated programs of the Administration on Aging should fall within the organizational arrangements of an Agency that is generally regarded as a welfare agency. An erosion of the Commissioner's authority over administration of the Older Americans' program was also noted. The Title IV Research and Demonstration Program had been placed under the Associate Administrator of the Social and Rehabilitation Service; the Title VI Retired Senior Volunteer Program and Foster Grandparent Program had been moved to the new Action Agency, and many of the operational responsibilities for Title III had been delegated to the Social and Rehabilitation Service regional offices. Thus as late as 1971, an Advisory Council to the U. S. Special Committee on Aging reported that:

> "the AoA falls far short of being the Federal 'focal
> point on aging' sought by Congress. Instead its concerns
> are splintered and scattered; there are limited, if any,
> policies and few clear-cut goals. Recent reorganizations
> have not strengthened Federal programs and commitment
> in aging in any way. Rather, they have fragmented an
> already flawed and feeble agency still further. This
> situation has created chaos as well as a lack of direction
> in Federal and State programs."[7]

To strengthen the Commissioner's position, Congress included in the 1975 Amendments language prohibiting delegation of the Commissioner's functions to any officer not responsible to the Commissioner, and providing that the Commissioner would be responsible only to the Secretary of Health, Education, and Welfare.[8]

2.2 Duties and Functions of the Administration on Aging

A detailed description of the duties and functions of the Administration on Aging is included in the Act. Sixteen categories of activities for performance by the Administration are mentioned. With respect to matters concerning the aged and involvements of aging, the administration is directed to:[9]

1. Serve as a clearinghouse for information
2. Administer grants
3. Develop plans, conduct and arrange for research
4. Assist the Secretary of Health, Education, and Welfare
5. Provide technical assistance and consultation services
6. Prepare, publish, and disseminate materials
7. Gather statistics
8. Stimulate more effective use of resources and services
9. Develop policies and set priorities
10. Coordinate Federal programs and activities
11. Coordinate and assist in planning and development by public and private non-profit organizations to establish a nationwide network of comprehensive services
12. Hold conferences of public and nonprofit private organizational officials
13. Develop and operate programs not otherwise provided by existing programs
14. Continually evaluate programs and activities, paying particular attention to Medicare, Medicaid, Age Discrimination Act of 1967, and the National Housing Act
15. Provide information and assistance to private non-profit organizations
16. Develop plans for education and training, and in consultation with the Director of Action, encourage the participation of voluntary groups including youth organizations

2.3 National Information and Resource Clearing House

As contemplated by the Act, the Commissioner would establish and operate a National Clearing House that would provide information to older persons directly or through State information and referral sources on a wide range of subjects pertaining to the aged, aging processes, or of interest to older people. The Commissioner would also arrange for the coordination of information and referral activities of other departments and agencies of the Federal government having information relevant to older persons.[10]

2.4 Authorization to Appropriate Funds for National Clearing House

Authorization is extended to appropriate funds to carry on the functions of the National Clearing House.[11] The 1975 Amendments to the Older Americans Act extended authorization for the program through fiscal year 1978.

2.5 Federal Council on the Aging

The 1973 Amendments authorized the establishment of a Federal Council on the Aging to consist of 15 members appointed by the President, with the advice and consent of the Senate for terms of 3 years, for the purposes

of advising the President on the needs of Older Americans and assisting
the Commissioner in appraising the need for personnel in the field of
aging.[12] In addition to advising the President and the Commissioner,
the Federal Council on Aging has extensive duties relating to review and
evaluation of policy and programs affecting older people, serving as a
spokesman for the elderly, informing the public, and providing forums
for discussing and publicizing problems. Not later than March 31st of
each year, the Council is required to submit a report to the President,
who is required to furnish a copy to Congress, on its findings and recommendations. The Council is also directed to undertake a study of the
interrelationship of Federal, State and local benefit programs for the
elderly, and to undertake a study of the combined impact of all taxes
on the elderly, and to undertake a study of the combined impact of all
taxes on the elderly. (Sec. 205h) Originally the study was to be completed within 18 months of the date of enactment of the 1973 Amendments.
Several extensions were granted to complete the study. A report of 64
pages, together with appendices, encompassing the results of both of these
studies was submitted by the Federal Council in 1976, and is now available
through the United States Government Printing Office.

The Council was also directed to undertake a study, and submit a
report, on the formula for apportioning Federal funds to the States for
area planning and social services under Title III. (Sec 205i) This study
was completed, and the results incorporated into a report of the Federal
Council on Aging dated December 30, 1974.

2.6 1975 Amendments (Application of Other Laws)

Sec. 102 of the 1975 Amendments (PL 94-135) added a new provision
(Section 211) to the Act. This new provision states that the Act of
December 5, 1974, (PL 95-510; 88 Stat. 1604) shall not apply to the
administration of the Older Americans Act or to the administration of
any program or activity under the Act. The Act of December 5, 1974,
mentioned in new Section 211, is the Joint Funding Simplification Act,
which absent the exclusion added to the Older Americans Act by new Section
211, would allow the transfer of programs from one Federal Agency or
Department to another Federal Agency or Department by mutual agreement
reached between the Federal agencies. In the Conference Report (HR 94-670)
that accompanied the 1975 Amendments, the conferees explained their reasons
for the Section 211 addition to the Act by saying at page 36:

> "The amendment made by the conference substitute is included
> to reaffirm the intent of the Older Americans Act that the
> Administration on Aging be the focal point and advocacy point
> for aging within the Federal government. Permitting the
> Commissioner on Aging to enter into such agreements which
> could result in a transfer of program and financial authority
> for Older Americans Act programs from the Administration on
> Aging to another Federal agency would seriously erode the
> purpose of the Act."

2.7 Administrative Reports

Annually the Secretary of Health, Education, and Welfare is to make
available to Congress and the public the results of evaluative research
conducted under the Act, and his findings and conclusions on the effectiveness of programs and projects conducted under the Act (Sec. 207(d)).
Not later than 120 days after the close of each fiscal year, the
Commissioner is to submit an annual report on activities carried out
under the Act (Sec. 208).

2.8   Joint Funding of Projects

Where Federal funds are provided for a single project by more than one Federal agency--to any agency or organization assisted under the act-- the Federal agency principally involved may be designated to act for all in administering the funds, if such arrangements conform to regulations prescribed by the President, and are consistent with other provisions of the Act (Sec. 209).   This provision was added to Title II by the 1973 Amendments.   The language of this provision is in many respects similar to the language of former Section 805, Title VIII.   Title VIII was repealed by the 1973 Amendments.   Although the new provision is patterned on former Section 805, the qualification that joint funding principles be employed only where "consistent with other provisions of the Act" was added in 1973.   Other language of this provision makes it clear that where more than one Federal agency is supplying funds to a project, a single non-Federal share may be established, and any technical requirements of an Federal agency inconsistent with those of the administering Federal agency may be waived.

2.9   Appropriation Authorization for Administration on Aging

Such sums as may be necessary are authorized to be appropriated for the Administration on Aging's functions in carrying out the purposes of the Act.   (Sec. 206(c)).

Title III.   Grants for State and Community Programs on Aging
3.1   Purpose

Amendments that became law in 1973 completely revised Title III of the Older Americans Act.[13]   Extensive revisions were made to give State Agencies on Aging a more dynamic role in solving the problems and meeting the needs of older people.   Motivation for the amendments is summed up in this House Report comment that accompanied the bill (H.R. 71) on which the amendments are based:

"The purpose of this new Title III would be to encourage
and assist State or local agencies to concentrate resources
in order to develop greater capacity for, and foster the
development of comprehensive and coordinated service systems
to serve older persons by entering into new cooperative
arrangements with each other and with providers of social
services for planning for the provision of, and providing,
social services and, where necessary to reorganize or
reassign functions, in order to
---secure and maintain maximum independence and dignity
   in a home environment for older persons capable of
   self-care with appropriate supportive services; and
---remove individual and social barriers to economic and
   personal independence for older persons."[14]

Even before the enactment of the 1975 Amendments to Title III, the effects of Title III funds under the old program were being felt at the local level.   With the assistance of Title III money nearly all the States and Territories had prior to the 1973 Amendments established state offices on aging, and 395 local agencies on aging had been funded.[15]   In 1972 there were about one million persons being served by over 1,500 projects funded under Title III.   More than 300 community programs were designed to maintain independent living arrangements for the elderly, and 466 programs were being conducted that involved older volunteers.   To help provide a balanced diet, meals or home delivered meals were being served to 60,000 to 70,000 older persons. Attention was being directed to the transportation needs of the elderly through 428 projects, some having as their principal purpose the actual furnishing of transportation to the elderly and others involving transportation only as a component of the program. Health and health-related services were being delivered through 337 projects designed to make available nurses and in-home health aides for the home-bound elderly. State agencies drawing on Title III funds provided support for 623 senior centers that were being operated in public low-rent housing, churches, public and private buildings and institutions. Among their accomplishments these senior centers listed the training of 14,708 elderly for employment that provided opportunities for an active role in community life.

Consequently it was in a climate of some already proven successes that Congress was considering amendment of the Title III program. As modified by the 1973 Amendments the law is directed to building upon and expanding the accomplishments of the old program by designing a system that would hopefully act as a more effective catalyst in drawing upon and organizing local resources to make living conditions better and improve the quality of life for older people.

3.2 Area Planning and Social Service Program

As a result of the 1973 Amendments each State is required to adopt a plan for supplying social services to the elderly that meets criteria set out in the Act.[16] A single agency must be designated at the sole State agency charged with the development and administration of the State plan.[17]

Furthur engrafted upon the Act is a requirement that the State Agency determine the areas for which an area plan will be developed, and a public or nonprofit private organization must be designated as the area agency on aging to serve such area. [18] In turn the Area Agency on Aging must develop an area plan that complies with the requirements of the Act, and which must be submitted to the State Agency for approval.[19] To help with the operational expenses of the Area Agency, the State Agency contributes to the support of the Area Agency, and the State Agency determines how much of the funds allotted to the State are to be apportioned among the various planning and service areas.[20]

Those areas for which a plan has been developed will need, and will receive more favorable funding from the State Agency; and funds can be made available to them on a matching basis of 90% Federal to 10% non-Federal as compared with 75% Federal and 25% non-Federal in areas that have not been selected for development of an area plan. Not more than 15% of the State's allotment for area planning and social services can be used for the cost of administration of area plans, and not more than 20% of such allotment can be used for social services that are not delivered as a part of a coordinated and comprehensive system for which there is an area plan.[21]

Area Agencies on Aging are not usually direct providers of services. As to functions that might properly be performed by Area Agencies, the following comment extracted from the report of the Senate Committee that held hearings on the 1973 Amendments is illustrative:

"It is not intended, however, that the area agencies on aging shall be primary providers of services. In many communities existing organizations may already be engaged in providing services and the entry of the area agencies

into the position of providing services is likely to result
in duplication and overlap. Their primary concern must be to
coordinate existing services and to stimulate the expansion
of such services and the introduction of new services by
other providers. State and area agencies alike are
authorized to provide services though when it is determined, in the judgment of the state agencies, that such
action is necessary to assure an adequate supply of
services."[22]

3.3 1975 Amendments to Title III
3.310 Grants to Indian Tribes

Again in 1975 extensive changes were made in Title III. It was
sensed that not enough attention was being given to Indians as potential
participants in programs for the aged. A provision was added to the
law which in part provides that if the Commissioner determines that members of an Indian tribe are not receiving benefits under Title III which
are equivalent to benefits provided to other older persons in the State
or Area involved, and further determines that they would be better served
by direct Federal grants, a proportionate sum of the States allotment
(in accordance with a prescribed formula) shall be reserved by the
Commissioner to make grants to the tribal organization, or other entity
having the capacity to provide services under Title III.

3.320 Area Plan Requirements   (Transportation)

Both the House and Senate recognized that the transportation needs
of the elderly were generally provided only on an uncoordinated and fragmented basis, and that eligibility requirements of other Federal programs
might make it difficult to integrate these other programs with transportation programs being conducted under Titles III and VII of the Older
Americans Act. Nevertheless, to the extent that such pooling might be
possible, the legislative committees thought that transportation components
available in various programs should be brought together. With this
thought in mind, a provision was added to Title III that authorized State
and Area Agencies to enter into agreements with agencies administering
programs under the Rehabilitation Act of 1973, and Titles VI, XIX, and
XX of the Social Security Act for the purpose of developing and implementing
plans for meeting the common need for transportation services of persons
receiving benefits under such Acts and older persons participating in
programs under Titles III and VII of the Older Americans Act.[23]

3.330 National Priority Services

Four national priority areas (transportation, home care, legal services,
and home renovation and repair) are established by the 1975 Amendments
to the Act.[24] As to the manner of providing such services, it seems
clear that Congress did not intend that services in the priority areas
be provided directly by Area Agencies on Aging. On this point the conferees said:

"The conferees wish to stress that requiring the funds
allotted to a State be used for these purposes does not
mean that State and area agencies on aging must provide
them directly. Their funds may continue to be used for
stimulating and coordinating the provision of services
so long as the required amounts are used in the four
service areas described above. Moreover, area agencies
are required by an amendment to section 304(c)(2) of the
Act to develop their area plans consistent with the

provision of the State plan regarding the four national priority service areas."[25]

Interest in concentrating more resources in the four priority areas was apparently stimulated by the results of a Congressional Research Survey. The survey showed that some States had not devoted much effort to supplying transportation, homemaker, legal and home repair and renovation services. The conferees summarized the results of the survey by saying:

"Finally, the conferees note that the conference substitute is based in part upon a survey taken by the Congressional Research Service at the direction of the House Committee on Education and Labor. The survey inquired of State agencies on aging as to how their funds are being used. With 49 of 56 States and jurisdictions responding, it was found that 10 States are currently spending less than 20 percent of their funds in the four priority areas designated in the House bill. Eight states are spending more than 20 percent but less than 33-1/3 percent. Thirty-one of the States are already spending more than 33-1/3 percent of their State plan allotment to provide the four priority services and thus presumably will not be affected by the conference substitute language. Many of the States that are spending heavily in these four areas are concentrating their resources primarily on transportation for the elderly. While the conferees are in agreement that transportation is a vitally important service to older people, it is hoped that all States will also expand their activities to cover the other three priority services as well, to the extent that funds permit."[26]

3.340 Deletion of Prior Plan Requirement on Legal Services

Prior to the 1975 amendments, the Act required Area Agencies on Aging where necessary and feasible, to enter into arrangements to provide legal services to older persons residing in the planning and service area.[27] Because other provisions for meeting the needs of the elderly for legal services were made in the 1975 amendments, the language directing the provision of legal services where "necessary and feasible" was no longer considered appropriate, and was deleted.[28]

3.350 Apportionment of Funds for Administration of State Plans: Minimum Allotment

Federal funds for administration of State plans are apportioned in accordance with a formula. Each State that has adopted a State plan is allowed from the funds appropriated a percentage that is based on the ratio of the State's population aged 60 or over to the population aged 60 or over in all States.[29] In the 1973 amendments a provision was added that entitled each State to receive for State administration at least one-half of 1% or $160,000 (even though the State may have been entitled to less under the apportionment formula).[30] The 1975 Amendments changed the minimum for State Administration to $200,000.[31] Other language of the 1975 Amendments provided that in any fiscal year no State shall receive from Federal funds for administration of its State plan less than its 1975 allotment; and further provided that if additional funds are needed

for State administration, the Commissioner may, if certain conditions
are met, approve the use of additional funds for State administration
even though such funds would normally be available under Sec. 303 only
for other purposes.[32] The Commissioner's discretionary authority to
approve the use of additional funds is subject to the limitation that
any additional amount that the Commissioner may elect to approve for
State administration cannot exceed three-quarters of 1% of the amount
of the State's allotments under Section 303(b) (planning and social service program) and Section 703(a)(nutrition program). The Act has always
required a contribution from the State to pay part of the cost of State
Administration. Since 1969 Federal funds may be used to pay no more
than 75% of the cost of State Administration.[33]

3.4 Model Projects

The Committees having legislative jurisdiction over the Older Americans Act recognized that there was a need for special projects, in addition
to projects being operated by the States and by Area agencies. Prior
to the 1973 amendments, provisions for model projects were included under
Sec. 305 of the Act (Areawide Model Projects). The 1969 Amendments authorized the Commissioner to make grants for model projects "upon such terms
as he deemed appropriate" while the 1973 amendments interjected the requirement that such grants should be made "after consultation with the
State agency."[34] Model project grants could be made only to the State
agencies under the 1969 Amendments, but the 1973 Amendments broadened
the eligible group to include public or nonprofit private agencies or
organizations. Matching funds for model projects were required under the
1969 Amendments with the Federal share not to exceed 75% of the project
cost, but the 1973 amendments eliminated the matching requirement. Up
to the time of the 1973 Amendments, no target areas were specified for
model projects, however, the 1973 amendments named four areas of concentration, (1) special housing needs, (2) continuing education, (3) preretirement education, and (4) services that meet particular needs of
physically and mentally impaired older persons.[35]

3.5 1975 Model Project Requirements

Three additional objectives for model project funds are named in
the 1975 Amendments.[36] These objectives are:
1. "ombudsmen services for residents of nursing homes",
2. needs of those "not receiving adequate services under other
    provisions" of the Act with emphasis on the needs of low income
    minorities and the rural elderly, and
3. assisting older persons to maintain independent living arrange-
    ments by providing assistance for senior ambulatory care day
    centers, and maintaining or initiating arrangements with the
    Agency of the State that administers or supervises the State
    Plan under Title XIX (Medicaid).[36]

3.6 Authorization for Appropriations

From 1969 until the 1973 Amendments, the Act contained separate
clauses to authorize appropriations for (1) project support, and (2) for
planning, coordination, evaluation and administration of State plans.
The 1973 Amendments placed these authorizations for appropriations in a
single clause, Section 303, covering both the funding of (1) social
services under Area plans, and (2) the expenses of State administration.
Another Section of the Act, Section 306, refers back to Section 303 in

citing appropriation authority for "Planning, Coordination, Evaluation and Administration of State Plans". Thus it is necessary to refer to Section 303, the general appropriation authorization clause for Title III, to find appropriation authority for Section 306, State administration.

Funds for State administration are distributed in accordance with a formula,[37] and certain limitations are placed on the use of these Federal funds. For instance, such percentage as the State agency determines, but not more than 75 percentum of the cost of administration of the State plan may come from Federal funds.[38]

Federal funds allotted for State administration, which are not used for administration of the State plan, may be used by the State to cover part of the cost of administration of Area plans.[39] If the Commissioner determines that all of a State's allotment will not be needed for a particular year, the part that will not be needed may be apportioned among other States in accordance with the formula provided for such distribution.[40] Federal funds to help support area plans for social services are also allocated among the States as provided by a statutory formula.[41] As contemplated by the Act, the State will decide what amount of funds from its Federal allotment should be apportioned to each planning and service area. Written into the law, however, are certain restrictions that limit the amount that can be spent for administrative costs, and also limits the amount that can be spent for social services that are not made available as a part of an area plan.[42] With respect to each category of activity (administrative, social services) carried on in a planning and service area, only a percentage of the costs may be absorbed by Federal funds, and the law specifies what that percentage is.[43]

Authorization for appropriation of funds to carry out the purposes of the Act have been available since the Act's inception, with a gradual escalating—of the amounts authorized, however, within the past few years amounts actually appropriated for functions of the Older Americans Act have remained fairly static.[44]

3.7 Transportation Projects

The 1974 Amendments added a special program to help solve some of the transportation problems, and meet some of the transportation needs of older people.[45] Similar to other grant provisions of the Older Americans Act, this program also requires a local contribution to match a Federal contribution of 75%. Sums appropriated for transportation projects under this Section are to be apportioned to the States in accordance with the Title III distribution formula (Sec. 303(b) of the Act). Unlike other Title III programs that have a common source of authority for making appropriation, this transportation program has a separate clause authorizing appropriations for special projects.[46]

Title IV. Training and Research
4.1 Legislative Development

The authors of the Older Americans Act believed that older people must frequently draw upon kinds of services that are necessitated by their own peculiar conditions and circumstances. Services of this character were not always generally available. And the framers of the legislation wished to fill this void by establishing a program that would encourage those looking for careers to acquire the kinds of skills that would be beneficial to the elderly.

At the time of the 1973 Amendments to the Act, research and development programs were covered under Title IV, and training activities under

Title V. Because these programs were closely related, it was decided
to bring both "research" and "training" under Title IV. The new Title IV
was then divided into three parts, Training, Research, and Multidisciplinary
Centers of Gerontology. In the 1967 Amendments a study was authorized
of the need for trained personnel in the field of aging. Results of the
study pointed up the necessity for multidisciplinary centers of gerontology, both to provide higher visibility to the field of aging, and
to afford opportunities for those acquiring skills that are helpful to
older people to have some contact with their clientele during training
and to acquaint themselves with the personnel and facilities that serve
older people.[47] Motivated at least in part by these considerations, and
perhaps in part by similar recommendations made by the 1971 White House
Conference on Aging, Congress in 1973 decided to add multidisciplinary
centers of gerontology as a Title IV program to be supported by Federal
funding.[48]

4.2 Training (Purpose)

The training program is intended to improve the kinds of services
that are needed by the elderly. And in this area a variety of approaches
is contemplated by the legislation, some designed to draw people into
the field of aging, and others directed to promoting education, broadening
and perfecting the kinds of skills that are most beneficial to the elderly.[49]

4.3 Training (Appraisal of Needs)

The Commissioner is required to appraise the needs of skilled personnel in the field of aging, and, as a part of the Administration's
annual report, to publish his findings.[50]

4.4 Training (Attracting Qualified Persons)

To encourage entry into the field of aging, the Commissioner may
make grants to public or nonprofit private agencies, organizations, or
institutions. The grantees may employ a variety of means to achieve their
objective, including the dissemination of materials, publicizing opportunities, and the use of part-time assignments for craftsmen, artists,
and scientists to induce them to apply at least a part of their talents
and skills in ways that help older people.[51]

4.5 Training Programs for Personnel

To further the purposes of the training program, grants may be made
by the Commissioner to appropriate organizations, institutions, and agencies
to assist them in teaching personnel employed or preparing for employment
in fields related to the purposes of the Older Americans Act.[52]

4.6 1975 Amendments (Training)

For the purposes of attracting qualified persons to the field of
aging, the 1975 amendments made it clear that higher educational institutions may have programs of less than 4 years and still be eligible for
grants from the Commissioner. As amended in 1975, the Act provides that
any school is eligible under the Act which provides "not less than a 1
year program" of training to prepare students for gainful employment in
a recognized occupation.[53]

The Senate Report that dealt with the 1975 Amendments expressed concern about "the Administration's efforts to phase out longterm training
programs." Language was added to the Act specifying that the Commissioner
may make grants to assist those pursuing "post-secondary education courses
of training or study related to the purposes of the Act."[53a]

Authority was also added by the 1975 Amendments for the Commissioner to make grants for the training of lawyers and paraprofessionals to provide legal (including tax and financial) counseling and services to older persons, the training of personnel to monitor the administration of programs affecting older persons, and the training of persons associated with public or private nonprofit agencies to identify and develop solutions to problems affecting older persons.[53b]

4.7 Research and Development

At the discretion of the Commissioner, a wide variety of research projects to benefit the elderly may qualify for federal assistance, including projects that are intended to identify wholesome and harmful factors in the environment of older people, promote the enrichment of their lives, aid in the coordination of community services, and make available better methods of dealing with problems of the elderly.[54]

4.8 Special Study and Demonstration Projects on Transportation

An all too pervasive problem of the elderly has been the unavailability of transportation. Inaccessibility frequently prevents older people from reaching even those services that are particularly targeted for them. The 1971 White House Conference on Aging pointed up the need for ways to increase the mobility of older people. In response Congress in 1973 added to Title IV of the Older Americans Act a separate section authorizing a study, and demonstration projects on methods that might be employed to expand the transportation capability for older people.[55] Incident to the study, the Commissioner is required to consult with the Secretary of Transportation and the Secretary of Housing and Urban Development and the Secretary of Transportation. At least half of the projects were required to be conducted in a predominantly rural area.[56] Not later than January of 1975, the Commissioner is required to transmit the results of the study to the Secretary of Health, Education, and Welfare, the President, and Congress.[57]

4.9 Multidisciplinary Centers of Gerontology

Federal support of multidisciplinary centers of gerontology was a recommendation of the 1971 White House Conference on Aging. It seems probable that the 1971 recommendation, at least in part, motivated Congress to make provisions for multidisciplinary centers of gerontology in the 1973 Amendments. Under the 1973 Amendments the Commissioner is authorized to make grants for the purpose of establishing or supporting multidisciplinary centers of gerontology.[58] In describing the contribution that these centers might make, the House report that accompanied the prospective legislation (H.R. 71) says:[58a]

> "The multidisciplinary centers authorized by this bill
> would: recruit and train personnel; conduct research
> into a variety of matters which affect the elderly,
> ranging from education to living arrangements; provide
> consultation and technical assistance regarding the
> planning of services for older persons; act as a reposi-
> tory of information related to its area of basic and
> applied research, encourage the incorporation of aging
> information into the teaching of biological, behavioral
> and social sciences in institutions of higher education;
> develop and operate short course training sequences for

staff of State, area and local aging agencies; develop
training programs on aging in schools of social work,
public health, health care administration, education;
and create opportunities for multidisciplinary efforts
in teaching, research and demonstration projects related
to aging.

4.10 Authorization of Appropriations--Part D
Part D contains all of the authorization to make appropriations
for the principal parts of Title IV, Training (Part A), Research and
Development (Part B), and Multidisciplinary Centers of Gerontology (Part
C). Such sums are authorized for appropriation as may be necessary.[59]

Title V. Multipurpose Senior Centers
5.1 Purpose
According to the authors of Title V, the purpose of the "senior
centers" federal assistance program is "to provide a focal point in communities for the development and delivery of social services and nutritional services designed primarily for older persons."[60] The term
"multipurpose senior center" means "a community facility for the organization and provision of a broad spectrum of services" including health,
social, nutritional, and educational services for the benefit of older
persons."[61] Developed in Title V are four concepts to promote senior
centers. One of the concepts is concerned with providing grants for the
alteration, acquisition, and renovation of senior centers. A second
concept also included in Part A of Title V is intended to authorize the
use of federal mortgage insurance to guarantee loans on senior centers.
The third concept, also finance-related, is directed to reducing the
mortgage interest payments on loans by allowing the Commissioner to pay
a part of the interest that the Senior Center would be required to pay.
The fourth concept (Part B of Title V) involves an authorization to the
Commissioner to make grants to help with the initial staffing costs of
senior centers. Each of these concepts will be discussed in more detail
in subsequent paragraphs.

5.2 Acquisition, Alteration, or Renovation of Multipurpose Senior Centers
To assist with the establishment and continuation of "senior centers",
the Commissioner is authorized to make grants to units of local government,
public and private nonprofit agencies and organizations, and to enter
into contracts, to pay not to exceed 75% of the cost of acquiring, al-
tering or renovating existing facilities.[62] Grants or contracts in any
one State shall not exceed 10% of the total amount appropriated for the
year. Before making grants or contracts, the Commissioner is required to
obtain reasonable assurances that the facility will be used as a senior
center for at least 10 years. Applications must also contain assurances
that those performing work on the facility will be paid not less than
the prevailing labor rate as determined by the Secretary of Labor in
accordance with the Davis-Bacon Act (40 USC 276a--276a5).[63] The Commissioner
is directed in making grants and entering into contracts to give preference to areas where a comprehensive and coordinated system for delivery
of services to older people is being developed under Title III.[64] If within
10 years after receiving a grant or entering into a contract, the agency
or organization loses its non-profit character, or the facility ceases
to be used for the purpose for which it was acquired, a provision in
Title V enables the United States to recapture its payments.[65]

5.3 Authorization for Appropriations for Acquisition, Alteration, Renovation
      For acquisition, alteration, and renovation of "multipurpose senior
centers" as contemplated in Title V, there are authorized to be appropriated such sums as may be necessary.[66]

5.4 Mortgage Insurance for Multipurpose Senior Centers
      To make available urgently needed facilities for programs for the
elderly, the Secretary of Health, Education, and Welfare is authorized
to insure mortgages on "new multipurpose senior centers," and their equipment, in accordance with terms and conditions established by him.[67]
Amount of the principal obligation being insured may not exceed $250,000.[68]
The Secretary has authority to fix the amortization terms, and must determine and collect a mortgage insurance premium.[69] Interest shall be at a
rate not in excess of the amount that the Secretary finds necessary "to
meet the mortgage market."[70] In administering this section, the Secretary
of Health, Education, and Welfare is given certain functions, powers,
and duties identical to those exercised by the Secretary of Housing and
Urban Development under Title II of the National Housing Act, and some
of the subsections of the National Housing Act are to be applied in carrying
out this mortgage insurance program for multipurpose senior centers.[71]
Incident to administration of the mortgage insurance provisions, a MULTI-
PURPOSE SENIOR CENTER INSURANCE FUND (a revolving fund) is to be brought
into existence.[72]

5.5 Authorization for Mortgage Insurance for Multipurpose Senior Centers
      To provide initial capital for the Multipurpose Senior Center Insur-
ance Funds, there are authorized to be appropriated such sums as may be
necessary.[73]

5.6 Annual Interest Grants
      The Secretary may make annual interest grants to reduce for the
borrower the expense of maintaining loans incurred in connection with
the acquisition, alteration, or renovation of senior centers.[74] The period
for which such grants shall be made shall not exceed 40 years.[75] The
interest grant cannot exceed the difference between the amount required
to service the loan and the amount that would be required if the loan
rate were 3%.[76] No State may receive more that 12½% of the funds appropriated.

5.7 Authorization for Annual Interest Grants
      Such sums as may be necessary are authorized to be appropriated for
annual interest grants.[77] Contracts for annual interest grants may not
exceed the amount authorized by the appropriation.[78]

5.8 Initial Staffing of Multipurpose Senior Centers (Sec. 511(b))
      To assist with the cost of initial staffing of "senior centers,"
the Commissioner is authorized to make grants. Grants may not be for a
longer period of time than 3 years. The amount of Federal assistance
for initial staffing is decreased with each year of operation, and is
limited to 75% for the first year, 66 and 2/3% for the second year, and
50% for the third year.

5.9 Authorization for Initial Staffing of Senior Centers
      Such sums as may be necessary are authorized to be appropriated for
"initial staffing of senior centers."

Title VI. Repealed (Formerly National Older Americans Volunteer Program)
     Title VI of the Older Americans Act, formerly "National Older Ameri-
cans Volunteer Program," was added to the Act by the 1969 Amendments
(Public Law 91-69, 9/17/69). Title VI was repealed by the "Domestic
Volunteer Service Act of 1973" (PL 93-113, Oct. 1, 1973). Title II of the
Domestic Volunteer Service Act of 1973 incorporated many of the features
of Title VI of the Older Americans Act. From the time Title VI was enacted in 1969 until July 1, 1971, the Retired Senior Volunteer Program
and Foster Grandparent Program was administered by the Administration on
Aging. On that date, Foster Grandparents and Senior Volunteer Programs
were transferred to the new ACTION agency in accordance with the President's reorganization Plan No. 1 of 1971. Treated as a part of related
legislation in the 1975 Amendments to the Older Americans Act, Title II
of the Domestic Volunteer Service Act of 1973 (Older Americans Volunteer
Program) was extended for 2 fiscal years.[80]

Title VII. Nutrition Program for the Elderly
     Title VII, the legislative vehicle for the nutrition program for
the elderly, was added by the 1972 Amendments.[81] Prior to the enactment
of Title VII, nutrition for the elderly received some limited attention
through research and development projects conducted under Title IV of the
Older Americans Act.

7.1 Administration
     Responsibility for seeing that the Nutrition Program is providing
the benefits Congress intended rests with the Administration on Aging.
In furthering the purposes of Title VII, the Commissioner, as the chief
administrative officer of the Administration on Aging, is directed to
consult with the Secretary of Agriculture, and to use the technical assistance that might be supplied by the Department of Labor, Office of Economic
Opportunity, the Department of Housing and Urban Development, the Department of Transportation, and other appropriate Federal Departments and
Agencies.[82]

7.2 Allotment of Funds
     From the sums appropriated, each State is allotted an amount that
bears the same ratio to the sums appropriated as the population 60 and
over of that State bears to the population 60 and over in all States,
subject to certain statutory guarantees that assure each State and Territory at least a minimum of the funds available for distribution.[83] The
Allotment of any State may be used to pay up to 90 percent of the cost
of projects in the State, and is made upon the condition that the State
will match the Federal grant with a 10 percent contribution.[84]

7.3 State Plans
     Federal assistance to State nutrition projects for the elderly will
be supplied only if the State submits to the Commissioner (of the Administration on Aging) a State plan for the projects. The plan must conform
to Title VII standards and criteria, and must be submitted in the form
of an amendment to the State's plan for Social Services as required by
Title III.[85] A single State agency must be designated as the only agency
to administer and supervise the State's nutrition plan, and the Agency
designated must be the same agency that is responsible for the State's
Title III plan unless the Governor, with the approval of the Commissioner
of the Administration on Aging, designates another agency.[86] The State

plan must, among other requirements, contain assurances that the Federal allotment to the State will be used to make grants for nutrition projects to public or private nonprofit institutions, organizations, or agencies to provide up to 90% of the costs of food and food service, and up to 90% of the cost of supportive social and transportation services.[87] Up to 1973 a State was allowed to use up to 10% of its nutrition plan allotment to pay administrative costs. The 1973 Amendments provided that funds allotted for State administrative costs under Title III may be used for administration of the State's nutrition plan,[88] with the limitation that if any organization other than the State Agency on Aging has been designated to administer the nutrition program, the Commissioner shall determine how much of the State's Title III funds can be used for administration of the State's nutrition program. Insight into the purpose of the Amendment can be obtained from the following Committee comment:

> "Third, wherever Title VII is a part of a Title III comprehensive system, funds for planning for Title VII may come from Title III appropriations. It is the Committee's intent that by having wherever possible only one planning authority for such funding, Title VII funds can be used for providing additional nutritional services. The Committee is disturbed by reports that several States have assigned administration of Title VII programs to agencies other than the state office of aging and suggests that the Commissioner has authority under section 705(a) of the Act to disapprove such practices."[89]

Subject to guidelines established by the Commissioner, recipients of grants of contracts to sponsor a nutrition project may require those elderly persons receiving a meal to contribute something toward defraying the cost of the meal.[90]

Another provision of the 1975 Amendments permitted nutrition projects to be made a part of the Title III social services system when mutually agreed upon by Area Agencies and those receiving nutrition grants.[91] In explaining the purpose of the Amendment, the following comment appears in the House Committee Report:

> "Second, provision is made for the integration of Title VII nutrition program into comprehensive and coordinated social service systems funded under Title III, but only, it should be emphasized, when such an arrangement is mutually agreed upon by both the Title III and the Title VII grantees. It is not the intention of the Committee to remove the special identity that the Title VII programs have already achieved, although we do encourage the integration of such projects with the comprehensive Title III programs."[92]

7.4 Nutrition and Other Program Requirements

Those receiving grants or contracts for nutrition projects must administer the projects in accordance with the statutory provisions and the Commissioner's regulations. Included in the law and regulations are requirements that nutrition project sponsors must agree to provide at least one hot meal a day for five or more days per week for individuals 60 and over, and their spouses; and to include, as a part of such project, recreational activities, informational, health, and welfare counseling, at least where such services are otherwise not available.[93]

7.5 Surplus Commodities

The Secretary of Agriculture must donate commodities to the Title VII nutrition projects, and must give special emphasis to furnishing high protein foods, meats, and meat alternates. When the program was established, authority was given to the Secretary of Agriculture to donate for the purposes of the Title VII projects commodities purchased by him under authority of Sec. 32 of the Act of Aug. 24, 1935.[94] In 1973, language was added to Title VII (Sec. 707(a) (2) and (3)) to make it clear that the Secretary of Agriculture had authority to make donations to the Title VII Nutrition Program under two other agricultural commodity purchase and disposal systems.[95] Again in 1974 the Older Americans Act was amended; this time to require the Secretary to maintain "an annually programmed level of assistance of not less than 10 cents per meal."[96] Another feature of the 1974 Amendments required the Secretary of Agriculture to issue regulations clarifying the use of food stamps under Title VII.

7.6 1975 Amendments to Nutrition Program for Elderly

In addition to making technical changes in Title VII, the 1975 Amendments added a subparagraph to Section 707 (surplus commodities) that directs the Secretary of Agriculture to purchase meat and high protein food for use in the Title VII projects.[97] Such sums as may be necessary are authorized to be appropriated for the new authority.[98] The 1975 Amendments to Title VII also expressly state that the Secretary's donations under the new authority (high protein foods) shall not be considered donated commodities for the purpose of meeting the requirement of maintaining through donation of commodities the statutory level of assistance required per meal (initially 10 cents per meal, but raised to 15 cents per meal for 1976, to be supplied by the Secretary of Agriculture through the donation of commodities)".[99] Also the 1975 Amendments raised the annually programmed level of assistance from "10 cents per meal" to "15 cents per meal" during fiscal year ending September 30, 1976, and 25 cents per meal during the fiscal year ending September 30, 1977.[100] Another modification made the donation of commodities by the Secretary of Agriculture mandatory rather than permissive. For States that had phased out their commodity distribution facilities before June 30, 1974, relief from the consequences of the phase-out is provided in the 1975 Amendments by a provision that allows the State to receive cash, in lieu of donated commodities, to further the purposes of the State's nutrition program.

7.7 Appropriations Authorized

Authority to appropriate funds to carry out the purposes of the nutrition program is contained in Section 708 of the Act, except for newly created authority for the donation of commodities by the Secretary of Agriculture which is contained in Sec. 707(c) of the Act, as amended. For Section 708, the 1974 Amendments authorized appropriations for fiscal years 1975, 1976, and 1977; and the 1975 Amendments authorized appropriations for the transitional quarter, July 1 to September 30, 1976, and Fiscal Year 1978.[101]

Title VIII. Repealed (Formerly the "General" Title)

From the inception of the Older Americans Act, the last Title of the Act was the "General" title. When the Older Americans Act was signed into law in 1965, the last Title, or "General" Title, was Title VI. In 1969 Title VI became the "National Older Americans Volunteer Program," and the "General" Title was moved to Title VIII. When the "Nutrition

Program for the Elderly" was added in 1972, the "General" Title was moved to Title VIII and the "Nutrition Program" was included under Title VII. When the 1973 Amendments were enacted, Title VIII was repealed, and new sections were added to Title II that covered the same subjects that were formerly covered in Title VIII.

Title IX. Older American Community Service Employment Act
9.1 Legislative Development of "Older Workers Program"
        When the Older Americans Act was amended in 1975, Title IX, the "older workers program," was added to the Act.[102] At the same time former authorization for an almost identical program contained in another legislative enactment was repealed.[103] Title IX is patterned on an employment and job training program popularly known as Operation Mainstream which was first authorized by the Economic Opportunity Act of 1964.[104] The program was subsequently continued as a part of the Comprehensive Employment and Training Act of 1973,[105] and supplemented by the Older American Community Service Employment and Training Act of 1973.[106] Some further insight into the historical development of the program can be obtained from this comment that appeared in U. S. Code Congressional and Administrative News at the time of the enactment of Title IX, Older American Comprehensive Service Amendments of 1973:

>"The program of Community Service Employment for older workers provided in this Title is modeled after the pilot program successfully conducted by the Department of Labor under operation mainstream. The operation mainstream program—which was delegated to the Department of Labor—as part of the reorganization of the office of Economic Opportunity—provides for contracts with private organizations to establish community service employment programs for workers 55 or older.... This Title is intended to provide the needed opportunities by establishing an identifiable program within the Department of Labor to continue and expand upon the pilot program conducted under "operation mainstream."[107]

9.2 Project Qualification, Matching Fund Requirement
        To promote part-time work opportunities for "unemployed low income persons who are fifty-five years or older and who have poor employment prospects," the Secretary of Labor is authorized to enter into agreements with public or private nonprofit agencies or organizations to pay (except in cases of emergency or disaster or in some economically depressed areas) not more than 90% of the cost of qualified projects.[108]

        One of the more important project qualifications requires that services of workers employed in the program be performed in connection with publicly owned and operated facilities and projects, or projects sponsored by organizations exempt from taxation under the Internal Revenue Code, however, in ay event services may not be performed in and around religious houses of worship.[109] Transportation cost of workers enrolled in the program are an allowable item.[110] Workers must be paid not less than the higher of the Federal minimum wage, State or local minimum wage, or the prevailing rates of pay for persons employed in similar public occupations by the same employer.[111] The Secretary of Labor is authorized to determine the amount of the Federal share, which may not exceed 90% of the project cost.[112] The non-Federal share may be in cash or in kind.

9.3 Administration of Older Workers Program

In awarding contracts the Secretary of Labor is authorized to consult with the State and Area Agencies on Aging, through the Commissioner on Aging, to help him assess where the need is greatest for community service projects.[113] And the Secretary is directed to require those receiving Federal assistance to coordinate Title IX projects and activities with other related manpower and unemployment programs if such coordination would increase job opportunities. Workmen's compensation insurance shall be provided for older workers participating in the Title IX program, and no contract may be entered into with anyone who does not provide workmen's compensation coverage equal to that required by law.[114]

9.4 Interagency Cooperation

In administering the older workers program, the Secretary of Labor is required to consult with and obtain the cooperation of other Federal agencies. The Secretary is also directed to enlist the assistance of other Federal Agencies and Departments in disseminating information about the older workers employment program. Among the agencies and departments specifically named are the Administration on Aging and the Department of Health, Education, and Welfare.

9.5 Apportionment of Federal Funds

When the older workers program, formerly authorized by the Older American Community Service Employment Act, was transferred to the Older Americans Act in 1975, changes were made in the apportionment formula. Prior to the 1975 Amendments, the law required that appropriations be divided among the States in the same proportion that the population 55 and over in a State bore to the population 55 years and over in all States with assurances that each State or protectorate would receive not less than a statutorily guaranteed amount. As amended in 1975, Title IX of the Older Americans Act requires the Secretary of Labor to initially reserve from the appropriation for the older workers program sufficient funds to maintain the 1975 level of activities conducted by national contractors under the Older Americans Community Service Employment program and related work programs.[115] In making awards to national contractors, preference is to be given to organizations of proven ability. After making reservations for national contracts, any remainder of appropriated funds is to be apportioned among the States on the basis of a formula which takes into account the number of persons 55 years or over in a State, and the per capita income of the State, as compared with the number of persons 55 years and over in all States and the National per capita income with further provision that all States and protectorates will be guaranteed certain minimum amounts.[116] More specifically the remainder of appropriated funds will be distributed by giving each State an amount which bears the same ratio to the remaining funds as the product of persons aged 55 or over in the State times the "allotment percentage" of that State bears to the sum of corresponding products for all States.[117] However, no state shall be allotted less than one-half of one percent of the funds remaining or $100,000, and the allotment percentage shall in no case be more than 75% or less than 33-1/3%. There is a requirement that projects carried on by national contractors be distributed among areas within each State in an equitable manner, taking into consideration the proportion of eligible persons in a given area as compared with the total number of such eligible persons in the State, and the relative distribution of rural and urban elderly within the State.[118] And the same requirements apply to any sums remaining, after reservation of funds for national contracts, which the Secretary of Labor might allow for projects within each State.

9.6 Authorization to Appropriate

Authorization is extended to appropriate funds for the older workers program for fiscal year 1976, the transitional quarter, 1977, and 1978. There is a further proviso that money appropriated for the Title IX program, included in the Older American Comprehensive Service Amendments of 1973, may be used for "operation mainstream" projects carried on under Title III of the Comprehensive Employment Training Act.[119]

9.7   1975 Amendments

In the 1975 Amendments, there is some amplification of the Act's language requiring older worker projects to produce an increase in employment. What was implied in the old law is spelled out in the new provisions. In this connection there are prohibitions against substituting Federal funds for local funds that would otherwise have been used in the performance of a project, employing an eligible individual to do substantially the same work as a person who is on layoff, and using an eligible individual to decrease overtime work of other employees.[120]

Formerly there was a requirement that in carrying out the purposes of Title IX, and particularly in locating suitable localities for employment projects, the Secretary of Labor should consult with representatives of States and their political subdivisions. The 1975 Amendments require that such consultation be with State Agencies on Aging, and appropriate Area Agencies on Aging, with the consultations to be carried on through the Commissioner of the Administration on Aging.[121]

At the time of the 1975 Amendments, the Act required the Secretary of Labor to consult and cooperate with certain Federal agency officials, including representatives of the Administration on Aging, in promoting and furthering the older workers program. The 1975 Amendments added some new language that requires the Secretary of Labor to "obtain the written views of, the Commissioner of the Administration on Aging prior to the establishment of rules or the establishment of general policy in the administration of this title."[122]

The 1975 Amendments require a reservation of appropriated funds for National contracts sufficient to maintain the 1975 level of activities carried on under National contracts before any formula allocation of appropriated funds is made among the States.[123] A new factor was introduced into the formula for allocating funds to the States, the "allotment percentage," which provides that the per capita income of the State as compared with National per capita income, shall be given weight in the allocation formula.[124]

At the time of the 1975 Amendments, there was, and still is, a requirement that funds for employment projects be apportioned among areas within the State in an equitable manner, considering the ratio of eligible persons in the area to eligible persons in the State.[125] The 1975 Amendments engrafted upon this provision the additional requirement that the relative "distribution of such individuals in rural and urban areas" should be considered in allocating funds within the State.[126]

And since the 1975 Amendments transferred the "older workers program" to Title IX of the Older Americans Act, the enabling legislation of the predecessor program, Title IX of the Older American Comprehensive Service Amendments of 1973 (42 USC 3061 et seq.) was repealed.[127]

Added by the 1975 Amendments was a provision that sums appropriated for Title IX of the Older American Comprehensive Services Amendments of 1973 may be used for Older American employment projects conducted as a part of Operation Mainstream under Title III of the Comprehensive Employment and Training Act of 1973.[128]

The 1975 Amendments expanded the then existing definition of "community service" to make "legal and other counseling services and assistance, including tax counseling and assistance and financial counseling, eligible areas for Federally assisted older worker projects.[129]

Conclusion

As envisioned by the framers of the legislation, the Older Americans Act was intended to be the tool that would provide assistance, direction, guidance, and even advocacy, for older Americans. The purposes of the Act are broadly stated, and so encompassing that if the objectives were fully realized, the lives of nearly all older Americans would be touched upon and enriched. Yet as a National program the funding and organizational machinery have never assumed any massive proportions. Modest funding, and the minimal array of organizational machinery, do not accurately reflect the effectiveness of the program. And this is true because the program's delivery system is designed to magnify the effects of dollars spent. Instead of providing services and assistance directly, the State and Area Agencies on Aging in a catalytic way draw upon and coalesce the benefits of other programs and the resources of local public and non-profit private organizations. Multiplication of benefits through cooperation and coordination is the key concept in the older Americans program. While Congress has in the past, and will in the future examine, and re-examine, the older American program for conceptual and mechanical weaknesses, for the moment the basic idea, structure, and delivery system appear sound.

Footnotes

1. Public Law 89-73 (July 14, 1965) (42 USC 3001 et seq.), as amended by:
    Public Law 90-42 (July 1, 1967)
    Public Law 91-69 (Sept. 17, 1969)
    Public Law 92-258 (March 22, 1972)
    Public Law 93-29 (May 3, 1973)
    Public Law 93-351 (July 12, 1974)
    Public Law 94-135 (Nov. 28, 1975)
2. Federal Council on the Aging, "Report on Study of State Formulae for Funding Programs Under the Older Americans Act, p. 2 (Dec. 30, 1974)
2a. Public Law 89-73, July 14, 1965
3. U. S. Senate, "Developments in Aging 1965: A Report of the Special Committee on Aging," p. 39 (March 15, 1966). The House passed the measure (HR 3708, as amended) on March 31, 1965, and the bill was passed in the Senate with amendments on May 27, 1965. The House agreed unanimously to the Senate amendments on July 6, 1965.
4. U. S. Senate, Special Committee on Aging, "Developments in Aging 1966," Appendix E, "The Administration on Aging 1966" by Wm. D. Bechill
5. Public Law 90-42 (July 1, 1967)
    Public Law 91-69 (September 17, 1969)
    Public Law 92-258 (March 22, 1972)
    Public Law 93-29 (May 3, 1973)
    Public Law 93-351 (July 12, 1974)
    Public Law 94-135 (Nov. 28, 1975)

6.   Sec. 101 of the Act
7.   U. S. House of Representatives, Committee on Education and Labor, Report No. 93-43, p. 8 (March 2, 1973)
8.   Sec. 201(a) of the Act
9.   Sec. 202(a) of the Act
10.   Sec. 204 of the Act
11.   Sec. 204(c) of the Act. For authorization and appropriation levels see Appendix I
12.   Sec. 205 of the Act
13.   Public Law 93-29, May 3, 1973
14.   U. S. House of Representatives, Report No. 93-43, March 2, 1973, p. 12
15.   U. S. Senate Report, Feb 14, 1973, Report No. 93-19, p. 3
16.   Sec. 305 of the Act
17.   Sec. 304(a) (1) of the Act. Note, however, that the language of this provision is affected by application of the "Intergovernmental Cooperation Act of 1968" (PL 90-577) which states: Notwithstanding any other Federal law which provides that a single State agency or multimember board or commission multimember board or commission must be established or designated to administer or supervise the administration of any grant-in-aid program, the head of any Federal department or agency administering such program may, upon request of the Governor or other appropriate executive or legislative authority of the State responsible for determining or revising the organizational structure of State government, waive the single State agency or multimember board or commission provision upon adequate showing that such provision prevents the establishment of the most effective and efficient organizational arrangements within the State government and approve other State administrative structure or arrangements: Provided, That the head of the Federal department or agency determines that the objectives of the Federal statute authorizing the grant-in-aid program will not be endangered by the use of such other State structure or arrangements.
18.   Sec. 304 of the Act
19.   Sec. 304 of the Act
20.   Sec. 303(e) of the Act
21.   Sec. 303(c) of the Act
22.   United States Senate, Report No. 93-19, p.9 (Feb. 14, 1973)
23.   Sec. 304(d)(1) of the Act; PL 94-135, Sec. 105
24.   Sec. 305(a)(10) and (b); 42 USC 3025(a) and (b); PL 94-135, Sec. 106
25.   U. S. House of Representatives, Report No. 94-670, p. 28 (November 17, 1975)
26.   U. S. House of Representatives, Report No. 94-670, p. 28 (November 17, 1975)
27.   Sec. 304(c)(4)(C) of the Act
28.   P.L. 94-135, Sec. 105 (November 28, 1975)
29.   Sec. 306(b)(1) of the Act which provides in part: "From the sums appropriated for any fiscal year under Section 303 for carrying out the purposes of this section, each State shall be allotted an amount which bears the same ratio to such sum as the population aged sixty or over in such State bears to the population aged sixty or over in all States...."
30.   Sec. 306(b)(1) of the Act
31.   Public Law 94-135, Sec. 107

32. Public Law 94-135, Sec. 107(b)(2); House of Representatives of the United States, Conference Report No. 94-670, p. 42, (Nov. 17, 1975)-- The conferees note that this provision is based on a substitute for a Senate amendment, saying: "The remainder of the Senate amendment is omitted by the conference substitute, and in lieu thereof the conference substitute authorizes States to apply to the Commissioner for authority to use funds allotted to the State under Sec. 303 for State administrative purposes."

33. Sec. 306(a)(1) of the Act; PL 91-69, Sec. 4(b), Sept. 17, 1969; the 1965 Act limited the Federal contribution for State plan administration to 50 percent (PL 89-73, Sec. 304)

34. Sec. 308(a) of the Act

35. Sec. 308(a) of the Act

36. PL 94-135, Sec. 108; 42 USC 1396

37. Sec. 306(b)(1) of the Act provides for an allocation of funds for State administration in accordance with a formula that allows each State to receive the same proportionate part of such funds as the ratio of the population aged 60 and over in a given State bears to the population aged 60 and over in all States with the qualification that no State shall receive less than $200,000 or other eligible governmental entities less than $62,500.

38. Sec. 306(a)(1) of the Act. The 1965 Act (Sec. 304) limited the Federal matching percentage for the State plan administration to 50 percent. The 1969 amendments (Sec. 4b; PL 91-69) raised the limit to 75 percent.

39. Sec. 306(a)(2) of the Act

40. Sec. 306(c) of the Act

41. Sec. 303(b)(2) of the Act. The allotment formula provides for a distribution principally based upon the ratio a State's population 60 and over bears to the population 60 and over in all States with floors, however, to assure that each State and Territory will receive a minimum allotment.

42. Sec. 303(e) of the Act. Not more than 15% of the State's allotment can be used for the cost of administration of area plans, and not more than 20% can be used for social services not provided as a part of a system for which there is an area plan approved by the State agency. The remainder of the allotment may be used for social services provided as a part of a system for which there is an area plan approved by the State agency.

43. Sec 303(e) of the Act. Federal funds may be used to pay 75% of the cost of administration of area plans, 75% of the cost of social services not provided as a part of a system included in an area plan, 90% of the cost of social services provided as a part of a system included under an area plan.

44. Sec. 303(a) of the Act. See Appendix I for Title III authorization and appropriation levels.

45. Sec. 309 of the Act (Public Law 93-351; July 12, 1974)

46. Sec. 309(a) of the Act. See Appendix I for authorizations and appropriations for Sec. 309.

47. U. S. House of Representatives, Report No. 93-43, p. 20 (March 2, 1973)

48. Public Law 93-29, May 3, 1973 (Sec. 421 of the Act, as amended)

49. Sec. 401 of the Act

50. Sec. 402 of the Act. Customarily the Commissioner holds hearings to provide factual data for the preparation of his report on manpower

needs. Notice of the hearings are published in the Federal Register.
(Fed. Register, 3/30/76, p. 13388)

51. Sec. 403 of the Act

52. Sec. 404 of the Act, as amended

53. Sec. 109, P.L. 94-135; amended Sec. 403 of the Act by expanding
the language referring to the "institutions of higher education"
by adding "as defined in section 1201(a) of the Higher Education
Act of 1965."

53a. Sec. 110(b), P.L. 94-135; U. S. Senate Report 94-255 (June 25. 1975)
p. 26

53b. Sec. 110(c) of P.L. 94-135; Sec. 404(c) of the Act, as amended

54. Sec. 411 of the Act; this section is essentially the same as Sec. 401
of the Act as it read from 1965 until the 1973 amendments

55. Sec. 412(a) of the Act; Public Law 93-29, Section 401, May 3, 1973

56. Sec. 412(c) of the Act, as amended

57. Sec. 412(d) of the Act, as amended. In compliance with the Con-
gressional directive, the Commissioner submitted in January of 1975
the requested transportation study. The study is identified as
DHEW Publication No. (OHD) 75-20081, "Transportation for the Elderly--
The State of the Art." See also transportation report prepared by
Subcommittee on Federal, State and Community Services of the Select
Committee on Aging and approved for publication by full Committee
June, 1976

58. Sec. 421 of the Act, as amended; Public Law 93-29, May 3, 1973

58a. House Report 93-43, p. 20, March 2, 1973

59. Sec. 431 of the Act. See Appendix I for authorizations and appropriations for Title IV.

60. Sec. 501(a) of the Act

61. Sec. 501(c) of the Act

62. Sec. 501(a) of the Act. Title V was added to the Act by the 1973
Amendments (PL 93-29). Prior to the 1973 Amendments, Sec. 301 of
the Act prohibited the use of Title III funds for costs of construction other than minor alterations and repairs.

63. Sec. 502(a)(4) of the Act

64. Sec. 502(b)(1) of the Act

65. Sec. 504 of the Act

66. Sec. 505(a) of the Act. See Appendix I for authorizations and
appropriations for the Acquisition, Alteration, and Renovation of
Multipurpose Senior Centers

67. Sec. 506(d) of the Act

68. Sec. 506(d) of the Act

69. Sec. 506(e) of the Act

70. Sec. 506(d)(3)(B) of the Act

71. Sec. 506(g) and (h) of the Act; Subsections (e), (g), (h), (i),
(j), (k), (1) and (n) of Sec. 207 of the National Housing Act

72. Sec. 506(h) of the Act

73. Sec. 506(h)(5) of the Act

74. Sec. 507(a) of the Act

75. Sec. 507(b) of the Act

76. Sec. 507(b) of the Act

77. Sec. 507(c)(1)

78. Sec. 507(c)(2)

79. Sec. 511(d) of the Act

80. PL 94-135, Nov. 28, 1975. Title II of the Domestic Volunteer Ser-

vice Act of 1973 was extended for 2 years, or through fiscal year 1978, with authorizations as follows: R.S.V.P.--$22 million for fiscal years 1977 and 1978; Foster Grandparents--$35 million for fiscal years 1977 and 1978; and Senior Companions--$8 million for fiscal years 1977 and 1978

81. Public Law 92-258
82. Section 702 of the Act
83. Section 703(a)(1) of the Act
84. Sec. 703(c) of the Act
85. Sec. 705(a) of the Act
86. Sec. 705(a)(1) of the Act
87. Sec. 705(a)(2)
88. Sec. 705(a)(2)(B)
89. House of Representatives, Committee on Education and Labor, House report No. 93-43, March 2, 1973, p. 24
90. Sec. 705(a)(2)(A)(ii)
91. Sec. 705(a)(5) of the Act
92. U. S. House of Representatives, Committee on Education and Labor, House Report No. 93-43, March 2, 1973, p. 24
93. Section 706 of the Act
94. 7 USC 612c
95. Commodity Credit Corporation, Sec. 416 of the Agricultural Act of 1949, 7 USC 1431; Dairy Products, Sec. 709 of the Food and Agricultural Act of 1965, 7 USC 1446 a-1
96. Public Law 93-351, July 12, 1975; Sec. 707(a)(4) of the Act as amended
97. Sec. 111(a) of PL 94-135; Sec. 707(c)(1) of the Act
98. Sec. 111(a) of PL 94-135; Sec. 707(c)(2) of the Act
99. PL 94-135, Sec. 111(a); Sec. 707(c)(2) of the Act, as amended
100. Pl 94-135, Sec. 111(b); Sec. 707(a)(4) of the Act
101. See Appendix I for Nutrition Program authorizations and appropriations. Authorization to appropriate for the donation of commodities of the Secretary of Agriculture is contained in Sec. 111(a) of PL 94-135; Sec. 707(c)(3) of the Act.
102. Public Law 94-135, Sec. 113, Nov. 28, 1975 (42 USC 3056)
103. Public Law 93-29, May 3, 1973; Title IX of Older American Comprehensive Service Amendments; 42 USC 3061 et seq.
104. Public Law 88-452, Aug. 20, 1964
105. Public Law 93-203, Dec. 28, 1973, (29 USC 801 et seq.)
106. Public Law 93-29, May 3, 1973 (42 USC 3061 et seq.), Title IX
107. U. S. Code Congr. and Admin. News (1973), p. 1352
108. Sec. 902 of the Act; all of the program funds are currently being administered under five major contracts with the following organizations: Greenthumb, National Council on Aging, National Council of Senior Citizens, National Retired Teacher Association, Forest Service of U.S.D.A.
109. Sec. 902(b)(1)(C) of the Act
110. Sec. 902(b)(1)(L) of the Act
111. Sec. 902(b)(1)(J) of the Act; average benefit of participating workers is $2,407 (Catalog of Federal Domestic Assistance, O.M.B., p. 514 (1975); possible work activity includes management, development, and conservation of parks, highways, and recreational areas of Federal, State and Local governments; the improvement and rehabilitation of community facilities; supplying social, health, and educational services to the poor.

112.   Sec. 902(c)(1) of the Act
113.   Sec. 903(a) of the Act
114.   Sec. 904(b) of the Act
115.   Sec. 906(a)(1) of the Act; Public Law 94-135, Sec. 113, Nov. 28, 1975
116.   Sec. 906(a)(2) of the Act; Public Law 94-135, Sec. 113
117.   Sec. 906(a)(3) of the Act; Public Law 94-135, Sec. 113
118.   Sec. 906(c) of the Act; Public Law 94-135; November 28, 1975
119.   Sec. 908 of the Act; Public Law 94-135, Sec. 113, Nov. 28, 1975. For appropriation and authorization levels, see APPENDIX I.
120.   Sec. 902(b)(F) and (G) of the Act, as amended
121.   Sec. 903(a) of the Act, as amended
122.   Sec. 905(a) of the Act, as amended
123.   Sec. 906(a) of the Act, as amended. This provision provides in part that the remainder is to be allotted among the States "so that each State will receive an amount which bears the same ratio to the remainder as the product of the number of persons aged 55 or over in the State and the allotment percentage of such State bears to the corresponding product for all States...."
124.   Section 906(a)(3) of the Act, as amended: "...the allotment percentage of each State shall be 100 per centum less that percentage which bears the same ratio to 50% as the per capita income of such State beats to the per capita income of the United States, except that (i) the allotment percentage shall in no case be more than 75 per centum or less than 33-1/3 per centum...."
125.   Sec. 906(c)(1) of the Act, as amended
126.   Sec. 906(c)(2) of the Act, as amended
127.   Sec. 908(b) of the Act, as amended
128.   Sec. 908(c) of the Act, as amended
129.   Sec. 907(3) of the Act, as amended

Appendix I

| | | Authorization to Appropriate (in millions) | | | | |
	***Section	1975	1976	TQ	1977	1978
Title II						
Ntl. Information & Resource Clrng. House	204c	*	*	*	*	*
Administration on Aging	206c	*	*	*	*	*
Title III						
State & Community Programs on Aging	303a	$130	$180	$57.75	$231	$287.20
Model Projects	308b	*	*	*	*	*
Transportation Projects	309a	$35				
Title IV						
Training & Research	431	*	*	*	*	*

***Section	1975	1976	TQ	1977	1978

Title V
Multipurpose Senior
Centers:

A--Acquisition, alter- ation, renovation	505a	*	*	*	*	*
B--Mortgage Insurance,	506h5	*	*	*	*	*
Interest Grants	507c1	*	*	*	*	*
C--Initial Staffing	511d	*				

Title VI (Repealed)

Title VII
Nutrition Program:

Meals & Services	708	$150	$200	$62.5	$200	$275
Commodities(protein)	707c3	*	*	*		
Meals Assistance(707c3)	707a4	**	**	**	**	

Title VIII (Repealed)

Title IX

Community Service Employment	908	$100	$100	$37.5	$150	$200

---

  * "such sums as may be necessary"
 ** Mandated level of assistance to be furnished by the Secretary of
    Agriculture is 10 cents per meal for 1975; 15 cents per meal for
    Fiscal Year ending Sept. 30, 1976, and 25 cents per meal for fiscal
    year ending September 30, 1977.
*** Sec. 112 of Public Law 94-135, November 28, 1975, extended authorizations
    to appropriate for Fiscal Years 1976 through 1978, and the transitional
    quarter (July 1, 1976 through September 30, 1976); and Section 113 of
    Public Law 94-135 extended authorizations to appropriate for Fiscal
    Years 1976 through 1978, and the transitional quarter.

Appendix I (Continued)

	Author- izing Section	Appropriations (in millions)					
		1975	1976[1]	1976[2]	T.Q.[2]	1977	1978
Title II							
Ntl. Information & Resource Clearing House	204c						
Administration on Aging	206c	$4.9	$4.9				
Federal Council . .		.5	.575	.575	.150		

	Section	1975	1976[1]	1976[2]	T.Q.[2]	1977	1978
Title III							
State & Community Programs on Aging:	303a						
State Administration		$15	$15	17.035	4.25		
Area Planning & Social Services		$82	$76	93.0	31.25		
Model Projects	308b	$ 8	$ 5	13.8	2.5		
		105	96	123.835	38.0		
Title IV							
Training & Research:	431						
A. Training		$ 8	$ 8	10.0	4.0		
B. Research		$ 7	$ 7	8.0	2.0		
C. Multi-Disciplinary Centers of Gerontology				1.0	1.0		
		15	15	19.0	7.0		
Title V							
Multipurpose Sr. Centers							
A. Acquisition, alteration, renovation	505a				5.0		
B. Mtg. Ins., Interest Grants	506h5 507c1						
C. Initial Staffing	511d						
Title VII							
Meals & Supportive Services	708	$125	$125[3]		31.25[3]		
Commodities[5]	707						
Title IX							
Older Americans Community Service Employment	908	$12	$30			$55.9[4]	

---

1. Public Law 94-41 (HJ Res 499) Permitted continued operation of program pending specific appropriations at lower of Admin. budget request or operating level of 1975, except for Title IVA and IX which had specific levels to be maintained, and Title VII which had an authorization for FY '76.
2. Second Supplemental Appropriation, H.R. 13172, P.L. 94-303(June 1, 1976).
3. Public Law 94-206; Jan. 28, 1976 (HR 8069)(Labor-HEW Appropriation)
4. Public Law 94-266 (H.J. Res. 890) Amendment to Swine Flu Immunization Bill; to remain available until June 30, 1977(12 month period)
5. Funds made available annually to the Dept. of Agriculture from duties collected under the customs laws, as authorized by the Agricultural Adjustment Act of 1935, Ch. 641, Sec. 32(7 USC 612c) have been sufficient, without the necessity for any additional appropriations, to support a number of special nutrition projects promoting domestic consumption of agricultural products, including donation of commodities to the Title VII program.

Amendments to the Older Americans Act of 1965 (P.L.95-478)

Oct. 18, 1978
[H.R. 12255]

Comprehensive
Older Americans
Act Amendments
of 1978.
42 U.S.C. 3001
note.

42 USC 3001
note.

To amend the Older Americans Act of 1965 to provide for improved programs for older persons, and for other purposes.

Be it enacted by the Senate and House of Representatives of the United States of America in Congress assembled, That (a) this Act may be cited as the "Comprehensive Older Americans Act Amendments of 1978".

(b) Except as otherwise specifically provided, whenever in this Act an amendment or repeal is expressed in terms of an amendment to, or repeal of, a section or other provision, the reference shall be considered to be made to a section or other provision of the Older Americans Act of 1965.

TITLE I—AMENDMENTS TO THE OLDER AMERICANS ACT OF 1965

OBJECTIVES

42 USC 3001.

SEC. 101. Section 101(8) is amended by inserting after "provide" the following: "a choice in supported living arrangements and".

ADMINISTRATION

42 USC 3012.

SEC. 102. (a)(1) Section 202(a) is amended by redesignating clauses (1), (2), (3), (4), (5), (6), (7), (8), (9), (10), (11), (12), (13), (14), (15), and (16) as clauses (2), (3), (4), (5), (6), (7), (8), (9), (10), (11), (12), (13), (14), (15), (16), and (17), respectively, and by inserting after the dash the following new clause:

"(1) serve as the effective and visible advocate for the elderly within the Department of Health, Education, and Welfare and with other departments, agencies, and instrumentalities of the Federal Government by maintaining active review and commenting responsibilities over all Federal policies affecting the elderly;".

42 USC 3012.

(2) Section 202 is amended by redesignating subsection (b), and all references thereto, as subsection (c), and by inserting after subsection (a) the following new subsection:

"(b) In order to strengthen the involvement of the Administration in the development of policy alternatives in long-term care and to insure that the development of community alternatives is given priority attention, the Commissioner shall—

"(1) develop planning linkages with health systems agencies designated under section 1515 of the Public Health Service Act (42 U.S.C. 300l–4);

"(2) participate in all departmental and interdepartmental activities which concern issues of institutional and noninstitutional long-term health care services development; and

"(3) review and comment on all departmental regulations and policies regarding community health and social service development for the elderly.".

42 USC 3013.

(b) Section 203 is amended to read as follows:

"FEDERAL AGENCY CONSULTATION

"SEC. 203. (a) The Commissioner, in carrying out the purposes and provisions of this Act, shall advise, consult, and cooperate with the head of each Federal agency or department proposing or administering programs or services substantially related to the purposes of this Act, with respect to such programs or services. The head of each Federal agency or department proposing to establish programs and services substantially related to the purposes of this Act shall consult with the Commissioner prior to the establishment of such programs and services. The head of each Federal agency administering any program substantially related to the purpose of this Act, particularly administering any program set forth in subsection (b), shall, to achieve appropriate coordination, consult and cooperate with the Commissioner in carrying out such program.

"(b) For the purposes of subsection (a), programs related to the purpose of this Act shall include—

29 USC 801 note.
42 USC 5001.
42 USC 1395, 1396, 1397.
12 USC 1715v, 1715w.
42 USC 1437 note.
12 USC 1701q.
42 USC 5301.
42 USC 2809.

20 USC 821 note.

49 USC 1602, 1604, 1607a, 1612.
42 USC 3014.

"(1) the Comprehensive Employment and Training Act of 1973,
"(2) title II of the Domestic Volunteer Service Act of 1973,
"(3) titles XVIII, XIX, and XX of the Social Security Act,
"(4) sections 231 and 232 of the National Housing Act,
"(5) the United States Housing Act of 1937,
"(6) section 202 of the Housing Act of 1959,
"(7) title I of the Housing and Community Development Act of 1974,
"(8) section 222(a)(8) of the Economic Opportunity Act of 1964,
"(9) the community schools program under the Elementary and Secondary Education Act of 1965, and
"(10) sections 3, 5, 9, and 16 of the Urban Mass Transportation Act of 1964.".

(c) Section 204(a)(1) is amended by inserting before the semicolon a comma and the following: "including information related to transportation services for older individuals offered by Federal, State, and local public agencies".

(d) Section 204(c) is amended to read as follows:

"(c) There are authorized to be appropriated to carry out the provisions of this section, for fiscal years 1979, 1980, and 1981, such sums as may be necessary.".

42 USC 3015.

(e)(1) Section 205(a) is amended by inserting "rural and urban" after "of" in the second sentence, and by adding at the end thereof the following new sentence: "No full-time officer or employee of the Federal Government may be appointed as a member of the Council.".

(2) Section 205(c) is amended by striking out the last sentence thereof.

(3) Section 205(e) is amended to read as follows:

"(e) The Council shall have staff personnel, appointed by the Chairman, to assist it in carrying out its activities. The head of each Federal department and agency shall make available to the Council such information and other assistance as it may require to carry out its activities.".

(4)(A) Section 205(g) is amended to read as follows:

"(g)(1) The Council shall undertake a thorough evaluation and study of programs conducted under this Act.

"(2) The study required in this subsection shall include—

"(A) an examination of the fundamental purposes of such programs, and the effectiveness of such programs in attaining such purposes;

"(B) an analysis of the means to identify accurately the elderly population in greatest need of such programs; and

"(C) an analysis of numbers and incidence of low-income and minority participants in such programs.

"(3) The study required under this subsection may include—

"(A) an exploration of alternative methods for allocating funds under such programs to States, State agencies on aging, and area agencies on aging in an equitable and efficient manner, which will accurately reflect current conditions and insure that such funds reach the areas of greatest current need and are effectively used for such areas;

"(B) an analysis of the need for area agencies on aging to provide direct services within the planning and service area; and

"(C) an analysis of the number of nonelderly handicapped in need of home delivered meal services.".

42 USC 3015. (B) Section 205 is amended by striking out subsections (h) and (i) and inserting in lieu thereof the following new subsection:

"(h) There are authorized to be appropriated to carry out the provisions of this section, for fiscal years 1979, 1980, and 1981, such sums as may be necessary.".

42 USC 3016. (f) Section 206 is amended by redesignating subsection (b) and subsection (c), and all references thereto, as subsection (c) and subsection (d), respectively, and by inserting after subsection (a) the following new subsection:

Post, p. 1535. "(b) The Commissioner shall prepare and submit to the Congress not later than September 30, 1980 a report on the effectiveness of programs conducted under part B of title III relating to legal services and an analysis of the need for a separate program of legal services under this Act and of factors which may prohibit the funding of legal services under this Act without such a separate program, together with such recommendations, including recommendations for additional legislation, as the Commissioner deems appropriate.".

42 USC 3017. (g)(1) Section 207(c) is amended by inserting before the period a comma and the following: "and conduct, where appropriate, evaluations which compare the effectiveness of related programs in achieving common objectives".

(2) Section 207(d) is amended—

(A) by inserting after "summaries" the following: "and analyses";

(B) by striking out "be available" and inserting in lieu thereof "be transmitted"; and

(C) by inserting before "the public" the following: "be accessible to".

42 USC 3020a. (h)(1) Section 211 is amended by inserting "(a)" after the section designation and by adding at the end thereof the following new subsection:

"(b) No part of the costs of any project under any title of this Act may be treated as income or benefits to any eligible individual (other than any wage or salary to such individual) for the purpose of any other program or provision of Federal or State law.".

(2) Section 211(a), as so redesignated in paragraph (1), is amended by inserting after "88 Stat. 1604)" the following: ", and of title V **48 USC 1469a.** of the Act of October 15, 1977 (Public Law 95–134; 91 Stat. 1164),".

(i) Title II is amended by adding at the end thereof the following new sections:

"REDUCTION OF PAPERWORK

42 USC 3020b. "SEC. 212. In order to reduce unnecessary, duplicative, or disruptive demands for information, the Commissioner, in consultation with State agencies designated under section 305(a)(1), and other appropriate agencies and organizations, shall continually review and evaluate all requests by the Administration on Aging for information under this Act and take such action as may be necessary to reduce the paperwork required under this Act. The Commissioner shall request only such information as the Commissioner deems essential to carry out the purposes and provisions of this Act.

"CONTRACTING AND GRANT AUTHORITY

42 USC 3020c. "SEC. 213. None of the provisions of this Act shall be construed to prevent a recipient of a grant or a contract from entering into an agreement, subject to the approval of the State agency, with a profitmaking organization, where such organization demonstrates clear superiority with respect to the quality of services covered by such contract to carry out the provisions of this Act and of the appropriate State plan.

42 USC 3020d.

42 USC 601, 1397.
42 USC 2701 note.

"SURPLUS PROPERTY ELIGIBILITY

"SEC. 214. Any State or local government agency, and any nonprofit organization or institution, which receives funds appropriated for programs for older individuals under this Act, under title IV or title XX of the Social Security Act, or under the Economic Opportunity Act of 1964, shall be deemed eligible to receive for such programs, property which is declared surplus to the needs of the Federal Government in accordance with laws applicable to surplus property.".

GRANTS FOR STATE AND COMMUNITY PROGRAMS ON AGING

42 USC 3021 note.

42 USC 3001 note.

SEC. 103. (a) (1) The Congress finds that—
(A) approximately 3 percent of the eligible population is presently served under community services programs authorized under the Older Americans Act of 1965, 17 percent of whom are minority group members;
(B) approximately 1 percent of the eligible population is presently served by the nutrition program authorized under the Older Americans Act of 1965, 21 percent of whom are minority group members;
(C) there is program fragmentation at the national, State, and local levels which inhibits effective use of existing resources; and
(D) coordination and consolidation of services provided under the Older Americans Act of 1965 allowing greater local determination to assess the need for services will facilitate achieving the goals of the Older Americans Act of 1965.

Post, p. 1517.
42 USC 3041, 3045.

Infra.

(2) It is the purpose of the amendments made by subsection (b) to combine within a consolidated title, subject to the modifications imposed by the provisions and requirements of the amendments made by subsection (b), the programs authorized by title III, title V, and title VII of the Older Americans Act of 1965 in the fiscal year 1978, and funds appropriated to carry out such consolidated title shall be used solely for the purposes and for the assistance of the same types of programs authorized under the provisions of such titles.
(b) Title III is amended to read as follows:

"TITLE III—GRANTS FOR STATE AND COMMUNITY PROGRAMS ON AGING

"PART A—GENERAL PROVISIONS

"PURPOSE; ADMINISTRATION

42 USC 3021.

"SEC. 301. (a) It is the purpose of this title to encourage and assist State and local agencies to concentrate resources in order to develop greater capacity and foster the development of comprehensive and coordinated service systems to serve older individuals by entering into new cooperative arrangements in each State with State and local agencies, and with the providers of social services, including nutrition services and multipurpose senior centers, for the planning for the provision of, and for the provision of, social services, nutrition services, and multipurpose senior centers, in order to—
"(1) secure and maintain maximum independence and dignity in a home environment for older individuals capable of self care with appropriate supportive services;
"(2) remove individual and social barriers to economic and personal independence for older individuals; and
"(3) provide a continuum of care for the vulnerable elderly.
"(b) (1) In order to effectively carry out the purpose of this title, the Commissioner shall administer programs under this title through the Administration on Aging.

"(2) In carrying out the provisions of this title, the Commissioner may request the technical assistance and cooperation of the Department of Labor, the Community Services Administration, the Department of Housing and Urban Development, the Department of Transportation, and such other agencies and departments of the Federal Government as may be appropriate.

"DEFINITIONS

42 USC 3022.

"SEC. 302. For the purpose of this title—
"(1) The term 'comprehensive and coordinated system' means a system for providing all necessary social services, including nutrition services, in a manner designed to—
"(A) facilitate accessibility to, and utilization of, all social services and nutrition services provided within the geographic area served by such system by any public or private agency or organization;
"(B) develop and make the most efficient use of social services and nutrition services in meeting the needs of older individuals; and
"(C) use available resources efficiently and with a minimum of duplication.
"(2) The term 'information and referral source' means a location where the State or any public or private agency or organization—
"(A) maintains current information with respect to the opportunities and services available to older individuals, and develops current lists of older individuals in need of services and opportunities; and
"(B) employs a specially trained staff to inform older individuals of the opportunities and services which are available, and to assist such individuals to take advantage of such opportunities and services.
"(3) The term 'long-term care facility' means any skilled nursing facility, as defined in section 1861(j) of the Social Security

42 USC 1395x.
42 USC 1396d.
42 USC 1396g.

Act, any intermediate care facility, as defined in section 1905(c) of the Social Security Act, any nursing home, as defined in section 1908(e) of the Social Security Act, and any other similar adult care home.
"(4) The term 'legal services' means legal advice and representation by an attorney (including, to the extent feasible, counseling or other appropriate assistance by a paralegal or law student under the supervision of an attorney), and includes counseling or representation by a nonlawyer where permitted by law, to older individuals with economic or social needs.
"(5) The term 'planning and service area' means an area specified by a State agency under section 305(a)(1)(E).
"(6) The term 'State' means each of the several States, the District of Columbia, the Commonwealth of Puerto Rico, Guam, American Samoa, the Virgin Islands, the Trust Territory of the Pacific Islands and the Northern Mariana Islands.
"(7) The term 'State agency' means the State agency designated by a State under section 305(a)(1).
"(8) The term 'unit of general purpose local government' means—
"(A) a political subdivision of the State whose authority is general and not limited to only one function or combination of related functions; or
"(B) an Indian tribal organization.

"AUTHORIZATION OF APPROPRIATIONS; USES OF FUNDS

42 USC 3023.

Post, p. 1535.

"SEC. 303. (a) There are authorized to be appropriated $300,000,000 for fiscal year 1979, $360,000,000 for fiscal year 1980, and $180,000,000 for fiscal year 1981 for the purpose of making grants under part B of this title (relating to social services).
"(b)(1) There are authorized to be appropriated $350,000,000 for fiscal year 1979, $375,000,000 for fiscal year 1980, and $400,000,000

Post, p. 1536.

for fiscal year 1981 for the purpose of making grants under subpart 1 of part C of this title (relating to congregate nutrition services).

"(2) There are authorized to be appropriated $80,000,000 for fiscal year 1979, $100,000,000 for fiscal year 1980, and $120,000,000 for fiscal year 1981 for the purpose of making grants under subpart 2 of part C of this title (relating to home delivered nutrition services).

"(c) Grants made under parts B and C of this title may be used for paying part of the cost of—

"(1) the administration of area plans by area agencies on aging designated under section 305(a)(2)(A), including the preparation of area plans on aging consistent with section 306 and the evaluation of activities carried out under such plans; and

"(2) the development of comprehensive and coordinated systems for social services, congregate and home delivered nutrition services, the development and operation of multipurpose senior centers, and the delivery of legal services.

"ALLOTMENT; FEDERAL SHARE"

42 USC 3024.
Post, pp. 1535, 1536.

"Sec. 304. (a)(1) From the sums appropriated under parts B and C for fiscal years 1979, 1980, and 1981, each State shall be allotted an amount which bears the same ratio to such sums as the population aged 60 or older in such State bears to the population aged 60 or older in all States, except that (A) no State shall be allotted less than one-half of 1 percent of the sum appropriated for the fiscal year for which the determination is made; (B) Guam, the Virgin Islands, and the Trust Territory of the Pacific Islands, shall each be allotted not less than one-fourth of 1 percent of the sum appropriated for the fiscal year for which the determination is made; (C) American Samoa and the Northern Mariana Islands shall each be allotted not less than one-sixteenth of 1 percent of the sum appropriated for the fiscal year for which the determination is made; and (D) no State shall be allotted an amount less than the State received for fiscal year 1978. For the purpose of the exception contained in clause (A) only, the term 'State' does not include Guam, American Samoa, the Virgin Islands, the Trust Territory of the Pacific Islands, and the Northern Mariana Islands.

"(2) The number of individuals aged 60 or older in any State and in all States shall be determined by the Commissioner on the basis of the most recent satisfactory data available to him.

"(b) Whenever the Commissioner determines that any amount allotted to a State under part B or C for a fiscal year under this section will not be used by such State for carrying out the purpose for which the allotment was made, he shall make such allotment available for carrying out such purpose to one or more other States to the extent he determines that such other States will be able to use such additional amount for carrying out such purpose. Any amount made available to a State from an appropriation for a fiscal year in accordance with the preceding sentence shall, for purposes of this title, be regarded as part of such State's allotment (as determined under subsection (a)) for such year, but shall remain available until the end of the succeeding fiscal year.

"(c) If the Commissioner finds that any State has failed to qualify under the State plan requirements of section 307, the Commissioner shall withhold the allotment of funds to such State referred to in subsection (a). The Commissioner shall disburse the funds so withheld directly to any public or private nonprofit institution or organization, agency, or political subdivision of such State submitting an approved plan under section 307, which includes an agreement that any such payment shall be matched in the proportion determined under subsection (d)(1)(B) for such State, by funds for in-kind resources from non-Federal sources.

"(d)(1) From any State's allotment under this section for any fiscal year—

"(A) such amount as the State agency determines, but not more than 8.5 percent thereof, shall be available for paying such percentage as the agency determines, but not more than 75 percent, of the cost of administration of area plans; and

"(B) the remainder of such allotment shall be available to such State only for paying such percentage as the State agency determines, but not more than 90 percent in fiscal years 1979 and 1980, and 85 percent in fiscal year 1981, of the cost of social services and nutrition services authorized under parts B and C provided in the State as part of a comprehensive and coordinated system in planning and service areas for which there is an area plan approved by the State agency.

Post, pp. 1535, 1536.

"(2) The non-Federal share shall be in cash or in kind. In determining the amount of the non-Federal share, the Commissioner may attribute fair market value to services and facilities contributed from non-Federal sources.

"ORGANIZATION

42 USC 3025.

"Sec. 305. (a) In order for a State to be eligible to participate in programs of grants to States from allotments under this title—

"(1) the State shall, in accordance with regulations of the Commissioner, designate a State agency as the sole State agency to—

State plan, development and approval.

"(A) develop a State plan to be submitted to the Commissioner for approval under section 307;

"(B) administer the State plan within such State;

"(C) be primarily responsible for the coordination of all State activities related to the purposes of this Act;

"(D) serve as an effective and visible advocate for the elderly by reviewing and commenting upon all State plans, budgets, and policies which affect the elderly and providing technical assistance to any agency, organization, association, or individual representing the needs of the elderly; and

"(E) divide the State into distinct areas, in accordance with guidelines issued by the Commissioner, after considering the geographical distribution of individuals aged 60 and older in the State, the incidence of the need for social services, nutrition services, multipurpose senior centers, and legal services, the distribution of older individuals who have low incomes residing in such areas, the distribution of resources available to provide such services or centers, the boundaries of existing areas within the State which were drawn for the planning or administration of social services programs, the location of units of general purpose local government within the State, and any other relevant factors; and

"(2) the State agency designated under clause (1) shall—

"(A) determine for which planning and service area an area plan will be developed, in accordance with section 306, and for each such area designate, after consideration of the views offered by the unit or units of general purpose local government in such area, a public or private nonprofit agency or organization as the area agency on aging for such area;

"(B) provide assurances, satisfactory to the Commissioner, that the State agency will take into account, in connection with matters of general policy arising in the development and administration of the State plan for any fiscal year, the views of recipients of social services or nutrition services, or individuals using multipurpose senior centers provided under such plan;

"(C) develop a formula, in accordance with guidelines issued by the Commissioner, for the distribution within the State of funds received under this title, taking into account, to the maximum extent feasible, the best available statistics on the geographical distribution of individuals aged 60 and older in the State, and publish such formula for review and comment;

"(D) submit its formula developed under subclause (C) to the Commissioner for review and comment; and

"(E) provide assurances that preference will be given to providing services to older individuals with the greatest economic or social needs and include proposed methods of carrying out the preference in the State plan.

Planning and service area, designation.

"(b) (1) In carrying out the requirement of clause (1) of subsection (a), the State may designate as a planning and service area any unit of general purpose local government which has a population of 100,000 or more. In any case in which a unit of general purpose local government makes application to the State agency under the preceding sentence to be designated as a planning and service area, the State agency shall, upon request, provide an opportunity for a hearing to such unit of general purpose local government. A State may designate as a planning and service area under clause (1) of subsection (a), any region within the State recognized for purposes of areawide planning which includes one or more such units of general purpose local government when the State determines that the designation of such a regional planning and service area is necessary for, and will enhance, the effective administration of the programs authorized by this title. The State may include in any planning and service area designated under clause (1) of subsection (a) such additional areas adjacent to the unit of general purpose local government or regions so designated as the State determines to be necessary for, and will enhance the effective administration of the programs authorized by this title.

"(2) The State is encouraged in carrying out the requirement of clause (1) of subsection (a) to include the area covered by the appropriate economic development district involved in any planning and service area designated under such clause, and to include all portions of an Indian reservation within a single planning and service area, if feasible.

"(3) The chief executive officer of each State in which a planning and service area crosses State boundaries, or in which an interstate Indian reservation is located, may apply to the Commissioner to request redesignation as an interstate planning and service area comprising the entire metropolitan area or Indian reservation. If the Commissioner approves such an application, he shall adjust the State allotments of the areas within the planning and service area in which the interstate planning and service area is established to reflect the number of older individuals within the area who will be served by an interstate planning and service area not within the State.

Appeal.

"(4) Whenever a unit of general purpose local government, a region, a metropolitan area or an Indian reservation is denied designation under the provisions of clause (1) of subsection (a), such unit of general purpose local government, region, metropolitan area, or Indian reservation may appeal the decision of the State agency to the Commissioner. The Commissioner shall afford such unit, region, metropolitan area, or Indian reservation an opportunity for a hearing. In carrying out the provisions of this paragraph, the Commissioner may approve the decision of the State agency, disapprove the decision of the State agency and require the State agency to designate the unit, region, area, or Indian reservation appealing the decision as a planning and service area, or take such other action as the Commissioner deems appropriate.

Area agency on aging.

"(c) An area agency on aging designated under subsection (a) shall be—

"(1) an established office of aging which is operating within a planning and service area designated under subsection (a);

"(2) any office or agency of a unit of general purpose local government, which is designated for the purpose of serving as an area agency by the chief elected official of such unit;

"(3) any office or agency designated by the appropriate chief elected officials of any combination of units of general purpose local government to act on behalf of such combination for such purpose; or

"(4) any public or nonprofit private agency in a planning and service area which is under the supervision or direction for this purpose of the designated State agency and which can engage in the planning or provision of a broad range of social services, or nutrition services within such planning and service area;

and shall provide assurance, determined adequate by the State agency, that the area agency will have the ability to develop an area plan and to carry out, directly or through contractual or other arrangements, a program in accordance with the plan within the planning and service area. In designating an area agency on aging within the planning and service area or within any unit of general purpose local government designated as a planning and service area the State shall give preference to an established office on aging, unless the State agency finds that no such office within the planning and service area will have the capacity to carry out the area plan.

"AREA PLANS

42 USC 3026.

"SEC. 306. (a) Each area agency on aging designated under section 305(a)(2)(A) shall, in order to be approved by the State agency, prepare and develop an area plan for a planning and service area for a 3-year period with such annual adjustments as may be necessary. Each such plan shall be based upon a uniform format for area plans within the State prepared in accordance with section 307(a)(1). Each such plan shall—

"(1) provide, through a comprehensive and coordinated system, for social services, nutrition services, and, where appropriate, for the establishment, maintenance, or construction of multipurpose senior centers, within the planning and service area covered by the plan, including determining the extent of need for social services, nutrition services, and multipurpose senior centers in such area (taking into consideration, among other things, the number of older individuals with low incomes residing in such area), evaluating the effectiveness of the use of resources in meeting such need, and entering into agreements with providers of social services, nutrition services, or multipurpose senior centers in such area, for the provision of such services or centers to meet such need;

Post, p. 1535.

"(2) provide assurances that at least 50 percent of the amount allotted for part B to the planning and service area will be expended for the delivery of—

"(A) services associated with access to services (transportation, outreach, and information and referral);

"(B) in-home services (homemaker and home health aide, visiting and telephone reassurance, and chore maintenance); and

"(C) legal services;

and that some funds will be expended for each such category of services;

"(3) designate, where feasible, a focal point for comprehensive service delivery in each community to encourage the maximum collocation and coordination of services for older individuals, and give special consideration to designating multipurpose senior centers as such focal point;

"(4) provide for the establishment and maintenance of information and referral services in sufficient numbers to assure that all older individuals within the planning and service area covered by the plan will have reasonably convenient access to such services;

"(5)(A) provide assurances that preference will be given to providing services to older individuals with the greatest economic or social needs and include proposed methods of carrying out the preference in the area plan; and

"(B) assure the use of outreach efforts that will identify individuals eligible for assistance under this Act, with special emphasis on rural elderly, and inform such individuals of the availability of such assistance;

"(6) provide that the area agency on aging will—

"(A) conduct periodic evaluations of activities carried out under the area plan;

"(B) furnish appropriate technical assistance to providers of social services, nutrition services, or multipurpose senior centers in the planning and service area covered by the area plan;

"(C) take into account in connection with matters of general policy arising in the development and administration of the area plan, the views of recipients of services under such plan;

"(D) serve as the advocate and focal point for the elderly within the community by monitoring, evaluating, and commenting upon all policies, programs, hearings, levies, and community actions which will affect the elderly;

"(E) where possible, enter into arrangements with organizations providing day care services for children so as to provide opportunities for older individuals to aid or assist on a voluntary basis in the delivery of such services to children;

"(F) where possible, enter into arrangements with local educational agencies, institutions of higher education, and nonprofit private organizations, to use services provided for older individuals under the community schools program under the Elementary and Secondary Education Act of 1965;

20 USC 821 note.
Advisory council, establishment.

"(G) establish an advisory council consisting of older individuals who are participants or who are eligible to participate in programs assisted under this Act, representatives of older individuals, local elected officials, and the general public, to advise continuously the area agency on all matters relating to the development of the area plan, the administration of the plan and operations conducted under the plan;

"(H) develop and publish methods by which priority of services is determined, particularly with respect to the delivery of services under clause (2); and

"(I) establish effective and efficient procedures for coordination between the programs assisted under this title and programs described in section 203(b).

Ante, p. 1514.
Waiver.

"(b)(1) Each State, in approving area agency plans under this section, may, for fiscal years 1979 and 1980, waive any particular requirement relating to the delivery of services or the establishment or operation of multipurpose senior centers which such agency cannot meet because of the consolidation authorized by the Comprehensive Older Americans Act Amendments of 1978, except that the State agency may grant such a waiver only if the area agency demonstrates to the State agency that it is taking steps to meet the requirements of this title, but in any event the State agency may not grant a waiver for any requirement of this Act in effect on September 30, 1978.

Ante, p. 1513.

"(2) Each State, in approving area agency plans under this section, may waive the requirement described in clause (2) of subsection (a) for any category of services described in such clause if the area agency on aging demonstrates to the State agency that services being furnished for such category in the area are sufficient to meet the need for such services in such area. If the State agency grants a waiver under the preceding sentence with respect to any category, then the area agency shall expend under clause (2) of subsection (a) a percentage of the amount allotted for part B to the planning and service area, for the categories with respect to which such waiver does not apply, that is agreed upon by the State agency and the area agency.

"(c)(1) Subject to regulations prescribed by the Commissioner, an area agency on aging designated under section 305(a)(2)(A) or, in areas of a State where no such agency has been designated, the State agency, may enter into agreements with agencies administering programs under the Rehabilitation Act of 1973, and titles XIX and XX of the Social Security Act for the purpose of developing and implementing plans for meeting the common need for transportation services of individuals receiving benefits under such Acts and older individuals participating in programs authorized by this title.

29 USC 701 note.
42 USC 1396, 1397.

Transportation services, funds.

"(2) In accordance with an agreement entered into under paragraph (1), funds appropriated under this title may be used to purchase transportation services for older individuals and may be pooled with funds made available for the provision of transportation services under the Rehabilitation Act of 1973, and titles XIX and XX of the Social Security Act.

"STATE PLANS

42 USC 3027.

"SEC. 307. (a) Except as provided in section 309(a), each State, in order to be eligible for grants from its allotment under this title for

Requirements.

any fiscal year, shall submit to the Commissioner a State plan for a 3-year period, with such annual revisions as are necessary, which meets such criteria as the Commissioner may by regulation prescribe. Each such plan shall—

"(1) contain assurances that the State plan will be based upon area plans developed by area agencies on aging within the State designated under section 305(a)(2)(A) and that the State will prepare and distribute a uniform format for use by area agencies in developing area plans under section 306;

"(2) provide that each area agency on aging designated under section 305(a)(2)(A) will develop and submit to the State agency for approval an area plan which complies with the provisions of section 306;

"(3)(A) provide that the State agency will evaluate the need for social services (including legal services), nutrition services, and multipurpose senior centers within the State and determine the extent to which existing public or private programs meet such need; and

42 USC 3041, 3045.

"(B) provide assurances that the State agency will spend in each fiscal year, for services to older individuals residing in rural areas in the State assisted under this title, an amount equal to not less than 105 percent of the amount expended for such services (including amounts expended under title V and title VII) in fiscal year 1978;

"(4) provide for the use of such methods of administration (including methods relating to the establishment and maintenance of personnel standards on a merit basis, except that the Commissioner shall exercise no authority with respect to the selection, tenure of office, or compensation of any individual employed in accordance with such methods) as are necessary for the proper and efficient administration of the plan, and, where necessary, provide for the reorganization and reassignment of functions to assure such efficient administration;

Hearing.

"(5) provide that the State agency will afford an opportunity for a hearing upon request to any area agency on aging submitting a plan under this title, to any provider of a service under such a plan, or to any applicant to provide a service under such a plan;

Reports.

"(6) provide that the State agency will make such reports, in such form, and containing such information, as the Commissioner may require, and comply with such requirements as the Commissioner may impose to insure the correctness of such reports;

Accounting procedures.

"(7) provide satisfactory assurance that such fiscal control and fund accounting procedures will be adopted as may be necessary to assure proper disbursement of, and accounting for, Federal funds paid under this title to the State, including any such funds paid to the recipients of a grant or contract;

"(8) provide that the State agency will conduct periodic evaluations of activities and projects carried out under the State plan;

"(9) provide for establishing and maintaining information and referral services in sufficient numbers to assure that all older individuals in the State who are not furnished adequate information and referral services under section 306(a)(4) will have reasonably convenient access to such services;

"(10) provide that no social services, including nutrition services, will be directly provided by the State agency or an area agency on aging, except where, in the judgment of the State agency, provision of such services by the State agency or an area agency on aging is necessary to assure an adequate supply of such services;

"(11) provide that subject to the requirements of merit employment systems of State and local governments, preference shall be given to individuals aged 60 or older for any staff positions (full time or part time) in State and area agencies for which such individuals qualify;

Ombudsman program.

"(12) provide assurances that the State agency will—

"(A) establish and operate, either directly or by contract or other arrangement with any public agency or other appropriate private nonprofit organization which is not responsible for licensing or certifying long-term care services in the State or which is not an association (or an affiliate of such an association) of long-term care facilities (including any other residential facility for older individuals), a long-term care ombudsman program which will—

"(i) investigate and resolve complaints made by or on behalf of older individuals who are residents of long-term care facilities relating to administrative action which may adversely affect the health, safety, welfare, and rights of such residents;

"(ii) monitor the development and implementation of Federal, State, and local laws, regulations, and policies with respect to long-term care facilities in that State;

"(iii) provide information as appropriate to public agencies regarding the problems of older individuals residing in long-term care facilities;

"(iv) provide for training volunteers and promote the development of citizen organizations to participate in the ombudsman program; and

"(v) carry out such other activities as the Commissioner deems appropriate;

Record access and disclosure. "(B) establish procedures for appropriate access by the ombudsman to long-term care facilities and patients' records, including procedures to protect the confidentiality of such records and ensure that the identity of any complainant or resident will not be disclosed without the written consent of such complainant or resident, or upon court order;

Reporting system. "(C) establish a statewide uniform reporting system to collect and analyze data relating to complaints and conditions in long-term care facilities for the purpose of identifying and resolving significant problems, with provision for submission of such data to the agency of the State responsible for licensing or certifying long-term care facilities in the State and to the Commissioner on a regular basis; and

"(D) establish procedures to assure that any files maintained by the ombudsman program shall be disclosed only at the discretion of the ombudsman having authority over the disposition of such files, except that the identity of any complainant or resident of a long-term care facility shall not be disclosed by such ombudsman unless—

"(i) such complainant or resident, or his legal representative, consents in writing to such disclosure; or

"(ii) such disclosure is required by court order;

Nutrition services. "(13) provide with respect to nutrition services that—

"(A) each project providing nutrition services will be available to individuals aged 60 or older, and to their spouses;

"(B) each project will provide meals in a congregate setting, except that each such project may provide home delivered meals based upon a determination of need made by the recipient of a grant or contract entered into under this title;

"(C) (i) each project will permit recipients of grants or contracts to charge participating individuals for meals furnished in accordance with guidelines established by the Commissioner, taking into consideration the income ranges of eligible individuals in local communities and other sources of income of the recipients of a grant or contract; and

"(ii) such charges will be used to increase the number of meals served by the project involved;

"(D) a site for such services and for comprehensive social services is furnished in as close proximity to the majority of eligible individuals' residences as feasible, with particular attention upon a multipurpose senior center, a school, a church, or other appropriate community facility, preferably within walking distance where possible, and where appropriate, transportation to such site is furnished or home delivered meals are furnished to eligible individuals who are homebound;

"(E) each project will establish outreach activities which

assure that the maximum number of eligible individuals may have an opportunity to participate;

"(F) each project may establish and administer the nutrition project with the advice of persons competent in the field of service in which the nutrition project is being provided, older individuals who will participate in the program, and of persons who are knowledgeable with regard to the needs of older individuals;

"(G) each project will provide special menus, where feasible and appropriate, to meet the particular dietary needs arising from the health requirements, religious requirements, or ethnic backgrounds of eligible individuals;

"(H) each area agency will give consideration, where feasible, in the furnishing of home delivered meals to the use of organizations which (i) have demonstrated an ability to provide home delivered meals efficiently and reasonably; and (ii) furnish assurances to the area agency that such an organization will maintain efforts to solicit voluntary support and that funds made available under this title to the organization will not be used to supplant funds from non-Federal sources; and

Post, p. 1536.

"(I) each State agency may, only for fiscal years 1979 and 1980, use not to exceed 20 percent of the amounts allotted under part C to the State for supportive services, including recreational activities, informational services, health and welfare counseling, and referral services, directly related to the delivery of congregate or home delivered meals, except that the Commissioner may approve an application from a State to use not to exceed 50 percent of its amount allotted under part C in areas with unusually high supportive services costs;

Multipurpose senior centers, facilities.

"(14) provide, with respect to the acquisition (in fee simple or by lease for 10 years or more), alteration, or renovation of existing facilities (or the construction of new facilities in any area in which there are no suitable structures available, as determined by the State agency, after full consideration of the recommendations made by area agencies, to be a focal point for the delivery of services assisted under this title) to serve as multipurpose senior centers, that—

"(A) the plan contains or is supported by reasonable assurances that (i) for not less than 10 years after acquisition, or not less than 20 years after the completion of construction, the facility will be used for the purpose for which it is to be acquired or constructed, unless for unusual circumstances the Commissioner waives the requirement of this division; (ii) sufficient funds will be available to meet the non-Federal share of the cost of acquisition or construction of the facility; (iii) sufficient funds will be available when acquisition or construction is completed, for effective use of the facility for the purpose for which it is being acquired or constructed; and (iv) the facility will not be used and is not intended to be used for sectarian instruction or as a place for religious worship;

"(B) the plan contains or is supported by reasonable assurances that, in the case of purchase or construction, there are no existing facilities in the community suitable for leasing as a multipurpose senior center;

"(C) the plans and specifications for the facility are in accordance with regulations relating to minimum standards of construction, promulgated with particular emphasis on securing compliance with the requirements of the Act of August 12, 1968, commonly known as the Architectural Barriers Act of 1968;

42 USC 4151 note.

"(D) the plan contains or is supported by adequate assurance that any laborer or mechanic employed by any contractor or subcontractor in the performance of work on the facility will be paid wages at rates not less than those prevailing for similar work in the locality as determined by the Secretary of Labor in accordance with the Act of March 3, 1931 (40

U.S.C. 276a—276a-5; commonly known as the Davis-Bacon Act), and the Secretary of Labor shall have, with respect to the labor standards specified in this clause, the authority and functions set forth in reorganization plan numbered 14 of 1950 (15 F.R. 3176; 64 Stat. 1267), and section 2 of the Act of June 13, 1934 (40 U.S.C. 276c) ; and

"(E) the plan contains assurances that the State agency will consult with the Secretary of Housing and Urban Development with respect to the technical adequacy of any proposed alteration or renovation;

Legal services.

"(15) provide that with respect to legal services—

"(A) the plan contains assurances that area agencies on aging will (i) enter into contracts with providers of legal services which can demonstrate the experience or capacity to deliver legal services; (ii) include in any such contract provisions to assure that any recipient of funds under division (i) will be subject to specific restrictions and regulations pro-

42 USC 2996 note.

mulgated under the Legal Services Corporation Act (other than restrictions and regulations governing eligibility for legal assistance under such Act and governing membership of local governing boards) as determined appropriate by the Commissioner; and (iii) attempt to involve the private bar in legal services activities authorized under this title, including groups within the private bar furnishing services to older individuals on a pro bono and reduced fee basis;

"(B) the plan contains assurances that no legal services will be furnished unless the grantee—

"(i) is a recipient of funds under the Legal Services Corporation Act; or

"(ii) administers a program designed to provide legal services to all older individuals with social or economic need and has agreed to coordinate its services with existing Legal Services Corporation projects in the area in order to concentrate the use of funds provided under this title on individuals with the greatest such need but who are not eligible for legal assistance under the Legal Services Corporation Act;

42 USC 2996 note.

and the area agency makes a finding after assessment, pursuant to standards for service promulgated by the Commissioner, that any grantee selected is the entity best able to provide the particular services;

"(C) the State agency will provide for the coordination of the furnishing of legal services to older individuals within the State, and provide advice and technical assistance in the provision of legal services to older individuals within the State and support the furnishing of training and technical assistance for legal services for older individuals; and

"(D) the plan contains assurances, to the extent practicable, that legal services furnished under the plan will be in addition to any legal services for older individuals being furnished with funds from sources other than this Act and that reasonable efforts will be made to maintain existing levels of legal services for older individuals; and

Post, p. 1535.

"(16) provide that the State agency, from funds allotted under section 304(a) for part B will use an amount equal to an amount not less than 1 percent of such allotment or $20,000, whichever is greater, for the purpose of carrying out the provisions of clause (12), except that (A) the requirement of this clause shall not apply in any fiscal year in which a State spends from State or local sources an amount equal to the amount required to be spent by this clause; and (B) the provisions of this clause shall not apply to American Samoa, Guam, the Virgin Islands, the Trust Territory of the Pacific Islands, and the Northern Mariana Islands.

"(b) (1) The Commissioner shall approve any State plan which he finds fulfills the requirements of subsection (a).

Waiver.

"(2) The Commissioner, in approving any State plan under this section may, for the fiscal years 1979 and 1980, waive any particular requirement relating to the delivery of services or the establishment or operation of multipurpose senior centers which the State agency cannot meet because of the consolidation authorized by the Comprehensive Older Americans Act Amendments of 1978 or because meeting such requirement would reduce or jeopardize the quality of services under this Act, except that the Commissioner may grant such a waiver only if the State agency demonstrates that it is taking steps to meet the requirements of this title, but in any event the Commissioner may not grant a waiver for any requirement of this Act in effect on September 30, 1978. The Commissioner may not disapprove any State plan under paragraph (1) solely on the ground that a State requested a waiver under the preceding sentence.

Ante, p. 1513.

"(3) The Commissioner, in approving any State plan under this section, may waive the requirement described in clause (3)(B) of subsection (a) if the State agency demonstrates to the Commissioner that the service needs of older individuals residing in rural areas in the State are being met, or that the number of older individuals residing in such rural areas is not sufficient to require the State agency to comply with the requirement described in clause (3)(B) of subsection (a).

Hearing.

"(c) The Commissioner shall not make a final determination disapproving any State plan, or any modification thereof, or make a final determination that a State is ineligible under section 305, without first affording the State reasonable notice and opportunity for a hearing.

State plan, failure to comply.

"(d) Whenever the Commissioner, after reasonable notice and opportunity for a hearing to the State agency, finds that—

"(1) the State is not eligible under section 305,

"(2) the State plan has been so changed that it no longer complies substantially with the provisions of subsection (a), or

"(3) in the administration of the plan there is a failure to comply substantially with any such provision of subsection (a),

the Commissioner shall notify such State agency that no further payments from its allotments under section 304 and section 308 will be made to the State (or, in his discretion, that further payments to the State will be limited to projects under or portions of the State plan not affected by such failure), until he is satisfied that there will no longer be any failure to comply. Until he is so satisfied, no further payments shall be made to such State from its allotments under section 304 and section 308 (or payments shall be limited to projects under or portions of the State plan not affected by such failure). The Commissioner shall, in accordance with regulations he shall prescribe, disburse the funds so withheld directly to any public or nonprofit private organization or agency or political subdivision of such State submitting an approved plan in accordance with the provisions of section 307. Any such payment shall be matched in the proportions specified in section 304.

Appeal.

"(e)(1) A State which is dissatisfied with a final action of the Commissioner under subsection (b), (c), or (d) may appeal to the United States court of appeals for the circuit in which the State is located, by filing a petition with such court within 30 days after such final action. A copy of the petition shall be forthwith transmitted by the clerk of the court to the Commissioner, or any officer designated by him for such purpose. The Commissioner thereupon shall file in the court the record of the proceedings on which he based his action, as provided in section 2112 of title 28, United States Code.

Petition filing.

"(2) Upon the filing of such petition, the court shall have jurisdiction to affirm the action of the Commissioner or to set it aside, in whole or in part, temporarily or permanently, but until the filing of the record, the Commissioner may modify or set aside his order. The findings of the Commissioner as to the facts, if supported by substantial evidence, shall be conclusive, but the court, for good cause shown, may remand the case to the Commissioner to take further evidence, and the Commissioner shall, within 30 days, file in the court the record of those further proceedings. Such new or modified findings of fact shall likewise be conclusive if supported by substantial evidence. The judgment of the court affirming or setting aside, in whole or in part, any action of the Commissioner shall be final, subject to review by the

Supreme Court of the United States upon certiorari or certification as provided in section 1254 of title 28, United States Code.

"(3) The commencement of proceedings under this subsection shall not, unless so specifically ordered by the court, operate as a stay of the Commissioner's action.

"PLANNING, COORDINATION, EVALUATION, AND ADMINISTRATION OF STATE PLANS

Grants.
42 USC 3028.

"SEC. 308. (a)(1) Amounts appropriated under section 303 may be used to make grants to States for paying such percentages as each State agency determines, but not more than 75 percent, of the cost of the administration of its State plan, including the preparation of the State plan, the evaluation of activities carried out under such plan, the collection of data and the carrying out of analyses related to the need for social services, nutrition services, and multipurpose senior centers within the State, and dissemination of information so obtained, the provision of short-term training to personnel of public or nonprofit private agencies and organizations engaged in the operation of programs authorized by this Act, and the carrying out of demonstration projects of statewide significance relating to the initiation, expansion, or improvement of services assisted under this title.

"(2) Any sums received by a State under this section for part of the cost of the administration of its State plan which the State determines is not needed for such purpose may be used by the State to supplement the amount available under section 304(d)(1)(A) to cover part of the cost of the administration of area plans.

"(3) Any State which has designated a single planning and service area under section 305(a)(1)(E) covering all, or substantially all, of the older individuals in such State, as determined by the Commissioner, may elect to pay part of the costs of the administration of State and area plans either out of sums received under this section or out of sums made available for the administration of area plans under section 304(d)(1)(A), but shall not pay such costs out of sums received or allotted under both such sections.

Funds, allocation.

"(b)(1) From the sums appropriated for any fiscal year under section 303 for carrying out the purposes of this section, each State shall be allotted an amount which bears the same ratio to such sums as the population aged 60 or older in such State bears to the population aged 60 or older in all States, except that (A) no State shall be allotted less than one-half of 1 percent of the sum appropriated for the fiscal year for which the determination is made, or $300,000, whichever is greater; and (B) Guam, American Samoa, the Virgin Islands, the Trust Territory of the Pacific Islands, and the Northern Mariana Islands shall be each allotted no less than one-fourth of 1 percent of the sum appropriated for the fiscal year for which the determination is made, or $75,000, whichever is greater. For the purpose of the exception contained in clause (A), the term 'State' does not include Guam, American Samoa, the Virgin Islands, the Trust Territory of the Pacific Islands, and the Northern Mariana Islands.

"State."

Applications for additional funds.

"(2)(A) Any State which desires to receive amounts, in addition to amounts allotted to such State under paragraph (1), to be used in the administration of its State plan in accordance with subsection (a) may transmit an application to the Commissioner in accordance with this paragraph. Any such application shall be transmitted in such form, and according to such procedures, as the Commissioner may require, except that such application may not be made as part of, or as an amendment to, the State plan.

"(B) The Commissioner may approve any application transmitted by a State under subparagraph (A) if the Commissioner determines, based upon a particularized showing of need, that—

"(i) the State will be unable to fully and effectively administer its State plan and to carry out programs and projects authorized by this title unless such additional amounts are made available by the Commissioner;

"(ii) the State is making full and effective use of its allotment under paragraph (1) and of the personnel of the State agency and area agencies designated under section 305(a)(2)(A) in the administration of its State plan in accordance with subsection (a) ; and

"(iii) the State agency and area agencies of such State designated under section 305 are carrying out, on a full-time basis, programs and activities which are in furtherance of the purposes of this Act.

"(C) The Commissioner may approve that portion of the amount requested by a State in its application under subparagraph (A) which he determines has been justified in such application.

Limitation. "(D) Amounts which any State may receive in any fiscal year under this paragraph may not exceed three-fourths of 1 percent of the sum of the amounts allotted under section 304(a) to such State to carry out the State plan for such fiscal year.

"(E) No application by a State under subparagraph (A) shall be approved unless it contains assurances that no amounts received by the State under this paragraph will be used to hire any individual to fill a job opening created by the action of the State in laying off or terminating the employment of any regular employee not supported under this Act in anticipation of filling the vacancy so created by hiring an employee to be supported through use of amounts received under this paragraph.

State allotments. "(3) Each State shall be entitled to an allotment under this section for any fiscal year in an amount which is not less than the amount of the allotment to which such State was entitled under paragraph (1) for the fiscal year ending June 30, 1975.

"(4) The number of individuals aged 60 or older in any State and in all States shall be determined by the Commissioner on the basis of the most recent satisfactory data available to him.

"(5) Notwithstanding any other provision of this title, with respect to funds received under section 303(b) (1) and (2), a State may elect in its plan under section 307(a) (13) regarding part C of this title, to transfer a portion of the funds appropriated between subpart 1 and *Post*, p. 1536. subpart 2 of part C, for use as the State considers appropriate to meet the needs of the area served. The Commissioner shall approve any such transfer unless he determines that such transfer is not consistent with the purposes of this Act.

"(c) The amounts of any State's allotment under subsection (b) for any fiscal year which the Commissioner determines will not be required for that year for the purposes described in subsection (a)(1) *Post*, pp. 1535, shall be available to provide services under part B or part C, or both, 1536. in the State.

"PAYMENTS

42 USC 3029. "SEC. 309. (a) Payments of grants or contracts under this title may be made (after necessary adjustments resulting from previously made overpayments or underpayments) in advance or by way of reimbursement, and in such installments, as the Commissioner may determine. From a State's allotment for a fiscal year which is available under section 308 the Commissioner may pay to a State which does not have a State plan approved under section 307 such amounts as he deems appropriate for the purpose of assisting such State in developing a State plan.

"(b) (1) For each fiscal year, not less than 25 percent of the non-Federal share of the total expenditures under the State plan which is required by section 304(d) shall be met from funds from State or local public sources.

"(2) Funds required to meet the non-Federal share required by section 304(d) (1) (B), in amounts exceeding the non-Federal share required prior to fiscal year 1981, shall be met from State sources.

"(c) A State's allotment under section 304 for a fiscal year shall be reduced by the percentage (if any) by which its expenditures for such year from State sources under its State plan approved under section 307 are less than its expenditures from such sources for the preceding fiscal year.

"DISASTER RELIEF REIMBURSEMENTS

42 USC 3030. "SEC. 310. (a) (1) The Commissioner may provide reimbursements to any State, upon application for such reimbursement, for funds such State makes available to area agencies in such State for the delivery of

42 USC 5121
note.

Post, p. 1539.

social services during any major disaster declared by the President in accordance with the Disaster Relief Act of 1974.

"(2) Total payments to all States under paragraph (1) in any fiscal year shall not exceed 5 percent of the total amount appropriated and available for carrying out the purposes of section 421.

"(b)(1) At the beginning of each fiscal year the Commissioner shall set aside, for payment to States under subsection (a), an amount equal to 5 percent of the total amount appropriated and available for carrying out the purposes of section 421.

"(2) Amounts set aside under paragraph (1) which are not obligated by the end of the third quarter of any fiscal year shall be made available for carrying out the purposes of section 421.

"(c) Nothing in this section shall be construed to prohibit expenditures by States for disaster relief for older individuals in excess of amounts reimbursable under this section, by using funds made available to them under other sections of this Act or under other provisions of Federal or State law, or from private sources.

"AVAILABILITY OF SURPLUS COMMODITIES

Nutrition services.
42 USC 3030a.

"SEC. 311. (a)(1) Agricultural commodities and products purchased by the Secretary of Agriculture under section 32 of the Act of August 24, 1935 (7 U.S.C. 612c), shall be donated to a recipient of a grant or contract to be used for providing nutrition services in accordance with the provisions of this title.

"(2) The Commodity Credit Corporation shall dispose of food commodities under section 416 of the Agricultural Act of 1949 (7 U.S.C. 1431) by donating them to a recipient of a grant or contract to be used for providing nutrition services in accordance with the provisions of this title.

Dairy products.

"(3) Dairy products purchased by the Secretary of Agriculture under section 709 of the Food and Agriculture Act of 1965 (7 U.S.C. 1446a–1) shall be used to meet the requirements of programs providing nutrition services in accordance with the provisions of this title.

"(4) In donating commodities under this subsection, the Secretary of Agriculture shall maintain an annually programmed level of assistance of not less than 15 cents per meal during fiscal year 1976, 25 cents per meal during fiscal year 1977 and fiscal year 1978, and 30 cents per meal during the three succeeding fiscal years. The amount specified in this paragraph shall be adjusted on an annual basis for each fiscal year after June 30, 1975, to reflect changes in the series for food away from home of the Consumer Price Index published by the Bureau of Labor Statistics of the Department of Labor. Such adjustment shall be computed to the nearest one-fourth cent. Among the commodities delivered under this subsection, the Secretary shall give special emphasis to high protein foods, meat, and meat alternates. The Secretary of Agriculture, in consultation with the Commissioner, is authorized to prescribe the terms and conditions respecting the donating of commodities under this subsection.

High protein foods, meat, and meat alternates.

"(b)(1) During each of the fiscal years ending before October 1, 1981, the Secretary of Agriculture shall purchase high protein foods, meat, and meat alternates on the open market, at prices not in excess of market prices, out of funds appropriated under this section, as determined under paragraph (3), for distribution to recipients of grants or contracts to be used for providing nutrition services in accordance with the provisions of this title. High protein foods, meat, and meat alternates purchased by the Secretary of Agriculture under this subsection shall be grown and produced in the United States.

"(2) High protein foods, meat, and meat alternates donated under this subsection shall not be considered donated commodities for purposes of meeting the requirement of subsection (a)(4) with respect to the annually programmed level of assistance under subsection (a).

"(3) There are authorized to be appropriated such sums as may be necessary in order to carry out the program established by paragraph (1).

Cash payments.

"(c)(1) Notwithstanding any other provision of law, a State may, for purposes of the programs authorized by this Act, elect to receive cash payments in lieu of donated foods for all or any portion of its project. In any case in which a State makes such an election, the Secretary of Agriculture shall make cash payments to such State in an amount equivalent in value to the donated foods which the State otherwise would have received if such State had retained its commodity distribution.

"(2) When such payments are made, the State agency shall promptly and equitably disburse any cash it receives in lieu of commodities to recipients of grants or contracts. Such disbursements shall only be used by such recipients of grants or contracts to purchase United States agricultural commodities and other foods for their nutrition projects.

"(3) Nothing in this subsection shall be construed to authorize the Secretary of Agriculture to require any State to elect to receive cash payments under this subsection.

"MULTIPURPOSE SENIOR CENTERS: RECAPTURE OF PAYMENTS

42 USC 3030b.

"SEC. 312. If, within 10 years after acquisition, or within 20 years after the completion of construction, of any facility for which funds have been paid under this title—

"(1) the owner of the facility ceases to be a public or nonprofit private agency or organization; or

"(2) the facility ceases to be used for the purposes for which it was acquired (unless the Commissioner determines, in accordance with regulations, that there is good cause for releasing the applicant or other owner from the obligation to do so);

the United States shall be entitled to recover from the applicant or other owner of the facility an amount which bears to the then value of the facility (or so much thereof as constituted an approved project or projects) the same ratio as the amount of such Federal funds bore to the cost of the facility financed with the aid of such funds. Such value shall be determined by agreement of the parties or by action brought in the United States district court for the district in which such facility is situated.

"AUDIT

42 USC 3030c.

"SEC. 313. The Commissioner and the Comptroller General of the United States or any of their duly authorized representatives shall have access for the purpose of audit and examination to any books, documents, papers, and records that are pertinent to a grant or contract received under this title.

"PART B—SOCIAL SERVICES

"PROGRAM AUTHORIZED

Grant program.
42 USC 3030d.

"SEC. 321. (a) The Commissioner shall carry out a program for making grants to States under State plans approved under section 307 for any of the following social services:

"(1) health, continuing education, welfare, informational, recreational, homemaker, counseling, or referral services;

"(2) transportation services to facilitate access to social services or nutrition services, or both;

"(3) services designed to encourage and assist older individuals to use the facilities and services available to them;

"(4) services designed to assist older individuals to obtain adequate housing, including residential repair and renovation projects designed to enable older individuals to maintain their homes in conformity with minimum housing standards or to adapt homes to meet the needs of older individuals suffering from physical disabilities;

"(5) services designed to assist older individuals in avoiding institutionalization, including preinstitution evaluation and screening and home health services, homemaker services, shopping services, escort services, reader services, letter writing services, and other similar services designed to assist such individuals to continue living independently in a home environment;

"(6) services designed to provide legal services and other counseling services and assistance, including tax counseling and assistance and financial counseling, to older individuals;

"(7) services designed to enable older individuals to attain and maintain physical and mental well-being through programs of regular physical activity and exercise;

"(8) services designed to provide health screening to detect or prevent illness, or both, that occur most frequently in older individuals;

"(9) services designed to provide preretirement and second career counseling for older individuals;

"(10) services of an ombudsman at the State level to receive, investigate, and act on complaints by older individuals who are residents of long-term care facilities and to advocate the well-being of such individuals;

"(11) services which are designed to meet the unique needs of older individuals who are disabled; or

"(12) any other services;

if such services meet standards prescribed by the Commissioner and are necessary for the general welfare of older individuals.

Facilities.

"(b)(1) The Commissioner shall carry out a program for making grants to States under State plans approved under section 307 for the acquisition, alteration, or renovation of existing facilities, including mobile units, and, where appropriate, construction of facilities to serve as multipurpose senior centers which shall be community facilities for the organization and provision of a broad spectrum of services, including provision of health, social, nutritional, and educational services and provision of facilities for recreational activities for older individuals.

Professional and technical personnel, compensation.

"(2) Funds made available to a State under this part may be used, for the purpose of assisting in the operation of multipurpose senior centers, to meet all or part of the costs of compensating professional and technical personnel required for the operation of multipurpose senior centers.

"Part C—Nutrition Services

"Subpart 1—Congregate Nutrition Services

"Program Authorized

Grants.
42 USC 3030e.

"Sec. 331. The Commissioner shall carry out a program for making grants to States under State plans approved under section 307 for the establishment and operation of nutrition projects—

"(1) which, 5 or more days a week, provide at least one hot or other appropriate meal per day and any additional meals which the recipient of a grant or contract under this subpart may elect to provide, each of which assures a minimum of one-third of the daily recommended dietary allowances as established by the Food and Nutrition Board of the National Academy of Sciences-National Research Council;

"(2) which shall be provided in congregate settings; and

"(3) which may include nutrition education services and other appropriate nutrition services for older individuals.

"Subpart 2—Home Delivered Nutrition Services

"Program Authorized

Grants.
42 USC 3030f.

"Sec. 336. The Commissioner shall carry out a program for making grants to States under State plans approved under section 307 for the establishment and operation of nutrition projects for older individuals which, 5 or more days a week, provide at least one home delivered hot, cold, frozen, dried, canned, or supplemental foods (with a satisfactory storage life) meal per day and any additional meals which the recipient of a grant or contract under this subpart may elect to provide, each of which assures a minimum of one-third of the daily recommended dietary allowances as established by the Food and Nutrition Board of the National Academy of Sciences-National Research Council.

"CRITERIA

Efficiency and quality standards. 42 USC 3030g.

"SEC. 337. The Commissioner, in consultation with organizations of and for the aged, blind, and disabled, and with representatives from the American Dietetic Association, the Association of Area Agencies on Aging, the National Association of Title VII Project Directors, the National Association of Meals Programs, Incorporated, and any other appropriate group, shall develop minimum criteria of efficiency and quality for the furnishing of home delivered meal services for projects described in section 336. The criteria required by this section shall take into account the ability of established home delivered meals programs to continue such services without major alteration in the furnishing of such services.".

TRAINING, RESEARCH, AND DISCRETIONARY PROJECTS AND PROGRAMS

42 USC 3031.

SEC. 104. (a)(1) Section 401 is amended to read as follows:

"STATEMENT OF PURPOSE

National manpower policy.

"SEC. 401. (a) The purpose of this part is to develop and implement a national manpower policy for the field of aging. Such a policy shall reflect the present and future needs for training personnel, including personnel involved in advocacy and leadership, in all programs serving the elderly recognizing the unique health, transportation, and housing problems of the elderly, the continual growth of the elderly population of the United States, and the high incidence of disabilities within such population. The national manpower policy established under this part shall require that training programs shall give priority to training personnel responsible for carrying out projects relating to multipurpose senior centers under part B of title III and for carrying out programs under part C of title III.

Ante, p. 1535.
Ante, p. 1536.
Implementation.

"(b) The policy required by this title shall be developed and implemented by the Commissioner in cooperation with other departments and agencies of the Federal Government, including the Public Health Service, the Health Care Financing Administration, the Social Security Administration, the National Institutes of Health, and in particular the National Institute on Aging, the Administration for Public Services, the Rehabilitation Services Administration, the Veterans' Administration, the Department of Labor, the Department of Housing and Urban Development, and the Department of Transportation, State employment agencies, State and area agencies on aging, and other appropriate agencies.".

42 USC 3032.

(2) Section 402 is amended to read as follows:

"APPRAISING PERSONNEL NEEDS IN THE FIELD OF AGING

"SEC. 402. (a) The Commissioner shall, at such times as he deems appropriate and in cooperation with representatives referred to in section 401(b), assess the Nation's existing and future personnel needs in the field of aging, including as part of such assessment, the needs for personnel in both institutional and non-institutional long-term care settings, and evaluate all programs, including institutional and non-institutional long-term care programs, serving the elderly at all levels of government recognizing the continual growth of the elderly population. The assessment required by this section shall be conducted in accordance with the national manpower policy developed under section 401.

Report to Congress.

"(b) The assessment required by this section shall be submitted biennially to the Congress. Each such report shall indicate the impact of the assessment on the national manpower policy and plans for the future.".

42 USC 3033.

(3)(A) Section 403 is amended by striking out "The" and inserting in lieu thereof the following: "In accordance with the requirements set forth in the national manpower policy, the".

42 USC 3033.

(B) Section 403(4) is amended by striking out "to the purposes of this Act" and inserting in lieu thereof "to the field of aging".

42 USC 3034.

(4)(A) Section 404(a) is amended—
(i) by striking out "The" and inserting in lieu thereof the

following: "In accordance with the requirements set forth in the national manpower policy, the"; and

(ii) by striking out "fields related to the purposes of this Act" and inserting in lieu thereof "the field of aging".

(B) Section 404(a)(1) is amended by striking out "purposes of this Act" and inserting in lieu thereof "field of aging".

(C) Section 404(a) is further amended by redesignating clauses (1), (2), (3), (4), (5), and (6) as clauses (2), (3), (4), (5), (6), and (7), respectively, and by inserting after the dash the following new clause:

"(1) to coordinate the training efforts of all programs serving the elderly at the Federal, State, and local levels recognizing the continual growth of the elderly population,".

(D) Section 404(a) is further amended by redesignating clauses (6) and (7), as so redesignated in subparagraph (C), as clauses (8) and (9), respectively, and by inserting after clause (5), as so redesignated in subparagraph (C), the following new clauses:

"(6) to assess future national personnel needs, including the need for training of advocates, with respect to the elderly with special emphasis on the needs of elderly minority group individuals and the need for the training of minority group individuals to meet such needs,

"(7) to assist in paying the costs, in whole or in part, of special courses of training designed to meet the needs of service providers in rural areas,".

42 USC 3035. (b)(1)(A) Section 411 is amended by inserting "(a)" after the section designation.

(B) Section 411(a), as so redesignated in subparagraph (A), is amended by striking out "The" and inserting in lieu thereof "To support research efforts related to the implementation of this Act together with areas of concern relating to the living conditions of the elderly, the".

(2) Section 411 is further amended by adding at the end thereof the following new subsections:

Grants and contracts. "(b) In accordance with the purposes of this part, the Commissioner shall make grants to any public agency or nonprofit private organization or institution and contracts with any agency, organization, or institution or with an individual for the purpose of—

Study. "(1) conducting a study related to the problems experienced by State and area agencies on aging and other service providers in operating transportation services, with particular emphasis on the difficulties of continually rising insurance costs and restrictions being placed upon the operation of such services by insurance underwriters;

"(2) revising existing Federal transportation programs for older individuals to—

"(A) provide more coordinated and comprehensive services to such individuals;

"(B) eliminate unnecessary duplication among such programs;

"(C) eliminate disparities in eligibility requirements among Federal transportation programs for older individuals; and

"(D) study the possibility of transferring to a single administrative unit the responsibility for the administration of all Federal transportation programs for older individuals; and

Study. "(3) conducting a study related to the differences in unit costs, service delivery, and access between rural areas and urban areas for services assisted under this Act and the special needs of the elderly residing in rural areas.

Submittal of study results to Congress. "(c) Upon completion of the studies described in subsection (b), but not later than 2 years after the date of the enactment of the Comprehensive Older Americans Act Amendments of 1978, the Commissioner shall submit to the Congress and make available through the National Information and Resource Clearing House for the Aging the results of the studies, together with such recommendations as he deems necessary.".

Repeal. (3) Section 412 is hereby repealed.

42 USC 3035a.
42 USC 3031.
42 USC 3036, 3037.
42 USC 3036, 3037, 3037a.

(c) (1) Title IV is amended—

(A) by redesignating part C and part E as part D and part F, respectively;

(B) by redesignating sections 421, 431, and 432 of sections 441, 451, and 452, respectively; and

(C) by inserting after part B the following new parts:

"PART C—DISCRETIONARY PROJECTS AND PROGRAMS

"DEMONSTRATION PROJECTS

Grants and contracts.
42 USC 3035b.

"SEC. 421. (a) The Commissioner may, after consultation with the State agency in the State involved, make grants to any public agency or nonprofit private organization or enter into contracts with any agency or organization within such State for paying part or all of the cost of developing or operating nationwide, statewide, regional, metropolitan area, county, city, or community model projects which will demonstrate methods to improve or expand social services or nutrition services or otherwise promote the well-being of older individuals. The Commissioner shall give special consideration to the funding of rural area agencies on aging to conduct model projects devoted to the special needs of the rural elderly. Such projects shall include alternative health care delivery systems, advocacy and outreach programs, and transportation services.

"(b) In making grants and contracts under this section, the Commissioner shall give special consideration to projects designed to—

Housing assistance.

"(1) assist in meeting the special housing needs of older individuals by—

"(A) providing financial assistance to such individuals, who own their own homes, necessary to enable them to make the repairs or renovations to their homes, which are necessary for them to meet minimum standards;

"(B) studying and demonstrating methods of adapting existing housing, or construction of new housing, to meet the needs of older individuals suffering from physical disabilities; and

"(C) demonstrating alternative methods of relieving older individuals of the burden of real property taxes on their homes;

Continuing education.

"(2) provide continuing education to older individuals designed to enable them to lead more productive lives by broadening the educational, cultural, or social awareness of such older individuals, emphasizing, where possible, free tuition arrangements with colleges and universities;

Preretirement education information.

"(3) provide preretirement education information, and relevant services (including the training of personnel to carry out such programs and the conducting of research with respect to the development and operation of such programs) to individuals planning retirement;

Special services.

"(4) provide services to assist in meeting the particular needs of physically and mentally impaired older individuals, including special transportation and escort services, homemaker, home health and shopping services, reader services, letter writing services, and other services designed to assist such individuals in leading more independent lives;

"(5) meet the special needs of, and improve the delivery of services to, older individuals who are not receiving adequate services under other provisions of this Act, with emphasis on the needs of low-income, minority, Indian, and limited English-speaking individuals and the rural elderly;

"(6) assist older individuals to remain within their communities and out of institutions and to maintain their independent living, in their own residences or in a family living arrangement, by—

"(A) providing financial assistance for the establishment and operation of senior ambulatory care day centers (providing a planned schedule of health, therapeutic, education, nutrition, recreational, rehabilitation, and social services at least 24 hours per week, transportation arrangements at low or no cost for participants to and from the center, a mid-day meal, outreach and public information programs, and opportunities for maximum participation of senior participants and senior volunteers in the planning and operation of the center) ; and

"(B) maintaining or initiating arrangements (or providing reasonable assurances that such arrangements will be maintained or initiated) with any agency of the State involved which administers or supervises the administration of a State plan approved under titles XIX and XX of the Social Security Act, and with other appropriate social services agencies receiving, or reimbursed through, Federal financial assistance, for the payment of all or a part of the center's costs in providing services to eligible individuals;

Rural areas. "(7) meet the special needs of older individuals residing in rural areas; or

"(8) develop or improve methods of coordinating all available social services for the homebound elderly, blind, and disabled by establishing demonstration projects in 10 States, in accordance with subsection (c).

Procedures. "(c)(1) The Commissioner shall consult with the Commissioner of the Rehabilitation Services Administration, the Commissioner of the Social Security Administration, and the Surgeon General of the Public Health Service, to develop procedures for—

"(A) identifying elderly, blind, and disabled individuals who need social services;

"(B) compiling a list in each community of all services available to the elderly, blind, and disabled; and

"(C) establishing an information and referral service within the appropriate community agency to—

"(i) inform those in need of the availability of such services; and

"(ii) coordinate the delivery of such services to the elderly, blind, and disabled.

The Commissioner shall establish procedures for administering demonstration projects under subsection (b)(8) no later than 6 months after the effective date of this subsection. The Commissioner shall **Report to Congress.** report to the Congress with respect to the results and findings of the demonstration projects at the end of fiscal year 1979. In such report, the Commissioner shall make such recommendation, based upon the findings, as may be appropriate to improve the delivery of social services to such elderly, blind, and disabled individuals.

Appropriation authorization. "(2)(A) There are authorized to be appropriated for fiscal years 1979, 1980, and 1981, such sums as may be necessary for the purpose of implementing the demonstration projects under subsection (b)(8).

"(B) For the purpose of carrying out this subsection, there are authorized to be appropriated such sums as may be necessary for fiscal year 1979.

"SPECIAL PROJECTS IN COMPREHENSIVE LONG-TERM CARE

Grants.
42 USC 3035c. "SEC. 422. (a)(1) The Commissioner may make grants to selected State agencies designated under section 305(a)(1), and, in consultation with State agencies, selected area agencies on aging designated under section 305(a)(2)(A), institutions of higher education, and other public agencies and private nonprofit organizations, associations, and groups to support the development of comprehensive, coordinated systems of community long-term care for older individuals, with special emphasis upon—

"(A) services designed to support alternatives to institutional living; and

"(B) the assessment of need, the development of a plan of care, and the referral of individuals, in the delivery of long-term care services, including non-institutional and institutional services, where appropriate.

"(2) A grant under this section may be made to pay part or all of the estimated cost of a program (including start-up cost) for a period of not more than 3 years, except that no funds may be used to pay for direct services which are eligible for reimbursement under title XVIII, title XIX, or title XX of the Social Security Act.

42 USC 1395, 1396, 1397.

"(3) A grant made under this section shall be used for the development of programs which provide a full continuum of services. Such services may include—

"(A) adult day health;

"(B) monitoring and evaluation of service effectiveness;

"(C) supported living in public and private nonprofit housing;

"(D) family respite services;

"(E) preventive health services;

"(F) home health, homemaker, and other rehabilitative and maintenance in-home services;

"(G) geriatric health maintenance organizations; and

"(H) other services which the Commissioner determines are appropriate, which were previously unavailable to the individuals to be served and which, at a minimum, provide for identification and assessment of the long-term care needs of older individuals, referral of such individuals to the appropriate services, and follow-up and evaluation of the continued appropriateness of such services with provision for re-referral as appropriate.

"(4) A grant under this section may be used to encourage the development of manpower training programs designed to further the purposes described in paragraph (3).

"(b)(1) In making grants to States under this section preference shall be given to applicants which demonstrate that—

"(A) adequate State standards have been developed to ensure the quality of services provided;

"(B) the State has made a commitment to carry out the program assisted under this section with the State agency responsible for the administration of title XIX of the Social Security Act or title XX of the Social Security Act, or both such agencies;

"(C) the State will develop plans to finance the comprehensive program assisted under this section; and

"(D) the State agency has a plan for statewide or designated regions of the State containing provisions designed to maximize access to older individuals for long-term care services.

Preference of applicants.

"(2) In awarding grants to agencies and organizations under this section, preference shall be given to applicants that—

"(A) possess the capability to establish community-based long-term care programs; and

"(B) demonstrate that a need exists for the establishment of such programs in the area to be served.

Program evaluation procedures.

"(3) Agencies and organizations assisted under this section shall establish procedures for evaluating the program assisted under this section, with respect to the benefits accruing to persons receiving assistance, the feasibility of the administrative model used for comprehensive coordination of services including coordination with other local programs, and the comparative costs and quality of services provided, and shall submit such evaluation to the Commissioner on a periodic basis.

Report to Congress.

"(c) The Secretary shall involve appropriate Federal departments and agencies in carrying out the provisions of this section in order to assure coordination at the Federal level and to avoid duplication and shall report to the Congress annually on the impact of grants made, on the experiences of grantees in meeting the requirements of this section, and on the comparative benefits and costs of projects assisted under this section.

"(d) Sums appropriated to carry out this section shall, to the extent feasible, be used to support programs equitably distributed throughout the Nation between urban and rural areas.

"SPECIAL DEMONSTRATION PROJECTS ON LEGAL SERVICES FOR OLDER AMERICANS

42 USC 3035d.

"SEC. 423. (a) The Commissioner may make grants to and enter into contracts with public and private nonprofit agencies or organizations in order to—

utilization, preretirement and retirement, and long-term care and alternatives)".

(2) Section 441(1)(A), as so redesignated in subsection (c)(1), is amended by inserting before the comma the following: "in accordance with the national manpower policy as described in section 401".

(3) Section 441, as so redesignated in subsection (c)(1), is amended by striking out "and" at the end of clause (2), by striking out the period at the end of clause (3) and inserting in lieu thereof a semicolon and "and", and by adding at the end thereof the following new clause:

"(4) provides for making biennial reports to the Commissioner summarizing the training, research, and special demonstration efforts of the centers which shall then be made available through the National Information and Resource Clearing House for the Aging, where appropriate.".

42 USC 3037.

(e)(1) Section 451, as so redesignated in subsection (c)(1)(B), is amended to read as follows:

"AUTHORIZATION OF APPROPRIATIONS

"SEC. 451. (a) Except as otherwise specifically provided in this title, there are authorized to be appropriated to carry out the provisions of this title such sums as may be necessary for each fiscal year ending prior to October 1, 1981.

"(b) No funds appropriated under this section—

"(1) may be transferred to any office or other authority of the Department of Health, Education, and Welfare which is not directly responsible to the Commissioner; or

"(2) may be used for any research program or activity which is not specifically authorized by this title.".

42 USC 3037a.

(2) Section 452, as so redesignated in subsection (c)(1), is amended by redesignating subsection (c) as subsection (d) and inserting after subsection (b) the following new subsection:

Grants and contracts.

"(c) The Commissioner may make multicategorical grants or contracts under any or all sections of this title by making grants or contracts for the purpose of supporting extensive research and demonstration of particular areas of need.".

COMMUNITY SERVICE EMPLOYMENT

42 USC 3056.
42 USC 3056–3056f, 3001 note.

SEC. 105. (a) The Act is amended by redesignating title IX as title V, and by redesignating section 901 through section 908 as section 501 through section 508, respectively.

(b)(1) Section 502(b) is amended by adding at the end thereof the following new paragraphs:

"(3) The Secretary shall develop alternatives for innovative work modes and provide technical assistance in creating job opportunities through work sharing and other experimental methods to prime sponsors, labor organizations, groups representing business and industry and workers as well as to individual employers, where appropriate.

Senior Environmental Employment Agency.
42 USC 3056.
Review.

"(4) The Secretary may enter into an agreement with the Administrator of the Environmental Protection Agency to establish a Senior Environmental Employment Corps.".

(2) Section 502, as so redesignated in subsection (a), is amended by adding at the end thereof the following new subsections:

"(d)(1) Whenever a national organization or other program sponsor conducts a project within a State such organization or program sponsor shall submit to the State agency on aging a description of such project to be conducted in the State, including the location of the project, 30 days prior to undertaking the project, for review and comment according to guidelines the Secretary shall issue to assure efficient and effective coordination of programs under this title.

Notice and opportunity for hearing.

"(2) The Secretary shall review on his own initiative or at the request of any public or private nonprofit agency or organization, or an agency of the State government, the distribution of programs under this title within the State including the distribution between urban and rural areas within the State. For each proposed reallocation of programs within a State, the Secretary shall give notice and

"(1) support legal research, technical assistance, training, information dissemination, and other support activities to agencies, organizations, institutions, and private law firms that are providing, developing, or supporting pro bono or reduced-fee legal services to older individuals; and

"(2) support demonstration projects to expand or improve the delivery of legal services to older individuals with social or economic need.

"(b) Any grants or contracts entered into under subsection (a)(2) shall contain assurances that the requirements of section 307(a)(15) are met.

"(c) From the sums appropriated under section 451 for each fiscal year, not less than $5,000,000 shall be reserved to carry out the provisions of this section.

"NATIONAL IMPACT DEMONSTRATIONS

42 USC 3035e.

"SEC. 424. (a) The Commissioner may carry out directly or through grants or contracts—

"(1) innovation and development projects and activities of national significance which show promise of having substantial impact on the expansion or improvement of social services, nutrition services, or multipurpose senior centers or otherwise promoting the well-being of older individuals; and

"(2) dissemination of information activities related to such programs.

"(b) An amount not to exceed 15 percent of any sums appropriated under section 451 may be used for carrying out this section.

"UTILITY AND HOME HEATING COST DEMONSTRATION PROJECTS

42 USC 3035f.

"SEC. 425. The Secretary may, after consultation with the appropriate State agency designated under section 305(a)(1), make grants to pay for part or all of the costs of developing model projects which show promise of relieving older individuals of the excessive burdens of high utility service and home heating costs. Any such project shall give special consideration to projects under which a business concern engaged in providing home heating oil to the public, or a public utility, provides home heating oil or utility services to low-income older individuals at a cost which is substantially lower than providing home heating oil or utility services to other individuals.

"PART D—MORTGAGE INSURANCE AND INTEREST GRANTS FOR MULTIPURPOSE SENIOR CENTERS

"MORTGAGE INSURANCE AUTHORIZED

42 USC 3035g.

"SEC. 431. (a) It is the purpose of this part to assist and encourage the provision of urgently needed facilities for programs for the elderly.

"(b) For the purpose of this part the terms 'mortgage', 'mortgagor', 'mortgagee', 'maturity date', and 'State' shall have the meanings respectively set forth in section 207 of the National Housing Act.

"(c) The Secretary of Health, Education, and Welfare is authorized to insure any mortgage (including advances on such mortgage during acquisition, alteration, renovation, or construction) in accordance with the provisions of this section upon such terms and conditions as he may prescribe and make commitments for insurance of such mortgage prior to the date of its execution or disbursement thereon.

"(d) In order to carry out the purpose of this section, the Secretary is authorized to insure any mortgage which covers a new multipurpose senior center, including equipment to be used in its operation, subject to the following conditions:

"(1) The mortgage shall be executed by a mortgagor, approved by the Secretary, who demonstrates ability successfully to operate one or more programs for the elderly. The Secretary may in his discretion require any such mortgagor to be regulated or restricted as to minimum charges and methods of financing, and in addition thereto, if the mortgagor is a corporate entity, as to capital structure and rate of return. As an aid to the regulation or restriction of any mortgagor with respect to any of the foregoing matters, the Secretary may make such contracts with and acquire for not to exceed $100 such stock interest in such mortgagor as he may deem necessary. Any stock or interest so purchased shall be paid for out of the Multipurpose Senior Center Insurance Fund, and shall be redeemed by the mortgagor at par upon the termination of all obligations of the Secretary under the insurance.

"(2) The mortgage shall involve a principal obligation in an amount not to exceed $250,000 and not to exceed 90 percent of the estimated replacement cost of the property or project, including equipment to be used in the operation of the multipurpose senior center, when the proposed improvements are completed and the equipment is installed.

"(3) The mortgage shall—

"(A) provide for complete amortization by periodic payments within such term as the Secretary shall prescribe, and

"(B) bear interest (exclusive of premium charges for insurance and service charges, if any) at not to exceed such per centum per annum on the principal obligation outstanding at any time as the Secretary finds necessary to meet the mortgage market.

"(4) The Secretary shall not insure any mortgage under this section unless he has determined that the center to be covered by the mortgage will be in compliance with minimum standards to be prescribed by the Secretary.

"(5) In the plans for such multipurpose senior center, due consideration shall be given to excellence of architecture and design, and to the inclusion of works of art (not representing more than 1 percent of the cost of the project).

Mortgage insurance premium charges. "(e) The Secretary shall fix and collect premium charges for the insurance of mortgages under this section which shall be payable annually in advance by the mortgagee, either in cash or in debentures of the Multipurpose Senior Center Insurance Fund issued at par plus accrued interest. In the case of any mortgage such charge shall not be less than an amount equivalent to one-fourth of 1 percent per annum nor more than an amount equivalent to 1 percent per annum of the amount of the principal obligation of the mortgage outstanding at any one time, without taking into account delinquent payments or prepayments. In addition to the premium charge provided for in this subsection, the Secretary is authorized to charge and collect such amounts as he may deem reasonable for the appraisal of a property or project during acquisition, alteration, or renovation; but such charges for appraisal and inspection shall not aggregate more than 1 percent of the original principal face amount of the mortgage.

"(f) The Secretary may consent to the release of a part or parts of the mortgaged property or project from the lien of any mortgage insured under this section upon such terms and conditions as he may prescribe.

"(g)(1) The Secretary shall have the same functions, powers, and duties (insofar as applicable) with respect to the insurance of mortgages under this section as the Secretary of Housing and Urban Development has with respect to the insurance of mortgages under title II of the National Housing Act.

12 USC 1707.

12 USC 1713. "(2) The provisions of subsections (e), (g), (h), (i), (j), (k), (l), and (n) of section 207 of the National Housing Act shall apply to mortgages insured under this section; except that, for the purposes of their application with respect to such mortgages, all references in such provisions to the General Insurance Fund shall be deemed to refer to the Multipurpose Senior Center Insurance Fund, and all references in such provisions to 'Secretary' shall be deemed to refer to the Secretary of Health, Education, and Welfare.

Multipurpose Senior Center Insurance Fund. "(h)(1) There is hereby created a Multipurpose Senior Center Insurance Fund which shall be used by the Secretary as a revolving fund for carrying out all the insurance provisions of this section. All mortgages insured under this section shall be insured under and be the obligation of the Multipurpose Senior Center Insurance Fund.

"(2) The general expenses of the operations of the Department of

Health, Education, and Welfare relating to mortgages insured under this section may be charged to the Multipurpose Senior Center Insurance Fund.

"(3) Moneys in the Multipurpose Senior Center Insurance Fund not needed for the current operations of the Department of Health, Education, and Welfare with respect to mortgages insured under this section shall be deposited with the Treasurer of the United States to the credit of such fund, or invested in bonds or other obligations of, or in bonds or other obligations guaranteed as to principal and interest by, the United States. The Secretary may, with the approval of the Secretary of the Treasury, purchase in the open market debentures issued as obligations of the Multipurpose Senior Center Insurance Fund. Such purchases shall be made at a price which will provide an investment yield of not less than the yield obtainable from other investments authorized by this section. Debentures so purchased shall be canceled and not reissued.

"(4) Premium charges, adjusted premium charges, and appraisal and other fees received on account of the insurance of any mortgage under this section, the receipts derived from property covered by such mortgages and from any claims, debts, contracts, property, and security assigned to the Secretary in connection therewith, and all earnings as the assets of the fund, shall be credited to the Multipurpose Senior Center Insurance Fund. The principal of, and interest paid and to be paid on, debentures which are the obligation of such fund, cash insurance payments and adjustments, and expenses incurred in the handling, management, renovation, and disposal of properties acquired or constructed in connection with mortgages insured under this section, shall be charged to such fund.

"(5) There are authorized to be appropriated to provide initial capital for the Multipurpose Senior Center Insurance Fund, and to assure the soundness of such fund thereafter, such sums as may be necessary.

"ANNUAL INTEREST GRANTS

42 USC 3035h.

"SEC. 432. (a) To assist nonprofit private agencies to reduce the cost of borrowing from other sources for the acquisition, alteration, renovation, or construction of facilities for multipurpose senior centers, the Secretary may make annual interest grants to such agencies.

"(b) Annual interest grants under this section with respect to any facility shall be made over a fixed period not exceeding forty years, and provision for such grants shall be embodied in a contract guaranteeing their payment over such period. Each such grant shall be in an amount not greater than the difference between (1) the average annual debt service which would be required to be paid, during the life of the loan, on the amount borrowed from other sources for the acquisition, alteration, renovation, or construction of such facilities, and (2) the average annual debt service which the institution would have been required to pay, during the life of the loan, with respect to such amounts if the applicable interest rate were 3 percent per annum, except that the amount on which such grant is based shall be approved by the Secretary.

"(c)(1) There are hereby authorized to be appropriated to the Secretary such sums as may be necessary for payment of annual interest grants in accordance with this section.

Limitation.

"(2) Contracts for annual interest grants under this section shall not be entered into in an aggregate amount greater than is authorized in appropriation Acts.

Limitation.

"(d) Not more than 12½ per centum of the funds provided for in this section for grants may be used within any one State.".

(2) The heading of title IV is amended to read as follows:

"TITLE IV—TRAINING, RESEARCH, AND DISCRETIONARY PROJECTS AND PROGRAMS".

42 USC 3036.

(d)(1) The first sentence of section 441, as so redesignated in subsection (c)(1), is amended by inserting before the period a comma and the following: "and gerontology centers of special emphasis (including health, income maintenance, housing, service delivery and opportunity for a hearing on the record by all interested individuals and make a written determination of his findings and decision.

"(e) The Secretary, in addition to any other authority contained in this title, may enter into agreements designed to assure the transition of individuals employed in public service jobs under this title to employment opportunities with private business concerns. The Secretary, from amounts reserved under section 506(a)(1)(B) in any fiscal year, may pay all of the costs of any agreement entered into under the provisions of this subsection.".

42 USC 3056d.

(c)(1) Section 503(a), as so redesignated in subsection (a), is amended by striking out "304" each place it appears therein and inserting in lieu thereof "305".

42 USC 3056a.

42 USC 3056a.

(3) Section 503, as so redesignated in subsection (a), is amended by adding at the end thereof the following new subsection:

"(f) In carrying out the provisions of this title, the Secretary may fund and expand projects concerning the Senior Environmental Employment Corps and energy conservation from sums appropriated under section 508 for such fiscal year.".

42 USC 3056f.
42 USC 3056c.

(d) Section 505, as so redesignated in subsection (a), is amended by adding at the end thereof the following new subsection:

"(c) In administering projects under this title concerning the Senior Environmental Employment Corps and energy conservation, the Secretary shall consult with the Administrator of the Environmental Protection Agency and the Secretary of Energy and shall enter into an agreement with the Administrator and the Secretary of Energy to coordinate programs conducted by them with such projects.".

42 USC 3056d.

(e)(1) Section 506(a)(1), as so redesignated in subsection (a), is amended—

(A) by inserting "(A)" after "(1)" and by adding at the end thereof the following new subparagraph:

"(B) From sums appropriated under this title for each fiscal year after September 30, 1978, the Secretary may reserve an amount not to exceed one per centum of the amount appropriated in excess of the amount appropriated for fiscal year 1978 for the purpose of entering into agreements under section 502(e), relating to improved transition to private employment.";

(B) by striking out "From" and inserting in lieu thereof "Subject to the provisions of paragraph (2), from"; and

(C) by striking out "the fiscal year ending June 30, 1975" and inserting in lieu thereof "fiscal year 1978".

(2) Section 506(a), as so redesignated in subsection (a), is amended by redesignating paragraph (2) and paragraph (3) as paragraph (3) and paragraph (4), respectively, and by inserting after paragraph (1) the following new paragraph:

"(2) For each fiscal year in which the sums appropriated under this title exceed the amount appropriated for fiscal year 1978, the Secretary shall reserve not more than 45 per centum of such excess amount for the purpose described in paragraph (1). The remainder of such excess shall be allotted pursuant to paragraph (3).".

(3) Section 506(a)(3), as so redesignated in subsection (a) and in paragraph (2), is amended by striking out "908" and inserting in lieu thereof "508".

42 USC 3056e.

(f) Section 507(2), as so redesignated in subsection (a), is amended by inserting "(including any such individual whose income is not more than 125 per centum of the poverty guidelines established by the Bureau of Labor Statistics)" after "low income".

(g) Section 508, as so redesignated in subsection (a), is amended by striking out "and" the second place it appears therein, and by inserting before the period at the end thereof the following: ", $350,000,000 for the fiscal year ending September 30, 1979, $400,000,000 for the fiscal year ending September 30, 1980, and $450,000,000 for the fiscal year ending September 30, 1981".

GRANTS FOR INDIAN TRIBES

SEC. 106. The Act is amended by adding after title V the following new title:

"TITLE VI—GRANTS FOR INDIAN TRIBES

"STATEMENT OF PURPOSE

42 USC 3057.

Ante, p. 1517.

"SEC. 601. It is the purpose of this title to promote the delivery of social services, including nutritional services, for Indians that are comparable to services provided under title III.

"ELIGIBILITY

42 USC 3057a.

"SEC. 602. (a) A tribal organization of an Indian tribe is eligible for assistance under this title only if—

"(1) the tribal organization represents at least 75 individuals who have attained 60 years of age or older;

"(2) the tribal organization demonstrates the ability to deliver social services, including nutritional services; and

"(3) individuals to be served by the tribal organization will not receive for the year for which application under this title is made, services under title III.

"(b) The terms 'Indian tribe' and 'tribal organization' for the purposes of this title are defined as in section 4 of the Indian Self-Determination and Education Assistance Act (25 U.S.C. 450b).

"GRANTS AUTHORIZED

42 USC 3057b.

"SEC. 603. The Commissioner may make grants to eligible tribal organizations to pay all of the costs for delivery of social services and nutritional services for Indians who are aged 60 and older.

"APPLICATIONS

Approval criteria.
42 USC 3057c.

"SEC. 604. (a) No grant may be made under this title unless the eligible tribal organization submits an application to the Commissioner which meets such criteria as the Commissioner may by regulation prescribe. Each such application shall—

"(1) provide that the eligible tribal organization will evaluate the need for social and nutritional services among older Indians to be represented by the tribal organization;

"(2) provide for the use of such methods of administration as are necessary for the proper and efficient administration of the program to be assisted;

"(3) provide that the tribal organization will make such reports in such form and containing such information, as the Commissioner may reasonably require, and comply with such requirements as the Commissioner may impose to assure the correctness of such reports;

"(4) provide that a nonprofit private organization selected by the tribal organization will conduct periodic evaluation of activities and projects carried out under the application;

"(5) establish objectives consistent with the purposes of this title toward which activities under the application will be directed, identify obstacles to the attainment of such objectives, and indicate the manner in which the tribal organization proposes to overcome such obstacles;

"(6) provide for establishing and maintaining information and referral services to assure that older Indians to be served by the assistance made available under this title will have reasonably convenient access to such services;

"(7) provide a preference for Indians aged 60 and older for full- or part-time staff positions wherever feasible;

"(8) provide assurances that either directly or by way of grant or contract with appropriate entities nutritional services will be delivered to older Indians represented by the tribal organization substantially in compliance with the provisions of part C of title III;

Ante, p. 1536.

Ante, p. 1524.

"(9) contain assurances that the provisions of sections 307 (a)(14)(A)(i) and (iii), 307(a)(14)(B), and 307(a)(14)(C) will be complied with whenever the application contains provisions for the acquisition, alteration, or renovation of facilities to serve as multipurpose senior centers;

"(10) provide assurances that either directly or by way of grant or contract with appropriate entities legal and ombudsman services will be made available to older Indians represented by the tribal organization substantially in compliance with the provisions of title III relating to the furnishing of similar services; and

Ante, p. 1517.

"(11) provide satisfactory assurance that fiscal control and fund accounting procedures will be adopted as may be necessary to assure proper disbursement of, and accounting for, Federal funds paid under this title to the tribal organization, including any funds paid by the tribal organization to a recipient of a grant or contract.

Population statistics development.

"(b) For the purpose of any application submitted under this title, the tribal organization may develop its own population statistics, with certification from the Bureau of Indian Affairs, in order to establish eligibility.

"(c) The Commissioner shall approve any application which complies with the provisions of subsection (a).

Ante, p. 1519.

"(d) Whenever the Commissioner approves an application under this title he shall withhold from the allotment of the appropriate State made under section 304 an amount attributable to the Indians to be served under the application who were also counted for the purpose of allotments under title III. The Commissioner shall reallot sums withheld under this subsection in accordance with the provisions of section 304(b).

"(e) Whenever the Commissioner determines not to approve an application submitted under subsection (a) he shall—

"(1) state his objections in writing to the tribal organization within 60 days after such decision;

"(2) provide to the extent practicable technical assistance to the tribal organization to overcome his stated objections; and

"(3) provide the tribal organization with a hearing, under such rules and regulations as he may prescribe.

"(f) Whenever the Commissioner approves an application of a tribal organization under this title, funds shall be awarded for not less than 12 months, during which time such tribal organization may not receive funds under title III.

"ADMINISTRATION

42 USC 3057d.

"SEC. 605. (a) In establishing regulations for the purpose of this title the Commissioner shall consult with the Secretary of the Interior.

Regulations.

"(b) The Commissioner shall prescribe final regulations for the administration of this title not later than 90 days after the date of the enactment of the Comprehensive Older Americans Act Amendments of 1978.

"SURPLUS EDUCATIONAL FACILITIES

Available for use as multipurpose senior centers. 42 USC 3057e.

"SEC. 606. (a) Notwithstanding any other provision of law, the Secretary of the Interior through the Bureau of Indian Affairs shall make available surplus Indian educational facilities to tribal organizations, and nonprofit organizations with tribal approval, for use as multipurpose senior centers. Such centers may be altered so as to provide extended care facilities, community center facilities, nutritional services, child care services, and other social services.

"(b) Each eligible tribal organization desiring to take advantage of such surplus facilities shall submit an application to the Secretary of the Interior at such time and in such manner, and containing or accompanied by such information, as the Secretary of the Interior determines to be necessary to carry out the provisions of this section.

"PAYMENTS

42 USC 3057f.

"SEC. 607. Payments may be made under this title (after necessary adjustments, in the case of grants, on account of previously made overpayments or underpayments) in advance or by way of reimbursement in such installments and on such conditions, as the Commissioner may determine.

"AUTHORIZATION OF APPROPRIATIONS

42 USC 3057g.

"SEC. 608. (a) Except as provided in subsection (c), there are authorized to be appropriated such sums as may be necessary for fiscal years 1979, 1980, and 1981, to carry out the provisions of this title.

"(b) For any fiscal year in which less than $5,000,000 is appropriated under subsection (a) tribal organizations are authorized to receive assistance in accordance with the provisions of title III.

Ante, p. 1517.

"(c) There are authorized to be appropriated such sums as may be necessary for fiscal years 1979, 1980, and 1981, to carry out the provisions of section 606.".

1981 White House Conference on Aging Act.

TITLE II—WHITE HOUSE CONFERENCE ON AGING

SHORT TITLE

42 USC 3001 note.

SEC. 201. This title may be cited as the "1981 White House Conference on Aging Act".

FINDINGS AND POLICY

42 USC 3001 note.

SEC. 202. (a) The Congress finds that—

(1) the number of individuals fifty-five years of age or older was approximately 43,000,000 in 1976, and will, by the end of this century, be over 57,000,000;

(2) nearly 5,200,000 individuals fifty-five years of age or older had incomes below the poverty level in 1976, as determined by the Federal Government;

(3) there is a great need to improve the economic well-being of older individuals;

(4) there is a great need to make comprehensive and quality health care more readily available to older individuals;

(5) there is a great need for expanding the availability of suitable and reasonably priced housing for older individuals, together with services needed for independent or semi-independent living;

(6) there is a great need for a more comprehensive and effective social service delivery system for older individuals;

(7) there is a great need for a more comprehensive long-term care policy responsive to the needs of older patients and their families;

(8) there is a great need to promote greater employment opportunities for middle-aged and older individuals who want or need to work;

(9) there is a great need to develop a national retirement policy that contributes to the fulfillment, dignity, and satisfaction of retirement years for older individuals;

(10) there is a great need for a national policy with respect to increasing, coordinating, and expediting biomedical and other appropriate research directed at determining the causes of the aging process; and

(11) false stereotypes about aging and the process of aging are prevalent throughout the Nation and policies should be developed to overcome such stereotypes.

(b)(1) It is the policy of the Congress that the Federal Government should work jointly with the States and their citizens to develop recommendations and plans for action to meet the challenges and needs of older individuals, consistent with the objectives of this title.

(2) In developing programs for the aging pursuant to this title, emphasis should be placed upon the right and obligation of older individuals to free choice and self-help in planning their own futures.

AUTHORITY OF THE PRESIDENT AND SECRETARY; FINAL REPORT

White House Conference on Aging, 1981. 42 USC 3001 note.

SEC. 203. (a) The President may call a White House Conference on Aging in 1981 in order to develop recommendations for further research and action in the field of aging which will further the policies set forth in section 202. The Conference shall be planned and conducted under the direction of the Secretary in cooperation with the Commissioner on Aging and the Director of the National Institute on Aging, and the heads of such other Federal departments and agencies as are appropriate. Such assistance may include the assignment of personnel.

(b) For the purpose of arriving at facts and recommendations concerning the utilization of skills, experience, and energies and the improvement of the conditions of older individuals, the Conference shall bring together representatives of Federal, State, and local governments, professional and lay people who are working in the field of aging (including researchers on problems of the elderly and the process of aging), and representatives of the general public, including older individuals.

Report to President.

(c) A final report of the Conference, which shall include a statement of a comprehensive coherent national policy on aging together with recommendations for the implementation of the policy, shall be submitted to the President not later than 180 days following the date on which the Conference is adjourned. The findings and recommendations included in the report shall be immediately available to the public. The Secretary shall, within 90 days after submission of the report, transmit to the President and to the Congress his recommendations for administrative action and the legislation necessary to implement the recommendations contained in the report.

Report to President and Congress.

ADMINISTRATION

42 USC 3001 note.

SEC. 204. (a) In administering this title the Secretary shall—

(1) request the cooperation and assistance of the heads of such other Federal departments and agencies as may be appropriate in carrying out the provisions of this title;

(2) render all reasonable assistance, including financial assistance, to State agencies on the aging and to area agencies on aging, and to other appropriate organizations to enable them to organize and conduct conferences on aging prior to the Conference;

(3) prepare and make available background materials for the use of delegates to the Conference which he deems necessary, and prepare and distribute any such report of the Conference as may be necessary and appropriate; and

(4) engage such additional personnel as may be necessary to carry out the provisions of this title without regard to the provisions of title 5, United States Code, governing appointments in the competitive service, and without regard to chapter 51 and subchapter III of chapter 53 of such title relating to classification and General Schedule pay rates.

5 USC 5101 *et seq.*, 5331.

(b) In carrying out his functions under clause (2) of subsection (a) the Secretary shall assure that conferences will be so conducted as to assure broad participation of older individuals.

(c) In carrying out his responsibilities under this title the Secretary shall assure that current and adequate statistical data and other information on the well-being of older individuals in the United States are readily available, in advance of the Conference, to participants in the Conference, together with such information as may be necessary to evaluate Federal programs and policies relating to aging. In carrying out the requirements of this subsection the Secretary may make grants to, and enter into contracts with, public agencies and nonprofit private organizations.

Statistics and information availability.

Grants and contracts.

ADVISORY COMMITTEES

Establishment. 42 USC 3001 note.

SEC. 205. (a) The Secretary shall establish an advisory committee to the Conference which shall include representation from the Federal Council on Aging and other public agencies and private nonprofit organizations as appropriate. The Secretary shall establish such other committees, including technical committees, as may be necessary to assist in planning, conducting, and reviewing the Conference. Each such committee shall be composed of professional and public members and shall include individuals from low-income families and from minority groups. A majority of the public members of each such committee shall be 55 years of age or older.

Membership.

(b) Appointed members of any such committee (other than any officers or employees of the Federal Government), while attending conferences or meetings of the committee or otherwise serving at the

Compensation.

request of the Secretary, shall be entitled to receive compensation at a rate to be fixed by the Secretary but not to exceed the daily rate prescribed for GS–18 under section 5332 of title 5, United States Code (including travel time). While away from their homes or regular places of business, such members may be allowed travel expenses, including per diem in lieu of subsistence, as authorized under section 5703 of such title for persons in Federal Government service employed intermittently.

5 USC 5703.

DEFINITIONS

42 USC 3001 note.
Ante, p. 1520.

SEC. 206. For the purpose of this title—

(1) The term "area agency on aging" means the agency designated under section 305(a)(2)(A) of the Older Americans Act of 1965.

(2) The term "State agency on aging" means the agency designated under 305(a)(1) of the Older Americans Act of 1965.

(3) The term "Secretary" means the Secretary of Health, Education, and Welfare.

(4) The term "Conference" means the White House Conference on Aging authorized in section 203(a).

(5) The term "State" includes the District of Columbia, the Commonwealth of Puerto Rico, Guam, American Samoa, the Virgin Islands, the Trust Territory of the Pacific Islands, and the Northern Mariana Islands.

AUTHORIZATION OF APPROPRIATIONS

42 USC 3001 note.

SEC. 207. There are authorized to be appropriated such sums as may be necessary, for fiscal years 1979, 1980, and 1981, to carry out the provisions of this title.

TITLE III—STUDY OF RACIAL AND ETHNIC DISCRIMINATION IN PROGRAMS FOR OLDER AMERICANS

STUDY AUTHORIZED

42 USC 1975c note.

SEC. 301. (a) The Commission on Civil Rights shall (1) undertake a comprehensive study of discrimination based on race or ethnic background in any federally-assisted programs and activities which affect older individuals; and (2) identify with particularity any such federally-assisted program or activity in which evidence is found of individuals or organizations who are otherwise qualified being, on the basis of race or ethnic background, excluded from participation in, denied the benefits of, refused employment or contracts with, or subject to discrimination under, such program or activity.

Hearings.

(b) As part of the study required by this section, the Commission shall conduct public hearings to elicit the views of interested parties, including the heads of Federal departments and agencies, on issues relating to racial or ethnic discrimination in programs and activities affecting older individuals receiving Federal financial assistance, and particularly with respect to discrimination among potential participants in, or beneficiaries of, specific federally-assisted programs.

ADMINISTRATIVE PROVISIONS

Independently prepared analyses, research and studies.
42 USC 1975c note.

Voluntary or uncompensated personnel, utilization.
42 USC 1975d.

SEC. 302. (a)(1) The Commission may obtain, through grant or contract, analyses, research, and studies by independent experts of issues relating to racial and ethnic discrimination in aging programs and activities and publish the results thereof.

(2) For purposes of the study required by section 301, the Commission may accept and utilize the services of voluntary or uncompensated personnel, without regard to the provisions of section 105(b) of the Civil Rights Act of 1957 (42 U.S.C. 1975(b)).

(b) The head of each Federal department or agency shall cooperate in all respects with the Commission with respect to the study required by section 301, and shall provide to the Commission such data, reports, and documents in connection with the subject matter of such study as the Commission may request.

REPORTS

42 USC 1975c
note.

SEC. 303. (a) Not later than 18 months after the date of the enactment of this Act, the Commission shall transmit a report of its findings and its recommendations for any statutory changes and administrative action, including suggested general regulations, to the Congress and to the President. The Commission shall provide a copy of its report to the head of each Federal department or agency with respect to which the Commission makes findings or recommendations.

(b) Not later than 45 working days after receiving a copy of the report required by subsection (a), the head of each Federal department or agency with respect to which the Commission makes its recommendations or findings shall submit his comments and recommendations regarding such report to the President and to the appropriate committees of the Congress.

AUTHORIZATION OF APPROPRIATIONS

42 USC 1975c
note.

SEC. 304. There are authorized to be appropriated such sums as may be necessary to carry out the provisions of this title.

TITLE IV—AMENDMENTS TO OTHER LAWS

AMENDMENTS TO AGE DISCRIMINATION ACT OF 1975

42 USC 6101.

SEC. 401. (a) Section 302 of the Age Discrimination Act of 1975 is amended by striking out "unreasonable".

(b) (1) The last sentence of section 304(a) (4) of the Age Discrimination Act of 1975 is amended to read as follows: "Such regulations shall be consistent with the final general regulations issued by the Secretary, and shall not become effective until approved by the Secretary.".

42 USC 6103.

(2) Section 304(a) (5) of the Age Discrimination Act of 1975 is amended by striking out "January 1, 1979" and inserting in lieu thereof "July 1, 1979".

42 USC 6104.

(c) Section 305 of the Age Discrimination Act of 1975 is amended by striking out subsection (e) and inserting in lieu thereof the following new subsections:

Notice of
violations.

"(e) (1) When any interested person brings an action in any United States district court for the district in which the defendant is found or transacts business to enjoin a violation of this Act by any program or activity receiving Federal financial assistance, such interested person shall give notice by registered mail not less than 30 days prior to the commencement of that action to the Secretary of Health, Education, and Welfare, the Attorney General of the United States, and the person against whom the action is directed. Such interested person may elect, by a demand for such relief in his complaint, to recover reasonable attorney's fees, in which case the court shall award the costs of suit, including a reasonable attorney's fee, to the prevailing plaintiff.

"(2) The notice referred to in paragraph (1) shall state the nature of the alleged violation, the relief to be requested, the court in which the action will be brought, and whether or not attorney's fees are being demanded in the event that the plaintiff prevails. No action described in paragraph (1) shall be brought (A) if at the time the action is brought the same alleged violation by the same defendant is the subject of a pending action in any court of the United States; or (B) if administrative remedies have not been exhausted.

"(f) With respect to actions brought for relief based on an alleged violation of the provisions of this title, administrative remedies shall be deemed exhausted upon the expiration of 180 days from the filing of an administrative complaint during which time the Federal department or agency makes no finding with regard to the complaint, or upon the day that the Federal department or agency issues a finding in favor of the recipient of financial assistance, whichever occurs first.".

42 USC 6104.

(d) Section 305(b) of the Age Discrimination Act of 1975 is amended by adding at the end thereof the following new sentence: "Whenever the head of any Federal department or agency who prescribes regulations under section 304 withholds funds pursuant to subsection (a), he may, in accordance with regulations he shall prescribe, disburse the funds so withheld directly to any public or nonprofit private organization or agency, or State or political subdivision thereof, which demonstrates the ability to achieve the goals of the Federal statute authorizing the program or activity while complying with regulations issued under section 304.".

42 USC 6106, 6107.

(e) The Age Discrimination Act of 1975 is amended by redesignating section 308 as section 309, and by inserting after section 307 the following new section:

"REPORTS

42 USC 6106a.

"SEC. 308. (a) Not later than December 31 of each year (beginning in 1979), the head of each Federal department or agency shall submit to the Secretary of Health, Education, and Welfare a report (1) describing in detail the steps taken during the preceding fiscal year by such department or agency to carry out the provisions of section 303; and (2) containing specific data about program participants or beneficiaries, by age, sufficient to permit analysis of how well the department or agency is carrying out the provisions of section 303.

"(b) Not later than March 31 of each year (beginning in 1980), the Secretary of Health, Education, and Welfare shall compile the reports made pursuant to subsection (a) and shall submit them to the Congress, together with an evaluation of the performance of each department or agency with respect to carrying out the provisions of section 303.".

AMENDMENTS TO DOMESTIC VOLUNTEER SERVICE ACT OF 1973

42 USC 5001.

SEC. 402. (a) Section 201 of the Domestic Volunteer Service Act of 1973 is amended—

(1) in subsections (a) and (c), by striking out "section 304 (a)(1)" and inserting in lieu thereof "section 305(a)(1)" and by striking out "section 3024(a)(1)" and inserting in lieu thereof "section 3025(a)(1)";

(2) in subsection (c), by striking out "sixty" and inserting in lieu thereof "forty-five"; and

(3) by inserting at the end thereof the following new subsection:

"(d) Notwithstanding any other provision of law, volunteer service under this part shall not be deemed employment for any purpose which the Director finds is not fully consistent with the provisions and in furtherance of the purpose of this part.".

42 USC 5011.

Domestic Volunteer Service, allowances and stipends.

(b) Section 211 of the Domestic Volunteer Service Act of 1973 is amended by adding at the end thereof the following new subsections:

"(e) The Director, in accordance with regulations he shall prescribe, may provide to persons serving as volunteers under this part, such allowances, stipends, and other support as he determines are necessary to carry out the purpose of this part. Any stipend or allowance provided under this subsection shall not be less than $2 per hour, except that (1) no increase in the stipend or allowance shall be made pursuant to this sentence unless the funds appropriated for carrying out this part are sufficient to maintain for the fiscal year in question a number of participants to serve under this part at least equal to the number of such participants serving during the preceding fiscal year, and (2) in the event that sufficient appropriations for any fiscal year are not available to increase any such stipend or allowance provided to $2 per hour, the Director shall increase the stipend or allowance to such amount as appropriations for such year permit consistent with clause (1) of this exception.

"Low-income person" and "person of low income."

"(f) For the purposes of this part, the terms 'low-income person' and 'person of low income' mean (1) any person whose income is not more than 125 percent of the poverty line set forth in section 625 of the Economic Opportunity Act of 1964, as amended (42 U.S.C. 2971d); and (2) any person considered a poor or low-income person under section 421(4) of this Act, with special consideration for participation in projects under this part provided to persons described in clause (2).".

42 USC 5012.

Grants and
contracts.

(c) Section 212(a) of the Domestic Volunteer Service Act of 1973 is amended by striking out paragraphs (2) and (3) and inserting in lieu thereof the following new paragraph:

"(2)(A) The Director shall award a grant or contract under this part for a project to be carried out over an area in a State more comprehensive than one community, to the State agency established or designated pursuant to section 305(a)(1) of the Older Americans Act of 1965, as amended (42 U.S.C. 3025(a)(1)), unless (i) the State has not established or designated such an agency; or (ii) such agency has been afforded at least 45 days to (I) review the project application made by a prospective grantee or contractor other than such agency for a project to be carried out in such State; and (II) make recommendations thereon. In the event that such an established or designated State agency is not awarded the grant or contract, any application approved for a project in such State shall contain or be supported by satisfactory assurances that the project has been developed, and will, to the extent feasible, be conducted, in consultation with, or with the participation of, such agency.

"(B) The Director shall award a grant or contract under this part for a project to be carried out entirely in a community served by a community action agency, to such agency unless such agency and the State agency established or designated pursuant to section 305(a)(1) of the Older Americans Act of 1965, as amended (42 U.S.C. 3025 (a)(1)) have been afforded at least 45 days to (i) review the project application made by a prospective grantee or contractor other than either such agency for a project to be carried out in such community; and (ii) make recommendations thereon. In the event that such a community action agency or such an established or designated State agency is not awarded the grant or contract, any application approved for a project to be carried out entirely in such community shall contain or be supported by satisfactory assurances that the project has been developed, and will, to the extent feasible, be conducted, in consultation with, or with the participation of, such community action agency.".

42 USC 5082.

(d) Section 502 of the Domestic Volunteer Service Act of 1973 is amended—

(1) in subsection (a), by striking out "and" after "September 30, 1976", and by inserting "$25,000,000 for the fiscal year ending September 30, 1979, $30,000,000 for the fiscal year ending September 30, 1980, and $35,000,000 for the fiscal year ending September 30, 1981," after "September 30, 1978,"; and

(2) in subsection (b)(2), by adding at the end thereof the following new sentence: "There are further authorized to be appropriated $55,000,000 for the fiscal year ending September 30, 1979, $62,500,000 for the fiscal year ending September 30, 1980, and $70,000,000 for the fiscal year ending September 30, 1981, for the purpose of carrying out programs under part B of such title.".

TITLE V—MISCELLANEOUS PROVISIONS
REPEALERS; EXISTING PROJECTS

42 USC 3056
note.
42 USC
3041–3041f,
3042,
3045–3045i.

42 USC 3045
note.

SEC. 501. (a) Effective at the close of September 30, 1978, title V and title VII are repealed. The Commissioner on Aging may complete any project which was undertaken under either such title, or under title V, as so redesignated in section 105(a), before such date, and which is unfinished on such date, with funds obligated but unexpended on such date.

(b) Any project receiving funds under title VII of the Older Americans Act of 1965, as in effect on the day before the effective date of this Act, shall continue to receive funds under part C of title III of such Act, as amended by this Act, if such project meets the requirements and criteria established in such title III, as amended by this Act, except that a State, pursuant to regulations prescribed by the Commissioner on Aging, shall not discontinue the payment of such funds to a project unless such State, after a hearing (if requested by the person responsible for administering such project), determines that such project has not carried out activities supported by such funds with demonstrated effectiveness.

LIMITATIONS ON PAYMENTS

Sec. 502. No authorization of appropriations in this Act shall be effective for any fiscal year beginning before October 1, 1978. Notwithstanding any other provision of this Act, no payment under this Act, or authorization to make payments or to enter into contracts under this Act, shall be effective except to such extent, or in such amounts, as are provided in advance in appropriations Acts.

CONFORMING AND TECHNICAL AMENDMENTS

42 USC 3002.

Sec. 503. (a) (1) Section 102(1) is amended by inserting ", other than for purposes of title V" before the period at the end thereof.

(2) Section 102 is amended by redesignating paragraph (4), the second place it appears therein, as paragraph (5), and by redesignating paragraphs (5) and (6) as paragraphs (6) and (7), respectively.

42 USC 3011.

(b) (1) Section 201(a) is amended by striking out "VI and as otherwise specifically provided by the Older Americans Comprehensive Services Amendments of 1973" and inserting in lieu thereof "V".

42 USC 3012.

(2) Section 202(a)(15), as so redesignated in section 102(b)(1), is amended by inserting after "Discrimination" the following: "in Employment".

42 USC 3015.

(3) Section 205(d)(3) is amended by striking out "and" at the end thereof.

42 USC 3012, 3014, 3015.

(4) (A) Sections 202, 204, and 205 are amended by striking out "older persons" each place it appears therein and inserting in lieu thereof "older individuals".

(B) Section 202(a)(12), as so redesignated in section 102(b)(1), is amended by striking out "such persons" and inserting in lieu thereof "such individuals".

42 USC 3034.

(c) (1) Section 404(a)(6), as so redesignated in section 104(a)(4) (C), is amended by striking out "curricula" the second place it appears therein and inserting in lieu thereof "curriculum".

(2) Section 404(b) is amended by striking out "federally supported" and inserting in lieu thereof "federally-supported".

42 USC 3034, 3035.

(3) Sections 404 and 411 are amended by striking out "older persons" each place it appears therein and inserting in lieu thereof "older individuals".

42 USC 3056b.

(d) Section 504(b), as so redesignated in section 105(a), is amended by striking out the comma after "contract" the second place it appears therein.

EFFECTIVE DATE

42 USC 3001 note.

Sec. 504. This Act, and the amendments made by this Act, shall take effect at the close of September 30, 1978.

Approved October 18, 1978.

LEGISLATIVE HISTORY:

HOUSE REPORTS: No. 95–1150 (Comm. on Education and Labor) and No. 95–1618 (Comm. of Conference).
SENATE REPORTS: No. 95–855 accompanying S. 2850 (Comm. on Human Resources) and No. 95–1236 (Comm. of Conference).
CONGRESSIONAL RECORD, Vol. 124 (1978):
    May 15, considered and passed House.
    July 24, considered and passed Senate, amended, in lieu of S. 2850.
    Oct. 4, House agreed to conference report.
    Oct. 6, Senate agreed to conference report.
WEEKLY COMPILATION OF PRESIDENTIAL DOCUMENTS, Vol. 14, No. 42:
    Oct. 18, Presidential statement.

Part three:
Statistics

Demographic Aspects of Aging and the Older Population in the United States

U.S. Bureau of the Census, Current Population Reports, Special Studies, Washington, D.C., 1977.

INTRODUCTION

The Nature of Demographic Aging

Aging marks the inexorable running out of the biological time clock for the individual, given the limited life span of possibly 100 years for humans.[1] Although the aging process goes on steadily throughout life, the term is commonly employed to refer to the changes in later life, following the reproductive age period. Aging proceeds at different rates for different individuals if we define it in physiological or functional terms rather than merely chronological terms. For some, the signs of physiological deterioration or the ability not to function independently come earlier than for others, but they inevitably appear for all as time passes. Demographically, however, aging is defined essentially in terms of chronological age, on the assumption that for large populations the aging process, functional age, and physiological age follow chronological age closely.

A discussion of the demographic aspects of aging could be concerned with how the numbers, composition, and characteristics of the population vary with age over the whole age range. The present report does deal with such age variation to some extent, but it focuses on the older ages, namely those over 55 and particularly those over 60, 65, and 75. At these ages the impact of aging in terms of changes in the individual's physical condition (e.g., life, health) and social and economic characteristics (e.g., labor force participation, income, living arrangements) is most pronounced and of special public concern. These individual changes are collectively reflected in the data on the demographic characteristics of the population.

Since the older ("gerontic") population is not a single homogeneous mass and its characteristics tend to vary sharply with age within the band 55 and over, or even 65 and over, it is desirable in any analysis of the older population to consider the group in terms of component age groups. In this report we distinguish at times the older population (55 and over or 60 and over), the elderly (65 and over), the aged (75 and over), and the extreme aged (85 and over). For convenience and simplicity in the discussion, however, the single broad group 65 and over is often selected for detailed consideration. The attainment of age 65 marks the point of retirement for many workers and a common age of qualification for Social Security benefits and "Medicare" coverage, and figures in several other important pieces of legislation affecting the older population, including Federal and State tax laws. After age 65, the level of many characteristics of the population changes very rapidly (e.g., numbers, proportions, sex composition, living arrangements) and hence differs greatly from that for the ages just below.

A distinction should be made between the aging of individuals and the aging of populations. The demographer is interested in both aspects of aging. His interest in the former is limited to the general experience of population groups with respect to the aging of individuals. This experience is reflected in such measures as life expectancy and the probability of survival from one age to another. Aging of this kind is a function of changes in mortality rates. The aging of a population refers to the fact that a population is "getting older." It may be measured variously in terms of the median age, the proportion of persons 65 years old and over, the ratio of persons 65 and over to children under 15, the

[1] Hayflick maintains that the phenomenon of a limited life span is general for animal life, even **in vitro;** see Leonard Hayflick, "The Strategy of Senescence," **The Gerontologist,** Vol. 14, No. 1, Feb. 1974, pp. 37-45, esp. pp. 38-39. See also Zhores A. Medvedev, "Aging and Longevity: New Approaches and New Perspectives," **The Gerontologist,** Vol. 15, No. 3, June 1975, pp. 196-201, esp. pp. 199-200; and P. R. J. Burch, "What Limits Life Span?", pp. 31-56, in B. Benjamin, P. R. Cox, and J. Peel (eds.), **Population and the New Biology,** Academic Press, New York, 1974.

proportion of the population above the age corresponding to a life expectancy of, say, 10 years,[2] etc. The various measures of aging may indicate different degrees of aging for the same population, and a population may be described as "aging" and "younging" at the same time if, as may occur, the proportion of aged persons and the proportion of children are both increasing.[3] Aging of populations is a function of changes in their mortality, fertility, and migration rates, particularly fertility rates (see below).

Sources and Accuracy of the Data

For the most part, the present study employs official statistics. They come principally from the following sources: Decennial censuses; the program of nonsurvey population estimates and projections carried out by the U.S. Bureau of the Census; the Current Population Survey, the continuing national sample survey conducted by the U.S. Bureau of the Census; and the vital statistics registration system and life tables prepared by the National Center for Health Statistics, U.S. Public Health Service. In addition, use has been made of the statistics of "Medicare" enrollment and death rates from the Social Security ("Medicare") data system.

In general, the figures for the older ages are subject to a substantial degree of error. For some categories of information the degree of error may be much greater than for the younger ages. The figures are affected not only by the failure to count everyone or to register all vital events and migratory movements, but also by the misreporting of age and other characteristics. The nonsurvey population estimates and projections, which are

derived by the methods of demographic accounting and demographic analysis, are subject to errors of the measurement model (that is, the general methodological design and the assumptions), in addition to the errors of coverage, response, and processing of the census data and the other data (e.g., birth statistics, death statistics, immigration data) employed in their preparation. The census data, the population estimates and projections, and the death statistics have not been adjusted for coverage errors or errors in reporting. Since these limitations apply to both the population figures and the figures on deaths, they apply also to the death rates and the life table values, although the errors may offset one another wholly or partly.

In addition to coverage, response, and processing errors, the estimates based on the Current Population Survey are subject to sampling error. Like the nonsurvey estimates and projections to which they are adjusted, the estimates from the Current Population Survey are at a level consistent with the census counts by age, sex, and race; that is, they do not contain corrections for census net undercounts in these categories. Further information regarding the derivation of the Current Population Survey estimates and the quality of the data from the Current Population Survey is given in Appendix A of this report and in the original sources cited.

In spite of the stated limitations of the reported data on the older population, it is believed that the general magnitudes, relations, and patterns are reflected satisfactorily by the reported figures, except perhaps for the figures at the very extreme ages. In any case, small differences should be disregarded or at least viewed with caution.

[2] The last measure was recently proposed by Norman Ryder in "Notes on Stationary Populations," **Population Index,** Vol. 41, No. 1, Jan. 1975, pp. 3-28, esp. pp. 16-17.

[3] U.S. Bureau of the Census, **The Methods and Materials of Demography,** Henry S. Shryock, Jacob S. Siegel, and Associates, U.S. Government Printing Office, Washington, D.C., 1975 (third printing, rev.), pp. 234-235.

NUMBERS AND PROPORTIONS OF OLDER PERSONS

Number of Older Persons

The older ("gerontic") population of the United States is large and continues to grow rapidly. There are now 42 million persons over 55 years of age, 32 million over 60, 22 million over 65, 8.5 million over 75, and 1.9 million over 85 (table 2-1). The latest population projections suggest that the numbers in all of these age categories will be considerably larger by the end of this century and will continue to grow in the early part of the next century.

The population 60 and over numbered 4.9 million in 1900. By 1930, the group had more than doubled in

size to 10.5 million. It approximately tripled again to 31.6 million in 1975. In the year 2000, the number is expected to be about 42 million, or about one-third greater than at present. Decennial growth rates for the population 60 and over approximated 30 percent between 1920 and 1960, but then they began a declining trend which is expected to bring the figure down to about 4 percent in the decade 1990-2000.

The population 65 and over numbered 3.1 million in 1900. By 1940, the group had nearly tripled in size to 9.0 million. It more than doubled again to 20.1 million

Table 2-1. **TOTAL POPULATION IN THE OLDER AGES AND DECENNIAL INCREASES: 1900 TO 2040**

(Numbers in thousands.   Estimates and projections as of July 1. Total resident population of the 48 States and District of Columbia (excluding Alaska and Hawaii) for 1900 to 1930.   Estimates for 1940 and later years refer to the total population of the 50 States and District of Columbia and include Armed Forces overseas. A minus sign (-) denotes a decrease)

Year	55 years and over			60 years and over			65 years and over			75 years and over			85 years and over		
	Number	Increase in preceding decade		Number	Increase in preceding decade		Number	Increase in preceding decade		Number	Increase in preceding decade		Number	Increase in preceding decade	
		Amount	Percent		Amount	Percent		Amount	Percent		Amount	Percent		Amount	Percent
ESTIMATES															
1900....................	7,125	(X)	(X)	4,901	(X)	(X)	3,099	(X)	(X)	899	(X)	(X)	[1]122	(X)	(X)
1910....................	9,087	1,962	27.5	6,274	1,373	28.0	3,986	887	28.6	1,170	271	30.1	[1]167	45	36.9
1920....................	11,548	2,461	27.1	7,952	1,678	26.7	4,929	943	23.7	1,449	279	23.8	[1]210	43	25.7
1930....................	15,182	3,634	31.5	10,484	2,532	31.8	6,705	1,776	36.0	1,945	496	34.2	[1]272	62	29.5
1940....................	19,725	4,543	29.9	13,822	3,338	31.8	9,031	2,326	34.7	2,664	719	37.0	370	[2]98	[2]36.0
1950....................	25,793	6,068	30.8	18,500	4,678	33.8	12,397	3,366	37.3	3,904	1,240	46.5	590	220	59.5
1960....................	32,299	6,506	25.2	23,828	5,328	28.8	16,675	4,278	34.5	5,621	1,717	44.0	940	350	59.3
1970....................	38,749	6,450	20.0	28,751	4,923	20.7	20,085	3,410	20.4	7,598	1,977	35.2	1,432	492	52.3
1975....................	42,180	(X)	(X)	31,643	(X)	(X)	22,400	(X)	(X)	8,527	(X)	(X)	1,877	(X)	(X)
PROJECTIONS[3]															
1980....................	45,570	6,821	17.6	34,267	5,516	19.2	24,523	4,438	22.1	9,112	1,514	19.9	2,071	639	44.6
1990....................	49,412	3,842	8.4	39,127	4,860	14.2	28,933	4,410	18.0	11,402	2,290	25.1	2,487	416	20.1
2000....................	53,537	4,124	8.3	40,589	1,462	3.7	30,600	1,667	5.8	13,521	2,119	18.6	3,217	730	29.4
2010....................	65,733	12,196	22.8	48,012	7,423	18.3	33,239	2,640	8.6	13,893	372	2.7	3,841	624	19.4
2020....................	79,481	13,749	20.9	60,664	12,652	26.4	42,791	9,552	28.7	15,381	1,488	10.7	3,826	-15	-0.4
2030...........(II)..	82,546	3,065	3.9	} 67,037	6,373	10.5	51,590	8,798	20.6	20,716	5,335	34.7	4,409	583	15.2
Range........{ (III)..	82,418	2,937	3.7												
(I)..	82,730	3,249	4.1												
2040...........(II)..	84,783	2,237	2.7	65,854	-1,183	-1.8	50,266	-1,324	-2.6	} 24,218	3,503	16.9	5,993	1,584	35.9
Range........{ (III)..	79,809	-2,610	-3.2	63,822	-3,215	-4.8	50,149	-1,441	-2.8						
(I)..	91,053	8,323	10.1	68,318	1,281	1.9	50,431	-1,158	-2.2						

X Not applicable.
[1] Estimates for 1900-30 as of April 1.
[2] Pertains to 10 1/4 year period.
[3] Base date of projections is July 1, 1974.

Source: Census of Population, 1930, Population Vol. II, General Report; and Current Population Reports, Series P-25, Nos. 311, 519, 614, and 601.

Figure 2-2. **PERCENT OF THE TOTAL POPULATION IN THE OLDER AGES:**
1900 TO 2040

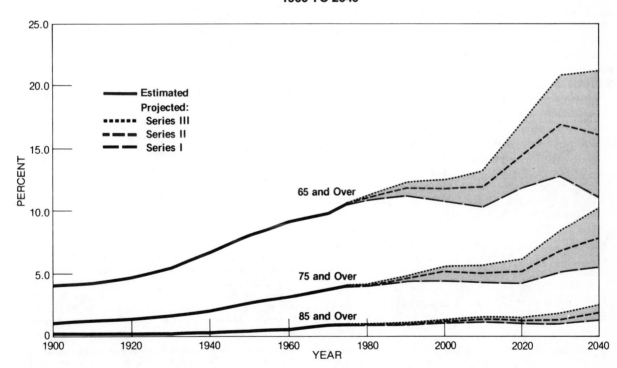

Note: Estimates and projections as of July 1, except for 85 and over, 1900-1930, which relate to April 1.
Points are plotted for years ending in zero except for 1975.
Source: Table 2-4 and text p. 6.

by 1970. In the year 2000, the number of persons 65 and over is expected to be about 31 million. The number has been rising in recent decades by about 3 to 4 million per decade, or roughly 300,000 to 400,000 per year, and is expected to continue rising in the next few decades at the same "rate." The estimated 22.4 million persons over 65 on July 1, 1975, exceeded the July 1, 1970 figure by 2.3 million, a quinquennial increase corresponding to an annual average gain of 460,000 persons.

The population 65 and over increased rapidly during the 1960-70 period (20 percent), much more rapidly than the population as a whole (13 percent). (See table 2-2 and figure 2-1.) Yet, the growth rate of this age group during the 1960's was well below its growth rate during the 1950's (35 percent) and the preceding decades (35 to 37 percent for 1920 to 1950). The population 65 and over is expected to continue to show substantial percentage increases during the 1970's and 1980's (22 percent and 18 percent, respectively), albeit much smaller increases than before 1960.

These changes principally reflect increases in the number of births 65 to 84 years or so before the particular reference date. As these numbers shift, the rate of growth of the elderly population in the appropriate later years fluctuates. The general rise in the number of births in the 19th century and in the first few decades of this century largely accounts for the past and prospective rapid increases in the number of elderly persons up to about 1990.

Of particular interest is the impact of the shift in the trend in the number of births since World War I. As a result of the rapid drop in the number of births during the 1920-30 and 1930-40 decades, we can expect a sharp drop in the amount and rate of increase of the population 65 and over after about 1990, lasting about two decades (6 percent for 1990-2000 and 9 percent for 2000-2010). The births of the post-war "baby boom," 1945-1959, which may be seen moving through the age distribution on the basis of decennial population data (e.g., under 15 years old in 1960 and 10 to 24 years old in 1970), will ultimately have their impact on the size of the aged population. Early in the next century (2010 to 2020) the number of persons 65 and over will leap forward (by 9.6 million, or 29 percent), as these cohorts attain age 65. After about 2020, again the growth rate may be expected to fall off sharply, principally as a result of the rapid deflation in the size of birth cohorts during the 1960's. In fact, the number of persons 65 and over may decline slightly between 2030 and 2040. In the latter year the group is expected to number over 50 million.

The projected numbers of elderly persons cited here should be close to the mark because they are unaffected by future fertility. The people who will be over 65 in the year 2000 or even the year 2020 are now all living; and so are all the people who will be over 65 in the year 2040. The fact that projected fertility is not involved in the projection for this age group is fortunate; fertility is a component of population change that cannot be predicted closely because it tends to fluctuate widely.

Mortality and immigration have an effect on the size of the older population also, however, deaths reducing the initial cohorts of births and net immigration typically increasing it. Mortality is subject to less variation than fertility and has rather steadily removed smaller and smaller proportions of the initial cohorts of births. During the first part of this century, from about 25 to 45 percent of the initial births survived to ages 65 to 84. Population projections assuming a "slight" reduction in future mortality indicate that about 55 percent of the initial births will survive to ages 65 to 84 (e.g., births 1975 to 1995 surviving to ages 65-84 in 2060).[1]

Whether immigration contributes to the **growth** of the older population depends on the fluctuations in the volume of immigration. These have sometimes resulted in an acceleration of population growth rates and at other times in a deceleration. The large and increasing volume of immigration prior to World War I, particularly of youth, contributed greatly to the rapid increase in the number of persons 65 and over up to about 1960. Because of the general reduction in immigration since World War I, however, this factor has been much less important in the growth of the elderly population since 1960 (even having a negative effect on growth) and is expected to play a minor role in the future.

The past general decline in death rates has contributed to the rapid increase in the number of aged persons, but its effect has been much less than the rise in the number of births. Death rates are expected to continue to decline, albeit only slightly. There is the possibility, nevertheless, of substantial future reductions in death rates of the older population. Such a trend could mean a somewhat larger elderly population and greater increases than we have projected. The projection of the population 65 and over for the year 2000 (30.6 million) would be larger by about 2 million, or 7 percent, for example, if "rapidly declining" mortality rates had been used in the calculations rather than "slightly declining" mortality rates.[2]

---

[1] Estimated from data in U.S. Bureau of the Census, **Current Population Reports,** "Projections of the Population of the United States: 1975 to 2050," by Campbell Gibson and Signe Wetrogan, Series P-25, No. 601, Oct. 1975, tables F-1, F-2, G-1, and B-1. The projections of mortality in Series P-25, No. 601, assume an "ultimate" life expectation at birth of 73.8 years, as compared with 71.7 years in 1972.

[2] Estimated from data in **Current Population Reports,** Series P-25, No. 381, Dec. 1967, table Z, and **Current Population Reports,** Series P-25, No. 601, Oct. 1975, table 8. Expectation of life at age 40 under "rapidly declining" mortality is 2.4 years greater than under "slightly declining" mortality in the year 2000.

Table 2-2. **DECENNIAL PERCENT INCREASE OF POPULATION BY BROAD AGE GROUPS: 1950 TO 2010**

(A minus sign (–) denotes a decrease. Periods extend from July 1 of initial year to June 30 of terminal year)

Age and projection series	1950 to 1960	1960 to 1970	1970 to 1980	1980 to 1990	1990 to 2000	2000 to 2010
All ages................II..	18.7	13.4	8.7	10.0	7.1	6.2
Range.............{ III..			7.6	6.9	4.0	2.1
I..			10.2	14.2	11.4	12.2
Under 15 years................II..	36.8	3.2	-11.6	13.4	0.8	-0.4
Range....................{ III..			-15.7	-0.1	-3.8	-8.3
I..			-6.5	30.2	7.6	10.2
15 to 24 years................II..	9.9	48.5	13.7	-16.2	11.8	5.7
Range.................{ III..				-16.6	-4.0	0.5
I..				-15.8	31.2	13.6
25 to 44 years................II..	3.2	2.7	27.7	25.5	-2.3	-3.5
Range....................{ III..					-2.5	-10.6
I..					2.1	5.5
45 to 54 years.....................	17.9	13.3	-2.9	11.4	41.8	13.1
55 to 64 years.....................	16.6	19.4	12.8	-2.7	12.0	41.7
65 to 74 years.....................	30.1	13.0	23.4	13.8	-2.6	13.3
75 to 84 years.....................	41.2	31.7	14.2	26.6	15.6	-2.4
85 years and over..................	59.3	52.3	44.6	20.1	29.4	19.4

Source: Current Population Reports, Series P-25, Nos. 311, 519, and 601.

Net and Gross Changes

Because of the relatively high death rates of the older population, membership in the group is relatively short in duration and the identity of the members changes rapidly over relatively short periods of time. "Population turnover" in this group may be measured in several ways. Consider the period of a decade. Most simply, we may examine the percentage of the total population 65 and over at the end of the decade falling in the 65-to-74-year group, the surviving new entrants. Of the population 65 and over in 1970, 62 percent joined after 1960 (table 2-3). We may also examine estimates of the components of change in population during the 1960-70 decade in relation to the initial size of the population. The gross increase rate during the decade 1960-70 was 87 percent. The gross increase rate is the number of persons reaching age 65 during the decade (14.4 million for 1960-70) plus the number of (net) immigrants (0.1 million), expressed as a percentage of the initial population (16.6 million). The gross loss rate—the number of deaths during the decade (11.0 million) expressed as a percent of the initial population—was 66 percent. The difference between the gross increase rate and the gross loss rate is the rate of net increase, or 21 percent.

The percent of the initial population 65 and over who died during the decade was 53 percent. In addition, the new arrivals in the group (i.e., persons reaching age 65 during the decade) sustained a loss of 15 percent by 1970. The resulting gross loss rate for the initial population and the new arrivals combined was 36 percent.

A more sensitive measure of the turnover, or "growth effectiveness," of the elderly population is given by the ratio of (a) the net increase in the population 65 and over to (b) the gross change in this age group (i.e., the sum of the components of change without regard to sign). The lower the ratio, the greater the turnover. For the 1960-70 decade this ratio was 0.14, that is, there was a net addition to the population 65 and over of only 14 persons for every 100 demographic events (additions through aging; net immigration; and deaths) affecting that age group.

During the course of the present decade, 1970-80, the rate of gross gain and the rate of gross loss of the population 65 and over are expected to remain at about the same levels as during the 1960-70 period (88 percent and 65 percent, respectively) although the number of persons reaching age 65 and the number of deaths are expected to increase sharply. The 10-year mortality rate for the initial population aged 65 and over (in 1970) is expected to be about the same as during the 1960-70 decade (55 percent), but the population reaching age 65 during the decade will experience a substantially smaller loss (12 percent, or about 2½ percentage points less) than persons reaching age 65 during the 1960-70 decade.

The rate of turnover for the male population aged 65 and over is much higher than for the female population at these ages, and the rate of turnover for the white population is higher than for the black population. The growth effectiveness ratio of the female population for 1970-80 will be about three-quarters greater than that of the male population (0.178 vs. 0.102) as a result of the higher male mortality. For blacks and whites the figures are expected to be closer, 0.183 and 0.138, respectively.

Proportion of Older Persons

The older population has been growing steadily as a share of the total U.S. population. From 1900 to 1975, the proportion of the population 60 years of age and over more than doubled. Persons in these ages now approximate 14.8 percent of the total population as compared with 6.4 percent in 1900 (table 2-4). Whether this group's share will decline, remain about the same, or continue to increase in the future depends principally on the future course of fertility. The proportion is now expected to fall between 14.1 percent and 16.6 percent at the end of this century. The first figure corresponds to the "high" fertility series (Series I) and the second figure corresponds to the "low" fertility series (Series III);[3] both series incorporate slight decreases in future death rates and a small allowance for net immigration (400,000 annually).

The proportion of the population 65 years and over has been increasing even more rapidly (figure 2-2). It grew 2½ times between 1900 and 1975, from 4.1 percent in 1900 to 10.5 percent in 1975. The proportion may then rise and fall again, or rise steadily, between 1975 and the year 2000, depending mainly on the course of fertility. For example, the proportion may reach a peak of nearly 11.7 percent in 1990 and then stay at about this level to the year 2000 (Series II); it may rise to only 11.1 percent in 1990 and then fall back to 10.7 percent in 2000 (Series I); or it may rise steadily to 12.5 percent in 2000 (Series III). The era of the rapid rise in the proportion 65 and over is past. Even the steady rise in the proportion 65 and over that we have seen in the past cannot be taken for granted for the future. Nevertheless, it now seems more likely that the proportion will rise in the next few decades than that it will fall.

The percent of the population 65 years and over as recorded at decennial intervals from 1900 to 1970 and as projected to 2050 is as follows:[4]

Year (July 1)	Percent	Year (July 1)	Percent (range)
1900....	4.1	1980...	11.0 (10.9-11.1)
1910....	4.3	1990...	11.7 (11.1-12.2)
1920....	4.6	2000...	11.7 (10.7-12.5)
1930....	5.4	2010...	11.9 (10.3-13.3)
1940....	6.8	2020...	14.6 (11.8-17.0)
1950....	8.1	2030...	17.0 (12.8-20.9)
1960....	9.2	2040...	16.1 (11.0-21.1)
1970....	9.8	2050...	16.1 (11.3-20.7)
1975....	10.5		

A rise in the proportion of the total population in the 75-and-over age group between now and the year 2000 is even more probable. The proportion is expected to fall between 4.7 percent (Series I) and 5.5 percent (Series III) in the year 2000, as compared with 4.0 percent in 1975.

Even as the proportion of elderly persons in the total population has been rising, so the elderly population itself has been aging and is expected to continue to age (table 2-5). The proportion 65 to 69 of the group 65 and over is getting smaller, while the proportion 75 and over is getting larger, and the trend is expected to continue at least to the end of the century. In 1900 the proportion 75 and over was 29 percent; by 1975 this proportion had risen to 38 percent. We may expect about 44 percent of the 65-and-over group to fall in the 75-and-over

---

[3] Series I, Series II (the central series of projections), and Series III are the principal series of population projections presented in **Current Population Reports,** Series P-25, No. 601. Series I assumes a total fertility rate of 2,700, Series II a total fertility rate of 2,100 (replacement level), and Series III a total fertility rate of 1,700.

[4] **Ibid,** tables 7 to 12, for the projections.

Table 2-5. **PERCENT DISTRIBUTION OF THE POPULATION 65 YEARS OLD AND OVER BY AGE: 1900 TO 2010**

(Estimates and projections as of July 1)

Age	1900	1930	1950	1960	1970	1975	Projections			
							1980	1990	2000	2010
65 years and over........	100.0	100.0	100.0	100.0	100.0	100.0	100.0	100.0	100.0	100.0
65 to 69 years...............	42.3	41.7	40.7	37.7	35.0	36.2	35.3	34.1	29.5	34.3
70 to 74 years...............	28.7	29.3	27.8	28.6	27.2	25.8	27.5	26.5	26.3	23.9
75 to 79 years...............	29.0	29.0	17.4	18.5	19.2	17.9	17.5	18.7	20.3	17.2
80 to 84 years...............			14.1	9.6	11.5	11.8	11.2	12.1	13.3	13.0
85 years and over............				5.6	7.1	8.4	8.4	8.6	10.5	11.6

Source: Current Population Reports, Series P-25, Nos. 311, 321, 519, 614, and 601. See table 2-1.

Table 2-3. ESTIMATES AND PROJECTIONS OF THE DEMOGRAPHIC COMPONENTS OF CHANGE IN THE POPULATION 65 YEARS OLD AND OVER, BY RACE AND SEX: 1970-80, 1960-70, AND 1950-60

(Numbers in thousands. Figures from the 1970 census have been adjusted for the misclassification of some persons of Spanish origin as Negro-and-other-races rather than white and for the overstatement of the number of centenarians)

Item and period	All classes	White		Negro and other races[1]	
		Male	Female	Male	Female
JULY 1, 1970 TO JULY 1, 1980[2]					
Population 65 years and over, 1980..........................	24,523	8,938	13,276	855	1,209
Population 65 years and over, 1970..........................	20,087	7,649	10,723	673	883
Net increase..	4,436	1,289	2,553	181	326
Number reaching age 65....................................	17,564	7,206	8,585	715	916
Net migrants 65 years and over............................	29	1	6	2	5
Deaths 65 years and over..................................	13,157	5,919	6,038	536	595
Deaths to initial population 65 years and over...........	10,988	4,689	5,346	421	484
Deaths to persons reaching age 65.......................	2,169	1,230	692	114	110
Gross change[3]..	30,749	13,127	14,630	1,253	1,516
Rate of gross gain[4]......................................	87.6	94.2	80.1	106.5	104.3
Rate of gross loss[4]......................................	65.5	77.4	56.3	79.5	67.4
Population 65 to 74 years as percent of population 65 years and over, 1980....................................	62.8	66.9	59.5	70.4	66.9
Ratio, net change to gross change[3].......................	.144	.098	.175	.145	.215
Mortality rate of population 65 years and over[5]..........	34.9	39.8	31.3	38.6	33.1
Mortality rate of initial population 65 years and over[4]..	54.7	61.3	49.9	62.6	54.9
Mortality rate for persons reaching age 65..............	12.3	17.1	8.1	16.0	12.0
APRIL 1, 1960 TO APRIL 1, 1970					
Population 65 years and over, 1970..........................	19,972	7,615	10,657	752	949
Population 65 years and over, 1960..........................	16,560	6,908	8,396	595	661
Net increase..	3,412	707	2,261	157	288
Number reaching age 65....................................	14,388	6,044	7,009	636	699
Net migrants 65 years and over............................	68	22	38	3	5
Deaths 65 years and over..................................	10,979	5,254	4,848	468	409
Deaths to initial population 65 years and over...........	8,833	4,115	4,127	310	281
Deaths to persons reaching age 65.......................	2,146	1,139	721	158	128
Gross change[3]..	25,435	11,320	11,895	1,107	1,113
Rate of gross gain[4]......................................	87.3	87.8	83.9	107.4	106.5
Rate of gross loss[4]......................................	66.3	76.1	57.7	78.7	61.9
Population 65 to 74 years as percent of population 65 years and over, 1970....................................	62.3	64.7	59.8	68.5	66.2
Ratio, net change to gross change[3].......................	.138	.065	.192	.158	.273
Mortality rate of population 65 years and over[5]..........	35.5	40.6	31.5	38.0	30.1
Mortality rate of initial population 65 years and over[4]..	53.3	59.6	49.2	52.1	42.5
Mortality rate for persons reaching age 65..............	14.9	18.8	10.3	24.8	18.3
APRIL 1, 1950 TO APRIL 1, 1960					
Population 65 years and over, 1960..........................	16,560	6,908	8,396	595	661
Population 65 years and over, 1950..........................	12,295	5,365	6,016	448	466
Net increase..	4,265	1,543	2,380	147	195
Number reaching age 65....................................	12,564	5,622	5,973	181	486
Net migrants, 65 years and over...........................	62	26	36		
Deaths 65 years and over..................................	8,714	4,282	3,810	339	283
Deaths to initial population 65 years and over...........	6,636	3,163	3,082	211	180
Deaths to persons reaching age 65.......................	2,078	1,119	728	128	103
Gross change[3]..	21,340	9,930	9,821	820	769
Rate of gross gain[4]......................................	102.7	105.3	99.9	107.4	104.3
Rate of gross loss[4]......................................	70.9	79.8	63.3	75.7	60.7
Population 65 to 74 years as percent of population 65 years and over, 1960....................................	66.4	68.1	64.6	69.5	68.5
Ratio, net change to gross change[3].......................	.200	.155	.242	.180	.254
Mortality rate of population 65 years and over[5]..........	35.1	39.0	31.8	36.5	29.7
Mortality rate of initial population 65 years and over[4]..	54.0	59.0	51.2	47.0	38.6
Mortality rate for persons reaching age 65..............	16.5	19.9	12.2	26.6	21.2

- Represents zero.

[1]Black only for the 1970-80 period.

[2]Current data to July 1, 1973.

[3]Gross change represents the sum of persons reaching age 65, net migrants, and deaths 65 years and over. It does not include the "error of closure," the residual (0.3 million for all classes, 1960-70, and 0.4 million for 1950-60) representing the difference between net increase based on the census counts and the net change based on the components. "Net increase" or "net change" in the table represents the difference between census counts, including the "error of closure."

[4]Per 100 initial population.

[5]Per 100 initial population 65 years and over plus persons reaching age 65 during the period.

Source: Population data from Census of Population, 1960 and 1970, PC(1)-1B; and Current Population Reports, Series P-25, Nos. 519 and 601.

Table 2-4. **PERCENT OF THE TOTAL POPULATION IN THE OLDER AGES, BY RACE AND SEX: 1900 TO 2010**

(Estimates and projections as of July 1. After 1930 percent includes Armed Forces overseas)

Age, race, and sex	1900	1930	1960	1970	1975	1980 II	1980 Range I-III	1990 II	1990 Range I-III	2000 II	2000 Range I-III	2010 II	2010 Range I-III
ALL RACES													
Both Sexes													
55 years and over	9.4	12.3	17.9	18.9	19.7	20.5	20.2-20.7	20.0	19.1-20.8	20.4	18.7-21.8	23.6	20.1-26.3
60 years and over	6.4	8.5	13.2	14.0	14.8	15.4	15.2-15.6	16.0	15.2-16.6	15.5	14.1-16.6	17.2	14.9-19.2
65 years and over	4.1	5.4	9.2	9.8	10.5	11.0	10.9-11.1	11.7	11.1-12.2	11.7	10.7-12.5	11.9	10.3-13.3
75 years and over	1.2	1.6	3.1	3.7	4.0	4.1	4.0-4.1	4.7	4.4-4.8	5.2	4.7-5.5	5.0	4.3-5.6
Male													
55 years and over	9.4	12.5	16.9	17.2	17.8	18.3	18.0-18.5	17.8	16.9-18.6	18.0	16.4-19.4	21.2	18.2-23.8
60 years and over	6.4	8.5	12.3	12.4	12.9	13.3	13.1-13.5	13.7	13.0-14.3	13.1	11.9-14.1	14.9	12.8-16.7
65 years and over	4.0	5.4	8.4	8.4	8.8	9.1	9.0-9.2	9.7	9.2-10.1	9.4	8.6-10.2	9.7	8.4-10.9
75 years and over	1.1	1.5	2.7	2.9	3.0	3.0	3.0-3.0	3.3	3.2-3.5	3.6	3.3-3.9	3.5	3.0-3.9
Female													
55 years and over	9.4	12.2	18.8	20.6	21.6	22.5	22.2-22.8	22.4	21.3-23.2	22.7	20.8-24.2	25.8	22.5-28.6
60 years and over	6.5	8.5	14.1	15.6	16.6	17.3	17.1-17.5	18.1	17.3-18.8	17.7	16.2-18.9	19.4	16.9-21.5
65 years and over	4.1	5.5	10.0	11.2	12.1	12.8	12.6-12.9	13.8	13.2-14.4	13.7	12.6-14.7	14.0	12.2-15.5
75 years and over	1.2	1.7	3.5	4.4	4.9	5.1	5.0-5.2	5.9	5.6-6.1	6.6	6.0-7.0	6.4	5.6-7.1
WHITE													
Both Sexes													
55 years and over	9.7	12.8	18.5	19.6	20.6	21.4	21.1-21.7	21.1	20.1-22.0	21.3	19.5-22.8	24.6	21.2-27.4
65 years and over	4.2	5.7	9.6	10.2	11.0	11.6	11.4-11.7	12.5	11.8-13.0	12.3	11.2-13.1	12.5	10.8-13.9
75 years and over	1.2	1.6	3.3	3.9	4.2	4.3	4.3-4.4	5.0	4.7-5.2	5.5	5.0-5.9	5.3	4.6-5.9
Male													
55 years and over	9.6	12.9	17.4	17.8	18.5	19.1	18.8-19.3	18.6	17.6-19.4	18.8	17.0-20.2	22.1	18.9-24.8
65 years and over	4.2	5.6	8.8	8.7	9.1	9.5	9.4-9.6	10.1	9.6-10.6	9.9	9.0-10.6	10.1	8.7-11.4
75 years and over	1.2	1.6	2.8	3.1	3.1	3.2	3.1-3.2	3.5	3.3-3.7	3.9	3.5-4.2	3.7	3.1-4.1
Female													
55 years and over	9.7	12.8	19.6	21.5	22.7	23.7	23.4-23.9	23.5	22.4-24.4	23.8	21.8-25.4	27.0	23.4-29.9
65 years and over	4.3	5.8	10.5	11.7	12.7	13.5	13.3-13.6	14.7	14.0-15.3	14.6	13.4-15.6	14.8	12.8-16.4
75 years and over	1.3	1.7	3.7	4.7	5.2	5.5	5.4-5.5	6.3	6.0-6.6	7.1	6.5-7.6	6.8	5.9-7.6
BLACK[1]													
Both Sexes													
55 years and over	6.8	7.8	13.1	14.0	14.4	14.9	14.7-15.1	15.3	14.6-15.9	16.0	14.7-17.2	19.5	16.9-21.8
65 years and over	3.0	3.1	6.2	6.9	7.4	7.8	7.7-7.9	8.5	8.1-8.8	8.8	8.1-9.5	9.5	8.2-10.7
75 years and over	1.0	1.0	1.9	2.3	2.5	2.5	2.4-2.5	2.9	2.8-3.1	3.3	3.0-3.5	3.4	3.0-3.8
Male													
55 years and over	7.2	8.5	12.8	13.2	13.2	13.5	13.3-13.7	13.8	13.1-14.4	14.4	13.1-15.6	17.7	15.3-20.1
65 years and over	3.0	3.2	5.9	6.3	6.5	6.8	6.7-6.9	7.2	6.9-7.5	7.5	6.8-8.1	8.0	6.9-9.1
75 years and over	0.9	1.0	1.8	2.0	2.1	2.0	2.0-2.0	2.3	2.2-2.4	2.5	2.3-2.7	2.6	2.2-3.0
Female													
55 years and over	6.4	7.1	13.4	14.8	15.4	16.1	15.9-16.3	16.6	15.9-17.3	17.5	16.1-18.7	21.0	18.4-23.4
65 years and over	2.9	3.0	6.4	7.5	8.1	8.8	8.7-8.9	9.6	9.2-10.0	10.1	9.2-10.8	10.8	9.5-12.1
75 years and over	1.0	1.0	2.0	2.5	2.9	2.9	2.9-2.9	3.5	3.4-3.7	4.0	3.7-4.3	4.2	3.6-4.6

[1]Estimates for 1900 and 1930 as of April 1.

Source: Negro Population in the United States: 1790-1915; Negroes in the United States: 1920-1932; Current Population Reports, Series P-25, Nos. 311, 519, 614, and 601; and unpublished calculations.

group in the year 2000. After the year 2000, the aging trend of the population 65 and over should reverse because of the shift in the trend of fertility after World War I. The greater concentration of the elderly at the higher ages has important implications for the general status of the 65-and-over group and for planning for their needs in view of the different health conditions and living arrangements of the various segments of the older population.

It is of interest to note that, if the population of the United States moves toward and attains a stationary level as a result of, say, replacement-level fertility combined with zero net immigration and "slightly declining" mortality rates, the proportion of elderly persons in the population would rise steadily, or almost steadily, and in the stationary condition about 17 percent of the total population would be 65 or over and about 8 percent would be 75 or over.[5] Under the assumptions cited, the population would first reach a near-stationary condition about the year 2025 and there would be about 46 million persons 65 and over, or twice as many as at present. These proportions are far above the corresponding proportions in 1975 and even well above the high (Series III) proportions projected for 2000. They approximate the proportions projected in Series II (replacement-level fertility) for 2030. (The allowance for net immigration in these series has the effect of slightly depressing the proportion of older persons.) If fertility remains well below the replacement level (Series III), the proportion would eventually slide up to 21 percent in 2030 and then maintain this level.

Obviously, statements sometimes made in the press and elsewhere that over one-third of the population of the United States will be over 65 years of age in another quarter to half century are unfounded. This would be "possible" only if fertility continued at replacement or subreplacement levels and death rates at the higher ages were reduced to zero or near zero in the next few years. (See the discussion of statistical immortality in a later section.)

In comparison with several other countries in the world, the proportion of persons 65 and over in the United States is relatively low. Countries such as Sweden, France, Belgium, Austria, Norway, and Great Britain have much larger proportions of aged, even as high as 14 percent. The countries of Asia, Africa, and Latin America tend to have much smaller proportions of aged persons, even as low as 3 percent.[6] Again, the principal demographic factor which accounts for these wide differences is the level of fertility. Where, as in the Western world, fertility is relatively low, the proportion of the aged tends to be high and where, as in the less developed countries, fertility is high, the proportion of aged will tend to be low.

Contribution of Fertility, Mortality, and Immigration

As has been stated, the general rise in the numbers of births up to the early 1920's, declines in age-specific death rates, and the heavy volume of immigrants, especially prior to World War I, have contributed to the increase in the **number** of persons over 65 in this century and the first two factors will continue to contribute to this increase. The first of these factors, the rise in the number of births, has been of primary importance. However, it has been the general decline in the birth rate which has contributed to the increase in the **proportion** of persons 65 and over. The historical

decline in the birth rate, extending up to the mid-thirties, has been reinforced by the recent decline in the rate (that is, from 1957 on) in contributing to the rise in the proportion 65 and over. A decline in fertility always contributes to a rise in the proportion of the older population but, contrary to intuitive judgment, declines in mortality rates do not contribute to a rise in the proportion of older persons unless the declines have been concentrated at the older ages.[7] Between 1900 and 1974, reductions in mortality have been as great at the younger ages as at the older ages; hence, the changes in mortality in this period have had little effect on age composition and the proportion of elderly persons. In fact, improvements in mortality may have contributed to a slight younging of the population, as Hermalin's empirical analysis covering 1900-1960 suggests.[8]

The immigration factor operates like the mortality factor, i.e., it tends to reduce the proportion of older persons unless the migrants are concentrated in the older ages. The empirical analysis by Hermalin also shows that immigration led to a younger population in the United States in the first 60 years of this century.[9] The data on immigration between 1960 and 1975 suggest that this finding could be extended to cover the whole period 1900-1975.

Such theoretical and historical analyses point to the likelihood that fertility levels will be the principal determinant of the future age composition of the U.S. population. Hence, the proportion of the population in the older ages projected for future years will be most importantly affected by the assumptions made regarding future fertility. The proportion will be affected only slightly by changes in mortality unless the improvements are mainly confined to the older ages and are relatively large. Uniform changes in the level of age-specific death rates over time (that is, without changes in the age pattern of death rates) would have no effect on the age structure of the population and under such circumstances the proportion of the elderly would tend to remain unchanged.[10] Because of the relatively low level of mortality at the ages below 50, future substantial reductions in mortality can only occur at the ages above 50. If such substantial reductions do occur—and they are not anticipated—they will contribute to a perceptible aging of the population. Illustrative figures for

[5] **Current Population Reports**, Series P-25, No. 601, table F-2.
[6] United Nations, **Demographic Yearbook, 1974**, Department of Economic and Social Affairs, Statistical Office, New York, 1976 (forthcoming), table 6.

[7] Ansley J. Coale, "The Effects of Changes in Mortality and Fertility on Age Composition," **Milbank Memorial Fund Quarterly**, Vol. XXXIV, No. 1, January 1956, pp. 79-114.
[8] Albert I. Hermalin, "The Effect of Changes in Mortality Rates on Population Growth and Age Distribution in the United States," **Milbank Memorial Fund Quarterly**, Vol. XLIV, No. 4, Part I, October 1966, pp. 451-469.
[9] Hermalin, op. cit., p. 461.
[10] In the mathematical relations, this uniformity must apply to the factor by which the age-specific proportions surviving from one date to another change.

the proportion 65 and over in the year 2000, assuming Series II or replacement-level fertility with an allowance for net immigration (400,000 per year), are as follows: With constant mortality, 11.5 percent; with "slightly declining" mortality, 11.7 percent; and with "rapidly declining" mortality, 12.2 percent.[11]

The proportion in the older ages will be affected only slightly by the net immigration anticipated in future years. Future net immigration is expected to have a slightly minifying effect on the proportion over 65. For example, the proportion 65 and over in the year 2000, assuming Series II fertility, will be 12.1 percent for the population without immigration, as compared with 11.7 percent for the population with immigration (400,000 per year).[12]

With the already low levels of mortality and immigration, and the prospect of little significant change in these components, fertility will become even more determinative of future changes in age composition than it has been of past changes. For example, under the assumptions of "slightly declining" mortality and 400,000 annual net immigration, the percent 65 and over in the year 2000 would vary from 10.7 to 12.5, depending on whether the high (Series I) or low (Series III) series of fertility prevails. Since fertility is largely under voluntary control, fertility levels may fluctuate widely and, as a result, periods of aging of the population and periods of younging of the population may succeed one another. This possibility is reflected in the combined trends of the various series of population projections for the next half century.

An Index of Aging in Terms of Years Until Death

As a final note in this chapter, it seems of interest to

---

[11] Estimated from data in **Current Population Reports,** Series P-25, No. 601, table 8, and No. 381, table B-2. Series II corresponds to a total fertility rate of 2,100. Expectation of life at age 5 under "rapidly declining" mortality is 3.8 years greater than under "slightly declining" mortality in the year 2000.

[12] **Current Population Reports,** Series P-25, No. 601, tables 8 and F-2.

examine also the indications of an alternative measure of population aging suggested by Ryder, the proportion of the population above the age corresponding to a life expectancy of 10 years.[13] In effect, this measure defines old age in terms of years until death and 10 years is arbitrarily selected as the point of entry into old age. Ryder applied the measure to a variety of theoretical stable conditions of fixed mortality and growth rates, excluding immigration.

Interpretation of the results for actual populations is less clear. Under circumstances of declining mortality at the older ages, and hence of rising life expectation at these ages, any upward trend, however slight, in the proportion of the total population above the age with 10 years of average life remaining could be taken as an indication of an aging population, since the rise in the minimal age of the group tends to militate against a rise in the proportion above that age. In fact, the proportions have shown a steady substantial rise from 1900 to 1970 in the United States as the age corresponding to a life expectancy of 10 years in current life tables has risen:

Year	Age at which average remaining lifetime equals 10.0 years	Proportion of total population above this age
1900...	68.6	.0274
1930...	69.1	.0352
1960...	72.5	.0416
1970...	73.7	.0436

The actual population has been subject to changing mortality as well as changing fertility and net immigration. Use of generation life tables to determine life expectancy at various ages and dates would be more realistic and precise.

---

[13] Norman Ryder, "Notes on Stationary Populations," **Population Index,** Vol. 41, No. 1, Jan. 1975, pp. 3-28, esp. pp. 16-17.

SEX AND RACE COMPOSITION

Sex Composition

A large majority of older persons in the United States are women, whereas at the younger ages there is an excess of males or a small excess of females. The characteristic pattern of sex ratios by age is a generally progressive decline throughout the age span, from a small excess of boys among young children to a massive

deficit of men in extreme old age. At the present time there are only 69 males for every 100 females 65 and over in the United States (table 3-1 and figure 3-1). Only forty years ago just as many males as females were reported at ages 65 and over, but there has been a steady decline in the proportion of men and an increasing excess of women since that time. It is now anticipated that the sex ratio of the population 65 and

Figure 3-1. SEX RATIOS IN THE OLDER AGES: 1900 TO 2010

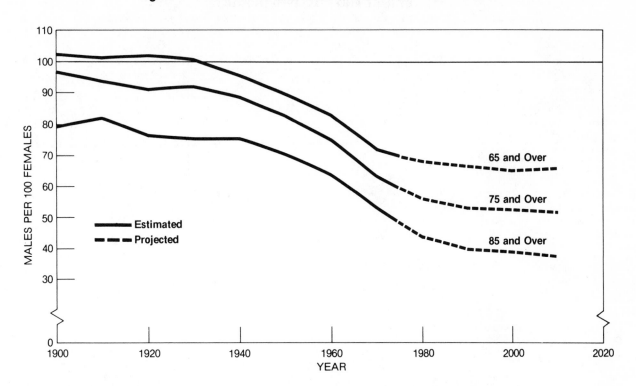

Note: Estimates and projections as of July 1, except for 85 and over, 1900-30, which relate to April 1.
Points are plotted for years ending in zero except for 1975.
Source: Table 3-1.

over will continue to fall, reaching 65 males per 100 females in the year 2000. These facts—the low sex ratio of the older population as compared with the sex ratios at the younger ages and the decline in the sex ratio of the older population over time—call for somewhat different but related explanations.

The sex ratio at some age group in the resident population of the United States may be viewed as determined by four factors: the sex ratio at birth, differences between the sexes in age-specific survival rates from birth, the balance of males and females among net "migrants," and the balance of the sexes among other net "movers" overseas (e.g., movement to outlying areas, movement of Armed Forces personnel, and Federal civilian employees outside the United States). The proportion of males and females in an age group, as shown by census data or extensions of census data, is also affected by net coverage errors and age reporting errors in census data. These factors operate on specific cohorts of births as they progress through life from birth to their extinction.

The pattern of sex ratios by age noted above reflects essentially the persistent excess of boys among the newborn and the progressive effect of higher death rates for males than for females over the entire age range, both in recent years and in the historical past. This explains the

low sex ratio of the older population. Furthermore—in explanation of the second fact, the decline in the sex ratio of the older population over time—males have benefited less than females from the declines in death rates, with the result that there has been a more rapid reduction in the sex ratio over the age span from birth to old age in more recent years than in the past and the sex ratios of the aged have steadily fallen over time. The heavy, predominantly male immigration prior to World War I is still reflected in the sex ratio of the population 65 and over but its influence is small now except in the 75-and-over group. The latest projections of population imply a continuation of the divergence of male and female death rates.

These factors are also reflected in the much more rapid growth of the female population 65 and over than of the male population at these ages (table 3-2). Between 1960 and 1970, for example, the female population grew more than twice as rapidly (28 percent) as the male population (11 percent), and during the present decade the female population is expected to grow nearly 1½ times as rapidly. Since the growth rates for the two sexes during recent decades are more nearly equal at the younger ages, the proportion 65 and over among females has moved well above that for males (figure 3-2). While the proportions for the two sexes were nearly

Table 3-2. **DECENNIAL PERCENT INCREASE OF THE POPULATION IN THE OLDER AGES, BY RACE AND SEX: 1960 TO 2010**

(Periods extend from July 1 of initial year to June 30 of terminal year. A minus sign (-) denotes a decrease)

Age, race, and sex	1960 to 1970	1970 to 1980	1980 to 1990	1990 to 2000	2000 to 2010
65 YEARS AND OVER					
All classes........................	20.4	22.1	18.0	5.8	8.6
Male...............................	11.4	18.0	16.2	4.5	9.3
Female.............................	27.9	25.1	19.2	6.6	8.2
White..............................	19.3	20.9	17.2	4.2	6.8
Male...............................	10.2	16.9	15.5	3.0	7.7
Female.............................	26.7	23.8	18.3	4.9	6.3
Black..............................	30.9	32.7	23.6	15.3	17.9
Male...............................	21.9	27.0	21.2	14.7	17.8
Female.............................	38.6	37.0	25.3	15.7	18.1
75 YEARS AND OVER					
All classes........................	35.2	19.9	25.1	18.6	2.7
Male...............................	22.3	10.9	21.9	16.8	1.8
Female.............................	44.8	25.6	27.0	19.6	3.2
White..............................	34.5	18.6	24.2	17.7	0.6
Male...............................	21.6	9.4	21.0	16.2	-0.2
Female.............................	44.2	24.4	25.9	18.6	1.0
Black..............................	38.0	28.6	35.5	23.2	14.7
Male...............................	26.5	20.3	30.5	20.7	14.6
Female.............................	48.3	34.4	38.7	24.7	14.7
85 YEARS AND OVER					
All classes........................	52.3	44.6	20.1	29.4	19.4
Male...............................	35.8	27.4	11.9	26.2	17.8
Female.............................	62.9	53.7	23.7	30.6	20.0
White..............................	51.2	42.9	19.6	28.9	18.5
Male...............................	34.3	26.0	10.6	26.2	17.2
Female.............................	62.3	51.5	23.5	30.0	19.1
Black..............................	55.2	61.8	14.8	34.5	20.0
Male...............................	39.3	40.2	8.0	29.3	19.7
Female.............................	71.1	74.8	18.1	36.8	20.1

Source: Current Population Reports, Series P-25, Nos. 519 and 601.

Figure 3-2. **PERCENT OF THE TOTAL POPULATION 65 YEARS OLD AND OVER, BY SEX AND BY RACE: 1900 TO 2010**

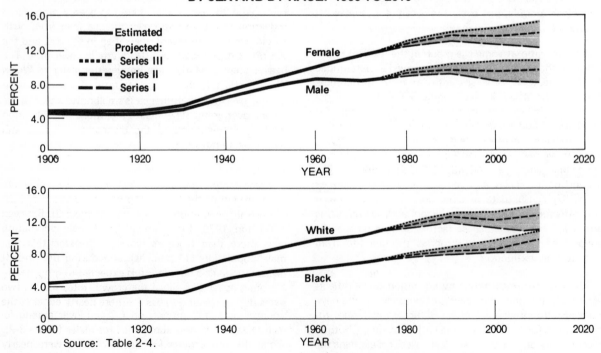

Source: Table 2-4.

Table 3-1. **SEX RATIOS FOR BROAD AGE GROUPS, BY RACE: 1900 TO 2010**

(Males per 100 females. Estimates and projections as of July 1. Figures for 1960 and later years include Armed Forces overseas)

Age, race, and projection series	1900	1930	1960	1970	1975	Projections			
						1980	1990	2000	2010
ALL RACES									
All ages............II..						94.9	94.6	94.5	94.4
Range..........{ I..	104.4	102.5	97.8	95.8	95.3	95.0	95.1	95.3	95.7
{ III..						94.8	94.2	93.8	93.3
Under 15 years..................	102.1	102.8	103.4	103.9	104.1	104.5	105.0	105.2	105.2
15 to 24 years..................	98.3	98.1	101.4	102.2	102.2	102.0	102.4	103.1	103.2
25 to 44 years..................	109.1	101.7	96.9	96.9	97.3	97.4	97.6	97.3	97.7
45 to 54 years..................	113.9	109.4	97.2	93.3	93.6	94.4	94.5	95.4	95.2
55 to 64 years..................	106.5	108.3	93.7	89.7	89.6	89.2	90.3	90.7	91.6
65 to 74 years..................	104.5	104.1	86.7	77.7	76.8	75.8	75.4	76.3	77.0
75 to 84 years..................	(NA)	(NA)	77.4	65.9	61.5	59.8	58.1	57.4	57.9
85 years and over..............	(NA)	(NA)	63.8	53.2	48.5	44.1	39.9	38.5	37.8
65 years and over..............	102.0	100.4	82.6	72.0	69.3	67.9	66.1	64.9	65.5
75 years and over..............	96.3	91.8	75.0	63.3	58.4	56.0	53.7	52.5	51.8
WHITE									
All ages............II..						95.5	95.4	95.3	95.3
Range..........{ I..	104.9	102.9	98.1	96.3	95.8	95.6	95.9	96.2	96.6
{ III..						95.4	95.0	94.7	94.3
Under 15 years..................	102.4	103.2	104.0	104.5	104.7	105.0	105.4	105.5	105.5
15 to 24 years..................	99.1	99.1	102.2	103.0	103.1	102.9	103.3	103.8	103.7
25 to 44 years..................	109.9	102.5	98.0	98.6	99.2	99.6	100.0	99.8	100.3
45 to 54 years..................	113.6	108.8	97.4	94.0	94.4	95.6	96.1	97.4	97.2
55 to 64 years..................	105.6	106.9	93.4	89.9	89.9	89.7	91.2	92.0	93.3
65 to 74 years..................	103.9	103.5	86.3	77.2	76.4	75.7	75.5	76.7	77.8
75 to 84 years..................	(NA)	(NA)	76.6	65.2	60.6	58.8	57.3	56.9	57.5
85 years and over..............	(NA)	(NA)	62.9	52.0	47.4	43.3	38.8	37.6	37.0
65 years and over..............	101.9	100.1	82.0	71.3	68.7	67.3	65.8	64.6	65.5
75 years and over..............	97.1	92.0	74.2	62.6	57.6	55.0	52.9	51.9	51.2
BLACK[1]									
All ages............II..						91.2	91.1	91.0	91.1
Range..........{ I..	98.6	97.0	93.8	91.8	91.5	91.3	91.5	91.9	92.5
{ III..						91.1	90.6	90.2	89.8
Under 15 years..................	99.8	98.9	99.7	100.4	101.2	101.8	103.6	104.1	104.4
15 to 24 years..................	91.6	88.1	94.5	96.5	96.9	97.4	98.2	99.8	99.9
25 to 44 years..................	96.9	92.3	87.9	84.9	85.0	85.2	86.3	86.8	87.8
45 to 54 years..................	110.2	112.5	81.6	86.4	87.0	87.5	87.0	88.2	89.6
55 to 64 years..................	116.3	126.2	92.8	85.1	84.3	84.2	85.6	85.2	86.7
65 to 74 years..................	111.4	111.0	88.3	79.3	77.1	74.5	73.6	74.6	74.1
75 to 84 years..................	95.0	93.8	84.7	73.4	69.8	69.0	64.2	63.0	63.3
85 years and over..............	73.7	74.2	73.7	60.0	53.5	48.1	14.0	41.6	41.2
65 years and over..............	103.7	103.5	86.7	76.2	72.9	70.7	68.4	67.8	67.6
75 years and over..............	89.5	89.0	82.6	70.5	65.5	63.1	59.3	57.3	57.2

NA Not available.

[1]Estimates for 1900 and 1930 as of April 1.

Source: Negro Population in the United States: 1790-1915; Negroes in the United States: 1920-1932; and Current Population Reports, Series P-25, Nos. 311, 519, 614, and 601.

equal in 1930 (5.5 percent and 5.4 percent), in 1975 the proportions were far apart (12.1 percent and 8.8 percent). This pattern of differences is not likely to change much by the year 2000 and is expected to become more intensified (table 2-4).

Race and Ethnic Composition

A much smaller proportion of the black population is 65 and over (7.4 percent in 1975) than for the white population (11.0 percent in 1975). This difference results principally from the higher fertility of the black population and secondarily from the relatively greater concentration of declines in mortality at the younger ages among blacks and the large immigration of whites prior to World War I.

The black population also shows a low sex ratio at ages 65 and over even though the figures for this group have been substantially higher than those for the white population for many decades. In 1975 the comparative figures were 73 and 69 (table 3-1). The age pattern of sex ratios for the black population is very roughly like that for whites, but the decline with age is less regular and less steep. The "starting" level and the sex ratios at the younger ages are lower than for whites, largely because of the lower sex ratio of births; and the sex ratios as recorded at the older ages are higher, possibly because of the narrower gap between male and female mortality rates in the past and the relatively greater coverage of males than females at the ages above 65 in the census.

The sex ratio of the elderly population in 1975 corresponds to an excess of 4.1 million women, or 18 percent of the total population 65 and over. A quarter century earlier, in 1950, the excess was quite small, 0.7 million, or 5.4 percent of the total. A quarter century from now, in 2000, the excess is expected to grow to a huge 6.5 million, or 21 percent of the total.

The population of Spanish origin currently has a very low proportion of persons 65 and over (3.6 percent in 1975) and a very high sex ratio at these ages (87 males per 100 females in 1975), in comparison with the white population as a whole and even the black population. The relevant explanatory factors may be similar to those applicable in the comparison of the black and white populations. In addition, males have dominated among immigrants of Spanish origin.

GEOGRAPHIC DISTRIBUTION AND INTERNAL MIGRATION

Divisions, States, and Counties

Number of elderly persons. Elderly persons tend to be most numerous in the largest States, of course. New York and California have the largest number of people over 65, with nearly 2 million each in 1975 (table 4-1). They are followed by Pennsylvania, Florida, Illinois, Texas, and Ohio. Each of these five States has over a million people over age 65, and together the seven States account for about 45 percent of the population in this age range.

In all States the number of persons 65 years and over increased between April 1, 1970 and July 1, 1975 and between April 1, 1960 and April 1, 1970. The pattern of percentage increases is roughly similar in both periods but, as expected, the figures are generally about half as great in the more recent period.

For the 1960-70 period the population 65 and over in the District of Columbia, Iowa, Maine, Montana, and Vermont grew slowly (i.e., at less than 10 percent of the 1960 population), as compared with 21 percent for the United States as a whole. In other States the growth of the elderly population during this period was rapid (i.e., 30 percent or more of the 1960 population). The population 65 and over in Arizona, Florida, and Nevada grew more than 70 percent between 1960 and 1970. Florida experienced a tremendous growth in the number of elderly persons—432,000 or 78 percent. California

Figure 4-1. PERCENT 65 YEARS OLD AND OVER OF THE TOTAL POPULATION FOR STATES: 1975

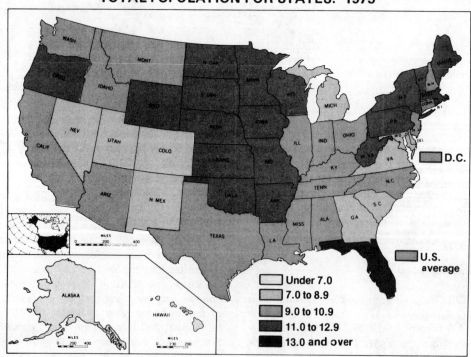

Source: Table 4-3.

Table 4-1. POPULATION 65 YEARS OLD AND OVER, 1960 AND 1970, BY RACE, AND 1975, AND POPULATION 75 YEARS OLD AND OVER, 1960 AND 1970, FOR REGIONS, DIVISIONS, AND STATES

(Numbers in thousands. Estimates as of April 1 for 1960 and 1970 and July 1 for 1975)

Region, division, and State	Population 65 and over — All classes			Increase 1970-75		Increase 1960-70		Population 65 and over — Black		Increase 1960-70		Population 75 and over — All classes		Increase 1960-70	
	1975	1970	1960	Amount	Percent	Amount	Percent	1970	1960	Amount	Percent	1970	1960	Amount	Percent
United States, total.	22,400	19,972	16,560	2,428	12.2	3,412	20.6	1,544	1,168	376	32.2	7,530	5,563	1,967	35.4
Regions:															
Northeast	5,545	5,176	4,498	369	7.1	678	15.1	246	156	89	57.3	1,935	1,463	472	32.3
North Central	6,119	5,703	5,078	416	7.3	625	12.3	281	190	90	47.4	2,251	1,752	499	28.5
South	7,145	6,014	4,582	1,131	18.8	1,432	31.2	936	777	160	20.6	2,162	1,531	631	41.2
West	3,592	3,080	2,401	512	16.6	679	28.3	81	44	37	83.3	1,182	817	365	44.7
Northeast:															
New England	1,370	1,264	1,122	106	8.4	142	12.7	18	13	5	41.8	499	390	109	28.0
Middle Atlantic	4,174	3,911	3,377	263	6.7	534	15.8	227	143	84	58.6	1,435	1,073	363	33.8
North Central:															
East North Central	4,077	3,793	3,358	284	7.5	435	13.0	225	146	80	54.7	1,466	1,131	335	29.6
West North Central	2,042	1,909	1,720	132	6.9	189	11.0	55	45	11	23.6	785	621	164	26.4
South:															
South Atlantic	3,595	2,922	2,099	673	23.0	823	39.2	433	343	90	26.1	1,028	677	351	51.9
East South Central	1,440	1,263	1,052	177	14.0	211	20.1	243	217	27	12.3	464	364	101	27.7
West South Central	2,109	1,828	1,430	281	15.4	398	27.8	260	217	44	20.1	670	491	180	36.6
West:															
Mountain	847	692	527	155	22.4	165	31.3	9	6	3	46.6	261	178	83	46.8
Pacific	2,746	2,389	1,873	357	15.0	516	27.5	72	38	34	89.2	921	639	282	44.1
New England:															
Maine	125	114	107	11	9.8	7	6.7	(Z)	(Z)	(Z)	(B)	45	40	5	12.5
New Hampshire	87	78	68	9	12.0	10	14.8	(Z)	(Z)	(Z)	(B)	30	25	6	23.3
Vermont	52	47	44	4	9.3	3	7.6	(Z)	(Z)	(Z)	(B)	19	17	2	12.7
Massachusetts	672	633	572	38	6.0	61	10.7	9	7	2	28.9	252	198	54	27.1
Rhode Island	113	104	90	9	8.9	14	15.4	1	1	1	54.4	40	30	10	31.9
Connecticut	321	288	243	33	11.6	45	18.3	7	5	3	58.8	113	80	33	41.3
Middle Atlantic:															
New York	2,030	1,951	1,688	79	4.0	263	15.6	112	65	46	70.9	706	525	181	34.4
New Jersey	767	694	560	74	10.6	134	23.8	40	27	13	49.9	253	175	79	44.9
Pennsylvania	1,377	1,267	1,129	111	8.7	138	12.2	75	51	24	47.6	476	372	104	27.8
East North Central:															
Ohio	1,066	993	897	73	7.4	96	10.7	65	44	21	46.6	388	311	77	24.7
Indiana	531	492	446	39	8.0	46	10.2	23	16	7	40.2	193	160	33	20.6
Illinois	1,153	1,089	975	64	5.9	114	11.7	79	53	26	49.2	416	320	97	30.2
Michigan	815	749	638	66	8.8	111	17.4	55	31	25	80.4	282	203	79	38.9
Wisconsin	512	471	403	41	8.8	68	16.8	4	2	2	100.4	186	137	49	36.1
West North Central:															
Minnesota	440	407	354	32	7.9	53	15.1	2	2	(Z)	30.9	167	121	46	38.0
Iowa	364	349	328	15	4.2	21	6.5	2	2	(Z)	20.6	149	122	26	21.7
Missouri	601	558	503	43	7.6	55	11.0	39	31	8	25.6	221	184	37	20.4
North Dakota	73	66	59	7	10.6	7	12.1	(Z)	(Z)	(Z)	(B)	27	21	6	30.1
South Dakota	85	80	72	5	6.3	8	11.5	(Z)	(Z)	(Z)	(B)	33	24	9	36.8
Nebraska	194	183	164	12	6.4	19	11.4	2	2	(Z)	14.1	77	59	18	31.2
Kansas	285	265	240	19	7.2	25	10.6	9	8	1	17.5	111	91	20	22.3
South Atlantic:															
Delaware	50	44	36	7	14.9	8	21.2	5	4	1	28.0	16	12	4	34.5
Maryland	340	298	227	42	14.0	71	31.4	39	27	12	46.3	106	74	32	42.8
District of Columbia	71	70	69	1	1.6	1	1.9	29	20	10	49.4	25	23	3	11.7
Virginia	424	364	289	59	16.3	75	26.0	64	54	10	18.4	131	98	33	33.9
West Virginia	211	194	173	17	8.9	21	12.0	10	9	1	15.1	73	61	12	19.1
North Carolina	492	412	312	81	19.6	100	32.0	79	62	17	28.0	143	102	42	40.8
South Carolina	229	190	151	39	20.8	39	25.7	53	47	6	12.6	65	47	17	36.9
Georgia	430	365	291	64	17.6	74	25.5	88	76	12	16.0	130	96	34	35.7
Florida	1,347	985	553	362	36.8	432	78.2	66	46	20	42.9	338	164	174	106.3
East South Central:															
Kentucky	368	336	292	32	9.6	44	15.0	24	22	2	8.1	129	104	25	23.7
Tennessee	441	382	309	59	15.5	73	23.6	56	46	10	22.5	140	107	33	30.8
Alabama	378	324	261	53	16.4	63	24.2	85	75	10	12.6	116	87	29	33.1
Mississippi	253	221	190	32	14.6	31	16.4	79	74	5	6.9	80	66	14	21.6
West South Central:															
Arkansas	271	237	194	35	14.6	43	22.0	43	38	5	12.2	90	67	23	34.6
Louisiana	346	305	242	41	13.6	63	26.0	89	77	11	14.8	105	80	25	30.8
Oklahoma	334	299	249	35	11.8	50	19.9	18	15	3	17.5	116	91	24	26.6
Texas	1,158	988	745	170	17.2	243	32.6	111	86	25	28.7	359	252	107	42.6
Mountain:															
Montana	75	68	65	6	9.4	3	5.4	(Z)	(Z)	(Z)	(B)	30	22	7	32.2
Idaho	79	67	58	12	17.3	9	16.2	(Z)	(Z)	(Z)	(B)	27	21	7	32.3
Wyoming	33	30	26	3	11.3	4	15.7	(Z)	(Z)	(Z)	(B)	12	8	3	41.4
Colorado	210	187	158	23	12.5	29	18.4	3	2	1	38.6	76	57	18	31.5
New Mexico	90	70	51	20	28.5	19	37.7	1	1	(Z)	71.0	25	16	9	54.4
Arizona	223	161	90	63	38.9	71	78.8	4	2	1	44.6	53	27	26	99.3
Utah	91	77	60	14	18.1	17	28.4	(Z)	(Z)	(Z)	(B)	29	21	8	40.3
Nevada	44	31	18	13	43.6	13	71.0	1	(Z)	(Z)	(B)	10	6	4	74.9
Pacific:															
Washington	365	320	279	44	13.8	41	14.8	3	2	1	48.9	129	99	30	29.7
Oregon	259	226	184	33	14.6	42	22.7	1	1	1	79.1	90	63	27	42.3
California	2,056	1,792	1,376	265	14.8	416	30.2	68	36	32	91.5	686	465	220	47.3
Alaska	9	7	5	2	25.1	2	36.0	(Z)	(Z)	(Z)	(B)	2	2	(Z)	27.7
Hawaii	57	44	29	13	30.5	15	51.7	(Z)	(Z)	(Z)	(B)	14	10	5	51.8

B Base of percent (population in 1960) less than 500.   Z Less than 500.

Source: Census of Population, 1960 and 1970, and Current Population Reports, Series P-25, No. 619.

added 416,000; but since it has nearly twice the population of Florida, its growth rate was far smaller (30 percent). Texas added 243,000 in absolute numbers, a gain which represented 33 percent of the 1960 population. Other States showing high growth rates for the population 65 and over during the 1960's are Maryland (31 percent), North Carolina (32 percent), and New Mexico (38 percent). Finally, New York showed a large absolute gain (263,000) but only a small relative gain (16 percent).

Rapid growth of the number of elderly persons also occurred between 1970 and 1975 in Arizona, Florida, Nevada, and Hawaii; each of these States experienced a gain of over 30 percent of its 1970 population, as compared with 12 percent for the entire country. Florida added 362,000, Texas 170,000, and California 265,000. Other States with high growth rates (over 15 percent) in the 1970-75 period are South Carolina, New Mexico, and Alaska. Slow growth (under 5 percent) was experienced by New York, Iowa, and the District of Columbia. All four geographic divisions in the North had growth rates well below the national average, and all divisions of the South and West, especially the South Atlantic Division and the Mountain Division, had growth rates above the national average.

Proportion of elderly persons. In 1975 the proportion of elderly persons in the States varied from 2.4 percent (Alaska) to 16.1 percent (Florida), as compared with 10.5 percent for the United States as a whole. Such midwestern States as Iowa, Kansas, Missouri, Nebraska, and South Dakota (that is, much of the midwestern farm belt), as well as Oklahoma, Arkansas, and Rhode Island, show high proportions (i.e., 12.0 percent or more) of elderly persons in 1975 (table 4-2 and figure 4-1). Florida is outstanding as the State to which the elderly migrate in order to retire, drawn by a very favorable climate. The following factors have contributed to a relatively large proportion of older persons in the States: Continued heavy out-migration of young persons, substantial in-migration of older persons in recent years, heavy immigration of foreign-born persons in the years prior to World War I, and relatively low fertility.

The States with low proportions (e.g., 8.5 percent or less) of elderly persons in 1975 fall mainly in the South and West. The list includes several States which have relatively high fertility (i.e., South Carolina, New Mexico, and Utah) and several States which have typically experienced a large net in-migration of persons well under 65 (i.e., Maryland, Virginia, Nevada, and Colorado, and the outlying States of Alaska and Hawaii).

Counties show a much wider variation in the proportion of elderly persons than States. Many counties with extremely high proportions may be found in the States of the West North Central Division. One-fifth of the 105 counties in Kansas had proportions of 20 percent or more in 1970, and nearly one-fifth of the 115 counties of Missouri had proportions of this magnitude.[1] In forty-five percent of the 619 counties in the West North Central Division, 15 percent or more of the population was 65 years old or over.

Internal migration. Although it would have been desirable to develop estimates of net migration for States between 1960 and 1970 and between 1970 and 1975 for the **age group** 65 and over, it would have taken considerable work to prepare satisfactory estimates of this kind.[2] Instead, estimates of net migration for States between 1960 and 1970 for the **age cohort** 65 and over in 1965 (i.e., 60 and over in 1960 and 70 and over in 1970) were prepared. For this purpose national census survival rates (rather than death statistics or life table survival rates) were employed in combination with the decennial census data in a residual method. Estimates of net migration derived by "surviving" the age cohort 60 and over in 1960 from 1960 to 1970 (70 and over in 1970) includes the net migration of some persons aged 60 to 64 in the early part of the decade prior to reaching age 65 and excludes the net migration of some persons aged 65 to 69 in the later part of the decade after reaching age 65. The two "error terms" would be expected to offset one another to a substantial degree in many States and, hence, net migration for this cohort during the decade should roughly approximate the net migration during the decade for the age group 65 and over.

---

[1] See U.S. Bureau of the Census, 1970 census, United States Maps, GE-50, No. 36, "Older Americans by Counties of the United States, 1970."

[2] If the number of persons 65 and over grew rapidly in a State during a period (e.g., 1960-70)—much more rapidly, say, than the national population in this age group (21 percent in 1960-70)—one would expect that, in addition to the "natural increase" during the period (i.e., persons reaching age 65 less deaths at ages 65 and over in 1960-70), there was a net influx of elderly persons into the State at this age during the period. Hence, estimates of net migration rates for States between 1960 and 1970 could be obtained simply by subtracting 0.21, the U.S. growth rate, from the decennial growth rate for each State. The results would be too rough for general use, however. This method assumes that birth rates 65 or more years earlier, survival rates for these birth cohorts to age 65, and death rates during the 1960-70 decade for the States were similar to the United States rates—conditions which are true only within wide limits—and that net interstate migration since birth has affected the number reaching age 65 between 1960 and 1970 to a similar degree in each State—a condition which is not true even within wide limits.

One could derive much more accurate estimates of the net migration of elderly persons for each State between 1960 and 1970 by subtracting direct estimates of "natural increase" 65 and over for each State from the change in the number of persons 65 and over during the period. Such estimates would require compiling deaths at ages 65 and over for the intercensal years and estimating the number of persons reaching age 65 during these years. It was not possible to complete such estimates in time for inclusion in this report.

Table 4-2. PERCENT 65 YEARS OLD AND OVER OF THE TOTAL POPULATION; 1960 AND 1970 BY RACE, AND 1975, AND PERCENT 75 YEARS OLD AND OVER, 1960 AND 1970, FOR REGIONS, DIVISIONS, AND STATES

(Numbers in thousands. Estimates as of April 1 for 1960 and 1970 and July 1 for 1975)

Region, division, and State	Population 65 years and over					Percent 65 years and over							Percent 75 years and over	
	All classes, 1975	1970				All classes, 1975	1970				1960		All classes	
		All classes	White	Black	Persons of Spanish language[1]		All classes	White	Black	Persons of Spanish language	All classes	Black	1970	1960
United States, total	22,400	19,972	18,272	1,544	382	10.5	9.8	10.3	6.8	4.1	9.2	6.2	3.7	3.1
Regions:														
Northeast	5,545	5,176	4,911	246	31	11.2	10.6	11.1	5.7	2.5	10.1	5.2	3.9	3.3
North Central	6,119	5,703	5,404	281	23	10.6	10.1	10.5	6.1	2.7	9.8	5.5	4.0	3.4
South	7,145	6,014	5,054	936	141	10.5	9.6	10.0	7.8	4.9	8.3	6.9	3.4	2.8
West	3,592	3,080	2,903	81	188	9.5	8.8	9.2	4.8	4.3	8.6	4.1	3.4	2.9
Northeast:														
New England	1,370	1,264	1,242	18	5	11.2	10.7	10.9	4.7	3.1	10.7	5.3	4.2	3.7
Middle Atlantic	4,174	3,911	3,669	227	26	11.2	10.5	11.1	5.7	2.4	9.9	5.1	3.9	3.1
North Central:														
East North Central	4,077	3,793	3,558	225	17	9.9	9.4	9.8	5.8	2.5	9.3	5.0	3.6	3.1
West North Central	2,042	1,909	1,847	55	5	12.2	11.7	11.9	7.9	3.4	11.2	8.0	4.8	4.0
South:														
South Atlantic	3,595	2,922	2,481	433	39	10.7	9.5	10.3	6.8	6.1	8.1	5.9	3.3	2.6
East South Central	1,440	1,263	1,018	243	2	10.6	9.9	10.0	9.5	3.5	8.7	8.0	3.6	3.0
West South Central	2,109	1,828	1,555	260	100	10.1	9.5	9.6	8.6	4.6	8.4	7.8	3.5	2.9
West:														
Mountain	847	692	670	9	53	8.8	8.4	8.6	5.0	4.7	7.7	5.0	3.2	2.6
Pacific	2,746	2,389	2,233	72	135	9.7	9.0	9.4	4.8	4.2	8.8	4.0	3.5	3.0
New England:														
Maine	125	114	114	(Z)	(Z)	11.8	11.5	11.5	4.3	4.6	11.0	1.9	4.5	4.2
New Hampshire	87	78	78	(Z)	(Z)	10.7	10.6	10.6	2.8	2.6	11.2	2.6	4.1	4.1
Vermont	52	47	47	(Z)	(Z)	11.0	10.6	10.7	6.0	5.5	11.2	6.0	4.3	4.3
Massachusetts	672	633	622	9	2	11.5	11.1	11.3	5.3	3.3	11.1	6.5	4.4	3.9
Rhode Island	113	104	102	1	(Z)	12.2	10.9	11.1	5.7	3.4	10.4	5.1	4.2	3.5
Connecticut	321	288	280	7	2	10.4	9.5	9.8	4.0	2.8	9.6	4.2	3.7	3.1
Middle Atlantic:														
New York	2,030	1,951	1,829	112	23	11.2	10.7	11.5	5.1	2.6	10.1	4.6	3.9	3.1
New Jersey	767	694	651	40	2	10.5	9.7	10.2	5.2	1.4	9.2	5.2	3.5	2.9
Pennsylvania	1,377	1,267	1,189	75	1	11.6	10.7	11.1	7.4	1.6	10.0	6.0	4.0	3.3
East North Central:														
Ohio	1,066	993	927	65	3	9.9	9.3	9.6	6.7	2.9	9.2	5.6	3.6	3.2
Indiana	531	492	468	23	2	10.0	9.5	9.7	6.3	2.4	9.6	6.0	3.7	3.4
Illinois	1,153	1,089	1,007	79	9	10.3	9.8	10.5	5.5	2.4	9.7	5.1	3.7	3.2
Michigan	815	749	691	55	4	8.9	8.4	8.8	5.6	3.0	8.2	4.3	3.2	2.6
Wisconsin	512	471	465	4	1	11.1	10.7	10.9	3.2	2.1	10.2	2.8	4.2	3.5
West North Central:														
Minnesota	440	407	404	2	1	11.2	10.7	10.8	5.8	2.4	10.4	6.9	4.4	3.5
Iowa	364	349	347	2	1	12.7	12.4	12.4	7.1	3.9	11.9	7.5	5.3	4.4
Missouri	601	558	518	39	2	12.6	11.9	12.4	8.2	4.0	11.7	8.0	4.7	4.2
North Dakota	73	66	65	(Z)	(Z)	11.5	10.7	10.9	0.8	1.5	9.3	1.0	4.4	3.3
South Dakota	85	80	78	(Z)	(Z)	12.5	12.0	12.4	3.1	1.8	10.5	5.1	5.0	3.6
Nebraska	194	183	180	2	1	12.6	12.3	12.5	6.0	2.8	11.6	7.1	5.2	4.2
Kansas	285	265	255	9	2	12.6	11.8	12.0	8.7	3.6	11.0	8.6	4.9	4.2
South Atlantic:														
Delaware	50	44	39	5	(Z)	8.7	8.0	8.3	6.1	3.8	8.0	6.1	2.9	2.7
Maryland	340	298	258	39	2	8.3	7.6	8.1	5.6	2.9	7.3	5.2	2.7	2.4
District of Columbia	71	70	40	29	1	10.0	9.3	19.1	5.5	4.9	9.1	4.8	3.3	3.0
Virginia	424	364	299	64	1	8.5	7.8	8.0	7.4	2.5	7.3	6.6	2.8	2.5
West Virginia	211	194	184	10	(Z)	11.7	11.1	11.0	14.5	5.9	9.3	9.5	4.2	3.3
North Carolina	492	412	331	79	(Z)	9.0	8.1	8.5	7.0	1.9	6.9	5.5	2.8	2.2
South Carolina	229	190	137	53	(Z)	8.1	7.3	7.6	6.7	2.2	6.3	5.7	2.5	2.0
Georgia	430	365	277	88	1	8.7	8.0	8.2	7.4	3.0	7.4	6.7	2.8	2.4
Florida	1,347	985	917	66	34	16.1	14.5	16.0	6.4	7.5	11.2	5.3	5.0	3.3
East South Central:														
Kentucky	368	336	312	24	(Z)	10.8	10.4	10.5	10.3	3.0	9.6	10.1	4.0	3.4
Tennessee	441	382	325	56	(Z)	10.5	9.7	9.9	9.0	3.2	8.7	7.8	3.6	3.0
Alabama	378	324	239	85	(Z)	10.4	9.4	9.4	9.4	3.4	8.0	7.7	3.4	2.7
Mississippi	253	221	142	79	(Z)	10.8	10.0	10.2	9.6	4.7	8.7	8.0	3.6	3.0
West South Central:														
Arkansas	271	237	193	43	(Z)	12.8	12.3	12.4	12.1	4.3	10.9	9.8	4.7	3.7
Louisiana	346	305	216	89	4	9.1	8.4	8.5	8.1	5.3	7.4	7.4	2.9	2.5
Oklahoma	334	299	272	18	1	12.3	11.7	11.9	10.3	3.5	10.7	9.8	4.5	3.9
Texas	1,158	988	874	111	95	9.5	8.8	9.0	8.0	4.6	7.8	7.3	3.2	2.6
Mountain:														
Montana	75	68	67	(Z)	(Z)	10.0	9.9	10.1	4.6	3.2	9.7	7.6	4.3	3.3
Idaho	79	67	67	(Z)	1	9.6	9.5	9.5	4.0	2.9	8.7	8.4	3.8	3.1
Wyoming	33	30	30	(Z)	1	9.0	9.0	9.2	5.6	3.9	7.8	6.1	3.6	2.5
Colorado	210	187	183	3	13	8.3	8.5	8.6	4.7	4.7	9.0	5.7	3.4	3.3
New Mexico	90	70	66	1	22	7.9	6.9	7.2	4.7	5.4	5.4	3.2	2.5	1.7
Arizona	223	161	153	4	14	10.0	9.1	9.5	6.6	4.2	6.9	5.6	3.0	2.0
Utah	91	77	76	(Z)	1	7.5	7.3	7.3	4.9	2.6	6.7	4.7	2.3	1.9
Nevada	44	31	29	1	1	7.5	6.3	6.5	3.1	4.0	6.4	2.9	2.0	1.9
Pacific:														
Washington	365	320	313	3	2	10.3	9.4	9.6	3.9	2.6	9.8	3.9	3.8	3.5
Oregon	259	226	222	1	1	11.3	10.8	10.9	5.1	3.0	10.4	4.1	4.3	3.6
California	2,056	1,792	1,681	68	131	9.7	9.0	9.4	4.9	4.2	8.8	4.0	3.4	3.0
Alaska	9	7	5	(Z)	(Z)	2.4	2.3	1.9	1.1	0.6	2.4	0.7	0.7	0.7
Hawaii	57	44	12	(Z)	1	6.6	5.7	4.1	0.9	3.2	4.6	0.7	1.8	1.5

Z Less than 500.

[1] For New York, New Jersey, and Pennsylvania, persons of Puerto Rican birth and parentage only; for five Southwestern States includes other persons of Spanish surname. Note that persons of Spanish origin may be of any race.

Source: Census of the Population, 1960 and 1970; Supplementary Report PC (S1)-29 (persons of Spanish language); and Current Population Reports, Series P-25, No. 619.

These estimates of net migration reflect a considerable movement of elderly persons out of the Middle Atlantic States and the East North Central States, and a considerable movement of elderly persons into the South Atlantic States, the West South Central States, and Pacific States, during the 1960-70 decade (table 4-3). New York, Pennsylvania, Ohio, Illinois, and Michigan were big losers, and Florida, Texas, and California were big gainers. In relative terms the District of Columbia, Alaska, and Hawaii were the largest losers, and Florida and Arizona were the largest gainers.

In spite of the fact that several States showed relatively high net in- or out-migration rates for the elderly population between 1960 and 1970, this age group moves relatively little. Mobility rates and migration rates show a generally downward progression with advancing age from age group 20 to 24, as may be seen for the years 1970-71 (one-year period) and 1970-75 (5-year period) in table 4-4.[3]

In the year 1970-71 the migration rate of interstate migrants 65 and over was only 1.4 percent, or only two-fifths as great as the migration rate for the population one and over (3.4 percent). (See table 4-5 and figure 4-2.) Similar differences appeared for other classes of movers. Mobility rates appear to rise around age 75 as a result, possibly, of institutionalization, changes in marital and household status, and movement to retirement centers.[4]

---

[3] As suggested earlier, mobility rates and migration rates for age cohorts for a span of calendar years, defined by the terminal ages, may not represent the experience at these ages satisfactorily because migration experience at younger ages is included. Therefore, rates for one-year time periods, particularly a series of one-year rates for several years, are preferable for analysis of mobility and migration for age groups. The last one-year time period for which national mobility and migration rates by age are available is 1970-71.

[4] For further discussion of this point, see Lynne R. Heltman, "Mobility of the Aged in the United States," paper presented at the annual meeting of the Population Association of America, Seattle, Washington, April 17-19, 1975.

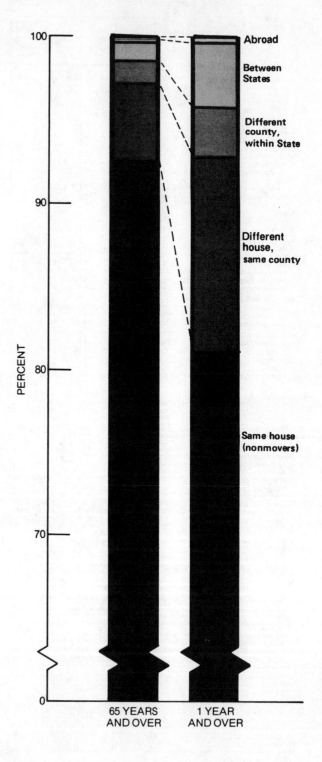

Figure 4-2. MOBILITY AND MIGRATION RATES FOR THE POPULATION 65 YEARS OLD AND OVER AND ONE YEAR OLD AND OVER: 1970-71

Abroad

Between States

Different county, within State

Different house, same county

Same house (nonmovers)

PERCENT

65 YEARS AND OVER   1 YEAR AND OVER

Source: Table 4-5.

Table 4-3. ESTIMATED NET MIGRATION OF THE POPULATION COHORT 65 YEARS OLD AND OVER IN 1965, BY RACE, FOR REGIONS, DIVISIONS, AND STATES: 1960-70

(Numbers in thousands. Rate represents net migration between 1960 and 1970 of the cohort 60 and over in 1960, 65 and over in 1965, and 70 and over in 1970 as percent of the population 65 and over in 1965 (average of the populations 60 and over in 1960 and 70 and over in 1970). Net migration was computed by the residual method using national census survival rates. No adjustment has been made to independent estimates of net immigration for the United States. A plus sign (+) denotes net in-migration and a minus sign (-) denotes out-migration)

Region, division, and State	All classes		White		Black	
	Amount	Rate	Amount	Rate	Amount	Rate
United States, total...............	+26	+0.1	+24	+0.1	+5	+0.4
Regions:						
Northeast.........................	-228	-4.6	-236	-5.0	+6	+3.2
North Central.....................	-128	-2.3	-136	-2.6	+7	+3.1
South.............................	+249	+4.8	+263	+6.1	-18	-2.2
West..............................	+133	+4.9	+134	+5.2	+10	+16.6
Northeast:						
New England......................	-19	-1.6	-21	-1.8	+1	+8.9
Middle Atlantic..................	-209	-5.6	-215	-6.1	+5	+2.8
North Central:						
East North Central..............	-138	-3.8	-145	-4.2	+7	+3.7
West North Central..............	+10	+0.5	+9	+0.5	+1	+1.0
South:						
South Atlantic...................	+195	+8.0	+204	+9.9	-11	-2.8
East South Central..............	+3	+0.3	+11	+1.2	-8	-3.7
West South Central..............	+50	+3.2	+48	+3.6	+1	+0.3
West:						
Mountain.........................	+36	+6.0	+38	+6.5	(Z)	+6.0
Pacific..........................	+98	+4.6	+96	+4.8	+9	+18.1
New England:						
Maine............................	-3	-2.7	-3	-2.7	(Z)	(B)
New Hampshire....................	+1	+0.9	+1	+0.8	(Z)	(B)
Vermont..........................	(Z)	-1.0	(Z)	-1.0	(Z)	(B)
Massachusetts....................	-14	-2.3	-16	-2.6	+1	+8.5
Rhode Island.....................	-2	-1.7	-2	-1.9	(Z)	+10.7
Connecticut......................	(Z)	(Z)	-1	-0.3	(Z)	+8.7
Middle Atlantic:						
New York.........................	-137	-7.3	-141	-7.9	+4	+4.4
New Jersey.......................	-9	-1.4	-11	-1.8	+1	+3.3
Pennsylvania.....................	-63	-5.1	-64	-5.5	(Z)	+0.3
East North Central:						
Ohio.............................	-35	-3.7	-37	-4.1	+2	+3.2
Indiana..........................	-13	-2.7	-14	-3.1	+1	+2.9
Illinois.........................	-62	-5.9	-62	-6.3	+1	+0.9
Michigan.........................	-29	-4.2	-33	-5.0	+3	+8.4
Wisconsin........................	+3	+0.6	+2	+0.5	(Z)	+16.2
West North Central:						
Minnesota........................	+5	+1.4	+5	+1.3	(Z)	+7.2
Iowa.............................	(Z)	(Z)	(Z)	(Z)	(Z)	-1.7
Missouri.........................	-4	-0.7	-5	-1.0	(Z)	+0.9
North Dakota.....................	(Z)	-0.4	(Z)	-0.1	(Z)	(B)
South Dakota.....................	(Z)	+0.5	+1	+1.1	(Z)	(B)
Nebraska.........................	+4	+2.2	+4	+2.3	(Z)	-3.3
Kansas...........................	+4	+1.7	+4	+1.7	(Z)	+2.2
South Atlantic:						
Delaware.........................	(Z)	+1.0	(Z)	+1.0	(Z)	-2.6
Maryland.........................	+4	+1.4	+3	+1.4	+1	+2.2
District of Columbia.............	-12	-16.6	-12	-25.0	(Z)	+1.5
Virginia.........................	+2	+0.6	+4	+1.5	-2	-4.0
West Virginia....................	-8	-4.4	-7	-4.0	-1	-9.1
North Carolina...................	+6	+1.6	+7	+2.6	-2	-2.3
South Carolina...................	-3	-2.0	+1	+0.7	-4	-8.5
Georgia..........................	+2	+0.6	+5	+1.9	-3	-4.0
Florida..........................	+205	+29.3	+203	+31.3	+1	+1.1
East South Central:						
Kentucky.........................	-1	-0.4	(Z)	-0.2	-1	-3.7
Tennessee........................	+5	+1.4	+5	+1.8	(Z)	-0.7
Alabama..........................	+3	+1.2	+5	+2.4	-3	-3.3
Mississippi......................	-4	-1.8	+1	+0.8	-5	-6.1
West South Central:						
Arkansas.........................	+9	+4.2	+9	+5.1	(Z)	-0.1
Louisiana........................	-3	-1.0	-1	-0.4	-2	-3.1
Oklahoma.........................	+8	+2.8	+7	+2.6	+1	+4.4
Texas............................	+37	+4.3	+34	+4.5	+3	+2.6
Mountain:						
Montana..........................	-1	-1.5	-1	-1.0	(Z)	(B)
Idaho............................	+1	+1.7	+1	+2.0	(Z)	(B)
Wyoming..........................	-1	-3.5	-1	-3.3	(Z)	(B)
Colorado.........................	+6	+3.7	+6	+3.7	(Z)	+8.1
New Mexico.......................	+2	+2.5	+2	+3.3	(Z)	+4.6
Arizona..........................	+24	+21.2	+25	+23.5	(Z)	+4.7
Utah.............................	+2	+3.3	+2	+3.4	(Z)	(B)
Nevada...........................	+2	+9.0	+2	+9.6	(Z)	+11.4
Pacific:						
Washington.......................	+3	+1.2	+4	+1.3	(Z)	+3.5
Oregon...........................	+10	+4.8	+10	+4.9	(Z)	+14.9
California.......................	+92	+5.9	+83	+5.6	+9	+19.0
Alaska...........................	-2	-30.6	-1	-33.3	(Z)	(B)
Hawaii...........................	-6	-17.3	+1	+9.9	(Z)	(B)

B Base of percent (average of population 60 and over in 1960 and 70 and over in 1970) less than 500.   Z Less than 500 or 0.05 percent.

Table 4-4. **MOBILITY RATES AND MIGRATION RATES, BY AGE: 1970-75 AND 1970-71**

Terminal age	Percent of population with different residence			
	Different house, same county		Different county	
	1970-75	1970-71	1970-75	1970-71
Total[1]	24.2	11.4	17.1	6.5
1 to 4 years	(X)	17.8	(X)	10.3
5 to 13 years	28.2	10.2	19.5	5.9
14 to 17 years	20.9	8.2	13.1	4.2
18 and 19 years	24.3	16.0	13.9	7.7
20 to 24 years	36.1	24.7	26.0	16.4
25 to 34 years	36.1	17.1	30.4	10.4
35 to 44 years	23.4	8.7	16.4	4.8
45 to 64 years	15.4	6.2	9.0	3.0
65 to 74 years	12.3	5.4	8.6	2.9
75 years and over	11.9	6.8	6.8	2.3

X Not applicable.
[1]For 1970-75, total is for persons five years old and over; for 1970-71, total is for persons one year old and over.
Source: Current Population Reports, Series P-20, Nos. 235 and 285.

Table 4-5. **MOBILITY RATES AND MIGRATION RATES FOR THE POPULATION 65 YEARS OLD AND OVER AND ONE YEAR OLD AND OVER, BY SEX: 1970-71**

(Data relate to the period March 1970 to March 1971)

Mobility status	Both sexes			Male			Female		
	65 years old and over	1 year old and over	Ratio, 65 and over to 1 and over	65 years old and over	1 year old and over	Ratio, 65 and over to 1 and over	65 years old and over	1 year old and over	Ratio, 65 and over to 1 and over
Total population	100.0	100.0	1.00	100.0	100.0	1.00	100.0	100.0	1.00
Same house (nonmovers)	91.2	81.3	1.12	91.8	80.6	1.14	90.8	81.9	1.11
Different house	8.7	17.9	.49	8.1	18.3	.44	9.1	17.6	.52
Same county	6.0	11.4	.53	5.4	11.5	.47	6.4	11.3	.57
Different county	2.7	6.5	.42	2.7	6.7	.40	2.7	6.3	.43
Within State	1.3	3.1	.42	1.4	3.2	.44	1.2	3.0	.40
Between States	1.4	3.4	.41	1.2	3.5	.34	1.5	3.4	.44
Contiguous	0.5	1.0	.50	0.3	1.0	.30	0.7	1.0	.70
Noncontiguous	0.9	2.5	.36	0.9	2.6	.35	0.8	2.4	.33
Abroad	0.1	0.8	.12	0.1	1.1	.09	0.1	0.5	.20

Source: Current Population Reports, Series P-20, No. 235.

Size of Place and Urban-Rural Residence

The 1970 census showed a gradation in the proportion of persons 65 and over according to the size of the place of residence, excluding the farm population ("other rural" areas) and the urban fringe; the larger the place, the lower the percentage of elderly people. The highest proportion of elderly persons (13.6 percent) is found in small towns, i.e., rural places of 1,000 to 2,500 inhabitants (table 4-6). The next highest proportion is found in urban places of 2,500 to 10,000, followed in order by urban places of 10,000 to 50,000, central cities of urbanized areas, "other rural" areas, and the urban fringe. In the urban fringe young families with children predominate. One of the lowest percentages (9.6 percent) is found in "other rural" areas (i.e., the farm population).

The high percentage of aged persons in rural places of 1,000 to 2,500 may result from the high rate of out-migration of young people to the larger places. We should expect this reason to apply also to the "other rural" areas but apparently other factors are dominant. A higher birth rate in the farm population may account for some of the difference. More important, many farmers over 65 can no longer operate their farms and so they migrate, not to Florida or other distant States, but to the town closest to their farm.

Of the 20.1 million persons 65 and over in April 1970, over half (55 percent) lived in urbanized areas. Of the latter group about three-fifths (62 percent) lived in central cities and two-fifths (38 percent) in the urban fringe. Thus, about one-third (34 percent) of all aged persons lived in central cities. About one-quarter (27 percent) lived in rural areas.

The distribution of blacks diverged sharply from that for the population as a whole, principally in their concentration in central cities within urbanized areas. Of the 1.6 million blacks 65 and over in 1970, about 950,000, or three-fifths (61 percent), lived in urbanized

Table 4-6. **DISTRIBUTION OF THE WHITE, BLACK, AND SPANISH-HERITAGE POPULATION 65 YEARS OLD AND OVER BY URBAN AND RURAL RESIDENCE AND BY SIZE OF PLACE: 1970**

Race	1970										1960		
		Urban						Rural					
			Urbanized areas			Other places of--							
	Total	Total	Total	Central cities	Urban fringe	10,000 or more	2,500 to 10,000	Total	Places of 1,000 to 2,500	Other rural	Total	Urban	Rural
NUMBER (thousands)													
Total..................	20,066	14,631	11,106	6,842	4,264	1,788	1,737	5,434	903	4,532	16,560	11,526	5,033
White..................	18,330	13,309	10,049	5,950	4,100	1,641	1,619	5,021	852	4,169	15,304	10,672	4,632
Negro and other races........	1,735	1,322	1,056	892	164	147	118	413	51	362	1,256	854	402
Black.................	1,559	1,192	949	812	137	136	107	367	44	323	(NA)	(NA)	(NA)
Spanish heritage[1]............	382	330	271	194	77	29	30	52	(NA)	(NA)	(NA)	(NA)	(NA)
PERCENT OF ALL AGES													
Total..................	9.9	9.8	9.4	10.7	7.8	10.8	12.2	10.1	13.6	9.6	9.2	9.2	9.3
White..................	10.3	10.3	10.0	12.0	8.0	11.1	12.5	10.3	13.9	9.7	9.6	9.7	9.6
Negro and other races........	6.8	6.4	6.0	6.2	5.3	8.3	9.3	8.4	9.9	8.2	6.1	5.8	7.1
Black.................	6.9	6.5	6.0	6.2	5.4	8.7	9.7	8.7	10.4	8.5	(NA)	(NA)	(NA)
Spanish heritage[1]............	4.1	4.0	3.9	4.2	3.4	4.3	5.0	4.6	(NA)	(NA)	(NA)	(NA)	(NA)
PERCENT OF ALL AREAS													
Total..................	100.0	72.9	55.3	34.1	21.2	8.9	8.7	27.1	4.5	22.6	100.0	69.6	30.4
White..................	100.0	72.6	54.8	32.5	22.4	9.0	8.8	27.4	4.6	22.7	100.0	69.7	30.3
Negro and other races........	100.0	76.2	60.9	51.4	9.5	8.5	6.8	23.8	2.9	20.9	100.0	68.0	32.0
Black.................	100.0	76.5	60.9	52.1	8.8	8.7	6.9	23.5	2.8	20.7	(NA)	(NA)	(NA)
Spanish heritage[1]............	100.0	86.3	70.9	50.8	20.2	7.7	7.7	13.7	(NA)	(NA)	(NA)	(NA)	(NA)

NA Not available.

[1] For New York, New Jersey, and Pennsylvania, persons of Puerto Rican birth and parentage only; for five Southwestern States, persons of Spanish language or Spanish surname; for remaining States, persons of Spanish language. Note that persons of Spanish origin may be of any race.

Source: Census of Population: 1970, General Population Characteristics, Final Report, PC(1)-B1, United States Summary, table 52, and PC(1)-C1, United States Summary, table 118.

areas. Of the latter group 86 percent lived in central cities and 14 percent lived in the urban fringe. Thus, over half (52 percent) of all blacks 65 and over lived in a central city. About one-quarter (24 percent) lived in rural areas, mostly on farms.

The population of Spanish heritage 65 and over is very largely an urban population (86 percent in 1970), much more urban than whites as a whole or blacks at this age. Like the black population the population of Spanish heritage is heavily concentrated in central cities of urbanized areas (51 percent in 1970) and like the white population in general an important share lives in the urban fringe (20 percent). Correspondingly, the share in rural areas is much smaller (14 percent) than for the white population as a whole or the black population. Data from the Current Population Survey suggest

that the urban-rural distribution of the elderly Spanish-heritage population is about the same in 1975 as in 1970.

Summary Note

The following generalizations seem to describe the migration tendencies of the elderly in the United States. Their migration rates are relatively low; with increasing age, people migrate less. If the elderly do migrate, they generally go to various retirement areas within the United States, particularly Florida, or to rural places or small towns (from farms), the country of origin (if foreign-born), or other areas abroad (e.g., Mexico) to retire. On the other hand, they may remain "stuck" in rural hinterlands or large urban centers, particularly the deteriorated parts of these areas.

MORTALITY AND SURVIVAL

Quantity vs. Quality of Life

Progress in the "control" or management of the aging process from a demographic point of view is measured principally in terms of the increase in the "quantity" of life, as shown, for example, by reductions in mortality rates and increases in survival rates or in average years of remaining life. Progress may also be measured in terms of improvements in the "quality" of life, as shown, for example, by reductions in the incidence rates and prevalence rates for morbidity, mental illness, and disability, in the proportions of the population hospitalized and institutionalized, and in proportions widowed or living alone. The discussion here is largely concerned with the quantity dimension, and gives little direct consideration to the quality dimension. Some attention is devoted to marital status and living arrangements as social characteristics of the population but health status is not discussed.[1]

The preoccupation with mortality, survival, and longevity should not be interpreted to imply that the quality of life is less important, only that it is a less appropriate and common area of demographic study, which has as its primary interest population size, geographic distribution, and structure. In fact, a principal concern of public and private effort should be to make the later years of life vigorous, healthy, and satisfying, not merely to add additional years of life. Hayflick has suggested that, given a human life span of about 100 years, society's goal might be that all persons should live healthy and active lives until their 100th birthdays and then die peacefully in their sleep as they begin their 101st year.[2]

---

[1] Few satisfactory summary studies giving national analyses of the health, living arrangements, and kinship network of the older population from a demographic point of view are available. Some references which present and analyze basic data relating to health are: Erdman Palmore (ed.), **Normal Aging: Reports from the Duke Longitudinal Study, 1955-1969**, Duke University Press, Durham, N.C., 1970, esp. Chapters 2 and 3; U.S. Bureau of the Census, 1970 Census of Population, Subject Report PC(2)-4E, **Persons in Institutions and Other Group Quarters**, 1973, and Subject Report PC(2)-6C, **Persons with Work Disability**, 1973; U.S. Public Health Service, National Center for Health Statistics, **Vital and Health Statistics**, "Current Estimates from the Health Interview Survey, United States, 1974", by Peter W. Ries, Series 10, No. 100, September 1975, and "Age Patterns in Medical Care, Illness, and Disability, United States, 1968-1969", by Christy Namey and Ronald W. Wilson, Series 10, No. 70, April 1972; and U.S. Public Health Service, National Center for Health Statistics, **Health in the Later Years of Life**, 1971, and **Health in the United States, 1975**, 1976.

[2] Leonard Hayflick, "The Strategy of Senescence," **The Gerontologist**, Vol. 14, No. 1, Feb. 1974, pp. 37-45, esp. p. 40 and p. 43.

Life Expectancy

Progress in the reduction of mortality or in extending length of life is often measured by life expectancy at birth. Life expectancy at birth is a capsulized indicator ("standardized" for differences in age composition to a limited degree) of progress in the elimination of premature death at all ages. It has shown a tremendous increase since the beginning of this century, having risen from 49 years in 1900-02 (Original Death Registration States) to 69.5 years in 1955, 71.3 years in 1973, and 71.9 years in 1974. (See table 5-1.) These figures imply a total gain of about 20 years in life expectancy in the first 55 or so years of this century, or an average annual gain of 0.4 year in this period. A plateau was reached about 1954-55, and in the 19 years from 1955 to 1974, life expectancy at birth has advanced haltingly and slowly, with the gain amounting to about 2½ years in this whole period or 0.13 year annually.

Since life expectation at birth is a function of death rates at all ages, it does not tell us at what ages the improvement occurred. We want particularly to distinguish progress in "life expectation" or survival at the ages under 65 from progress at the ages over 65. We can summarize changes in death rates in these and other age ranges in terms of life table survival rates and in terms of "age-bounded expectancy values." According to the life table of 1900-02, 41 percent of the newborn babies would reach age 65, but according to the life table for 1974, 74 percent would reach age 65—a gain of 33 persons aged 65 per 100 babies. The proportion of persons surviving from age 65 to age 80 was 33 percent in 1900-02 and 51 percent in 1974—a gain of 18 persons aged 80 per 100 persons aged 65. Accordingly, the chance of survival from birth to age 65 and the chance of survival from age 65 to age 80 are both much higher than earlier; but the increase in the survival rate of persons above age 65 has been notably smaller than at the younger ages. The corresponding survival rates for 1955 (71 percent and 45 percent) were, respectively, only a little lower, and substantially lower, than those for 1974.

Changes in "life expectation" for ages below 65, represented here by the average years of life lived between birth and age 65,[3] may be compared with changes in life expectation at age 65, to illustrate these differences further. Average years of life lived below age 65, which can have a peak value of 65, increased from 44 years in 1900-02 to 60 years in 1974 (i.e., by 16 years), while average years of life remaining at age 65

---

[3] The value for average years of life lived between birth and age 65 is computed by the formula $T_0 - T_{65}$ from the life table.

Table 5-1. AVERAGE REMAINING LIFETIME, AVERAGE YEARS LIVED IN INTERVAL, AND PROPORTION SURVIVING, FOR VARIOUS AGES AND AGE INTERVALS, BY RACE AND SEX: 1900 TO 1974

Measure, exact age, race, and sex	1974	1969-71	1965	1959-61	1955	1949-51	1939-41	1929-31	1900-02
ALL CLASSES									
Average remaining lifetime									
0 years	71.9	70.8	70.2	69.9	69.5	68.1	63.6	59.3	49.2
65 years	15.6	15.0	14.6	14.4	14.2	13.8	12.8	12.3	11.9
75 years	9.8	9.5	9.0	8.7	8.7	8.4	7.6	7.3	7.1
80 years	7.6	7.2	6.7	6.4	6.6	6.3	5.7	5.4	5.3
Average years lived in interval									
0 to 65 years	60.4	60.0	59.7	59.7	59.5	58.7	55.9	52.9	44.4
65 to 80 years	11.7	11.5	11.4	11.4	11.2	11.1	10.6	10.4	10.1
Proportion surviving									
0 to 65 years	.738	.719	.714	.711	.707	.676	.604	.538	.409
65 to 80 years	.510	.490	.480	.472	.454	.434	.379	.350	.331
WHITE									
Male									
Average remaining lifetime									
0 years	68.9	68.0	67.6	67.6	67.3	66.3	62.8	59.1	48.2
65 years	13.4	13.1	12.9	13.0	12.9	12.8	12.1	11.8	11.5
75 years	8.3	8.3	8.0	7.9	8.0	7.8	7.2	7.0	6.8
80 years	6.4	6.4	6.0	5.9	6.1	5.9	5.4	5.3	5.1
Average years lived in interval									
0 to 65 years	59.8	59.3	59.1	59.0	58.8	58.2	55.8	52.9	43.7
65 to 80 years	10.8	10.6	10.6	10.6	10.6	10.5	10.2	10.1	9.9
Proportion surviving									
0 to 65 years	.685	.663	.659	.658	.657	.635	.583	.530	.392
65 to 80 years	.405	.391	.391	.395	.386	.378	.341	.325	.313
Female									
Average remaining lifetime									
0 years	76.6	75.4	74.7	74.2	73.6	72.0	67.3	62.7	51.1
65 years	17.6	16.9	16.3	15.9	15.5	15.0	13.6	12.8	12.2
75 years	10.7	10.2	9.6	9.3	9.2	8.9	7.9	7.6	7.3
80 years	8.1	7.5	6.9	6.7	6.7	6.6	5.9	5.6	5.5
Average years lived in interval									
0 to 65 years	62.0	61.7	61.5	61.4	61.2	60.5	58.0	54.9	45.7
65 to 80 years	12.6	12.5	12.2	12.2	12.0	11.7	11.1	10.7	10.3
Proportion surviving									
0 to 65 years	.827	.816	.811	.807	.800	.768	.687	.605	.438
65 to 80 years	.613	.592	.575	.553	.528	.495	.420	.381	.350
NEGRO AND OTHER RACES [1]									
Male									
Average remaining lifetime									
0 years	62.9	61.0	61.1	61.5	61.2	58.9	52.3	47.6	32.5
65 years	13.4	12.9	12.6	12.8	13.2	12.8	12.2	10.9	10.4
75 years	9.6	10.2	9.8	8.9	10.4	8.8	8.2	7.0	6.6
80 years	8.3	9.4	8.3	6.9	8.9	7.1	6.6	5.4	5.1
Average years lived in interval									
0 to 65 years	55.8	54.6	54.7	54.9	54.6	53.1	47.9	44.4	30.6
65 to 80 years	10.3	9.8	9.7	10.2	9.8	10.1	9.9	9.3	9.1
Proportion surviving									
0 to 65 years	.529	.492	.504	.514	.500	.452	.354	.293	.190
65 to 80 years	.374	.338	.353	.389	.372	.374	.345	.281	.254
Female									
Average remaining lifetime									
0 years	71.2	69.0	67.4	66.5	65.9	62.7	55.6	49.5	35.0
65 years	16.7	16.1	15.5	15.1	15.1	14.5	13.9	12.2	11.4
75 years	11.8	12.1	11.2	10.1	12.0	10.2	9.8	8.6	7.9
80 years	9.9	10.1	9.0	7.7	10.1	8.2	8.0	6.9	6.5
Average years lived in interval									
0 to 65 years	59.5	58.5	57.7	57.3	56.8	55.1	49.9	45.7	32.5
65 to 80 years	11.6	11.1	11.0	11.3	10.8	10.8	10.6	9.8	9.4
Proportion surviving									
0 to 65 years	.699	.657	.626	.608	.589	.524	.405	.309	.220
65 to 80 years	.517	.487	.493	.498	.468	.453	.421	.351	.305

[1] Black only for 1929-31 and 1900-02.

Source: Life table published by the National Center for Health Statistics, U.S. Public Health Service, and the U.S. Bureau of the Census. For 1974, see "Final Mortality Statistics, 1974", Monthly Vital Statistics Report, Vol. 24, No. 11, February 1976. Derived figures prepared by the U.S. Bureau of the Census.

Figure 5-1. AVERAGE REMAINING LIFETIME AT BIRTH AND AT AGE 65 AND AGE 75: 1900-02, 1929-31, 1949-51, AND 1974

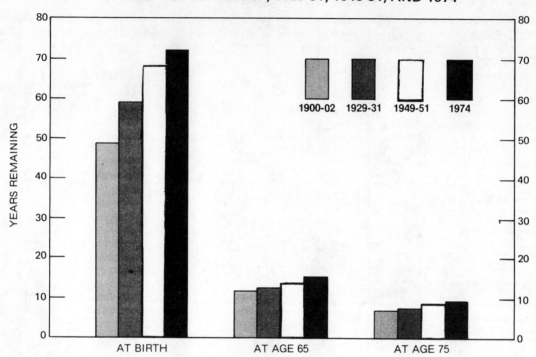

Source: Table 5-1 and National Center for Health Statistics, *Monthly Vital Statistics Reports*, V . 23, No. 13.

has moved ahead more slowly, from 11.9 years in 1900-02 to 15.6 years in 1974 (i.e., by 3.7 years). According to these measures, "life expectation" values increased relatively little between 1955 and 1974, both for ages under 65 and at age 65. Most or nearly all of the progress in life expectation recorded for the period 1900-02 to 1974 at the younger ages, occurred by 1955, therefore. The modest progress at the older ages was more evenly distributed over the period since 1900. (See figure 5-1.)

Age-specific death rates at the older ages for the years 1940 to 1974 reflect a sharp deceleration of the reduction in mortality among the older population in the late 1950's and the 1960's, as compared with earlier years (table 5-2 and figure 5-2). For example, the death rate at ages 55 to 64, 65 to 74, and 75 to 84 each dropped about 22 percent between 1940 and 1954 but remained nearly unchanged between 1954 and 1968. The annual data for the late sixties and early seventies suggest that another turning point in the trend of mortality at the older ages was reached about 1968 and that mortality at these ages may be on its way down again. The reasons for the fluctuations of the death rates for the older population are not well known. An initial understanding of these changes may be pursued in terms of an examination of death rates specific by sex, race, and cause of death.[4]

Sex Differences

Mortality rates of males in the United States, as well as in other economically developed countries, are now well above those of females throughout the age scale. For the leading causes of death males tend to be the sex more likely to die, although a higher percentage of females have one or more chronic conditions, females have higher disability (restricted activity) rates when ill, and females suffer excess morbidity from acute conditions.[5] Diseases in which males show an excess predominate as causes of death and those for which females show an excess predominate as causes of sickness. As a

[4] Analysis of mortality data in terms of real birth cohorts, particularly by sex, race, and cause, should provide even more insight into the trends of mortality and the real prospects for survivorship of persons at various ages. Cohort analysis of mortality refers to analysis in terms of the death rates at successive ages in successive years for each group born in the same year or group of years, as contrasted with analysis in terms of the rates at a given age over time, called period analysis. See U.S. Public Health Service, National Center for Health Statistics, "Cohort Mortality and Survivorship: U.S. Death-Registration States, 1900-1968," by Iwao M. Moriyama and Susan O. Gustavus, **Vital and Health Statistics**, Series 3, No. 16, 1972.

[5] Based on data from the National Health Interview Survey; see National Center for Health Statistics, **Vital and Health Statistics**, Series 10, **op. cit.** See also Lois M. Verbrugge, "Sex Differentials in Morbidity and Mortality: A Riddle," paper presented at the annual meeting of the Population Association of America, Seattle, Wash., April 17-19, 1975; abstract published in **Population Index**, July 1975, pp. 410-411.

Table 5-2. **DEATH RATES FOR THE POPULATION 55 YEARS OLD AND OVER, BY AGE: 1940 TO 1974**

Year and period	55 to 64 years	65 to 74 years	75 to 84 years	85 years and over	65 years and over
RATES PER 1,000 POPULATION					
1940..........................	22.2	48.4	112.0	235.7	72.2
1954..........................	17.4	37.9	86.0	181.6	58.6
1968..........................	17.2	38.5	80.8	196.1	62.1
1973 (prov.)..................	16.1	34.4	79.8	174.5	58.8
1973..........................	16.1	34.4	79.3	174.3	58.7
1974 (prov.)..................	15.4	33.4	76.4	164.9	56.8
PERCENT CHANGE					
1940-54.......................	-21.6	-21.7	-23.2	-23.0	-23.2
1954-68.......................	-1.1	+1.6	-6.0	+8.0	+5.6
1968-74.......................	-10.5	-13.2	-5.4	-15.9	-9.3

Source: National Center for Health Statistics, U.S. Public Health Service, various annual volumes of Vital Statistics of the United States; National Center for Health Statistics, U.S. Public Health Service, various issues of Monthly Vital Statistics Report.

result, life expectation for females far exceeds that for males; in 1974 there was a difference of nearly eight years (table 5-1). Expectation of life at birth in the United States in 1974 was 68.2 years for males and 75.9 years for females. A large part of this difference is accounted for by the difference in death rates between the sexes over age 65. Expectation of life at age 65 was 13.4 years for males and 17.5 years for females in 1974. The difference in average years of life lived under age 65 is about 2½ years while the difference in average years of remaining life at age 65 is about 4 years.

Males and females have not shared equally in the progress in mortality reduction in this century, particularly at the older ages. In 1900-02 females had only a small advantage over males in life expectation at birth (2.9 years). Between 1900-02 and 1974 expectation of life at birth increased 20 years for males and 25 years for females, so that about 5 years were added to the original difference of almost 3 years.

As shown by the ratios of male death rates to female death rates for various years since 1900-02 given in table 5-3, reductions in death rates for females have far outpaced those for males at the older ages. In 1900-02 death rates of males at the older ages were only slightly above those for females; the excess averaged 10 percent for ages 65 and over. The progressive divergence of the rates brought the relative difference to over 70 percent in 1974. Death rates for the two sexes at these ages have been moving farther apart for both whites and Negroes-and-other-races. The divergence of the death rates of the sexes has been greater for the white population than for the Negro-and-other-races population, however, so that there is a greater relative difference between the sexes for the whites in 1974.

Life expectation at age 65 showed gains between 1900-02 and 1974 of 1.9 years for males and 5.3 years for females. As a result, 3.4 years were added to the original difference of less than 1 year. The differential

gains in life expectation by sex at age 65 for the Negro-and-other-races population have been similar to those for whites. As a result, life expectation for Negro-and-other-races women at age 65 is also well above that for Negro-and-other-races men (16.7 vs. 13.4).

The life expectation for males and females for 1974 imply that the male-female difference in life expectation at birth and at age 65 remained at about the same level between 1970 and 1974, i.e., about 7.7 years and 4.1 years, respectively. The figures also reflect a one-year increase in life expectancy at birth for males and females equal to or larger than any recorded in the last two decades (0.6 year).

The relative importance of "hereditary" (genetic and nongenetic) and "environmental" factors in influencing the relative longevity of males and females is unknown. The tendency of women to live longer than men may result largely or even wholly from differences in the environment, roles, and life-styles of men and women.[6] Generally males are engaged in the more stressful, physically demanding, and dangerous occupations. Many of the changes over time in the differences between male and female death rates are associated with social and environmental factors.[7] There is also strong evidence supporting a biological basis for the difference between the death rates of the sexes. For example, male fetal and

[6] Erdman Palmore and Frances C. Jeffers (eds.), **Prediction of Life Span,** Heath Lexington Books, D.C. Heath and Co., Lexington, Mass., 1971, esp. pp. 283 and 285.

[7] Philip E. Enterline, "Causes of Death Responsible for Recent Increases in Sex Mortality Differentials in the United States," **Milbank Memorial Fund Quarterly,** Vol. 39, No. 2, 1961, pp. 312-328; Frank Godley and David O. Kruegel, "Cigarette Smoking and Differential Mortality: New Estimates from Representative National Samples," paper presented at the annual meeting of the Population Association of America, Seattle, Wash., April 17-19, 1975; and Robert D. Retherford, "Tobacco Smoking and the Sex Mortality Differential," **Demography,** Vol. 9, No.2, 1972, pp. 203-216.

Figure 5-2. DEATH RATES FOR THE POPULATION 55 YEARS OLD AND OVER, BY AGE: 1950 TO 1974

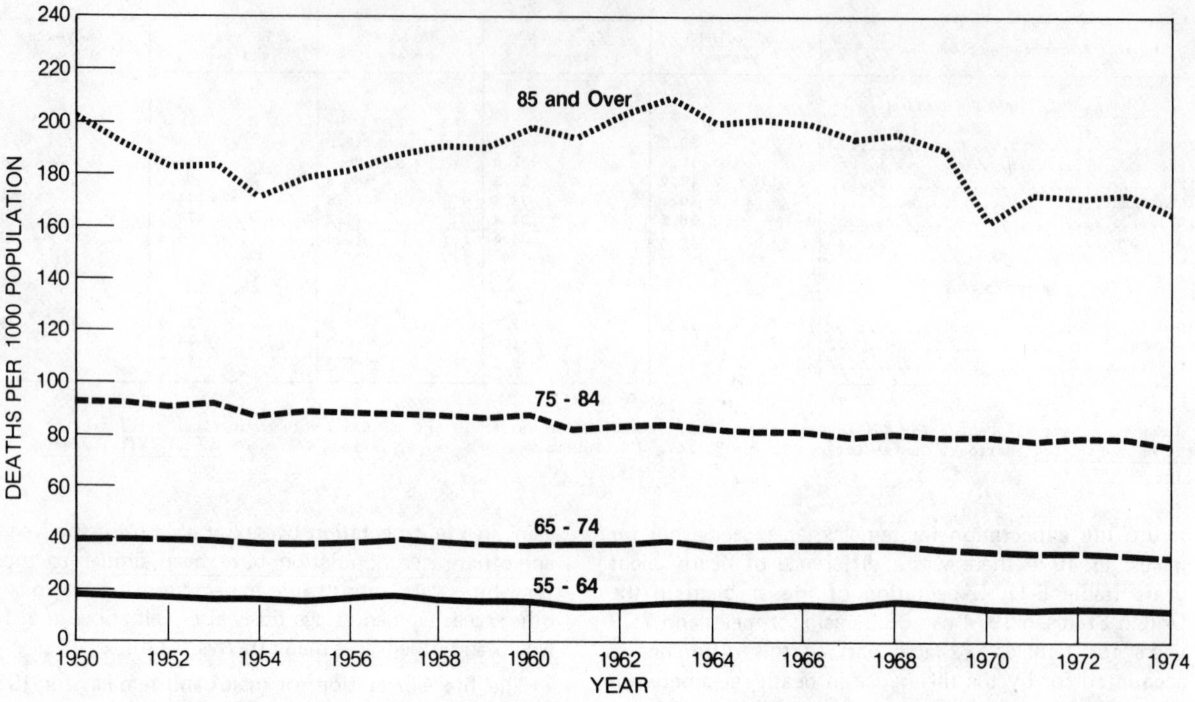

Source: National Center for Health Statistics, *Vital Statistics of the United States,* 1960 and 1970, Vol. II, Part A; *Monthly Vital Statistics Reports,* "Final Monthly Statistics, 1973," and "Annual Summary for the United States, 1974."

Table 5-3. RATIOS OF MALE TO FEMALE DEATH RATES FOR THE POPULATION 55 YEARS OLD AND OVER, BY AGE AND RACE: 1900 TO 1974

Race and year	55 to 64 years	65 to 74 years	75 to 84 years	85 years and over	65 years and over
ALL CLASSES					
1900[1]	1.14	1.11	1.08	1.05	1.06
1940	1.45	1.29	1.17	1.08	1.17
1954	1.82	1.57	1.29	1.06	1.30
1968	2.08	1.86	1.45	1.06	1.42
1974[2]	2.07	1.95	1.55	1.23	1.46
WHITE					
1900[1]	1.12	1.11	1.08	1.05	1.06
1940	1.50	1.30	1.16	1.07	1.17
1954	1.91	1.59	1.29	1.04	1.31
1968	2.19	1.92	1.45	1.08	1.43
1974[2]	2.14	2.02	1.56	1.25	1.47
NEGRO AND OTHER RACES					
1900[3]	1.00	1.08	1.16	1.27	1.06
1940	1.11	1.22	1.29	1.25	1.18
1954	1.33	1.35	1.29	1.30	1.24
1968	1.57	1.47	1.40	1.05	1.36
1974[2]	1.73	1.54	1.40	1.17	1.38

[1] For the original Death Registration States.
[2] Provisional data.
[3] For the original Death Registration States; black population only.

Source: U.S. Bureau of the Census, United States Life Tables, 1930, 1936; National Center for Health Statistics, U.S. Public Health Service, annual volumes of Vital Statistics of the United States, 1940, 1954, and 1968; and Monthly Vital Statistics Report, "Provisional Statistics, 1974."

infant mortality is greater than female fetal and infant mortality. A study of mortality in male and female Catholic teaching orders, whose living conditions are nearly equal, tends to support a biological hypothesis.[8] We may secure an answer to the question as to why women live longer than men if the present tendencies for the environment, roles, and life-styles of men and women to be more similar and the present tendencies for sexual differentiation to diminish continue.[9] In the U.S.S.R., where there is less differentiation in the occupational roles of men and women than in the United States, however, there is an even greater gap in life expectation at birth (9.2 years in 1970) in favor of females than here.

One tenable hypothesis regarding the basis of the difference in life expectation of the sexes is that women have superior vitality and, with the virtual elimination of the infectious and parasitic illnesses and maternal mortality and the consequent emergence of the "chronic degenerative" diseases, such as diseases of the heart, cerebrovascular diseases, and malignant neoplasms, as the leading causes, this vital superiority has

been increasingly evidenced. Males succumb more frequently and more readily to most of these diseases for reasons that are not well understood. This divergence of male and female death rates is occurring in spite of the fact that the differences in the life styles and roles of men and women have diminished. Social factors continue to account for an important part of the difference directly, or indirectly by their influence on and interaction with genetic or biological factors. For example, women are more likely to secure earlier diagnosis and appropriate treatment for health conditions, including particularly the serious illnesses.

Race Differences

Life expectation at birth of whites in 1974 (72.7 years) is well above that for Negroes-and-other-races (67.0 years) and most of this difference is accounted for by the lower death rates of whites at the ages below 65. The difference between the races in average years of life lived between birth and age 65 in 1974 is about 3.2 years. For ages 65 and over as a whole, it would appear from the slightly higher life expectancy of whites at age 65 that whites have slightly lower death rates at these ages (table 5-1). Death rates of whites are, in fact, substantially lower at ages 65-69 and 70-74. By ages 75-79, however, the reported death rates have nearly converged

---

[8] Francis C. Madigan, "Are Sex Mortality Differentials Biologically Caused?", **Milbank Memorial Fund Quarterly**, Vol. 35, No. 2, 1957, pp. 202-223.

[9] Palmore and Jeffers, **op. cit.**, p. 285.

Table 5-4. **RATIOS OF NEGRO-AND-OTHER-RACES TO WHITE DEATH RATES FOR THE POPULATION 55 YEARS OLD AND OVER, BY AGE AND SEX: 1900 TO 1974**

Sex and year	55 to 64 years	65 to 74 years	75 to 84 years	85 years and over	65 years and over
ALL CLASSES					
1900[1]	1.56	1.23	0.98	0.82	1.13
1940	1.79	1.08	0.85	0.73	1.01
1954	1.70	1.33	0.82	0.53	0.98
1968	1.69	1.56	0.87	0.54	1.08
1974[2]	1.54	1.32	0.91	0.66	0.98
MALE					
1900[1]	1.48	1.21	1.02	0.93	1.13
1940	1.47	1.16	0.89	0.79	1.02
1954	1.49	1.08	0.80	0.56	0.95
1968	1.49	1.39	0.85	0.54	1.05
1974[2]	1.43	1.17	0.84	0.63	0.94
FEMALE					
1900[1]	1.65	1.24	0.95	0.76	1.13
1940	1.97	1.26	0.80	0.68	1.00
1954	2.13	1.27	0.81	0.60	1.00
1968	2.07	1.82	0.88	0.55	1.10
1974[2]	1.77	1.53	0.94	0.67	1.00

[1] For the original Death Registration States; black population only.
[2] Provisional data.

Source: U.S. Bureau of the Census, United States Life Tables, 1930, 1936; National Center for Health Statistics, U.S. Public Health Service, annual volumes of Vital Statistics of the United States, 1940, 1954, and 1968; and Monthly Vital Statistics Report, "Provisional Statistics, 1974."

and, from ages 80-84 on, blacks appear to have the lower rates. At ages 65-74 in 1974 the recorded death rate for Negroes-and-other-races was a third greater than the death rate for whites, but at ages 75-84 the recorded death rate for Negroes-and-other-races was 10 percent below the death rate for whites (table 5-4).

The magnitude, and possibly even the direction, of differences between the death rates of the races at the older ages are subject to uncertainty. The basic data, especially for blacks, are subject to major errors. The differences in recorded death rates of blacks and whites at these higher ages may be in part a result of reporting errors in the census, especially misreporting of age of blacks, and in part a result of reporting errors in death registration, especially misreporting of age on death certificates for blacks. Calculations of death rates based wholly on Social Security ("Medicare") data agree with death rates based on vital statistics in indicating a "crossover" of the rates for the two races at ages 80-84 and a steady divergence of the rates thereafter.[10] On the other hand, the Social Security data reflect smaller differences between the races at the older ages than the vital registration statistics.

At least some, if not most, of the difference between death rates for whites and blacks not explainable by errors in the data may be accounted for by differences in the socioeconomic status (occupation, education, and income) of the race groups. There is evidence of differences in mortality rates according to socio-economic status. Analysis of deaths and death rates in the four-month period, May-August 1960, based on a match of death certificates and census records, indicates that, in general, death rates vary inversely with educational attainment, income, and occupational level, even considering whites and blacks separately.[11] The pattern is rather consistent among persons aged 25 to 64 but hardly applies to persons 65 and over. The chances of reaching age 65 are clearly better for the more affluent, better educated, and more highly placed persons. In addition to socioeconomic status, other social, economic, and cultural factors may contribute to the difference between the death rates for the races. Genetic factors may also play a significant part; recent investigations have revealed that specific gene-linked diseases have an affinity for certain ethnic and racial groups.[12] The relatively favorable mortality position of

blacks as compared with whites above age 65 suggests that socioeconomic differences do not "operate" at the older ages as they do at the ages below 65. One explanatory hypothesis is that those blacks who have survived the excessive environmental stresses of their younger years may be destined by natural selection to live an especially long life.

Cause of Death

"Diseases of the heart" far outranks any other cause of death among persons 65 and over. Rates (per 100,000 population) at ages 65 and over for the 10 leading causes of death in 1973 are shown in table 5-5. Malignant neoplasms (cancer) and cerebrovascular diseases (mainly stroke) hold second and third place, respectively. Taken together, these three causes accounted for three out of four deaths at ages 65 and over in 1973. Other leading causes, in rank order, are: influenza and pneumonia; arteriosclerosis; accidents; diabetes; bronchitis, emphysema, and asthma; cirrhosis of the liver; and infections of the kidney. These are all far less frequent than the leading three, however.

Rates for males 65 years and over as a whole for diseases of the heart and malignant neoplasms are far above those for women, as shown by the sex ratios of death rates for the leading causes of death in 1973 (table 5-6). There is a considerable excess of male mortality also for influenza and pneumonia, accidents, and "bronchitis, emphysema, and asthma." The cerebrovascular diseases, arteriosclerosis, and infections of the kidney show little preference for one sex or the other. On the other hand, the rate for diabetes is somewhat higher for women. For all 10 leading causes except diabetes and infections of the kidney, the rates for males at ages 65-74 are well above those for females.

Death rates for several leading causes for the ages 65 and over as a whole are rather similar for Negroes-and-other-races and for whites. The rate for Negroes-and-other-races is considerably lower for arteriosclerosis and "bronchitis, emphysema, and asthma" and considerably higher for diabetes and infections of the kidney, but for the other leading causes the rates for whites and Negroes-and-other-races differ relatively little (table 5-7). A striking difference appears for ages 65-74 and 75-84. The rates at ages 65-74 are substantially higher for Negroes-and-other-races than for whites for all the major causes of death except "bronchitis, emphysema, and asthma," and cirrhosis of the liver. At ages 75-84, however, the opposite appears to be the case; recorded death rates for the older age group are lower for Negroes-and-other-races for most major causes. Rates for cerebrovascular diseases, influenza and pneumonia, arteriosclerosis, diabetes, and infections of the kidney are far higher for Negroes-and-other-races at ages 65-74 than for whites and then the differences drop sharply at ages 75-84. As suggested earlier, because of errors of reporting in the census and in the death registration, the real shift from ages 65-74 to 75-84 may be less pronounced than is indicated by these figures.

[10] Francisco Bayo, "Mortality of the Aged," **Transactions,** Society of Actuaries, Vol. 24, Part I, No. 3, March 1972, pp. 1-24.

[11] Evelyn M. Kitagawa and Philip M. Hauser, **Differential Mortality in the United States: A Study in Socioeconomic Epidemiology,** Harvard Univ. Press, Cambridge, Mass., 1973, esp. pp. 11, 14, and 157.

[12] Ailon Shiloh and Ida Cohen Selavan (eds.), **Ethnic Groups of America: Their Morbidity, Mortality, and Behavior Disorders,** Vol. I, **The Jews,** 1974, esp. pp. xv and xvi, and Vol. II, **The Blacks,** Charles C. Thomas, Publisher, Springfield, Ill., 1975.

Table 5-5. **DEATH RATES FOR THE TEN LEADING CAUSES OF DEATH, FOR AGES 65 AND OVER, BY AGE: 1973**

Rank	Cause of death	65 years and over	65 to 74 years	75 to 84 years	85 years and over
	All causes......................	5,874.4	3,440.0	7,932.1	17,429.4
1	Diseases of heart....................	2,643.2	1,461.6	3,609.2	8,382.1
2	Malignant neoplasms..................	946.7	768.1	1,187.9	1,435.3
3	Cerebrovascular diseases.............	839.3	355.1	1,233.5	3,197.9
4	Influenza and pneumonia..............	210.3	82.1	295.6	910.4
5	Arteriosclerosis.....................	146.0	32.4	190.6	890.2
6	Accidents............................	127.7	77.5	160.6	404.2
	Motor vehicle.....................	33.2	29.4	40.7	34.7
	All other........................	94.5	48.1	119.8	369.5
7	Diabetes mellitus....................	126.3	85.4	179.7	245.9
8	Bronchitis, emphysema, and asthma.....	97.7	79.4	126.2	133.2
9	Cirrhosis of liver...................	37.9	44.6	28.8	19.9
10	Infections of kidney.................	22.9	11.1	32.2	81.6
	All other causes.................	676.4	442.7	887.8	1,728.7

Source: Prepared on basis of data from U.S. Public Health Service, National Center for Health Statistics, Vital Statistics of the United States, Mortality, Part A, 1973 (forthcoming). (See table 5-8.)

Table 5-6. **RATIOS OF MALE DEATH RATES TO FEMALE DEATH RATES FOR THE TEN LEADING CAUSES OF DEATH, FOR AGES 65 AND OVER, BY AGE: 1973**

Cause of death	65 years and over	65 to 74 years	75 to 84 years
All causes...................................	1.455	1.935	1.540
Diseases of heart..................................	1.434	2.080	1.488
Malignant neoplasms................................	1.779	1.834	1.878
Cerebrovascular diseases...........................	1.028	1.411	1.146
Influenza and pneumonia............................	1.555	2.248	1.890
Arteriosclerosis...................................	0.952	1.519	1.201
Accidents..	1.516	2.055	1.575
Motor vehicle....................................	2.295	2.085	2.483
All other.......................................	1.313	2.036	1.352
Diabetes mellitus..................................	0.860	0.920	0.889
Bronchitis, emphysema, and asthma..................	5.422	5.361	6.394
Cirrhosis of liver.................................	2.662	2.678	2.354
Infections of kidney...............................	1.063	1.065	1.248
All other causes...................................	1.734	2.084	1.861

Source: Prepared on basis of data from U.S. Public Health Service, National Center for Health Statistics, Vital Statistics of the United States, Mortality, Part A, 1973 (forthcoming). (See table 5-8.)

Table 5-7. **RATIOS OF NEGRO-AND-OTHER-RACES DEATH RATES TO WHITE DEATH RATES FOR THE TEN LEADING CAUSES OF DEATH, FOR AGES 65 AND OVER, BY AGE: 1973**

Cause of death	65 years and over	65 to 74 years	75 to 84 years
All causes.....................................	0.993	1.340	0.930
Diseases of heart..................................	0.888	1.208	0.838
Malignant neoplasms................................	1.019	1.167	0.944
Cerebrovascular diseases...........................	1.101	1.937	1.016
Influenza and pneumonia............................	0.931	1.641	0.915
Arteriosclerosis...................................	0.759	1.669	0.840
Accidents..	0.980	1.400	0.896
Motor vehicle....................................	1.033	1.282	0.769
All other.......................................	0.962	1.474	0.941
Diabetes mellitus..................................	1.511	2.141	1.217
Bronchitis, emphysema, and asthma..................	0.449	0.457	0.462
Cirrhosis of liver.................................	0.826	0.841	0.728
Infections of kidney...............................	1.416	2.240	1.295
All other causes...................................	1.305	1.613	1.212

Source: Prepared on basis of data from U.S. Public Health Service, National Center for Health Statistics, Vital Statistics of the United States, Mortality, Part A, 1973 (forthcoming). (See table 5-8.)

Table 5-8. DEATH RATES FOR SELECTED CAUSES OF DEATH FOR THE POPULATION 55 YEARS OLD AND OVER, BY AGE, RACE, AND SEX: 1940, 1954, AND 1973

(Rates per 100,000 population)

Cause of death, race, and sex	55 to 64 years			65 to 74 years			75 to 84 years			85 years and over		
	1940	1954	1973	1940	1954	1973	1940	1954	1973	1940	1954	1973
All causes...................	2,215.5	1,737.4	1,611.9	4,838.3	3,785.1	3,440.0	11,203.9	8,603.5	7,932.1	23,565.1	18.157.5	17,429.4
Male.....................	2,612.0	2,254.2	2,206.6	5,462.3	4,673.8	4,731.5	12,126.4	9,800.6	10,108.1	24,639.0	18,741.1	19,809.4
Female...................	1,800.4	1,236.7	1,079.8	4,222.2	2,979.1	2,445.5	10,368.6	7,625.9	6,562.5	22,759.1	17,740.0	16,234.0
White:												
Male....................	2,521.9	2,170.7	2,118.2	5,399.9	4,645.8	4,653.9	12,202.3	9,936.3	10,214.3	25,135.1	19,081.2	20,436.1
Female..................	1,684.4	1,137.8	1,000.7	4,153.6	2,918.8	2,324.7	10,482.6	7,716.0	6,582.2	23,495.3	18,284.5	16,685.8
Negro and other races:												
Male....................	3,710.7	3,227.1	3,069.5	6,283.2	5,006.0	5,456.7	10,876.9	7,995.0	8,965.7	19,972.0	14,381.8	13,605.7
Female..................	3,318.3	2,426.5	1,821.7	5,227.5	3,700.5	3,662.0	8,413.7	6,219.8	6,291.8	15,971.0	11,053.1	11,115.9
DISEASES OF THE HEART												
Male.............................	[1]931.8	1,008.9	954.6	[1]2,129.2	2,112.5	2,068.2	4,962.3	4,405.3	4,519.5	[1]10,343.6	8,300.0	9,308.6
Female...........................	[1]505.1	426.1	332.0	[1]1,490.3	1,262.0	994.5	4,221.8	3,460.2	3,036.4	[1]9,661.3	8,089.9	7,916.8
White												
Male.............................	[1]921.8	996.9	943.7	[1]2,146.6	2,134.5	2,068.2	5,060.8	4,502.8	4,609.4	[1]10,846.7	8,522.3	9,664.1
Female...........................	[1]472.4	389.3	300.8	[1]1,483.9	1,244.9	948.3	4,308.6	3,520.9	3,061.4	[1]10,240.5	8,388.1	8,156.1
Negro and Other Races												
Male.............................	[1]1,054.2	1,150.3	1,061.2	[1]1,901.9	1,851.7	2,064.7	3,345.7	3,106.7	3,551.6	[1]5,601.9	5,450.0	5,826.4
Female...........................	[1]935.5	868.4	625.7	[1]1,585.9	1,635.1	1,459.6	2,730.7	2,512.0	2,709.9	[1]4,324.8	4,428.2	5,205.7
MALIGNANT NEOPLASMS												
Male.............................	352.2	433.0	513.3	737.2	839.4	1,033.7	1,275.2	1,371.6	1,665.7	1,467.0	1,688.8	2,018.0
Female...........................	384.1	348.9	355.4	664.9	589.4	563.7	1,047.1	972.5	887.0	1,276.0	1,275.3	1,142.7
White												
Male.............................	357.1	424.7	493.4	759.5	846.0	1,017.6	1,320.3	1,403.9	1,671.8	1,569.9	1,740.8	2,062.5
Female...........................	385.4	341.8	348.6	677.1	598.8	556.5	1,080.5	994.8	895.2	1,348.5	1,327.5	1,174.0
Negro and Other Races												
Male.............................	291.9	530.6	707.5	445.0	761.1	1,184.0	532.2	942.0	1,600.0	499.1	1,022.7	1,566.0
Female...........................	367.6	434.8	419.2	486.1	475.1	636.7	473.7	623.8	781.2	608.2	634.4	787.5
CEREBROVASCULAR DISEASES (Vascular lesions affecting central nervous system)												
Male.............................	218.3	185.8	125.9	593.6	550.9	425.0	1,475.7	1,514.9	1,338.5	2,617.4	2,887.2	3,133.8
Female...........................	205.0	158.6	90.0	554.2	461.2	301.3	1,416.9	1,414.6	1,167.6	2,614.5	3,179.1	3,230.1
White												
Male.............................	200.8	163.1	109.2	579.1	530.6	397.9	1,485.6	1,530.1	1,342.9	2,684.9	2,941.5	3,228.6
Female...........................	180.1	132.6	75.2	531.4	436.1	272.2	1,423.9	1,424.1	1,162.9	2,705.4	3,276.8	3,324.4
Negro and Other Races												
Male.............................	432.1	450.2	289.6	784.2	791.5	680.5	1,312.8	1,313.4	1,291.1	1,983.2	2,190.9	2,192.5
Female...........................	531.1	472.0	228.5	888.1	764.0	593.6	1,298.0	1,265.9	1,222.9	1,775.6	1,978.1	2,162.5
INFLUENZA AND PNEUMONIA												
Male.............................	119.3	38.4	43.9	253.5	92.3	119.6	719.4	258.9	415.7	2,041.9	774.0	1,124.0
Female...........................	76.2	17.2	20.6	203.2	51.4	53.2	659.4	189.2	220.0	1,945.5	669.6	803.0
White												
Male.............................	107.3	33.4	39.2	240.4	86.7	113.4	720.2	258.7	417.8	2,091.3	782.3	1,167.7
Female...........................	65.6	14.2	18.9	194.3	46.9	50.0	663.4	189.4	222.7	2,015.5	683.2	835.3
Negro and Other Races												
Male.............................	265.8	96.6	90.7	426.6	158.8	178.2	706.4	261.3	392.5	1,577.3	668.2	696.2
Female...........................	214.5	53.2	36.6	332.7	105.2	85.5	590.6	186.5	184.6	1,299.8	503.1	437.5
ARTERIOSCLEROSIS												
Male.............................	19.2	12.9	8.0	96.5	70.9	40.1	464.8	367.9	212.5	1,664.6	1,374.8	890.1
Female...........................	13.0	7.8	4.2	67.9	48.6	26.4	370.8	298.9	176.9	1,472.3	1,401.8	890.3
White												
Male.............................	17.3	11.4	7.6	95.6	68.0	38.3	474.2	373.5	215.9	1,757.4	1,451.4	930.6
Female...........................	11.2	6.2	3.6	66.9	45.8	24.5	378.3	303.3	178.8	1,558.1	1,477.2	927.6
Negro and Other Races												
Male.............................	44.0	30.4	12.0	106.5	110.1	56.7	309.7	289.7	175.6	792.0	650.0	496.2
Female...........................	37.7	27.2	9.9	81.7	89.6	46.2	242.9	228.7	152.4	681.8	620.5	468.2

See footnotes at end of table.

There were increases in the last few decades in the death rates at the older ages from some causes of death and decreases in the death rates for others. The rates for diabetes, "bronchitis, emphysema, and asthma," and cirrhosis of the liver showed increases, while the rates for diseases of the heart, cerebrovascular diseases, influenza and pneumonia, and arteriosclerosis showed decreases. The rates for malignant neoplasms, influenza and pneumonia, and accidents have not changed much. Death rates from some leading causes for men have risen in the last few decades (e.g., malignant neoplasms and diabetes), while the death rates for women from these causes have declined. For some other leading causes, the death rates for females have fallen more rapidly than the death rates for men (e.g., diseases of heart and cerebrovascular diseases) or the death rates for men have risen more rapidly than the death rates for women (e.g., "bronchitis, emphysema, and asthma," and cirrhosis of the liver). As a result, the gap between the death rates of men and women aged 65 and over for malignant neoplasms, "bronchitis, emphysema, and asthma," cirrhosis of the liver, diseases of the heart, and cerebrovas-

cular diseases has widened; and the gap between the death rates for diabetes has narrowed. Death rates for specific age groups 55 and over for selected causes by sex and race for 1940, 1954, and 1973 are shown in table 5-8.[13]

Some diseases have all but been eliminated statistically speaking, since their actual elimination would add little to life expectancy. For instance, according to life tables for 1969-71 to be published by the National Center for Health Statistics, if tuberculosis were eliminated completely, there would be a mere 0.04 year gain in life expectancy at birth (table 5-9). On the other hand, if the major cardiovascular-renal diseases (principally, diseases of the heart, cerebrovascular diseases,

---

[13] See also U.S. Public Health Service, National Center for Health Statistics, **Vital and Health Statistics,** "Mortality Trends for Leading Causes of Death, United States—1950-69," by A. J. Klebba, J.D. Maurer, and E.J. Glass, Series 20, No. 16, March 1974, and "The Change in Mortality Trend in the United States," by Iwao M. Moriyama, Series 3, No. 1, March 1964.

Table 5-8. DEATH RATES FOR SELECTED CAUSES OF DEATH FOR THE POPULATION 55 YEARS OLD AND OVER, BY AGE, RACE, AND SEX. 1940, 1954, AND 1973—Continued

(Rates per 100,000 population)

Cause of death, race, and sex	55 to 64 years			65 to 74 years			75 to 84 years			85 years and over		
	1940	1954	1973	1940	1954	1973	1940	1954	1973	1940	1954	1973
MOTOR VEHICLE ACCIDENTS												
Male	62.4	38.2	35.6	85.4	50.3	41.7	119.1	77.8	64.3	125.3	71.1	68.4
Female	18.7	14.7	15.1	28.6	19.4	20.0	37.2	24.8	25.9	26.9	23.5	17.8
White												
Male	62.8	36.7	33.3	86.5	50.4	39.7	121.1	79.1	65.1	127.3	69.1	71.4
Female	18.9	14.5	15.2	29.4	19.9	20.3	38.6	25.2	26.8	27.1	23.9	13.5
Negro and Other Races												
Male	57.8	54.8	57.9	72.1	50.0	60.5	85.5	60.5	56.3	106.5	95.5	39.6
Female	15.7	16.8	14.2	17.7	13.9	17.5	13.7	19.8	14.0	24.5	18.8	10.2
ALL OTHER ACCIDENTS												
Male	88.5	55.9	52.7	135.6	86.2	67.4	335.9	205.9	142.6	967.6	616.4	406.2
Female	30.4	17.3	18.4	110.4	50.1	33.1	485.8	228.5	105.5	1,521.3	822.6	351.1
White												
Male	87.8	54.3	48.9	135.7	84.9	64.6	342.9	209.1	142.6	1,014.5	634.8	421.5
Female	29.2	16.1	18.0	111.3	48.7	31.9	501.0	232.8	106.6	1,625.6	865.4	365.4
Negro and Other Races												
Male	96.5	74.6	89.2	133.8	102.6	94.4	221.0	163.0	143.2	525.8	381.8	256.6
Female	45.9	32.3	22.7	97.8	66.7	46.0	226.2	161.1	91.4	559.2	296.9	188.6
DIABETES MELLITUS												
Male	60.2	29.4	33.7	140.4	70.0	81.4	231.3	131.0	167.0	217.4	143.1	234.9
Female	114.6	46.9	34.4	240.5	112.5	88.5	311.4	172.5	187.8	223.2	164.0	251.4
White												
Male	61.2	28.6	30.2	145.6	70.9	76.5	238.8	135.4	166.0	229.2	147.2	242.8
Female	114.2	43.6	27.5	246.3	113.2	77.8	322.6	177.2	183.4	236.2	168.4	251.1
Negro and Other Races												
Male	47.6	38.4	67.8	73.0	59.9	126.9	108.1	72.3	177.5	106.5	90.9	156.6
Female	120.3	86.9	98.9	156.8	103.4	196.3	118.4	99.2	242.5	103.0	109.4	255.7

[1] Approximation derived as follows: Rate for major cardiovascular-renal diseases, excluding vascular lesions affecting the central nervous system, non-cardiac hypertensive disease (1949), and chronic and unspecified nephritis and other renal sclerosis.

Source: National Center for Health Statistics, U.S. Public Health Service, Vital Statistics Rates in the United States, 1940-1960, table 63; and Vital Statistics of the United States, Mortality, Part A, 1973 (forthcoming).

Table 5-9. **GAIN IN EXPECTATION OF LIFE AT BIRTH AND AT AGE 65 DUE TO ELIMINATION OF VARIOUS CAUSES OF DEATH, BY RACE AND SEX: 1969-71**

Cause of death	Total		White				Negro and other races			
			Male		Female		Male		Female	
	At birth	At age 65	At birth	At age 65	At birth	At age 65	At birth	At age 65	At birth	At age 65
Major cardiovascular-renal diseases..........	11.8	11.4	10.5	9.5	12.0	12.2	10.4	10.4	15.3	15.1
Diseases of the heart..	5.9	5.1	6.1	4.9	5.2	5.0	5.3	4.8	6.3	5.8
Cerebrovascular diseases..............	1.2	1.2	0.9	0.9	1.4	1.3	1.4	1.3	2.2	1.9
Malignant neoplasms[1].....	2.5	1.4	2.3	1.4	2.6	1.2	2.3	1.7	2.4	1.2
Motor vehicle accidents..	0.7	0.1	0.9	0.1	0.4	0.1	1.0	0.1	0.4	(Z)
All accidents excluding motor vehicles..........	0.6	0.1	0.8	0.1	0.4	0.1	1.2	0.2	0.5	0.1
Influenza and pneumonia..	0.5	0.2	0.4	0.2	0.4	0.2	0.8	0.3	0.7	0.3
Diabetes mellitus........	0.2	0.2	0.2	0.1	0.3	0.2	0.2	0.2	0.6	0.4
Infective and parasitic diseases................	0.2	0.1	0.1	(Z)	0.1	(Z)	0.4	0.1	0.3	0.1
Tuberculosis..........	(Z)	(Z)	(Z)	(Z)	(Z)	(Z)	0.1	0.1	0.1	(Z)

Z Less than 0.05 percent.

[1]Including neoplasms of lymphatic and hematopoietic tissues.

Source: U.S. Public Health Service, National Center for Health Statistics, "U.S. Life Tables by Causes of Death: 1969-71," by T.N.E. Greville, U.S. Decennial Life Tables for 1969-71, Vol. I, No. 5, 1976 (forthcoming).

arteriosclerosis, hypertension, and nephritis and nephrosis) were eliminated, there would be an 11.8 year gain in life expectancy at birth, and even an 11.4 year gain in life expectation at age 65. The corresponding figures for heart diseases, the principal component of this category, are 5.9 years and 5.1 years. Second in rank with respect to the possible gain in expectation of life at birth that would be realized if a category of diseases were eliminated is malignant neoplasms, with a gain of 2.5 years, but since these diseases affect a wide span of ages, the gain at age 65 would be only about half as great (1.4 years). The gain at birth from eliminating any other major category amounts to less than one year, e.g., 0.5 year for influenza and pneumonia.

According to the life tables by cause for 1969-71, a newborn infant has a 59 percent chance of eventually dying from a major cardiovascular-renal disease and a 16 percent chance of eventually dying from cancer (table 5-10). The probabilities of eventually dying from diseases of the heart and cerebrovascular diseases, the major components of the former category, are 41 percent and 12 percent, respectively. The probability of eventually dying from any other particular cause is less than 5 percent.

Death rates at ages below 65, except infancy, have fallen so low that the chances of eventually dying from most of the major causes are not grossly different at age 65 from the chances of eventually dying from them at birth. The chance of eventually dying from the major cardiovascular-renal diseases is somewhat higher (67 percent), and the chance of eventually dying from cancer is a little lower (15 percent), at age 65 than at birth. Roughly speaking, a 65-year old has a 50 percent chance of eventually dying from diseases of the heart.

The life tables by cause of death for 1969-71 to be published by the National Center for Health Statistics, in combination with the corresponding tables for 1959-61, imply little change between 1959-61 and 1969-71 in the gains in life expectancy from eliminating such leading causes of death as the major cardiovascular-renal diseases, neoplasms, and "influenza, pneumonia, and bronchitis," and in the probability of eventually dying from these causes.[14] The gains in life expectancy from eliminating the major cardiovascular-renal diseases for 1959-61 are 10.9 years at birth and 10.0 years at age 65, both figures being about a year less than for 1969-71. The gain for malignant neoplasms for 1959-61 was about the same as for 1969-71—2.3 years.

Because of the low death rates at ages under 65 and the rather large proportion of older persons, the average age of persons dying from each of the leading causes is quite high. In 1973 the median age at death of persons dying from cardiovascular diseases was 75 years. The median age at death was 67 for malignant neoplasms, 76 for influenza and pneumonia, 71 for diabetes, and 70 for "bronchitis, emphysema, and asthma." It was somewhat lower for cirrhosis of the liver (56) and much lower for accidents (37). For all causes combined, the median age of persons dying is now 70; in 1900, when infectious

[14]U.S. Public Health Service, National Center for Health Statistics, "United States Life Tables by Causes of Death: 1959-61," by T.N.E. Greville, **Life Tables, 1959-61**, Vol. 1, No. 6, 1968. See also Samuel Preston, Nathan Keyfitz, and Robert Schoen, **Causes of Death: Life Tables for National Populations**, Seminar Press, New York, 1972, pp. 768-771; corrective adjustments have to be made in these life tables, particularly in the table eliminating cardiovascular diseases, for the procedure used to "close out" the table.

Table 5-10. PROBABILITY AT BIRTH AND AT AGE 65 OF EVENTUALLY DYING FROM VARIOUS CAUSES, BY RACE AND SEX: 1969-71

Probability for persons at the indicated exact age of eventually dying from the specified cause	Total	White		Negro and other races	
		Male	Female	Male	Female
AT BIRTH					
Infective and parasitic diseases...........	.007	.007	.006	.017	.012
Tuberculosis............................	.002	.003	.001	.008	.004
Malignant neoplasms[1].....................	.163	.169	.159	.154	.135
Diabetes................................	.020	.015	.024	.017	.037
Major cardiovascular-renal diseases........	.588	.565	.632	.472	.593
Diseases of the heart....................	.412	.422	.421	.317	.372
Cerebrovascular diseases.................	.122	.095	.151	.106	.160
Influenza and pneumonia....................	.034	.032	.035	.040	.035
Motor vehicle accidents....................	.020	.028	.012	.032	.011
All accidents excluding motor vehicles.....	.026	.030	.021	.043	.022
AT AGE 65					
Infective and parasitic diseases...........	.005	.006	.004	.013	.008
Tuberculosis............................	.002	.003	.001	.007	.003
Malignant neoplasms[1].....................	.145	.164	.128	.168	.112
Diabetes................................	.021	.016	.025	.018	.035
Major cardiovascular-renal diseases........	.672	.640	.706	.606	.694
Diseases of the heart....................	.460	.460	.468	.401	.436
Cerebrovascular diseases.................	.149	.122	.171	.146	.190
Influenza and pneumonia....................	.037	.037	.037	.041	.034
Motor vehicle accidents....................	.006	.007	.004	.008	.003
All accidents excluding motor vehicles.....	.018	.016	.019	.018	.017

[1]Including neoplasms of lymphatic and hematopoietic tissues.

Source: U.S. Public Health Service, National Center for Health Statistics, "U.S. Life Tables by Causes of Death: 1969-71," by T.N.E. Greville, U.S. Decennial Life Tables for 1969-71, Vol. I, No. 5, 1976 (forthcoming).

and parasitic illnesses were much more common and the population had a much younger age distribution, it was only about 36.

Geographic Variations

Death rates for States have shown a steady, rapid convergence from at least 1929-31 (when the first complete set of life tables for States was prepared) to 1959-61, but little change in their degree of variation since that date. By 1959-61 the variation in life expectation at birth and at age 65 between the States had already become rather small (except possibly for Negroes at birth). The figures indicate a greater State variation for "blacks" than whites in death rates below age 65 but about the same small variation for each race group above age 65. In 1969-71 the variations in life expectation around the U.S. average were very similar to those in 1959-61 and, hence, were rather small. This variation may be represented by the average (mean) deviation of the values for States around the (unweighted) average (mean) of all the values. The mean deviation in life expectation at birth for States in 1969-71 was about 0.7 year for whites and 1.0 years for blacks (table 5-11); the corresponding figures at age 65 were 0.4 and 0.5 year.

For life expectancy at birth the West North Central Division appears to have the most favorable position and the South Atlantic Division the least favorable one, even though the geographic differences are small (table 5-12).

The leading States are Hawaii, Minnesota, Utah, North Dakota, and Nebraska, and lagging States are District of Columbia, South Carolina, Mississippi, Georgia, and Louisiana. For expectation of life at age 65, most States in the West Region, the West North Central Division, and the West South Central Division exceeded the national average, while most States in the Northeast Region, and in the East North Central, the South Atlantic, and East South Central Divisions fell below the national average.

By 1969-71 expectation of life at birth for the leading State had reached 77.3 years for white females and 69.6 years for white males. The corresponding figures for blacks were much lower, 72.3 years for females and 63.7 years for males. As in the case of the United States as a whole, the "best" State showed little difference between the races in life expectancy at age 65: 18.2 years for white females vs. 17.5 years for black females, 14.2 years for white males vs. 14.3 years for black males. Depending on sex and race, expectation values for the worst State were 3½ to 5½ years lower at birth, and 2 to 2½ years lower at age 65, than for the best State (table 5-11).

Prospects for Mortality Reduction

The future number of elderly persons will depend directly on the progress in reducing death rates at the older ages as well as at the younger ages. We are interested, therefore, in the prospects for reduction of

Table 5-11. **VARIATION IN LIFE EXPECTATION AT BIRTH AND AT AGE 65, BY RACE AND SEX, FOR STATES: 1969-71 AND 1959-61**

Area and age	All classes	White		Black[1]	
		Male	Female	Male	Female
1969-71					
At Birth					
High State.............................	73.6	[2]69.6	[2]77.3	[3]63.7	[3]72.3
United States..........................	70.8	67.9	75.5	61.0	69.1
Low State.............................	65.7	[2]65.8	[2]73.7	[3]58.3	[3]67.0
Mean deviation[4].....................	1.15	0.80	0.58	1.09	0.93
At Age 65					
High State.............................	16.2	[2]14.2	[2]18.2	[3]14.3	[3]17.5
United States..........................	15.0	13.0	16.9	12.9	16.0
Low State.............................	14.4	[2]12.2	[2]16.1	[3]11.7	[3]15.1
Mean deviation[4].....................	0.46	0.44	0.45	0.43	0.51
1959-61					
At Birth					
High State.............................	72.0	[2]69.2	[2]75.7	[5]64.3	[5]67.9
United States..........................	69.9	67.6	74.2	61.5	66.5
Low State.............................	66.4	[2]64.6	[2]72.7	[5]57.3	[5]63.4
Mean deviation[6].....................	1.06	0.68	0.62	1.13	0.90
At Age 65					
High State.............................	15.7	[2]14.3	[2]17.4	[5]13.7	[5]16.3
United States..........................	14.4	13.0	15.9	12.8	15.1
Low State.............................	13.6	[2]12.1	[2]15.0	[5]11.7	[5]13.9
Mean deviation[6].....................	0.41	0.44	0.47	0.47	0.53

[1]Data actually relate to Negro-and-other-races but Negroes represent over 90 percent of the total Negro-and-other-races population in the United States.
[2]Forty-eight States, excluding Alaska, Hawaii, and District of Columbia.
[3]Twenty-three States and District of Columbia, excluding California, Hawaii, and Oklahoma.
[4]Mean deviation around U.S. unweighted average; 23 States and District of Columbia for "black," excluding California, Hawaii, and Oklahoma.
[5]Twenty-one States and District of Columbia, excluding California, Hawaii, and Oklahoma.
[6]Mean deviation around U.S. unweighted average; 21 States and District of Columbia for "black," excluding California, Hawaii, and Oklahoma.

Source: National Center for Health Statistics, U.S. Public Health Service, State Life Tables, 1959-61, and 1969-71 (forthcoming). (See table 5-12.)

death rates at all ages. In this connection it is useful to consider the prospects for reducing the gap between the rates for the sexes, the races and ethnic groups, socioeconomic groups, and geographic areas in our population.

A number of different approaches may be taken to the task of projecting death rates, survival rates, or life expectation for the United States. One is to extrapolate past trends in mortality experience in the United States in terms of age-sex-race-specific death rates, either on a period or cohort basis.[15] Another is to consider the components of death rates in more analytical terms, for example, in terms of cause of death or, at a more basic level, in terms of the factors affecting specific causes

(e.g., morbidity rates by cause; smoking practices; working conditions; atmospheric pollution; dietary habits); and to bring judgment to bear on the possibilities of reducing the rates for particular causes of death or the influence of particular disease-related conditions. Some reductions could be achieved, for example, by extending the application of present medical knowledge relating to the diagnosis and treatment of the major illnesses through public information campaigns, a change in the organization of medical care, mass screening and follow-up, etc.; and by developing new diagnostic and treatment procedures, etc.

In this connection it is important to consider the competing risks of death. Because of the interdependence of the risks of death from various causes, changes in the pattern of mortality rates by cause would result from eliminating or sharply reducing certain causes. Multiple causes are often involved in the event of death;

[15]See footnote 4 in this chapter.

Table 5-12. **LIFE EXPECTATION AT BIRTH AND AT AGE 65, BY RACE, FOR REGIONS, DIVISIONS, AND STATES: 1969-71**

Region, division, and State	All races		White		Negro and other races	
	At birth	65 years and over	At birth	65 years and over	At birth	65 years and over
United States, total................	70.8	15.0	71.4	15.1	65.0	14.5
Regions:						
Northeast........................	70.9	14.7	71.6	14.7	64.9	14.5
North Central...................	71.2	15.0	71.8	15.1	64.5	14.2
South...........................	69.8	15.1	71.3	15.3	64.0	14.3
West............................	71.6	15.5	71.7	15.4	70.7	16.4
Northeast:						
New England.....................	71.9	15.1	72.1	15.0	67.5	15.8
Middle Atlantic.................	70.6	14.6	71.4	14.6	64.7	14.4
North Central:						
East North Central.............	70.8	14.8	71.5	14.8	64.6	14.2
West North Central.............	72.1	15.5	72.5	15.5	63.9	14.3
South:						
South Atlantic.................	69.5	15.1	71.3	15.4	63.3	14.2
East South Central............	69.5	14.8	70.9	15.0	64.1	14.1
West South Central............	70.5	15.2	71.6	15.4	65.4	14.7
West:						
Mountain.......................	71.2	15.5	71.6	15.5	(S)	(S)
Pacific........................	71.8	15.5	70.3	15.3	70.7	16.4
New England:						
Maine..........................	70.9	14.7	70.9	14.7	(S)	(S)
New Hampshire..................	71.2	14.7	71.2	14.7	(S)	(S)
Vermont........................	71.6	14.8	71.6	14.8	(S)	(S)
Massachusetts..................	71.8	15.1	72.0	15.1	67.7	15.8
Rhode Island...................	71.9	15.0	72.1	14.9	(S)	(S)
Connecticut....................	72.5	15.3	72.9	15.3	67.2	15.9
Middle Atlantic:						
New York.......................	70.5	14.7	71.5	14.7	65.1	14.8
New Jersey.....................	70.9	14.6	71.8	14.7	64.4	14.2
Pennsylvania...................	70.4	14.4	71.2	14.4	63.8	13.8
East North Central:						
Ohio...........................	70.8	14.6	71.4	14.7	65.3	14.1
Indiana........................	70.9	14.7	71.3	14.8	65.4	14.2
Illinois.......................	70.1	14.6	71.2	14.7	63.7	14.0
Michigan.......................	70.6	14.7	71.5	14.8	65.0	14.6
Wisconsin......................	72.5	15.3	72.6	15.3	(S)	(S)
West North Central:						
Minnesota......................	73.0	15.7	73.0	15.7	(S)	(S)
Iowa...........................	72.6	15.6	72.6	15.6	(S)	(S)
Missouri.......................	70.7	15.0	71.6	15.1	63.9	14.3
North Dakota...................	72.8	15.8	73.1	15.8	(S)	(S)
South Dakota...................	72.1	15.8	73.0	15.9	(S)	(S)
Nebraska.......................	72.6	15.9	72.9	15.9	(S)	(S)
Kansas.........................	72.6	15.8	72.9	15.8	(S)	(S)
South Atlantic:						
Delaware.......................	70.1	14.4	71.4	14.6	(S)	(S)
Maryland.......................	70.2	14.5	71.6	14.7	64.6	13.8
District of Columbia...........	65.7	14.6	70.6	15.5	63.6	13.6
Virginia.......................	70.1	14.7	71.6	15.0	64.1	13.6
West Virgina...................	69.5	14.5	69.8	14.6	(S)	(S)
North Carolina.................	69.2	14.8	71.1	15.1	63.2	14.0
South Carolina.................	68.0	14.5	70.3	14.6	62.6	14.6
Georgia........................	68.5	14.7	70.6	14.9	62.9	14.5
Florida........................	70.7	16.1	72.2	16.2	62.9	14.5
East South Central:						
Kentucky.......................	70.1	14.8	70.7	14.9	63.6	13.4
Tennessee......................	70.1	14.9	71.2	15.7	64.5	13.9
Alabama........................	69.1	14.8	70.9	15.0	63.9	14.2
Mississippi....................	68.1	14.6	70.5	14.9	64.0	14.3
West South Central:						
Arkansas.......................	70.7	15.4	71.7	15.5	65.9	15.0
Louisiana......................	68.8	14.4	70.7	14.7	64.4	13.9
Oklahoma.......................	71.4	15.5	71.8	15.4	67.8	16.0
Texas..........................	70.9	15.4	71.7	15.5	65.5	14.9
Mountain:						
Montana........................	70.6	15.3	71.0	15.4	(S)	(S)
Idaho..........................	71.9	15.7	72.0	15.7	(S)	(S)
Wyoming........................	70.3	15.3	70.5	15.3	(S)	(S)
Colorado.......................	72.1	15.7	72.2	15.7	(S)	(S)
New Mexico.....................	70.3	15.5	71.0	15.4	(S)	(S)
Arizona........................	70.6	15.5	71.3	15.5	(S)	(S)
Utah...........................	72.9	15.7	73.0	15.6	(S)	(S)
Nevada.........................	69.0	14.4	69.4	14.3	(S)	(S)
Pacific:						
Washington.....................	71.7	15.3	71.9	15.2	(S)	(S)
Oregon.........................	72.1	15.6	72.2	15.5	(S)	(S)
California.....................	71.7	15.5	71.9	15.5	70.1	16.4
Alaska.........................	69.3	14.7	(S)	(S)	(S)	(S)
Hawaii.........................	73.6	16.2	(S)	(S)	73.7	16.5

S Not computed because fewer than 1,600 female or male deaths of these races were registered in the 3-year period 1969-71.
Source: National Center for Health Statistics, U.S. Public Health Service, State Life Tables, 1969-71 (forthcoming); figures for divisions and regions derived by the Census Bureau by weighting the official figures for States.

Table 5-13. **COMPARISON OF ACTUAL VALUES FOR AVERAGE REMAINING LIFETIME AND AVERAGE YEARS LIVED IN INTERVAL WITH VALUES PROJECTED BY THE SOCIAL SECURITY ADMINISTRATION FOR 1970-75**

Age, sex, and mortality assumption	Average years of life remaining or in interval			Change	
	Actual, 1953 (base year)	Actual, 1972	Projected, 1970-75	Actual, 1953 to 1972	Projected, 1953 to 1970-75
BIRTH					
Male					
Low......................................	66.0	67.4	70.3	+1.4	+4.3
High.....................................			68.0		+2.0
Female					
Low......................................	72.0	75.1	76.5	+3.1	+4.5
High.....................................			74.4		+2.4
0 TO 64 YEARS					
Male					
Low......................................	58.0	58.9	60.1	+0.9	+2.1
High.....................................			59.2		+1.2
Female					
Low......................................	60.4	61.4	62.0	+1.0	+1.6
High.....................................			61.4		+1.0
65 YEARS					
Male					
Low......................................	12.9	13.1	14.3	+0.2	+1.4
High.....................................			13.4		+0.5
Female					
Low......................................	15.3	17.0	17.2	+1.7	+1.9
High.....................................			16.2		+0.9

Source: Prepared on basis of data from U.S. Public Health Service, National Center for Health Statistics, Life Tables of the United States, 1953 and 1972, and U.S. Social Security Administration, Division of the Actuary, "Illustrative United States Population Projections," Actuarial Study, No. 46, by T.N.E. Greville, May 1957.

with the elimination of one cause, the other(s) may account for death, though possibly with some lag. Moreover, if deaths from a particular cause (e.g., cancer) were eliminated or sharply reduced, those saved would be subject to death from other causes (e.g., diseases of the heart) and, conceivably but not necessarily, the rates from these causes could rise as a result.

Still another procedure for projecting death rates is to postulate that the United States will attain the level of the most advanced areas, either a State of the United States or foreign country, or some analytical extension of that level, at some specified future date. This concept can be extended, probably with less merit, to encompass socioeconomic class differences and even race differences. Further, one can consider composite mortality patterns combining the record of the "best" State or foreign country at each age.

In spite of the difficulties and uncertainties, the projections of death rates made in 1956 by the Office of

the Actuary, Social Security Administration, proved to be rather consistent with actual developments to date, particularly in following a very conservative course. Nevertheless, the projections generally overstated the actual figures, as shown in table 5-13. The actual changes in expectation of life at birth between 1953 and 1972 were below the low projected value for males and just above it for females. Actual changes in "average years lived" at ages under 65 and "average years of life remaining" at age 65 also tended to fall below or close to the low projected values.

More recent projections of death rates for the United States were published by the Office of the Actuary in 1966 and 1974.[16] In each case death rates specific in

[16] U.S. Social Security Administration, Office of the Actuary, "United States Population Projections for OASDHI Cost Estimates," **Actuarial Study** No. 62, by Francisco Bayo, December 1966; and U.S. Social Security Administration, Office of the Actuary, "United States Population Projections for OASDHI Cost Estimates," **Actuarial Study** No. 72, by Francisco Bayo and Steven F. McKay, July 1974.

terms of age, sex, and cause of death (10 classes) were analyzed in making the projections. Judgments were then made as to the expected reduction in these rates by the year 2000, taking into account the past trends in the rates and recent and prospective medical and related socioeconomic developments. The projections published in 1974 show little increase in life expectation at birth or at age 65 between 1972 and 2000:

Age and sex	1972 (base period)	2000	Increase, 1972 to 2000
BIRTH			
Male..........	67.4	69.0	1.6
Female........	75.1	76.9	1.8
65 YEARS			
Male..........	13.1	13.6	0.5
Female........	17.0	18.1	1.1

They imply an increase of only about 1½ years in life expectation at birth and of only ¾ year in life expectation at age 65 in this period. The assumption of modest future reductions in mortality reflects the trends during the past few decades. The outlook is now assumed to be somewhat less favorable for males, and slightly more favorable for females, than in 1966, when the previous projections were made.

In considering the record of the "best" State as a guide to possible progress for the United States, we may refer to the life tables for States for 1969-71 and 1959-61 published by the National Center for Health Statistics.[17] Life expectation at birth was highest in Hawaii (73.6 years). The figure for Hawaii exceeds the U.S. average (70.8 years) by 2.8 years. The best expectation at age 65 (16.2 years), which relates to Hawaii also, exceeds the U.S. average (15.0 years) by merely 1.2 years. This difference suggests little room for improvement before the United States is as well off as the best State. A similar comparison for sex-race groups indicates that the differences between life expectation at birth in the United States and the best State are only about 1½ years for white males and white females (48 States, excluding Alaska, Hawaii, and District of Columbia) and 2½ to 3 years for black males and black females (23 States, excluding California, Hawaii, and Oklahoma). At age 65 the differences for white males and white females (1¼ years), and for black males and black females (1½ years), are also small and about equal for the sexes. Actual changes in the sixties did not move the

[17]See sources of table 5-11 and table 5-12.

values any closer to the "targets" for males, but some progress was made for females. Although these figures suggest that progress in reducing U.S. average mortality toward the level of the leading States would not result in a continuation of the historical trend of increasing disparity between the death rates of males and females, no substantial convergence is suggested either.

Greater possible improvement is suggested by the experience of the countries of very low mortality, principally countries of northwestern Europe and Oceania. Sweden may be selected as the single country with the best overall record, although its death rates are not the lowest at some ages (table 5-14). Expectation of life at birth for females in Sweden in 1973 was 77.7 years, as compared with 75.3 years for females in the United States in 1973 (table 5-15). The difference is only 2.4 years. Most of the difference in death rates occurs at ages under 65, however, since expectation of life at age 65 is about the same. The United States disadvantage is much greater for males, especially at birth. Life expectancy at birth for males in Sweden, 72.1 years, exceeds the United States figure, 67.6 years, by 4.5 years; at age 65, the Swedish figure, 14.0 years, is only 0.9 years higher.

If, further, we combine the lowest death rates at each age in recent years (1969 to 1971) for the countries with reliable data (principally in northern and western Europe, and Oceania) into a single hypothetical life table, the possibility of additional increases in life expectation in the United States is suggested. The differences between the United States and the best-country composite are only moderate ones, however. The values for life expectation for females in the composite table are 78.7 years at birth and 18.0 years at age 65, implying differences of 3.4 years and 0.8 years over the corresponding United States values (table 5-15). Differences for males are a little larger although, of course, the expectancy values themselves for the United States and the composite are much lower than for females. The best-country composite figures for males are 73.5 years at birth and 15.2 years at age 65.

We can hypothesize, on the basis of the foreign data and the State data, that with present knowledge a life expectancy at birth of 78 years for females and 72 years for males, and at age 65 of 18 years for females and 15 years for males, is attainable in the United States in the near future. Even so, reaching the target cited for males "at birth" will be quite difficult.

There is implicit in these figures as well as in the figures in table 5-15 the prospect that the male-female gap in life expectation for the United States will continue to remain large even though it will narrow somewhat. Male-female differences in life expectation are substantial in all countries with low mortality (table 5-14). Sweden showed a difference of 5.6 years in 1973 and the best-country composite showed a difference of 5.2 years. Differences for States in the United States in

Table 5-14. **DEATH RATES FOR THE POPULATION 55 YEARS OLD AND OVER OF VARIOUS COUNTRIES, BY SEX AND AGE, BETWEEN 1969 AND 1971**

(Deaths per 1,000 population in specified group)

Country and year	Male							Female						
	55 to 59 years	60 to 64 years	65 to 69 years	70 to 74 years	75 to 79 years	80 to 84 years	85 years and over	55 to 59 years	60 to 64 years	65 to 69 years	70 to 74 years	75 to 79 years	80 to 84 years	85 years and over
Austria, 1970	16.0	28.4	46.2	71.3	107.6	157.7	261.3	8.1	13.3	23.1	42.1	72.3	122.5	225.3
Belgium, 1969	17.0	28.4	44.8	67.2	100.5	152.6	247.4	7.9	12.8	22.5	39.9	69.0	118.1	211.2
Czechoslovakia, 1970	18.0	29.6	48.8	74.5	112.2	163.7	258.9	8.7	14.6	25.2	45.9	80.3	131.1	222.2
Denmark, 1970	12.8	20.6	33.5	54.2	77.3	119.4	210.7	7.4	12.1	18.7	32.2	55.4	96.5	183.3
Finland, 1970	21.0	31.4	46.3	72.4	103.8	178.4		7.5	13.0	22.5	40.7	74.6	154.0	
France, 1970	15.1	23.8	36.3	55.0	83.0	131.7	225.5	6.6	10.0	16.5	28.6	52.0	89.8	181.6
Germany, East, 1970	15.7	26.7	44.5	68.2	137.6			8.2	13.8	24.4	44.5	79.5	136.3	244.1
Germany, West, 1970	15.0	25.5	43.8	69.4	104.4	159.2	267.1	7.9	12.8	22.6	40.1	107.1		
Hungary, 1971	16.1	25.9	43.3	69.8	106.9	157.8	254.7	8.8	14.5	24.7	44.8	80.0	131.5	231.6
Iceland, 1970	14.8	22.2	27.3	44.4	65.8	109.8	196.8	5.9	10.5	18.5	28.3	47.3	98.8	216.6
Italy, 1969	14.7	25.4	40.9	63.2	89.4	158.3		7.4	12.4	21.6	38.1	65.7	133.4	
Netherlands, 1971	13.1	21.9	34.6	53.4	81.5	124.0	220.0	6.1	9.8	17.1	31.6	56.0	102.0	196.5
Norway, 1970	12.3	19.5	32.8	52.1	77.9	123.8	221.4	5.9	8.9	16.9	30.5	53.1	100.1	186.5
Poland, 1971	16.1	26.8	44.1	70.6	129.4			7.8	13.2	22.9	42.1	101.4		
Sweden, 1971	10.7	18.0	29.7	49.2	79.2	125.0	218.4	5.9	9.5	15.8	29.2	53.6	94.7	180.0
England and Wales, 1971	15.2	25.8	42.2	66.7	103.1	147.2	243.1	8.0	12.4	20.0	34.4	62.2	102.1	193.0
Yugoslavia, 1971	15.5	24.9	39.7	65.4	104.4	151.0	209.0	8.9	15.1	24.9	47.8	79.8	127.2	192.7
Australia, 1971	16.8	26.4	41.9	64.1	99.9	147.3	240.5	8.4	13.0	20.7	35.9	62.7	102.6	197.2
New Zealand, 1971	16.1	26.0	40.2	61.3	92.9	147.0	243.3	8.4	12.8	19.6	33.2	58.4	98.5	198.8
Japan, 1971	12.3	20.3	34.6	55.6	89.7	143.0	226.1	6.9	11.2	19.8	33.7	60.7	108.2	195.0
Canada, 1971	14.6	22.9	34.7	51.9	79.0	118.8	198.6	7.2	11.0	17.3	28.4	48.1	82.4	163.3
United States, 1970[1]	18.6	27.9	41.2	58.9	86.8	123.9	178.2	9.1	13.2	20.4	32.4	53.8	87.7	155.2
United States, 1973[2]	17.8	27.0	39.3	58.7	88.1	122.4	198.1	8.9	12.9	19.0	31.6	53.4	83.4	162.3

[1]From National Center for Health Statistics, U.S. Public Health Service, Vital Statistics of the United States, Part A, 1970 Volume II.
[2]From National Center for Health Statistics, U.S. Public Health Service, Monthly Vital Statistics Report, Volume 23, No. 11 (supplement 2), "Summary Report, Final Mortality Statistics, 1973," table 3.

Source: United Nations, Demographic Yearbook, 1972, table 25.

1969-71 are consistently high, varying only negligibly around the national average of 7.6 years.

Historical and comparative analysis suggests, therefore, no great convergence of male and female mortality or life expectation in the United States in the near future. This analysis is also consistent with the view that at least a substantial part of the difference reflects the vital superiority of women. A tenable hypothesis regarding the prospects for convergence of male and female death rates, therefore, is that the difference will shortly reach a maximum at about its present level or decline only a small amount, and then remain essentially unchanged, barring sucessful genetic intervention favoring males or widespread deleterious environmental influences particularly affecting women.[18] In any case, substantial convergence of male and female death rates in the foreseeable future is now considered highly unlikely.[19]

Bourgeois-Pichat has extrapolated the trends in endogeneous mortality in the countries with the lowest recorded rates as an approach to the measurement of the limit of the decline in mortality imposed by the human constitution.[20] The extrapolation takes account of recent and prospective medical developments in the most advanced countries. On this basis, in 1952 Bourgeois-Pichat calculated life expectations at birth of 78.2 years for females and 76.3 years for males, and expectations at age 65 of 17.6 years for females and 16.3 years for males. Bourgeois-Pichat's projections for females have already been achieved, even exceeded, by the best-county composite. His projections for males suggest that much progress is still possible, both below and above age 65. The figures imply a considerable convergence of male and female death rates—a development previously noted as highly unlikely.

What appears attainable with respect to reduction in mortality is clearly a shifting thing, as the scope and level of exogenous and endogenous mortality shift. A new calculation of the same type prepared currently would undoubtedly raise Bourgeois-Pichat's figures. Calculations such as those of Bourgeois-Pichat are subject to question because of the impossibility of making an exact separation between endogenous and exogenous mortality and because some exogenous causes of mortality (e.g., accidents) cannot be assumed to decline.

[18]Charles L. Rose, "Critique of Longevity Studies," pp. 13-29, in Palmore and Jeffers, op. cit., esp. p. 19.
[19]George C. Myers, "Changing Mortality Patterns and Sex Imbalances Among the Aged," paper presented at the 10th International Congress of Gerontology, Jerusalem, Israel, June 22-27, 1975.

[20]Jean Bourgeois-Pichat, "Essai sur la mortalité 'biologique' de l'homme," **Population** (Paris), Vol. 7, No. 3, pp. 381-394, July-Sept. 1952. Endogenous causes of death are those which have a typically genetic or biological basis and are presumably less amenable to control, as contrasted with the exogenous causes, which are typically environmentally caused.

Table 5-15. **COMPARISON OF AVERAGE REMAINING LIFETIME AND AVERAGE YEARS LIVED IN INTERVAL FOR THE UNITED STATES, SWEDEN, AND BEST-COUNTRY COMPOSITE**

Area	Male			Female			Excess of female over male		
	e_0	$^1e_{0-64}$	e_{65}	e_0	$^1e_{0-64}$	e_{65}	e_0	$^1e_{0-64}$	e_{65}
United States, 1973[2].................	67.6	59.0	13.1	75.3	61.5	17.2	7.7	2.5	4.1
Sweden, 1973[3]......................	72.1	61.4	14.0	77.7	62.8	17.1	5.6	1.4	3.1
Best-country composite[4]...............	73.5	61.6	15.2	78.7	63.0	18.0	5.2	1.4	2.8
Difference, U.S. and best-country composite..........................	5.9	2.6	2.1	3.4	1.5	0.8	-2.5	-1.1	-1.3

[1]Computed by $(T_0 - T_{65}) \div l_0$.
[2]U.S. Public Health Service, National Center for Health Statistics, <u>Vital Statistics of the United States</u>, <u>Mortality</u>, <u>Part A</u>, <u>1973</u> (forthcoming).
[3]Best single country; based on data in United Nations, <u>Demographic Yearbook</u>, <u>1974</u>, table 18 (forthcoming).
[4]Composite of lowest age-specific death rates for countries with reliable data for the years, 1969 to 1971.

The fact that persons at age 65 would live 10 years longer on the average than they are now slated to live if the major cardiovascular-renal diseases were eliminated does not provide a useful basis for projections of mortality. It should be clearly recognized that the cause-of-death life tables which provide such estimates of gains in life expectation are merely analytical tools, providing guides as to where it may be most important and effective to apply effort in extending life expectation. The major cardiovascular-renal diseases are not likely to be eliminated in the foreseeable future although death rates from these causes may be moderately reduced.[21] In sum, there is no sound reason for expecting major increases in life expectation or any significant extension of the life span in the foreseeable future.[22]

Some Theoretical Considerations

Persons who are saved from death due to a particular cause or class of causes (e.g., malignant neoplasms) must die of some other causes, including possibly some new causes to be identified. Nevertheless, death rates at each age by cause may continue to decline indefinitely. With a decline in age-specific death rates more individuals will survive to the older ages and, hence, more persons will die at these later ages (wholly or largely from particular established causes) even though death rates at these ages are lower than they had been.[23] This combination of facts explains the seeming paradox that general age-specific death rates and cause-specific death rates by age may continue to decline while the chances of eventually dying from a particular disease (i.e., the number dying from that disease per 100 persons in the original cohort) may increase.

Reference was made earlier to the effect of reductions in mortality on the growth of the elderly population in the United States. Consider now an extreme situation: How much faster would the elderly population and the proportion of elderly persons grow if no one died? The immediate effect on the growth rate of the total population would be quite pronounced if life expectancy at birth were infinite rather than about 71, as at present—an increase in the growth rate equal to the death rate—but in the long run the rate of population growth would hardly be increased.[24] Under conditions of replacement-level fertility and a small regular flow of immigrants, such as now roughly characterize the United States population, the immediate achievement of zero death rates would result in a growth rate of about 1.7 percent in the first projection year, 1.3 percent in the year 2000, and 1.1 percent in the year 2025, as

[21]See P.R.J. Burch, "What Limits Life Span?", pp. 31-56, in B. Benjamin, P. R. Cox, and J. Peel (eds.), **Population and the New Biology**, Academic Press, New York, 1974.

[22]This generalization is directly contrary to the premise of Richard A. Kalish, "Added Years: Social Issues and Consequences," pp. 273-280, in Erdman Palmore and Frances C. Jeffers (eds.), **Prediction of Life Span**, Heath Lexington Books, D.C. Heath and Co. Lexington, Mass., 1971.

[23]This fact may be illustrated by a hypothetical life table in which no one dies before age 85 and in which death rates between age 85 and some age such as 120 rise from 0 to 1.0, being always below the present rates until age 120. The fact that death rates below age 85 have fallen to zero means that 100,000 persons survive to age 85. Then, even with lower death rates above age 85, much larger numbers of persons die at the higher ages from the various diseases of later life than in current life tables, until the cohort is extinct by about age 120.

[24]See also Ansley J. Coale, "Increases in Expectation of Life and Population Growth," **International Population Conference**, Vienna 1959, International Union for the Scientific Study of Population, pp. 36-41.

compared with 0.8 percent in 1975.[25] Similarly, after the initial tremendous impact of the shift to zero mortality, the growth rate of the elderly population would begin to revert to its former level. The population 65 and over is currently increasing at 2.4 percent annually; with zero death rates the growth rate would jump to 8.3 percent in the first projection year and then gradually fall back to 2.9 percent in 2000, and 2.8 percent in 2025.

Of more importance in the present context is the effect on age composition of the elimination of deaths. Since, with a life expectancy of 71 years, any large reductions in death rates would be limited to ages over 60, the elimination of deaths would tend to add greatly to the proportion of the population in the older ages. The conditions stated above would result in a rise of the proportion 65 years and over to 24 percent in 2000, 38 percent in 2025, and 47 percent in 2050. If zero death rates are achieved more gradually (i.e., by the year 2000 for the white population and by the year 2020 for the black population), the proportion 65 and over would rise to about 18 percent in 2000, 33 percent in 2025, and 44 percent in 2050. Once mortality had been eliminated or had been reduced to very low levels—such that variable changes in mortality by age would have a negligible effect in any case—further changes in age structure would depend almost wholly on the level of fertility.[26] With low fertility (e.g., a total fertility rate of 1.0) the proportion of the aged would tend to rise sharply; with high fertility (e.g., a total fertility rate of 4.0) the proportion would tend to be depressed and, over a long period, would be quite small.

[25]These calculations were made by the author on the same basis as the Series II projections of the U.S. Bureau of the Census given in **Current Population Reports,** Series P-25, No. 601, except for the modification in the mortality assumption.

[26]Ansley J. Coale, "Age Composition in the Absence of Mortality and in Other Odd Circumstances," **Demography,** Vol. 10, No. 4, Nov. 1973, pp. 537-542.

SOCIAL AND ECONOMIC CHARACTERISTICS

In this chapter we consider the principal social and economic characteristics of the older population. These characteristics are treated under the following four headings: (1) marital status and living arrangements; (2) educational attainment; (3) labor force participation; and (4) income level. We conclude with a note on the relation of the age composition of the population to intergenerational dependency in families and to economic dependency in our society.

Marital Status and Living Arrangements

The marital distribution and living arrangements of elderly men differ sharply from those of elderly women (figures 6-1 and 6-2). Most men 65 and over are married and live with their wives; few live alone. In March 1975 three out of four men in this age range were married and living with their wives (table 6-1). Only one out of seven men 65 and over was widowed and only one out of seven was living alone (table 6-2). Women 65 and over are much more likely to be widowed than married and a substantial portion of them live alone. In March 1975 only one out of three women 65 and over was married and living with her husband. Over half of the women were widowed and over one out of three women was living alone. While the distribution of elderly persons by marital status changed little during the 1960's, in the

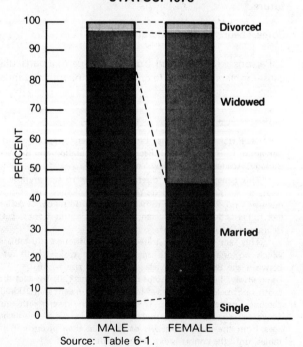

Figure 6-1. PERCENT DISTRIBUTION OF THE MALE AND FEMALE POPULATION 65 YEARS OLD AND OVER BY MARITAL STATUS: 1975

Source: Table 6-1.

last quarter century, from 1950 to 1975, the cumulative changes have been substantial, especially for men. The proportion married has greatly increased and the proportions single and widowed have fallen sharply.

Several factors explain the higher proportion of widows among elderly women. The principal one is the much higher mortality rates of married men as compared with their wives—a joint effect of the higher mortality rates of men than women and the fact that husbands are typically older than their wives by a few years. An indication of the difference may be secured by comparing the annual death rates (per 100,000) for married females at various older ages with those for married males at slightly higher ages for a recent year (1959-61):[1]

Figure 6-2. PERCENT DISTRIBUTION OF THE MALE AND FEMALE POPULATION 65 YEARS OLD AND OVER BY LIVING ARRANGEMENTS: 1975

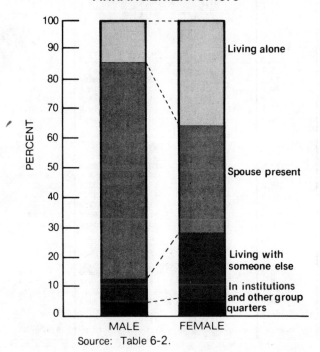

Source: Table 6-2.

As a result of these differences in death rates, most married women outlive their husbands and they tend to outlive them by many years. Currently in the United States, women who become widowed at age 65 outlive their husbands, on the average, by about 16 years. Men who become widowed at age 70 outlive their wives by about 10 years. On the other hand, the expectation of

life at age 65 of married women exceeds that of their husbands at age 70 by about 9 years (without specification of a particular age at death or the sex of the first decedent.)[2]

A second factor accounting for the higher proportion of widows than widowers is the higher remarriage rates of widowers, who often take wives from among women under 65 and single or divorced women over 65 as well as widows over 65. An indication of the difference in the remarriage rates of the sexes may be secured by comparing the marriage rates of males 65 and over with those for females at these ages. In 1971 the annual marriage rate (per 1,000 unmarried persons) for females 65 and over was 2.4 while the rate for males was 16.7; these figures reflect a 7 to 1 difference in the rate.[3] They also indicate the relative rarity of marriage of elderly persons. The vast majority of marriages at these ages are marriages of widowed persons. The higher remarriage rate of widowers is a result of social norms supporting marriage to younger women (and discouraging the opposite), a stronger motivation to remarry, and a male demographic advantage in the fact of a surplus of women in the marriage market. In 1975 the proportion of unmarried women 65 and over was three times as great as the proportion of unmarried men 65 and over (table 6-1).

Female		Male		Ratio
Age	Rate	Age	Rate	Male/Female
60-64..	1291.2	65-69.	3663.5	2.837
65-69..	1998.9	70-74.	5236.5	2.620
70 and over..	4646.7	75 and over.	9905.9	2.132

[2] The first figure is approximated by the expectation of life of females at age 65, adjusted for the difference between the mortality level of widowed women and all women; the second figure is approximated in the same way for males; and the third figure is approximated by the difference between the expectation of life of females at age 65 and the expectation of life of males at age 70, the male expectation being adjusted for the difference between the mortality level of married males and all males and the female expectation for the corresponding difference and the shift from married status to widowhood. See also Robert J. Myers, "Statistical Measures in the Marital Life Cycles of Men and Women," **International Population Conference, Vienna, 1959**, International Union for the Scientific Study of Population, pp. 229-233.

[3] U.S. Public Health Service, National Center for Health Statistics, **Vital Statistics of the United States**, 1971, Vol. III, **Marriage and Divorce**, 1975, table 1-7. See also Judith Treas and Anke Van Hilst, "Marriage and Remarriage Among the Older Population," paper presented at the Annual Meeting of the Gerontological Society, Oct. 27, 1975, Louisville, Ky.

[1] U.S. Public Health Service, National Center for Health Statistics, "Mortality from Selected Causes by Marital Status, United States," **Vital and Health Statistics**, Series 20, No. 8a and 8b, by A. Joan Klebba, 1970.

Table 6-1. DISTRIBUTION OF THE POPULATION 55 YEARS OLD AND OVER BY MARITAL STATUS, BY AGE AND SEX: 1950 TO 1990

(Total resident population excluding members of the Armed Forces on post, 1950 to 1970. Noninstitutional population excluding members of the Armed Forces on post, 1975 and 1990. Figures are for March of year indicated)

Marital status and year	Male				Female			
	55 to 64 years	65 to 74 years	75 years and over	65 years and over	55 to 64 years	65 to 74 years	75 years and over	65 years and over
1950								
Percent, total.....	100.0	(NA)	(NA)	100.0	100.0	(NA)	(NA)	100.0
Single..................	8.9	(NA)	(NA)	8.0	7.2	(NA)	(NA)	8.0
Married.................	81.8	(NA)	(NA)	66.2	65.0	(NA)	(NA)	36.0
Spouse present.........	79.2	(NA)	(NA)	63.3	62.8	(NA)	(NA)	34.3
Spouse absent..........	2.7	(NA)	(NA)	2.9	2.2	(NA)	(NA)	1.7
Widowed.................	7.1	(NA)	(NA)	23.6	25.5	(NA)	(NA)	55.3
Divorced................	2.1	(NA)	(NA)	2.2	2.2	(NA)	(NA)	0.7
1960								
Percent, total.....	100.0	100.0	100.0	100.0	100.0	100.0	100.0	100.0
Single..................	7.9	6.7	7.8	7.1	6.5	8.4	8.6	8.5
Married.................	82.5	78.9	59.1	72.5	65.8	45.6	21.8	37.1
Spouse present.........	79.0	76.2	56.5	69.8	62.9	43.5	20.6	35.3
Spouse absent..........	3.4	2.7	2.6	2.6	2.9	2.1	1.2	1.8
Widowed.................	6.2	12.7	31.6	18.8	24.5	44.4	68.3	52.9
Divorced................	3.5	1.7	1.5	1.6	3.2	1.7	1.2	1.5
1970								
Percent, total.....	100.0	100.0	100.0	100.0	100.0	100.0	100.0	100.0
Single..................	7.8	8.0	6.6	7.5	6.8	7.8	7.5	7.7
Married.................	85.2	78.0	64.3	73.1	67.4	45.2	21.0	35.6
Spouse present.........	82.3	75.2	60.4	69.9	63.8	43.5	19.1	33.9
Spouse absent..........	2.9	2.8	3.9	3.2	3.6	1.6	1.9	1.7
Widowed.................	4.1	11.3	27.7	17.1	21.2	44.0	70.3	54.4
Divorced................	3.0	2.7	1.4	2.3	4.6	3.0	1.3	2.3
1975								
Percent, total.....	100.0	100.0	100.0	100.0	100.0	100.0	100.0	100.0
Single..................	6.5	4.3	5.5	4.7	5.1	5.8	5.8	5.8
Married.................	85.0	83.9	70.0	79.3	69.3	49.0	23.4	39.1
Spouse present.........	81.8	81.8	68.2	77.3	66.7	47.3	22.3	37.6
Spouse absent..........	3.2	2.0	1.8	2.0	2.6	1.8	1.1	1.5
Widowed.................	4.0	8.8	23.3	13.6	20.3	41.9	69.4	52.5
Divorced................	4.5	3.1	1.2	2.5	5.3	3.3	1.5	2.6
1990								
Percent, total.....	100.0	100.0	100.0	100.0	100.0	100.0	100.0	100.0
Single................	4.4	6.7	4.4	5.9	4.5	6.8	5.7	6.3
Range.................	(3.7-5.9)	(7.2-5.7)	(3.8-5.6)	(6.0-5.6)	(4.2-5.3)	(6.7-6.9)	(5.3-6.4)	(6.1-6.7)
Married, spouse present..	85.1	77.1	65.3	73.0	70.4	46.1	20.2	35.1
Range.................	(86.4-82.6)	(76.3-78.6)	(66.8-62.5)	(73.0-73.1)	(71.8-67.6)	(46.4-45.6)	(19.8-20.8)	(35.1-35.0)
Other ever married.......	10.5	16.2	30.2	21.1	25.1	47.1	74.2	58.6
Range.................	(10.0-11.5)	(16.5-15.7)	(29.4-31.9)	(21.0-21.3)	(24.0-27.1)	(46.9-47.6)	(74.9-72.8)	(58.8-58.3)

NA Not available.

Source: Current Population Reports, Series P-20, Nos. 33, 105, 255, and 287, and Series P-25, No. 607.

The distribution of the population by marital status and by living arrangements shifts notably with increasing age. For women the proportion married falls sharply and the proportion widowed rises sharply in the age range 55 and over. Corresponding to these changes, there are increases in the proportions living alone or with someone other than one's spouse (son, daughter, other relative, nonrelative). In March 1975 only one out of five women 75 and over was married and living with her husband, as compared with two out of three for ages 55 to 64 years. Two out of five women 75 and over lived alone, as compared with one out of six for ages 55 to 64 years. For men the changes are similar but not as dramatic. About seven out of ten men 75 and over were married and living with their wives, and only one out of seven lived alone. At ages 55 to 64 the corresponding figures were four out of five and one out of thirteen.

About 80 percent of the men 65 and over and 56 percent of the women 65 and over were members of

Table 6-2. **LIVING ARRANGEMENTS OF THE POPULATION 55 YEARS OLD AND OVER, BY AGE AND SEX: 1965, 1970, AND 1975**

(Numbers in thousands. Total resident population excluding members of the Armed Forces on post. Figures are for March of year indicated)

Living arrangements and year	Male				Female			
	55 to 64 years	65 to 74 years	75 years and over	65 years and over	55 to 64 years	65 to 74 years	75 years and over	65 years and over
1975								
Number, total............	9,302	5,984	3,123	9,106	10,391	7,782	5,323	13,105
In households..................	9,122	5,809	2,893	8,702	10,271	7,585	4,791	12,376
Living alone.................	711	723	567	1,290	1,812	2,558	2,160	4,718
Spouse present...............	7,509	4,765	1,976	6,741	6,873	3,593	1,071	4,664
Living with someone else......	902	321	350	671	1,586	1,434	1,560	2,994
Not in households[1].............	180	175	230	404	120	197	532	729
Percent, total............	100.0	100.0	100.0	100.0	100.0	100.0	100.0	100.0
In households..................	98.1	97.1	92.6	95.6	98.8	97.5	90.0	94.4
Living alone.................	7.6	12.1	18.2	14.2	17.4	32.9	40.6	36.0
Spouse present...............	80.7	79.6	63.3	74.0	66.1	46.2	20.1	35.6
Living with someone else......	9.7	5.4	11.2	7.4	15.3	18.4	29.3	22.8
Not in households[1].............	1.9	2.9	7.4	4.4	1.2	2.5	10.0	5.6
1970								
Percent, total............	100.0	100.0	100.0	100.0	100.0	100.0	100.0	100.0
In households..................	97.6	96.4	93.7	95.5	98.4	97.6	91.1	95.0
Living alone.................	7.2	11.3	19.1	14.1	17.1	31.6	37.0	33.8
Spouse present...............	82.3	75.2	60.4	69.9	63.8	43.5	19.1	33.9
Living with someone else......	8.1	9.9	14.2	11.5	17.5	22.4	35.0	27.4
Not in households[1].............	2.4	3.6	6.3	4.5	1.6	2.4	8.9	5.0
1965								
Percent, total............	100.0	100.0	100.0	100.0	100.0	100.0	100.0	100.0
In households..................	97.5	97.5	93.6	96.2	98.4	97.4	92.0	95.3
Living alone.................	7.0	11.7	15.7	13.1	15.5	27.9	29.9	28.6
Spouse present...............	80.3	75.3	54.0	67.9	63.8	43.3	19.0	34.1
Living with someone else......	10.2	10.5	23.9	15.2	19.1	26.1	43.1	32.6
Not in households[1].............	2.5	2.5	6.4	3.8	1.6	2.6	8.0	4.7

[1]Population in institutions and other group quarters.

Source: Current Population Reports, Series P-20, Nos. 144 and 287, and unpublished data for March 1970 (revised).

Table 6-3. **FAMILY STATUS OF THE POPULATION 65 YEARS OLD AND OVER, BY SEX: 1965, 1970, AND 1975**

(Total resident population excluding members of the Armed Forces on post. Figures are for March of year indicated)

Family status	1975		1970		1965	
	Male	Female	Male	Female	Male	Female
Percent, total.............	100.0	100.0	100.0	100.0	100.0	100.0
In families......................	79.8	56.1	79.2	58.5	80.3	62.9
Head..........................	76.1	8.5	72.9	9.8	71.3	10.7
Wife..........................	(X)	35.0	(X)	33.3	(X)	33.3
Other relative................	3.7	12.7	6.3	15.4	9.0	18.9
Primary individual...............	14.8	37.3	14.9	35.2	13.9	30.6
Secondary individual.............	1.2	1.2	2.4	1.9	2.3	2.2
Inmate of institution............	4.2	5.3	3.6	4.4	3.5	4.3

X Not applicable.

Source: Current Population Reports, Series P-20, Nos. 144 and 287, and unpublished data for March 1970 (revised).

families in 1975 (table 6-3). Most men (76 percent) were family heads but only a minority of the women were wives of family heads (35 percent) or family heads themselves (9 percent). The distribution of the elderly by family status has shown marked shifts during recent years. The overall proportions of persons, especially women, living in families has been decreasing. The proportions of male heads was substantially lower (71 percent), and the proportions of female heads somewhat higher (11 percent), in 1965. The decrease of females in families between 1965 and 1975 resulted largely from the decrease in "other relatives" (i.e., persons in families other than the heads or their wives); for males the decrease in "other relatives" was offset by a rise in heads. The proportion of all men 65 years old and over who were "other relatives" in families dropped from 9 percent in 1965 to 4 percent in 1975, and the proportion for women dropped from 19 percent to 13 percent.

In the last decade there has been an increase in the proportion of elderly individuals who maintained their own households, living either alone or with nonrelatives. Such "primary" individuals represented about 15 percent of the men 65 years old and over and about 37 percent of the women 65 and over in 1975. During the same period there was a pronounced decline in the proportion of elderly persons living with relatives other than spouses. Nearly all (about 96 percent) primary individuals 65 years old and over occupied their own house or apartment entirely alone as "one-person households" in 1975.

Contrary to the popular view, only a small proportion of the elderly population lives in institutions. Slightly less than 5 percent of the population 65 and over resided in institutions in 1975. According to 1970 census data, the proportions of institutional residents are at a minimum at about ages 40 to 44 for males (1.0 percent) and at ages 20 to 29 for females (0.3 percent), and then rise steadily with increasing age. For example, the figures for males and females aged 75 and over are 6.9 percent and 10.9 percent, respectively. The proportion of the elderly population residing in institutions has been rising, as the proportions of widowed females and extreme aged among the elderly have been rising. In 1960 only 3.7 percent of the population 65 and over resided in institutions. In 1960 most institutionalized elderly persons lived in mental hospitals; today most live in homes for the aged.

Educational Attainment

The educational attainment of older persons is well below that of adults in general, as measured in terms of the percent of high school graduates and the median years of school completed. In March 1975 the percentage of the population 65 and over which had graduated from high school was only about three-fifths as great as the percentage of high school graduates in the entire

population 25 years and over (table 6-4). A little over one-third of the elderly population were high school graduates, as compared with three-fifths of all persons 25 and over. Half of those 65 and over had completed less than nine years of school, but over half of all adults 25 and over had completed 12 years of school or more.

The negative relationship between age and educational attainment reflects the widening opportunity available to each new cohort of students and the increasing aspiration for, and achievement of, greater education on the part of the new cohorts. These factors have been associated with the rising socioeconomic status of the United States population and the concomitant intergenerational influences. Another factor has been the special history of immigration to the United States, which now accounts for a much larger proportion of foreign-born persons among the older population than at the younger ages. In 1970, 15 percent of those 65 and over were foreign-born, with the proportion showing a steady rise with increasing ages among the older population. This group has higher proportions of illiteracy and lower educational attainment than the native population.

The level of educational attainment of the elderly population has been increasing rapidly, just as it has for the entire adult population, as younger persons with more education move into older age groups. The proportion of high school graduates among those 65 and over was only 18 percent as recently as 1952. By 1990 about half of the population over 65 is expected to be high school graduates and, in view of the slower rise in educational attainment expected for adults below 65, the relative gap between the educational attainment of the group 65 and over and the educational attainment of the total population 25 years and over will be substantially reduced. It is expected that in 1990 the percent of high school graduates 65 and over will be only about one-third below the percent for the entire adult population. The deficit in educational attainment is less for the elderly female population today than for the elderly male population and is expected to remain so in 1990.

Labor Force Participation

Labor force (worker) proportions for elderly males have been dropping rapidly over the past quarter century. In 1950 almost half of all men 65 and over was in the labor force, but by 1960 only one-third of the men in this age range was working or looking for work. Only about one-fifth of the men 65 and over (22 percent) works today (table 6-5). The decline reflects the joint effect of the increase in voluntary retirement programs, the implementation of more stringent retirement rules by employers, and the drop in self-employment. A secular decline already appears at ages as low as 55 to 59 and is reflected in each older age group with

Table 6-4. **EDUCATIONAL ATTAINMENT OF THE POPULATION 65 YEARS OLD AND OVER AND 25 YEARS OLD AND OVER, BY SEX: 1952 TO 1990**

(Figures are for March of year indicated)

Sex and year	Median school years completed			Percent high school graduates		
	65 years old and over	25 years old and over	Ratio, 65 and over to 25 and over	65 years old and over	25 years old and over	Ratio, 65 and over to 25 and over
BOTH SEXES						
1952..........................	8.2	10.1	0.81	18.4	38.4	0.48
1959..........................	8.3	11.0	0.75	19.4	42.9	0.45
1965..........................	8.5	11.8	0.72	23.5	49.0	0.48
1970..........................	8.7	12.2	0.71	28.3	55.2	0.51
1975..........................	9.0	12.3	0.73	35.2	62.6	0.56
1980..........................	9.7	12.4	0.78	37.9	65.4	0.58
1985..........................	10.9	12.5	0.87	44.0	70.2	0.63
1990..........................	11.9	12.6	0.94	49.4	74.2	0.67
MALE						
1952..........................	8.0	9.7	0.82	15.3	36.4	0.42
1959..........................	8.2	10.7	0.77	18.1	41.3	0.44
1965..........................	8.3	11.7	0.71	21.8	48.0	0.45
1970..........................	8.6	12.2	0.70	25.9	55.0	0.47
1975..........................	8.9	12.4	0.72	33.4	63.1	0.53
1980..........................	9.4	12.5	0.75	36.3	66.5	0.55
1985..........................	10.7	12.6	0.85	43.0	71.9	0.60
1990..........................	11.8	12.7	0.93	48.7	76.3	0.64
FEMALE						
1952..........................	8.3	10.4	0.80	21.1	40.2	0.52
1959..........................	8.4	11.2	0.75	20.4	44.4	0.46
1965..........................	8.6	12.0	0.72	24.7	49.9	0.49
1970..........................	8.8	12.1	0.73	30.1	55.4	0.54
1975..........................	9.4	12.3	0.76	36.5	62.1	0.59
1980..........................	9.9	12.4	0.80	38.9	64.4	0.60
1985..........................	11.1	12.4	0.90	44.7	68.7	0.65
1990..........................	12.0	12.5	0.96	49.9	72.3	0.69

Source: Current Population Reports, Series P-20, Nos. 45, 99, 158, 207, and forthcoming report for 1975; and Series P-25, No. 476 (projections).

increasing intensity. Still, six out of seven men (84 percent) at ages 55 to 59 and two out of three men (66 percent) at ages 60 to 64 work today. At ages 70 and over, on the other hand, only about one out of six men (15 percent) are working. These trends are expected to continue, so that by 1990 only 17 percent of the male population 65 and over and only 10 percent of the male population 70 and over are expected to be in the labor force.

The worker proportions for older women, on the other hand, have experienced little change. The proportions for women 65 and over have fluctuated over the past quarter century at around 8 to 11 percent although a steady decline seems to have occurred in the last decade; today 1 out of 12 women (8.3 percent) 65 and over work. The prospects are for a moderate decline in this proportion to 7.5 percent in 1990. On the other hand, during the 1950-75 period women 55 to 64, especially those 55 to 59, have left their homes in generally increasing proportions to join the work force.

The worker proportion for women 55 to 64 has risen from 27 percent in 1950 to 41 percent in 1975 and is expected to climb to 43 percent in 1990. Many women who have completed rearing a family or who have become divorced or widowed are returning to the work force; some of these formerly would simply have remained as homemakers.

Worker proportions for older blacks have been historically distinguished by the higher level of the proportions for black women over those for white women. The worker proportions for black women for ages 55 to 64 have been converging so rapidly with those for white women during the past quarter century, however, that by 1975 the difference was rather small. For ages 65 and over the difference became quite small after a sharp convergence at the beginning of the period. Worker proportions for black males 65 and over are similar to and have been changing in the same pattern as those for white males. The proportions at ages 55 to 64 have also been changing in the same pattern as those for whites but they are substantially lower.

Table 6-5. **WORKER PROPORTIONS FOR THE POPULATION 55 YEARS OLD AND OVER, BY AGE, RACE, AND SEX: 1950 TO 1990**

(Figures are monthly averages. Total noninstitutional population)

Age, race, and sex	1950	1955	1960	1965	1970	1975	1980	1990
ALL CLASSES								
Male								
55 to 64 years..................	86.9	87.9	86.8	84.7	83.0	75.8	74.7	70.1
55 to 59 years.................	(NA)	92.5	91.6	90.2	89.5	84.4	83.0	80.8
60 to 64 years.................	(NA)	82.5	81.2	78.0	75.0	65.7	63.0	57.2
65 years and over................	45.8	39.6	33.1	27.9	26.8	21.7	20.1	16.8
65 to 69 years.................	(NA)	57.0	46.8	43.0	41.6	31.7	29.9	26.1
70 years and over..............	(NA)	28.1	24.4	19.1	17.7	15.1	12.9	10.3
Female								
55 to 64 years..................	27.0	32.5	37.2	41.1	43.0	41.0	42.0	42.6
55 to 59 years.................	(NA)	35.6	42.2	47.1	49.0	47.9	48.9	51.1
60 to 64 years.................	(NA)	29.0	31.4	34.0	36.1	33.3	33.4	33.4
65 years and over................	9.7	10.6	10.8	10.0	9.7	8.3	8.0	7.5
65 to 69 years.................	(NA)	17.8	17.6	17.4	17.3	14.5	14.4	13.9
70 years and over..............	(NA)	6.4	6.8	6.1	5.7	4.9	4.4	4.1
NEGRO AND OTHER RACES								
Male								
55 to 64 years..................	81.9	83.1	82.5	78.8	79.2	68.7	(NA)	(NA)
55 to 59 years.................	(NA)	(NA)	(NA)	(NA)	83.5	76.9	(NA)	(NA)
60 to 64 years.................	(NA)	(NA)	(NA)	(NA)	73.6	59.3	(NA)	(NA)
65 years and over................	45.5	40.0	31.2	27.9	27.4	20.9	(NA)	(NA)
65 to 69 years.................	(NA)	(NA)	(NA)	(NA)	(NA)	(NA)	(NA)	(NA)
70 years and over..............	(NA)	(NA)	(NA)	(NA)	(NA)	(NA)	(NA)	(NA)
Female								
55 to 64 years..................	40.9	40.7	47.3	48.9	47.1	43.8	(NA)	(NA)
55 to 59 years.................	(NA)	(NA)	(NA)	(NA)	53.4	52.1	(NA)	(NA)
60 to 64 years.................	(NA)	(NA)	(NA)	(NA)	39.0	34.6	(NA)	(NA)
65 years and over................	16.5	12.1	12.8	12.9	12.2	10.5	(NA)	(NA)
65 to 69 years.................	(NA)	(NA)	(NA)	(NA)	(NA)	(NA)	(NA)	(NA)
70 years and over..............	(NA)	(NA)	(NA)	(NA)	(NA)	(NA)	(NA)	(NA)

NA Not available.

Source: U.S. Department of Labor, Bureau of Labor Statistics, Employment and Earnings, Vol. 22, No. 7, January 1976; Special Labor Force Report 156, The U.S. Labor Force: Projections to 1990, 1973; and projections to be published in a forthcoming Special Labor Force Report.

(table 6-6). This ratio has fluctuated between about .49 and .57 for the last few decades. The sex of the head of the family makes an important difference in the relative position of families with heads 65 and over. Families headed by females 65 and over have higher median incomes than all female-headed families; but for families headed by males, median incomes are relatively much lower for families with heads 65 and over. The median income of families with heads 65 and over increased nearly 300 percent over the period 1950-74 and more than 100 percent over the period 1965-74 in current dollars, but grew much less rapidly in constant dollars.

Income Level

Families with heads 65 and over have relatively low incomes as compared with all families (figure 6-3). The median income of families with heads 65 and over in 1974 ($7,298) was less than three-fifths (.57) the median income for all families ($12,836) in 1974

The median income of unrelated individuals (i.e., those not living with any relatives) over 65 more than doubled in the 1965-74 period but is still quite low ($2,956 in 1974). Unrelated individuals over 65 have a median income only about two-fifths as great as families with heads over 65. Similarly, families headed by blacks 65 and over have much lower incomes than families headed by whites 65 and over. The median income of families with black heads over 65 ($4,909) is only two-thirds as large as that of families with white heads over 65 ($7,519).

A more realistic view of the relative income status of elderly persons is secured by adjusting the income data for families by the number of persons in the family. A comparison of the per-person income for families with heads 65 and over with the per-person income for all families provides a much more favorable picture of the relative position of elderly persons than a comparison based on the total income of families.

Table 6-6. MEDIAN INCOME OF FAMILIES WITH HEADS 65 YEARS OLD AND OVER, BY TYPE OF FAMILY AND RACE OF HEAD, AND OF UNRELATED INDIVIDUALS 65 YEARS OLD AND OVER, BY RACE AND SEX: 1950 TO 1974

(Persons as of March 1975, March 1971, March 1968, March 1966, March 1961, and March 1951)

Race and year	Families					Unrelated individuals		
	Total	Male head			Female head	Total	Male	Female
		Total	Married, wife present	Other marital status				
HEAD 65 YEARS OLD AND OVER								
All Races								
1974............................	$7,298	$7,234	$7,177	$9,281	$7,723	$2,956	$3,405	$2,869
1970............................	5,053	5,011	4,966	6,722	5,370	1,951	2,250	1,888
1967[1].........................	3,908	3,845	3,817	4,485	4,408	1,477	1,804	1,409
1965[1].........................	3,514	(NA)	(NA)	(NA)	(NA)	1,378	(NA)	(NA)
1960............................	2,897	2,857	2,813	4,063	3,139	1,053	1,313	960
1950............................	1,903	(NA)	(NA)	(NA)	(NA)	646	(NA)	(NA)
White								
1974............................	7,519	7,387	7,315	10,609	8,525	3,073	3,730	2,959
1970............................	5,263	5,177	5,107	7,320	5,909	2,005	2,365	1,937
1967[1].........................	4,043	3,949	3,907	4,965	4,766	1,514	1,897	1,437
Black								
1974............................	4,909	5,066	5,075	5,005	4,602	2,152	2,385	1,998
1970............................	3,282	3,393	3,359	(B)	2,878	1,443	1,708	1,357
1967[1].........................	2,609	2,551	2,556	(B)	2,808	1,127	1,299	1,058
ALL FAMILIES OR UNRELATED INDIVIDUALS								
All Races								
1974............................	12,836	13,788	13,847	11,737	6,413	4,439	5,998	3,493
1970............................	9,867	10,480	10,516	9,012	5,093	3,137	4,540	2,483
1967[1].........................	7,933	8,358	8,398	6,804	4,269	2,379	3,514	1,917
1965[1].........................	6,957	7,310	7,330	6,515	3,535	2,153	3,194	1,767
1960............................	5,620	5,857	5,873	4,860	2,968	1,720	2,480	1,377
1950............................	3,319	3,435	3,446	3,115	1,922	1,045	1,539	846
White								
1974............................	13,356	14,055	14,099	12,438	7,363	4,636	6,357	3,723
1970............................	10,236	10,697	10,723	9,524	5,754	3,283	4,864	2,615
1967[1].........................	8,234	8,557	8,588	7,353	4,855	2,470	3,881	1,998
Black								
1974............................	7,808	10,365	10,530	7,942	4,465	3,059	4,627	2,343
1970............................	6,279	7,766	7,816	6,751	3,576	2,117	3,320	1,651
1967[1].........................	4,875	5,737	5,808	4,478	3,004	1,760	2,756	1,358
RATIO, HEAD 65 YEARS OLD AND OVER TO ALL FAMILIES OR UNRELATED INDIVIDUALS								
All Races								
1974............................	0.569	0.525	0.518	0.791	1.204	0.666	0.568	0.821
1970............................	0.512	0.478	0.472	0.746	1.054	0.622	0.496	0.760
1967[1].........................	0.493	0.460	0.455	0.659	1.033	0.621	0.513	0.735
1965[1].........................	0.505	(NA)	(NA)	(NA)	(NA)	0.640	(NA)	(NA)
1960............................	0.515	0.488	0.480	0.836	1.058	0.612	0.529	0.697
1950............................	0.573	(NA)	(NA)	(NA)	(NA)	0.618	(NA)	(NA)
White								
1974............................	0.563	0.526	0.519	0.853	1.158	0.663	0.587	0.795
1970............................	0.514	0.484	0.476	0.769	1.027	0.611	0.486	0.741
1967[1].........................	0.491	0.461	0.455	0.675	0.982	0.613	0.489	0.719
Black								
1974............................	0.629	0.489	0.482	0.630	1.031	0.703	0.515	0.853
1970............................	0.523	0.437	0.430	(X)	0.805	0.682	0.514	0.825
1967[1].........................	0.535	0.445	0.440	(X)	0.935	0.640	0.471	0.779

B Base less than 75,000.   NA Not available.   X Not applicable.
[1]Revised.

Source: Current Population Reports, Series P-60, Nos. 9, 37, 59, 97, and 101.

Since families headed by persons over 65 are smaller in size than families headed by persons under 65, the family income has to be spread over fewer persons in the former group of families than in the latter group. In 1974 the per-person income of the families with heads 65 and over was only about 18 percent below the corresponding figure for all families (table 6-7 and figure 6-3), as compared with the 43 percent disadvantage shown by data on total family income. This more favorable situation pertains whether the family is headed by a male or female or by a black or white. The relative advantage of families headed by females 65 and over, over all families headed by females, noted earlier is increased by the adjustment; persons in families headed by females 65 and over had an average income 42 percent greater than persons in all families headed by females.

The adjustment of family income data to a per-person basis magnified the observed gap between the income of whites and blacks in families headed by persons 65 and over. The income of blacks in "elderly" families now appears to be only one-half (52 percent) as large as the income for "elderly" families of all races. The disadvantage is particularly great when the family is headed by a female; in this case the income of blacks is only 45 percent as great as the income of all races.

A substantial segment of family heads 65 and over (9.5 percent in 1974) have incomes below the poverty level (table 6-8). The sex and race of the family head is an important factor in the poverty status of families. Over a third of black female family heads 65 and over have incomes below the poverty level. A far greater proportion of black female unrelated individuals (about two-thirds) have incomes below the poverty line. In fact, for each sex-race group the percent below the poverty level for unrelated individuals 65 and over is about two to three times as great as that for heads of families in the corresponding sex-race category. The percent below the poverty level for black family heads over 65 (28 percent) is between three and four times that for white family heads (8 percent). Yet, because of the very great difference in the age distribution of the two races, elderly family heads and elderly unrelated individuals comprised about 31 percent of all poor white family heads and unrelated individuals in 1974, but only about 21 percent of all poor blacks of this family status.

The proportion of the elderly population below the poverty level has been falling sharply in the last decade and a half. In 1974 only 16 percent of the elderly were poor, as compared with 35 percent in 1959, and for those living in families the proportions fell from 27

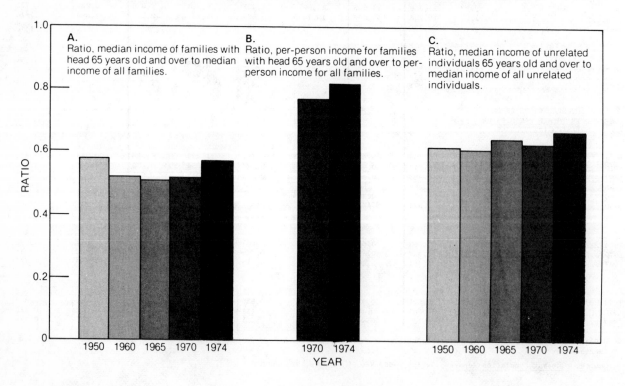

Figure 6-3. RATIO OF MEDIAN INCOME FOR FAMILIES WITH HEADS 65 YEARS OLD AND OVER TO MEDIAN INCOME FOR ALL FAMILIES: 1950 TO 1974

Table 6-7. INCOME PER PERSON BASED ON MEDIAN INCOME OF FAMILY, FOR ALL FAMILIES AND FAMILIES WITH HEADS 65 YEARS OLD AND OVER, BY TYPE OF FAMILY AND RACE OF HEAD: 1960 TO 1974

(Persons as of March 1975, March 1971, March 1968, and March 1961)

| Race and year | Total families | Male head | | | Female head |
		Total	Married, spouse present	Other	
HEAD 65 YEARS OLD AND OVER					
All Races					
1974..............................	$3,054	$3,105	$3,094	$3,387	$2,839
1970..............................	2,088	2,114	2,131	2,263	2,004
1967[1]..............................	(NA)	(NA)	1,611	(NA)	(NA)
1960..............................	(NA)	(NA)	1,141	(NA)	(NA)
White					
1974..............................	3,255	3,226	3,222	3,944	3,410
1970..............................	2,230	2,231	2,220	2,624	2,308
Black					
1974..............................	1,584	1,778	1,787	1,691	1,275
1970..............................	1,049	1,135	1,183	(NA)	834
ALL FAMILIES					
All Races					
1974..............................	3,731	3,973	3,968	4,162	1,998
1970..............................	2,726	2,863	2,858	3,055	1,548
1967[1]..............................	2,144	2,229	2,222	2,396	1,314
1960..............................	1,531	1,566	1,558	1,723	939
White					
1974..............................	3,951	4,098	4,087	4,556	2,496
1970..............................	2,892	2,971	2,962	3,438	1,931
Black					
1974..............................	1,992	2,631	2,639	2,482	1,148
1970..............................	1,457	1,789	1,789	1,713	847
RATIO, HEAD 65 YEARS OLD AND OVER TO ALL FAMILIES					
All Races					
1974..............................	0.819	0.782	0.780	0.814	1.421
1970..............................	0.766	0.738	0.746	0.741	1.295
1967[1]..............................	(NA)	(NA)	0.725	(NA)	(NA)
1960..............................	(NA)	(NA)	0.732	(NA)	(NA)
White					
1974..............................	0.824	0.787	0.788	0.866	1.366
1970..............................	0.771	0.751	0.749	0.763	1.195
Black					
1974..............................	0.795	0.676	0.677	0.681	1.111
1970..............................	0.720	0.634	0.661	(NA)	0.985

NA Not available.
[1] Based on revised median income.

Source: Current Population Reports, Series P-20, Nos. 33, 106, 173, 218, 276, and 287, and Series P-60, Nos. 9, 37, 59, 97, and 101.

Table 6-8. FAMILY HEADS AND UNRELATED INDIVIDUALS 65 YEARS OLD AND OVER BELOW THE POVERTY LEVEL, BY RACE AND SEX: 1974

(Numbers in thousands. Persons as of March 1975)

Family status and sex	All races			White			Black		
	Total	Below poverty level		Total	Below poverty level		Total	Below poverty level	
		Number	Percent		Number	Percent		Number	Percent
FAMILY HEADS									
Total...................	8,034	760	9.5	7,319	567	7.7	641	177	27.6
Male.......................	6,925	616	8.9	6,410	493	7.7	454	108	23.9
Female.....................	1,108	144	13.0	909	74	8.1	187	69	36.8
UNRELATED INDIVIDUALS									
Total...................	6,502	2,065	31.8	5,874	1,697	28.9	577	349	60.5
Male.......................	1,455	390	26.8	1,233	292	23.7	195	86	44.3
Female.....................	5,047	1,675	33.2	4,641	1,405	30.3	381	262	68.8

Note: The weighted average nonfarm threshold at the poverty level in 1974 is $2,364 for an unrelated individual 65 years of age or over and $2,982 for a family of two persons with a head 65 years or over.

Source: Current Population Reports, Series P-60, No. 99, July 1975, table 17.

percent in 1959 to 8.5 percent in 1974 (table 6-9). On the other hand, 36 percent of elderly blacks were still below the poverty level in 1974.

Familial and Societal Dependency

Much interest has been expressed in the relative size of the dependent-age population, particularly the elderly, and the productive-age population, and the effect of changing dependency ratios on the support of the elderly population. The implication is that the older segment of the population constitutes an economic burden on the younger segment; that is, each "generation" is obliged to support a previous "generation," which was obliged to support a still earlier generation, etc. This note identifies some of the facets of this question and presents some pertinent data.

A number of different types of dependency ratios can be distinguished. First, intergenerational familial dependency ratios can be distinguished from societal dependency ratios. The former represent essentially the relative numbers of "dependents" in one generation defined by an age range at a given date to a specific age group in a later generation, presumably their children. This measure is analogous to a fertility measure "in reverse." Instead of relating children to parents, we relate parents to children; in this case, of course, the parents are elderly or aged, and their children adults. Dependency may be measured more analytically in terms of actual economic and social dependency. Psychological, social, and economic support (e.g., kinship network) of the older generation by their children is represented by such measures.

Ratios relating persons 65 to 84 to their children 45 to 49 and persons 80 and over to their children 60 to 64 can be used to illustrate intergenerational familial age-dependency ratios. The "burden" on their children of supporting the extreme aged (80 and over) increased greatly in the last quarter century after only a slight increase in the first four decades of this century (table 6-10). The series is expected to move irregularly in the next several decades, with peaks in the year 2000 and 2030. There were about 21 to 24 persons 80 or over for every 100 persons 60 to 64 in 1900 and in 1940, but by 1975 the ratio had approximately doubled to 49 for every 100. By the year 2000 the ratio will have increased by another quarter to 73 persons 80 and over for every 100 persons 60 to 64. The past trend in the ratio of younger parents (65 to 84) to their children (45 to 49) has been roughly similar, with the increase between 1900 and 1940 being somewhat greater and the increase between 1940 and 1975 somewhat smaller. Peaks will be reached in 1980 at 200 persons 65 to 84 per 100 persons 45 to 49 and in the year 2020 with "235 per 100," as compared with 174 in 1975.

Societal dependency ratios represent essentially the relative burden of older "dependents," defined either by age or economic status, on "productive" persons, also defined either by age or economic status. When we are considering economic support by the community, a relatively wide band of ages must be used to represent "producers." Age-dependency ratios, relating the number of persons of "dependent" ages to the number of persons of "productive" ages, are intended to show how age composition contributes to economic dependency in a given population. A number of different

Table 6-9. **FAMILY STATUS AND RACE OF PERSONS 65 YEARS OLD AND OVER BELOW THE POVERTY LEVEL: 1959 TO 1974**

(Numbers in thousands. Persons as of March 1975, March 1971, March 1967, and April 1960)

Family status and race	Number below poverty level				Percent below poverty level			
	1974	1970	1966	1959	1974	1970	1966	1959
All persons 65 years old and over..............	3,308	4,793	5,114	5,481	15.7	24.6	28.5	35.2
In families.....................	1,243	2,013	2,507	3,187	8.5	14.8	19.2	26.9
Head........................	760	1,188	1,450	1,787	9.5	16.5	20.9	29.1
Male......................	616	980	1,218	1,507	8.9	15.9	20.9	29.1
Female....................	144	209	231	280	13.0	20.1	20.4	28.8
Other family members...........	483	825	1,057	1,400	7.3	13.0	17.2	24.6
Unrelated individuals...........	2,065	2,779	2,607	2,294	31.8	47.2	53.8	61.9
Male......................	390	549	563	703	26.8	38.9	44.5	59.0
Female....................	1,675	2,230	2,044	1,591	33.2	49.8	57.0	63.3
White.........................	2,642	4,011	4,357	4,744	13.8	22.6	26.4	33.1
Black.........................	626	735	722	711	36.4	47.7	55.1	62.5

Source: Current Population Reports, Series P-60, Nos. 86, 91, and 99, and unpublished data for 1966.

Table 6-10. **FAMILIAL INTERGENERATIONAL DEPENDENCY RATIOS AND SOCIETAL AGE AND ECONOMIC DEPENDENCY RATIOS: 1900 TO 2010**

(Figures are for July of year except as noted. Ratios for 1940 and later years include Armed Forces overseas)

Year	Familial dependency ratios		Societal dependency ratios			
	Population 80 years and over / Population 60 to 64 years	Population 65 to 84 years / Population 45 to 49 years	Population 65 years and over / Population 18 to 64 years	Population 60 years and over / Population 20 to 59 years	Population 65 years and over / Males 20-64 yrs. and females 35-59 yrs.	Nonworkers 65 years and over / Workers 20 to 59 years
ESTIMATES						
1900.............................	[2]0.21	[2]0.86	0.07	0.13	0.11	(NA)
1910.............................	[2]0.22	[2]0.85	0.07	0.13	0.11	(NA)
1920.............................	[2]0.21	[2]0.82	0.08	0.14	0.11	(NA)
1930.............................	[2]0.22	[2]0.90	0.09	0.16	0.13	(NA)
1940.............................	[2]0.24	[2]1.05	0.11	0.19	0.15	[2]0.21
1950.............................	[2]0.28	[2]1.30	0.13	0.23	0.18	[2]0.25
1960.............................	0.36	1.44	0.17	0.27	0.23	[3]0.28
1970.............................	0.43	1.54	0.17	0.29	0.25	[3]0.29
1975.............................	0.49	1.74	0.18	0.29	0.26	[3]0.29
PROJECTIONS[1]						
1980.............................	0.49	2.04	0.18	0.29	0.26	[3]0.29
1990.............................	0.59	1.91	0.19	0.30	0.27	[3]0.30
2000.............................	0.73	1.44	0.19	0.28	0.25	(NA)
2010.............................	0.55	1.46	0.19	0.32	0.26	(NA)
2020.............................	0.45	2.35	0.24	0.40	0.33	(NA)
2030.............................	0.70	2.33	0.29	0.44	0.39	(NA)

NA Not available.
[1]Series II projections.
[2]Figures are census data for April 1.
[3]Labor force data are monthly averages based on or consistent with the Current Population Survey.

Source: Based on Current Population Reports, Series P-25, Nos. 311, 519, 614, and 601; Census of Population, 1950, 1960, and 1970; Special Labor Force Report 119, The U.S. Labor Force: Projections to 1985, 1970; Special Labor Force Report 156, The U.S. Labor Force: Projections to 1990, 1973; and projections to be published in a forthcoming Special Labor Force Report.

age-dependency ratios may be considered. For example, the age factor in economic dependency may be represented by the ratio of persons 65 and over to persons 18 to 64. This ratio showed a nearly steady rise between 1900 and 1975, having more than doubled, but is expected to level off or increase slowly in the next several decades. The ratio was 0.07 in 1900 and 0.18 in 1975, and is expected to be about 0.19 in the year 2010 (Series II projections). A sharp rise in the ratio is then anticipated in the next few decades (to 0.29 in 2030) as the large postwar birth cohorts reach 65 years of age.

In view of the trend toward later entry into the labor force, the trend toward earlier retirement, and the large proportion of part-time workers under 20 and over 60, it is useful to examine also the trend in the ratio of persons 60 and over to persons 20 to 59. The upward progression in this series is roughly about the same as that for the series just discussed; the values are much larger, however, since there are more "dependents" and fewer "producers." We see again the sharp net rise in the ratio, from 0.29 in 1975 to 0.44 in 2030.

At many ages the proportions of women in the labor force are low (less than 50 percent) and a large share of those who work work part-time. Accordingly, a dependency ratio has been constructed relating persons 65 and over to the sum of males 20 to 64 and females 35 to 59. This "sex-adjusted" measure shows nearly the same fluctuations as the last two series considered and approximates the second of these closely in magnitude.

Measures relating actual workers and nonworkers may be viewed as more realistic for measuring economic dependency than are age-dependency ratios. For this purpose, the ratio of nonworkers 60 and over to workers 20 to 59 has been examined. This series has shown a moderate rise in recent past decades, but is expected to remain relatively unchanged to 1990. Currently there are about three nonworkers 60 and over for every ten workers 20 to 59 years of age. This series is almost identical to the age-dependency series based on the same ages and may be expected to show a similar pattern of increase after 1990, barring sharp changes in worker proportions.

In theory, the difference between an economic dependency ratio and the corresponding age-dependency ratio represents the net contribution of the proportions of nonworkers at each age of each sex to economic de-pendency. Specifically, the difference reflects the extent to which persons of working age are not actually workers and to which persons of nonworking age are workers. These adjustments may balance out, as in the present case. Even the economic dependency ratio as we have defined it excludes the effect of weeks worked in a year, hours worked in a week, and productivity—all of which affect the economic product available for supporting the dependent population—and it excludes the economic contribution of homemakers in rearing children and managing the affairs of the home and of volunteer workers.

It may be maintained that the concepts of age dependency and even economic dependency of the elderly will become increasingly less significant as more and more workers participate in effective retirement plans, in addition to Federal Social Security, to which they contribute a share of their income. These plans represent a postponement of current satisfactions of goods and services, so that the retiree has a claim on goods and services at a future period; and this "claim" should be gradually augmented by the current market interest rate (including an adjustment for inflation). The contributions to retirement funds and the size of the retirement funds will increasingly reflect the changing size of the cohorts of retirees since larger elderly cohorts will have made larger contributions to the funds when they worked. Such larger cohorts will also have saved larger sums in pursuit of their own "personal" retirement plans.

Increases in life expectation and the continuation of the trend of a rising age of entry into the labor force and a falling age of retirement are other demographic changes which have actuarial implications for the conduct of the Social Security program and should be considered when decisions are being made about the level of contributions; these demographic changes are expected to be modest, however. The trend of expanding public services to the elderly may also create special demands on the retirement system if the level of such services is not correctly anticipated. Prospective changes can be financially covered by an additional period of work before or after "retirement," higher general taxes, or larger contributions to the retirement system on the basis of a higher rate of worker contributions or a broader income base for the present rate of contributions.[4] Opportunities for productive work on the part of the elderly may also be expanded.

[4] James N. Morgan, "Welfare Economic Aspects of Prolongation of Life," **Congress Abstracts**, Vol. I, 10th International Congress of Gerontology, Jerusalem, Israel, June 22-27, 1975, pp. 25-27.

Nevertheless, because of the difficulties of anticipating the total consumption requirements of the elderly and because of changes in the age composition of the population, particularly a sharp rise in the ratio of elderly persons to persons of working age, subsidies from the current crop of workers (i.e., intergenerational transfers) may be necessary through general taxation and an increase in payroll contributions. However, the view that changes in the age distribution of the population will be the dominant factor affecting the condition of the Social Security System, and specifically the view that an increase in the age-dependency ratio will necessarily have a seriously adverse affect on the system, are misleading, if not erroneous. Finally, it may be maintained that the Social Security System is not to be viewed strictly as an insurance fund and that it is "backed up" by the taxing power and economic solvency of the U.S. Government.

Guide to Census Data on the Elderly
Excerpts

U.S. Bureau of the Census and the Administration on Aging, Washington, D.C., 1978.

Preface

In mid-1975, the Administration on Aging distributed to its National Network on Aging a publication entitled Guide to Sources and Uses of Current Data on the Aging. This earlier guide contains some similiarities to the current guide, but also exhibits many differences. The earlier guide contains a section which describes the statistical programs of the Bureau of the Census and the National Center for Health Statistics. Other sections include brief descriptions of State and local sources of data, criteria for evaluating secondary data sources, potential uses of secondary data for program planning (including the derivation of State-level estimates from National-level data), uses for planning and validating sample surveys, and limitations on the use of secondary data. An appendix contains an inventory of selected State-level data on the aging in a variety of Federal publications. The inventory is quite similar to the one in the current guide, but is not limited to State-level data sources. The earlier inventory also excludes many 1970 census publications which were published after its release.

The current guide is limited essentially to 1970 census data but describes some data available from selected annual surveys conducted by the Bureau of the Census since 1970. It is anticipated that similar census information on the elderly will be made available from the 1980 Census at small-area levels such as census tracts, counties, towns, and metropolitan areas but will not be published until the early 1980's.

Introduction

This report is a guide to data on the elderly available from the 1970 Census of Population and Housing. It has been prepared in response to many requests concerning the availability of statistics on the social, demographic, economic, and housing characteristics of the elderly population.

The Bureau of the Census collects, tabulates, and makes available substantial data on the elderly in the form of printed reports, computer tapes, and special tabulations. However, because these data are found in many sources and for many geographic levels, this guide should serve to lessen the amount of time necessary to search for data on the elderly.

The Bureau of the Census has published two other guides to data for selected sub-populations: racial groups and persons of Spanish ancestry. 1/ This guide differs from these two guides in three important ways:

- This guide provides information on two sub-populations -- the elderly racial groups and elderly Spanish Americans - this guide might be considered as a guide to data on minority elderly populations.

- This guide provides information on more characteristics of the elderly by including many characteristics that are cross-classified with others, thus providing more detailed information than would have been the case if general categories of data or characteristics had been used.

- This guide combines information on data available in both printed reports and on computer tapes into single tables, thus emphasizing in many cases, that the same data item is available in two sources for the same geographic level.

These features make this guide a comprehensive, yet detailed reference to sources of information on the elderly population.

The sources of data available for the elderly are shown in tables 1 and 2 - one on population data sources and the other on housing data sources. The population data are divided into two subject matter sections: (1) general and social characteristics, and (2) economic characteristics. Most, but not all, of the characteristics in the tables are cross-classified. For example, if employment status is cross-classified with marital status, this cross-classification may be listed under

either economic characteristics or general and social characteristics but not necessarily under both.

Racial groups covered in this guide are White, Black, and other races as defined by the Bureau of the Census for use in the 1970 decennial census. The Spanish Americans are considered to be persons of Spanish origin or descent, Spanish language, Spanish surname, or Puerto Rican birth or parentage. The availability of racial and ethnic information on the elderly is indicated by special symbols in tables 1 and 2.

The following geographic areas are used in the source tables to indicate the availability of census data on the elderly: Nation, region, State, Standard Metropolitan Statistical Area (SMSA), county, place, and census tract. The definitions of these geographic areas can be found in any report on the 1970 Census of Population and Housing. If data are needed for multistate regions that do not conform to census regions, State data can be aggregated. Should data be needed for multicounty areas, county data can be aggregated. The reports and tapes referenced in tables 1 and 2 provide additional information on many of the geographic areas for which census data are available.

Almost 500 data items are referenced in tables 1 and 2. Although the majority of these data items pertain to the population 65 years and older, some of the data are available for population 60 or 62 years and older. The specific age cutoff for each data item is indicated in the sources cited.

The data may be available in more or less detail than indicated in the guide. At times, housing reports and tapes

1/ Bureau of the Census, Data on Selected Racial Groups Available from the Census, Washington, DC: U.S. Department of Commerce, DAD No. 40 (rev.), May 1977; and Bureau of the Census, Data on the Spanish Ancestry Population Available from the 1970 Census of Population and Housing, Washington, DC: U.S. Department of Commerce, DAD No. 41, May 1975.

provide detailed data for SMSAs and parts of SMSAs; in other instances, the data are restricted to areas meeting a minimum population-size criterion. For example, a particular characteristic may be shown for SMSAs with a population 250,000 or more, but not for all SMSAs. The minimum size criterion also applies to specific sub-populations such as Blacks, Spanish Americans, American Indians, Japanese, Chinese, and Filipinos, and persons living in group quarters, condominiums or cooperatives, and mobile homes. The reports and tapes referenced in tables 1 and 2 indicate the various geographic and size restrictions on availability for given data items.

Some of the less well known but highly useful sources of detailed data on the elderly are discussed following tables 1 and 2. Such sources include public use samples, special tabulations, the Current Population Survey, the Annual Housing Survey, and the 1976 Survey of Income and Education.

To enhance the usefulness of this guide and to provide the reader with a better understanding of the sources referenced, general descriptions of the major printed reports and computer tapes with 1970 Census of Population and Housing data follow in the next section.

Description of the Printed Reports

The printed reports from the 1970 census and the data for the elderly population available in the reports are discussed in this section. Data available on computer tapes are discussed in the following section. The major report series from the 1970 census are summarized in figure 2. Sources for additional data on the elderly are described in the last section of this guide .

Population Reports

Data available for the elderly found in the population reports are referenced in detail in table 1.

Volume I, Characteristics of the Population (series PC(1)) - This volume contains four chapters, A - D. Chapter A, Number of Inhabitants (series PC(1)-A), contains no data on the elderly or racial and ethnic groups. Chapter B, General Population Characteristics (series PC(1)-B), presents some basic or "100-percent" population data for the elderly. These data are not available for Spanish American elderly but are generally available for the total, White, and Black elderly. Chapter C, General Social and Economic Characteristics (series PC(1)-C), covers data for the elderly from both the complete-count and the sample questionnaires. 1/ Some of these data include sex, labor force status, weeks worked, and poverty status. The data are generally available for the total, White, Black, and Spanish American elderly. Chapter D, Detailed Characteristics (series PC(1)-D), describes characteristics identical to those in Chapter C but with more detailed cross-classification. However, some of the 100-percent characteristics, such as household relationships which are not available by age in Chapter C, are available by age in Chapter D. In the Chapter D reports for States, data on the elderly are available for total, White, Black and Spanish American elderly with few exceptions. However, in the United States report, less than half the data items for the elderly are available for Whites. About three-fourths of the items are available for Blacks and Spanish American elderly. In Chapters A-D few data items are available for "other races" elderly.

Volume II, Subject Reports (series

1/ "Complete-counts, samples, and percentages" refer to the size of the population base enumerated. For additional information on the sampling used for the 1970 Census, see U.S. Bureau of the Census, 1970 Census Users' Guide, Part I, Washington, DC, 1970, page 21.

PC(2)) - Each report in this series concentrates on a particular subject (see figure 1). Thirty-three of these 40 reports contain data on the elderly with the data availability for Black and Spanish Americans varying from one report to another. Detailed information and cross-classification generally are provided on a national and regional level; in some reports, data for States and SMSAs are shown. An asterisk (*) in figure 1 indicates which subject reports are available on computer tape.

Housing Reports

Data for the elderly from this and the other housing reports are referenced in table 2.

Volume I, Housing Characteristics for States, Cities, and Counties (series HC(1)). This volume contains two chapters, A and B. Chapter A, General Housing Characteristics (series HC(1)-A) includes 100-percent data on general or housing characteristics. Chapter B, Detailed Housing Characteristics (series HC(1)-B), contains sample data on detailed characteristics. Neither of these chapters contains data on the elderly.

Volume II, Metropolitan Housing Characteristics (series HC(2)) - This volume contains 18 tables with data for the elderly, with household composition cross-classified with other items in all these tables. There are six tables each for total, Black, and Spanish American elderly. Three of these six tables are for SMSAs and three are for central cities of SMSAs.

Volume III, Block Statistics (series HC(3)) - These reports were published for each of the 236 urbanized areas defined at the time of the 1970 census and for selected areas in 42 States. Several 100-percent characteristics are indicated for each block. For the elderly, only one data item is available and then for the total elderly popula-

tion -- percent persons aged 62 years or over. This report is not referenced in table 2.

Volume IV, Components of Inventory Change (series HC(4)) - was issued for the United States and 15 selected SMSAs. Data for the elderly population are available in nine tables. No data are available for the Black and Spanish American elderly. The age-related data are for total elderly household heads cross-classified with housing tenure and selected characteristics of the housing inventory.

Volume V, Residential Finance (series HC(5)) - contains two chapters with age-related data for principal owners of one-unit properties. Chapter 1 has 75 tables for total elderly principal property owners for such characteristics as family income, mortgage status, government insurance status, mortgage debt, first and second mortgage characteristics and property value. The data in chapter 1 are for the United States, regions, and metropolitan residence (by size of SMSA). Chapter 3 contains two tables for Black elderly principal owners with data on mortgage status and government insurance status. The data in Volume V are estimates from a sample survey conducted in 1971.

Volume VI, Plumbing Facilities and Estimates of Dilapidated Housing (series HC(VI)) - contains information on plumbing facilities and estimates of dilapidated housing for owner- and renter-occupied housing units for the United States, regions, divisions, States, places of 50,000 or more or central cities, and SMSAs and constituent counties. No data are available for the elderly population.

Volume VII, Subject Reports (series HC(7))- consists of nine reports on selected topics such as housing of senior citizens, household composition, space utilization, structural characteristics, mobile homes, and cooperatives and condominiums (see figure 1). Seven of

FIGURE 1: 1970 CENSUS OF POPULATION AND HOUSING SUBJECT REPORTS

Report Title	Series	Nation	Region	Division	State	SMSA	City
POPULATION							
National Origin and Language*	PC(2)-1A	x	x			o	
Negro Population*	PC(2)-1B	x	x		x	o	o
Persons of Spanish Origin	PC(2)-1C	x	x			o	o
Persons of Spanish Surname*	PC(2)-1D	x			1/	1/	1/
Puerto Ricans in the United States	PC(2)-1E	x	x		x	o	o
American Indians	PC(2)-1F	x	x			o	2/
Japanese, Chinese, and Filipinos in the United States	PC(2)-1G	x	x		x	o	o
State of Birth*	PC(2)-2A	x	x	x	x	3/	
Mobility for States and the Nation*	PC(2)-2B	x	x	x	x		
Mobility for Metropolitan Areas*	PC(2)-2C	x				4/	
Lifetime and Recent Migration*	PC(2)-2D	x		x	x		
Migration Between State Economic Areas*	PC(2)-2E	x				5/	
Women by Number of Children Ever Born*	PC(2)-3A	x	x				
Childspacing and Current Fertility	PC(2)-3B	x	x				
Family Composition*	PC(2)-4A	x	x				
Persons by Family Characteristics*	PC(2)-4B	x	x				
Marital Status*	PC(2)-4C	x	x				
Age at First Marriage*	PC(2)-4D	x	x		x		
Persons in Institutions and Other Group Quarters	PC(2)-4E	x	x	x	x	6/	6/
School Enrollment	PC(2)-5A	x	x				
Educational Attainment*	PC(2)-5B	x	x				
Vocational Training	PC(2)-5C	x					
Employment Status and Work Experience*	PC(2)-6A	x					
Persons Not Employed*	PC(2)-6B	x					
Persons with Work Disability*	PC(2)-6C	x					
Journey to Work	PC(2)-6D	x				7/	7/
Veterans*	PC(2)-6E	x					
Occupational Characteristics	PC(2)-7A	x					
Industrial Characteristics	PC(2)-7B	x					
Occupation by Industry*	PC(2)-7C	x					
Government Workers	PC(2)-7D	x					
Occupation and Residence in 1965*	PC(2)-7E	x	x				
Occupations of Persons with Higher Earnings	PC(2)-7F	x					
Sources and Structure of Family Income*	PC(2)-8A	x	x				
Earnings by Occupation and Education*	PC(2)-8B	x	x				
Income of the Farm-Related Population*	PC(2)-8C	x			x		
Low-Income Population	PC(2)-9A	x	x				
Low-Income Areas in Large Cities*	PC(2)-9B	x					8/
Americans Living Abroad*	PC(2)-10A	x					
State Economic Areas*	PC(2)-10B	x				5/	
HOUSING							
Housing Characteristics by Household Composition*	HC(7)-1	x					
Housing of Senior Citizens*	HC(7)-2	x			x	x	
Space Utilization of the Housing Inventory*	HC(7)-3	x					
Structural Characteristics of the Housing Inventory*	HC(7)-4	x	x				
Mover Households	HC(7)-5	x	x				
Mobile Homes*	HC(7)-6	x	x	x	x	o	
Geographic Aspects of the Housing Inventory*	HC(7)-7	x	x				
Cooperative and Condominium Housing	HC(7)-8	x	x		o	o	
Housing of Selected Racial Groups*	HC(7)-9	x	x		o	o	

* Available on summary computer tapes
1/ State, SMSA, and city data in California, Texas, New Mexico, Arizona, and Colorado only
2/ Also Indian reservations
3/ SMSAs 250,000+
4/ SMSAs 500,000+
5/ 510 SEA's including most large SMSAs as defined in 1960

6/ SMSAs 500,000+ and counties and places with 1,000+ inmates
7/ SMSAs 250,000+ and constituent counties and large places
8/ 50 largest cities and New York boroughs
x Data for all areas
o Data for selected areas only

FIGURE 2: 1970 CENSUS OF POPULATION AND HOUSING REPORTS

POPULATION

Series Number	Title	Description	Geographic Area	Unit of Issue
PC(1)	Volume I, Characteristics of the Population..........	This volume consists of separate reports described in Series PC(1)-A through PC(1)-D below.	(See Series PC(1)-A through PC(1)-D below.)	United States, each State, District of Columbia; Puerto Rico; Guam; Virgin Islands; American Samoa; Canal Zone; Trust Territory of the Pacific Islands.
PC(1)-A	Number of Inhabitants..........	Final official population counts.	States, counties (by urban-rural residence), SMSAs, urbanized areas, county subdivisions, all incorporated places, unincorporated places of 1,000+ population.	United States, each State, District of Columbia; Puerto Rico; Guam; Virgin Islands; American Samoa; Canal Zone; Trust Territory of the Pacific Islands.
PC(1)-B	General Population Characteristics	Data on age, sex, race, marital status and relationship to head of household (100% population subjects).	States, counties, (as above), SMSAs, urbanized areas, county subdivisions, places of 1,000+ population.	United States, each State, District of Columbia; Puerto Rico; Guam; Virgin Islands; American Samoa; Canal Zone; Trust Territory of the Pacific Islands.
PC(1)-C	General Social and Economic Characteristics..........	Data estimates on population subjects collected on a sample basis.	States (by urban, rural-nonfarm, and rural-farm residence), counties, SMSAs, urbanized areas, places of 2,500+ population.	United States, each State, District of Columbia; and Puerto Rico.

FIGURE 2: 1970 CENSUS OF POPULATION AND HOUSING REPORTS (CONT.)

Series Number	Title	Description	Geographic Area	Unit of Issue
POPULATION				
PC(1)-D	Detailed Characteristics.........	Data estimates on most population subjects collected on a sample basis, cross-classified by age, race, and other characteristics.	States (by urban, rural-nonfarm, and rural-farm residence), SMSAs, and large cities.	United States, each State, District of Columbia; and Puerto Rico.
PC(2)	Volume II, Subject Reports...... (See figure 1 for more detail)	Detailed information and tabulations for selected population characteristics.	United States, regions, States and SMSAs for some reports.	Forty reports on selected subjects. (See figure 1 for more detail)
HOUSING				
HC(1)	Volume I, Housing Characteristics for States, Cities, and Counties	This volume consists of the separate reports described in Series HC(1)-A and HC(1)-B below.	(See Series HC(1)-A and HC(1)-B below.)	United States, each State, District of Columbia; Puerto Rico, Guam; Virgin Islands; American Samoa; Canal Zone; Trust Territory of the Pacific Islands.
HC(1)-A	General Housing Characteristics...	Data on the housing subjects collected on a 100% basis.	States, counties, SMSAs (by urban-rural parts), urbanized areas, places of 1,000+ population.	United States, each State, District of Columbia; Puerto Rico, Guam; Virgin Islands; American Samoa; Canal Zone; Trust Territory of the Pacific Islands.

FIGURE 2: 1970 CENSUS OF POPULATION AND HOUSING REPORTS (CONT.)

Series Number	Title	Description	Geographic Area	Unit of Issue
HOUSING				
HC(1)-B	Detailed Housing Characteristics..	Data on the housing subjects collected on a sample basis.	States, counties (by urban, rural-nonfarm, and rural-farm parts), SMSAs, urbanized areas and places of 2,500+ population.	United States, each State, District of Columbia; and Puerto Rico.
HC(2)	Volume II, Metropolitan Housing Characteristics.............	Data covering most of the 1970 census housing subjects in considerable detail and cross-classification.	SMSAs and their component large cities.	United States, each SMSA.
HC(3)	Volume III, Block Statistics......	Selected 100% population and housing data.	Blocks.	Each urbanized area, contract block statistics areas by State.
HC(4)	Volume IV, Components of Inventory Change................	Data on components of change based on a sample survey conducted in late 1970 and early 1971.	Fifteen SMSAs, separately for central city and balance of SMSA.	United States and regions, each of 15 SMSAs.
HC(5)	Volume V, Residential Finance......	Data on financing characteristics of homeowner properties and rental and vacant properties. Based on a sample survey conducted in early 1971.	United States, regions, presented by size of place and by type of area.	One report.

FIGURE 2: 1970 CENSUS OF POPULATION AND HOUSING REPORTS (CONT.)

Series Number	Title	Description	Geographic Area	Unit of Issue
HOUSING				
HC(6)	Volume VI, Plumbing Facilities and Estimates of Dilapidated Housing..	Data on plumbing facilities reported in the 1970 census and estimates of dilapidation.	United States, regions, divisions, States, SMSAs, central cities and other cities of 50,000+ population, and constituent counties.	One report.
HC(7)	Volume VII, Subject Reports...... (See figure 1 for more detail)	Detailed information and cross-classifications for selected housing characteristics.	United States, regions, States and SMSAs for some reports.	Nine reports on selected subjects. (See figure 1 for more detail)
JOINT POPULATION HOUSING				
PHC(1)	Census Tract Reports............	Data for most 1970 census of Population and Housing subjects.	SMSAs by census tract.	Each SMSA.
PHC(2)	General Demographic Trends for Metropolitan Areas, 1960 to 1970..	Comparative 1960 and 1970 data on population counts and selected 100% population and housing subjects.	State, counties (population counts only), SMSAs and their central cities and constituent counties.	United States, each State, District of Columbia.
PHC(3)	Employment Profiles of Selected Low-Income Areas..............	Data on social and economic characteristics of residents of low-income areas based on sample surveys conducted during late 1970 and early 1971.	Selected poverty neighborhoods in cities.	Seventy-six reports, including at least one each for 51 cities, 7 rural areas, and one Indian reservation.

the reports contain information on the elderly population: HC(7)-1, HC(7)-2, HC(7)-4, HC(7)-5, HC(7)-6, HC(7)-8, and HC(7)-9. Of these seven reports, only HC(7)-8 and HC(7)-9 do not contain data for the total, Black, and Spanish American elderly. Report HC(7)-9, Housing of Selected Racial Groups, includes data for American Indians, Japanese, Chinese, Filipinos, Koreans, and other minority races. None of the housing subject reports contain information for the White elderly population. The data are available for the United States and sometimes for regions, States, and SMSAs. An asterisk (*) in figure 1 indicates which reports are available on computer tape. A housing subject report of special interest is report HC(7)-2, Housing of Senior Citizens, which has 48 tables of data on persons, household heads, and household members aged 60 years and over. Most of the tables provide information for three age categories of the elderly: 60 - 64 years, 65 - 74 years, and 75 years and over.

Joint Population and Housing Reports

Census Tract Reports (series PHC(1)) contains information from both the 1970 Census of Population and Housing. The data are published for 241 SMSAs. Seven tables of information are available for the elderly: 3 with age cross-classified with sex for the total, Black, and Spanish American elderly; three with data on the poverty status of total, Black, and Spanish American elderly persons, family heads, and unrelated individuals; and one table with information on total elderly males not in the labor force. No housing data for the elderly are available in this report series.

General Demographic Trends for Metropolitan Areas, 1960 to 1970 (series PHC(2)) focuses on population and housing trends from 1960 to 1970, drawing information largely from the advance reports for the 1970 census. Two tables present data on the number of elderly in 1960 and 1970 and the percent change from 1960 to 1970. The data are available for White and Black elderly only and for the United States, States, and SMSAs.

Employment Profiles of Selected Low-Income Areas (series PHC(3)) consists of 76 reports, including seven summary reports and 68 reports for selected low-income areas (60 in 51 cities, seven in rural areas, and one on an Indian reservation). Each of the reports has 22 tables of data on the elderly. Four tables have data for the total, White, Black, and Spanish elderly populations. Of the remaining 18 tables, nine have data for the total elderly and nine have data for Black elderly. Information available for the elderly in the selected low-income areas includes, but is not limited to, labor force status, employment status, place of work and means of transportation to work, job training, job-seeking methods, earnings and income, residential mobility, and indebtedness. The PHC(3) reports were produced from the 1970 Census Employment Survey. The data from these reports are not referenced in the data sources tables because they are available for groups of, rather than individual, census tracts and/or counties. The data are available from the Customer Service Branch, Data User Services Division, Bureau of the Census, Washington, DC, 20233.

Description of Summary Tapes

Data on the elderly from the 1970 Census of Population and Housing are available on the 1970 Census Summary Tapes. These computer tapes can be obtained by users for the cost of reproduction as part of the Bureau's data products program. Information on the data on the elderly available on computer tape is presented in this section.

Computer tapes containing basic data about individual persons or housing units (basic record tapes) were used to create tapes containing summary data or totals of characteristics or estimates of totals at various geographic levels. These summary tapes were produced in six tabulation series -- referred to as counts -- which yielded the statistics presented in most of the printed reports (see figure 3). The first three series, the First, Second, and Third Counts, contain only complete-count or 100-percent data, derived from the census questions asked of all households. The Fourth, Fifth, and Sixth Count Summary Tapes present tabulations which include the 20-, 15-, and 5-percent sample population and housing characteristics such as occupation, income, education, value, rent, plumbing facilities, and so on.

Many of the characteristics contained on the summary tapes are cross-classified by race and ethnicity. All of the summary tape counts have tabulations of data for the Black population; but data for other detailed racial categories (Indian, Japanese, Chinese, Filipino, Hawaiian, Korean, and "other race" populations) are limited mainly to population counts in the first two summary tape series and to several basic population characteristics on the Sixth Count Summary Tapes. Only the Fourth, Fifth, and Sixth County Summary Tapes contain information for Spanish Americans since the items identifying this population group appeared only on questionnaires received by sample households.

First Count Summary Tapes

These tapes contain 6 tables which present data for the elderly cross-tabulated by complete-count or 100-percent items. Only one of the six tables provides information by race. These tapes are the source of the PC(1)-A reports, Number of Inhabitants. The total contents of the First Count tapes are available on microfilm.

Second Count Summary Tapes

Also derived from the 100-percent items,

these tapes contain 14 tables which present data on the elderly covering the same subjects as the First Count tapes but in greater detail. All 14 tables present complete-count population and housing characteristics for the total, White, and Black populations. Counts of persons by sex are shown for the White, Black, Indian, Japanese, Chinese, Filipino, Hawaiian, Korean, and "other race" populations. These tapes are the source of the PC(1)-B reports, General Population Characteristics, HC(1)-A reports, General Housing Characteristics, and one source of the Census Tract Reports, series PHC(1). The Second Count tapes, however, contain more data items for tracts and other selected areas than do the printed reports.

Third Count Summary Tapes

Including one table of data cross-classified by age, these tapes contain 100-percent population and housing data at the block level (the smallest geographic area for which the Bureau publishes statistics). That table provides no race detail. These tapes, the source of the Block Statistics reports, series HC(3), contain more data than are presented in the reports. They contain less data, however, than the First and Second Count Summary Tapes. Computer programs have been developed to create microfilm versions of the Third Count tapes on a customized basis.

Fourth Count Summary Tapes

These tapes are the primary source of sample data for small areas based on the questions asked of a sample of the total population. Ten tables in the Fourth Count population files present data for the total, White, Black and Spanish American elderly. Twenty-two of the housing tables have information on the elderly. None of the housing data are available for the White elderly. Seventeen of the tables have data for Spanish Americans while only seven have data for Blacks. Fourteen tables have data for Spanish Americans only. No data are available for the elderly of other races or ethnic groups. The Fourth Count tape is the source of the Social and Economic Characteristics reports, PC(1)-C, the Detailed Housing Characteristics reports, HC(1)-B, and part of the Census Tract Reports, PHC(1).

Fifth Count Summary Tapes

These are the only tapes organized by ZIP code areas. File C was produced as a special tabulation and is now available with data at the census tract and other small-area levels. These tapes include two tables which show population characteristics cross-tabulated by age, one table being for the total elderly only. No housing data are available for the elderly population.

Sixth Count Summary Tapes

The Sixth Count tapes contain data for large areas such as States and SMSAs and include more detailed tabulations and cross-classifications of sample population and housing characteristics for the elderly than any of the other summary tapes. Forty-five of the tables for population characteristics have data for the elderly. Three of those tables include data for "other races" elderly. Forty-two of the tables have data for the total, White, Black, and Spanish American elderly. Fifty tables contain housing data for the total, White, Black, and Spanish American elderly. These tapes were the sources of the PC(1)-D reports, Detailed Characteristics of the Population, and the HC(2) reports, Metropolitan Housing Characteristics.

FIGURE 3:   SUMMARY CHART OF THE 1970 CENSUS SUMMARY TAPES

Summary Tape Series		Geographic Areas Covered	Complete Count or Sample	Related Printed Report
1st Count	File A	Block Group or Enumeration District	Complete Count	PC(1)-A PHC(2)
	File B	State, County, Minor Civil Division (MCD) or Census County Division (CCD), MCD-Place, Place, Congressional District		
2nd Count	File A	Tract	Complete Count	PC(1)-B HC(1)-A PHC(1)
	File B	State, County, Minor Civil Division or Census County Division, Place SMSA, and Component Areas		
3rd Count		Block	Complete Count	HC(3)
4th Count Pop.	File A	Tract	Sample	PC(1)-C HC(1)-B PHC(1)
	File B	Minor Civil Division or Census County Division		
	File C	State, County, Place, SMSA, and Component Areas		
4th Count Hous.	File A	Tract		
	File B	Minor Civil Division or Census County Division		
	File C	State, County, Place, SMSA, and Component Areas		
5th Count	File A	3 digit ZIP areas	Sample	NONE
	File B	5 digit ZIP areas (in SMSAs)		
	File C	Block Groups or Enumeration Districts, Tracts, MCDs/CCDs in Non-tracted Areas		
6th Count	Pop.	State, SMSA, Metropolitan County, City 50,000+, Central City	Sample	PC(1)-D HC(2)
	Hous.	State, SMSA, Metropolitan County, Nonmetropolitan County 50,000+, City 50,000+, Central City		

Data Sources for Population Characteristics of the Elderly

This section of the guide references in table 1 those reports or computer tapes from the 1970 census that contain population characteristics data on the elderly (data sources pertaining to housing characteristics of the elderly are presented in table 2, page 49). Because of space limitations and the amount of detail presented, reports, computer tapes, and the availability of racial and ethnic data were necessarily abbreviated. The key to references in table 1 follows (for further information on the following report series or computer tapes, see pages 3 and 13 respectively).

Each source reference for the population characteristics in table 1 is shown in two parts: first, the particular report or summary tape, and, second, following the colon, the table or tabulation number or numbers. For example, the source "US(B):53" means table 53 of the U.S. Summary Report, Chapter B. "PHC(1):P-1" means table P-1 of the Census Tract Report; and "T2:2" means tabulation 2 of the Second Count Summary Tape. The report and summary tape designations or keys are as follows:

US: United States Summary, 1970 Census of Population, Volume I, Part I, Characteristics of the Population, Chapters A-D

ST: The individual State reports of the 1970 Census of Population, Volume I, Parts 2-52, Characteristics of the Population, Chapters A-D

PHC(1): The individual standard metropolitan statistical area reports of the 1970 Census of Population, Census Tracts, Parts 1-24, Report numbers 1-241

PHC(2): General Demographic Trends for Metropolitan Areas, 1960 to 1970 (one report)

SP: United States Summary, 1970 Census of Population, Volume II, Subject Reports, 40 reports concentrating on selected subjects2/:

SP1A National Origin and Language
SP1B Negro Population
SP1C Persons of Spanish Origin
SP1D Persons of Spanish Surname
SP1E Puerto Ricans in the United States
SP1F American Indians
SP1G Japanese, Chinese, and Filipinos in
       the United States

SP2A State of Birth
SP2B Mobility for States and the Nation
SP2C Mobility for Metropolitan Areas

2/ Summary tape files are available for these reports, providing data at the national regional, State, and SMSA levels. Copies of these tapes are obtainable from: Customer Services Branch, Data User Services Division, Bureau of the Census, Washington, DC, 20233.

SP: United States Summary (CONT.)

SP2D	Lifetime and Recent Migration
SP2E	Migration Between State Economic Areas
SP3A	Women by Number of Children Ever Born
SP3B	Childspacing and Current Fertility
SP4A	Family Composition
SP4B	Persons by Family Characteristics
SP4C	Marital Status
SP4D	Age at First Marriage
SP4E	Persons in Institutes and Other Group Quarters
SP5A	School Enrollment
SP5B	Educational Attainment
SP5C	Vocational Training
SP6A	Employment Status and Work Experience
SP6B	Persons Not Employed
SP6C	Persons with Work Disability
SP6D	Journey to Work
SP6E	Veterans
SP7A	Occupational Characteristics
SP7B	Industrial Characteristics
SP7C	Occupation by Industry
SP7D	Government Workers
SP7E	Occupation and Residence in 1965
SP7F	Occupations of Persons with Higher Earnings
SP8A	Sources and Structure of Family Income
SP8B	Earnings by Occupation and Education
SP8C	Income of the Farm-Related Population
SP9A	Low-Income Population
SP9B	Low-Income Areas in Large Cities
SP10A	Americans Living Abroad
SP10B	State Economic Areas

T: Census summary Tapes, "counts" 1-6

Racial/Ethnic Characteristics

Data on the elderly are available for a number of racial and ethnic populations, most notably Blacks and Spanish Americans. The data items in table 1 are keyed to their availability for selected racial and ethnic populations as follows:

('') Whites

(*) Blacks

(+) Spanish Americans

(o) other races

Additional Sources of Data on the Elderly

There are several other major sources of data on the elderly available from the Bureau of the Census. Public use samples and special tabulations derived from 1970 Census of Population and Housing basic records allow the user to cross-tabulate and analyze 1970 Census data by age whereas the printed reports and tapes do not. The Current Population Survey, particularly the March supplement, provides data on a monthly basis while the Annual Housing Survey provides data on an annual basis. The Survey of Income and Education provides data for 1976.

Public Use Samples

Public use samples are subsamples of the basic census data for individuals and households with identifying information removed. These samples are created from the basic records and are available on computer tapes. The basic public use sample is a 1/100 sample of the 1970 basic Census records. Also available are 1/1,000 and 1/10,000 subsamples which are drawn from the original 1/100 sample.

There are six public use samples drawn from the basic records of the 1970 census. Two long-form census questionnaires were used in the 1970 census: one for the 15-percent sample, the other for the 5-percent sample of the population. Three of the public use samples were prepared from the 15-percent sample and three from the 5-percent sample, each providing one of the following three levels of geographic identification for each sample record: county groups, States, and divisions. The files which furnish only division - level geographic identification also provide a set of socioeconomic and housing characteristics for the neighborhood in which each sample household or group quarter is located.

The public use samples for county groups and States contain nonaggregated data for persons, households, and housing units. Thus, characteristics of individuals, households, and housing units can be cross-tabulated as the user requires. Any of the data included in the public use samples can be tabulated for the elderly. Figure 4 lists the items in the public use samples for county groups, States, and neighborhoods (by division).

Certain considerations must be taken into account before using these samples. Those considerations include greater sampling variability than in corresponding tabulations in the printed reports and the summary tapes; cost of the tapes, statistical analysis, programming, and computer time; and various geographic limitations.

For further information on the public use samples, inquiries should be addressed to: Data Access and Use Staff, Data User Services Division, Bureau of the Census, Washington, DC, 20233.

Special Tabulations

Tabulations can be obtained from the basic individual and household records from the 1970 census to provide any number of cross-tabulations of variables or data for any geographic area of interest. These tabulations can be performed for the complete-count as well as the sample items in the 1970 census. However, the data for the tabulations would be only for those individuals that constituted the 20-percent subsample in the census. As such, those data are subject to sampling variability but not to the extent of the data in the public use samples previously described. Another advantage of special tabulations is that they are not limited to specific geographic areas as are the public use samples. The flexibility of the special tabulations in terms of cross-tabulations of variables and wide choice of geographic areas of aggregation must be weighed

FIGURE 4: ITEMS ON THE 1970 PUBLIC USE SAMPLE TAPES

PERSON CHARACTERISTICS

Basic relationship
Detailed relationship
Subfamily number
Type of group quarters
Sex
Color or race
Spanish surname
Age
Quarter of birth
Marital status
Widow
State or country of birth
Highest grade attended
Finished grade
Children ever born
Hours worked
Years last worked
Current industry
Current occupation
Class of worker
Working 5 years ago
Residence of 5 years ago
State of residence 5 years ago
Public or private school
Veteran
Veteran of Vietnam
Veteran of Korean War
Veteran of World War II
Veteran of World War I
Veteran of other time
Place of work: SMSA
Place of work: State
Means of transportation to work
Puerto Rican stock
Spanish mother tongue

Number of times married
Quarter of first marriage
Metropolitan residence 5 years ago
Spanish descent
Citizenship
Year of immigration
In armed forces 5 years ago
In college 5 years ago
Worked last year
Weeks worked
Earnings: Wages, etc.
Earnings: Business, etc.
Earnings: Farm, etc.
Social Security income
Welfare income
Other income
Chief income recipient
Person's total income
Poverty cutoff
Persons in family or subfamily
Subfamily relationship
Type of subfamily
Family unit membership
Family relationship summary
Parent's country of birth
Mother tongue
Year moved in
Age at first marriage
Vocational training
Field of training
Disability
Prevent any work
Duration of disability
Industry 5 years ago
Occupation 5 years ago

HOUSEHOLD CHARACTERISTICS

Race of head
Age of head
Spanish surname head
Persons under 18 years of age
  in household
Related children under 18 years of
  age in household

Other nonrelatives in household
Relatives other than child or
  wife of head
Persons per room
Total income of family or
  primary individual
Gross rent/income ratio

FIGURE 4: ITEMS ON THE 1970 PUBLIC USE SAMPLE TAPES (CONT.)

Related children under 6 years
  of age in household
Persons 65 years of age or over
  in household
Persons 60 years of age or over
  in household
Roomers, boarders, or lodgers in
  household

Value/income ratio
Year head moved into unit
Puerto Rican stock (head)
Spanish mother tongue (head)
Spanish descent
Household type

HOUSING UNIT CHARACTERISTICS

Persons in household or group
  quarters
Units at this address
Vacancy status
Duration of vacancy
Telephone available
Access to unit
Complete kitchen facilities
Rooms
Hot and cold piped water
Flush toilet
Bathtub or shower
Plumbing facilities
Basement
Tenure
Commercial Use
Value
Monthly contract rent
Gross monthly rent
Electricity
Gas
Water
Fuel
UHF-TV

Second home
Heating equipment
Year structure built
Units in structure
Location of structure
Sales of farm products
Source of water
Sewage disposal
Bathrooms
Air conditioning
Automobiles
Number of stories
Passenger elevator
Cooking fuel
Heating fuel
Water heating fuel
Bedrooms
Washing machine
Clothes dryer
Dishwasher
Food freezer
Television set
Battery radio

against the substantial increase in costs over the public use samples or the census summary tapes discussed in previous sections of this report. Another potential disadvantage of the special tabulations is that several months may be required to perform them. Special tabulations data are available in a wide variety of media: tape, punched cards, computer printouts, type-written copy, hand-posted copy, or microfilm/microfiche.

Four examples of special tabulations are abstracted as follows:

- Title: Minority Elderly Study
  Source: 1970 Census of Population and Housing
  Subject Content: A wide range of population and housing variables for eight elderly populations: Blacks, Spanish Americans, Russians, Italians, Czechoslovakians, Polish, Whites, and foreign stock.

- Title: Detailed Race by Age by Sex
  Source: 1970 Census of Population
  Subject Content: Age by sex for detailed minority races not shown on standard summary tapes. Eighteen age intervals by sex are shown for six specified races: White, Black, American Indian, Japanese, Chinese, and other races.

  Geographic Areas Covered: The United States, States, counties, specified SMSAs and census tracts within them.

- Title: Cross Tabulation of Housing Characteristics for Selected Census Summary Areas
  Source: 1970 Census of Population and Housing
  Subject Content: Count of occupied units by tenure and race of head, inadequate and adequate conditions, oldest person's age, household size, and household income.

  Geographic Areas Covered: The United States, Region, Division, State, SMSA, County and Place.

- Title: West Virginia: The Elderly Population Information on Selected Characteristics and Conditions.
  Source: 1970 Census of Population and Housing
  Subject Content: Poverty status, race, below poverty, living in problem housing, living alone, without access to auto, without access to phone, ethnicity, tenure status, and living arrangement status by age and by sex.

  Geographic Areas Covered: Planning and Service Areas (PSAs) of the State of West Virginia.

For further information on special tabulations of 1970 Census data, inquiries should be addressed to: Customer Service Branch, Data User Services Division, Bureau of the Census, Washington, DC, 20233.

Current Population Survey

The Current Population Survey is a monthly sample survey conducted by the Census Bureau for the Bureau of Labor Statistics to obtain monthly labor force statistics. Approximately 65,000 households are eligible for interviews. 4/ Supplemental questions are added to the survey each month, the March supplement being the major source of demographic data contained in the Current Population Survey. The subject content of the monthly supplements remains relatively constant from year to year, with some questions being added or deleted.

The data collected in the March supplement are available not only in printed reports but also on computer tapes. These data files, one for each year, are known as Annual Demographic Files. They are microdata files, like the 1970 Public Use Sample, and contain such data as age, sex, race, ethnic origin, family characteristics, educational attainment, mobility, employment, and income.

The Bureau of the Census publishes current demographic, social, and economic statistics in its Current Population Reports. There are eight series of Current Population Reports, four of which contain data from the Current Population Survey: Population Characteristics (P-20), Special Studies (P-23), Farm Population (P-27), and Consumer Income (P-60).

One example of a report which would be germane to the study of the elderly population is the Special Studies (P-23), Report No. 57, "Social and Economic Characteristics of the Older Population". This report presents selected economic and social data for the elderly population primarily from the 1970 Census and the March 1974 demographic supplement

to the Current Population Survey. Specifically, this report includes data for the elderly on family composition, marital status, fertility, the institutionalized population, nativity and parentage, mobility and residence, education, vocational training, literacy, voting and veterans, labor force participation, employment status, occupation and industry, income and earnings, low-income status of persons and families, housing, health and health services, and crime victimization. Also included are the growth in the size of the elderly population from 1900 to 1974 and projections of the elderly population from 1975 to 2000.

For further information on the Current Population Survey, inquiries should be addressed to: Population Division or Demographic Surveys Division, Bureau of the Census, Washington, DC, 20233.

Annual Housing Survey

The Annual Housing Survey is a joint undertaking of the Bureau of the Census and the Department of Housing and Urban Development. The survey consists of two parts: a national sample of housing units from urban and regional areas whose residents are interviewed every year, and metropolitan area samples from 60 standard metropolitan statistical areas (SMSAs) divided into 3 groups with one group of 20 SMSAs interviewed each year on a rotating basis.

The survey includes, but is not limited to, the following general items: number and characteristics of residential living units, measures of losses and new construction, presence of plumbing facilities, frequency of mechanical and utility breakdowns in housing units, characteristics of recent movers into housing units, indicators of physical

---

4/ During 1978 the sample size may be expanded to provide State level data. Currently, data are for the United States only.

condition of housing units, neighborhood conditions, financial characteristics of housing inventory, and characteristics of occupants. Some specific items in the survey include the following: age, sex, race, and ethnic origin of household head; number of rooms, bedrooms, and bathrooms; number of persons in household; type of living quarters; property value; rent; family income; utilities; and presence of and objections to neighborhoods conditions.

The data from the Annual Housing Survey are available in printed reports for 1973, 1974, and 1975; on microfilm for 1974; and on public use microdata tapes for the SMSAs surveyed in 1974. Six printed reports were prepared for the 1974 and 1975 national survey. The individual SMSA reports for each of those years have four parts corresponding to the first four reports for the national samples. The six reports or part are:

- Part A: General Housing Characteristics
- Part B: Indicators of Housing and Neighborhood Quality
- Part C: Financial Characteristics of the Housing Inventory
- Part D: Housing Characteristics of Recent Movers
- Part E: Urban and Rural Housing Characteristics
- Part F: Financial Characteristics by Indicators of Housing and Neighborhood Quality

The national survey data for 1973 were published for Parts A-D and F. SMSA surveys were not conducted during 1973.

Public use microdata tapes and microfilm copies of data from the surveys are available through the Customer Service Branch, Data User Services Division, Bureau of the Census, Washington, DC, 20233. For further information on the Annual Housing Survey, inquiries should be addressed to: Housing Division, Bureau of the Census, Washington, DC, 20233.

Survey of Income and Education

The purpose of the 1976 Survey of Income and Education was to provide to Congress a count, by State, of the school-aged children who lived in families at or below the poverty level. In addition, the survey was designed to provide, by State, the count of persons who, because of a multilingual background, were not proficient in speaking or understanding English. Finally, the survey included items to help in the redefinition of the concept of poverty and to meet a number of programmatic needs of the Department of Health, Education, and Welfare for whom the survey was conducted by the Bureau of the Census.

This one-time survey collected information on about 151,000 households. The survey was conducted during the months of April, May, and June 1976. The survey's design and size permitted the development of State-level estimates from the sample information collected.

Some of the data items included in the survey were: age, race, sex, and ethnicity of household head; household realtionships; educational attainment; labor force activities; level and sources of income; languages spoken in the home; mobility; health conditions limiting activities; health insurance coverage; food stamp recipiency; housing tenure; housing costs; household and family size; age of and payments for support of persons in institutions and hospitals; and wage earners in family.

Several reports have been prepared from the survey data. A report on children in poverty was submitted to Congress in 1977. A report on persons with English language difficulty was delivered to the Department of Health, Education, and Welfare in 1977. In November 1977, the

Bureau of the Census published the first of five reports on income distribution and poverty. The first report was entitled "Household Money Income in 1975, by Housing Tenure and Residence, for the United States, Regions, Divisions and States", Current Population Reports, Series P-60, No. 108. The other reports will appear in the Bureau's Current Population Reports P-60 Series. These reports may be obtained from the U.S. Government Printing Office.

Data from the Survey of Income and Education are available on computer tape from the Bureau of the Census.

The data are available for the entire United States and census geographic divisions. Data files are not available for individual states. These data files can be manipulated in the same manner as the public use sample files. Users can create their own cross-tabulations and estimates from the basic records information in the files. These files are available from: Customer Services Branch, Data User Services Division, Bureau of the Census, Washington, DC, 20233. For further information on this survey, inquiries should be addressed to: Population Division or Demographic Surveys Division, Bureau of the Census, Washington, DC, 20233

Prospective Trends in the Size and Structure of the Elderly Population, Impact of Mortality Trends, and Some Implications

Jacob S. Siegel*

U.S. Department of Commerce, Bureau of the Census, Washington, D.C., January 1979.

Editor's note: For space reasons, the introductory paragraph and footnote one were moved to the end of this article (page 296).

SIZE AND STRUCTURE OF THE ELDERLY POPULATION

Numbers and Proportions

Change in numbers. Between now and the end of the century the population 65 and over is expected to grow at only about half the rate of the past quarter century, but this growth will still be considerable:

Period	Percent increase			
	65 and over	65 to 74	75 to 84	85 and over
1950 to 1976....	85	67	104	233
1976 to 2000....	39	23	57	91
2000 to 2020....	42	61	15	27

During this period, this age group will increase by nearly 40 percent, from 23 million in 1976 to 32 million in 2000 (table 1). The age group is expected approximately to double between 1976 and 2020, when we should have about 45 million elderly persons. In this period, all age segments of the elderly population are expected to grow rapidly, particularly the extreme aged. In fact, the percent changes show a regular progression with age for the 1976-2000 period. The population 65 to 74 should increase by about 23 percent, the population 75 to 84 by about 57 percent, and the population 85 and over by about 91 percent.

---

*The author wishes to acknowledge the professional assistance of Maria Davidson, Jerome Glynn, and J. Gregory Robinson in the preparation of the materials employed in this document.

We can have a fair degree of confidence in the projections of the general level of the population and the growth rates shown, since the accuracy of projections of population *numbers* for the older age groups is dependent essentially on the accuracy of the projections of mortality, particularly for the older ages. Reasonable alternative projections of mortality would not seriously alter the population projections (see below).

The general rise in the numbers of births, particularly up to the early 1920's, is the principal factor that accounts for the large past and prospective increases in the number of elderly persons. Past and prospective declines in death rates, and immigration, particularly the heavy volume of immigrants prior to World War I, serve also to augment the number of elderly persons but they play a distinctly secondary role. The sharp drop in the rate of increase in the 65-and-over population after about 1990, lasting about two decades, is a result of the rapid drop in the number of births during the 1920-30 and 1930-40 decades. The baby boom cohorts cause the leap forward in the elderly population after 2010.

Change in the proportion of elderly persons. The proportion of elderly persons in the total population is likely to continue to rise, but more slowly than in the past. The rise may not be a steady one because of the probable fluctuations in future fertility, but two of the three series of projections published by the Census Bureau (those having lower fertility) show a general rise in the proportion and all of the projected range for the proportion is above the level of 1976. Changes in the proportion of the elderly are directly affected by projections of the total population, and hence of fertility, as well as by projections of the elderly population. Hence, we can have much less confidence in these figures.

If fertility moves toward replacement level (fertility somewhat above the level of 1976) between 1976 and 1990,

Table 1. Total Population in the Older Ages and Decennial Increases: 1950 to 2040

(Numbers in thousands. Estimates and projections as of July 1. Figures refer to the total population of the 50 States and District of Columbia. A minus sign (-) denotes a decrease. See text for explanation of Series I, II, and III)

Year	60 years and over			65 years and over			70 years and over			75 years and over			85 years and over		
		Increase in preceding decade			Increase in preceding decade			Increase in preceding decade			Increase in preceding decade			Increase in preceding decade	
	Number	Amount	Percent	Number	Amount	Percent	Number	Amount	Percent	Number	Amount	Percent	Number	Amount	Percent
ESTIMATES															
1950....................	18,500	(X)	(X)	12,397	(X)	(X)	7,348	(X)	(X)	3,904	(X)	(X)	590	(X)	(X)
1960....................	23,828	5,328	28.8	16,675	4,278	34.5	10,394	3,046	41.5	5,621	1,717	44.0	940	350	59.3
1970....................	28,753	4,925	20.7	20,087	3,412	20.5	13,065	2,671	25.7	7,600	1,979	35.2	1,432	492	52.3
1976....................	32,244	(X)	(X)	22,934	(X)	(X)	14,654	(X)	(X)	8,741	(X)	(X)	1,966	(X)	(X)
PROJECTIONS[1]															
1980....................	34,724	5,971	20.8	24,927	4,840	24.1	16,227	3,162	24.2	9,434	1,834	24.1	2,294	862	60.2
1990....................	40,184	5,460	15.7	29,824	4,897	19.6	19,803	3,576	22.0	12,021	2,587	27.4	2,881	587	25.6
2000....................	41,973	1,789	4.5	31,822	1,998	6.7	22,630	2,827	14.3	14,386	2,365	19.7	3,756	875	30.4
2010....................	49,850	7,877	18.8	34,837	3,015	9.5	23,211	581	2.6	15,060	674	4.7	4,575	819	21.8
2020....................	63,265	13,415	26.9	45,102	10,265	29.5	29,126	5,915	25.5	16,975	1,915	12.7	4,776	201	4.4
2030....................	70,737	7,472	11.8	55,024	9,922	22.0	37,936	8,810	30.2	23,170	6,195	36.5	5,681	905	18.9
2040.............(II)..	69,806	-931	-1.3												
Range { (III)..	68,566	-2,171	-3.1	54,925	-99	-0.2	40,774	2,838	7.5	27,907	4,737	20.4	7,980	2,299	40.5
(I)..	71,445	708	1.0												

(X) Not applicable.
[1]Base date of projections is July 1, 1976.

Source: U.S. Bureau of the Census, Current Population Reports, Series P-25, Nos. 311, 519, 614, 643, and 704.

as in the Series II Census Bureau projections,[2] we can expect about 12 percent of the population to be aged 65 and over in the year 2000 and about 15½ percent in 2020, as compared with 10.7 percent in 1976 (table 2 and figure 1). The proportions 65 and over in 2020 corresponding to the population projections based on below-replacement fertility (Series III Census Bureau projections) and above-replacement fertility (Series I Census Bureau projections) are 18 and 13 percent, respectively. As fertility decreases, with a given level of mortality, the proportion of the older population tends to increase. The Bureau of the Census series of projected percents 65 and over at 10-year intervals to 2040, including the projected range, is as follows:

Year	Percent
1976..............	10.7
1980..............	11.2 (11.1 - 11.3)
1990..............	12.2 (11.7 - 12.6)
2000..............	12.2 (11.3 - 12.9)
2010..............	12.7 (11.1 - 13.9)
2020..............	15.5 (12.7 - 17.8)
2030..............	18.3 (14.0 - 22.1)
2040..............	17.8 (12.5 - 22.8)

[2] The basic fertility assumptions employed in developing the three series of population projection relate to the average numbers of children born to a woman in her lifetime:

Series I   2.7 children per woman
Series II   2.1 children per woman
Series III 1.7 children per woman

Only one mortality assumption (moderate declines) and one immigration assumption (400,000 net immigration per year) are combined with these three fertility assumptions in the Census Bureau population projections.

If fertility continues at current levels and mortality declines moderately, as is assumed, the percentage of elderly persons can be expected to fall just below the highest percentage (18 percent) shown for the year 2020. A sharp rise will occur in the 2010-25 period (unless fertility rises well above replacement level) because of the entry of the 1945-60 baby-boom cohorts into the 65-and-over population. There may be only a modest rise or a decline in the proportion after 2025, as a result mainly of the decline in the number of births after 1960.

Fertility has been and will continue to be a more important determinant of shifts in the proportion of the older population than mortality. Both recent changes in the birth rate and shifts in the numbers of births 65 years earlier jointly affect the proportion of elderly. Changes in death rates affect the proportion also but their influence is quite limited.[3] Furthermore, as appears to have occurred in the earlier part of this century, declines in death rates may tend to retard or contribute only slightly to the rise in the proportion of elderly persons.[4] When, as for the Census Bureau projections, the greater declines in death rates are assumed to occur at the older ages, the effect is to raise the proportion. At low levels of fertility, only extremely large future reductions in mortality occurring mainly at the older ages could

[3] Ansley J. Coale, "The Effects of Changes in Mortality and Fertility on Age Composition," **Milbank Memorial Fund Quarterly**, Vol. 34, No. 1, January 1956, pp. 79-114.
[4] Albert I. Hermalin, "The Effect of Changes in Mortality Rates on Population Growth and Age Distribution in the United States," **Milbank Memorial Fund Quarterly**, Vol. 44, No. 4, Part 1, October 1966 pp. 451-469.

Table 2. Percent of the Total Population in the Older Ages, by Sex: 1950 to 2020

(Estimates and projections as of July 1. Based on totals including Armed Forces overseas. See text for explanation of Series I, II, and III)

Age and sex	1950	1960	1970	1976	Projections[1] 1980 II	1980 Range I to III	2000 II	2000 Range I to III	2020 II	2020 Range I to III
ALL RACES										
Both sexes										
60 years and over..............	12.1	13.2	14.1	15.0	15.6	15.5 to 15.7	16.1	14.8 to 17.1	21.8	17.9 to 25.0
65 years and over..............	8.1	9.3	9.9	10.7	11.2	11.1 to 11.3	12.2	11.3 to 12.9	15.5	12.7 to 17.8
70 years and over..............	4.8	5.8	6.4	6.8	7.3	7.2 to 7.4	8.7	8.0 to 9.2	10.0	8.2 to 10.2
75 years and over..............	2.6	3.1	3.7	4.1	4.2	4.2 to 4.3	5.5	5.1 to 5.9	5.9	4.8 to 6.7
85 years and over..............	0.4	0.5	0.7	0.9	1.0	1.0 to 1.0	1.4	1.3 to 1.5	1.6	1.3 to 1.7
Male										
60 years and over..............	11.8	12.4	12.6	13.1	13.6	13.5 to 13.7	13.8	12.7 to 14.7	19.3	15.7 to 22.3
65 years and over..............	7.7	8.5	8.5	9.0	9.3	9.3 to 9.4	10.0	9.2 to 10.7	13.2	10.7 to 15.2
70 years and over..............	4.5	5.2	5.3	5.5	5.8	5.7 to 5.8	6.8	6.2 to 7.2	8.0	6.5 to 9.2
75 years and over..............	2.3	2.7	3.0	3.1	3.1	3.1 to 3.2	4.0	3.7 to 4.2	4.3	3.4 to 4.9
85 years and over..............	0.3	0.4	0.5	0.6	0.7	0.6 to 0.7	0.8	0.8 to 0.9	0.9	0.8 to 1.1
Female										
60 years and over..............	12.5	14.1	15.6	16.8	17.6	17.4 to 17.7	18.3	16.9 to 19.3	24.1	20.0 to 27.5
65 years and over..............	8.6	10.0	11.2	12.3	13.0	12.9 to 13.1	14.3	13.2 to 15.1	17.8	14.7 to 20.3
70 years and over..............	5.2	6.3	7.5	8.1	8.8	8.7 to 8.8	10.5	9.7 to 11.1	12.0	9.9 to 13.6
75 years and over..............	2.8	3.5	4.4	5.0	5.3	5.3 to 5.3	7.0	6.5 to 7.4	7.4	6.1 to 8.4
85 years and over..............	0.5	0.6	0.9	1.2	1.4	1.4 to 1.4	2.0	1.9 to 2.1	2.3	1.9 to 2.6

[1]Base date of projections is July 1, 1976.

Source: U.S. Bureau of the Census, Current Population Reports, Series P-25, Nos. 311, 519, 614, 643, and 704.

contribute to substantial increases in the future percentage of the elderly. If fertility turns up and mortality declines only moderately, as is possible, the proportion of elderly persons in the population may stop rising and may even decline (e.g., Series I Census Bureau projections, 1990 to 2010).

Age and Sex Composition

Age pattern of the older population. The older population has been getting older and is expected to continue doing so for a few decades. For example, the proportion of persons in the age group 65 and over who are 75 and over is now rising and will generally continue to rise until at least the year 2000. In 1976, the proportion in the older age group was 38 percent. In the year 2000, we can expect the proportion to be about 45 percent (table 3). It is then likely to fall back to about 38 percent again in 2020 as the larger cohorts born in the high fertility period following World War II enter the younger segment of the group (65 to 74 years).

Change in sex balance. Rates of increase are expected to be generally greater for elderly females than elderly males in the next few decades, but the tremendous differences in the growth rates of the sexes seen in the last few decades will not be repeated:

For each sex for the 1976-2000 period growth rates progress upward with increasing age.

There were 69 males for every 100 females in the age group 65 and over in 1976 (table 3). The deficit of males

Sex and period	Percent increase 65 and over	Percent increase 65 to 74	Percent increase 75 to 84	Percent increase 85 and over
Male				
1950 to 1976..	60	51	69	159
1976 to 2000..	36	24	55	69
2000 to 2020..	45	63	17	25
Female				
1950 to 1976..	108	82	135	286
1976 to 2000..	41	22	58	101
2000 to 2020..	39	60	14	28

increases sharply with advancing age. At birth, the sex ratio has consistently been about 105-106. By ages 70-74 the sex ratio has fallen below 75 and by ages 85 and over it has fallen below 50.

The sex ratio at ages 65 and over is expected to fall to 67 per 100 by the year 2000 and then to rise, reaching 69 again by the year 2020. The sex ratio at ages 75 and over and 85 and over will also tend to continue declining for the next few decades.

The large excess of females over males among the elderly is also reflected in differences in the age distribution of the sexes. In 1976, 12.3 percent of the female population was over 65, as compared with 9.0 percent of the male popula-

Figure 1. Percent of the Total Population in the Older Ages: 1920 to 2020

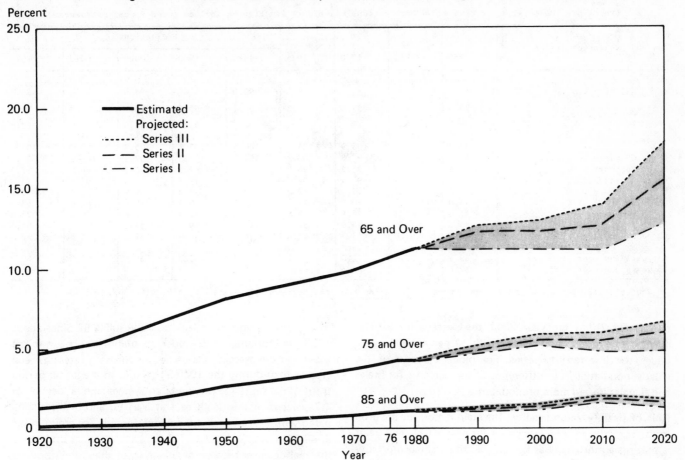

Note: Points are plotted for years ending in zero except for 1976.
Source: Table 2 and **Current Population Reports**, Series P-25, No. 311, 519, 614, 643, and 704.

Table 3. Percent Distribution of the Population 65 Years Old and Over, by Age: 1950 to 2020

Age	1950	1960	1970	1976	Projections				
					1980	1990	2000	2010	2020
65 years and over........	100.0	100.0	100.0	100.0	100.0	100.0	100.0	100.0	100.0
65 to 69 years.................	40.7	37.7	35.0	36.1	34.9	33.6	28.9	33.4	35.4
70 to 74 years.................	27.8	28.6	27.2	25.8	27.3	26.1	25.9	23.4	26.9
75 to 79 years.................	17.4	18.5	19.2	17.7	17.3	18.4	20.1	17.0	16.8
80 to 84 years.................	9.3	9.6	11.5	11.9	11.3	12.2	13.3	13.1	10.2
85 years and over.............	4.8	5.6	7.1	8.6	9.2	9.7	11.8	13.1	10.6

Source: U.S. Bureau of the Census, Current Population Reports, Series P-25, No. 311, 519, 614, 643, and 704.

Table 4. Sex Ratios of the Population, by Broad Age Groups: 1950 to 2020

(Males per 100 females. Estimates and projections as of July 1. Figures include Armed Forces overseas)

Age and projection series	1950	1960	1970	1976	Projections				
					1980	1990	2000	2010	2020
All ages............II..	99.3	97.0	94.8	94.8	95.0	94.8	94.6	94.4	93.8
Range.......... I..					95.1	95.2	95.4	95.7	95.7
III..					94.9	94.5	94.0	93.5	92.4
Under 15 years.................	103.8	103.4	103.9	104.2	104.5	105.1	105.2	105.1	105.1
15 to 29 years.................	98.7	97.7	97.8	100.3	101.3	101.3	102.1	102.1	102.1
30 to 44 years.................	97.4	95.5	95.2	95.8	96.6	97.2	96.7	96.8	97.3
45 to 59 years.................	99.8	96.9	93.4	94.8	95.3	95.1	95.9	95.4	95.3
60 to 64 years.................	100.4	91.2	87.7	87.9	87.9	98.8	89.9	91.1	90.9
65 to 69 years.................	94.0	87.8	80.7	79.3	79.7	80.5	82.4	82.4	83.2
70 to 74 years.................	91.3	85.3	73.9	73.5	72.4	72.9	74.6	74.8	75.9
75 to 84 years.................	85.0	77.4	65.9	61.0	60.3	59.6	59.9	60.7	61.4
85 years and over..............	70.0	63.8	53.2	47.0	44.7	40.9	39.4	38.8	38.5
65 years and over..............	89.5	82.6	72.0	69.0	68.2	67.3	66.6	67.0	69.3
75 years and over..............	82.6	75.0	63.3	57.7	56.2	54.7	54.0	53.4	54.2

Source: U.S. Bureau of the Census, Current Population Reports, Series P-25, Nos. 311, 519, 614, 643, and 704.

tion (table 2). In the year 2000, the percent for females may be as high as 15, compared with 11 percent for males, under the low fertility series. For older segments of the elderly population, the difference in the percents for males and females is even more pronounced.

Role of fertility and mortality. The main reason for the drop in the sex ratio *with increasing age* for past and current years is that male mortality has been higher than female mortality at each age of life for many decades in the United States.[5] This pattern is expected to continue. The main factor determining the declining trend in the sex ratios at each age *over time* is the relative level of male and female mortality, or more precisely, the relative levels of male and female survival rates. The death rates for the sexes at the various age groups have been steadily diverging, to the greater and greater disadvantage of males. The further decline or slight rise in the sex ratio of the population at the older ages projected for future years is a result of the assumption made in the Census Bureau projections that there will be a further slight divergence of male and female mortality rates.

MORTALITY AND SURVIVAL

Past General Trends

We can describe the 1940-54 period as one of generally rapid mortality declines in terms of age, sex, race, and cause-of-death categories. From 1954 until 1968, however, there was little progress in this regard. The expectation of life at birth and at age 65 remained nearly the same over

the 14-year period from 1954 to 1968 (table 5). Since about 1968 the mortality of the older population has begun to fall again and the average rate of decline in death rates has been greater than during the 1940-54 period. In the 9-year period from 1968 to 1977, there was an average annual decline of 1.7 percent in the death rate at ages 65 and over, as compared with a decline of 1.5 percent for this age group in the 1940-54 period (table 6). The observed declines understate the real declines because of the aging of the elderly population itself.[6] As a result of the declines in death rates, life expectancies at birth and at age 65 have been climbing steadily upward; life expectancy at birth is estimated at 73.5 years in 1977 as compared with 70.2 years in 1968.

Sex Differences

Past trends. As stated previously, the difference between the sexes in mortality levels is quite large and has been growing until recently. By 1976 the difference in the life expectancy at birth of males (69.0 years) and females (76.7 years) reached 7.7 years (table 5). It was only 4.3 years in 1940. An increasing part of the difference is accounted for by the difference in life expectancy at age 65. According to the death rates of 1976, the male-female difference in the average number of years lived in the age interval 0-64 years was 2.3 years, as compared with 4.3 years for age 65 and over.[7] By 1976

---

[5] U.S. Bureau of the Census, **Current Population Reports**, Series P-23, No. 59 (rev.), op. cit., esp. p. 13-14.

[6] Mary Grace Kovar and Lois Fingerhut, "Recent Trends in U.S. Mortality Among the Aged," unpublished paper presented at the annual meeting of the Gerontological Society, San Francisco, California, November 21, 1977.

[7] The maximum number of years of life that may be lived in the interval under age 65 is, of course, 65 years. The "actual" figures for 1976 are 59.6 for males and 61.9 for females. The average number of years lived above age 65 is equal to life expectancy at age 65. Life expectancy at age 65 for 1976 is 13.7 years for males and 18.0 years for females.

the death rate of males 65 and over exceeded the corresponding rate for females by nearly 50 percent (table 7).

Basis of the gap. Because of the magnitude, durability, and pervasive consequences for our society of the gap between male and female death rates, the basis for the gap is a matter of serious social concern. The gap is evidence of a considerable inequality between the sexes in the effects of environmental and/or genetic influences on mortality rates.

The evidence for the basis of the large and growing difference is conflicting, as suggested by a number of facts and studies. Social factors appear to exercise an important influence on the difference, but in combination with and in interaction with genetic and biological factors. Studies and analyses by Enterline,[8] Godley and Kruegel,[9] Retherford,[10] and Waldron[11] favor explanations primarily in terms of "environmental" factors. Others, such as the Madigan study,[12] favor explanations primarily in terms of (genetic and nongenetic) hereditary factors.

The study of Madigan, relating to mortality differences between brothers and nuns in Catholic teaching orders, concludes that the excess male mortality can be attributed to biological factors since the men and women can be assumed to have essentially the same life styles. Male fetal and infant mortality is markedly greater than female fetal and infant mortality. There is evidence that the female reproductive period is highly protective for women and, accordingly, the lengthening of the female reproductive period in the past centry, presumably due to improved nutrition and hygiene, has apparently afforded an increasing biological advantage to women.

The changes in recent decades in the male-female mortality gap appear to be more associated with social and environmental factors. The Retherford study concluded that two-thirds of the divergence between the male and female death rates of adults in most of this century was due to smoking. Yet, females have taken up smoking in large and increasing numbers during this period, especially since World War II. Furthermore, during the same period larger and larger proportions of women have been joining the labor force.

Presumably we should have seen some convergence of the death rates of men and women. The divergence observed has been occurring, therefore, in spite of the fact that the differences in the life styles and roles of men and women have diminished. It is notable that we find the largest difference in life expectancy at birth, some 10 years, in the USSR, where men and women occupy much more equal occupational roles than in the United States.[13] A major change in the relative mortality levels of the sexes is not expected to occur in the United States, if at all, until a whole generation of women is reared in the work ethic of males—that is, socialized from childhood with a "work-or-perish" life design.

The increasing male-female mortality difference may also be interpreted as a result of a major shift of the cause-pattern of mortality in this century, involving a sharp reduction in the relative importance of the infectious and parasitic diseases and maternal mortality and a rise in the relative importance of the chronic "degenerative" diseases, e.g., diseases of the heart, malignant neoplasms, cerebrovascular diseases. For the second group of causes, male rates tend to be much higher than female rates whereas, for many categories in the first group of causes, female rates tend to be more similar to those of male rates. Even for the second group, male-female differences have widened over the last several decades, however.

Race Differences

There is still a difference of several years in life expectancy at birth between the races (White, Black-and-other-races). The difference has been reduced sharply over the last several decades, from about 11 years in 1940 to 5 years in 1976 (table 5). The difference in life expectancy at age 65 is small, however, and has been small throughout this whole period. The magnitude of the male-female differences in life expectancy and the evolution of the differences are similar for Whites and Blacks.

Death rates for the Black-and-other-races population are higher than for Whites below age 65 and at ages 65-74. There is then a crossover of the rates at ages 75-79 in the U.S. death registration data. The crossover is not to be viewed merely as a statistical artifact since the crossover phenomenon appears in many other paired comparisons, often involving data of high quality.[14] For example, it

[8] Philip E. Enterline, "Cause of Death Responsible for Recent Increases in Sex Mortality Differentials in the United States," **Milbank Memorial Fund Quarterly**, Vol. 39, No. 2, 1961, pp. 312-328.

[9] Frank Godley and David Q. Kruegel, "Cigarette Smoking and Differential Mortality: New Estimates from Representative National Samples," unpublished paper presented at the annual meeting of the Population Association of America, Seattle, Washington, April 17-19, 1975.

[10] Robert D. Retherford, "Tobacco Smoking and the Sex Mortality Differential," **Demography**, Vol. 9, No. 2, 1972, pp. 203-216, and **The Changing Sex Differential in Mortality**, Greenwood Press, Westport, Conn. 1975.

[11] Ingrid Waldron, "Why Do Women Live Longer Than Men?", **Journal of Human Stress**, Vol. 2, March 1976, pp. 2-13, and Ingrid Waldron and Susan Johnston, "Why Do Women Live Longer Than Men?", **Journal of Human Stress**, Vol. 2, June 1976, pp. 19-29.

[12] Francis C. Madigan, "Are Sex Mortality Differentials Biologically Caused?", **Milbank Memorial Fund Quarterly**, Vol. 35, No. 2, 1957, pp. 203-223.

[13] Jacques Vallin and Jean-Claude Chenais, "Evolution Récente de la Mortalité en Europe dans les Pays Anglo-Saxons et en Union Soviétique, 1960-1970," **Population**, Vol. 29, Nos. 4-5, July-Oct. 1974, pp. 862-898, esp. p. 863; Institut National d'Etudes Démographiques, "Sixième Rapport sur la Situation Démographique de la France," **Population**, Vol. 32, No. 2, March-April 1977, pp. 253-338, esp. 293-294.

[14] Charles B. Nam and Kathleen A. Ockay, "Factors Contributing to the Mortality Crossover Pattern: Effects of Developmental Level, Overall Mortality Level, and Causes of Death," unpublished paper submitted to the XVIII General Conference of the International Union for the Scientific Study of Population, Mexico City, August 8-13, 1977.

Table 5. Life Expectancy at Birth and at Age 65, by Race and Sex: 1900 to 1976

Race and year	At birth				At age 65			
	Both sexes	Male	Female	Difference	Both sexes	Male	Female	Difference
ALL RACES								
1900–02	49.2	47.9	50.7	2.8	11.9	11.5	12.2	0.7
1939–41	63.6	61.6	65.9	4.3	12.8	12.1	13.6	1.5
1954	69.6	66.7	72.7	5.0	14.4	13.1	15.7	2.2
1968	70.2	66.6	74.0	7.4	14.6	12.8	16.3	3.5
1976	72.8	69.0	76.7	7.7	16.0	13.7	18.0	4.3
WHITE								
1900–02	49.7	48.2	51.1	2.9	11.9	11.5	12.2	0.7
1939–41	64.9	62.8	67.3	4.5	12.8	12.1	13.6	1.5
1954	70.5	67.4	73.6	6.2	14.4	13.1	15.7	2.6
1968	71.1	67.5	74.9	7.4	14.7	12.8	16.4	3.6
1976	73.5	69.7	77.3	7.6	16.1	13.7	18.1	4.4
BLACK AND OTHER RACES								
1900–02	33.8	32.5	35.0	2.5	10.9	10.4	11.4	1.0
1939–41	53.9	52.3	55.6	3.3	13.0	12.2	13.9	1.7
1954	63.4	61.0	65.8	4.8	14.6	13.5	15.7	2.2
1968	63.7	60.1	67.5	7.4	13.7	12.1	15.1	3.0
1976	68.3	64.1	72.6	8.5	15.8	13.8	17.6	3.8
WHITE–BLACK DIFFERENCE								
1900–02	15.9	15.7	16.1	(X)	1.0	1.1	0.8	(X)
1939–41	11.0	10.5	11.7	(X)	-0.2	-0.1	-0.3	(X)
1954	7.1	6.4	7.8	(X)	-0.2	-0.4	–	(X)
1968	7.4	7.4	7.4	(X)	1.0	0.7	1.3	(X)
1976	5.2	5.6	4.7	(X)	0.3	-0.1	0.5	(X)

(X) Not applicable.

Source: National Center for Health Statistics (U.S. Public Service) and the U.S. Bureau of the Census. For 1976, "Advance Report–Final Mortality Statistics, 1976," Monthly Vital Statistics Report, Vol. 26, No. 12, Supplement (2), March 1978.

Table 6. Death Rates for the Population 55 Years Old and Over, by Age: 1940 to 1977

Year and period	55 to 64 years	65 to 74 years	75 to 84 years	85 years and over	65 years and over
RATES PER 1,000 POPULATION					
1940	22.2	48.4	112.0	235.7	72.2
1954	17.4	37.9	86.0	181.6	58.6
1968[1]	17.0	37.2	82.9	195.8	61.4
1976 (prov.)	14.8	31.4	73.2	156.1	54.2
1976	14.8	31.3	73.3	155.7	54.3
1977 (prov.)	14.3	30.5	71.5	145.9	52.6
PERCENT CHANGE					
1940 to 1954	-21.6	-21.7	-23.2	-23.0	-18.8
1954 to 1968	-2.3	-1.8	-3.6	+7.8	+4.8
1968 to 1977	-15.9	-18.0	-13.8	-25.5	-14.3

[1]Official estimates for 1968 have been revised by the Census Bureau on the basis of revised population estimates.

Source: National Center for Health Statistics (U.S. Public Health Service), various annual volumes of Vital Statistics of the United States and various issues of Monthly Vital Statistics Report.

Table 7. Ratios of Male to Female Death Rates for the Population 55 Years Old and Over, by Age: 1900 to 1976

Year	55 to 64 years	65 to 74 years	75 to 84 years	85 years and over	65 years and over
ALL CLASSES					
1900.....................	1.14	1.11	1.08	1.05	1.06
1940.....................	1.45	1.29	1.17	1.08	1.17
1954.....................	1.82	1.57	1.29	1.06	1.30
1968.....................	2.07	1.88	1.46	1.18	1.44
1976.....................	1.99	1.97	1.58	1.26	1.46

Source: U.S. Bureau of the Census, United States Life Tables, 1930, 1936; National Center for Health Statistics (U.S. Public Health Service), annual volumes of Vital Statistics of the United States, for 1940 and 1954, and "Advance Report – Final Mortality Statistics," Monthly Vital Statistics Report, Vol. 26, No. 12, Supplement (2), March 1978.

appears in death rates based on U.S. Social Security Administration ("Medicare") data, albeit at a higher age (ages 80-84). The Social Security data also reflect smaller differences between the races than the registration statistics.

Little attention has been given to the relative contribution of genetic and environmental influences to the White-Black mortality gap. The Kitagawa and Hauser study suggests that most of the difference may be accounted for by the difference in the socioeconomic status of the racial groups.[15]

Causes of Death

The cause-pattern for deaths of the elderly has continued to shift toward the chronic "degenerative" causes and away from the infectious-parasitic causes. The major chronic causes are moving in opposite directions, however, death rates from cancer have been rising sharply and death rates from the cardiovascular diseases have been falling sharply in the last decade.

Only a few categories of causes account for most deaths over age 65. In 1976 diseases of the heart accounted for 44 percent of all deaths at these ages, and diseases of the heart, malignant neoplasms, and cerebrovascular diseases accounted for three-quarters of the deaths (table 8). The rates for the remaining "leading" causes are so low that each cause, taken separately, accounts for less than 5 percent of the total number of deaths over age 65.

Additional insight into the current cause-pattern of mortality is secured by examining the possible gain in life expectancy from eliminating various causes of death and the chance of eventually dying from various causes. If all deaths from cardiovascular diseases were eliminated and if the chance of dying from the various causes is assumed to be independent, the gain in life expectancy at birth would be 12 years and the gain at ages 65 would be 11 years according to the 1969-71 death rates (table 9). Diseases of the heart account for about half of these additions to life expectancy. Roughly speaking, a 65-year old has a two-thirds chance of eventually dying from a cardiovascular disease—a 50 percent chance of dying from a disease of the heart and a one-seventh chance of dying from a cerebrovascular disease.

If all deaths from cancer were eliminated, 2½ years of life would be added at birth and 1½ years of life would be added at age 65. The elimination of cancer would have a much smaller effect on life expectancy at age 65 than the elimination of cardiovascular diseases because the cancer rate is much lower generally and because cancer is less concentrated at the older ages. A 65-year old has a one-sixth chance of eventually dying from cancer.

If all cancer mortality were eliminated, the total number of deaths would not be greatly reduced after a while since the persons saved would be subject to the residual death rate for all other causes, albeit at older ages.[16] Death rates at each age would fall but the chance of eventually dying from the other causes would rise. On the other hand, the saving of lives would be greater both initially and for a longer

---

[15] Evelyn M. Kitagawa and Philip M. Hauser, **Differential Mortality in the United States: A Study in Socioeconomic Epidemiology**, Harvard University Press, Cambridge. Mass.. 1973.

[16] Nathan Keyfitz, "What Difference Would it Make if Cancer Were Eradicated? An Examination of the Taeuber Paradox," **Demography**, Vol. 14, No. 4, Nov. 1977, pp. 411-418, esp. p. 417.

U.S. Bureau of the Census, "Demographic Aspects of Aging and the Older Population in the United States," **op. cit.**, esp. p. 43.

Table 8. Death Rates for the 10 Leading Causes of Death for Ages 65 and Over, by Age: 1976

(Deaths per 100,000 population)

Cause of death by rank	65 years and over	65 to 74 years	75 to 84 years	85 years and over
All causes...............	5,428.9	3,127.6	7,331.6	15,486.9
1 Diseases of the heart.......	2,393.5	1,286.9	3,263.7	7,384.3
2 Malignant neoplasms.........	979.0	786.3	1,248.6	1,441.5
3 Cerebrovascular diseases....	694.6	280.1	1,014.0	2,586.8
4 Influenza and pneumonia.....	211.1	70.1	289.3	959.2
5 Arteriosclerosis............	122.2	25.8	152.5	714.3
6 Diabetes mellitus...........	108.1	70.0	155.8	219.2
7 Accidents...................	104.5	62.2	134.5	306.7
Motor vehicle.............	25.2	21.7	32.3	26.0
All other.................	79.3	40.4	102.2	280.7
8 Bronchitis, emphysema and asthma....................	76.8	60.7	101.4	108.5
9 Cirrhosis of liver.........	36.5	42.6	29.3	18.0
10 Nephritis and nephrosis....	25.0	15.2	34.1	64.6
All other causes...........	677.5	427.8	908.6	1,683.8

Source: National Center for Health Statistics (U.S. Public Health Service), "Advance Report-Final Mortality Statistics, 1976," Monthly Vital Statistics Report, Vol. 26, No. 12, Supplement (2), March 1978; and unpublished data provided by the National Center of Health Statistics.

period if the cardiovascular diseases were eliminated, because the residual death rate would be reduced much more sharply.

It should be recognized that these figures have no *direct* implications for the future since complete elimination of the cardiovascular diseases or of cancer has not been projected or predicted. They mainly elucidate the current cause-pattern of mortality and hence may aid in planning current health programs.

Projections of Mortality and Population

Prospects for mortality reduction. A number of different approaches may be taken in projecting death rates for the United States. One is to extrapolate past trends in age-sex-race-cause specific death rates. Another is to consider the rates in more analytic terms, for example, in terms of the factors affecting specific causes of death (e.g., dietary habits, smoking practices). An even more analytical step is to take account of competing risks and joint causes of death. Guides for extrapolation may be derived from the experience of countries with the lowest death rates at each age and from available studies of the biological "limit" of mortality.

Historical and comparative international demographic analysis suggests only moderate reductions in death rates in the United States in the next several decades. There is little basis for anticipating major increases in life expectation in this period,[17] and it is visionary to anticipate any extension of human life span.[18] Life expectation at birth for Sweden ("best" single country) in 1974 and life expectation for a composite "country" derived from the lowest death rates at each age for various countries around 1974 are only 3 to 5 years greater than for the United States in 1974 (table 10). At present mortality levels, even major (percentage) declines in death rates would correspond to only moderate (per-

[17] Jean Bourgeois-Pichat, "Future Outlook for Mortality Decline in the World," unpublished paper presented at the meeting of the United Nations, Ad Hoc Group of Experts on Demographic Projections, New York, November 1977.
Nathan Keyfitz, "Cause of Death in Future Mortality," **Proceedings of the International Population Conference,** Vol. 1, pp. 483-503, International Union for the Scientific Study of the Population, Mexico City, Aug. 8-13, 1977.

[18] For a summary comment, see Bernice L. Neugarten, "The Future and the Young-Old," in Lissy F. Jarvik (ed.), **Aging into the 21st Century: Middle-Agers Today,** Gardner Press, Inc., New York, 1978.

Table 9. Gain in Life Expectancy from Eliminating Specified Causes of Death and Chance of Eventually Dying from These Causes: 1969 to 1971

Cause of death	Gain in life expectancy (in years)		Chance of eventually dying	
	At birth	At age 65	At birth	At age 65
Major cardiovascular-renal diseases	11.8	11.4	.588	.672
Diseases of the heart	5.9	5.1	.412	.460
Cerebrovascular diseases	1.2	1.2	.122	.149
Malignant neoplasms	2.5	1.4	.163	.145
Motor vehicle accidents	0.7	0.1	.020	.006
All other accidents	0.6	0.1	.026	.018
Influenza and pneumonia	0.5	0.2	.034	.037
Diabetes mellitus	0.2	0.2	.020	.021
Infective and parasitic diseases	0.2	0.1	.007	.005

[1] Including neoplasms of lymphatic and hematopoietic tissues.

Source: National Center for Health Statistics, (U.S. Public Health service), "U.S. Life Tables by Cause of Death: 1969-71," by T.N.E. Greville, U.S. Decennial Life Tables for 1969-71, Vol. 1, No. 5, 1976.

centage) increases in life expectancy.[19] For example, if present death rates at each age were reduced by half, life expectation at birth would rise by only about 15 percent, that is, from 73 years to about 84 years. In the light of the present age structure of mortality, if large (absolute) reductions are to occur in mortality at all they would have to be concentrated at the older ages since death rates at the younger ages are already quite low.

Demographic analysis also suggests no great convergence of male and female mortality or life expectancy in the United States in the near future.[20] When the U.S. values for 1974 are compared with the figures for Sweden in 1974 and the country composite for "1974", the U.S. figures are found to be much closer to the attained best levels for females than for males (table 10). The comparison suggests that the possibilities for improvement for males in the United States are greater than for females and that some

convergence of the values for males and females may be realized. This analysis also suggests that the male-female difference may have a substantial, irreducible minimum in post-industrial society.

As noted earlier, the present large difference presumably reflects both a biological advantage of women and the persistent, sizeable differentiation of the life styles, roles, and personal habits of the sexes. Even if men are afforded improved environmental "opportunities" or the environmental circumstances for females become more prejudicial to their health, a substantial difference in favor of women is expected to remain for several decades.

The projections of mortality incorporated in the Census Bureau's latest projections of population are adaptations of mortality projections prepared by the Social Security Administration that took explicit account of past trends in death rates for age, sex, and cause categories. They imply moderate reductions in death rates[21] and a modest increase in expectation of life at birth and at age 65 between 1976 and 2020. For the year 2020, the projected figure for average life expectancy for both sexes is 75.0 years, as compared with the

[19] Nathan Keyfitz and Antonio Golini, "Mortality Comparisons: The Male-Female Ratio," **Genus**, Vol. 31, No. 1-4, 1975, pp. 1-34; Keyfitz, "What Difference Would it Make if Cancer were Eradicated? An Examination of the Taeuber Paradox," **op. cit.**; Jacob S. Siegel and Edwin Fonner, Jr., "Effect of Changes in Age-Specific Death Rates on Life Expectancy," unpublished paper presented at the annual meeting of the American Public Health Association, Miami Beach, Florida, Oct. 17-19, 1976.

[20] Bourgeois-Pichat, **op. cit.**; George C. Myers, "Changing Mortality Patterns and Sex Imbalances among the Aged," unpublished paper presented at the 10th International Congress of Gerontology, Jerusalem, Israel, June 1975.

[21] Death rates were assumed to decline at different rates at different ages between 1976 and 2050. It is estimated that the average percent decline in age-specific death rates for this period was 17 percent. This figure was obtained as the difference between the age-adjusted death rates calculated on the complements of 5-year survival rates in 1976 and 2050.

Table 10. Recent and Projected Values for Life Expectancy at Birth and at Age 65 for the United States and Comparative International Values

Year	At birth				At age 65			
	Both sexes	Male	Female	Difference[1]	Both sexes	Male	Female	Difference[1]
1973[a].............	71.3	67.6	75.3	7.7	15.3	13.1	17.2	4.1
1974[b].............	71.9	68.2	75.9	7.7	15.6	13.4	17.5	4.1
1975[c].............	72.5	68.7	76.5	7.8	16.0	13.7	18.0	4.3
1976[d].............	72.8	69.0	76.7	7.7	16.0	13.7	18.0	4.3
PROJECTIONS[e]								
1976 (Base).............	73.1	69.1	77.0	7.9	16.0	13.8	18.4	4.6
2000.............	74.1	70.0	78.3	8.3	16.8	14.2	19.0	4.8
2020.............	75.0	70.7	79.4	8.7	17.2	14.5	19.8	5.3
2050.............	76.4	71.8	81.0	9.2	18.0	15.0	20.7	5.7
Best country composite, 1974..	76.6	73.8	79.4	5.6	17.4	15.5	18.8	3.3
Sweden, 1974.............	75.1	72.2	78.0	5.8	16.0	14.1	17.5	3.4
Difference, United States and best country composite, 1974.	-4.7	-5.6	-3.5	2.1	-1.8	-2.1	-1.3	0.8

[1]Excess of female over male value.

Sources:

   a. National Center for Health Statistics, "Final Mortality Statistics, 1973," Monthly Vital Statistics Report, Vol. 23, No. 11, Supplement (2), February 1975.
   b. National Center for Health Statistics, "Final Mortality Statistics, 1974," Monthly Vital Statistics Report, Vol. 24, No. 11, Supplement, February 1976.
   c. National Center for Health Statistics, "Final Mortality Statistics, 1975," Monthly Vital Statistics Report, Vol. 25, No. 11, Supplement, February 1977.
   d. National Center for Health Statistics, "Final Mortality Statistics, 1976," Monthly Vital Statistics Report, Vol. 26, No. 12, Supplement (2), March 30, 1978.
   e. U.S. Bureau of the Census, "Projections of the Population of the United States: 1977 to 2050," Current Population Reports, Series P-25, No. 704, July 1977, and unpublished data.

base estimate of 73.1 years in 1976 (table 10). For males separately, the life expectancy value set for 2020 is 70.7 years, as compared with 69.1 years for 1976. The corresponding figures for females are 79.4 and 77.0. These figures imply a modest continuation of the divergence between male and female death rates and life expectancies that has been observed so far in this century.

Evaluation of earlier official projections of mortality and the older population. In view of the widespread use of the Census Bureau's projections of the older population, it is useful to review the "accuracy" of past projections of the older population and the underlying projections of mortality. For this purpose the projections of the number of elderly persons for 1975 and 2000, included in the sets of projections published in the last 25 years or so by the Census Bureau, have been compared with the current estimate for 1975 and with the latest projections for the year 2000 (table 11).

The projections of the population 65 years and over for 1975 published at various dates from August 1953 to December 1972 varied from 20.7 million (August 1953 and October 1955) to 22.2 million (December 1972). These figures differed from the current estimate for 1975 (22.4 million) by 7.9 percent and 1.1 percent, respectively. In all cases the projections fell below the current estimate. One of the earliest projections in this series (November 1958) showed a relatively low deviation from the current estimate, 2.4 percent. Except for this figure, the percent deviation generally declined as the publication date approached 1975. The corresponding percent "errors" for the projections of the population 70 and over were generally similar or somewhat smaller. The differences between the past projections and the current estimate for 1975 represent a combination of the difference in the allowance for immigration and in the census counts for the adult population (the census counts being in error also) as well as in allowances for mortality.

There is presumably great interest now in the accuracy of the projections for the year 2000. We do not, of course, have current figures for evaluating the projections for this year, but we can examine the deviation of the projections published in July 1964 to October 1975 from the latest projection for 2000, 31.8 million, published in July 1977. All projections fell below the latest figure and generally

Table 11. Comparison of Estimates and Projections of Populations 65 Years and Over and 70 Years and Over: 1975 to 2000

(Numbers in thousands. Estimates and projections as of July 1)

Age group and projection	1975			2000		
	Population	Difference from current estimate		Population	Difference from latest projection[1]	
		Amount	Percent		Amount	Percent
65 YEARS AND OVER						
Current estimate[2]....................	22,420	(X)	(X)	(X)	(X)	(X)
Projections (P-25 report number and date of issue):[3]						
704 (July, 1977)...................	(X)	(X)	(X)	31,822	(X)	(X)
601 (Oct., 1975)...................	22,330	-90	-0.4	30,600	-1,222	-3.8
493 (Dec., 1972)...................	22,170	-250	-1.1	28,842	-2,980	-9.4
470 (Nov., 1971)...................	21,859	-561	-2.5	28,839	-2,983	-9.4
448 (Aug., 1970)...................	21,503	-917	-4.1	28,837	-2,985	-9.4
381 (Dec., 1967)...................	21,160	-1,260	-5.6	28,184	-3,638	-11.4
286 (July, 1964)...................	21,172	-1,248	-5.6	28,199	-3,623	-11.4
187 (Nov., 1958)...................	21,872	-548	-2.4	(NA)	(NA)	(NA)
123 (Oct., 1955)...................	20,665	-1,765	-7.9	(NA)	(NA)	(NA)
78 (Aug., 1953)...................	20,689	-1,731	-7.7	(NA)	(NA)	(NA)
70 AND OVER						
Current estimate[2]....................	14,319	(X)	(X)	(X)	(X)	(X)
Projections (P-25 report number and date of issue):[3]						
704 (July, 1977)...................	(X)	(X)	(X)	22,630	(X)	(X)
601 (Oct., 1975)...................	14,233	-86	-0.6	21,577	-1,053	-4.7
493 (Dec., 1972)...................	14,484	165	1.2	20,310	-2,320	-10.3
470 (Nov., 1971)...................	14,169	-150	-1.0	20,226	-2,404	-10.6
448 (Aug., 1970)...................	13,983	-336	-2.3	20,306	-2,324	-10.3
381 (Dec., 1967)...................	13,690	-629	-4.4	19,859	-2,771	-12.2
286 (July, 1964)...................	13,688	-631	-4.4	19,866	-2,764	-12.2
187 (Nov., 1958)...................	14,089	-230	-1.6	(NA)	(NA)	(NA)
123 (Oct., 1955)...................	13,117	-1,202	-8.4	(NA)	(NA)	(NA)
78 (Aug., 1953)...................	13,131	-1,188	-8.3	(NA)	(NA)	(NA)

X Not applicable.
NA Not available.

[1] Current Population Reports, Series P-25, No. 721, April 1978.
[2] Latest projection is 31,822,000, published in Current Population Reports, Series P-25, No. 704, July 1977.
[3] Base date may be a few months to one and a half years prior to publication date and final death statistics used may relate to a calendar year two to three years before the publication date.

the projections had to be revised upward when a new set of projections was prepared. The differences between the various projections and the 31.8 million varied from 4 percent to 11 percent. The projections approximated 28-29 million until 1975 and 30½ million in 1975, when the Census Bureau introduced a new set of mortality projections. The various projections for ages 70 and over in 2000 show a similar pattern of differences from the latest projection.

The latest projection of the population 65 and over for the year 2000 (31.8 million) is 4 percent greater than the last previous projection (30.6 million), and the latest projection of the population 65 and over for the year 2020 (45.1 million) is 5 percent greater (42.8 million). These differences reflect mainly the lower-than-anticipated mortality of the 1972-76 period and the use of more favorable mortality rates for future years.

Mortality trends are difficult to predict although they present a much smaller problem for projections of population than do projections of fertility trends. Employing a single assumption of regular small declines in mortality rates at the older ages is no longer a safe course to follow. Death rates may decline at different rates in successive periods or even rise, as they have in the last several decades and as fertility has done, although the reasonable bounds are much narrower for mortality than fertility in the short term. These new uncertainties suggest the desirability of making alternative assumptions regarding future mortality, as has been done for fertility.

Although it would be desirable to hit the future population on target, this is not to be expected. Happily, the kinds of errors in the projections of mortality that the Census Bureau has made are far smaller in their impact on population size and structure, and hence less problematic, than the kind of errors normally associated with projections of fertility, the young population, and even the total population. In spite of the errors in the mortality projections, the Census Bureau projections of the elderly population have tended to reflect the future size of this group, its fluctuations, and its rate of increase reasonably well. Policy formulation and administrative action based on the population numbers as projected would not be seriously prejudiced by their "errors".

The percentage of the population 65 and over projected today for the year 2000 is substantially higher than was projected for this group in past years. The principal reason for the earlier understatement of the percentage has been the failure to project fertility satisfactorily for the intervening period. If the lower fertility assumptions employed now for the year 2000 were combined with the earlier projections of the number of elderly persons, the resulting percentages of elderly persons for the year 2000 would be much closer to the latest projections of the percentage.

Alternative analytical and theoretical models of mortality. It is of value in understanding the possible influence of future changes in mortality on population size and structure to posit various alternative mortality assumptions, including some which are relatively unrealistic or even highly theoretical. The purpose of such an exercise is not primarily to make alternative predictions; it is to aid in elucidating the role of mortality declines as a factor affecting population size and structure. Such mortality series may also serve to measure the adequacy and "robustness" of the principal series of mortality projections. Four analytical or theoretical series of projections were developed for these purposes. They are:

1. Death rates of 1976 remain unchanged.
2. Death rates decline twice as rapidly between 1976 and 2050 as in Census Bureau projections.
3. Death rates of 1976 are reduced by one-half in 2050.
4. Death rates of 2050 are zero ("gradual immortality").

In all series, the death rates were derived for intermediate years by geometric interpolation. These death rates were combined with the three fertility assumptions and the single immigration assumption of the Census Bureau projections to derive new population projections. The effect of still different fertility, mortality, and net immigration assumptions (e.g., 300,000 net immigration per year) may be derived by interpolation of the appropriate population series or of the appropriate summary measures.

The first series provides an analytic (zero) base for measuring the number of lives saved by the improvement in death rates assumed in the various other series. Series (2) and (3), representing much more extreme assumptions than the Census Bureau series, are viewed as somewhat unrealistic. They are designed to evaluate the sensitivity of the population parameters to alternative mortality assumptions. The

fourth series, gradual immortality, aids in focusing on a possible trajectory of mortality and population change resulting from radical declines in mortality in the next several decades.

The effect of these alternative fertility and mortality assumptions on a range of measures bearing on the size and structure of the future elderly population in 2000 and 2020 has been examined. These measures are: The number of persons 65 and over and 75 and over and their percent increases, the proportion of persons 65 and over, the proportion of 75-year-olds among 65-year-olds, the numerical gap between the sexes, the relative number of elderly males and females, and so-called societal and familial aged dependency ratios. For several of these measures the choice of fertility assumption has no effect in the next half century, such as the number 65 and over, the number 75 and over, the male-female difference, the sex ratio of the population 65 and over, and the ratio of persons 65-79 to persons 45-49 (familial dependency ratio). For the proportion 65 and over and the ratio of persons 65 and over to persons 18-64 (societal dependency ratio), both the fertility assumption and the mortality assumption affect the measure. We focus particularly on the comparative variation resulting from the three different fertility series, on the one hand, and the Census Bureau series on mortality, the series doubling the Census Bureau rate of decline in death rates, and the series reducing the initial death rates by one-half in 2050, on the other.

The projected decline in death rates in the Census Bureau series added some 900,000 persons (3 percent) to the population 65 and over in the year 2000 and some 2.8 million (7 percent) in the year 2020 (table 12). As a result of the net immigration assumed, some 370,000 persons (1.2 percent) were added to the number in 2000 and 1.7 million persons (4 percent) were added in 2020. If the assumed decline in death rates were twice as rapid, the elderly population would be substantially larger at both dates; the additions to the Census Bureau projections would be 1.5 million in 2000 and 4.4 million in 2020. Reducing the current rates by half would add even more elderly persons.

The percent 65 and over would also be raised under the alternative mortality series, but the increases tend to be small. If death rates were assumed to decline twice as rapidly as originally, the percent would be 12.6 instead of 12.2 in 2000, and 16.5 instead of 15.5 in 2020, under the middle fertility series. The fertility assumption has a much greater effect on the percent 65 and over than the mortality assumption; the original projections for 2000 vary from 11.3 to 12.9. In fact, the effect of the immigration assumption is as great as the effect of the mortality assumption, albeit in the opposite direction.

Note, however, that lower mortality per se does not account for the higher percent of elderly; rather it is the secondary assumption that larger mortality declines, and hence larger increases in survival rates, will occur at the older ages, than at the younger ages. This assumed pattern of

Table 12. Parameters for the Elderly Population Under Alternative Fertility and Mortality Assumptions: 1976, 2000, and 2020

(Numbers in thousands)

Population parameter	1976	2000[2] Census[1] Bureau	2000[2] Mortality assumption Set 1	Set 2	Set 3	Set 4	2020[2] Census[1] Bureau	2020[2] Mortality assumption Set 1	Set 2	Set 3	Set 4
1) Population, 65 years and over.........	22,934	31,822	30,923	33,278	33,855	65,799	45,102	42,327	49,483	51,301	129,691
2) Percent increase over 1976............	(X)	38.8	34.8	45.1	47.6	186.9	96.7	84.6	115.8	123.7	465.5
3) Population, 75 years and over........	8,741	14,386	13,791	15,224	15,916	42,583	16,975	15,316	19,458	21,495	90,607
4) Percent increase over 1976............	(X)	64.6	57.8	74.2	82.1	387.2	94.2	75.2	112.6	145.9	936.6
PERCENT 65 AND OVER											
5) Series I (High).....................	10.7	11.3	11.0	11.6	11.9	20.1	12.7	12.1	13.6	14.1	28.3
6) Series II (Medium).................		12.2	11.9	12.6	12.9	21.6	15.5	14.8	16.5	17.2	33.0
7) Series III (Low)..................		12.9	12.7	13.3	13.6	22.8	17.8	17.0	18.9	19.6	36.6
8) Percent, 75 years and over / 65 years and over...........	38.1	45.2	44.6	45.7	47.0	64.7	37.6	36.2	39.3	41.9	69.9
9) Excess of females over males, 65 years and over....................	4,207	6,388	6,151	6,915	6,181	5,221	8,166	7,544	9,217	7,462	3,865
10) Sex ratio, 65 years and over.........	69.0	66.6	66.8	65.6	69.1	85.3	69.3	69.7	68.6	74.6	94.2
11) Ratio (per 100) 65 to 79 years / 45 to 49 years........	156.4	125.5	123.3	128.9	129.5	172.0	215.9	207.6	229.1	229.4	303.1
RATIO (PER 100) 65 YEARS AND OVER / 18 TO 64 YEARS											
12) Series I (High)..................	18.1	19.5	19.0	20.3	20.7	38.7	22.7	21.5	24.5	25.6	60.8
13) Series II (Medium).................		19.9	19.4	20.7	21.1	39.5	26.0	24.6	28.0	29.2	69.1
14) Series III (Low).................		20.2	19.7	21.0	21.5	40.1	28.6	27.1	30.8	32.2	75.7

X Not applicable.
[1]Current Population Reports, Series P-25, No. 704, July 1977.
[2]Set 1 Death rates of 1976 remain unchanged.
 Set 2 Death rates decline twice as rapidly between 1976 and 2050 as in latest Census Bureau projections.
 Set 3 Death rates of 1976 are reduced by one-half in 2050.
 Set 4 Death rates of 2050 are zero.

declines in mortality would result in larger percent increases in the population at the older ages than at the younger ages and, hence, a rise in the proportion of the population at the older ages.

Uniform *percentage* reductions in death rates, such as are implied in sets (3) and (4), consistently result in higher proportions of the elderly. They necessarily produce larger *absolute* decreases in death rates, and larger *percentage* increases in survival rates, at the older ages than at the younger ages. The rise in the proportion of the elderly would be reinforced by declining fertility. Under the assumption that death rates are cut in half by 2050, the percent over 65 would rise to 12 to 13½ (depending on the fertility assumption) in 2000 (as compared with the Census Bureau projection of 11½ to 13), and to 14 to 19½ in 2020 (as compared with the Census Bureau projection of 12½ to 18). Under an assumption of "gradual immortality" some 20 to 23 percent of the population would be over 65 in the year 2000; for 2020 the percents are higher and the range is wider, 28 to 37. It seems clear that the proportion of elderly persons in future years will not be greatly affected by the choice of mortality assumption, unless that assumption is a radical one, but that the choice of fertility assumption can have a significant effect.

The alternative assumptions on mortality have little effect on the proportion of 75-year-olds of all 65-year-olds in 2000, and only an extreme reduction in death rates (e.g., 50-percent reduction) would substantially change the proportion in 2020. The immigration assumption has practically no effect on this ratio.

The ratio of elderly persons to "working-age" persons would tend to be slightly higher with lower mortality rates. Mortality would share with fertility much of the influence in affecting the ratio in 2000, but would have relatively little effect in 2020. This shifting role of mortality is a result of the fact that the numerator of the ratio at both these dates is influenced only by the mortality level while the denominator is influenced by fertility in an increasing degree as time passes.

The excess of elderly females over elderly males is not seriously affected by the mortality assumption to 2000, but in the long run the pattern of declines in mortality by age and sex and the extent of the decline have a large effect on the size of the difference. Similarly the sex ratio of the elderly may fall or rise in the long run, depending on the age-sex pattern of the declines in death rates and the rate of decline.

In sum, reasonable alternative possibilities for declines in death rates (i.e., barring the most extreme assumptions), with allowance for alternative levels of fertility, do not substantially change the picture with regard to the parameters of the elderly population for the next 25 years, but may do so over a longer period, such as 40 to 50 years.[22]

SOME SOCIOECONOMIC IMPLICATIONS

The demographic changes mentioned have many important social and economic implications. I focus here on some of these, particularly those relating to the current and future requirements for health services.

Societal and Familial Aged Dependency Ratios

Societal dependency. The relative number of elderly persons (65 and over) and persons of the usual working ages (18 to 64), which roughly reflects the balance of elderly "dependents" to "producers", more than doubled between 1920 and 1960. The figure has been barely rising since then and is expected to continue increasing slowly in the next several decades (table 13). The ratio was 18 per 100 persons 18 to 64 in 1976; it may rise only slightly to 20 by 1990, where it may remain for a few decades, and then it would rise sharply (26 in 2020, Series II) as the postwar birth cohorts reach 65 years of age. This is the period when support of the elderly by public funds, whether secured as Social Security taxes or general revenue (both being disbursed as intergenerational transfers), may become a serious problem of public finance.

Familial dependency. The trend in the relative numbers of persons 65 to 79 and persons 45 to 49 can be used to illustrate roughly the prospective shifts in the ratio of elderly parents to the children who would "support" them. This measure increased sharply and steadily between 1920 and 1976, when there were 156 persons 65 to 79 per 100 persons 45 to 49. A peak will be reached in 1980 at 180, and again in the year 2020 with a still higher figure of 216. Thus, the ratio of the number of elderly persons to the number of younger persons of the next generation will become more favorable at times and less favorable at others, with the most rapid shift to an unfavorable balance occurring in the second decade of the next century.

The fluctuations in these familial dependency ratios reflect mainly past trends in the number of births, which have tended to move in a wavelike fashion in the last several decades. For example, the very high ratio in the year 2020 results from the combination of the relatively large (average annual) number of births in the postwar decade (population 65-74 years) and the small (average annual) number of births in the early seventies (population 45-49 years).

With declining or low fertility, elderly persons will have fewer brothers and sisters and fewer children than in the past to provide needed or desirable economic and psychological support. This will occur in spite of increasing survivorship of children and siblings. Past and prospective shifts in fertility, mortality, and age structure are obviously not the only factors affecting the problem of the support of the elderly, but the shifts in societal and familial dependency ratios suggest that the extent of the problem of familial and societal support of the aged will become greater at times than at present, and possibly serious after 2010.

There is the definite possibility of a condition of population stationarity (i.e., zero population growth) in the United States in the next 75 years resulting from recent and prospective low fertility. Such a stationary population will be characterized by a smaller proportion of elderly persons who have living relatives of the same or next generation, a higher proportion of elderly persons in the population, and a higher ratio of aged persons to persons of the usual working ages. This situation suggests that Government may be expected to play a bigger part in the support of the elderly, particularly in providing health and other services.[23]

Provision of Health Care

The demographic changes identified will mean that the needs of the elderly will account for larger and larger share of the health effort, resources, and budget. The aged are the largest users of health resources. They make more visits to physicians (per person) and use hospital facilities more frequently than any younger age group.[24] Given the great increase in the number of elderly persons expected in the next half century and assuming even the same per capita demand for health care for each age-sex group in the future as at present, the total demand for health care will tend to increase greatly. The expected rise in the proportion of elderly persons, reflecting the relatively more rapid increase in the number of elderly persons than of younger-age persons, will augment greatly the relative demand for health care on the part of

---

[22] Preston has also examined the possible changes in the U.S. population parameters with some extreme assumptions of declines in mortality in: Samuel H. Preston, **Mortality Patterns in National Populations**, New York, Academic Press, 1976, esp. Chapter 7. He shows that, if deaths due to cardiovascular diseases were immediately eliminated, the number and proportion of elderly people would increase sharply in the first few decades and then would continue to increase more slowly. Under conditions of replacement-level fertility, the proportion would reach about 25 percent in three-quarters of a century. The increase in the proportion of the elderly resulting from the elimination of cancer would be far less than the corresponding increase from the elimination of cardiovascular diseases. Elimination of any important cause, particularly cardiovascular diseases or cancer, would also tend to raise the sex ratio of the elderly. For example, the present sex ratio of 69 males to 100 females would rise by several points in a single decade if cardiovascular diseases were immediately eliminated.

[23] Ethel Shanas and Philip M. Hauser, "Zero Population Growth and the Family Life of Old People," **Journal of Social Issues**, Vol. 30, Number 4, 1974, pp. 79-91.

[24] U.S. Public Health Service, **Health, United States, 1976-77**, 1978, esp. chapter 1.

Table 13. Familial Aged Dependency Ratios and Societal Aged Dependency Ratios : 1920 to 2020

(Figures are shown for July 1 of the year indicated. Ratios for 1940 and later years include Armed Forces overseas)

Year	Population 65 to 79 years / Population 45 to 49 years	Population 65 years and over / Population 18 to 64 years
ESTIMATES		
1920.................................	0.76	.08
1930.................................	0.82	.09
1940.................................	0.95	.11
1950.................................	1.16	.13
1960.................................	1.29	.17
1970.................................	1.35	.17
1976.................................	1.56	.18
PROJECTIONS		
1980.................................	1.80	.18
1990.................................	1.68	.20
2000...................... II..		.20
Range............. { I..	1.25	.20
III..		.20
2010...................... II..		.20
Range............. { I..	1.27	.19
III..		.21
2020...................... II..		.26
Range............. { I..	2.16	.23
III..		.29

Source: U.S. Bureau of the Census, Census of Population, 1930, General Report, Vol. II, table 7, and Current Population Reports, Series P-25, Nos. 311, 519, 614, 643, and 704; unpublished data for age group 45-49 for years 2010 and 2020.

the elderly population in future years. The upward shift in the average age of the elderly, combined with the sharply increased demand for health care within the older age span, will add further to the increase in overall demand and to the elderly population's share.

We can anticipate increasing utilization of health care resources per capita among the elderly in part because of the expected increase in the educational and income level of the elderly and their increased participation in broad health insurance plans. A more educated and affluent population of prospective older patients will tend to seek more comprehensive health care services and advanced methods of treatment, resorting more often to specialists and use of specialized equipment.

The demand for mental health services may also be expected to rise sharply as a result of the effect of these same demographic factors. The incidence of emotional disorders rises with increasing age. Emotional disorders constitute an important factor accounting for a change in living arrangements (i.e., moving in with children, institutional care). They represent, therefore, an important share of the real total health care requirements of the elderly and the general population.

Given the relation of social isolation to emotional disorders and the prominence of emotional disorders among elderly persons, it may be possible to trace a logical nexus between the small family system (low fertility, "nucleation" of families, and "individuation" of households), a large male-female mortality gap, and high internal migration rates of younger relatives, on the one hand, and the prevalance of emotional disorders among the elderly, on the other. Of course, any such relation is reinforced by low income, loss of the work role, poor physical health, and limited ambulatoriness on the part of many elderly persons.

Issues Relating to Sex Differences in Mortality

The large sex difference in mortality has a considerable impact on many aspects of our social life. In addition to the fact that it results in a large excess of women at the older ages, it tends to produce a high rate of widowhood and paternal orphanhood, major economic losses to families and society, and loss of familial psychological and social support for the surviving women. Its ultimate price in life dissatisfactions are immense and incalculable.

In view of the considerable differences between the mortality levels of males and females and the tremendous demographic, social, and economic consequences that flow from these differences, it is essential that we try to understand better the relative etiological roles of genetic and environmental factors in producing the differences. More needs to be learned about those aspects of the behavior and genetic makeup of males that make them more vulnerable than females to serious illness. Are there, for example, male-female differences in recognizing the need for, seeking, and accepting medical care? The conduct of KAP (knowledge-attitude-practice) studies for mortality, as has been done for fertility, may help to provide an answer to this question. Can the physiological bases for the female advantage be more clearly identified?

Whether or not we can fully understand the underlying bases of the difference in · the mortality of the sexes, its great magnitude, its persistence, and its many and profound consequences justify a major assault on the problem. Imaginative and wide-ranging programs should be launched with the prevention of premature death of males as a specific goal. The goal of greater sex equality in length of life may be viewed as sufficiently important to call for a course of preferential treatment for men.

Other Issues Relating to Mortality

The same issues as just presented for male-female mortality differences may be considered in relation to Black-White differences *mutatis mutandis,* although here the differences are not as marked and have been declining over time, the disadvantage is not consistently in one direction over the age span, and the social consequences are not as profound. The issues here relate primarily to the substantial excess of the mortality of Blacks over Whites at the ages below about age 75.

Various bioethical and other nonmedical considerations are involved in decisions regarding the allocation of funds for health research and provision of health care to elderly people. In particular, there is a problem of making decisions about the allocation of limited resources where different applications will have different payoffs in lives ultimately saved. Available funds are always assigned on a discretionary basis to different public programs and, within the domain of health, to different programs for health prevention, maintenance, and treatment.[25]

One issue is whether it is more effective to allocate additional research funds for heart disease or cancer. One can begin to develop an answer to this question from available information. One should decide whether it is more desirable to maintain the life of very sick, extremely aged persons at all costs or to apply some of these funds for preventive purposes to younger adults. The latter course could, in the long run, be more effective in improving the average quality of life among the elderly and equalizing death rates of the sexes. For example, it might be more cost-effective (in terms of years of life added) to spend a larger share of community funds on mobile cardiac units, use of which might prevent the death of many middle-aged husbands and fathers, and less on drastic mechanical methods of life prolongation for extreme-aged persons who are already very seriously ill.

As increasing numbers of persons survive to the older ages and particularly as the proportion of older persons in the population increases, the relative frequency of persons with chronic, seriously debilitating conditions of later life, including incurable and intractable conditions, will increase. This development suggests the need for more widespread confrontation of the complex bioethical issues relating to "life with dignity" and the "right to die" and for exploration of these concepts in relation to the general issue of basic human rights.

---

[25] Victor R. Fuchs, **Who Shall Live? Health, Economics, and Social Change,** Basic Books, New York, 1974; Steven E. Rhoades, "How Much Should We Spend to Save a LIfe?" **The Public Interest,** No. 51, Spring 1978, pp. 74-92.

Editor's note: The following paragraph and footnote appeared on the first page of the original.

For convenience and simplicity, in the present discussion the age range 65 and over as a whole is employed as the principal basis for identifying and describing the elderly population. Although as a group the elderly population is markedly different in its demographic and socioeconomic characteristics from the population at the younger ages, it is not a homogenous group, and various age segments within it should be considered separately in any detailed analysis of the characteristics of the group. If we compare the population 85 and over with the population 65 to 74, for example, we find many sharp differences with respect to such characteristics as living arrangements, marital status, work status, income, education, health, kinship support, and use of leisure time.[1]

---

[1] For a more comprehensive treatment of this subject, see U.S. Bureau of the Census, "Demographic Aspects of Aging and the Older Population in the United States," by Jacob S. Siegel, **Current Population Reports,** Series P-23, No. 59 (rev.), May 1976.

A Demographic Profile of the Black Elderly

Robert Hill*

Aging, Nos. 287-288 (September-October 1978). U.S. Department of Health, Education, and Welfare, Administration on Aging.

Almost a decade ago, in 1970, the National Urban League assessed the socio-economic status of the black elderly.[1] Unfortunately, the main conclusion of that analysis was that the status of the black aged had not significantly improved in the 10 years since the pioneering study, *Double Jeopardy* had been issued.[2] How much has the social and economic situation of the black aged improved since 1970? To what extent have the disparities between elderly blacks and whites narrowed or widened in such areas as housing, income, education, health, and employment opportunities?

Population Size

Since 1970, the elderly black population has been increasing more than twice as fast as the overall black population. While the total black population increased by 11 percent, the number of blacks 65 and over increased by 25 percent— from 1.6 million to 1.9 million—raising the proportion of elderly persons in the total black population from 7 to 8 percent.[3]

Although the elderly white population had a somewhat smaller rate of increase (17 percent) than the elderly black population, it was much

This article was prepared with invaluable assistance from Esther Piovia, Research Associate and Joan Dupigny, Administrative Secretary in the National Urban League Research Department.

*Dr. Hill, who received his Ph.D. from Columbia University, is Director of Research at the National Urban Institute in Washington D.C. He has written a number of works relating to the black elderly including "Informal Adoption Among Black Families" and a "Profile of the Black Aged." Dr. Hill is a member of the National Caucus on the Black Aged and formerly served on the U.S. Senate Special Subcommittee on Aging and Aged Blacks.

greater than the 5 percent increase in the white population as a whole. Thus, the 21 million white persons 65 years and over in 1977 made up 11 percent of the total white population, compared to 18 million or 10 percent in 1970. About 60 percent of all elderly persons today, whether black or white, are women—the same proportion as in 1970.

Urbanization

There has been a sharp shift in the elderly black population from rural to metropolitan areas. Between 1970 and 1977, the proportion of all blacks 65 and over who lived in metropolitan areas jumped from 58 percent to 66 percent, while the proportion of elderly whites who lived in metropolitan areas edged up from 61 to 62 percent.

Well over half (55 percent) of all the black aged in 1977 lived in the central cities of the metropolitan areas, compared to only 29 percent of all the white aged. In 1970, a somewhat higher proportion (32 percent) of the white aged lived in central cities, compared to less than half (47 percent) of the black aged. Clearly, the white elderly have been moving to the suburbs, while the black elderly are moving to the central cities. One-third of all whites 65 and over live in suburban areas today, compared to only 11 percent of all black elderly. Thus, only one-third of all the black elderly now live in non-metropolitan or rural areas, compared to 38 percent of all the white elderly.[4]

Educational Attainment

The educational gap between elderly blacks and whites has narrowed among black men. In

1970, while only 8 percent of elderly black males had graduated from high school, 27 percent—or about three and a half times as many elderly white males—had finished high school. But by 1977, the proportion of elderly white males who had finished high school (38 percent) was only about two and a half times higher than the proportion of elderly black males completing high school (16 percent).

On the other hand, the gap between the educational levels of elderly black and white women has widened somewhat. The proportion of elderly white women completing high school in 1970 (31 percent) was three times higher than the proportion of high school graduates among elderly black women (10 percent). But by 1977, the proportion of high school graduates among elderly white women rose to 41 percent—well over three times the proportion (14 percent) among elderly black women.[5]

Marital Status

The proportion of elderly men living with their wives has increased among both blacks and whites. In 1970, 55 percent of elderly black men were living with their spouses, compared to 70 percent of elderly white men. But by 1977, almost three-fifths (57 percent) of all elderly black men lived with their wives, compared to almost four-fifths (76 percent) of all elderly white men.[6]

At the same time, the proportion of elderly men who were widowers declined, especially among blacks. While the proportion of widowed elderly white men declined from 17 to 13 percent between 1970 and 1977, the proportion of elderly black men who were widowed fell sharply from one-third to one-fourth. But the proportion of elderly black men who were separated or divorced increased from 8 to 14 percent between 1970 and 1977, while the proportion of separated and divorced elderly white men remained unchanged at 5 percent.

Because of their longer life spans, elderly women are much more likely than elderly men to be widowed. But even this group has declined among older women, especially blacks. While the proportion of elderly white women who were widowed edged down from 54 to 51 percent between 1970 and 1977, the proportion of widowed elderly black women plummeted from 67 to 58 percent. This decline among the widowed has resulted in an increase in the proportion of elderly women living with their husbands—from 22 to 28 percent among blacks and from 35 to 38 percent among whites. Clearly,

these findings suggest that the life spans of both men and women among black and white elderly have increased. How much in fact have they risen?

Life Expectancy

Since 1970, blacks have narrowed the life expectancy gap with whites by at least one full year. In 1970, white men were expected to live to 68.0 years from birth, while black men were expected to live only 61.3 years—a gap of 6.7 years. But by 1976, white men had a life expectancy of 69.7 years, compared to a life expectancy at birth of 64.1 years among black men—a gap of 5.6 years.[7]

A similar closing of the life expectancy gap occurred among black and white women. In 1970, white women had a life expectancy of 75.6 years at birth while the life expectancy for black women was 69.4 years—6.2 years lower. By 1976, white women were expected to live to 77.3 years, compared to 72.6 years for black women—a gap of 4.7 years.

Of course, among those reaching the age of 65, the life expectancies of both blacks and whites have traditionally been quite close. But even that gap has virtually closed. In 1969-71, the life expectancy of white men at age 65 was only slightly more (13.0 years) than the life expectancy of elderly black men (12.8), and by 1976, the life expectancies of elderly black and white men were even closer—13.7 years for whites and 13.8 years for blacks.

Similarly, while the life expectancy of white women at age 65 in 1969-71 was a full year higher (16.9 years) than the life expectancy (15.9 years) for elderly black women, this gap closed in half by 1976 between elderly white women (18.1 years) and elderly black women (17.6 years).

Family Composition

Some 69 percent of the 695,000 black families headed by persons 65 and over in 1977 were headed by men, compared to 88 percent of the 7.4 million elderly white families. In 1970, the proportion of male-headed elderly families among blacks and whites were 69 percent and 85 percent, respectively.

However, about 600,000 elderly blacks in 1977 were living alone or with nonrelatives compared to 6.4 million elderly whites. Two-thirds of the elderly blacks living alone were women, compared to four-fifths of the elderly whites living alone. The proportions of elderly women living alone in 1976 were not significantly different from the proportions living alone among elderly blacks (66 percent) and whites (76 percent) in 1970.

But one major difference between the composition of elderly black and white families remains: black families are much more likely than white families to have young children in them. This is especially true for elderly families headed by black women.

Two-fifths of all black families headed by women 65 and over had children under 18 years living with them, compared to only one-tenth of families headed by elderly white women. Similarly, while only 4 percent of white husband-wife families with heads 65 years and over had dependent children living with them, more than five times as many (22 percent) of elderly black two-parent families had dependent children living with them.[8] The majority of these children were grandchildren or children of other relatives.

The extended family pattern of providing informal foster care and adoption services to children continues to be widely prevalent among elderly black families, especially those headed by women. Consequently, while social service programs based on the presumption that the child-rearing responsibilities of the elderly are no longer operative may be applicable for most elderly white families, they are clearly not applicable for a sizable proportion of elderly black families, which vitally need quality child care services.[9]

It should be emphasized, however, that because of their desire to be as self-reliant as possible, black elderly are much more likely to take others into their households rather than permit themselves to be taken into the households of younger relatives. Among black families headed by persons under 65 in 1976, only 3 percent of the husband-wife families and 4 percent of the female-headed families had persons 65 and over living with them. Interestingly, white families are just as likely as black families to take elderly persons into their households. Among white families headed by persons under 65 in 1976, 3 percent of the husband-wife families and 7 percent of the female-headed families had elderly persons living with them.

Housing

A major reason that so many black elderly are able to take others into their families is because the overwhelming majority of them are homeowners. In 1977, 70 percent of all black families headed by elderly persons owned their homes, compared to 84 percent of all white families with elderly heads. Among the 31 percent of elderly black families who lived in rental units, only 6 percent lived in public housing and less than 1 percent lived in subsidized units.[10]

Even the majority of elderly black families who are poor own their homes and are least likely to live in public housing or subsidized rental units. About three-fifths of poor black families headed by elderly persons in 1977 owned their homes, while only 37 percent lived in rental units. Among poor elderly blacks 9 percent lived in public housing, while less than 1 percent lived in subsidized rental units. Somewhat similar patterns of residence held for poor white elderly families as well.

While the majority of elderly blacks living in families are homeowners, the overwhelming majority of elderly black persons living alone are renters. In 1977, 65 percent of elderly black men living alone and 51 percent of elderly black women living alone were renters. Those black elderly living alone were much more likely to live in public housing than those living in families. About one-fifth of the black elderly women who lived alone lived in public housing (19 percent), while a tenth of black elderly men who lived alone were in public housing (10 percent).

Amount of Income

The income of elderly blacks improved significantly during the 1970's, narrowing the income gap with elderly whites. Between 1969 and 1976, the median income of elderly husband-wife black families increased 105 percent (from $3,154 to $6,457), while the median income of elderly husband-wife families among whites increased 84 percent (from $4,827 to $8,902). Thus, the ratio of black to white income among husband-wife elderly families rose from 65 percent to 73 percent over that seven-year period.[11]

A more significant narrowing of the income gap occurred between black and white families headed by elderly females. While the median income of elderly families headed by white women increased 66 percent between 1969 and 1976, the median income of elderly families headed by black women rose 91 percent. Consequently, the black to white income ratio among families headed by women jumped from 44 to 51 percent.

But this improvement in the income status of elderly blacks was not confined to those living in families. Even among the elderly who lived alone, the median income of black men increased 120 percent (from $1,321 to $2,900) between 1969 and 1976, compared to an increase of 82 percent (from $2,336 to $4,245) among white males. But among elderly women living alone, the increase in income over this seven-year period was about the same for blacks (95 percent, from $1,263 to $2,547) and whites (90 percent, from $1,838 to $3,497). Thus, while the income ratio between elderly black and white women living alone remained unchanged at about 70 percent, the black to white income ratio among elderly males rose from 57 percent to 68 percent.

One reason for the disproportionate improvement in the economic status of elderly blacks is that their incomes were so abysmally low in 1969. And, despite this progress, the income of the average elderly black female-headed family today is only half that of the average elderly white female-headed family. Whether they are living in husband-wife families or alone, the incomes of elderly black men and women are only two-thirds that of their white counterparts.

Most important, however, is the fact that the median income of elderly black families is significantly below the *lowest* budget level that the government has defined as providing a minimum standard of living. In 1976, for example, the Bureau of Labor Statistics' lower budget standard for a retired couple was $4,695. Only 17 percent of elderly white couples had incomes below that level, compared to 37 percent of elderly black couples. Thus, poverty still characterizes elderly blacks disproportionately more than elderly whites. But what have been the recent poverty trends among elderly blacks and whites?[12]

Poverty

The extent of poverty dropped sharply during the 1970's among elderly blacks as well as whites. While the proportion of elderly whites who were poor fell from 23 to 12 percent between 1969 and 1977, the proportion of poor elderly blacks similarly fell from 50 percent to 36 percent. However, this sharp drop in poverty among the elderly did not occur among the rest of the black and white populations. In fact, the proportion of poor persons among all blacks remained essentially unchanged (from 32 to 31 percent) between 1969 and 1976, while the proportion of poor persons among all whites remained at about 9 percent over that seven-year interval.[13]

This decline in poverty occurred among elderly blacks living in central cities as well as those living in rural areas. Between 1969 and 1976, the rate of poverty among elderly blacks living in central cities decreased from 39 to 29 percent, while the poverty rate for elderly blacks living in nonmetropolitan areas fell sharply from 66 to 45 percent. Similar declines in poverty rates occurred among elderly whites living in metropolitan and nonmetropolitan areas.

But, once again, no such decline in poverty occurred among the rest of the blacks living in central cities. In fact, the proportion of all blacks living in central cities who were poor rose from 25 to 31 percent between 1969 and 1976. However, there was a significant decline in poverty among all blacks living in nonmetropolitan or rural areas (from 52 to 38 percent) over that period.

Consequently, it appears that the income supports provided to elderly blacks during the 1970's have been much more effective in improving their economic condition than have been the income supports to the rest of the black population. But what are the different sources of income for elderly blacks?[14]

Sources of Income

The overwhelming majority of elderly black families, whether headed by men or women, receive social security income. In 1976, 91 percent of the black families headed by elderly men and 85 percent of the black families headed by elderly women had income from social security benefits. The proportion of elderly white families receiving social security was somewhat higher among men (92 percent) and women (93 percent).

Earnings were the second most frequent source of income among elderly black families. While 57 percent of the black families headed by elderly women had income from earnings, 59 percent of the black families headed by elderly men had earnings income. About half (46 percent) of white families headed by elderly men had earnings income, compared to 60 percent of the white families headed by elderly women.

Female-headed black families were much more likely than male-headed black families to receive Supplemental Security Income (SSI)— the replacement for the former welfare program for the aged, Old Age Assistance. While only one-fifth of the black families headed by elderly men had income from SSI, twice as many (44 percent) black families headed by elderly women were SSI recipients. The proportions of elderly white families receiving SSI were much smaller among those headed by men (5 percent) and women (14 percent). Since elderly blacks were much more likely than elderly whites to have worked in occupations that were not covered by social security, they obviously have a greater need to supplement their minimal social security benefits with earnings or SSI.

On the other hand, significantly higher proportions of elderly white families than elderly black families received income from dividends, interest, or private pensions. For example, while only one-sixth of all elderly black families received income from dividends, interest, or rent in 1976, over two-thirds of the elderly white families had income from these sources. Similarly, while the proportions of elderly black families receiving income from private or government employee pensions were 21 percent among those headed by men and 16 percent among those headed by women, the proportions of elderly white families receiving income from such pensions were 43 percent among those headed by men and 32 percent among those headed by women.

Although almost all elderly blacks living alone received social security income, they were more likely than elderly whites to depend on SSI as their second major source of income. About 87 percent of the elderly black women living alone received social security, 39 percent received SSI payments, and 15 percent had earnings income. Among elderly black men living alone, the proportions receiving social security, SSI, and earnings were 87 percent, 28 percent, and 27 percent, respectively.

However, among elderly whites living alone, dividends and pensions were the second and third major sources of income, while very few depended on SSI. The proportions of elderly white males living alone who received income from social security, dividends, private pensions, earnings, and SSI were 90 percent, 52 percent, 33 percent, 21 percent, and 12 percent, respectively. Among elderly white women living alone, the comparable proportions receiving such income were 91 percent, 60 percent, 25 percent, 16 percent, and 11 percent.

In short, the three major sources of income for elderly blacks, whether living alone or in families, are social security, earnings, and SSI. But the three major sources of income for elderly whites living in families are social security, dividends, and earnings, while the top three sources of income for elderly whites living alone are social security, dividends, and pensions.

Employment Status

Since earnings are the second major source of

income for most elderly blacks, it is important to assess the nature and extent of their participation in the labor force.

During 1977, one-fifth (19.3 percent) of elderly black men and one-tenth (9.9 percent) of elderly black women were in the labor force. This was a decline from a labor force participation rate of 27.4 percent among elderly black men and 12.2 percent among elderly black women in 1970.

Elderly whites have similar levels of labor force participation as blacks. Between 1970 and 1977, while the labor force participation rates among elderly white men declined from 26.7 to 20.2 percent, the participation rates of elderly white women fell from 9.5 to 8.0 percent.[15]

Although elderly whites and blacks are about as likely to enter the labor force seeking work, their chances of obtaining employment vary significantly. While elderly black men have much higher unemployment rates than elderly white men, elderly black women have much lower jobless rates than elderly white women.

Elderly white men had an unemployment rate of 4.9 percent in 1977, but the jobless rate for elderly black men was 8.3 percent. While the jobless rate for elderly white women was also 4.9 percent in 1977, the unemployment rate for elderly black women was only 3.6 percent. Of course, the jobless rates among women in their pre-retirement years are higher for blacks than whites. Although these patterns of unemployment between elderly blacks and whites have held throughout the 1970's, their jobless rates were only about half as high at the beginning of this decade prior to the two recessions.[16]

Standard of Living

It should not be inferred that the significant improvement in the economic status of elderly blacks since 1970 means that their current income is adequate for such basic necessities as food, shelter, and clothing. On the contrary, several indepth studies have shown that the record-level inflation in this nation has disproportionately affected the elderly, especially minorities, to a much greater extent than the rest of the population because of their more relatively fixed incomes. The black elderly, in particular, pay a disproportionate share of their income for rent, utilities, and spiraling food prices.[17]

Moreover, contrary to popular belief, most elderly blacks do not receive some of the benefits of government programs that are supposed to be targeted to economically disadvantaged groups.

For example, three-fourths of poor elderly blacks living alone do not live in either subsidized or public housing. During the peak of the 1975 recession, only one-fifth of all elderly black couples and one-fourth of all elderly blacks living alone purchased food stamps, compared to 3 percent of all elderly white couples and 6 percent of all elderly whites living alone.[18] The majority of elderly blacks do not benefit from Medicare coverage because they cannot afford the payments,[19] and over half of all poor elderly blacks, whether living alone or in families, do not receive any Supplemental Security Income.[20] It should, therefore, be no surprise that over one-third of all elderly black couples have incomes below the government's lower budget level for maintaining a minimum standard of living. Consequently, the issue of income inadequacy continues to be the major area of concern among elderly blacks—and whites.

Conclusions

The social and economic status of elderly blacks today is significantly better than it was a decade ago. Between 1970 and 1975, the life expectancy of blacks increased by almost three years and the gap with whites narrowed by at least one year. Thus, there has been a sharp decline in the proportion of elderly blacks who are widowed.

Elderly blacks continue to provide vital informal foster care, adoption, and day care services to black children through the extended family network. However, there is some evidence that it has become increasingly difficult for elderly blacks to assume such responsibilities because of spiraling inflation and insensitive social policies. For example, despite the fact that the overwhelming majority of black working women depend on elderly relatives for day care services, current income tax regulations continue to exclude day care credits and deductions for sizable numbers of children who are cared for by their grandparents. No such exclusions prevail for children being cared for by non-relatives. Such policies serve to weaken and not strengthen the strong kinship bonds in many families—both black and white.[21]

Finally, although the economic gap between most elderly blacks and whites has narrowed since 1970, the incomes of elderly blacks are only two-thirds of the incomes of their white counterparts. Over one-third of all elderly black couples have incomes below the government's lower budget living standard. And because of the unrelenting, record-level inflation, elderly blacks pay disproportionate shares of their income for food, shelter, and other basic necessities. Consequently, although elderly blacks have made significant strides, they still have a long way to go in achieving an equitable and adequate quality of life.

REFERENCES

[1] Robert B. Hill, "A Profile of Black Aged," in *Minority Aged in America*, Institute of Gerontology, The University of Michigan-Wayne State University, Ann Arbor, 1972, pp. 35-50.

[2] National Urban League, *Double Jeopardy*, New York, 1964; Inabel Lindsay, *Multiple Hazards of Age and Race: The Situation of Aged Blacks in the U.S.*, a report for the U.S. Senate Special Committee on Aging, Nov. 12, 1971.

[3] The recent population figures were derived from the U.S. Bureau of the Census, *Current Population Reports*, "Estimates of the Population of the U.S. by Age, Sex and Race: 1970 to 1977," Series P.-25, No. 721, 1978.

[4] The recent data on the urbanization of the black elderly were derived from U.S. Bureau of the Census, *Current Population Reports*, "Characteristics of the Population Below the Poverty Level: 1976," Series P-60, No. 115, 1978.

[5] The educational attainment data were derived from U.S. Bureau of the Census, *Current Population Reports*, Ibid.

[6] The marital status data were derived from U.S. Bureau of the Census, *Current Population Reports*, "Marital Status and Living Arrangements, March 1977," Series P-20, No. 323, 1978.

[7] The life expectancy data were derived from U.S. Public Health Service, National Center for Health Statistics, *Monthly Vital Statistics Report*, Vol. 26, No. 12, Supplement (2), "Final Mortality Statistics, 1976," 1978.

[8] The family composition data were derived from U.S. Bureau of the Census, *Current Population Reports*, "Household and Family Characteristics, March 1976," Series P-20, No. 311, 1977.

[9] For an indepth analysis of the role of the child-rearing functions performed by elderly blacks in the extended families, see Robert B. Hill, *Informal Adoption Among Black Families*, Washington, D.C. Also see an excellent analysis of black extended families in Carol Stack, *All Our Kin: Strategies for Survival in A Black Community*, New York: Harper and Row, 1974.

[10] The housing data were derived from U.S. Bureau of the Census, *Current Population Reports*, "Characteristics of the Population Below the Poverty Level: 1976," Series P-60, No. 115, Table 24.

[11] The income data were derived from U.S. Bureau of the Census, *Current Population Reports*, "Money Income in 1976 of Familes and Persons in the U.S.," Series P-20, No. 114, 1978.

[12] A more detailed description of the Bureau of Labor Statistics' three budget levels for retired couples can be found in U.S. Labor Department, Bureau of Labor Statistics, *Three Budgets for a Retired Couple, Autumn 1976*, USDL 77-690.

[13] The poverty data were derived from U.S. Bureau of the Census, Series P-60, No. 115, *op. cit.*, and No. 116, "Money Income and Poverty Status of Families and Persons in the U.S.: 1977 (Advance Report)," 1978.

[14] See Robert B. Hill, "The Myth of Income Cushions During the 1974-75 Depression," *Urban League Review*, Vol. 2, No. 1 (Winter 1976), p. 53.

[15] The labor force data were derived from U.S. Department of Labor *Employment and Training Report of the President, 1977* and *Employment and Earnings, January 1978*.

[16] See also National Urban League Research Department, *NUL Quarterly Economic Report on the Black Worker*, Washington, D.C., 1978.

[17] See Robert B. Hill, *Inflation and the Black Consumer*, Washington, D.C., NUL Research Department, 1974; and David Caplovitz, *Making Ends Meet: How Families Cope With Inflation and Recession*, New York: Institute for Research on Human Affairs, The Graduate School and University Center, City University of New York, January 1978.

[18] See U.S. Bureau of the Census, *Current Population Reports*, "Characteristics of Households Purchasing Food Stamps," Series P-23, No. 61, 1976.

[19] According to the HEW Medicare Survey Report for 1972, over half (53 percent) of the nonwhites enrolled in Supplementary Medical Insurance (SMI) either received no services or were not able to meet the deductible. See Social Security Administration, Office of Research and Statistics, *Health Insurance Statistics*, "Current Medicare Report: Supplementary Medical Insurance—Utilization and Changes, 1972," Publication No. (SSA) 75-11702, September 30, 1975.

[20] See U.S. Bureau of the Census, Series P-60, No. 115, *op. cit.*

[21] See testimony by Robert B. Hill on "Tax Credits for Child Care Services by Relatives," before the U.S. Senate Finance Committee, June 19, 1978.

Perspective on American Husbands and Wives
Excerpts

U.S. Bureau of the Census, Department of Commerce, 1978.

Median Age at First Marriage, by Sex: 1890 to 1977

Year	Male[1]	Female	Year	Male[1]	Female
1977	24.0	21.6	1958	22.6	20.2
1976	23.8	21.3	1957	22.6	20.3
1975	23.5	21.1	1956	22.5	20.1
1974	23.1	21.1	1955	22.6	20.2
1973	23.2	21.0	1954	23.0	20.3
1972	23.3	20.9	1953	22.8	20.2
1971	23.1	20.9	1952	23.0	20.2
1970	23.2	20.8	1951	22.9	20.4
1969	23.2	20.8	1950	22.8	20.3
1968	23.1	20.8	1949	22.7	20.3
1967	23.1	20.6	1948	23.3	20.4
1966	22.8	20.5			
1965	22.8	20.6	1947	23.7	20.5
1964	23.1	20.5	1940	24.3	21.5
1963	22.8	20.5	1930	24.3	21.3
1962	22.7	20.3	1920	24.6	21.2
1961	22.8	20.3	1910	25.1	21.6
1960	22.8	20.3	1900	25.9	21.9
1959	22.5	20.2	1890	26.1	22.0

[1]Figures for 1947 to 1977 are based on Current Population Survey data supplemented by data from the Department of Defense on marital status by age for men in the Armed Forces. Figures for earlier dates are from decennial censuses.

Percent Distribution of Husbands and Wives, by Age: March 1977

Age	Husbands	Wives
Total.......(thousands)..	48,002	48,002
Percent...............	100.0	100.0
14 to 34 years.................	30.4	36.6
35 to 44 years.................	19.4	19.4
45 to 64 years.................	36.1	34.0
65 years and over.............	14.1	10.0
Median age...........(years)..	45.1	41.9

Age of Wife, by Age of Husband: March 1977

(For meaning of symbols, see text)

Husbands and wives, by age of husband	All couples		Age of wife					
	Number (thousands)	Percent	14 to 24 years	25 to 34 years	35 to 44 years	45 to 54 years	55 to 64 years	65 years and over
Husbands, all ages..............	48,002	100.0	11.4	25.2	19.4	19.2	14.8	10.0
14 to 24 years........................	3,257	100.0	91.0	8.8	0.2	-	-	-
25 to 34 years........................	11,339	100.0	21.2	75.4	3.1	0.2	-	-
35 to 44 years........................	9,323	100.0	1.0	31.6	62.9	4.2	0.2	-
45 to 54 years........................	9,460	100.0	0.2	2.9	29.6	61.7	5.4	0.2
55 to 64 years........................	7,846	100.0	0.1	0.4	3.2	34.6	56.6	5.1
65 years and over.....................	6,777	100.0	-	0.2	0.5	3.6	31.2	64.6
Wives, all ages.....(thousands)..	48,002	(X)	5,486	12,101	9,312	9,214	7,093	4,797
Percent.......................	...	100.0	100.0	100.0	100.0	100.0	100.0	100.0
Age of husband:								
14 to 24 years........................	...	6.8	54.0	2.4	0.1	-	-	-
25 to 34 years........................	...	23.6	43.7	70.7	3.8	0.3	-	-
35 to 44 years........................	...	19.4	1.7	24.3	63.0	4.3	0.3	-
45 to 54 years........................	...	19.7	0.3	2.2	30.1	63.3	7.2	0.5
55 to 64 years........................	...	16.3	0.1	0.3	2.7	29.5	62.6	8.3
65 years and over.....................	...	14.1	-	0.1	0.3	2.6	29.8	91.2

Difference Between Ages of Husband and Wife, by Age: March 1977

Age	All couples		Husband older					Same age	Husband younger
	Number (thousands)	Percent	10 years or more	5 to 9 years	3 or 4 years	2 years	1 year		
PERCENT DISTRIBUTION									
Age of Husband:									
All ages...........	48,002	100.0	7.2	19.6	20.2	13.2	13.2	12.1	14.4
Under 35 years...........	14,594	100.0	1.1	11.4	20.6	16.3	18.4	16.8	15.5
35 to 44 years...........	9,324	100.0	5.6	20.6	22.2	14.2	12.9	11.3	13.2
45 to 54 years...........	9,459	100.0	8.2	21.7	19.5	11.8	11.5	11.4	15.8
55 to 59 years...........	4,226	100.0	9.0	25.0	20.1	11.9	11.1	9.1	13.8
60 and 61 years...........	1,523	100.0	10.5	21.3	23.4	10.8	9.1	9.3	15.6
62 to 64 years...........	2,097	100.0	11.9	24.8	17.9	12.4	9.2	8.7	15.1
65 to 69 years...........	2,845	100.0	13.2	27.1	19.3	9.0	8.5	9.0	13.8
70 years and over........	3,933	100.0	21.5	28.3	16.9	8.7	8.0	7.0	9.7
Age of wife:									
All ages...........	48,002	100.0	7.2	19.6	20.2	13.2	13.2	12.1	14.4
Under 35 years...........	17,587	100.0	5.8	16.5	21.5	15.3	16.4	13.9	10.6
35 to 44 years...........	9,312	100.0	8.3	21.6	21.1	13.0	12.1	11.3	12.6
45 to 54 years...........	9,214	100.0	8.0	22.1	19.3	12.3	11.6	11.7	15.0
55 to 59 years...........	4,044	100.0	8.9	21.4	20.0	11.0	11.3	9.5	17.9
60 and 61 years...........	1,289	100.0	8.7	23.0	18.5	13.7	9.8	11.1	15.3
62 to 64 years...........	1,760	100.0	8.5	22.2	19.0	10.5	9.5	10.4	20.0
65 to 69 years...........	2,366	100.0	7.7	19.7	17.5	10.0	10.8	10.8	23.6
70 years and over........	2,431	100.0	5.3	18.8	16.5	10.8	10.9	11.4	26.3

Education of Husband 45 Years Old and Over, by Education of Wife: March 1977

Husband and wives, by education of husband	Total		Education of wife					
			Elementary	High school		College		
	Number (thousands)	Percent	0 to 8 years	1 to 3 years	4 years	1 to 3 years	4 years	5 years or more
Husbands, 45 years old and over	24,084	100.0	21.1	17.5	42.1	10.8	5.9	2.6
Elementary:								
0 to 8 years.....................	7,008	100.0	52.0	21.5	22.0	3.2	0.9	0.3
High school:								
1 to 3 years....................	3,897	100.0	16.4	35.4	40.8	5.5	1.4	0.4
4 years........................	7,181	100.0	8.5	13.6	62.6	10.3	3.6	1.4
College:								
1 to 3 years....................	2,631	100.0	5.0	8.8	50.9	24.1	8.4	2.9
4 years........................	1,835	100.0	2.0	4.0	40.1	24.3	23.4	6.3
5 years or more................	1,532	100.0	0.7	2.7	28.2	22.7	26.4	19.3

Earning Status of Husbands and Wives, by Mobility and Age: March 1977

Subject	All married-couple families	Husband and wife only earners	Husband only earner	Wife only earner
Total[1]........(thousands)..	47,497	17,278	12,204	1,699
Percent...................	100.0	36.4	25.7	3.6
MOBILITY				
Percent...................	100.0	100.0	100.0	100.0
Nonmovers........................	73.9	62.7	73.4	70.0
Movers...........................	26.1	37.3	26.6	30.0
Same county.....................	14.9	22.8	14.6	11.1
Same State......................	5.6	8.3	6.1	3.6
Different State.................	4.7	5.6	4.8	10.0
Other...........................	1.0	0.6	1.0	5.2
AGE OF SPOUSES				
Percent...................	100.0	100.0	100.0	100.0
Both 14 to 24 years.............	5.9	10.8	5.1	8.6
Husband only....................	0.6	1.1	0.6	1.0
Both 25 to 34 years.............	17.8	28.1	24.9	12.5
Husband only....................	5.7	9.6	6.2	4.7
Both 35 to 44 years.............	12.3	10.5	10.5	4.8
Husband only....................	7.2	9.6	9.6	4.1
Both 45 to 54 years.............	12.2	9.1	8.8	5.8
Husband only....................	7.6	5.5	6.4	3.2
Both 55 to 64 years.............	9.3	7.3	11.7	12.3
Husband only....................	7.1	4.9	7.3	10.0
Both 65 years and over..........	9.1	1.1	5.8	11.2
Husband only....................	5.0	2.4	3.0	21.7

[1]Includes 16,307,000 families not shown separately.

Family Size and Presence of Children for Married-Couple Families, by Joint Age Level of the Husband and Wife: March 1977

Size of family and presence of children	All married-couple families	Age of both husband and wife				
		14 to 24 or 25 to 34 years	35 to 44 years	45 to 54 years	55 to 64 years	65 years and over
Total..............(thousands)..	47,497	11,279	5,844	5,810	4,422	4,319
Percent.......................	100.0	100.0	100.0	100.0	100.0	100.0
SIZE OF FAMILY						
2 persons.............................	36.2	26.9	5.4	28.1	65.8	86.9
3 persons.............................	21.2	26.0	12.4	27.8	22.0	9.4
4 persons.............................	21.6	30.4	31.9	20.7	7.6	2.3
5 persons.............................	11.7	11.8	25.1	12.3	2.6	0.7
6 persons.............................	5.3	3.5	13.5	6.1	1.2	0.5
7 or more persons.....................	4.0	1.4	11.6	5.0	0.7	0.2
Average per family...................	3.42	3.40	4.66	3.61	2.57	2.22
PRESENCE AND AGE OF CHILDREN						
No children under 18 years.............	47.6	27.8	9.7	53.4	92.3	99.6
Some under 18 years....................	52.4	72.2	90.3	46.6	7.7	0.4
All under 6 years....................	12.5	34.7	2.6	0.3	-	-
Some under 6, some 6 to 17...........	10.9	22.4	16.2	1.3	0.1	-
All 6 to 17 years....................	28.9	15.1	71.5	45.1	7.6	0.4
Average number of children under 18:						
Per family..........................	1.06	1.36	2.24	0.76	0.10	0.01
Per family with children.............	2.02	1.88	2.48	1.63	1.26	1.37

Metropolitan-Nonmetropolitan Residence and Mobility of Married-Couple Families, by Joint Age Level of the Husband and Wife: March 1977

Residence and mobility	All married-couple families	Age of both husband and wife				
		14 to 24 or 25 to 34 years	35 to 44 years	45 to 54 years	55 to 64 years	65 years and over
Total..............(thousands)..	47,497	11,279	5,844	5,810	4,422	4,319
Percent.......................	100.0	100.0	100.0	100.0	100.0	100.0
RESIDENCE						
Metropolitan areas.....................	65.8	65.9	66.3	69.6	66.9	60.1
Nonmetropolitan areas..................	34.2	34.1	33.7	30.4	33.1	39.9
MOBILITY						
Nonmovers.............................	73.9	48.2	81.6	88.3	90.5	93.4
Movers................................	26.1	51.8	18.4	11.7	9.5	6.6
Same county..........................	14.9	29.9	9.6	6.7	4.6	3.7
Same State...........................	5.6	11.1	3.5	2.8	2.7	1.4
Different State......................	4.7	8.9	4.3	1.9	1.9	1.4
Other................................	1.0	1.9	1.0	0.3	0.2	0.1

Labor Force Status and Participation Rates of Wives, by Age and Presence of Own Children: March 1977

(Numbers in thousands)

Presence of own children and age of wife	All wives	In labor force		Not in labor force		Labor force partici- pation rate
		Number	Percent	Number	Percent	
Total wives[1]......................	47,984	22,377	100.0	25,607	100.0	46.6
16 to 24 years.........................	5,467	3,181	14.2	2,286	8.9	58.2
25 to 34 years.........................	12,101	6,315	28.2	5,787	22.6	52.2
35 to 44 years.........................	9,312	5,212	23.3	4,100	16.0	56.0
45 to 54 years.........................	9,214	4,773	21.3	4,440	17.3	51.8
55 years and over......................	11,890	2,896	12.9	8,994	35.1	24.4
Wives with no own children under 18 years[1].................	22,886	10,268	45.9	12,618	49.3	44.9
16 to 24 years.........................	2,584	1,988	8.9	596	2.3	76.9
25 to 34 years.........................	2,139	1,744	7.8	395	1.5	81.5
35 to 44 years.........................	1,420	915	4.1	505	2.0	64.5
45 to 54 years.........................	5,384	2,883	12.9	2,501	9.8	53.5
55 years and over......................	11,359	2,738	12.2	8,621	33.7	24.1
Wives with own children under 18 years[1].................	25,098	12,109	54.1	12,989	50.7	48.2
16 to 24 years.........................	2,883	1,193	5.3	1,690	6.6	41.4
25 to 34 years.........................	9,962	4,570	20.4	5,392	21.1	45.9
35 to 44 years.........................	7,892	4,297	19.2	3,595	14.0	54.4
45 to 54 years.........................	3,830	1,891	8.5	1,939	7.6	49.4
55 years and over......................	531	158	0.7	373	1.5	29.8

[1] Includes wives 16 years old and over.

Labor Force Status and Participation Rates of Wives, by Presence and Age of Own Children: March 1977

(Numbers in thousands)

Presence and age of own children	All wives	In labor force		Not in labor force		Labor force partici- pation rate
		Number	Percent	Number	Percent	
Total[1].........................	47,984	22,377	100.0	25,607	100.0	46.6
None under 18 years....................	22,886	10,268	45.9	12,618	49.3	44.9
Some under 18 years....................	25,098	12,109	54.1	12,989	50.7	48.2
All 6 to 17 years......................	13,800	7,674	34.3	6,126	23.9	55.6
All 14 to 17 years...................	3,924	2,247	10.0	1,677	6.5	57.3
All 6 to 13 years....................	5,313	2,842	12.7	2,471	9.6	53.5
Some 6 to 13 years, some 14 to 17 years...........................	4,563	2,584	11.5	1,979	7.7	56.6
Some 6 to 17 years, some under 6 years.	5,217	1,989	8.9	3,228	12.6	38.1
All under 6 years.....................	6,081	2,446	10.9	3,635	14.2	40.2
All 3 to 5 years....................	1,448	752	3.4	696	2.7	51.9
All under 3 years...................	3,053	1,210	5.4	1,844	7.2	39.6
Some 3 to 5 years, some under 3 years	1,580	485	2.2	1,096	4.3	30.7

[1] Includes wives age 16 years and over.

Education of Wife, by Education of Husband 45 Years Old and Over: March 1977

Education of wife	Total		Education of husband					
			Elementary	High school		College		
	Number (thousands)	Percent	0 to 8 years	1 to 3 years	4 years	1 to 3 years	4 years	5 years or more
All wives, husband 45 years old and over...............	24,084	100.0	29.1	16.2	29.8	10.9	7.6	6.4
Elementary:								
0 to 8 years.....................	5,079	100.0	71.7	12.6	12.1	2.6	0.7	0.2
High school:								
1 to 3 years....................	4,211	100.0	35.8	32.8	23.2	5.5	1.7	1.0
4 years.........................	10,135	100.0	15.2	15.7	44.4	13.2	7.3	4.3
College:								
1 to 3 years....................	2,608	100.0	8.7	8.2	28.4	24.3	17.1	13.3
4 years.........................	1,427	100.0	4.4	3.7	17.9	15.6	30.1	28.3
5 years or more.................	624	100.0	3.7	2.6	16.0	12.0	18.6	47.3

Labor Force Participation and Family Income for Married-Couple Families, by Joint Age Level of the Husband and Wife: March 1977

Labor force participation and family income	All married-couple families	Age of both husband and wife				
		14 to 24 or 25 to 34 years	35 to 44 years	45 to 54 years	55 to 64 years	65 years and over
Total..............(thousands)..	47,497	11,279	5,844	5,810	4,422	4,319
Percent......................	100.0	100.0	100.0	100.0	100.0	100.0
LABOR FORCE PARTICIPATION						
In Labor Force.......................						
Husband and wife.....................	42.2	50.6	54.1	50.0	31.0	2.9
Husband only.........................	38.5	42.8	41.5	43.5	43.8	13.4
Wife only............................	4.5	3.1	2.1	3.0	7.3	3.6
Neither spouse.......................	14.9	3.5	2.3	3.6	17.9	80.1
FAMILY INCOME						
Under $2,000.........................	1.0	1.0	1.0	1.0	1.3	1.1
$2,000 to $4,999.....................	5.3	3.3	1.9	1.9	5.1	18.8
$5,000 to $9,999.....................	17.4	17.9	8.0	8.4	17.0	42.8
$10,000 to $14,999...................	20.6	26.3	15.8	15.3	18.8	18.2
$15,000 to $19,999...................	20.8	25.7	23.8	19.6	20.2	8.7
$20,000 to $24,999...................	14.5	14.1	20.5	18.1	14.3	4.4
$25,000 to $49,999...................	18.1	11.1	25.5	31.6	19.9	5.0
$50,000 and over.....................	2.2	0.6	3.5	4.2	3.5	1.0
Median income...............(dollars)..	$16,013	$15,285	$19,878	$20,837	$16,543	$7,660

Major Pension and Retirement Programs
Life Expectancy

Life Insurance Fact Book 1978, American Council of Life Insurance, Washington, D.C.

It is estimated that at the end of 1977 over 50 million American workers were participants in major private and public pension and retirement programs other than Social Security.

About 43 million persons were members of private nongovernment plans. This includes both active workers and those presently retired, along with survivors and beneficiaries. There is some duplication, which may be significant but is unknown, as a result of a worker being covered by more than one plan. It is not possible to eliminate statistical duplication in or between the two major categories — those persons under plans with insurance companies and those under private plans administered by trustees, trust companies or banks.

Government-administered plans, including those for Federal civilian employees, state and local government employees and railroad workers, involved over 18 million persons at year-end 1977. This figure also includes some persons counted more than once who are covered by more than one plan, either private or some other government plan.

The Railroad Retirement System is unique in being a private system covering a single industry, but administered by the Federal government. The system is now actually a part of the Social Security program. It covers some 1.6 million persons. Figures for the railroad employees and the beneficiaries are separately maintained and generally are carried as a separate item under government-administered plans.

About 153 million persons had OASDI (Social Security) earnings credits at the end of 1977. Of these, 128 million had been in the Social Security program long enough to have fully insured status as of year-end 1977.

Nearly one-half of all workers in commerce and industry in the United States, and close to three-fourths of all government civilian personnel, are enrolled in retirement plans other than Social Security. Included are those enrolled in profit-sharing plans which provide for periodic benefits at retirement. This compares with fewer than one-fifth of all employees in commerce and industry and fewer than one-half of all government workers in 1940.

Retirement plans have an important effect on two major areas of American social and economic life:

1. They provide appreciable amounts of income to many retired workers and their dependents. As benefit payments and the number of retired workers receiving benefits have increased, private plans have shown the greatest gains.

In 1977, private plans paid some $14.1 billion to about 8.1 million persons who had retired because of age, length of service or disability, or to their beneficiaries. Of these benefits, private pension plans with life insurance companies paid $3.1 billion to 2.1 million persons. Government-administered retirement plans for civilian employees in the United States, including railroad plans, paid a total of $20.8 billion in benefits to 4.8 million retired persons or their beneficiaries. Of this amount, the Federal civilian

Number of Persons Covered by
Major Pension and Retirement Programs
in the United States *(000 Omitted)*

Year	Private Plans		Government-Administered Plans			
	With Life Insurance Companies	Other Private Plans	Railroad Retirement	Federal Civilian Employees†	State and Local Employees	OASDI‡
1940	695	3,565	1,349	745	1,552	27,622
1945	1,470	5,240	1,846	2,928	2,008	40,488
1950	2,755	7,500	1,881	1,873	2,894	44,477
1955	4,105	12,290	1,876	2,333	3,927	64,161
1960	5,475	17,540	1,654	2,707	5,160	73,845
1961	5,635	18,440	1,662	2,855	5,309	76,295
1962	5,770	19,370	1,643	2,943	5,654	78,953
1963	6,060	19,990	1,664	2,985	5,940	81,035
1964	6,710	20,350	1,650	3,069	6,330	83,400
1965	7,040	21,060	1,661	3,114	6,780	87,267
1966	7,835	21,710	1,666	3,322	7,210	91,768
1967	8,700	22,330	1,641	3,499	7,594	93,607
1968	9,155	22,910	1,625	3,565	8,012	95,862
1969	9,920	24,410	1,620	3,627	8,303	98,012
1970	10,580	25,520	1,633	3,625	8,591	98,935
1971	10,880	26,580	1,578	3,596	9,079	100,392
1972	11,545	27,400	1,575	3,737	9,563	103,976
1973	12,485	28,700	1,582	4,030	10,050	108,268
1974	13,335	29,240	1,589	4,052	10,835	108,854
1975	15,195	30,300	1,574	4,130	11,230	110,085
1976	16,985	31,400*	1,565	4,184	12,000*	113,724
1977	19,240	32,500*	1,572*	4,288*	12,500*	117,482

Note 1. It is not possible to obtain a total for number of persons covered by pension plans by adding together the figures shown by year. Each series has been derived separately and there are differences in amount of duplication within each series and among the various series and also differences in definition of "coverage" among the series. In addition, private plans with life insurance companies include persons covered by Keogh plans, tax-sheltered annuities and, after 1974, IRA plans, but other private plans do not include persons covered by these plans.

Note 2. These data represent various dates during the year, since the fiscal years of the plans are not necessarily the same. Trends from year to year within each series are not affected. The number of persons covered include survivors or dependents of deceased workers and beneficiaries as well as retired workers. Retirement arrangements for members of the armed forces, and provisions for veterans pensions, are not included. Persons covered by private plans and many persons covered by government-administered plans are also usually covered by Social Security. Data for "Other Private Plans", compiled by the Social Security Administration, exclude plans for the self-employed, those having vested benefits but not presently employed at the firm where benefits were accrued, and also exclude an estimated number who have vested benefits from employment other than from their current employment.

*Estimated.

†Includes members of the U.S. Civil Service Retirement System, the Tennessee Valley Retirement System, the Foreign Service Retirement System, and the Retirement System of the Federal Reserve Banks, which includes the Bank Plan and the Board of Governors' Plan.

‡Includes persons employed with coverage in effect at year-end including the self-employed, workers retired for age or disability, dependents of retired workers and survivors of deceased workers who are receiving periodic benefits.

Source: Compiled by the American Council of Life Insurance.

employee plans paid $9.7 billion, state and local government employee plans paid $7.3 billion, and the Railroad System paid $3.8 billion.

Social Security (OASDI) benefits paid to retired workers including those on disability amounted to $57.8 billion. There were 20.8 million such persons on the rolls at year-end, along with 13.3 million dependents and survivors. Just under $27 billion in benefits were paid in 1977 under OASDI to survivors and dependents. The majority of workers receiving benefits from private plans or government-administered plans also received OASDI payments.

2. As a result of the rapid accumulation of pension plan assets and reserves, pension funds have come to be a considerable source of capital for the nation's financial markets. At the end of 1977, the assets of all pension programs in the United States (including OASDI) amounted to over $504 billion.

Federal pension legislation enacted in 1974 was concerned with private plans, and various provisions became effective at different times. Under one provision, individual retirement accounts (IRAs) may be established by workers employed where there is no private retirement plan. The Pension Benefit Guarantee Corporation came into existence in 1975, and is now in full operation.

Old-Age, Survivors, and Disability Insurance *(000 Omitted)*

Year	Persons With Earnings Credits Year-End*	Persons Employed With Coverage in Effect Year-End	Employer and Worker Taxes in Year	Persons Fully Insured Year-End†	Persons Receiving Monthly Benefits Year-End	Monthly and Lump Sum Payments in Year
1945	72,400	39,200	$ 1,285,486	33,400	1,288	$ 273,885
1950	82,700	41,000	2,667,077	59,800	3,478	961,094
1955	98,600	56,200	5,713,045	70,500	7,960	4,968,155
1960	109,400	59,000	11,876,220	84,400	14,844	11,244,795
1965	121,300	66,400	17,205,372	94,800	20,867	18,310,676
1966	125,000	69,000	22,585,229	97,200	22,767	20,048,347
1967	127,900	69,900	25,423,792	99,900	23,707	21,406,455
1968	130,800	71,300	27,034,289	102,600	24,562	24,936,435
1969	133,500	72,700	31,545,608	105,400	25,314	26,750,841
1970	135,900	72,700	34,737,059	108,200	26,229	31,863,381
1971	138,200	73,100	38,342,721	110,600	27,291	37,170,726
1972	140,600	75,500	42,888,228	113,200	28,476	41,595,064
1973	142,900	78,100	51,907,100	116,400	29,868	51,459,310
1974	145,200	79,300	58,906,577	119,800	30,854	58,521,344
1975	148,300	78,300	64,259,394	122,800	32,085	66,922,707
1976	150,900	80,700	71,594,624	126,400	33,024	75,664,649
1977	153,000	83,400	78,710,397	128,200	34,082	84,575,800

Note: Data are revised.

*Social Security Administration estimate of persons who have ever had covered earnings.

†Beginning in 1965, figures include transitionally insured persons. Data represent number insured at beginning of following year.

Source: Social Security Administration, U.S. Department of Health, Education and Welfare. Data pertaining to the "Medicare" program are not included in this table. Data for 1977 pertaining to coverage and insured status are estimated.

Social Security. Social Security is financed through taxes to provide payments to those who have retired, but it also helps families whose breadwinners die or become disabled.

A total of $78.7 billion in OASDI taxes (not including those for Medicare) was paid in 1977, including $37.7 billion by employers, $37.4 billion by employees and $3.6 billion by self-employed persons. For 1977, payments from OASDI amounted to $84.6 billion. Combined assets of the OASDI trust funds totaled $35.9 billion at year-end 1977.

Private Pension Plans with Life Insurance Companies

The number of Americans covered by pension plans with life insurance companies totaled 19.2 million at year-end 1977, an increase of 2.3 million over last year. This figure includes retired people receiving pension benefits, those who have left employment with vested pension credits, and those still actively at work. There is some duplication due to persons being covered under more than one plan.

Pension reserves behind plans with life companies at year-end totaled $101.0 billion, an increase of 14% over year-end 1976, and more than three times greater than 10 years ago. These reserves include the funds behind pension plan variable annuities, which are based wholly or in part on equity investments.

Group annuities cover the largest number of people under pension plans with life insurance companies. The traditional type is the deferred group annuity, under which a paid-up annuity is purchased each year for each employee, with the sum of these benefits paid as monthly income upon retirement. Deposit administration type plans set up a single fund for all employees in the pension group; money is withdrawn to buy an annuity for an employee when he retires. Immediate participation guarantee plans are a variation of this type, with participation in gains or losses from mortality and investments as they occur, rather than being spread over the life of the contract.

Under terminal funded plans, reserves are usually not set up with the insurance company until the employee is about to retire. Funding for the prospective pension prior to retirement may be handled in a variety of ways.

Individual policy pension trusts, group permanent plans, and profit-sharing plans — often used by smaller firms — were in effect for 1.9 million persons. Individual policy pension trusts usually involve the purchase of a whole life or endowment policy for each person to provide retirement benefits. Group permanent plans use whole life or endowment policies on a group basis keyed to retirement. Profit-sharing plans generally provide for an individual fund for each participant annually.

In September 1974, comprehensive Federal pension legislation, the Employee Retirement Income Security Act of 1974 (ERISA), was signed into law. This law relates primarily to private pension and welfare plans, and various sections of the law became effective at different times. One important section which became effective in 1975 allowed individuals to set up their own Individual Retirement Accounts (IRAs) if there was no private pension plan where they work. Contributions and accruals are tax free until retirement, with limits set on the annual amount of contributions and penalties set for early withdrawals. Funding of these individual plans can be handled in a variety of ways, one being through contracts with life insurance companies, generally annuities or endowments. By year-end 1977, 935,000 persons had set up such plans with life insurance companies, and the average reserve per person was about $2,000. The maximum annual contribution allowed was 15% of salary or wage or $1,500, whichever was less. Beginning in 1977, a nonemployed spouse could be covered, with the maximum IRA contribution rising to $1,750.

Another provision of ERISA liberalized Keogh plans, increasing the maximum amount that self-employed persons could set aside for themselves and their employees

Relative Growth in Life Insurance Companies' Pension Reserves in the United States

350 Index   1967 = 100

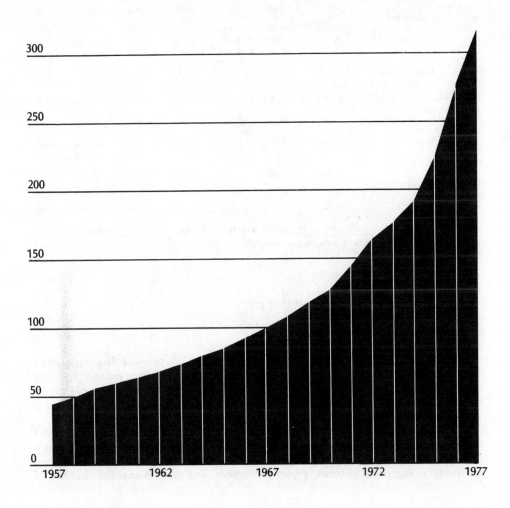

Private Pension Plans in the United States with Life Insurance Companies

Type of Plan	Number of Plans	Number of Persons Covered	Total Reserves Including Separate Accounts (000,000 Omitted)	Separate Account Reserves (000,000 Omitted)	Payments into Plans in Year (000,000 Omitted)	Number of Persons Receiving Payments	Pension Payments (000,000 Omitted)
			In Force at Year End			**Pension Payments during Year**	
			1975				
Group Annuities†	54,090	10,545,000	$ 54,625	$10,900	$ 6,735	1,440,000	$2,160
Terminal Funded Group Plans	3,250	145,000	1,950	60	340	85,000	110
Individual Policy Pension Trusts‡	176,410	1,960,000	5,550	440	1,075	100,000	140
HR 10 (Keogh) Plans	N.A.	450,000	1,300	150	345	10,000	10
Tax-Sheltered Annuities	N.A.	935,000	3,150	790	750	20,000	35
Individual Retirement Accounts	N.A.	440,000	375	40	355	*	**
Other Plans	N.A.	720,000	4,750	140	650	60,000	65
Total	—	15,195,000	$ 71,700	$12,520	$10,250	1,715,000	$2,520
			1976				
Group Annuities†	63,820	11,810,000	$ 67,275	$13,310	$10,195	1,640,000	$2,315
Terminal Funded Group Plans	3,700	165,000	2,500	60	540	100,000	145
Individual Policy Pension Trusts‡	187,530	1,975,000	5,975	620	1,120	120,000	155
HR 10 (Keogh) Plans	N.A.	460,000	1,650	210	435	10,000	15
Tax-Sheltered Annuities	N.A.	1,105,000	4,300	1,070	880	20,000	30
Individual Retirement Accounts	N.A.	685,000	1,125	60	755	*	**
Other Plans	N.A.	785,000	5,575	240	790	70,000	75
Total	—	16,985,000	$ 88,400	$15,570	$14,715	1,960,000	$2,735
			1977				
Group Annuities†	64,340	13,825,000	$ 76,650	$14,170	N.A.	1,770,000	$2,620
Terminal Funded Group Plans	3,970	170,000	2,800	60	N.A.	95,000	175
Individual Policy Pension Trusts‡	190,040	1,855,000	6,225	640	$ 1,205	105,000	145
HR 10 (Keogh) Plans	N.A.	465,000	1,950	220	420	10,000	25
Tax-Sheltered Annuities	N.A.	1,210,000	5,150	1,070	1,030	30,000	55
Individual Retirement Accounts	N.A.	935,000	1,875	70	980	*	5
Other Plans	N.A.	780,000	6,350	230	920	70,000	80
Total	—	19,240,000	$101,025	$16,460	—	2,080,000	$3,105

Note: 1976 data are revised. 1977 data are preliminary.

N.A.—Not available.

*Fewer than 5,000.

**Less than $2,500,000.

†Includes Immediate Participation Guarantee and Deposit Administration plans.

‡Includes Group Permanent plans and profit-sharing plans.

Source: American Council of Life Insurance.

— from $2,500 to $7,500 — so long as this did not exceed 15% of salary. The response to this action can be seen in the increase since 1974 in the number of persons covered under these plans and in the reserves held for them. Tax-sheltered annuities, permitted for use primarily in the academic community and nonprofit organizations, have also shown increases.

In 1977, payments of $3.1 billion were made under life company pension plans to 2.1 million persons. Of this amount, $2.8 billion was paid to 1.9 million persons with group annuity and terminal funded plans, and $310 million to 215,000 persons having individual policy pension trusts, group permanent, and other plans. The number of persons receiving payments has more than doubled in the past 10 years, and the total annual payments are more than three times as large.

Legislation in most states allows life insurance companies to maintain separate investment accounts for a given pension plan or group of plans. More latitude in equity investments is permitted for separate accounts than for life insurance company investments generally. Pension reserves in separate accounts were $16.5 billion at the end of 1977, an increase of 6% over last year. Some of the increase is attributable to increases in the valuation of securities, primarily common stocks, in these accounts.

LIFE EXPECTANCY

The average length of a person's life in the United States has increased by more than 50% during this century.

Most of the improvement in life expectancy took place during the first half of the century. Little change has occurred since the mid-1950s. Between 1900 and 1955, life expectancy increased by 22.3 years, but since 1955, it has increased by only 3.2 years to 72.8 years in 1976.

But while this century's advances in medicine, public health and safety have added to people's lives, the benefits have not been distributed equally. By far the largest increase in life expectancy has been among the newborn as a result of sharp reductions in mortality among infants and young children. Increases in life expectancy have been progressively smaller at older ages, and smaller for men than for women at all ages.

The measure of life expectancy results from the calculation of the average number of years of life that remain to a group of persons now at the same age, based on a particular mortality table. The measurement refers to the entire group and cannot be taken to indicate how long a particular individual may expect to live.

The gain in life expectancy for women since the turn of the century has been greater than for men at nearly all ages. Female life expectancy at birth has increased by 28.4 years since 1900, while male life expectancy has increased by 22.7 years. The difference in the average length of life between men and women has increased. Life expectancy at age 40 was about 1.4 years longer for a woman than for a man at the turn of the century; it is now 6.3 years longer.

Expectation of Life
at Birth in the United States (Years)

Year	White			All Other			Total		
	Male	Female	Total	Male	Female	Total	Male	Female	Total
1900	46.6	48.7	47.6	32.5	33.5	33.0	46.3	48.3	47.3
1910	48.6	52.0	50.3	33.8	37.5	35.6	48.4	51.8	50.0
1920	54.4	55.6	54.9	45.5	45.2	45.3	53.6	54.6	54.1
1930	59.7	63.5	61.4	47.3	49.2	48.1	58.1	61.6	59.7
1940	62.1	66.6	64.2	51.5	54.9	53.1	60.8	65.2	62.9
1950	66.5	72.2	69.1	59.1	62.9	60.8	65.6	71.1	68.2
1960	67.4	74.1	70.6	61.1	66.3	63.6	66.6	73.1	69.7
1961	67.8	74.5	71.0	61.9	67.0	64.4	67.0	73.6	70.2
1962	67.6	74.4	70.9	61.5	66.8	64.1	66.8	73.4	70.0
1963	67.5	74.4	70.8	60.9	66.5	63.6	66.6	73.4	69.9
1964	67.7	74.6	71.0	61.1	67.2	64.1	66.9	73.7	70.2
1965	67.6	74.7	71.0	61.1	67.4	64.1	66.8	73.7	70.2
1966	67.6	74.7	71.0	60.7	67.4	64.0	66.7	73.8	70.1
1967	67.8	75.1	71.3	61.1	68.2	64.6	67.0	74.2	70.5
1968	67.5	74.9	71.1	60.1	67.5	63.7	66.6	74.0	70.2
1969	67.8	75.1	71.3	60.5	68.4	64.3	66.8	74.3	70.4
1970	68.0	75.6	71.7	61.3	69.4	65.3	67.1	74.8	70.9
1971	68.3	75.8	72.0	61.6	69.7	65.6	67.4	75.0	71.1
1972	68.3	75.9	72.0	61.5	69.9	65.6	67.4	75.1	71.1
1973	68.4	76.1	72.2	61.9	70.1	65.9	67.6	75.3	71.3
1974	68.9	76.6	72.7	62.9	71.2	67.0	68.2	75.9	71.9
1975	69.4	77.2	73.2	63.6	72.3	67.9	68.7	76.5	72.5
1976	69.7	77.3	73.5	64.1	72.6	68.3	69.0	76.7	72.8

Source: National Center for Health Statistics, U.S. Department of Health, Education and Welfare.

In contrast, the difference in life expectancy between white and nonwhite Americans has been greatly reduced in this century. Generally, the gain for nonwhite males has exceeded that for white males at all ages. Nonwhite females showed the greatest gains at the younger and older ages. For white females, life expectancy improved most between the ages of about 45 and 65.

In 1976, the difference in life expectancy between white and nonwhite persons at birth was 4.7 years for females and 5.6 years for males, and this difference decreased with age.

Expectation of Life at Various Ages in the United States 1976

Age	White		All Other		Total	
	Male	Female	Male	Female	Male	Female
0- 1	69.7	77.3	64.1	72.6	69.0	76.7
1- 5	69.8	77.2	64.9	73.3	69.2	76.7
5-10	66.0	73.4	61.1	69.5	65.4	72.9
10-15	61.1	68.5	56.3	64.6	60.5	68.0
15-20	56.2	63.6	51.4	59.7	55.7	63.1
20-25	56.1	58.7	46.8	54.9	51.0	58.2
25-30	47.1	53.9	42.5	50.2	46.5	53.4
30-35	42.4	49.1	38.2	45.5	41.9	48.6
35-40	37.7	44.2	34.0	40.9	37.3	43.8
40-45	33.1	39.5	30.0	36.4	32.8	39.1
45-50	28.7	34.9	26.1	32.1	28.4	34.5
50-55	24.4	30.4	22.5	28.0	24.2	30.1
55-60	20.5	26.1	19.2	24.3	20.4	25.8
60-65	16.9	22.0	16.3	20.7	16.8	21.8
65-70	13.7	18.1	13.8	17.6	13.7	18.0
70-75	10.9	14.4	11.3	14.3	10.9	14.4
75-80	8.5	11.2	9.7	12.3	8.6	11.2
80-85	6.6	8.5	8.6	10.9	6.8	8.7
85 and Over	5.1	6.4	7.2	9.1	5.3	6.6

Source: National Center for Health Statistics, U.S. Department of Health, Education and Welfare.

Expectation of Life at Various Ages in the United States 1976

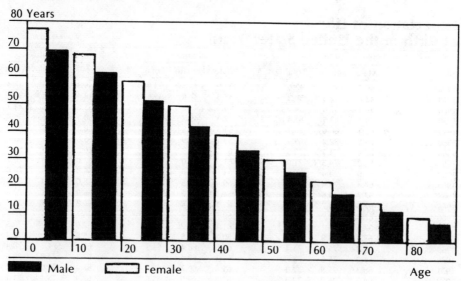

CAUSES OF DEATH

In recent decades, the overall death rate of the U.S. population has decreased due to medical developments, improvements in public health and job safety, and rising standards of living. The death rate continued to decline in 1977 to the lowest rate ever recorded.

Medical improvements and environmental changes have been more effective in reducing deaths from some causes than others. There has been increasing success in identifying and controlling contagious diseases, but there has been less success in controlling deaths from accidental causes.

Distribution of Ordinary Policyholder Deaths by Cause U.S. Life Insurance Companies

Cause of Death	1945	1950	1955	1960	1965	1970
NATURAL CAUSES						
Cardiovascular-renal Disease	49.3%	57.0%	57.2%	55.7%	53.9%	52.1%
Cancer	14.8	17.3	18.6	18.7	19.2	20.1
Pneumonia and Influenza	3.1	1.9	2.0	3.2	3.1	3.3
Tuberculosis (all forms)	2.8	1.3	.5	.3	.2	.1
Diabetes	1.5	1.3	.9	1.0	1.1	1.0
Other Diseases*	18.2	12.0	12.3	13.1	13.6	14.5
Total Natural Causes	89.7	90.8	91.5	92.0	91.1	91.1
EXTERNAL CAUSES						
Motor Vehicle Accidents	2.3	3.1	3.1	2.9	3.6	3.5
Other Accidents	5.9	3.6	3.2	3.1	3.2	3.1
Suicide	1.9	2.2	2.0	1.8	1.8	1.7
Homicide	.2	.3	.2	.2	.3	.6
Total External Causes	10.3	9.2	8.5	8.0	8.9	8.9
Total All Causes	100.0%	100.0%	100.0%	100.0%	100.0%	100.0%

Cause of Death	1972	1973	1974	1975	1976	1977
NATURAL CAUSES						
Cardiovascular-renal Disease						
Diseases of the Heart and Hypertension						
Ischemic Heart Disease and other Myocardial Insufficiencies	33.2%	32.9%	32.6%	32.3%	32.0%	31.6%
Hypertensive Heart Disease and Hypertension	1.8	1.8	1.4	1.3	1.3	1.2
Other Diseases of the Heart	4.1	4.1	4.5	4.6	5.3	5.7
Total Diseases of the Heart	39.1	38.8	38.5	38.2	38.6	38.5
Cerebrovascular Disease	7.1	7.1	7.0	6.7	6.5	6.4
Arteriosclerosis and other Diseases of Arteries, Arteriolas and Capillaries	3.2	3.4	3.3	3.3	2.9	2.9
Other	1.7	1.6	1.6	1.6	1.5	1.5
Total Cardiovascular-renal	51.1	50.9	50.4	49.8	49.5	49.3
Cancer	20.4	20.1	20.7	21.4	21.9	22.3
Pneumonia and Influenza	3.0	2.9	2.7	2.8	2.9	2.6
Diabetes	1.0	1.0	1.1	1.0	1.0	.9
Other Diseases						
Bronchitis and Other Respiratory Diseases	3.0	2.9	2.9	2.9	3.0	3.0
Cirrhosis	1.4	1.4	1.4	1.3	1.3	1.2
Other*	11.2	11.9	12.0	12.0	11.8	12.1
Total Other Diseases	15.6	16.2	16.3	16.2	16.1	16.3
Total Natural Causes	91.1	91.1	91.2	91.2	91.4	91.4
EXTERNAL CAUSES						
Motor Vehicle Accidents	3.5	3.5	3.0	3.0	3.1	3.1
Other Accidents	3.1	3.1	3.3	3.1	2.9	2.9
Suicide	1.6	1.6	1.7	1.8	1.8	1.8
Homicide	.7	.7	.8	.9	.8	.8
Total External Causes	8.9	8.9	8.8	8.8	8.6	8.6
Total All Causes	100.0%	100.0%	100.0%	100.0%	100.0%	100.0%

Note: A small number classified as "War Deaths" is included in "Other Diseases" in the data for 1960 and 1965; in other years the category is excluded. If "War Deaths" were included in the 1977 data this category would be .02% of the resulting distribution.

*Includes those causes not specified.

Source: American Council of Life Insurance.

In 1977, the deaths of nearly 3 out of 4 ordinary life insurance policyholders with U.S. life companies were due to two principal causes: cardiovascular-renal diseases and cancer.

Since the 1950s, deaths attributable to cardiovascular-renal diseases have decreased slightly, whereas cancer has been an increasing cause of death. These trends have followed those of the general population of the United States.

The percentage of deaths due to cardiovascular-renal diseases declined to 49.3% of all deaths in 1977. Deaths due to ischemic heart disease and chronic disease of endocardium and other myocardial insufficiencies dropped to 31.6% in 1977. Cerebrovascular diseases also declined to 6.4%. The decline in these latter causes of death in recent years has accounted for most of the decline in the percentage of deaths due to cardiovascular-renal disease. Heart disease has decreased significantly in recent years and has affected the overall declining death rate.

The proportion of deaths due to cancer continued to increase; 22.3% of policyholder deaths were attributed to this cause.

Motor vehicle accidents are another major cause of death. Between 1950 and 1970, there was a significant increase in the death rate, but in recent years it has declined. Much of this decrease is attributable to the lower speed limits on the nation's highways. In 1950 motor vehicle accidents accounted for 3.1% of policyholders' deaths, by 1973 they reached 3.5%, but in 1977 they were down to 3.1%.

Bronchitis and other respiratory diseases accounted for 3.0% of policyholder deaths. Pneumonia and influenza combined were responsible for 2.6% of deaths, while cirrhosis of the liver represented 1.2%.

The percentage of deaths attributable to accidents, other than those involving motor vehicles, has remained the same in the last two years and amounted to 2.9% of policyholder deaths in 1977. Two other external causes of death, suicide and homicide, represented 2.6% of deaths.

Over the years, the nation's life insurance companies have made significant contributions to basic research relating to causes of death. The recent focus of individual company contributions and research grants has been in the areas of delivery of health care services and preventive medicine. The Insurance Medical Scientist Scholarship Fund, supported by insurance company contributions, provides scholarships for students planning careers in medical research and teaching.

Death Rate

Mortality among Americans, as measured by the death rate, has decreased in recent years, after remaining at about the same level for more than a decade.

The age-adjusted death rate (technically adjusted for the changing proportion of people at each age in the U.S. population) was 6.3 per thousand in 1976 (the latest year for which data are available), the lowest rate ever recorded. In 1966 the age-adjusted rate was 7.4. From 1966 to 1971 there was a 5.4% drop to 7.0. The drop from 1971 to 1976 was even more significant — a decrease of 10.0%.

The decrease in mortality reflects continuing downtrends for three causes of death: diseases of the heart, cerebrovascular diseases and motor vehicle accidents. The first two causes, which accounted for 42.7% of the 1976 age-adjusted mortality rate, have decreased 17.6% from 1971 to 1976, compared to 9.8% from 1966 to 1971. These recent decreases were offset, in part, by increases in the rates for cancer, suicide and homicide.

For 1976 the age-adjusted death rate for the male population was 8.3 per thousand, compared with the female rate of 4.6 per thousand. Similarly, the rate for persons of races other than white was 8.3 per thousand, compared with a rate of 6.0 per thousand for white persons.

During the first half of this century there was a sharp decline in the death rate due to the advances in medicine. This decline resulted in a reduction of deaths at young and middle ages, so that many more people now live into their seventies and eighties.

Between 1950 and 1970, however, there was relatively little change in the overall death rate for the total population. As the seventies began, the death rate began to

Age-Adjusted Death Rate in the United States

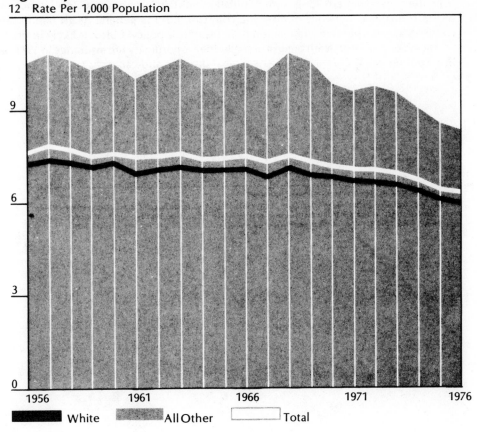

12 Rate Per 1,000 Population

| | White | | All Other | | Total |

decline more noticeably, falling from 7.3 per thousand in 1969 to 6.3 per thousand in 1976. During the same period, the death rate for nonwhites declined even more significantly, from 10.2 per thousand to 8.3 per thousand. Since 1969, the overall death rate for men has dropped more significantly than the death rate for women. The rate per thousand for men declined 1.2 per thousand to 8.3; for women the change was from 5.4 per thousand in 1969 to 4.6 per thousand in 1976.

Because life insurance policyholders as a group represent a large proportion of the total population, their overall mortality rates are likely to parallel those for the nation as

Death Rate in the United States
Age-Adjusted Rate Per 1,000 Population

Year	Male	Female	Total	Year	Male	Female	Total
1915	15.4	13.4	14.4	1964	9.4	5.7	7.4
1920	14.7	13.8	14.2	1965	9.5	5.6	7.4
1925	13.8	12.2	13.0	1966	9.5	5.6	7.4
1930	13.5	11.3	12.5	1967	9.4	5.5	7.3
1935	12.9	10.4	11.6	1968	9.7	5.6	7.4
1940	12.1	9.4	10.8	1969	9.5	5.4	7.3
1945	11.1	8.0	9.5	1970	9.3	5.3	7.1
1950	10.0	6.9	8.4	1971	9.2	5.2	7.0
1955	9.3	6.1	7.7	1972	9.2	5.2	7.0
1960	9.5	5.9	7.6	1973	9.1	5.1	6.9
1961	9.2	5.7	7.4	1974	8.8	4.9	6.7
1962	9.4	5.8	7.5	1975	8.5	4.7	6.4
1963	9.6	5.8	7.6	1976	8.3	4.6	6.3

Note: Some data are revised from previous editions.

Source: National Center for Health Statistics, U.S. Department of Health, Education and Welfare. Rates have been computed using the 1940 age distribution of the United States population as the standard population. Figures for 1915-1930 are for Death Registration States only; 1935-1976 are for the United States.

a whole. Even though the actual experience of a particular life company may differ from the general pattern, long-term population mortality trends are a useful indicator of the probable experience of most life companies. If the general death rate in the United States declines, the rate among life insurance policyholders is likely to drop.

The major causes of death among policyholders of ordinary life insurance in 1977, as in recent decades, were cardiovascular-renal diseases and cancer.

Health: United States 1978

U.S. Department of H.E.W., National Center for Health Statistics, December, 1978.

Mortality

The crude death rate in the United States attained the lowest level in its history in 1975 and 1976, 8.9 deaths per 1,000 population. The preliminary 1977 data indicate a further decrease to 8.8.

With the exception of epidemic years, death rates in the United States declined fairly steadily during the first half of this century. After a slight rise in the mid-1950's to mid-1960's, the rates resumed a downward trend. From 1970 to 1976, the greatest relative decreases in death rates were for children under 10 years of age and adults 30–44 years of age.

Death rates are lower for white people than for black people from infancy through 75–79 years of age. At 80–84 years of age an often-noted "crossover" occurs and death rates are higher for white people than for black people and appear to remain so through the oldest ages. Although various hypotheses have been offered to explain this phenomenon, none have been supported by conclusive evidence.

The Social Security Administration has prepared a set of mortality projections, and based on their assumptions, mortality decreases by the year 2000 will be greatest for infancy and early childhood. They also will be greater for females than for males, implying a continuation of the widening of the sex differential in mortality. By 2000, mortality rates for males 15–34 years of age are expected to rise as a result of a projected increase in deaths due to accidents, suicides, and homicides for these ages.[1] More certain is the projected rise in the crude death rate because of increasing proportions of the elderly in the total population. By the year 2000, the crude death rate is projected to reach 10.2 per 1,000 population.

Knowledge of changes in specific rates— that is, rates specific for any number of population characteristics, such as sex, race, and age—is useful for the health planner. Geographic differences in age or race specific mortality rates may signal a need for new or modified health care services and facilities and may direct attention to possible environmental problems associated with specific localities.

A large part of the change in the death rate from one calendar year to the next, however, is because of the changing age structure of the population. For an analysis of trends over time, it is advantageous to look at the age-adjusted death rate, a summary statistic useful for making annual compari-

NOTE: Unless otherwise noted, data are from the ongoing data-collection systems of the National Center for Health Statistics. In many instances the data have been published in the *Vital and Health Statistics* series.

[1] Office of the Actuary: United States population projections for OASDHI cost estimates, by F. R. Bayo, H. W. Shiman, and B. R. Sobus. *Actuarial Study No. 76.* DHEW Pub. No. (SSA)77–11522. Social Security Administration. Baltimore, Md., June 1977.

sons. The rate shows what the level of mortality would be if no changes occurred in the age composition of the population from year to year. From the beginning of this century, the age-adjusted death rate decreased by 53 percent from 17.8 in 1900 to 8.4 in 1950, and then by another 25 percent to 6.3 in 1976. If the decrease from 1950 to 1976 were measured only by the crude rate, however, the decrease would be about 7 percent, a figure that does not reflect the magnitude of the true mortality decline.

Ever since mortality statistics have been collected in most parts of the world, two phenomena have been evident. The age-adjusted death rates for males have been higher than the rates for females, and the death rates for white people have been lower than the rates for all other people.

In looking at U.S. data, the "all other" category is composed primarily of black people, and most of the deaths in the "all other" category refer to black deaths. The remaining races in the "all other" category include Indians, Chinese, Japanese, and others and when combined have a lower mortality rate than the white population.

The relative difference between the age-adjusted rates for males and females has been increasing over time. In 1900, death rates for males were only about 9 percent greater than for females; by 1950, the difference had grown to 45 percent. In 1976, mortality for males was 80 percent higher than for females. On the other hand, the difference between color groups had been narrowing slowly. Mortality rates for the white population were about 37 percent lower than rates for all other people in 1900; by 1976, the difference was reduced to about 28 percent.

The expectation of life at birth is an indicator that summarizes levels of mortality. For a person born in 1976, it was 25.5 years more than for someone born in 1900, with life expectancy increasing from 47.3 years to 72.8 years. More than 80 percent of this increase occurred between 1900 and 1950. The major factor related to the tremendous gain during the first 50 years of this century was the decrease in mortality from infectious and parasitic diseases which for the most part affected infants and young children. Since 1950, 4.6 years have been added to life expectancy at birth.

Expectation of life at birth is influenced heavily by mortality rates for infancy and childhood. Just as most of the selected industrialized countries had lower infant mortality rates, they also had higher life expectancies at birth than the United States. Of the 12 countries selected for comparison, only in the German Democratic Republic was life expectancy at birth in 1976 for men lower than in the United States. Only in England and Wales and the German Democratic Republic was life expectancy at birth for women in 1976 lower than it was for women in the United States. At 65 years of age, however, the position of the United States was practically reversed. Women at 65 years of age in the United States could expect to live as long as or longer than women in all other selected developed countries. Life expectancy for men at 65 years of age also compared more favorably with other countries than did life expectancy at birth. This reflects the fact that the excess in mortality rates for men in the United States, as compared to other countries, is greater in childhood and early adulthood but less marked at older ages.

Infant mortality rates are useful for identifying problems with the health status of infants and mothers and possible problems in the delivery of health care and related services to these groups in the community. At the beginning of the 20th century in the United States and as late as 1918, the available data indicate that 1 in 10 infants died in the first year of life. Not until 1950 did the infant mortality rate fall below 30 deaths per 1,000 live births. Although the black infant mortality rate was still almost twice as high as the white infant mortality rate in 1976, 25.5 versus 13.3, the rates for both races have been declining over the past quarter of a century.

Comparable decreases have been noted in late fetal mortality. The trend in perinatal mortality reflects the declining risks in both the late fetal and early infancy period. The perinatal mortality rate decreased by nearly 50 percent between 1950 and 1976 from 32.5 to 16.7 perinatal deaths per 1,000 live births and late fetal deaths.

A number of factors may have worked together to bring about the reductions in infant and perinatal mortality: (1) more women receiving prenatal care early in pregnancy, (2) a decreasing proportion of higher order, thus higher risk births, (3) advances in medical science, particularly in neonatalogy, (4) increasing availability of the most modern care through regional perinatal centers, (5) improvements in contraceptive utilization, allowing women to time and space their pregnancies more effectively, thereby reducing the proportion of high risk births, (6) increasing legal abortion rates, (7) the availability of programs to improve the nutrition of pregnant women and infants, and (8) general improvements in socioeconomic conditions.

Infant mortality rates in the United States do not compare favorably with rates in other selected industrialized nations. In both 1971 and 1976, 9 of the 12 selected industrialized countries had lower infant mortality rates than the United States. The 1976 rates in Sweden and in Japan were 8.7 and 9.3 infant deaths per 1,000 live births, respectively, and they were substantially lower than the U.S. rate of 15.2. Even if only the infant mortality rate for the U.S. white population is used, the rate is still higher than the rates in Sweden, the Netherlands, France, Switzerland, and Japan. The U.S. perinatal mortality ratio compared somewhat more favorably with other countries, but this may partly be the result of international differences in distinguishing between fetal and infant deaths.

For about the past three decades, heart disease and cancer have accounted for more than 50 percent of all deaths in the United States. In 1976, 58 percent of all deaths were caused by these two categories of diseases. The increase in the proportion of all mortality accounted for by heart disease and cancer can be attributed, in part, to the aging of the population, decreases in mortality from infectious and certain other categories of disease, changes in cause of death reporting, and, for some cancer sites, to a true increase in the incidence of the disease.

Heart disease continues to be the leading cause of death in the United States and as such is the dominant influence on total mortality rates. In 1976, there were 724,000 deaths from diseases of the heart, 35 percent more than in 1950 but almost 2 percent less than in 1970. Throughout the first half of this century, the death rate for heart disease rose continually and peaked in the early 1960's. It has since been declining. Between 1960 and 1976, despite an aging population, the death rate decreased 9 percent to 337 deaths per 100,000 population. During that period, the mortality rate for each 5-year age group from 25–69 years of age decreased by more than 25 percent, while for each succeeding age group through 85 years of age and over the decline was more than 19 percent.

Heart disease mortality, like total mortality, is higher for males than for females. Between 1950 and 1976, the ratio of age-specific heart disease death rates for white males to the rates for white females increased for nearly every age group. In 1976, the death rates for white males 40–44 through 50–54 years of age were more than 4 times the rates for white females in the same age groups.

Heart disease mortality also affects the white and black populations differently. In 1976, the mortality rate for white males was much higher than the rate for black males. Nearly all of the differences, however, could be accounted for by the older age distribution of the white population. That is, if the black population had had the same age distribution as the white population, the mortality rate for black people would have been fairly similar to the rate for white people.

Ischemic heart disease mortality, which includes about 90 percent of all heart disease mortality, decreased by 11 percent between 1968 and 1976.[2] Excluding changes in the age distribution of the population over the 8-year period, the decline would have been close to 28 percent. For persons 65 years of age and over, the rate decreased by 16 percent to 2,166 deaths per 100,000 population. The rate for white males 65–69 years of age decreased by 20 percent to 1,403 and for blacks males by 29 percent to 1,236 deaths per 100,000 population.

For each year 1970 through 1975, age-adjusted death rates for ischemic heart disease for males and females were higher in the United States than they were in other selected industrialized countries including Sweden, England and Wales, the Netherlands, Canada, the German Federal Republic, Switzerland, and Japan. Ischemic heart dis-

---

[2] Because of revisions in the International Classification of Diseases, time trend data for ischemic heart disease mortality are only available since 1968.

ease mortality rates in Japan are much lower than in the other selected countries. Some of the wide variation is attributed to the low cholesterol diet of the Japanese people, and some to the classification of sudden deaths as stroke rather than heart disease. Although for most selected countries the rates were relatively stable or showed a slight increase during the 5 years, the mortality rates from ischemic heart disease for the United States decreased.

Between 1950 and 1976, the death rate from all malignant neoplasms increased by 26 percent from 140 to 176 deaths per 100,000 persons, while the age-adjusted death rate increased by only 5.5 percent during these 26 years. It is apparent, therefore, that changes in the age distribution accounted for a large portion of the increase in the death rates. Cancer usually strikes middle-aged and older people, although relative to other causes of death, cancer still ranked in the leading three causes of death for children 1–4 and 5–14 years of age in 1976. From 1950 to 1976, cancer mortality for people under 45 years of age decreased, while for each succeeding 5-year age group, from 45–49 to 80–84 years of age, cancer mortality increased. For those 65 years of age and over, death rates for cancer increased 15 percent in the 26-year period from 851 to 979 deaths per 100,000 persons.

In 1976, the death rate for cancer was highest for white males (199) and lowest for females other than white (118). The risk of cancer mortality increased most notably among black males from 1950 to 1976. The age-specific death rates increased during the 26 years for each 5-year age group beginning with 35–39 years of age. At 65 years of age and over, the rate for black males more than doubled to 1,475 deaths per 100,000 population. Among females, on the other hand, from 1950 to 1976, the age-specific rates for white people decreased for all but one 5-year age group, and for black people the rates decreased for those under 65 years of age and increased for those 65 years of age and over.

Nearly one-fourth of all cancer mortality in 1976 was caused by cancer of the respiratory system, and more than 95 percent of the respiratory cancer was cancer of the trachea, bronchus, and lung. For deaths among males from cancer in the United States, lung cancer was the most prevalent cause. In the past quarter of a century, mortality from cancer of the respiratory system tripled, increasing from 14 deaths per 100,000 population in 1950 to 43 in 1976. The age-adjusted rate more than doubled during this period. Among black people, the death rate more than quadrupled during this period.

As with all cancer mortality, respiratory cancer mortality rises sharply with age. Between 1950 and 1976, the death rate for people 65 years of age and over increased threefold to 211 deaths per 100,000 people 65 years of age and over. Among black males 65 years of age and over, respiratory cancer mortality increased nearly sevenfold in the 26-year period, reaching 394 deaths per 100,000 in 1976.

The sex ratio in respiratory cancer mortality rates has narrowed during the past 15 years for both white and black people because of the faster rate of increase in rates for females. The rate in 1976 for white males, however, was still more than 3 times the rate for white females (68 versus 21), and the rate for black males was more than 4 times the rate for black females (63 versus 15).

The much higher respiratory cancer mortality among males can be attributed to, among other variables, the diversity of carcinogenic substances known to be associated with heavy industry. In the United States, it has been shown that men who are miners, laborers, and transportation workers have an increased risk of cancer (except skin cancer) when compared to men involved in agricultural occupations.[3] The effects of increased heavy cigarette smoking among women may be one of the factors involved in the narrowing of sex ratios in mortality rates for respiratory cancer.

International comparisons of cancer mortality between the United States and eight selected industrialized countries of Western Europe, Canada, Australia, Israel, Japan, and Mexico for the period 1961–76 show that the age-adjusted death rates for males in the United States were lower than the rates in all but four countries (Mexico, Sweden, Israel,

---

[3] National Cancer Institute: *Cancer Rates and Risks*, 2d ed., by D. L. Levin, et al. DHEW Pub. No. (NIH)76–691. Public Health Service. Washington. U.S. Government Printing Office, 1974.

Death rates, according to race, sex, and age: United States, 1976

(Data are based on the national vital registration system)

Age	All races			White			All other					
							Total			Black		
	Both sexes	Male	Female	Both sexes	Male	Female	Both sexes	Male	Female	Both sexes	Male	Female
	Number of deaths per 100,000 resident population											
All ages[1]	889.6	1,007.0	778.3	899.4	1,010.4	793.6	824.8	983.5	680.0	886.2	1,051.8	735.7
Under 1 year	1,595.0	1,762.6	1,419.0	1,356.2	1,511.8	1,192.1	2,781.5	3,012.4	2,542.2	3,014.2	3,282.8	2,738.1
1–4 years	69.9	78.2	61.3	64.1	71.9	55.9	96.9	107.5	86.1	102.5	112.9	92.1
5–9 years	34.8	41.0	28.3	32.7	38.3	26.9	45.1	54.8	35.4	47.0	57.0	37.0
10–14 years	34.6	44.0	25.0	33.7	42.8	24.2	39.5	49.9	29.0	39.9	50.7	29.0
15–19 years	97.1	139.9	53.2	96.0	138.1	52.6	103.3	149.8	56.9	102.2	147.3	57.3
20–24 years	131.3	198.4	64.4	120.0	182.4	57.0	199.5	300.1	107.2	208.8	316.7	110.7
25–29 years	129.3	187.2	72.4	110.9	159.8	61.8	254.8	389.9	139.3	276.3	422.3	150.5
30–34 years	144.8	196.5	94.5	122.4	164.2	80.9	297.8	436.6	180.7	328.6	486.5	196.3
35–39 years	198.4	261.6	138.6	168.4	219.2	119.2	405.0	580.5	261.8	435.8	629.0	278.0
40–44 years	313.4	406.0	225.3	271.9	352.2	194.0	601.1	811.3	426.1	650.7	883.9	456.9
45–49 years	498.1	647.8	356.3	450.0	586.6	319.0	863.6	1,138.3	625.6	945.4	1,240.1	687.6
50–54 years	767.7	1,017.3	536.8	706.8	940.9	488.4	1,280.3	1,683.3	928.6	1,389.1	1,828.0	1,009.0
55–59 years	1,175.0	1,578.0	807.2	1,107.7	1,496.4	751.0	1,796.6	2,352.8	1,312.6	1,917.7	2,522.4	1,396.0
60–64 years	1,822.8	2,496.3	1,230.5	1,743.6	2,407.9	1,157.7	2,579.2	3,371.4	1,917.0	2,710.7	3,569.3	2,005.7
65–69 years	2,541.5	3,586.9	1,712.8	2,488.7	3,542.9	1,651.5	2,990.0	3,963.4	2,229.2	3,072.7	4,118.2	2,281.3
70–74 years	3,948.3	5,433.7	2,856.4	3,824.1	5,340.8	2,721.9	5,335.2	6,394.1	4,452.1	5,750.6	6,932.8	4,803.8
75–79 years	6,186.7	8,263.3	4,850.6	6,102.6	8,246.8	4,745.3	7,131.4	8,428.5	6,132.6	7,916.8	9,426.9	6,800.6
80–84 years	9,034.4	11,521.1	7,632.5	9,183.4	11,774.4	7,743.4	7,394.7	9,010.0	6,333.6	7,812.5	9,555.1	6,698.4
85 years and over	15,486.9	17,983.9	14,312.1	16,068.5	18,767.6	14,823.3	10,018.5	11,519.1	9,175.2	10,511.5	12,375.0	9,554.1

[1] Includes unknown age.

NOTE: Excludes deaths of nonresidents of the United States.

SOURCE: National Center for Health Statistics: Vital Statistics of the United States, 1976, Vol. II, Part A. Washington. U.S. Government Printing Office, Public Health Service, DHEW, Hyattsville, Md. To be published; Data computed by the Division of Analysis from data compiled by the Division of Vital Statistics.

Death rates, life expectancy, and projections, according to sex and age: United States, 1976 and 2000

(Data are based on intercensal estimates and national vital registration system)

Age	Sex					
	Male			Female		
	1976[1]	2000	Percent change	1976[1]	2000	Percent change
	Number of deaths per 1,000 resident population			Number of deaths per 1,000 resident population		
All ages[2]	9.99	9.42	−5.7	7.44	6.75	−9.3
Under 1 year	18.96	15.04	−20.7	14.92	11.74	−21.3
1–4 years	0.79	0.71	−10.1	0.64	0.55	−14.1
5–9 years	0.43	0.40	−7.0	0.30	0.27	−10.0
10–14 years	0.47	0.45	−4.3	0.28	0.25	−10.7
15–19 years	1.49	1.55	4.0	0.55	0.53	−3.6
20–24 years	2.04	2.13	4.4	0.66	0.63	−4.5
25–29 years	1.90	1.95	2.6	0.77	0.72	−6.5
30–34 years	2.06	2.08	1.0	1.01	0.94	−6.9
35–39 years	2.74	2.68	−2.2	1.64	1.52	−7.3
40–44 years	4.16	3.94	−5.3	2.44	2.26	−7.4
45–49 years	6.82	6.41	−6.0	3.74	3.44	−8.0
50–54 years	10.31	9.64	−6.5	5.49	5.03	−8.4
55–59 years	16.27	15.17	−6.8	8.24	7.57	−8.1
60–64 years	24.94	23.14	−7.2	12.35	11.18	−9.5
65–69 years	36.52	34.18	−6.4	17.78	16.05	−9.7
70–74 years	55.04	51.78	−5.9	29.97	27.14	−9.4
75–79 years	81.86	77.37	−5.5	49.82	44.80	−10.1
80–84 years	114.14	109.11	−4.4	78.83	70.45	−10.6
85 years and over	183.61	183.20	−0.2	151.71	149.52	−1.4
	Remaining life expectancy in years			Remaining life expectancy in years		
At birth	68.7	69.6	1.3	76.1	77.4	1.7
1 year	69.0	69.6	0.9	76.2	77.3	1.4
5 years	65.2	65.8	0.9	72.4	73.5	1.5
10 years	60.3	60.9	1.0	67.5	68.6	1.6
20 years	50.9	51.5	1.2	57.8	58.8	1.7
30 years	41.8	42.4	1.4	48.2	49.2	2.1
40 years	32.7	33.3	1.8	38.7	39.7	2.6
50 years	24.2	24.8	2.5	29.8	30.7	3.0
60 years	16.8	17.3	3.0	21.5	22.3	3.7
65 years	13.7	14.2	3.6	17.7	18.5	4.5
70 years	11.0	11.3	2.7	14.1	14.8	5.0

[1] The 1976 death rates and expectation of life were estimated by the Social Security Administration; when the Social Security Administration study was underway, the 1976 figures were not final and were estimated by adjusting the 1974 rates.

[2] Age-adjusted rate computed by the direct method and standardized to the United States population in 1970 using 19 age groups.

SOURCE: Office of the Actuary: United States population projections for OASDHI cost estimates, by F. R. Bayo, H. W. Shiman, and B. R. Sobus. *Actuarial Study No. 76.* DHEW Pub. No. (SSA)77–11522. Social Security Administration. Baltimore, Md., June 1977; Division of Vital Statistics, National Center for Health Statistics: Selected data.

and Japan).[4] Between 1970 and 1975, the rate for males in the Netherlands was higher than that in any of the selected countries, and in 1975, it was 25 percent higher than the United States rate of 207 per 100,000

[4] If rates for only white males in the United States were compared, these differences might not have occurred.

population.

Mortality from cancer of the trachea, bronchus, and lung shows a different pattern. It has been exceedingly high in the United States among both males and females. Only England and Wales, the Netherlands, and Israel have had higher death rates from cancer at these sites.

Age-adjusted death rates, according to color and sex: United States, selected years 1900–1976

(Data are based on the national vital registration system)

Year	Color								
	Total			White			All other		
	Both sexes	Male	Female	Both sexes	Male	Female	Both sexes	Male	Female
	Number of deaths per 1,000 resident population								
1900[1]	17.8	18.6	17.0	17.6	18.4	16.8	27.8	28.7	27.1
1910[1]	15.8	16.9	14.6	15.6	16.7	14.4	24.1	24.8	23.2
1920[1]	14.2	14.7	13.8	13.7	14.2	13.1	20.6	20.4	21.0
1930[1]	12.5	13.5	11.3	11.7	12.8	10.6	20.1	21.0	19.2
1940	10.8	12.1	9.4	10.2	11.6	8.8	16.3	17.6	15.0
1945	9.5	11.1	8.0	9.1	10.7	7.5	13.1	14.5	11.9
1950	8.4	10.0	6.9	8.0	9.6	6.5	12.3	13.6	10.9
1955	7.7	9.3	6.1	7.4	9.1	5.7	10.4	11.9	9.1
1960	7.6	9.5	5.9	7.3	9.2	5.6	10.5	12.1	8.9
1965	7.4	9.5	5.6	7.0	9.1	5.3	10.1	12.2	8.3
1970	7.1	9.3	5.3	6.8	8.9	5.0	9.8	12.3	7.7
1971	7.0	9.2	5.2	6.7	8.8	4.9	9.6	12.1	7.5
1972[2]	7.0	9.2	5.2	6.7	8.8	4.9	9.7	12.3	7.5
1973	6.9	9.1	5.1	6.6	8.7	4.8	9.5	12.1	7.4
1974	6.7	8.8	4.9	6.4	8.4	4.7	9.0	11.5	6.9
1975	6.4	8.5	4.7	6.1	8.1	4.5	8.5	11.0	6.5
1976	6.3	8.3	4.6	6.0	8.0	4.4	8.3	10.7	6.4

[1] Death registration areas only. The death registration areas increased in number from 10 States and the District of Columbia in 1900 to the entire coterminous United States in 1933.

[2] Data are based on a 50-percent sample of deaths.

NOTE: Beginning 1970, deaths of nonresidents of the United States are excluded. Age-adjusted rates are computed by the direct method, using as the standard population the age distribution of the total population of the United States as enumerated in 1940. Adjustment is based on 11 age groups.

SOURCES: National Center for Health Statistics: *Vital Statistics of the United States,* Vol. II, for data years 1900–1973, Washington. U.S. Government Printing Office; for data years 1974–1976, Public Health Service, DHEW, Hyattsville, Md. To be published.

Life expectancy at specified ages, according to color and sex: United States, selected years 1900–1976

(Data are based on the national vital registration system)

Specified age and year	Total	White		All other	
		Male	Female	Male	Female
At birth	Remaining life expectancy in years				
1900[1]	47.3	46.6	48.7	32.5	33.5
1950	68.2	66.5	72.2	59.1	62.9
1960	69.7	67.4	74.1	61.1	66.3
1970	70.9	68.0	75.6	61.3	69.4
1971	71.1	68.3	75.8	61.6	69.7
1972[2]	71.1	68.3	75.9	61.5	69.9
1973	71.3	68.4	76.1	61.9	70.1
1974	71.9	68.9	76.6	62.9	71.2
1975	72.5	69.4	77.2	63.6	72.3
1976	72.8	69.7	77.3	64.1	72.6
At 20 years					
1900–1902[1]	42.8	42.2	43.8	35.1	36.9
1950	51.3	49.6	54.7	43.7	46.9
1960	52.4	50.1	56.2	45.5	49.9
1970	53.1	50.3	57.4	44.7	52.2
1971	53.3	50.5	57.5	44.9	52.3
1972[2]	53.3	50.4	57.5	44.6	52.5
1973	53.4	50.5	57.7	44.9	52.6
1974	53.9	51.0	58.1	45.7	53.6
1975	54.4	51.4	58.6	46.3	54.7
1976	54.6	51.6	58.7	46.8	54.9
At 65 years					
1900–1902[1]	11.9	11.5	12.2	10.4	11.4
1950	13.9	12.8	15.1	12.5	14.5
1960	14.3	12.9	15.9	12.7	15.2
1970	15.2	13.1	17.1	13.3	16.4
1971	15.2	13.2	17.2	13.2	16.3
1972[2]	15.2	13.1	17.1	13.1	16.3
1973	15.3	13.2	17.3	13.1	16.2
1974	15.2	13.4	17.6	13.4	16.8
1975	16.0	13.7	18.1	13.7	17.5
1976	16.0	13.7	18.1	13.8	17.6

[1] Death registration areas only. The death registration areas increased in number from 10 States and the District of Columbia in 1900 to the entire coterminous United States in 1933.

[2] Data are based on a 50-percent sample of deaths.

SOURCES: National Center for Health Statistics: *Vital Statistics of the United States,* Vol. II, for data years 1900–1973. Washington. U.S. Government Printing Office; for data years 1974–1976, Public Health Service, DHEW, Hyattsville, Md. To be published.

Life expectancy at birth and at 65 years of age, according to sex: Selected countries, selected years 1969–76

(Data are based on reporting by countries)

Country	Year	Life expectancy				Year	Life expectancy			
		At birth		At 65 years			At birth		At 65 years	
		Male	Female	Male	Female		Male	Female	Male	Female
		Remaining number of years					Remaining number of years			
Canada	1970	69.3	76.2	13.7	17.4	1974	69.6	77.1	13.8	18.0
United States	[1]1969–71	67.0	74.6	13.0	16.8	1976	69.0	76.7	13.7	18.0
Sweden	1970	72.3	77.4	14.4	17.2	1976	72.2	78.1	14.0	17.5
England and Wales	1970	68.8	75.2	12.0	16.0	1976	69.7	75.8	12.3	16.3
Netherlands	1970	70.9	76.6	13.6	16.6	1976	71.6	78.1	13.6	17.6
German Democratic Republic	1970	68.9	74.2	12.9	15.4	1976	68.9	74.5	12.1	14.8
German Federal Republic	1970	67.3	73.6	11.9	15.0	1975	68.1	74.7	12.2	15.7
France	1970	69.1	76.7	13.4	17.4	1974	69.5	77.6	13.6	17.8
Switzerland	[1]1968–73	70.3	76.2	13.3	16.3	1976	71.7	78.3	14.0	17.7
Italy	1970	68.5	74.6	13.0	16.1	1974	69.9	76.1	13.6	16.7
Israel[2]	1970	69.9	73.4	13.5	14.5	1975	71.0	74.7	14.0	15.5
Japan	1970	69.5	74.9	12.7	15.6	1976	72.3	77.6	14.1	17.0
Australia	1970	67.4	74.2	11.9	15.7	1975	69.3	76.4	13.1	17.1

[1] Average for the period.
[2] Jewish population only.

NOTE: Countries are grouped by continent.

SOURCES: World Health Organization: *World Health Statistics, 1970.* Vol. 1. Geneva. World Health Organization, 1973; *1978.* Vol. 1. Geneva. World Health Organization. To be published; United Nations: *Demographic Yearbook 1976.* Pub. No. ST/ESA/STAT/SER.R/4. New York. United Nations, 1977; National Center for Health Statistics: *U.S. Decennial Life Tables for 1969–1971,* Vol. 1, No. 1. DHEW Pub. No. (HRA) 75–1150. Health Resources Administration. Washington. U.S. Government Printing Office, May 1975; Final mortality statistics, 1976. *Monthly Vital Statistics Report,* Vol. 26, No. 12, supplement 2. DHEW Pub. No. (PHS) 78–1120. Public Health Service. Washington. U.S. Government Printing Office, Mar. 30, 1978.

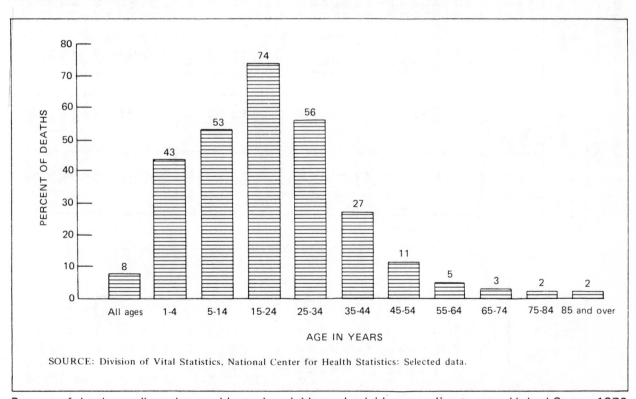

Percent of deaths attributed to accidents, homicide, and suicide, according to age: United States, 1976

Resident population, according to race, sex, and age: United States, July 1, 1976

(Data are based on decennial census updated by data from multiple sources)

Age	All races			White			All other				
							Total			Black	
	Both sexes	Male	Female	Both sexes	Male	Female	Both sexes	Male	Female	Male	Female
	Population in thousands										
All ages	214,649	104,472	110,177	186,225	90,909	95,315	28,424	13,563	14,862	11,787	12,976
Under 5 years	15,339	7,839	7,500	12,653	6,482	6,171	2,686	1,358	1,328	1,171	1,146
Under 1 year	3,026	1,550	1,476	2,519	1,293	1,226	507	258	249	221	215
1 year	3,066	1,556	1,500	2,534	1,297	1,237	532	269	263	230	226
2 years	2,938	1,504	1,434	2,415	1,239	1,176	524	265	259	227	222
3 years	3,039	1,552	1,488	2,492	1,275	1,217	547	276	271	239	234
4 years	3,270	1,668	1,602	2,693	1,378	1,315	576	290	286	253	249
5–9 years	17,349	8,848	8,501	14,460	7,397	7,063	2,889	1,451	1,438	1,273	1,263
5 years	3,568	1,826	1,742	2,956	1,517	1,439	612	309	303	268	264
6 years	3,512	1,787	1,724	2,926	1,494	1,432	585	293	292	256	256
7 years	3,440	1,752	1,687	2,864	1,465	1,400	575	288	287	253	253
8 years	3,353	1,710	1,643	2,803	1,434	1,369	550	276	274	243	241
9 years	3,477	1,772	1,705	2,910	1,487	1,423	567	285	282	252	249
10–14 years	19,819	10,106	9,713	16,612	8,491	8,121	3,207	1,615	1,592	1,441	1,423
10 years	3,721	1,899	1,822	3,085	1,579	1,506	636	320	316	283	279
11 years	3,808	1,940	1,868	3,187	1,628	1,560	621	312	309	278	275
12 years	4,005	2,046	1,959	3,364	1,723	1,641	641	324	318	289	285
13 years	4,071	2,074	1,997	3,428	1,750	1,678	643	323	320	290	287
14 years	4,213	2,147	2,066	3,547	1,811	1,736	666	335	330	301	297
15–19 years	21,165	10,722	10,443	17,934	9,107	8,827	3,231	1,615	1,616	1,431	1,438
15 years	4,286	2,187	2,099	3,618	1,850	1,768	668	337	331	300	296
16 years	4,184	2,132	2,053	3,534	1,805	1,729	651	327	323	292	289
17 years	4,212	2,140	2,072	3,556	1,810	1,746	656	330	326	293	291
18 years	4,237	2,135	2,102	3,607	1,822	1,785	630	314	316	277	281
19 years	4,246	2,128	2,118	3,619	1,820	1,799	626	307	319	268	281
20–24 years	19,440	9,705	9,735	16,690	8,390	8,300	2,750	1,315	1,435	1,135	1,248
20 years	4,156	2,087	2,070	3,540	1,784	1,756	616	303	314	264	278
21 years	3,983	2,003	1,980	3,412	1,725	1,686	572	278	294	241	259
22 years	3,852	1,920	1,932	3,308	1,661	1,647	544	258	286	224	249
23 years	3,709	1,840	1,869	3,197	1,600	1,598	512	241	271	206	232
24 years	3,739	1,855	1,884	3,233	1,620	1,613	506	235	271	200	230

25-29 years	17,710	8,776	8,934	15,437	7,729	7,708	2,272	1,047	1,225	1,911	885	1,025
30-34 years	14,181	6,989	7,192	12,373	6,161	6,212	1,809	828	981	1,498	683	815
35-39 years	11,872	5,775	6,097	10,366	5,098	5,267	1,507	677	830	1,295	582	713
40-44 years	11,140	5,432	5,708	9,735	4,795	4,940	1,405	637	769	1,203	546	657
45-49 years	11,656	5,672	5,983	10,298	5,042	5,256	1,357	630	727	1,166	544	622
50-54 years	11,980	5,758	6,222	10,704	5,165	5,539	1,275	593	683	1,114	517	597
55-59 years	10,754	5,132	5,622	9,703	4,643	5,060	1,051	489	562	937	434	503
60-64 years	9,310	4,355	4,956	8,431	3,952	4,478	880	402	477	794	358	436
65-69 years	8,281	3,662	4,619	7,408	3,279	4,129	873	383	490	806	346	461
70-74 years	5,913	2,505	3,408	5,427	2,284	3,143	486	221	265	425	189	236
75-79 years	4,051	1,586	2,465	3,720	1,442	2,278	331	144	187	280	119	161
80-84 years	2,724	982	1,742	2,497	892	1,605	227	90	137	200	78	122
85 years and over	1,966	629	1,337	1,777	561	1,216	189	68	121	165	56	109
1-4 years	12,313	6,289	6,024	10,134	5,189	4,945	2,179	1,100	1,079	1,881	949	931
5-13 years	32,955	16,807	16,148	27,525	14,077	13,448	5,430	2,730	2,700	4,801	2,412	2,389
14-17 years	16,896	8,606	8,290	14,255	7,276	6,979	2,640	1,330	1,311	2,359	1,186	1,173
18-24 years	27,922	13,968	13,954	23,916	12,032	11,884	4,006	1,935	2,070	3,490	1,680	1,810
18-21 years	16,622	8,353	8,269	14,178	7,151	7,027	2,444	1,202	1,243	2,149	1,050	1,099
22-24 years	11,300	5,615	5,685	9,738	4,881	4,857	1,562	734	828	1,342	630	711
15-44 years	95,508	47,399	48,109	82,534	41,280	41,254	12,974	6,119	6,855	11,159	5,263	5,897
14 years and over	166,355	79,826	86,529	146,047	70,351	75,696	20,308	9,475	10,833	17,645	8,204	9,441
16 years and over	157,855	75,492	82,364	138,881	66,689	72,192	18,974	8,802	10,172	16,451	7,603	8,848
18 years and over	149,459	71,220	78,239	131,791	63,075	68,717	17,668	8,145	9,523	15,286	7,018	8,268
21 years and over	136,821	64,871	71,950	121,025	57,649	63,376	15,795	7,222	8,574	13,637	6,209	7,428
62 years and over	28,402	11,902	16,500	25,770	10,756	15,014	2,632	1,146	1,486	2,354	1,001	1,353
65 years and over	22,934	9,364	13,571	20,829	8,457	12,372	2,105	906	1,199	1,876	787	1,089
Median age of population	29.0	27.9	30.2	29.8	28.6	31.2	24.0	22.8	25.1	23.8	22.6	24.9

Age in years

SOURCE: U.S. Bureau of the Census: Population estimates and projections, *Current Population Reports*. Series P-25, No. 643. Washington. U.S. Government Printing Office, Jan. 1977.

Population, dependency ratios, and projections under Series II fertility assumption (2.1 births per woman) and percent change from 1970 population, according to age: United States, selected years 1970–2000.

(Data are based on decennial census updated by data from multiple sources)

Age and dependency ratios	Year											
	Population in thousands		Projected population in thousands					Percent change from 1970 population				
	1970	1976	1980	1985	1990	1995	2000	1980	1985	1990	1995	2000
All ages	204,878	215,118	222,159	232,880	243,513	252,750	260,378	8.4	13.7	18.9	23.4	27.1
Under 5 years	17,148	15,339	16,020	18,803	19,437	18,775	17,852	-6.6	9.7	13.3	9.5	4.1
5-9 years	19,898	17,349	16,096	16,259	19,040	19,666	19,000	-19.1	-18.3	-4.3	-1.2	-4.5
10-14 years	20,835	19,819	17,800	16,567	16,718	19,527	20,153	-14.6	-20.5	-19.8	-6.3	-3.3
15-19 years	19,315	21,220	20,609	18,007	16,777	16,919	19,727	6.7	-6.8	-13.1	-12.4	2.1
20-24 years	17,184	19,630	20,918	20,510	17,953	16,728	16,898	21.7	19.4	4.5	2.7	-1.7
25-29 years	13,718	17,806	18,930	20,581	20,169	17,665	16,469	38.0	50.0	47.0	28.8	20.1
30-34 years	11,576	14,238	17,242	19,278	20,917	20,489	17,981	48.9	66.5	80.7	77.0	55.3
35-39 years	11,151	11,916	14,033	17,274	19,261	20,874	20,435	25.8	54.9	72.7	87.2	83.3
40-44 years	11,991	11,160	11,688	14,102	17,331	19,304	20,909	-2.5	17.6	44.5	61.0	74.4
45-49 years	12,147	11,662	11,030	11,526	13,889	17,052	18,990	-9.2	5.1	14.3	40.4	56.3
50-54 years	11,163	11,981	11,668	10,931	11,422	13,758	16,885	4.5	2.1	2.3	23.2	51.3
55-59 years	9,998	10,754	11,401	11,122	10,416	10,885	13,106	14.0	11.2	4.2	8.9	31.1
60-64 years	8,666	9,310	9,797	10,615	10,360	9,707	10,151	13.1	22.5	19.5	12.0	17.1
65-69 years	7,023	8,281	8,700	9,244	10,022	9,791	9,192	23.9	31.6	42.7	39.4	30.9
70-74 years	5,465	5,913	6,793	7,301	7,782	8,433	8,244	24.3	33.6	42.4	54.3	50.9
75-79 years	3,859	4,051	4,324	5,108	5,501	5,885	6,394	12.0	32.4	42.5	52.5	65.7
80-84 years	2,309	2,724	2,816	3,064	3,639	3,939	4,236	22.0	32.7	57.6	70.6	83.5
85 years and over	1,432	1,966	2,294	2,588	2,881	3,352	3,756	60.2	80.7	101.2	134.1	162.3
	Number per 100 population		Number per 100 projected population					Percent change from 1970 ratio				
Dependency ratio[1]	78.0	69.4	64.3	62.5	63.5	65.2	63.2	-17.6	-19.9	-18.6	-16.4	-19.0
Child dependency ratio[2]	60.6	51.3	45.8	43.5	43.5	44.7	43.2	-24.4	-28.2	-28.2	-26.2	-28.7
Aged dependency ratio[3]	17.5	18.1	18.4	19.1	20.0	20.5	19.9	5.1	9.1	14.3	17.1	13.7

[1] Population under 18 years of age and 65 years of age and over per 100 population 18-64 years of age.
[2] Population under 18 years of age per 100 population 18-64 years of age.
[3] Population 65 years of age and over per 100 population 18-64 years of age.

NOTE: Projected populations are based on U.S. Bureau of the Census Series II fertility assumption of an average 2.1 lifetime births per woman with continuation of mortality rates at current levels. Figures are for the total population, including Armed Forces abroad, as of July 1.

SOURCES: U.S. Bureau of the Census: Population estimates and projections. *Current Population Reports*. Series P-25, Nos. 614 and 704. Washington. U.S. Government Printing Office, Dec. 1975 and July 1977.

Death rates due to diseases of the heart, according to race, sex, and age: United States, selected years 1950–76

(Data are based on the national vital registration system)

Race, sex, and age	Year										
	1950	1955	1960	1965	1970	1971	1972[1]	1973	1974	1975	1976
	Number of deaths per 100,000 resident population										
Total[2]											
All ages	356.8	356.5	369.0	368.0	362.0	360.5	363.0	360.8	349.2	336.2	337.2
Under 25 years	5.0	3.2	2.4	2.1	2.2	2.4	2.5	2.6	2.5	2.4	2.5
Under 1 year	4.1	7.4	6.6	9.8	13.1	15.4	20.2	23.0	22.0	20.3	23.1
1–24 years	5.0	3.0	2.1	1.7	1.8	1.9	1.9	2.0	1.9	1.8	1.8
25–29 years	14.8	11.7	9.9	8.6	7.0	6.8	6.3	6.5	5.6	5.6	5.6
30–34 years	27.5	22.4	20.9	19.5	16.6	15.3	14.9	14.3	14.1	12.4	12.1
35–39 years	57.3	49.1	47.7	46.0	40.8	40.3	38.0	36.8	33.1	32.6	30.1
40–44 years	122.5	107.7	103.5	98.8	90.7	88.3	86.4	83.6	78.3	76.0	72.8
45–49 years	228.7	200.8	197.6	188.4	174.4	170.3	168.9	165.7	159.1	147.3	145.7
50–54 years	397.5	362.0	355.8	340.4	308.3	298.1	292.1	283.8	271.3	261.9	252.5
55–59 years	642.2	584.1	571.6	535.7	514.3	503.2	493.0	493.2	459.2	437.0	423.2
60–64 years	1,007.9	915.2	934.2	905.6	811.9	796.8	800.2	774.3	738.0	710.3	701.7
65 years and over	2,844.5	2,772.7	2,823.0	2,778.7	2,683.3	2,673.2	2,682.3	2,643.3	2,537.9	2,403.9	2,393.5
65–69 years	1,494.6	1,427.9	1,412.6	1,348.1	1,263.8	1,211.5	1,208.3	1,161.2	1,109.6	1,049.5	1,021.6
70–74 years	2,348.1	2,168.5	2,173.5	1,999.9	1,936.4	1,899.7	1,919.6	1,869.6	1,800.2	1,708.2	1,658.6
75–79 years	3,683.4	3,462.1	3,358.8	3,242.5	3,052.2	3,018.5	3,049.8	3,010.2	2,849.3	2,716.1	2,707.6
80–84 years	5,476.1	5,421.5	5,501.5	5,103.6	4,744.1	4,636.9	4,601.5	4,523.1	4,332.6	4,133.8	4,090.6
85 years and over	9,151.0	8,917.2	9,317.8	9,538.4	7,891.3	8,468.9	8,386.9	8,382.1	7,983.1	7,282.0	7,384.3
White male											
All ages	434.2	438.5	454.6	450.8	438.3	433.9	434.1	430.9	415.5	401.1	399.4
Under 25 years	4.2	2.8	2.1	1.8	2.2	2.2	2.3	2.4	2.4	2.3	2.5
Under 1 year	4.6	6.7	6.9	8.9	12.0	12.1	14.7	18.4	19.1	19.3	22.4
1–24 years	4.2	2.6	1.9	1.5	1.8	1.8	1.9	1.9	1.9	1.8	1.8
25–29 years	14.4	12.3	9.5	8.2	6.8	7.0	6.2	6.6	5.8	6.1	6.0
30–34 years	29.0	26.6	24.9	22.6	18.8	18.3	17.3	16.5	16.1	14.4	14.9
35–39 years	68.4	66.1	66.0	62.2	54.8	54.7	49.7	48.8	45.2	43.4	41.3
40–44 years	160.4	152.4	151.7	144.8	131.3	129.5	126.1	123.5	115.3	111.6	109.2
45–49 years	313.3	291.6	300.4	287.1	266.0	260.0	259.3	254.1	246.7	228.5	223.2
50–54 years	544.6	523.9	540.4	520.3	474.2	461.1	453.5	436.9	420.1	405.9	390.1
55–59 years	878.6	836.8	842.0	812.8	784.3	769.2	750.6	754.8	703.3	668.9	642.7
60–64 years	1,324.3	1,262.6	1,311.6	1,314.6	1,209.9	1,190.2	1,204.1	1,161.3	1,103.5	1,067.4	1,049.0
65 years and over	3,302.2	3,251.2	3,363.2	3,401.3	3,316.2	3,302.4	3,302.8	3,267.0	3,132.9	2,986.0	2,963.2
65–69 years	1,939.7	1,889.6	1,928.7	1,903.1	1,828.8	1,767.8	1,760.4	1,714.4	1,650.1	1,567.9	1,537.2
70–74 years	2,852.9	2,724.2	2,788.8	2,679.5	2,641.4	2,598.5	2,629.2	2,569.4	2,472.9	2,367.3	2,317.7
75–79 years	4,248.7	4,090.3	4,099.6	4,082.8	3,939.0	3,925.8	3,980.7	3,946.9	3,759.3	3,600.1	3,603.3
80–84 years	6,186.6	6,258.3	6,340.5	6,137.4	5,828.7	5,729.9	5,707.0	5,703.1	5,437.0	5,283.2	5,219.4
85 years and over	9,959.6	9,316.0	10,135.8	10,657.3	8,818.0	9,786.5	9,575.7	9,664.1	9,269.2	8,550.3	8,692.9

White female

	290.5	293.0	306.5	310.7	313.8	316.1	321.0	319.4	312.3	301.3	305.5
All ages	290.5	293.0	306.5	310.7	313.8	316.1	321.0	319.4	312.3	301.3	305.5
Under 25 years	4.2	2.4	1.7	1.5	1.4	1.6	1.7	1.8	1.7	1.7	1.6
Under 1 year	2.9	5.6	4.3	7.4	7.0	9.9	14.6	14.9	14.6	16.0	15.5
1–24 years	4.3	2.3	1.5	1.3	1.2	1.3	1.2	1.3	1.3	1.2	1.2
25–29 years	10.4	7.3	6.2	5.0	3.6	3.5	3.5	3.5	2.8	2.9	2.8
30–34 years	17.0	11.6	10.0	9.2	7.7	6.4	6.8	6.7	6.4	5.7	5.1
35–39 years	29.8	20.8	18.5	17.9	15.3	14.7	14.8	14.8	12.7	12.1	11.4
40–44 years	56.3	42.3	39.4	34.5	31.7	31.8	31.0	30.0	28.4	27.8	25.3
45–49 years	103.8	78.7	72.7	70.9	63.3	64.1	58.2	58.6	55.2	51.8	53.1
50–54 years	184.2	149.8	137.9	134.0	121.7	116.9	110.4	110.5	104.4	103.4	97.1
55–59 years	331.4	282.1	263.4	239.1	227.7	225.4	217.0	217.0	201.5	194.0	189.9
60–64 years	613.9	522.9	518.9	468.1	419.4	414.9	404.1	392.7	376.8	360.0	357.6
65 years and over	2,503.1	2,430.0	2,432.8	2,367.9	2,283.9	2,280.1	2,301.1	2,253.7	2,174.3	2,053.1	2,056.1
65–69 years	1,055.9	975.3	914.7	852.3	763.5	725.6	730.1	684.5	653.5	619.3	597.7
70–74 years	1,891.2	1,682.6	1,635.6	1,453.1	1,384.7	1,341.7	1,356.9	1,285.8	1,236.8	1,165.4	1,121.1
75–79 years	3,237.2	3,015.1	2,848.9	2,672.8	2,473.6	2,432.4	2,461.4	2,418.9	2,279.5	2,152.0	2,120.3
80–84 years	5,166.9	5,041.9	5,062.0	4,591.4	4,221.5	4,141.8	4,107.4	3,997.4	3,867.8	3,644.7	3,616.3
85 years and over	9,085.7	9,155.9	9,280.8	9,333.2	7,839.9	8,215.1	8,222.6	8,156.1	7,778.6	7,105.3	7,244.5

All other male

	342.0	319.4	320.5	318.4	310.2	303.9	308.4	305.9	291.0	277.1	276.5
All ages	342.0	319.4	320.5	318.4	310.2	303.9	308.4	305.9	291.0	277.1	276.5
Under 25 years	9.7	6.8	5.3	4.9	5.2	5.9	6.7	6.6	5.2	4.9	5.5
Under 1 year	5.9	12.6	13.1	20.4	32.2	38.4	53.3	63.4	47.2	35.4	44.6
1–24 years	9.9	6.5	4.9	4.1	4.1	4.5	4.8	4.4	3.7	3.8	4.0
25–29 years	31.2	28.8	26.2	27.4	26.5	20.6	20.7	21.9	20.1	19.1	18.0
30–34 years	71.9	51.1	53.7	55.1	49.9	46.1	47.4	42.8	43.7	41.7	37.6
35–39 years	129.0	106.7	112.5	118.7	112.3	109.7	105.3	98.6	88.1	96.3	88.5
40–44 years	261.8	232.3	211.3	233.6	230.2	203.4	203.2	185.6	173.6	178.2	163.6
45–49 years	428.9	414.1	365.6	374.5	376.1	353.2	380.1	361.9	330.4	301.6	298.3
50–54 years	813.9	676.2	631.0	627.2	585.0	560.3	575.7	561.1	533.5	507.9	510.8
55–59 years	1,196.4	999.4	912.1	876.2	891.0	882.4	891.0	888.5	836.1	758.8	767.5
60–64 years	1,663.9	1,522.6	1,540.7	1,499.1	1,267.5	1,232.7	1,255.0	1,244.4	1,188.9	1,126.5	1,168.7
65 years and over	2,637.9	2,562.6	2,752.1	2,715.7	2,680.1	2,673.8	2,700.4	2,700.5	2,569.5	2,431.5	2,382.0
65–69 years	1,856.9	1,811.7	1,983.3	1,864.3	1,816.9	1,692.3	1,726.7	1,662.9	1,565.9	1,446.6	1,416.7
70–74 years	2,518.1	2,467.6	2,562.5	2,429.8	2,540.9	2,594.0	2,582.2	2,686.1	2,638.8	2,437.6	2,341.6
75–79 years	3,578.1	3,066.3	3,098.6	3,277.0	3,359.3	3,317.1	3,415.2	3,352.7	3,214.4	3,152.2	3,171.5
80–84 years	3,845.9	4,064.3	4,489.1	3,973.0	3,948.9	3,887.7	3,890.9	3,869.5	3,519.0	3,589.5	3,478.9
85 years and over	6,152.6	5,720.8	6,128.6	6,929.4	4,983.6	5,808.2	5,725.5	5,826.4	5,501.8	4,917.2	4,826.5

See footnotes at end of table.

Death rates due to diseases of the heart, according to race, sex, and age: United States, selected years 1950–76—Continued

(Data are based on the national vital registration system)

Number of deaths per 100,000 resident population

Race, sex, and age	Year										
	1950	1955	1960	1965	1970	1971	1972[1]	1973	1974	1975	1976
Black male:											
All ages	348.4	- - -	330.6	331.7	330.3	319.9	326.1	324.4	308.6	296.1	296.9
Under 25 years	9.8	- - -	5.3	5.1	5.4	6.0	6.9	6.9	5.4	5.2	5.7
Under 1 year	- - -	- - -	13.9	21.3	33.5	37.5	55.8	68.4	46.9	37.2	46.6
1–24 years	- - -	- - -	4.8	4.3	4.3	4.7	5.0	4.6	3.9	4.0	4.3
25–29 years	32.5	- - -	28.1	28.4	28.0	22.8	22.0	23.6	22.0	21.2	20.1
30–34 years	73.8	- - -	57.7	59.7	57.4	52.5	53.4	48.8	49.3	47.9	43.6
35–39 years	133.7	- - -	120.0	127.7	124.5	121.2	113.3	107.1	95.2	104.2	97.6
40–44 years	271.4	- - -	222.1	250.1	253.4	220.2	220.6	203.3	190.7	194.3	180.6
45–49 years	442.3	- - -	386.0	397.3	412.8	381.3	413.6	391.1	358.6	329.7	327.8
50–54 years	841.2	- - -	667.0	661.6	626.1	593.5	621.1	600.8	569.5	547.8	553.8
55–59 years	1,225.8	- - -	973.2	931.4	954.3	930.0	947.7	946.4	888.2	804.5	826.0
60–64 years	1,717.3	- - -	1,593.9	1,613.1	1,354.6	1,307.4	1,328.2	1,318.8	1,248.5	1,189.7	1,238.0
65 years and over	2,680.8	- - -	2,798.4	2,790.4	2,836.7	2,802.5	2,842.2	2,852.2	2,726.3	2,580.9	2,527.4
65–69 years	1,894.9	- - -	2,030.4	1,937.9	1,934.9	1,782.0	1,810.4	1,745.0	1,631.1	1,509.7	1,464.7
70–74 years	2,570.3	- - -	2,661.2	2,547.8	2,694.5	2,733.9	2,752.7	2,908.0	2,866.0	2,636.9	2,539.7
75–79 years	{ 4,107.9	- - -	3,146.3	3,422.8	3,504.9	3,437.1	3,584.6	3,582.5	3,500.0	3,482.8	3,565.5
80–84 years	(combined)	- - -	4,409.5	4,078.6	4,305.1	4,147.6	4,215.2	4,122.5	3,798.6	3,826.7	3,721.8
85 years and over	(combined)	- - -	6,037.9	7,113.3	5,367.6	6,033.3	6,102.3	6,146.7	5,868.8	5,296.2	5,182.1
All other female											
All ages	283.0	256.8	255.5	248.6	241.0	236.7	237.6	239.7	227.9	214.7	215.9
Under 25 years	11.4	7.5	5.3	4.6	4.7	4.9	4.6	4.9	4.8	3.9	4.1
Under 1 year	6.4	16.3	11.7	17.4	31.4	39.5	44.7	45.8	48.4	31.3	42.6
1–24 years	11.7	6.9	4.9	3.9	3.5	3.5	3.1	3.4	3.3	2.9	2.7
25–29 years	37.3	26.7	23.1	19.8	14.2	15.9	14.2	13.0	9.8	7.6	9.7
30–34 years	66.1	51.1	43.8	36.7	31.6	27.5	24.1	24.6	25.1	17.5	17.6
35–39 years	129.1	91.2	83.2	73.5	59.6	58.6	59.3	52.9	44.6	45.2	32.7
40–44 years	245.5	177.2	158.2	147.8	118.8	112.4	107.4	99.7	91.5	80.0	76.1
45–49 years	397.6	319.1	257.9	227.0	203.2	188.1	188.2	179.2	169.7	146.3	145.5
50–54 years	667.9	542.7	455.1	390.1	342.0	318.8	308.5	297.4	276.5	247.5	247.6
55–59 years	998.8	789.2	712.6	592.7	535.5	487.8	523.2	493.8	455.1	436.3	410.1
60–64 years	1,421.7	1,143.2	1,170.6	1,100.9	828.7	770.5	804.3	764.0	718.1	686.7	662.9
65 years and over	2,158.2	2,075.8	2,197.2	2,090.8	2,094.4	2,094.6	2,070.9	2,117.5	1,999.6	1,864.5	1,866.4
65–69 years	1,366.7	1,394.6	1,393.3	1,251.3	1,226.8	1,168.1	1,112.9	1,073.1	977.6	892.9	833.7
70–74 years	2,160.0	1,879.6	2,006.4	1,765.9	1,836.4	1,894.7	1,930.5	2,081.9	1,980.4	1,867.0	1,782.3
75–79 years	3,059.7	2,712.3	2,507.5	2,503.7	2,492.6	2,492.2	2,400.0	2,483.7	2,368.4	2,382.9	2,597.9
80–84 years	2,955.0	3,045.1	3,730.2	3,570.1	3,353.5	3,105.8	3,133.3	3,034.2	2,870.4	2,638.9	2,698.5
85 years and over	5,350.0	4,811.8	5,564.1	5,912.2	4,784.7	5,159.2	5,029.3	5,205.7	4,882.5	4,181.8	4,160.3

Black female:

	289.9	268.5	263.8	261.0	253.5	256.1	259.4	247.6	235.7	237.4
All ages										
Under 25 years	11.4	5.4	4.8	4.8	5.0	5.0	5.2	5.0	4.2	4.2
Under 1 year	---	12.0	17.9	31.3	41.3	48.3	49.1	47.0	34.8	44.7
1–24 years	---	5.0	4.1	3.7	3.6	3.4	3.6	3.5	3.1	2.9
25–29 years	38.3	24.4	20.3	16.0	17.5	15.3	13.7	11.2	8.9	10.7
30–34 years	67.4	47.0	40.3	34.5	29.9	25.4	26.4	28.1	20.1	20.9
35–39 years	131.6	88.5	79.3	66.7	63.2	64.7	59.0	48.5	49.5	36.0
40–44 years	249.5	166.8	156.6	133.0	124.3	119.8	112.5	102.6	90.8	84.8
45–49 years	403.0	269.1	241.3	223.2	204.2	203.9	197.7	189.1	164.9	166.1
50–54 years	682.0	471.8	409.4	367.8	340.5	332.3	322.5	301.4	273.1	275.4
55–59 years	1,022.7	754.8	619.9	567.6	517.0	550.2	525.7	485.2	471.2	443.1
60–64 years	1,457.0	1,211.1	1,165.4	878.2	804.7	839.9	800.4	756.6	726.8	702.3
65 years and over	2,172.9	2,234.7	2,151.9	2,199.4	2,180.6	2,169.8	2,219.6	2,102.8	1,970.1	1,969.3
65–69 years	1,378.8	1,430.6	1,307.0	1,291.6	1,216.6	1,162.7	1,120.7	983.0	924.3	859.2
70–74 years	2,188.3	2,055.2	1,816.2	1,947.6	2,002.9	2,056.2	2,239.5	2,145.9	2,029.6	1,935.2
75–79 years	} 3,499.3	2,545.0	2,585.8	2,625.8	2,615.8	2,551.9	2,659.5	2,564.1	2,632.5	2,869.9
80–84 years	} 3,499.3	3,743.1	3,632.9	3,536.8	3,178.9	3,256.9	3,177.1	3,025.7	2,798.3	2,884.4
85 years and over	3,499.3	5,650.0	6,030.4	5,003.8	5,363.8	5,273.0	5,403.8	5,130.7	4,398.0	4,344.0

[1] Based on a 50-percent sample of deaths.
[2] Includes all races and both sexes.

NOTE: The ICDA revisions and code numbers are for 1950 and 1955, Sixth Revision, Nos. 400–402, 410–443; for 1960 and 1965, Seventh Revision, Nos.400–402, 410–443; and for 1970–76, Eighth Revision, Nos. 390–398, 402, 404, 410–414, 420–429.

SOURCES: National Center for Health Statistics: *Vital Statistics of the United States*, Vol. II, for data years 1950–1973, Washington. U.S. Government Printing Office; for data years 1974–1976, Public Health Service, DHEW, Hyattsville, Md. To be published; U.S. Bureau of the Census: Population estimates and projections. *Current Population Reports*. Series P–25, Nos. 310, 519, 529, and 643. Washington, U.S. Government Printing Office, June 1965, Apr. 1974, Sept. 1974, and Jan. 1977; General population characteristics, United States summary, 1960 and 1970. *U.S. Census of Population*. Final reports PC(1)–B1; *1950 Nonwhite Population by Race*, Special report P-E No. 3B. Washington, U.S. Government Printing Office, 1961, 1972, and 1951; National Center for Health Statistics: Data computed by the Division of Analysis from data compiled by the Division of Vital Statistics.

Death rates due to ischemic heart disease, according to race, sex, and age: United States, 1968–76

(Data are based on the national vital registration system)

Race, sex, and age	Year								
	1968	1969	1970	1971	1972[1]	1973	1974	1975	1976
	Number of deaths per 100,000 resident population								
Total[2]									
All ages	338.4	332.6	328.1	327.0	328.7	326.0	314.5	301.7	301.0
Under 25 years	0.3	0.3	0.3	0.4	0.3	0.3	0.2	0.2	0.2
25–29 years	2.8	2.9	3.1	2.9	2.5	2.4	2.0	2.0	2.1
30–34 years	10.4	10.1	10.0	9.9	8.4	8.3	8.3	7.4	7.4
35–39 years	32.4	32.1	30.4	30.2	28.2	27.6	24.1	23.8	22.0
40–44 years	79.3	76.6	73.7	72.6	71.0	68.4	64.4	62.3	59.8
45–49 years	158.3	153.2	148.6	146.0	144.6	141.6	136.1	126.3	123.2
50–54 years	283.8	275.7	269.6	262.4	256.2	248.7	236.7	228.6	218.6
55–59 years	479.2	463.2	457.9	448.0	436.1	438.2	406.8	385.5	370.4
60–64 years	781.5	744.4	733.1	718.2	719.6	694.8	660.1	633.8	622.1
65 years and over	2,573.1	2,527.1	2,470.4	2,461.2	2,467.1	2,424.1	2,319.1	2,186.7	2,166.2
65–69 years	1,213.6	1,178.0	1,151.9	1,105.9	1,098.3	1,053.3	1,001.9	944.5	912.8
70–74 years	1,862.8	1,813.2	1,785.3	1,749.5	1,764.7	1,713.7	1,640.2	1,547.5	1,495.1
75–79 years	2,932.7	2,835.6	2,824.2	2,787.9	2,817.7	2,768.7	2,612.9	2,481.6	2,458.1
80–84 years	4,581.0	4,519.8	4,383.5	4,292.5	4,254.1	4,168.4	3,978.2	3,777.4	3,716.2
85 years and over	8,483.0	8,284.5	7,249.4	7,780.4	7,712.0	7,692.6	7,315.5	6,640.0	6,715.0
White male									
All ages	419.3	411.9	404.9	400.6	400.1	396.1	380.3	366.3	362.5
Under 25 years	0.3	0.3	0.3	0.4	0.3	0.3	0.3	0.3	0.2
25–29 years	3.4	3.3	3.8	3.5	3.2	3.0	2.5	2.8	2.8
30–34 years	13.7	13.3	13.3	13.8	12.0	11.7	11.3	10.6	10.6
35–39 years	48.7	48.5	46.0	45.7	41.4	40.9	37.3	35.8	34.0
40–44 years	123.4	120.0	115.6	114.3	111.5	108.9	101.7	99.1	96.6
45–49 years	255.0	248.7	240.2	235.9	234.2	229.0	221.9	205.4	199.3
50–54 years	454.1	442.5	433.0	421.9	413.8	397.6	380.9	368.8	350.7
55–59 years	746.5	731.9	722.2	708.1	686.6	692.3	641.7	608.5	582.2
60–64 years	1,187.1	1,144.2	1,120.7	1,099.7	1,110.1	1,068.3	1,012.1	977.6	952.0
65 years and over	3,204.0	3,153.9	3,090.3	3,074.4	3,072.5	3,029.8	2,892.3	2,747.3	2,712.0
65–69 years	1,760.1	1,723.8	1,698.5	1,644.6	1,632.2	1,586.0	1,518.6	1,441.3	1,402.6
70–74 years	2,582.9	2,524.2	2,468.7	2,429.6	2,456.6	2,390.5	2,286.5	2,179.7	2,121.6
75–79 years	3,792.5	3,686.6	3,686.6	3,662.5	3,717.4	3,666.9	3,483.4	3,323.3	3,307.0
80–84 years	5,597.4	5,560.1	5,436.4	5,344.9	5,308.2	5,297.0	5,024.9	4,859.0	4,778.4
85 years and over	9,598.7	9,443.1	8,164.2	9,028.4	8,851.6	8,920.7	8,527.3	7,841.9	7,954.4

White female

	286.6	283.7	282.5	285.1	289.4	287.3	280.5	269.2	272.0
All ages	286.6	283.7	282.5	285.1	289.4	287.3	280.5	269.2	272.0
Under 25 years	0.2	0.2	0.1	0.2	0.2	0.2	0.1	0.1	0.1
25–29 years	1.1	1.0	1.2	1.2	0.8	1.1	0.7	0.6	0.8
30–34 years	3.4	3.0	3.5	3.0	2.7	3.0	2.9	2.3	2.1
35–39 years	8.7	9.2	8.4	8.6	8.8	8.9	7.3	7.1	6.3
40–44 years	23.3	22.4	21.1	21.8	21.3	20.1	19.0	18.8	17.5
45–49 years	48.6	46.0	45.8	47.2	43.4	43.7	40.9	38.9	39.5
50–54 years	99.3	95.8	96.1	93.2	88.0	87.8	82.5	81.7	76.5
55–59 years	200.1	188.5	189.6	187.5	178.9	181.0	168.9	161.6	155.8
60–64 years	381.3	358.2	364.1	360.5	350.5	339.1	325.3	308.9	306.9
65 years and over	2,174.5	2,139.7	2,093.4	2,092.4	2,110.1	2,060.8	1,983.2	1,863.6	1,858.0
65–69 years	731.0	700.3	685.3	650.6	651.9	609.4	578.5	546.5	522.5
70–74 years	1,315.4	1,280.1	1,269.0	1,227.8	1,237.4	1,169.2	1,118.6	1,046.5	1,004.2
75–79 years	2,372.5	2,289.1	2,276.3	2,239.3	2,265.4	2,218.6	2,085.3	1,963.3	1,922.0
80–84 years	4,095.3	4,025.6	3,889.7	3,826.6	3,796.9	3,681.7	3,549.0	3,331.1	3,284.9
85 years and over	8,311.6	8,118.8	7,192.3	7,553.2	7,564.6	7,486.0	7,143.4	6,484.7	6,596.1

All other male

	278.8	269.5	261.1	256.6	257.8	255.8	244.0	229.9	228.3
All ages	278.8	269.5	261.1	256.6	257.8	255.8	244.0	229.9	228.3
Under 25 years	0.9	0.7	0.7	0.9	0.9	0.7	0.3	0.5	0.3
25–29 years	10.6	11.5	10.9	9.5	7.0	7.6	7.3	6.5	6.1
30–34 years	31.9	36.6	28.5	29.4	23.7	22.7	23.2	20.9	20.9
35–39 years	87.6	81.9	75.0	77.1	72.1	66.9	57.0	61.1	59.7
40–44 years	182.9	180.4	174.0	156.7	151.9	140.1	134.4	135.2	122.8
45–49 years	328.9	318.9	304.5	284.8	302.3	288.2	267.8	245.4	234.8
50–54 years	521.9	521.7	483.5	471.4	481.5	468.0	443.9	421.5	422.9
55–59 years	820.6	766.7	750.1	742.7	751.3	749.7	700.2	633.8	637.4
60–64 years	1,222.9	1,128.2	1,084.7	1,061.9	1,066.3	1,063.7	1,006.7	950.4	985.6
65 years and over	2,469.4	2,421.0	2,349.4	2,336.8	2,351.7	2,344.0	2,238.8	2,086.8	2,034.8
65–69 years	1,655.5	1,630.6	1,568.2	1,460.8	1,472.7	1,422.2	1,349.4	1,223.3	1,200.8
70–74 years	2,318.5	2,213.8	2,234.3	2,246.3	2,254.5	2,344.0	2,289.0	2,096.3	1,985.5
75–79 years	2,979.0	3,010.0	2,966.7	2,929.5	3,013.6	2,922.1	2,806.1	2,712.3	2,723.6
80–84 years	3,535.8	3,661.8	3,471.9	3,458.9	3,392.2	3,372.0	3,120.2	3,117.4	2,984.4
85 years and over	5,958.5	5,259.1	4,418.8	5,110.2	5,023.5	5,090.6	4,831.6	4,245.3	4,176.5

See footnotes at end of table.

Death rates due to ischemic heart disease, according to race, sex, and age: United States, 1968–76—Continued

(Data are based on the national vital registration system)

Race, sex, and age	Year								
	1968	1969	1970	1971	1972[1]	1973	1974	1975	1976
	Number of deaths per 100,000 resident population								
Black male:									
All ages	290.8	282.0	277.2	269.3	271.9	270.4	258.1	244.9	244.2
Under 25 years	0.8	0.7	0.7	0.9	1.0	0.7	0.3	0.6	0.4
25–29 years	11.8	12.9	11.7	10.6	7.6	8.5	8.2	7.4	7.0
30–34 years	35.4	39.9	32.7	33.6	26.8	25.8	26.1	23.9	23.6
35–39 years	94.0	89.1	83.3	85.2	76.9	73.0	61.2	65.3	65.5
40–44 years	196.5	192.6	191.3	168.9	164.8	152.5	147.9	147.8	135.5
45–49 years	348.8	341.2	333.0	305.7	328.3	310.0	290.8	267.6	257.7
50–54 years	548.8	552.6	516.0	498.7	520.5	499.6	473.8	453.7	456.5
55–59 years	864.7	813.9	803.3	780.4	800.0	796.7	740.9	669.2	684.8
60–64 years	1,302.5	1,198.2	1,157.8	1,125.2	1,125.4	1,123.4	1,055.5	1,000.8	1,041.3
65 years and over	2,560.5	2,518.4	2,479.5	2,442.2	2,464.1	2,468.3	2,368.2	2,207.8	2,150.3
65–69 years	1,737.4	1,711.4	1,664.3	1,533.1	1,534.9	1,488.0	1,402.2	1,275.4	1,235.8
70–74 years	2,397.3	2,301.6	2,364.8	2,360.4	2,398.9	2,531.0	2,478.7	2,253.5	2,142.9
75–79 years	3,039.8	3,106.4	3,085.7	3,027.6	3,155.6	3,114.9	3,044.2	2,986.2	3,047.9
80–84 years	3,777.2	3,913.8	3,778.5	3,674.6	3,651.5	3,581.7	3,581.7	3,318.7	3,193.6
85 years and over	6,302.9	5,602.7	4,743.7	5,309.5	5,344.2	5,348.9	5,131.3	4,558.5	4,464.3
All other female									
All ages	213.4	204.2	200.4	197.5	197.7	200.7	188.9	177.7	176.9
Under 25 years	0.4	0.5	0.4	0.5	0.2	0.4	0.4	0.2	0.2
25–29 years	3.8	6.0	4.3	4.5	4.6	3.3	2.1	2.2	2.2
30–34 years	17.9	14.0	15.7	12.9	9.4	9.4	11.6	8.6	8.3
35–39 years	40.5	39.2	38.3	34.8	34.9	33.2	23.3	26.5	17.6
40–44 years	97.5	86.1	79.8	78.1	76.8	69.8	65.9	52.9	49.8
45–49 years	166.3	154.3	149.1	140.4	140.9	134.1	126.6	111.6	104.5
50–54 years	287.7	270.0	265.3	253.4	238.0	241.2	219.6	192.7	194.7
55–59 years	474.9	447.0	433.3	393.8	421.2	395.8	367.0	349.2	320.1
60–64 years	809.3	745.3	703.6	643.1	674.4	642.3	597.1	570.1	541.7
65 years and over	1,943.5	1,869.7	1,830.0	1,836.7	1,810.6	1,855.0	1,730.9	1,606.6	1,595.6
65–69 years	1,198.1	1,142.4	1,055.3	1,011.4	958.5	922.8	831.1	749.8	698.4
70–74 years	1,602.4	1,559.7	1,590.2	1,655.1	1,661.8	1,821.2	1,715.4	1,592.7	1,509.4
75–79 years	2,326.3	2,157.7	2,205.6	2,181.4	2,101.8	2,182.6	2,051.7	2,070.2	2,237.4
80–84 years	3,100.0	2,975.8	2,949.1	2,749.5	2,800.0	2,660.8	2,513.6	2,302.3	2,332.8
85 years and over	5,096.7	4,930.7	4,227.9	4,582.9	4,461.0	4,633.0	4,251.5	3,662.7	3,590.9

Black female:

Age	All ages 227.4	218.8	217.0	211.6	213.0	217.3	205.4	195.2	194.5
Under 25 years	0.5	0.5	0.5	0.6	0.2	0.5	0.4	0.2	0.3
25–29 years	4.1	6.5	4.9	5.1	5.1	3.7	2.5	2.5	2.6
30–34 years	19.8	15.9	17.5	14.1	10.6	10.7	13.0	9.9	9.8
35–39 years	44.0	42.5	43.5	38.2	38.9	37.1	25.7	29.6	19.8
40–44 years	107.2	94.8	89.1	86.8	86.0	79.4	74.6	60.7	55.9
45–49 years	179.4	167.1	163.6	152.4	154.1	148.1	142.4	126.6	118.8
50–54 years	303.7	288.7	285.5	271.5	255.7	262.1	239.2	212.6	216.8
55–59 years	500.0	472.5	459.2	420.1	443.2	421.3	391.2	377.1	345.1
60–64 years	849.5	785.8	747.7	672.5	706.0	671.5	628.7	605.0	573.4
65 years and over	2,012.4	1,947.8	1,920.2	1,909.4	1,893.9	1,944.9	1,819.0	1,696.1	1,682.8
65–69 years	1,250.4	1,200.3	1,111.8	1,053.4	998.9	964.7	856.1	777.3	721.3
70–74 years	1,678.1	1,627.4	1,683.5	1,747.7	1,768.5	1,960.1	1,858.4	1,731.3	1,638.1
75–79 years	2,411.3	2,258.3	2,320.0	2,280.9	2,233.8	2,331.4	2,217.6	2,282.2	2,491.9
80–84 years	3,158.0	3,120.5	3,110.5	2,810.5	2,907.8	2,785.3	2,650.4	2,439.8	2,490.2
85 years and over	5,269.6	5,070.0	4,418.2	4,760.9	4,666.2	4,831.3	4,462.5	3,843.4	3,747.7

[1] Based on a 50-percent sample of deaths.

[2] Includes all races and both sexes.

NOTE: The ICDA revision and code numbers are the Eighth Revision, Nos. 410–413.

SOURCES: National Center for Health Statistics: *Vital Statistics of the United States*, Vol. II, for data years 1968–1973. Washington. U.S. Government Printing Office; for data years 1974–1976. Public Health Service, DHEW, Hyattsville, Md. To be published; U.S. Bureau of the Census: Population estimates and projections. *Current Population Reports*. Series P–25, Nos. 519, 529, and 643. Washington. U.S. Government Printing Office, Apr. 1974, Sept. 1974, and Jan. 1977; National Center for Health Statistics: Data computed by the Division of Analysis from data compiled by the Division of Vital Statistics.

Death rates due to malignant neoplasms, according to race, sex, and age: United States, selected years 1950–76

(Data are based on the national vital registration system)

Number of deaths per 100,000 resident population

Race, sex, and age	1950	1955	1960	1965	1970	1971	1972[1]	1973	1974	1975	1976
Total[2]											
All ages	139.8	146.5	149.2	153.8	162.8	163.6	166.0	167.3	170.5	171.7	175.8
Under 25 years	8.5	8.6	8.1	7.5	7.0	6.7	6.4	6.4	6.0	5.7	5.7
Under 1 year	8.7	7.7	7.2	7.1	4.7	4.3	4.6	4.4	3.8	4.2	3.2
1–24 years	8.5	8.6	8.2	7.6	7.1	6.8	6.5	6.4	6.0	5.8	5.7
25–29 years	15.1	14.6	14.7	13.8	12.7	13.0	12.1	11.9	11.5	11.4	11.2
30–34 years	25.3	23.7	23.8	24.0	21.0	21.7	20.3	20.0	19.2	19.2	18.7
35–39 years	45.8	44.5	43.0	42.4	40.9	38.7	39.0	39.7	38.1	35.5	35.2
40–44 years	81.2	79.2	77.6	78.4	76.8	76.4	75.4	72.0	72.1	71.2	68.9
45–49 years	137.0	135.7	135.4	136.1	139.3	137.6	138.7	139.9	140.0	136.6	134.4
50–54 years	216.9	219.7	224.2	227.4	229.6	224.7	222.7	222.4	227.1	226.2	228.4
55–59 years	329.6	327.4	327.8	330.5	357.5	355.1	362.4	359.7	360.1	352.7	356.2
60–64 years	468.5	466.2	478.3	496.1	498.8	496.7	499.9	508.4	523.1	519.7	533.5
65 years and over	851.3	869.5	870.9	887.0	923.4	934.5	947.6	946.7	957.2	961.1	979.0
65–69 years	598.8	638.0	634.6	647.9	674.0	676.8	682.1	679.5	676.2	670.3	685.3
70–74 years	830.0	812.7	818.6	829.9	857.1	864.7	897.3	888.5	909.6	923.1	927.8
75–79 years	1,077.6	1,067.1	1,032.9	1,047.0	1,099.5	1,104.3	1,121.4	1,133.4	1,153.3	1,152.9	1,185.0
80–84 years	1,294.2	1,294.9	1,310.1	1,239.2	1,286.1	1,272.1	1,273.4	1,271.1	1,304.6	1,326.0	1,343.1
85 years and over	1,450.8	1,465.3	1,450.0	1,483.6	1,320.7	1,440.7	1,428.5	1,435.3	1,414.7	1,408.8	1,441.5
White male											
All ages	147.2	160.0	166.1	173.7	185.1	186.1	188.7	189.6	193.7	194.8	199.2
Under 25 years	9.7	10.4	9.7	8.8	8.5	8.1	7.8	7.6	7.1	6.8	6.8
Under 1 year	9.6	8.7	7.9	6.2	4.3	4.5	4.0	4.5	3.8	4.5	3.1
1–24 years	9.7	10.4	9.8	8.9	8.6	8.3	7.9	7.7	7.2	6.8	6.9
25–29 years	15.0	15.0	16.4	15.0	13.7	14.4	13.0	13.4	12.1	12.5	12.1
30–34 years	20.6	19.8	21.1	21.1	19.1	20.9	17.6	18.1	17.7	18.2	16.4
35–39 years	32.7	33.0	33.8	35.5	33.6	33.2	32.4	34.5	31.8	29.4	29.8
40–44 years	57.2	56.2	59.7	63.4	65.3	63.7	62.5	62.1	60.4	59.6	58.7
45–49 years	110.4	113.5	114.5	119.5	122.9	122.2	122.7	125.6	129.7	124.3	124.7
50–54 years	194.7	209.5	219.9	222.9	225.4	220.4	217.8	216.1	226.8	224.9	225.1
55–59 years	327.9	340.5	360.1	368.3	397.4	391.9	401.7	388.6	389.3	378.2	382.7
60–64 years	506.0	529.6	559.3	598.1	617.0	601.4	613.6	614.3	629.6	619.7	630.5
65 years and over	986.0	1,045.6	1,073.4	1,144.9	1,221.2	1,249.2	1,267.7	1,270.1	1,286.8	1,296.0	1,318.3
65–69 years	685.5	767.1	780.0	832.0	879.3	888.8	887.4	888.0	890.9	887.3	900.3
70–74 years	965.2	986.4	1,029.9	1,078.3	1,153.8	1,171.7	1,216.2	1,201.2	1,221.0	1,248.8	1,247.4
75–79 years	1,261.4	1,297.0	1,297.9	1,376.3	1,493.3	1,530.3	1,569.2	1,573.5	1,629.5	1,616.8	1,672.8
80–84 years	1,573.4	1,633.0	1,648.4	1,647.5	1,770.2	1,791.2	1,821.3	1,834.2	1,870.6	1,923.3	1,964.8
85 years and over	1,733.9	1,746.9	1,791.4	1,958.7	1,772.2	2,001.7	1,966.5	2,062.5	2,034.0	2,046.6	2,110.9

White female

Age	139.9	141.0	139.8	141.9	149.4	149.5	152.2	153.0	156.1	157.7	162.0
All ages	139.9	141.0	139.8	141.9	149.4	149.5	152.2	153.0	156.1	157.7	162.0
Under 25 years	7.8	7.4	7.0	6.7	6.0	5.6	5.5	5.3	5.0	4.9	4.7
Under 1 year	7.8	7.2	6.8	6.2	5.4	4.1	4.9	4.5	3.4	4.2	3.6
1–24 years	7.8	7.4	7.0	6.7	6.0	5.6	5.5	5.3	5.1	4.9	4.8
25–29 years	14.8	13.8	12.7	12.4	11.6	11.3	11.0	10.5	10.7	10.2	10.3
30–34 years	27.3	25.7	24.2	25.1	21.8	21.4	21.2	20.7	20.1	19.5	20.3
35–39 years	53.9	51.7	47.9	44.3	44.5	39.7	41.1	41.8	40.5	37.7	38.6
40–44 years	97.4	93.3	86.7	85.0	78.8	80.8	79.2	73.7	75.5	75.0	71.0
45–49 years	153.1	144.8	143.8	140.4	142.6	139.0	139.8	137.7	137.3	134.3	131.3
50–54 years	221.1	213.8	211.6	216.5	214.8	210.2	207.5	206.2	206.6	208.1	209.5
55–59 years	314.5	297.8	281.7	279.0	301.9	299.6	305.4	306.7	308.8	302.9	306.3
60–64 years	419.4	394.5	382.6	380.8	380.0	384.2	383.0	394.5	404.9	406.6	420.7
65 years and over	768.4	747.6	718.4	702.0	714.3	713.1	724.6	719.0	726.7	729.2	744.9
65–69 years	534.2	526.7	500.3	488.3	495.6	493.1	502.1	498.8	493.7	486.1	506.7
70–74 years	733.1	679.5	641.6	623.6	626.4	622.9	646.3	630.2	646.0	655.4	661.2
75–79 years	956.1	912.7	847.8	820.5	836.2	823.2	825.4	840.5	845.1	842.2	856.6
80–84 years	1,153.1	1,114.8	1,107.2	1,005.8	1,011.9	986.1	985.4	974.8	1,008.0	1,019.6	1,023.7
85 years and over	1,348.1	1,357.6	1,304.9	1,257.5	1,126.6	1,200.4	1,204.6	1,174.0	1,164.8	1,165.9	1,192.8

All other male

Age	106.1	119.1	134.1	144.3	161.0	161.8	165.2	170.1	173.5	175.3	179.2
All ages	106.1	119.1	134.1	144.3	161.0	161.8	165.2	170.1	173.5	175.3	179.2
Under 25 years	7.2	7.3	6.9	6.4	6.7	6.4	5.7	6.3	6.0	5.5	5.8
Under 1 year	10.4	6.9	6.5	6.1	4.7	3.9	6.7	3.5	5.6	3.8	4.7
1–24 years	7.0	7.3	6.9	6.4	6.8	6.5	5.7	6.4	6.0	5.6	5.8
25–29 years	14.8	12.0	14.7	13.1	11.4	13.9	11.7	11.0	10.6	11.6	10.6
30–34 years	21.5	21.8	21.7	19.5	23.6	20.2	25.1	19.9	16.7	18.5	17.6
35–39 years	39.7	38.3	47.3	48.8	44.1	47.3	50.4	43.6	43.1	45.6	37.1
40–44 years	74.4	84.9	99.3	103.6	108.1	101.1	110.3	94.0	98.9	100.5	99.7
45–49 years	144.6	170.3	169.9	184.6	213.9	200.7	217.3	220.7	208.7	208.8	204.4
50–54 years	282.3	277.6	308.8	327.2	373.7	356.8	359.1	376.0	385.7	382.1	385.0
55–59 years	421.1	447.6	433.7	485.9	553.3	570.1	612.0	612.9	619.3	612.7	618.8
60–64 years	571.6	643.2	710.6	754.8	750.3	783.5	757.9	807.8	830.3	863.0	909.7
65 years and over	691.6	810.4	982.4	1,073.8	1,221.1	1,240.4	1,270.7	1,319.0	1,349.2	1,351.5	1,377.7
65–69 years	579.2	722.0	864.1	901.4	988.8	987.5	1,012.4	1,020.7	1,022.5	1,035.1	1,017.5
70–74 years	720.7	818.7	1,021.2	1,119.3	1,266.3	1,300.5	1,359.6	1,436.6	1,518.7	1,503.2	1,568.8
75–79 years	896.9	891.6	1,038.0	1,217.7	1,504.5	1,496.9	1,568.2	1,648.1	1,668.2	1,700.7	1,813.9
80–84 years	751.4	957.1	1,195.5	1,252.4	1,593.8	1,534.2	1,470.1	1,523.2	1,625.0	1,654.7	1,671.1
85 years and over	900.0	1,045.8	1,211.7	1,458.8	1,268.4	1,493.9	1,458.8	1,566.0	1,535.1	1,479.7	1,473.5

See footnotes at end of table.

Death rates due to malignant neoplasms, according to race, sex, and age: United States, selected years 1950–76—Continued

(Data are based on the national vital registration system)

Number of deaths per 100,000 resident population

Race, sex, and age	1950	1955	1960	1965	1970	1971	1972[1]	1973	1974	1975	1976
Black male:											
All ages	106.6	...	136.7	149.2	171.6	170.6	174.2	180.7	184.4	188.5	193.5
Under 25 years	7.1	...	6.7	6.4	6.8	6.4	5.9	6.6	6.1	5.7	6.0
Under 1 year	...	...	6.8	6.0	5.3	4.0	5.8	3.5	6.3	3.1	4.5
1–24 years	...	...	6.7	6.4	6.9	6.5	5.9	6.7	6.1	5.8	6.0
25–29 years	15.3	...	15.0	13.9	12.8	14.5	12.4	12.1	11.6	12.5	11.4
30–34 years	21.1	...	21.7	20.3	25.9	20.9	25.9	20.6	17.6	19.9	18.4
35–39 years	39.3	...	47.7	51.1	46.6	50.4	52.8	47.2	46.1	48.1	40.0
40–44 years	74.3	...	101.2	107.5	115.7	109.0	120.7	102.4	106.9	110.3	108.8
45–49 years	147.5	...	177.9	195.3	229.2	216.8	231.3	238.7	227.2	229.3	223.2
50–54 years	288.5	...	324.4	344.6	404.1	381.8	383.4	403.0	414.3	416.1	418.2
55–59 years	425.2	...	461.4	511.9	595.7	606.9	652.8	653.6	654.6	657.8	666.6
60–64 years	580.1	...	740.1	802.8	802.3	826.6	805.5	857.3	881.2	915.8	970.4
65 years and over	696.1	...	980.4	1,097.4	1,297.6	1,303.9	1,332.7	1,395.8	1,433.4	1,441.6	1,475.0
65–69 years	581.2	...	886.5	939.5	1,049.4	1,041.4	1,063.7	1,060.0	1,068.9	1,086.9	1,062.7
70–74 years	733.3	...	1,017.1	1,136.5	1,349.1	1,365.1	1,437.6	1,557.2	1,641.0	1,621.9	1,714.3
75–79 years	}	...	1,012.6	1,247.5	1,580.6	1,572.4	1,651.3	1,776.3	1,809.7	1,875.0	2,026.1
80–84 years	853.5	...	1,145.2	1,246.4	1,707.7	1,611.1	1,536.4	1,615.5	1,766.7	1,784.0	1,783.3
85 years and over	}	...	1,155.2	1,456.7	1,387.0	1,528.6	1,507.0	1,653.3	1,604.2	1,573.6	1,614.3
All other female											
All ages	110.1	108.4	109.8	109.2	110.0	115.0	113.4	117.9	117.2	115.5	117.8
Under 25 years	6.4	5.5	5.9	5.3	4.9	5.5	4.4	5.4	4.7	4.6	4.2
Under 1 year	6.9	5.3	6.5	3.8	3.3	4.3	3.8	3.6	4.5	2.7	0.8
1–24 years	6.4	5.5	5.9	5.4	5.0	5.6	4.5	5.4	4.7	4.6	4.3
25–29 years	19.6	19.9	17.1	15.3	14.4	15.2	14.2	12.7	13.7	11.1	11.3
30–34 years	49.1	38.8	41.5	40.4	25.5	29.7	26.7	26.7	25.4	23.9	23.9
35–39 years	89.1	82.9	72.1	71.4	60.2	60.4	57.7	56.3	57.7	51.4	45.3
40–44 years	155.9	144.8	128.4	119.1	115.2	110.8	107.1	106.7	102.9	95.1	94.3
45–49 years	223.5	226.4	207.1	194.4	173.9	189.4	182.7	192.7	177.1	177.9	164.1
50–54 years	335.7	312.0	300.7	271.2	267.0	270.4	273.4	273.6	262.3	251.0	270.9
55–59 years	446.2	390.7	369.6	343.6	357.1	371.3	346.8	393.0	368.9	368.1	357.8
60–64 years	528.3	446.0	505.4	508.1	422.6	442.9	438.5	446.7	484.9	459.3	471.9
65 years and over	513.5	542.2	591.0	597.0	641.6	609.7	676.9	689.2	685.5	683.3	700.9
65–69 years	429.2	478.0	498.3	341.8	534.0	542.0	554.9	535.0	505.0	484.5	492.0
70–74 years	565.2	551.3	596.6	590.8	672.4	719.6	745.2	800.4	840.4	810.3	801.5
75–79 years	617.7	672.8	676.6	671.3	729.1	738.3	766.1	808.1	785.1	917.1	940.1
80–84 years	525.0	545.1	757.2	690.9	744.2	781.6	715.3	742.5	773.6	769.5	822.6
85 years and over	719.2	641.2	727.5	942.9	758.9	847.4	819.5	787.5	792.8	732.7	819.0

Black female:

Age	111.8	113.8	113.6	117.3	121.4	120.1	125.5	124.7	123.3	126.8
All ages	111.8	113.8	113.6	117.3	121.4	120.1	125.5	124.7	123.3	126.8
Under 25 years	6.5	6.0	5.4	5.1	5.6	4.6	5.4	4.7	4.7	4.2
Under 1 year	---	6.7	3.0	3.3	4.6	4.2	3.1	4.6	2.7	0.5
1–24 years	---	5.9	5.5	5.2	5.6	.46	5.5	4.7	4.8	4.3
25–29 years	19.7	18.4	16.6	15.4	16.6	15.3	13.6	14.9	11.2	12.3
30–34 years	50.6	43.1	43.9	27.0	30.8	22.7	28.9	26.9	25.4	25.8
35–39 years	89.2	75.9	73.9	64.6	61.8	62.6	59.3	60.6	54.8	48.4
40–44 years	156.6	132.4	124.6	124.7	118.9	117.1	115.2	111.6	101.4	100.3
45–49 years	227.3	210.7	201.8	183.2	202.6	193.8	208.8	190.6	191.3	177.3
50–54 years	339.5	308.4	278.4	280.3	284.2	287.8	290.4	279.6	270.6	290.6
55–59 years	449.9	384.8	355.0	370.7	388.0	361.1	407.7	382.0	385.5	377.7
60–64 years	530.1	518.5	527.4	444.7	455.3	450.5	463.4	501.1	472.7	491.1
65 years and over	513.0	591.4	601.2	668.4	623.0	695.2	713.4	709.7	704.4	730.3
65–69 years	428.4	505.0	515.5	558.3	554.3	563.8	545.8	513.6	489.0	497.8
70–74 years	569.5	596.5	593.5	702.3	749.0	778.7	852.4	897.9	860.1	855.5
75–79 years	} 605.3	673.4	670.1	762.5	761.2	792.2	848.4	831.4	989.8	1,028.6
80–84 years	}	745.1	672.6	764.7	785.3	719.6	764.2	791.2	789.0	871.3
85 years and over	}	728.9	934.8	791.5	873.9	851.4	810.0	813.6	733.0	844.0

(In column 111.8, the values for 75–79 years, 80–84 years, and 85 years and over are combined by a brace into a single figure: 605.3.)

¹ Based upon a 50-percent sample of deaths.

² Includes all races and both sexes.

NOTE: The ICDA Revisions and code numbers are for 1950 and 1955, Sixth Revision, Nos. 140–205, for 1960 and 1965, Seventh Revision, Nos. 140–205; and for 1970–76, Eighth Revision, Nos. 140–209.

SOURCES: National Center for Health Statistics: *Vital Statistics of the United States*, Vol. II, for data years 1950–1973, Washington. U.S. Government Printing Office; for data years 1974–1976, Public Health Service. DHEW, Hyattsville, Md. To be published; U.S. Bureau of the Census: Population estimates and projections. *Current Population Reports*. Series P–25, Nos. 310, 519, 529, and 643. Washington. U.S. Government Printing Office, June 1965, Apr. 1974, Sept. 1974, and Jan. 1977; General population characteristics, United States summary, 1960 and 1970. *U.S. Census of Population*. Final reports PC(1)–B1: *1950 Nonwhite Population by Race*. Special report P–E No. 3B. Washington. U.S. Government Printing Office, 1961, 1972, and 1951; National Center for Health Statistics: Data computed by the Division of Analysis from data compiled by the Divison of Vital Statistics.

Death rates due to cancer of the respiratory system, according to race, sex, and age: United States, selected years 1950-76

(Data are based on the national vital registration system)

Race, sex, and age	Year										
	1950	1955	1960	1965	1970	1971	1972	1973	1974	1975	1976
	Number of deaths per 100,000 resident population										
Total[2]											
All ages	14.1	18.2	22.2	26.9	34.2	35.4	37.0	37.8	39.5	40.7	42.5
Under 25 years	0.2	0.1	0.1	0.1	0.1	0.1	0.1	0.1	0.1	0.1	0.1
25–34 years	0.9	1.0	1.1	1.0	1.0	1.1	0.9	1.0	0.9	0.9	0.9
35–44 years	5.1	5.9	7.3	9.3	11.6	11.2	11.6	11.2	11.0	11.0	10.7
45–54 years	22.9	27.4	32.0	38.4	46.2	47.0	49.2	49.6	51.6	52.3	53.4
55–64 years	55.2	68.5	81.5	93.5	116.2	116.3	122.8	125.6	130.5	131.9	135.6
65 years and over	69.0	90.2	111.0	136.1	170.1	180.2	186.3	189.5	196.4	202.2	211.4
65–74 years	69.3	92.9	117.2	142.9	174.6	183.6	190.5	193.0	198.5	205.3	212.5
75–84 years	69.3	88.2	102.9	129.2	175.1	184.7	192.2	195.7	206.9	212.4	226.2
85 years and over	64.0	65.8	79.1	97.1	113.5	133.0	127.9	136.6	141.1	142.8	152.5
White male											
All ages	24.1	32.5	39.6	47.5	58.3	59.4	61.5	62.4	64.5	65.8	67.9
Under 25 years	0.2	0.2	0.1	0.1	0.1	0.1	0.1	0.1	0.1	0.1	0.1
25–34 years	1.2	1.4	1.6	1.4	1.4	1.5	1.0	1.1	1.1	1.3	1.0
35–44 years	7.9	8.9	10.4	12.9	15.4	14.7	14.9	14.7	14.2	13.4	13.4
45–54 years	39.1	47.2	53.0	60.7	67.6	67.1	69.9	69.5	72.9	73.0	72.7
55–64 years	95.9	125.3	149.8	169.7	199.3	195.3	202.8	204.1	208.4	206.3	209.3
65 years and over	116.1	164.4	211.7	270.8	341.7	361.2	371.7	377.4	387.1	398.0	411.3
65–74 years	119.5	172.1	225.1	282.5	344.8	358.6	366.7	371.3	374.0	385.2	391.8
75–84 years	109.1	155.2	191.9	259.2	360.7	385.7	405.9	411.1	438.4	452.0	477.5
85 years and over	102.8	105.1	133.9	181.5	221.8	269.7	260.4	285.2	294.2	298.2	329.6
White female											
All ages	5.4	5.7	6.4	8.6	13.1	14.2	15.5	16.0	17.5	18.8	20.5
Under 25 years	0.1	0.1	0.1	0.1	0.1	0.1	0.1	0.1	0.1	0.0	0.1
25–34 years	0.5	0.6	0.6	0.6	0.6	0.7	0.6	0.8	0.7	0.5	0.7
35–44 years	2.2	2.6	3.4	4.5	6.0	6.1	6.9	6.4	6.4	7.1	6.7
45–54 years	6.5	6.8	9.8	14.8	22.1	23.4	25.3	24.4	25.7	27.7	29.1
55–64 years	15.5	14.8	16.7	23.4	39.3	41.8	46.8	49.7	54.7	58.9	63.0
65 years and over	31.6	31.2	30.6	36.7	50.0	55.3	58.6	60.9	66.3	69.6	77.3
65–74 years	27.2	26.7	26.5	33.1	45.4	51.3	56.6	57.9	64.1	68.1	76.3
75–84 years	40.0	39.1	36.5	41.1	56.8	59.4	60.6	64.9	68.9	71.3	79.4
85 years and over	43.9	42.7	45.2	51.2	57.4	68.2	64.5	66.2	71.3	73.1	76.4

	14.5	20.6	30.5	36.0	47.6	48.7	51.8	54.2	56.4	56.7	58.3
All other male											
All ages	14.5	20.6	30.5	36.0	47.6	48.7	51.8	54.2	56.4	56.7	58.3
Under 25 years	0.2	0.1	0.1	0.2	0.1	0.1	0.1	0.1	0.1	0.1	0.1
25–34 years	2.1	2.2	2.5	1.7	2.4	1.9	2.5	1.9	1.6	1.6	1.5
35–44 years	9.3	12.9	19.8	24.5	29.3	27.5	28.0	25.2	26.7	27.3	23.8
45–54 years	40.5	56.3	70.4	84.7	113.1	113.2	115.1	130.6	128.7	122.9	129.0
55–64 years	79.1	108.0	154.2	171.0	231.5	241.8	263.9	275.4	283.8	290.0	295.4
65 years and over	60.7	93.7	170.2	219.6	285.3	299.4	326.3	332.9	357.8	358.4	369.1
65–74 years	67.6	100.6	183.4	240.2	301.2	310.6	343.9	343.6	378.1	378.2	384.3
75–84 years	48.5	83.2	145.4	177.8	278.7	301.0	313.9	331.9	340.7	346.9	372.2
85 years and over	10.5	45.8	114.8	147.1	158.8	117.6	192.2	218.9	221.1	218.8	223.5
Black male:											
All ages	14.3	---	31.1	37.6	51.2	51.8	55.5	58.3	61.0	61.8	63.3
Under 25 years	0.2	---	0.1	0.2	0.2	0.2	0.1	0.1	0.0	0.1	0.1
25–34 years	2.1	---	2.6	1.8	2.9	2.0	2.6	2.1	1.8	1.6	1.5
35–44 years	9.4	---	20.7	26.1	32.6	30.5	31.1	28.1	29.8	30.7	26.7
45–54 years	41.1	---	75.0	90.4	123.5	123.7	125.9	143.4	141.8	136.9	142.6
55–64 years	78.8	---	161.8	182.7	250.3	259.9	283.8	295.6	306.1	313.2	319.4
65 years and over	58.9	---	166.4	224.0	302.9	311.4	343.0	353.7	382.4	383.3	394.0
65–74 years	65.2	---	184.6	248.1	322.2	324.7	368.0	366.7	402.8	404.7	408.8
75–84 years	} 42.4	---	126.3	172.6	290.6	310.6	315.8	351.9	369.2	370.7	401.5
85 years and over		---	110.3	140.0	154.4	159.5	190.7	220.0	220.8	220.8	226.8
All other female											
All ages	3.4	4.5	4.9	6.3	9.5	10.5	10.5	11.5	12.1	12.5	13.4
Under 25 years	0.1	0.1	0.1	0.1	0.0	0.0	0.1	0.1	0.0	0.0	0.0
25–34 years	1.1	0.7	0.7	0.9	0.5	0.8	0.6	0.6	0.7	0.7	0.8
35–44 years	2.6	3.3	3.5	6.1	9.4	9.8	8.7	8.8	8.6	8.4	8.3
45–54 years	8.7	10.9	12.5	16.7	23.3	28.1	28.2	31.2	32.1	30.7	34.4
55–64 years	15.5	19.6	20.2	25.8	35.3	39.4	40.1	46.7	53.6	52.3	54.7
65 years and over	18.3	25.0	27.2	29.3	49.0	51.5	51.8	55.0	54.8	62.6	66.0
65–74 years	17.8	25.2	22.5	29.5	47.7	53.7	50.5	55.6	54.4	62.9	65.8
75–84 years	19.6	25.0	35.8	27.7	53.2	49.3	55.3	54.8	59.2	64.4	70.1
85 years and over	19.2	23.5	44.7	34.7	45.8	42.1	51.2	51.1	43.3	55.5	56.2

See footnotes at end of table.

Death rates due to cancer of the respiratory system, according to race, sex, and age: United States, selected years 1950-76—Continued

(Data are based on the national vital registration system)

Race, sex, and age	Year										
	1950	1955	1960	1965	1970	1971	1972[1]	1973	1974	1975	1976
	Number of deaths per 100,000 resident population										
All ages	3.4	---	4.9	6.3	10.1	11.1	10.9	12.1	12.7	13.4	14.5
Black female:											
Under 25 years	0.1	---	0.1	0.1	0.1	0.0	0.1	0.1	0.0	0.0	0.0
25-34 years	1.2	---	0.8	0.9	0.5	0.9	0.6	0.5	0.7	0.7	0.8
35-44 years	2.7	---	3.4	6.3	10.5	10.4	9.9	9.7	9.3	9.5	9.1
45-54 years	8.8	---	12.8	17.6	25.3	30.0	30.5	33.7	34.9	33.6	38.4
55-64 years	15.3	---	20.7	26.0	36.4	41.2	41.6	47.9	54.8	55.0	57.9
65 years and over	17.2	---	25.3	27.3	50.0	51.8	49.2	54.2	55.0	63.2	66.6
65-74 years	16.4	---	20.7	28.2	49.3	53.5	47.3	55.9	54.9	63.7	66.3
75-84 years		---	33.1	24.5	52.6	49.8	52.3	53.1	60.5	65.5	73.9
85 years and over	19.2	---	44.7	30.4	47.6	44.9	54.1	45.0	38.6	53.5	49.5

[1] Based upon a 50-percent sample of deaths.
[2] Includes all races and both sexes.

NOTE: The ICDA revisions and code numbers are for 1950 and 1955, Sixth Revision, Nos. 160-164; for 1960 and 1965, Seventh Revision, Nos. 160-164; and for 1970-76, Eighth Revision, Nos. 160-163.

SOURCES: National Center for Health Statistics: *Vital Statistics of the United States*, Vol. II, for data years 1950-1973. Washington. U.S. Government Printing Office; for data years 1974-1976, Public Health Service. DHEW, Hyattsville, Md. To be published; U.S. Bureau of the Census: Population estimates and projections. *Current Population Reports*. Series P-25, Nos. 310, 519, 529, and 643. Washington. U.S. Government Printing Office, June 1965, Apr. 1974, Sept. 1974, and Jan. 1977; General population characteristics, United States summary, 1960 and 1970. *U.S. Census of Population*. Final reports PC(1)-B1; *Nonwhite Population by Race*. Special report P-E No. 3B. Washington. U.S. Government Printing Office, 1961, 1972, and 1951; National Center for Health Statistics: Data computed by the Division of Analysis from data compiled by the Division of Vital Statistics.

Consumption of selected food groups, according to race, frequency of intake, type of food, and age: United States, 1971-74

(Data are based on interviews of a sample of the civilian noninstitutionalized population)

Percent of persons

Food group and age	Both races				White				Black			
	2 or more times per day	Once a day	1-6 times per week	Seldom or never	2 or more times per day	Once a day	1-6 times per week	Seldom or never	2 or more times per day	Once a day	1-6 times per week	Seldom or never
Whole milk												
All ages 1-74 years	36.4	21.2	21.9	20.5	37.5	21.2	21.0	20.3	27.9	21.3	29.3	21.5
1-5 years	74.4	11.6	7.8	6.3	75.3	11.0	7.1	6.5	68.0	15.2	11.9	4.9
6-11 years	69.6	19.1	7.5	3.8	72.8	17.4	5.9	3.9	50.7	28.9	17.3	3.2
12-17 years	56.5	20.1	15.7	7.7	59.8	18.0	14.3	8.0	36.0	33.3	24.5	6.1
18-44 years	26.2	22.4	27.4	24.0	27.6	22.9	26.0	23.4	13.8	18.3	38.5	29.3
45-64 years	15.8	23.4	28.1	32.7	16.3	24.3	27.4	32.0	9.9	14.6	35.6	39.9
65-74 years	15.5	25.7	26.0	32.8	16.0	26.3	25.7	32.0	10.5	20.2	28.9	40.3
Meat and poultry												
All ages 1-74 years	32.5	51.7	15.2	0.6	31.8	52.5	15.1	0.6	38.4	44.7	16.3	0.5
1-5 years	31.5	53.9	14.2	0.3	30.4	55.4	13.9	0.3	38.3	45.7	15.9	0.2
6-11 years	32.1	56.8	10.8	0.4	30.4	58.2	11.0	0.4	41.7	48.3	9.8	0.3
12-17 years	36.5	48.6	14.4	0.5	35.5	49.6	14.5	0.5	43.2	42.2	14.0	0.7
18-44 years	37.9	49.1	12.6	0.5	37.0	49.9	12.6	0.5	44.7	42.4	12.4	0.5
45-64 years	26.0	53.7	19.7	0.7	26.1	54.2	19.1	0.7	24.7	48.8	25.8	0.7
65-74 years	18.1	53.6	26.8	1.5	18.3	54.6	25.6	1.5	16.6	43.0	39.3	1.1
Fish and shellfish												
All ages 1-74 years	0.1	0.9	54.2	44.8	0.1	0.9	53.5	45.5	0.1	0.9	59.4	39.6
1-5 years	0.1	0.7	51.7	47.5	0.1	0.7	50.2	49.0	0.0	1.0	60.0	39.0
6-11 years	0.1	0.7	56.1	43.0	0.2	0.6	54.8	44.4	0.0	1.6	64.3	34.1
12-17 years	0.0	0.9	49.9	49.2	0.0	0.8	49.2	49.9	0.0	1.1	54.4	44.5
18-44 years	0.0	1.0	54.6	44.3	0.0	1.1	54.2	44.7	0.1	0.5	58.3	41.0
45-64 years	0.0	1.1	57.7	41.2	0.0	1.1	57.2	41.6	0.0	1.0	62.5	36.5
65-74 years	0.1	0.7	47.7	51.5	0.1	0.7	46.9	52.3	0.0	0.6	56.5	42.9
Eggs												
All ages 1-74 years	0.3	15.4	66.6	17.6	0.3	14.6	67.3	17.8	0.5	22.0	61.5	16.0
1-5 years	0.4	17.4	69.8	12.4	0.4	17.2	69.6	12.9	0.8	18.5	71.0	9.7
6-11 years	0.1	9.7	74.3	15.8	0.0	8.7	75.2	16.1	1.0	16.2	68.5	14.2
12-17 years	0.3	8.7	65.3	25.7	0.3	7.7	65.5	26.5	0.4	14.9	63.7	21.0
18-44 years	0.3	16.1	66.3	17.3	0.3	14.9	67.4	17.4	0.4	26.3	56.9	16.4
45-64 years	0.3	18.7	65.0	16.0	0.4	18.2	65.4	16.0	0.2	24.1	60.0	15.7
65-74 years	0.5	21.4	58.8	19.3	0.5	20.6	59.6	19.3	0.3	29.9	50.3	19.5

All fruits and vegetables

All ages 1–74 years	59.1	31.4	9.1	0.4	60.9	30.8	8.0	0.4	45.4	35.9	17.9	0.7
1–5 years	64.6	27.1	7.8	0.5	66.7	25.9	6.9	0.6	52.4	34.1	13.4	0.0
6–11 years	63.6	29.5	6.8	0.2	65.0	28.7	6.2	0.2	55.4	34.2	10.4	0.0
12–17 years	58.0	30.8	10.8	0.4	59.5	30.6	9.5	0.4	48.7	31.8	18.9	0.6
18–44 years	54.0	35.8	9.9	0.4	55.5	35.5	8.7	0.3	40.7	38.8	19.7	0.9
45–64 years	63.2	28.0	8.5	0.4	65.3	27.1	7.2	0.4	41.0	36.4	21.6	1.1
65–74 years	62.4	27.0	9.6	1.0	64.5	26.2	8.5	0.9	40.3	35.5	21.6	2.6

Cereals

All ages 1–74 years	0.8	15.9	44.8	38.5	0.7	16.2	44.6	38.5	1.2	13.8	46.8	38.2
1–5 years	2.4	32.6	56.7	8.4	2.3	32.1	56.8	8.7	2.3	35.2	55.9	6.6
6–11 years	1.9	28.8	60.9	8.4	2.0	29.2	60.4	8.4	1.7	26.1	63.8	8.4
12–17 years	1.4	16.0	51.8	30.9	1.1	16.6	50.7	31.6	3.2	12.2	58.4	26.1
18–44 years	0.1	8.0	38.1	53.8	0.1	8.2	38.3	53.3	0.1	6.0	36.2	57.7
45–64 years	0.3	13.2	40.1	46.3	0.3	13.8	40.1	45.9	1.0	7.3	40.9	50.7
65–74 years	0.7	25.4	41.3	32.6	0.6	26.5	41.7	31.0	0.7	13.1	37.3	48.9

Desserts

All ages 1–74 years	10.5	30.2	46.5	12.7	10.8	30.4	46.3	12.5	8.9	28.8	48.1	14.1
1–5 years	19.3	40.0	36.9	3.8	20.1	39.4	36.9	3.5	14.3	43.4	36.9	5.4
6–11 years	18.4	44.8	34.4	2.4	19.4	44.5	33.6	2.6	13.1	46.6	39.2	1.1
12–17 years	15.2	32.9	47.1	4.8	14.9	33.4	46.7	5.0	17.1	29.9	49.5	3.5
18–44 years	7.6	24.9	52.9	14.6	7.7	25.2	52.9	14.2	6.6	22.1	53.2	18.1
45–64 years	6.4	27.2	45.9	20.6	6.9	27.9	45.5	19.8	1.0	20.2	50.1	28.7
65–74 years	6.7	27.2	44.9	21.2	6.9	28.0	44.3	20.8	4.6	19.1	51.1	25.2

Salty snacks

All ages 1–74 years	1.3	10.1	51.5	37.1	1.1	9.6	51.7	37.7	2.7	14.8	50.2	32.4
1–5 years	2.2	12.6	65.3	19.9	2.2	10.7	64.9	22.1	2.0	24.0	67.3	6.7
6–11 years	2.3	19.6	66.0	12.0	1.9	18.6	66.6	12.9	4.9	26.1	62.6	6.4
12–17 years	2.5	15.8	65.8	16.0	1.7	14.4	66.1	17.8	7.5	24.0	63.4	5.2
18–44 years	0.9	9.6	55.5	34.0	0.9	9.6	56.0	33.6	1.2	9.2	51.7	37.8
45–64 years	0.2	4.1	32.3	63.4	0.2	3.8	33.1	62.8	0.1	6.6	23.6	69.6
65–74 years	0.5	2.5	21.4	75.6	0.6	2.6	21.9	74.9	0.6	1.3	16.0	82.1

NOTE: Data are based on findings over a 3-month period.

SOURCE: Division of Health Examination Statistics, National Center for Health Statistics: Data from the Health and Nutrition Examination Survey.

Persons 12–74 years of age on a special diet, according to reason for dieting, kind of diet, sex, race, age, and family income: United States, 1971–75

(Data are based on interviews of a sample of the civilian noninstitutionalized population)

Sex, race, age, and family income	Percent of population 12–74 years on a special diet	Reason for diet					Kind of diet				
		Over-weight	Diabetes	Ulcer	Heart trouble or high blood pressure	Other	Low fat	Low salt	Low carbo-hydrate	Low calorie	Other
		Percent of persons									
Total[1,2]	10.6	4.1	1.6	1.0	2.0	3.4	3.8	2.0	2.4	3.9	4.3
Sex											
Male	8.3	2.3	1.2	0.9	2.0	2.7	3.2	1.4	1.6	2.3	3.4
Female	12.8	5.7	2.0	1.0	1.9	4.0	4.3	2.5	3.1	5.3	5.0
Race											
White	10.9	4.2	1.6	1.0	1.9	3.5	3.9	2.0	2.6	4.0	4.5
Black	9.0	3.0	1.7	0.9	2.4	2.0	3.3	2.0	1.2	2.8	2.9
Age											
12–17 years	3.0	1.7	0.3	0.1	—	1.2	0.9	0.3	0.6	1.4	1.2
18–24 years	6.3	3.8	0.2	0.4	0.1	2.2	1.7	0.4	1.0	3.4	2.0
25–34 years	8.0	4.8	0.4	0.8	0.3	2.1	2.0	0.7	1.9	3.9	2.6
35–44 years	11.2	5.1	0.9	1.3	1.5	3.4	3.4	1.3	2.1	4.6	4.2
45–54 years	12.5	4.6	1.7	1.7	2.8	3.9	4.9	2.1	3.3	4.1	6.1
55–64 years	19.7	5.0	4.5	1.4	6.1	6.3	8.3	5.9	4.9	5.7	8.1
65–74 years	21.4	3.3	6.5	1.5	6.3	7.1	9.0	6.1	5.0	5.3	9.1
Family income											
Less than $4,000	12.5	3.2	3.1	1.5	3.3	3.9	4.5	3.1	2.6	3.6	5.3
$4,000–$6,999	11.9	4.6	2.0	0.9	2.8	3.4	3.6	3.2	2.4	4.4	3.8
$7,000–$9,999	11.0	4.2	1.8	1.0	2.1	3.3	3.9	2.1	2.4	4.6	4.3
$10,000–$14,999	9.4	3.8	1.2	1.0	1.2	3.2	3.5	1.4	2.5	3.1	4.3
$15,000 or more	9.3	4.3	0.8	0.5	1.2	3.3	3.3	1.1	2.0	3.9	3.7

[1] Includes all other races not shown separately.

[2] Excludes unknown family income.

SOURCE: Division of Health Examination Statistics, National Center for Health Statistics: Data from the Health and Nutrition Examination Survey.

Persons 12–74 years of age having trouble chewing or biting certain foods, according to type of food, sex, race, age, and family income: United States, 1971–75

(Data are based on interviews of a sample of the civilian noninstitutionalized population)

Sex, race, age, and family income	Population 12–74 years in thousands	Persons having trouble with—			
		Chewing steaks, chops, or other firm meats	Biting apples or corn on the cob	Biting or chewing any other food	Any of these
		Percent of population			
Total [1,2]	147,154	10.2	11.4	7.5	14.6
Sex					
Male	70,600	9.1	10.2	6.7	13.1
Female	76,554	11.2	12.6	8.2	16.0
Race					
White	129,973	9.6	11.1	6.9	14.2
Black	15,714	15.1	15.0	12.4	18.5
Age					
12–17 years	23,545	2.4	3.1	1.6	4.3
18–24 years	23,809	4.3	3.4	2.9	6.3
25–34 years	26,137	7.2	6.7	5.3	9.9
35–44 years	21,438	9.0	10.2	6.9	13.4
45–54 years	22,366	13.1	14.8	9.5	18.4
55–64 years	17,867	19.4	23.0	14.4	27.8
65–74 years	11,992	25.6	31.8	19.1	35.6
Family income					
Less than $4,000	22,316	21.3	22.4	15.8	27.0
$4,000–$6,999	20,867	14.0	15.5	11.6	19.8
$7,000–$9,999	34,695	9.7	11.1	7.3	14.5
$10,000–$14,999	35,869	6.9	7.5	4.3	10.1
$15,000 or more	33,407	5.3	6.3	3.7	8.7

[1] Includes all other races not shown separately.
[2] Excludes unknown family income.

SOURCE: Division of Health Examination Statistics, National Center for Health Statistics: Data from the Health and Nutrition Examination Survey.

Persons 17 years of age and over who assessed themselves as overweight, according to sex, race, age, and family income: United States, 1974

(Data are based on household interviews of a sample of the civilian noninstitutionalized population)

Age and family income	Sex					
	Male			Female		
	All races [1]	White	Black	All races [1]	White	Black
	Percent of persons					
All ages 17 years and over [2]	30.5	31.9	19.6	48.9	49.6	44.2
Less than $5,000	20.4	22.3	12.5	44.1	45.1	40.7
$5,000–$9,999	27.3	28.6	19.7	50.1	50.9	46.3
$10,000–$14,999	32.2	33.4	22.3	51.6	52.2	46.2
$15,000 or more	37.3	37.7	32.2	51.2	51.4	49.6
17–44 years [2]	28.1	29.4	18.6	48.4	49.1	45.0
Less than $5,000	17.6	18.4	14.2	46.4	47.0	45.3
$5,000–$9,999	25.4	26.7	18.8	49.1	50.5	42.5
$10,000–$14,999	30.1	31.4	19.5	50.8	51.3	46.2
$15,000 or more	32.9	33.4	28.7	48.4	48.6	49.9
45–64 years [2]	37.9	39.6	22.7	56.1	56.7	52.0
Less than $5,000	25.6	31.4	*8.5	51.0	51.5	48.8
$5,000–$9,999	34.7	36.7	23.7	57.7	57.7	59.9
$10,000–$14,999	37.2	38.3	27.5	56.7	57.7	48.6
$15,000 or more	45.3	45.4	40.8	60.0	60.3	49.8
65 years and over [2]	23.8	24.5	17.1	36.9	38.1	23.7
Less than $5,000	20.8	21.8	*14.0	37.0	39.6	17.4
$5,000–$9,999	23.3	24.0	*14.0	39.0	39.0	*39.0
$10,000–$14,999	29.3	29.2	*49.4	37.9	38.3	*23.8
$15,000 or more	32.2	32.1	*29.5	33.1	33.0	*32.9

[1] Includes all other races not shown separately.
[2] Includes unknown family income.

SOURCE: Division of Heath Interview Statistics, National Center for Health Statistics: Data from the Health Interview Survey.

Obesity among persons 20–74 years of age, according to sex, race, age, and poverty level: United States, 1971–74

(Data are based on physical examinations of a sample of the civilian noninstitutionalized population)

Age and poverty level	Sex					
	Male			Female		
	All races[1]	White	Black	All races[1]	White	Black
	Percent of persons					
All ages 20–74 years	13.0	13.3	11.6	22.7	21.8	31.2
Below poverty level	8.0	8.2	7.6	26.5	23.1	33.3
Above poverty level	13.8	13.9	13.4	22.6	22.1	30.0
20–44 years	14.2	14.2	13.3	19.7	18.4	25.6
Below poverty level	9.7	9.4	11.1	22.8	20.6	27.6
Above poverty level	14.7	14.9	14.6	18.8	18.3	24.0
45–64 years	12.1	12.2	10.2	29.0	27.6	43.0
Below poverty level	4.8	5.3	3.7	35.1	26.4	49.4
Above poverty level	13.2	13.2	12.4	29.2	28.5	40.0
65–74 years	11.0	11.5	5.8	20.5	19.8	27.7
Below poverty level	9.1	10.3	4.6	24.7	25.2	23.2
Above poverty level	10.8	11.1	7.0	20.1	19.2	36.3

[1] Includes all other races not shown separately.

NOTE: Obesity measure is based on triceps skinfold measurements and is defined as falling above the sex-specific 85th percentile measurements for persons 20–29 years of age.

SOURCE: Division of Health Examination Statistics, National Center for Health Statistics: Data from the Health and Nutrition Examination Suvey.

Sports participation status of persons 20 years of age and over, according to selected characteristics: United States, 1975

(Data are based on household interviews of a sample of the civilian noninstitutionalized population)

Selected characteristic	Population in thousands[1,2]	Sports participation during year prior to interview		
		In one or more sports	As team member	In tournament
		Percent of persons		
Total				
All persons 20 years and over[3]	135,655	41.6	11.2	6.7
Age				
20–44 years	71,084	58.1	16.5	9.5
45–64 years	43,145	30.3	7.3	4.9
65 years and over	21,426	9.9	1.5	0.7
Sex and age				
Male 20 years and over	63,665	47.4	14.4	10.2
20–44 years	34,268	62.4	20.7	14.2
45–64 years	20,567	35.7	8.8	7.3
65 years and over	8,830	16.6	2.7	*1.3
Female 20 years and over	71,990	36.5	8.4	3.5
20–44 years	36,816	54.0	12.5	5.1
45–64 years	22,579	25.4	5.9	2.8
65 years and over	12,595	5.2	*0.6	*0.2
Family income				
Less than $5,000	21,180	23.1	4.7	2.8
$5,000–$9,999	29,271	34.8	8.3	4.7
$10,000–$14,999	29,538	47.7	13.7	7.6
$15,000 or more	44,358	55.0	16.1	10.2

Selected characteristic	Population in thousands[1,2]	Sports participation during year prior to interview		
		In one or more sports	As team member	In tournament
		Percent of persons		
Color and age				
White 20 years and over	120,141	43.2	11.7	7.0
20–44 years	61,990	60.3	17.4	10.0
45–64 years	38,696	32.2	7.7	5.3
65 years and over	19,455	10.7	1.6	0.7
All other 20 years and over	15,515	29.2	7.1	4.0
20–44 years	9,094	42.7	10.3	6.2
45–64 years	4,450	14.0	3.6	*1.1
65 years and over	1,971	*1.7	–	–
Self-perceived physical activeness				
Less active	21,952	32.5	5.1	2.4
As active as others of same age	61,946	45.3	11.3	5.6
More active	36,666	54.8	17.8	12.6

[1] Includes unknown sports status.

[2] Population estimate based on July through December 1975.

[3] Includes unknown family income and unknown self-perception of physical activeness.

NOTE: Base of percentage is the population. For example, 41.6 percent of all persons 20 years of age and over participated in one or more sports.

SOURCE: National Center for Health Statistics: Exercise and participation in sports among persons 20 years of age and over, United States, 1975, by J. W. Choi. Advance Data from Vital and Health Statistics, No. 19. DHEW Pub. No. (PHS)78–1250. Public Health Service, Hyattsville, Md., Dec. 14, 1977.

Self-assessed exercise and activity status of persons 12–74 years of age, according to sex, race, age, and family income: United States, 1971–75

(Data are based on interviews of a sample of the civilian noninstitutionalized population)

Sex, race, age, and family income	Population 12–74 years in thousands	Self-assessed exercise and activity status		
		All statuses	Very active or much exercise	Somewhat active or some exercise	Inactive or little or no exercise
		Percent distribution			
Total[1,2]	147,154	100.0	56.9	37.0	6.1
Sex					
Male	70,600	100.0	63.6	31.1	5.3
Female	76,554	100.0	50.9	42.3	6.8
Race					
White	129,973	100.0	56.7	37.4	5.9
Black	15,714	100.0	58.8	33.1	8.1
Age					
12–17 years	23,545	100.0	78.8	19.7	1.5
18–24 years	23,809	100.0	57.9	37.9	4.2
25–34 years	26,137	100.0	59.3	35.6	5.1
35–44 years	21,438	100.0	54.1	39.0	6.9
45–54 years	22,366	100.0	51.1	40.8	8.1
55–64 years	17,867	100.0	50.4	41.2	8.4
65–74 years	11,992	100.0	33.8	53.7	12.5
Family income					
Less than $4,000	22,316	100.0	49.0	39.6	11.4
$4,000–$6,999	20,867	100.0	55.5	37.3	7.2
$7,000–$9,999	34,695	100.0	58.8	36.3	4.9
$10,000–$14,999	35,869	100.0	59.5	36.2	4.3
$15,000 or more	33,407	100.0	59.0	36.0	5.0

[1] Includes all other races not shown separately.
[2] Excludes unknown family income.

SOURCE: Division of Health Examination Statistics, National Center for Health Statistics: Data from the Health and Nutrition Examination Survey.

Cigarette smoking status of persons 20 years of age and over, according to sex, race, and age: United States, 1965 and 1976

(Data are based on household interviews of a sample of the civilian noninstitutionalized population)

Sex, race, and age	Cigarette smoking status, 1965				Cigarette smoking status, 1976			
	Total[1]	Never smoked	Former smoker	Current smoker[2]	Total[1]	Never smoked	Former smoker	Current smoker[2]
	Percent distribution							
MALE								
Total[3]								
All ages 20 years and over	100.0	27.1	20.5	52.4	100.0	29.2	28.9	41.9
20—24 years	100.0	31.8	9.0	59.2	100.0	41.9	12.2	45.9
25—34 years	100.0	24.6	14.7	60.7	100.0	33.1	18.3	48.5
35—44 years	100.0	21.2	20.6	58.2	100.0	25.1	27.3	47.5
45—64 years	100.0	24.0	24.1	51.9	100.0	21.6	37.1	41.3
65 years and over	100.0	43.4	28.1	28.5	100.0	32.7	44.4	23.0
White								
All ages 20 years and over	100.0	27.0	21.4	51.5	100.0	28.8	30.0	41.2
20—24 years	100.0	32.2	9.6	58.1	100.0	41.5	13.3	45.3
25—34 years	100.0	24.4	15.5	60.1	100.0	33.4	18.9	47.7
35—44 years	100.0	21.2	21.5	57.3	100.0	24.4	28.9	46.8
45—64 years	100.0	23.6	25.1	51.3	100.0	21.3	38.1	40.6
65 years and over	100.0	43.6	28.7	27.7	100.0	31.6	45.6	22.8
Black								
All ages 20 years and over	100.0	27.0	12.1	60.8	100.0	30.2	19.3	50.5
20—24 years	100.0	28.8	3.8	67.4	100.0	43.1	4.1	52.8
25—34 years	100.0	24.9	6.7	68.4	100.0	28.9	11.8	59.4
35—44 years	100.0	20.4	12.3	67.3	100.0	27.3	13.8	58.8
45—64 years	100.0	26.7	15.3	57.9	100.0	21.7	28.6	49.7
65 years and over	100.0	42.1	21.5	36.4	100.0	40.5	33.0	26.4

FEMALE

	100.0	57.7	8.2	34.1	100.0	54.3	13.8	32.0
Total³								
All ages 20 years and over	100.0	57.7	8.2	34.1	100.0	54.3	13.8	32.0
20–24 years	100.0	50.8	7.3	41.9	100.0	55.4	10.4	34.2
25–34 years	100.0	46.5	9.9	43.7	100.0	49.6	12.9	37.5
35–44 years	100.0	46.7	9.6	43.7	100.0	46.0	15.8	38.2
45–64 years	100.0	59.4	8.6	32.0	100.0	49.3	15.9	34.8
65 years and over	100.0	85.9	4.5	9.6	100.0	75.5	11.7	12.8
White								
All ages 20 years and over	100.0	57.3	8.5	34.2	100.0	53.8	14.4	31.8
20–24 years	100.0	50.1	8.0	41.9	100.0	54.2	11.4	34.4
25–34 years	100.0	46.3	10.3	43.4	100.0	49.2	13.7	37.1
35–44 years	100.0	46.2	9.9	43.9	100.0	44.9	17.0	38.1
45–64 years	100.0	58.5	8.8	32.7	100.0	49.0	16.4	34.7
65 years and over	100.0	85.8	4.5	9.8	100.0	75.4	11.5	13.2
Black								
All ages 20 years and over	100.0	59.6	6.0	34.4	100.0	55.0	9.9	35.1
20–24 years	100.0	53.3	2.5	44.2	100.0	60.1	5.0	34.9
25–34 years	100.0	45.5	6.7	47.8	100.0	48.6	8.9	42.5
35–44 years	100.0	50.1	7.0	42.8	100.0	49.1	9.6	41.3
45–64 years	100.0	67.6	6.6	25.7	100.0	50.0	11.9	38.1
65 years and over	100.0	88.4	4.5	7.1	100.0	77.4	13.3	9.2

¹ Excludes unknown smoking status.
² A current smoker is a person who has smoked at least 100 cigarettes and who now smokes cigarettes on a regular basis.
³ Includes all other races not shown separately.

SOURCE: Division of Health Interview Statistics, National Center for Health Statistics: Data from the Health Interview Survey.

Cigarettes smoked per day by persons 20 years of age and over, according to amount smoked, sex, race, and age: United States, 1965 and 1976

(Data are based on household interviews of a sample of the civilian noninstitutionalized population)

Sex, race, and age	Cigarettes smoked per day, 1965					Cigarettes smoked per day, 1976				
	Total[1]	Less than 15	15–24	25–44	45 or more	Total[1]	Less than 15	15–24	25–44	45 or more
	Percent of persons[2]									
MALE										
Total[3]										
All ages 20 years and over	52.4	14.4	23.5	11.4	1.5	41.9	10.0	18.6	11.2	1.7
20–24 years	59.2	19.9	28.3	8.1	0.7	45.9	14.3	22.7	7.9	*0.5
25–34 years	60.7	15.3	29.7	12.9	1.6	48.5	12.2	21.9	12.2	1.5
35–44 years	58.2	13.4	25.4	15.7	2.1	47.6	9.2	19.4	15.8	2.6
45–64 years	51.9	13.4	22.7	12.3	1.7	41.3	7.6	18.1	13.0	2.4
65 years and over	28.5	12.9	10.7	3.4	*0.4	23.0	8.9	9.7	3.6	*0.6
White										
All ages 20 years and over	51.5	13.0	23.5	12.2	1.6	41.2	8.7	18.3	11.9	1.9
20–24 years	58.1	18.1	28.5	8.7	0.8	45.3	12.3	23.6	8.3	*0.5
25–34 years	60.1	13.5	30.2	13.8	1.7	47.7	10.4	21.9	13.1	1.7
35–44 years	57.3	12.0	25.1	16.7	2.3	46.8	7.9	18.7	16.7	2.9
45–64 years	51.3	12.2	22.6	13.1	1.8	40.6	6.5	17.5	13.8	2.5
65 years and over	27.7	11.9	10.8	3.6	*0.4	22.8	8.5	9.5	3.9	*0.7
Black										
All ages 20 years and over	60.8	27.5	24.3	4.7	*0.6	50.5	21.6	22.1	5.4	*0.3
20–24 years	67.4	32.9	26.1	*3.3	*_	52.8	30.1	18.1	*4.7	*_
25–34 years	68.4	30.7	26.8	5.4	*1.3	59.4	25.9	24.5	5.5	*0.4
35–44 years	67.3	26.9	28.8	6.8	*0.8	58.8	22.4	26.1	9.7	*_
45–64 years	57.9	25.5	23.7	4.7	*0.4	49.7	17.6	24.8	5.8	*0.7
65 years and over	36.4	22.4	11.0	*1.1	*_	26.4	14.0	12.4	*_	*_

FEMALE

Total[3]										
All ages 20 years and over	34.1	14.7	14.2	4.5	0.3	32.0	11.5	13.8	5.8	0.4
20–24 years	41.9	19.8	17.2	3.7	*0.2	34.2	14.5	14.3	4.4	*0.5
25–34 years	43.7	17.9	18.6	6.3	0.4	37.5	12.6	16.6	7.0	0.6
35–44 years	43.7	16.9	18.9	6.9	0.5	38.2	12.7	16.7	7.7	*0.5
45–64 years	32.0	14.0	13.2	4.0	0.3	34.8	11.8	15.2	6.9	0.5
65 years and over	9.6	5.9	2.9	0.6	*0.0	12.8	6.2	4.9	1.4	*0.0
White										
All ages 20 years and over	34.2	13.8	14.8	4.8	0.3	31.8	10.4	14.2	6.3	0.5
20–24 years	41.9	18.6	18.2	4.0	*0.2	34.4	13.3	15.0	5.0	*0.5
25–34 years	43.4	16.3	19.5	6.7	0.4	37.1	11.2	17.1	7.6	0.7
35–44 years	43.9	15.7	19.7	7.4	0.6	38.1	11.1	17.0	8.8	*0.6
45–64 years	32.7	13.6	13.9	4.3	0.3	34.7	10.9	15.4	7.3	0.6
65 years and over	9.8	5.9	3.0	0.6	*0.0	13.2	5.9	5.4	1.6	*0.1
Black										
All ages 20 years and over	34.4	22.8	8.9	1.9	*0.1	35.1	20.8	11.7	2.1	*—
20–24 years	44.2	31.2	9.4	*1.4	*0.6	34.9	22.9	10.9	*1.1	*—
25–34 years	47.8	30.8	11.7	4.0	*0.1	42.5	24.1	13.8	*3.2	*—
35–44 years	42.8	26.8	12.8	*2.5	*0.1	41.3	24.6	15.6	0.6	*—
45–64 years	25.7	17.6	6.8	*0.9	*—	38.1	20.3	14.0	3.9	*—
65 years and over	7.1	5.8	1.2	*—	*—	9.2	9.2	*—	*—	*—

1 Includes unknown number of cigarettes smoked.

2 Excludes population with unknown smoking status from base of percentage.

3 Includes all other races not shown separately.

NOTE: A current smoker is a person who has smoked at least 100 cigarettes and who now smokes cigarettes on a regular basis.

SOURCE: Division of Health Interview Statistics, National Center for Health Statistics: Data from the Health Interview Survey.

Persons 12–74 years of age who had at least 1 drink of alcohol during the year prior to interview, according to frequency of drinking, sex, race, age, and family income: United States, 1971–75

(Data are based on household interviews of a sample of the civilian noninstitutionalized population)

Sex, race, age, and family income	Population 12–74 years in thousands	Frequency of drinking					
		Persons who had at least 1 drink	Every day	Just about every day	About 2 or 3 times per week	About 1 to 4 times per month	Less than once per month
		Percent of persons drinking					
Total[1,2] _____	147,154	72.0	7.5	3.8	11.6	25.3	23.8
Sex							
Male _____	70,600	77.6	11.5	5.7	15.5	26.8	18.1
Female _____	76,554	66.9	3.9	2.0	7.9	24.0	29.0
Race							
White _____	129,973	73.0	8.1	3.9	11.5	25.4	24.1
Black _____	15,714	63.6	3.2	2.9	12.2	23.8	21.5
Age							
12–17 years _____	23,545	38.9	0.1	0.2	1.2	8.7	28.6
18–24 years _____	23,809	84.9	2.8	3.0	12.8	40.2	26.2
25–34 years _____	26,137	85.8	7.3	4.7	15.8	35.9	22.2
35–44 years _____	21,438	81.2	11.6	5.4	14.8	29.5	19.9
45–54 years _____	22,366	78.4	11.5	6.2	15.7	22.5	22.6
55–64 years _____	17,867	70.1	12.5	4.0	10.4	18.9	24.4
65–74 years _____	11,992	56.2	9.6	2.5	8.5	13.9	21.8
Family income							
Less than $4,000 _____	22,316	61.6	4.1	2.2	9.8	21.9	23.5
$4,000–$6,999 _____	20,867	64.8	6.3	2.1	9.0	24.2	23.2
$7,000–$9,999 _____	34,695	72.0	6.6	3.6	10.6	25.6	25.7
$10,000–$14,999 _____	35,869	75.6	8.0	3.9	12.5	26.2	25.0
$15,000 or more _____	33,407	79.7	10.3	5.9	14.4	27.0	22.1

[1] Includes all other races not shown separately.
[2] Excludes unknown family income.

NOTE: Numbers and percents may not add to totals because of rounding.

SOURCE: Division of Health Examination Statistics, National Center for Health Statistics: Data from the Health and Nutrition Examination Survey.

Persons 20 years of age and over using sleeping aids, aspirins, coffee, or cigarettes, according to frequency of use, sex, and age: United States, 1976

(Data are based on household interviews of a sample of the civilian noninstitutionalized population)

Sex and age	Population in thousands	Substance				
		Sleeping aids,[1] once a week or more	Aspirins, once a week or more	Coffee, 5 or more cups per day	Cigarettes	
					Current smokers[2]	15 or more per day
Both sexes		Percent of persons with known use				
All ages 20 years and over	137,478	5.7	23.0	17.9	36.4	25.1
20–24 years	18,662	1.6	13.7	6.6	39.6	24.6
25–34 years	31,137	2.1	19.5	16.5	42.6	29.4
35–44 years	22,631	4.4	23.6	27.5	42.4	30.7
45–54 years	23,402	7.4	24.5	27.0	40.7	30.5
55–64 years	19,849	8.6	26.7	18.6	34.5	24.1
65–74 years	13,831	10.2	29.1	11.6	21.2	12.2
75 years and over	7,967	12.4	31.3	5.4	9.5	4.7
Male						
All ages 20 years and over	64,556	4.2	18.1	20.3	41.9	31.4
20–24 years	8,997	1.5	10.0	7.6	45.9	31.0
25–34 years	15,097	1.5	14.3	18.3	48.5	35.6
35–44 years	10,869	2.9	17.9	28.9	47.6	37.9
45–54 years	11,273	4.6	19.3	30.7	44.0	35.9
55–64 years	9,359	7.0	22.6	21.9	38.1	30.4
65–74 years	5,998	7.8	26.3	14.7	27.4	17.3
75 years and over	2,964	11.0	25.0	6.9	14.0	7.0
Female						
All ages 20 years and over	72,922	7.0	26.9	15.9	32.0	20.0
20–24 years	9,666	1.7	16.8	5.9	34.2	19.2
25–34 years	16,040	2.7	23.8	15.0	37.5	24.2
35–44 years	11,762	5.6	28.1	26.3	38.2	24.9
45–54 years	12,129	9.8	28.9	23.8	37.8	25.9
55–64 years	10,490	10.0	30.1	15.8	31.4	18.8
65–74 years	7,833	12.0	31.2	9.3	16.6	8.4
75 years and over	5,003	13.2	34.9	4.5	6.8	3.3

[1] Including any medicines for insomnia.

[2] A current smoker is a person who has smoked at least 100 cigarettes and who now smokes cigarettes on a regular basis.

SOURCE: Division of Health Interview Statistics, National Center for Health Statistics: Data from the Health Interview Survey.

Measures of Health

No one measure accurately reflects the health of the American people and, in fact, a determination of how healthy Americans really are depends to a large extent on how health is defined. With more people living longer than ever before, measures of health other than death are necessary to characterize the disease and disability patterns of an aging population.

Estimates of disease incidence may rise artificially as diagnostic procedures and reporting practices improve. Also, with increased accessibility to medical care, the measures of health status currently used may indicate an artificial "worsening" of health rather than an improvement. For example, as more people receive medical care it is likely that more people will be diagnosed, thereby increasing the number of conditions reported in health surveys. As people are told to cut down their activities because of diagnosed conditions, measures of disability will likely increase.

In the National Health Interview Survey, a large sample of the civilian noninstitutionalized population is asked to assess their own health status in comparison to others their same age. The survey also inquires into the number of acute or chronic conditions and the amount of activity limitation or disability incurred. In the National Health and Nutrition Examination Survey, actual examinations are made by physicians and dentists to assess the health of a sample of the civilian noninstitutionalized population. Local or State health agencies are responsible for reporting the incidence of notifiable diseases to the Center for Disease Control (CDC). From these and other sources, the health of people living in the United States is measured.

NOTE: Unless otherwise noted, data are from the ongoing data-collection systems of the National Center for Health Statistics. In many instances the data have been published in the *Vital and Health Statistics* series.

In 1976, an estimated 48 percent of the civilian noninstitutionalized population assessed themselves in excellent health. With increasing age and decreasing family income, the proportion of people feeling in excellent health declined. The perception of excellent health was characteristic of 70 percent of the population under 17 years of age in families with incomes of $15,000 per year or more, whereas feeling in excellent health was characteristic of less than a quarter of the population 65 years of age and over who had family incomes of less than $5,000.

Limitations in functional activities can become obstacles to a normal life. In 1976, 14 percent of the civilian noninstitutionalized population were limited in their usual activities because of chronic diseases or physical impairments. Nearly a third of the population 45 years of age and over was limited in activity compared with less than a tenth of the population under 45 years of age. Arthritis and rheumatism and heart conditions were the leading causes of limitation for those over 44 years of age, but impairments of the back and spine most often caused a limitation of activity for adults 17–44 years of age. Asthma was the primary limiting condition for children under 17 years of age.

Some chronic conditions were so severe that almost 4 percent of the civilian noninstitutionalized population were unable to carry on their major activity. For example, visual impairments limited more than 9 percent of the population 65 years of age and over to the extent that they were unable to carry on their major activity. Based on data from the Health and Nutrition Examination Survey from the early 1970's, nearly 90 percent of the population 65–74 years of age were found to have a significant eye abnormality, and about one-fifth of these people needed treatment for their problem. However, the poorer the population the less likely they were to be receiving needed care. More than half of the elderly with family incomes of less than $5,000 were not getting care compared with slightly more than a fifth of those with family incomes of $10,000 or more.

Data from the Health Interview Survey must be interpreted with caution. People can only report on the conditions they are aware of or think they have. Furthermore, since the data are limited to the noninstitutionalized population, the estimates of people limited in activity are lower than they would be if the institutionalized population were included.

People may be institutionalized when they become severely disabled or dependent on others for their daily activities. According to data from the Survey of Institutionalized Persons conducted by the Bureau of the Census, approximately 1.6 million people were in facilities other than long-stay hospitals or correctional facilities in 1976. Of these people, two-thirds were dependent upon others for at least some of their daily activities. Just over a third of those under 18 years of age needed some personal assistance compared with three-fourths of those 65 years of age and over. More people needed assistance for bathing or dressing than for other activities.

As measured by the Health Interview Survey, acute conditions are only temporarily disabling and result in either 1 day or more of restricted activity or the receiving of medical attention. In 1976, children under 17 years of age had an average of 308 acute conditions per 100 people, more than any other age group. It is probably more likely for a child to be kept home from school for 1 or 2 days than it would be for an adult to stay home from work. Also, parents are more apt to seek medical attention for their children than for themselves.

The incidence of acute conditions is higher for people in families with lower incomes than for people with higher incomes. People 17–44 years of age with family incomes of $15,000 or more had 196 acute conditions per 100 persons, while people in the same age group with family incomes of less than $5,000 had 279 acute conditions per 100 persons.

It is difficult to interpret the incidence of acute conditions for elderly people. Since the elderly are more likely to already have limited their usual activity or to be under medical care for a chronic condition, the onset of another condition may not further restrict an elderly person or cause him or her to seek further medical care.

The number of disability days per person provides some indication of the extent to which people have to cut down on activities as a result of an acute or chronic condition. In 1976, there was an average of 18 days of restricted activity per person including 7 days in bed and 5 days lost from work. There were more bed-disability days per person for the older than for the younger population. The number of work-loss days does not exhibit the same age differential as bed-disability days because as people become more ill they are more likely to drop out of the labor force and hence be excluded from the calculations of days of work lost.

Just as people with lower incomes had more acute conditions, they also had more disability days than the more affluent. People 45–64 years of age in families with less than $5,000 income had 3 times the number of restricted-activity days per person than those in families with incomes of $15,000 or more per year.

From the Health Interview Survey a comparison can be made between the health status of persons who reported working as their usual activity in the year prior to interview with those who reported some other usual activity. Based on selected measures of health (i.e., the percent reporting their health as fair or poor and the number of restricted-activity days and bed-disability days per person per year), people 25–44 and 45–64 years of age who classified themselves as usually working perceived themselves in better health and had fewer days of restricted activity, including days spent in bed, than those who reported some other usual activity. People 17–44 years of age who usually worked had more acute conditions than those who did not work. This is probably because the onset of a disabling condition may cause a worker to seek prompt medical care or to temporarily cut back on activities, while someone who does not work may have already cut back on activity.

The number of disability days for the currently employed population varied by occupation and by industry. In general, men in white-collar positions had the fewest days of restricted activity per person (10.5), and women in all other jobs (e.g., blue collar, service, farm workers) had the most (15.5). Employees in transportation and public utilities industries had more bed-disability and work-loss days than those in other industries, while employees in the construction industry had the fewest number of disability days.

Oral health is an important part of physical health that is often neglected. The presence of dental disease reflects both the condition of the teeth and gums and the extent of met or unmet needs. Dental treatment begun early in life can prevent future dental disease.

According to dental examinations of the civilian noninstitutionalized population during 1971–74, 64 percent needed some kind of dental care. About one-fifth needed to have their teeth cleaned, while two-fifths needed work on decayed teeth. There were pronounced age and family income differences in the need for dental care. For each age group, people with lower incomes had greater dental care needs than those who were more affluent. For example, 78 percent of children 12–17 years of age in families with incomes less than $5,000 needed dental care compared with 54 percent in families with incomes of $15,000 or more.

Periodontal disease and dental caries are two of the leading causes of tooth loss. Dental caries is a chronic destructive disease of the teeth that if left untreated results in loss of affected teeth. Periodontal disease designates a variety of conditions of the supporting structures of the teeth. In the early 1970's, about 16 percent of young children 1–5 years of age and more than 50 percent of children 6–17 years of age needed dental work on decayed teeth, according to findings of dental examinations. The need for periodontal treatment was greater for people 18 years of age and over than for younger people. Of the 54 percent of the population 65–74 years of age who had their natural teeth, 28 percent were found to need periodontal treatment and 33 percent to need work on decayed teeth.

State and local health departments are responsible for reporting the number of cases of certain diseases to the Center for Disease Control (CDC), although the reporting is voluntary. The completeness of reporting under such a system varies according to public concern and awareness of the importance of the disease. There is known to be serious underreporting of some diseases including the common childhood diseases.

In 1976, more than 93,000 cases of childhood diseases for which immunization is available were reported to CDC. In the 7 years following licensure of the rubella vaccine in 1969, the number of cases of the disease dropped by 78 percent to 12,000. The licensure of the measles vaccine in 1963 was followed by a dramatic drop in incidence of reported cases from nearly 400,000 to 22,000 cases in 1968. By 1976, reported measles incidence had again risen to 41,000 cases. Following introduction of the vaccine in 1968, the incidence of mumps declined by 75 percent from 152,000 reported cases in 1968 to 38,000 cases in 1976. The incidence of polio decreased precipitously after the introduction of the vaccine in 1955. Since 1973, fewer than 20 cases of polio have been reported annually.

One of the few childhood diseases for which there is no vaccination is chickenpox. National reporting of this disease to CDC began in 1972. From 1974 to 1976, the number of reported cases per 100,000 population increased from 72.2 to 96.1. Cyclical variation in the incidence of acute conditions often accounts for yearly increases or decreases. Trends in incidence of the disease are not always readily apparent.

As discussed in the "Mortality" section of this report, cancer is one of the leading causes of death in the United States. The annual cancer incidence rate is a measure of the number of newly diagnosed cases for a given period. Based on data from the Surveillance, Epidemiology, and End Results Reporting (SEER) Program, which covers about 10 percent of the U.S. population, the average annual cancer incidence rate for 1973–76 was 324.4 cases per 100,000 population. The rates varied from a low of 277.8 in Utah to a high of 358.0 in the San Francisco area. The cancer mortality rate for the SEER geographic areas was 167.7 per 100,000 population, ranging from a low of 122.6 in Utah to a high of 200.4 in New Orleans. There was considerable variation by site of cancer in the relationship between incidence and mortality. For cancers of the breast and prostate, for example, the incidence rate was approximately 3 times the mortality rate, while for lung cancer, incidence was only 25 percent higher than mortality. This differential can be explained in part by differences in survival rates for these various forms of cancer. Among those persons diagnosed with cancer of the lung in 1973, the percent surviving 3 years was only 12 percent compared with 78 percent for those with cancer of the breast and 68 percent for those with cancer of the prostate. Mortality for the SEER areas combined is remarkably similar to the total U.S. mortality for all cancer sites and for each of the selected sites.

Although tuberculosis was once a widespread disease in the United States, it has since become a relatively minor one. The rate has dropped from 80.5 to 15.0 cases per 100,000 population from 1950 to 1976. Tuberculosis is nearly 5 times more common in people other than white, and it is much more likely to occur in cities of at least 500,000 people than in smaller ones.

In 1976, gonorrhea ranked first among reportable communicable diseases in the United States. The number of cases per 100,000 civilian population has been increasing since the late 1950's. However, data for 1976 and 1977 suggest a possible reversal of the long-standing upward trend, particularly for people under 30 years of age. The incidence rates of other venereal diseases including syphilis have been decreasing.

The health of a newborn cannot be measured in the same way as the health of the general population. One of several indicators of infant health is birth weight. Infants weighing 2,500 grams or less at birth are considered to be low-birth-weight and are at a greater risk of future health problems than other infants. In 1976, 7.3 percent of all infants born were low-birth-weight. The proportion of low-birth-weight infants born to black women was nearly twice as high as the proportion born to white women (13.0 percent versus 6.1 percent).

The highest proportion of low-birth-weight infants were born to black teenagers with less than a high school education. A higher proportion of low-birth-weight infants were born to unmarried than to married women, regardless of educational attainment. Unmarried women who completed high school had twice the proportion of low-birth-weight infants when compared to married women who finished high school (11.6 percent versus 5.7 percent). Similarly, unmarried women without any high school education had about 1½ times the proportion of low-birth-weight infants when compared to married women without a high school education (13.6 percent versus 8.7 percent).

Lack of proper prenatal care has also been associated with the risk of having a low-birth-weight infant. Women who received prenatal care in the first or second month of pregnancy had a lower proportion of low-birth-weight infants than women who did not get care until later in their pregnancy. However, when both the educational attainment and age of the mother are taken into account, it appears that women 20–29 and those 30–39 years of age who had graduated from college had a lower proportion of low-birth-weight infants than women with lower educational attainment, regardless of the month in which their prenatal care began.

Self-assessment of health, according to age, sex, and family income: United States, 1976

(Data are based on household interviews of a sample of the civilian noninstitutionalized population)

Age, sex, and family income	Self-assessed level of health				
	All levels[1]	Excellent	Good	Fair	Poor
		Percent distribution			
ALL AGES					
Total[2]	100.0	48.2	38.9	9.6	2.8
Sex					
Male	100.0	51.3	37.1	8.5	2.7
Female	100.0	45.3	40.7	10.6	2.9
Family income					
Less than $5,000	100.0	31.9	42.0	18.0	7.6
$5,000–$9,999	100.0	40.4	43.4	12.2	3.7
$10,000–$14,999	100.0	49.7	40.3	8.0	1.6
$15,000 or more	100.0	59.6	33.8	5.3	1.1
UNDER 17 YEARS					
Total[2]	100.0	58.8	36.4	3.9	0.4
Sex					
Male	100.0	59.2	36.2	3.8	0.4
Female	100.0	58.4	36.6	4.0	0.4
Family income					
Less than $5,000	100.0	41.2	49.9	7.5	0.8
$5,000–$9,999	100.0	49.7	44.4	4.9	0.6
$10,000–$14,999	100.0	59.8	35.8	3.8	0.3
$15,000 or more	100.0	69.6	27.4	2.4	0.2
17–44 YEARS					
Total[2]	100.0	52.0	39.3	7.0	1.4
Sex					
Male	100.0	56.6	36.4	5.6	1.1
Female	100.0	47.7	42.1	8.3	1.6

Family income					
Less than $5,000	100.0	39.2	44.7	12.4	3.4
$5,000–$9,999	100.0	44.3	44.3	9.4	1.9
$10,000–$14,999	100.0	51.8	40.3	6.5	1.1
$15,000 or more	100.0	60.8	34.2	4.1	0.6
45–64 YEARS					
Total²	100.0	35.5	41.8	16.2	5.9
Sex					
Male	100.0	38.6	39.6	14.9	6.4
Female	100.0	32.8	43.8	17.5	5.5
Family income					
Less than $5,000	100.0	17.1	34.4	30.2	17.6
$5,000–$9,999	100.0	26.5	42.1	21.9	9.2
$10,000–$14,999	100.0	32.3	47.2	15.9	4.0
$15,000 or more	100.0	47.5	40.6	9.6	2.2
65 YEARS AND OVER					
Total²	100.0	29.0	39.0	22.3	9.0
Sex					
Male	100.0	29.5	37.4	23.2	9.3
Female	100.0	28.7	40.2	21.6	8.8
Family income					
Less than $5,000	100.0	24.1	36.6	26.4	12.4
$5,000–$9,999	100.0	29.7	40.6	22.0	7.4
$10,000–$14,999	100.0	34.4	41.5	18.0	5.5
$15,000 or more	100.0	37.8	39.1	16.8	6.1

¹ Includes unknown level of health.

² Includes unknown family income.

SOURCE: Division of Health Interview Statistics, National Center for Health Statistics: Data from the Health Interview Survey.

Selected chronic conditions causing limitation of activity, according to degree of limitation, sex, and age: United States, 1976

(Data are based on household interviews of a sample of the civilian noninstitutionalized population)

Activity limitation, sex, and age	Number of persons limited in activity	Chronic condition									
		Arthritis and rheumatism	Heart conditions	Hypertension without heart involvement	Diabetes	Mental and nervous conditions	Asthma	Impairments of back or spine	Impairments of lower extremities and hips	Visual impairments	Hearing impairments
		Percent of persons limited in activity because of specified condition									
All degrees of activity limitation											
Both sexes, all ages	30,175,062	16.8	15.7	6.9	5.1	4.9	4.8	7.5	6.1	5.4	2.5
Under 17 years	2,266,695	*1.0	2.4	*0.3	*1.0	6.7	20.1	3.2	6.9	3.7	5.2
17–44 years	7,512,474	6.8	4.8	3.4	2.3	5.9	5.9	13.9	8.0	4.2	2.7
45–64 years	10,504,689	19.6	19.0	9.0	6.8	5.7	3.4	7.9	5.6	4.0	1.9
65 years and over	9,891,204	24.9	23.4	8.9	6.3	3.0	2.1	3.3	5.0	8.2	2.4
Male, all ages	14,564,509	11.4	16.7	4.8	4.8	4.4	4.9	7.2	6.7	5.7	2.8
Under 17 years	1,279,389	*0.4	*2.5	*0.4	*1.1	8.1	21.2	*1.5	7.4	3.8	5.2
17–44 years	3,777,280	4.9	3.9	2.4	1.8	5.5	5.3	13.3	10.2	5.7	3.2
45–64 years	5,182,145	14.9	22.2	6.8	6.9	4.7	2.7	8.0	6.3	4.8	2.6
65 years and over	4,325,695	16.3	25.3	6.1	6.2	2.0	2.2	2.7	4.0	7.6	2.0
Female, all ages	15,610,553	21.7	14.8	8.9	5.2	5.4	4.8	7.9	5.5	5.0	2.2
Under 17 years	987,306	*1.9	*2.2	*0.2	*0.9	5.0	18.6	5.4	6.2	3.6	5.1
17–44 years	3,735,194	8.8	5.7	4.5	2.7	6.3	6.5	14.5	5.8	2.6	2.1
45–64 years	5,322,544	24.2	15.9	11.1	6.7	6.6	4.0	7.9	4.9	3.2	1.2
65 years and over	5,565,509	31.6	22.0	11.1	6.4	3.8	2.0	3.8	5.7	8.6	2.7
Limited but not in major activity											
Both sexes, all ages	7,495,791	13.0	6.7	5.2	3.2	3.4	7.2	8.0	8.2	6.1	4.6
Under 17 years	1,087,587	*1.3	*3.0	*0.5	*1.4	6.1	19.1	5.4	9.3	4.3	5.6
17–44 years	2,843,947	7.2	3.1	2.9	2.4	3.7	8.2	12.2	10.8	5.6	4.1
45–64 years	2,264,578	18.4	8.8	7.8	4.9	2.6	3.8	6.9	6.5	4.7	4.2
65 years and over	1,299,679	25.7	14.0	9.6	3.4	*1.6	*0.9	3.0	4.9	11.2	5.6

Limited in amount or kind of major activity

Both sexes, all ages	15,210,160	18.3	16.3	7.8	5.0	4.7	4.6	8.8	5.3	4.2	1.8
Under 17 years	1,058,928	*0.7	*1.9	*0.2	*0.7	7.5	22.6	*0.7	4.2	*1.7	4.9
17-44 years	3,721,693	6.8	5.4	4.0	2.3	5.4	4.7	16.5	6.6	3.2	1.8
45-64 years	5,671,034	20.7	19.9	9.5	6.9	5.3	3.4	9.3	4.8	3.2	1.2
65 years and over	4,758,505	28.4	23.9	10.5	5.9	2.9	1.9	4.1	5.0	6.5	1.7

Unable to carry on major activity

Both sexes, all ages	7,469,111	17.5	23.4	6.8	7.0	7.0	3.0	4.4	5.6	7.2	1.9
Under 17 years	120,180	*1.7	*1.4	*—	*—	*5.7	*7.1	*4.2	*9.0	*15.1	*3.2
17-44 years	946,834	5.8	7.5	*2.7	*1.9	14.5	*3.7	8.4	5.3	3.7	*1.8
45-64 years	2,569,077	18.2	26.2	8.7	8.1	9.1	2.9	5.8	6.5	5.0	1.4
65 years and over	3,833,020	20.4	26.1	6.8	7.7	3.6	2.7	2.5	5.0	9.2	2.2

SOURCE: Division of Health Interview Statistics, National Center for Health Statistics: Data from the Health Interview Survey.

Percent of population with significant eye abnormality and treatment status, according to age and family income: United States, 1971–72

(Data are based on examinations of a sample of the civilian noninstitutionalized population)

Treatment status and family income	All ages	Age				
		1–5 years	6–19 years	20–44 years	45–64 years	65–74 years
With significant eye abnormality		Percent of population				
All incomes[1]	39.2	12.2	23.5	34.5	61.7	88.9
Less than $5,000	49.3	18.2	29.3	32.4	71.2	88.2
$5,000–$9,999	36.6	9.5	22.3	33.7	60.6	88.9
$10,000 or more	36.5	12.3	22.9	34.7	59.3	88.3
Needing treatment for eye abnormality						
All incomes[1]	7.1	3.5	4.7	5.0	10.2	22.1
Less than $5,000	9.0	3.7	4.6	4.2	10.5	22.2
$5,000–$9,999	6.8	3.2	4.9	4.6	10.5	23.2
$10,000 or more	6.3	3.6	4.2	5.5	9.9	17.5
Not receiving treatment:		Percent of persons needing treatment				
All incomes[1]	47.9	71.4	46.8	52.0	47.1	43.0
Less than $5,000	57.8	91.9	43.5	81.0	58.1	54.1
$5,000–$9,999	48.5	62.5	38.8	56.5	52.4	37.1
$10,000 or more	42.9	72.2	50.0	43.6	38.4	21.7

[1] Includes unknown income.

SOURCE: Division of Health Examination Statistics, National Center for Health Statistics: Data from the Health and Nutrition Examination Survey: Data computed by the the Division of Analysis from data compiled by the Division of Health Examination Statistics.

Institutionalized population and their need for assistance in personal care, according to age, degree of assistance needed, and type of activity: United States, 1976

(Data are based on reporting by staff in a sample survey of institutions)

Population, degree of assistance needed, and type of activity	Age			
	All ages	Under 18 years	18–64 years	65 years and over
	Number of persons			
Institutionalized population	[1]1,550,100	151,530	334,120	1,027,850
	Percent distribution			
Total	100.0	100.0	100.0	100.0
Need no assistance[2,3]	25.3	56.0	40.9	16.3
Need regular assistance or are totally dependent[2]	67.5	36.3	50.1	77.3
Unknown	7.3	7.7	8.9	6.5
	Percent of persons			
Need regular help[2]	43.8	20.1	33.9	50.8
Getting in and out of bed	13.2	3.2	6.3	16.9
Eating or drinking	8.4	6.5	5.8	9.4
Bathing or dressing	33.7	13.4	26.7	39.2
Walking or getting about	11.5	3.3	5.8	14.6
Using toilet or bedpan	11.8	6.2	7.3	14.1
Totally dependent[2]	40.5	25.7	29.3	46.0
Getting in and out of bed	27.5	17.3	16.5	32.0
Eating or drinking	12.4	13.6	9.1	12.7
Bathing or dressing	35.1	24.6	24.7	39.5
Walking or getting about	29.7	16.3	18.5	34.9
Using toilet or bedpan	26.3	18.6	16.5	30.0

[1] Includes 2 percent for whom age is not stated.
[2] In one or more of the specified activities.
[3] Includes less than 1 percent who need occasional help.

NOTE: These data exclude persons in long-stay hospitals and penal and juvenile detention facilities.

SOURCE: U.S. Bureau of the Census: *Current Population Reports.* Series P–23, No. 69. Washington. U.S. Government Printing Office, June 1978.

Incidence of acute conditions, according to condition, age, sex, usual activity, and family income: United States, 1976

(Data are based on interviews of a sample of the civilian noninstitutionalized population)

Age, sex, usual activity, and family income	All acute conditions	Acute condition							
		Respiratory			Other[1]	Injuries	Infective and parasitic diseases	Digestive system conditions	All other
		Total	Upper	Influenza					
	Number of acute conditions per 100 persons per year								
All ages under 65 years[2]	231.9	126.9	64.4	56.1	6.4	33.4	26.6	11.0	34.0
Sex and usual activity									
Male	222.0	120.2	61.2	52.6	6.3	39.7	26.0	10.9	25.2
Working or going to school	207.1	113.3	55.2	52.9	5.1	39.3	22.8	10.9	20.9
All other activities[3]	290.7	152.4	89.6	51.5	11.4	41.2	41.4	11.1	44.6
Female	241.4	133.3	67.5	59.4	6.4	27.4	27.1	11.1	42.5
Working or going to school	241.9	137.6	69.5	61.3	6.8	27.9	25.7	12.0	38.6
All other activities[3]	240.8	127.5	64.9	56.6	6.0	26.7	29.2	9.9	47.5
Family income									
Less than $5,000	266.0	151.4	79.1	65.1	7.1	35.1	27.0	14.5	38.0
$5,000–$9,999	238.2	125.2	63.8	55.0	6.3	35.5	26.8	13.1	37.7
$10,000–$14,999	239.3	132.1	60.9	62.9	8.2	33.2	30.5	9.4	34.1
$15,000 or more	222.5	122.1	64.6	51.8	5.7	33.1	26.4	9.8	31.1
Under 17 years[2]	307.8	169.8	98.2	61.1	10.4	37.0	45.4	15.1	40.5
Sex and usual activity									
Male	304.8	159.1	91.2	57.5	10.4	44.5	47.4	15.4	38.4
Working or going to school	268.8	140.1	73.7	58.8	7.7	43.5	40.6	17.4	27.2
All other activities[3]	381.6	199.8	128.7	54.8	16.2	46.6	61.8	11.1	62.3
Female	310.9	180.9	105.5	64.9	10.5	29.2	43.4	14.7	42.7
Working or going to school	283.2	169.1	91.2	67.9	10.0	26.4	36.0	15.8	35.8
All other activities[3]	370.4	206.1	136.1	58.5	11.6	35.1	59.3	12.4	57.5
Family income									
Less than $5,000	316.1	179.8	112.2	56.3	11.4	30.9	48.1	15.6	41.7
$5,000–$9,999	291.9	156.1	92.4	56.2	7.5	35.3	46.7	17.4	36.5
$10,000–$14,999	311.6	173.3	92.2	66.4	14.7	37.6	46.4	11.9	42.5
$15,000 or more	321.8	175.1	103.1	62.1	9.8	41.1	48.3	15.1	42.2

	218.7	119.5	54.9	59.9	4.7	35.6	20.5	10.2	33.0
17–44 years[2]									
Sex and usual activity									
Male	201.3	113.0	52.7	56.2	4.2	44.4	18.3	9.2	16.4
Working or going to school	203.9	115.0	53.7	57.1	4.2	44.5	18.5	9.0	16.8
All other activities[3]	166.5	84.8	40.4	42.5	*1.9	41.9	*16.5	*11.9	*11.4
Female	235.1	125.6	57.1	63.4	5.1	27.4	22.5	11.1	48.5
Working or going to school	237.7	128.8	63.7	59.7	5.4	31.2	21.7	11.0	45.0
All other activities[3]	231.5	121.0	47.9	68.3	4.7	21.9	23.9	11.3	53.4
Family income									
Less than $5,000	279.3	156.7	77.6	71.8	7.3	42.6	22.4	17.1	40.3
$5,000–$9,999	231.8	122.3	56.6	60.2	5.5	40.4	17.6	12.4	39.1
$10,000–$14,999	229.3	126.1	52.6	68.5	4.9	34.8	27.6	8.7	32.0
$15,000 or more	195.9	108.0	51.0	53.2	3.7	32.1	18.6	8.2	29.1
45–64 years[2]	150.7	80.9	35.4	41.5	4.0	24.2	12.0	6.9	26.8
Sex and usual activity									
Male	138.4	75.7	33.1	38.3	4.3	23.2	9.3	7.4	22.8
Working or going to school	137.4	75.9	35.8	36.0	4.1	22.2	10.2	6.8	22.4
All other activities[3]	139.6	76.0	21.0	49.5	5.5	25.6	*5.2	*10.3	22.5
Female	161.8	85.6	37.5	44.4	3.7	25.0	14.4	6.4	30.5
Working or going to school	167.8	95.4	39.8	52.0	*3.7	22.5	14.9	6.8	28.1
All other activities[3]	156.9	77.9	35.5	38.7	*3.7	27.0	14.1	6.0	31.7
Family income									
Less than $5,000	172.1	102.4	37.9	63.6	*0.9	25.7	*7.7	*7.9	28.4
$5,000–$9,999	168.1	83.0	34.3	42.6	*6.1	25.7	15.2	7.7	36.6
$10,000–$14,999	142.4	77.4	27.9	44.3	*5.3	22.1	10.9	*6.9	25.2
$15,000 or more	144.7	80.4	40.6	35.9	3.9	24.8	12.7	6.2	20.5

[1] Includes pneumonia, bronchitis, and other respiratory conditions not shown separately.

[2] Includes unknown family income and unknown usual activity.

[3] Includes persons keeping house (females only), retired persons 45–64 years of age (both sexes), persons with other activities not specified (both sexes), and persons under 6 years of age for whom no activity is specified.

SOURCE: Division of Health Interview Statistics, National Center for Health Statistics: Data from the Health Interview Survey.

Disability days, according to type of disability day, age, sex, and family income: United States, 1976
(Data are based on household interviews of a sample of the civilian noninstitutionalized population)

Age, sex, and family income	Civilian noninstitutionalized population		Type of disability day		
	Total	Currently employed, 17 years and over	Restricted activity	Bed disability	Work loss[1]
	Number in thousands		Days per person per year		
ALL AGES					
Total[2]	210,643	87,119	18.2	7.1	5.3
Sex					
Male	101,626	52,177	16.4	6.1	5.2
Female	109,018	34,942	19.9	8.1	5.6
Family income					
Less than $5,000	28,987	6,891	32.5	12.1	5.8
$5,000–$9,999	42,543	15,603	20.3	8.2	6.1
$10,000–$14,999	44,471	19,748	15.7	5.9	5.5
$15,000 or more	75,797	38,212	12.8	5.1	4.7
UNDER 17 YEARS					
Total[2]	60,891	...	11.0	5.1	...
Sex					
Male	31,039	...	10.7	4.9	...
Female	29,852	...	11.3	5.3	...
Family income					
Less than $5,000	6,547	...	12.2	6.5	...
$5,000–$9,999	12,202	...	11.2	5.1	...
$10,000–$14,999	14,125	...	11.0	4.6	...
$15,000 or more	22,511	...	10.5	4.9	...
17–44 YEARS					
Total[2]	84,701	57,268	14.2	5.6	5.0
Sex					
Male	40,991	33,725	12.6	4.3	4.7
Female	43,710	23,543	15.7	6.8	5.5

Family income				
Less than $5,000	9,789	21.6	8.6	5.0
$5,000–$9,999	16,363	16.1	6.5	5.9
$10,000–$14,999	19,533	14.4	5.5	5.6
$15,000 or more	33,202	10.8	4.2	4.2
45–64 YEARS				
Total²	43,253	25.4	8.9	6.1
Sex				
Male	20,633	23.6	7.9	6.3
Female	22,620	27.0	9.9	5.9
Family income				
Less than $5,000	4,876	53.6	18.9	7.6
$5,000–$9,999	7,842	30.6	11.8	7.2
$10,000–$14,999	8,506	22.3	7.6	5.6
$15,000 or more	17,443	17.5	5.8	5.8
65 YEARS AND OVER				
Total²	21,799	40.0	15.1	4.0
Sex				
Male	8,962	36.8	14.3	3.2
Female	12,837	42.2	15.6	5.7
Family income				
Less than $5,000	7,775	50.3	16.9	7.5
$5,000–$9,999	6,136	36.4	14.6	3.6
$10,000–$14,999	2,308	31.5	11.4	*1.9
$15,000 or more	2,641	28.0	13.1	*0.8

¹ Work-loss rates are based on the currently employed population 17 years of age and over.
² Includes unknown family income.

SOURCE: Division of Health Interview Statistics, National Center for Health Statistics: Data from the Health Interview Survey.

Self-assessment of health, limitation of activity, restricted-activity days, and bed-disability days, according to usual activity, sex, age, and family income: United States, 1976 (Data are based on household interviews of a sample of the civilian noninstitutionalized population)

Sex, age, and family income	Percent feeling fair or poor[4]			Usual activity								
				Percent limited in activity			Restricted-activity days per person per year			Bed-disability days per person per year		
	Total[1]	Working[2]	All other[3]	Total[1]	Working[2]	All other[3]	Total[1]	Working[2]	All other[3]	Total[1]	Working[2]	All other[3]
Both sexes 25–44 years[5]	9.4	7.1	15.3	10.2	7.8	16.2	15.5	13.3	21.1	5.9	4.9	8.4
Less than $5,000	23.2	13.6	33.2	21.4	13.3	29.8	28.4	19.1	38.3	10.6	5.7	15.8
$5,000–$9,999	13.6	10.1	21.7	13.1	8.7	23.0	18.0	15.3	23.9	6.7	5.7	8.8
$10,000–$14,999	8.6	7.4	11.5	9.8	8.8	12.4	15.9	14.2	20.4	6.0	5.2	8.1
$15,000 or more	5.2	4.6	7.3	7.2	6.3	10.0	11.8	11.1	13.9	4.3	4.1	5.2
Male 25–44 years[5]	7.7	5.9	33.9	10.5	8.2	44.8	13.9	11.9	43.1	4.7	4.0	15.0
Less than $5,000	21.0	12.2	39.3	23.6	13.5	44.8	29.0	20.1	47.8	8.9	4.7	18.0
$5,000–$9,999	12.0	8.8	36.7	13.8	9.3	49.6	17.2	14.4	39.9	5.5	4.9	*10.3
$10,000–$14,999	7.0	6.4	24.0	10.1	9.2	36.4	13.5	12.3	48.5	5.0	4.6	*19.1
$15,000 or more	4.0	3.7	21.9	7.3	6.8	37.1	10.1	9.7	35.4	3.2	3.1	*7.5
Female 25–44 years[5]	11.1	9.0	13.1	10.0	7.2	12.8	17.0	15.6	18.5	7.0	6.3	7.6
Less than $5,000	24.7	15.3	30.9	19.8	13.0	24.2	28.0	17.9	34.8	11.8	7.0	15.0
$5,000–$9,999	15.1	12.0	18.5	12.4	7.9	17.5	18.6	16.8	20.6	7.6	6.8	8.5
$10,000–$14,999	10.1	9.5	10.7	9.6	8.2	10.8	18.4	18.1	18.6	7.0	6.7	7.4
$15,000 or more	6.4	6.1	6.7	7.0	5.5	8.9	13.4	13.7	13.0	5.5	5.8	5.1
Both sexes 45–64 years[5]	22.2	14.2	35.5	24.3	15.1	39.6	25.4	16.2	40.6	8.9	5.4	14.9
Less than $5,000	47.8	26.5	57.6	49.0	26.5	59.5	53.6	27.4	65.8	18.9	10.1	23.0
$5,000–$9,999	31.1	21.2	42.7	31.3	18.3	46.4	30.6	17.6	45.5	11.8	6.1	18.4
$10,000–$14,999	19.8	15.6	28.2	22.5	16.8	33.8	22.3	17.8	31.3	7.6	5.5	11.6
$15,000 or more	11.8	9.2	18.7	15.7	12.3	24.8	17.5	14.3	25.8	5.8	4.6	9.1
Male 45–64 years[5]	21.3	14.2	55.0	25.1	16.3	66.8	23.6	15.4	61.9	7.9	4.7	23.1
Less than $5,000	53.1	29.7	67.6	59.1	30.8	76.6	55.4	32.5	69.6	19.5	12.2	24.1
$5,000–$9,999	35.5	24.1	58.6	37.1	20.9	69.7	32.5	17.4	62.6	12.3	5.2	26.7
$10,000–$14,999	20.5	16.4	47.2	24.7	18.8	63.3	22.7	17.0	59.4	7.0	4.9	20.8
$15,000 or more	10.7	9.0	35.1	15.7	13.4	50.2	16.2	13.8	53.1	5.0	4.1	18.1
Female 45–64 years[5]	23.0	14.1	30.0	23.5	13.0	31.8	27.0	17.5	34.5	9.9	6.5	12.5
Less than $5,000	45.0	24.3	53.2	43.8	23.6	51.8	52.7	23.9	64.1	18.6	8.6	22.5
$5,000–$9,999	28.0	18.0	35.8	27.1	15.5	36.3	29.2	17.9	38.2	11.4	7.1	14.9
$10,000–$14,999	19.2	14.2	23.5	20.2	13.1	26.5	22.0	19.3	24.4	8.1	6.7	9.4
$15,000 or more	13.1	9.5	16.5	15.8	10.0	21.3	19.0	15.6	22.1	6.7	5.5	7.8

[1] Includes unknown activity status.
[2] Includes 1.5 percent of persons 25–64 years of age going to school.
[3] Includes keeping house (females only), retired persons (over 44 years of age), and other activities not specified.
[4] The complement of the percent feeling fair or poor is the percent feeling excellent or good.
[5] Includes unknown family income.

SOURCE: Division of Health Interview Statistics, National Center for Health Statistics: Data from the Health Interview Survey.

Disability days for the currently employed population, according to occupation, type of disability day, sex, and industry: United States, 1976

(Data are based on household interviews of a sample of the civilian noninstitutionalized population)

Sex and industry	Currently employed persons in thousands[1]	Occupation								
		Total[2]			White collar			All other[3]		
		Restricted activity	Bed disability	Work loss	Restricted activity	Bed disability	Work loss	Restricted activity	Bed disability	Work loss
		Number of days per currently employed person per year								
Both sexes										
All industries[4]	87,119	12.5	4.4	5.3	11.6	4.3	4.5	13.6	4.5	6.2
Agriculture	2,971	12.3	3.3	5.2	*11.4	*3.7	*6.7	12.3	3.2	5.1
Mining	722	14.7	*3.5	5.5	*21.3	*2.0	*3.0	11.8	*4.1	*6.6
Construction	5,203	10.1	2.9	4.2	10.5	*4.1	3.7	9.9	2.4	4.3
Manufacturing	20,297	13.7	4.2	6.0	11.7	3.8	4.8	14.8	4.4	6.6
Transportation and public utilities	5,540	14.9	5.2	7.3	11.2	4.3	4.0	17.7	5.9	9.8
Wholesale and retail trade	17,178	10.8	4.0	4.8	10.5	4.0	4.1	11.2	4.2	6.0
Finance, insurance, and real estate	4,871	12.1	4.4	4.6	11.9	4.4	4.5	15.0	*4.0	*5.8
Service and miscellaneous	24,065	12.6	5.1	4.8	11.6	4.6	4.3	14.2	5.7	5.7
Public administration	5,433	13.4	4.6	6.7	14.4	5.1	6.8	11.4	3.7	6.5
Male										
All industries[4]	52,177	11.7	3.7	5.2	10.5	3.3	4.0	12.7	3.9	6.0
Agriculture	2,495	12.5	3.3	5.7	*13.4	*4.8	*10.9	12.4	3.2	5.4
Construction	4,849	9.3	2.6	4.0	8.0	*3.0	*3.5	9.6	2.4	4.1
Manufacturing	14,166	12.8	3.7	5.6	11.5	3.3	4.6	13.6	3.9	6.1
Transportation and public utilities	4,334	15.6	4.9	7.7	12.0	4.1	3.8	17.4	5.4	9.6
Wholesale and retail trade	9,499	9.7	3.1	4.4	9.4	2.7	3.4	10.0	3.5	5.6
Finance, insurance, and real estate	2,250	12.5	3.5	3.9	12.0	3.2	3.4	*15.9	*4.8	*7.0
Service and miscellaneous	9,763	10.7	4.3	4.5	8.8	3.6	3.8	13.6	5.3	5.6
Public administration	3,652	12.5	3.7	6.1	13.7	4.0	5.9	11.0	*3.2	6.3
Female										
All industries[4]	34,942	13.7	5.5	5.6	12.7	5.3	5.0	15.5	5.8	6.7
Manufacturing	6,131	15.7	5.3	7.0	12.2	4.8	5.3	18.0	5.6	8.0
Wholesale and retail trade	7,679	12.1	5.2	5.4	11.5	5.2	4.8	13.4	5.4	6.7
Finance, insurance, and real estate	2,621	11.8	5.1	5.3	11.8	5.3	5.4	*11.0	*0.6	*0.6
Service and miscellaneous	14,302	13.9	5.6	5.1	13.4	5.3	4.7	14.6	6.0	5.8
Public administration	1,781	15.2	6.7	8.0	15.3	6.6	8.0	*14.9	*7.7	*7.9

[1] Data refer to persons 17 years of age and over.
[2] Includes occupation not specified.
[3] Includes blue collar, service, and farm workers.
[4] Includes industry not specified and industries in which less than 1.5 million persons were employed for which data are not shown separately.

SOURCE: Division of Health Interview Statistics. National Center for Health Statistics: Data from the Health Interview Survey.

Persons 1–74 years of age needing dental care, according to age and selected needs: United States, 1971–74

(Data are based on dental examinations of a sample of the civilian noninstitutionalized population)

Selected dental needs	All ages 1–74 years	Age					65–74 years	
		1–5 years	6–11 years	12–17 years	18–44 years	45–64 years	Total	With natural teeth only
	Number of persons in thousands							
Total	193,976	16,949	23,356	24,654	73,882	42,362	12,774	6,939
	Percent needing specified care							
Cleaning	19.1	2.4	28.2	27.5	22.4	13.5	8.4	15.5
Gingivitis treatment	8.9	*0.1	1.9	13.4	13.8	6.9	3.5	6.4
Periodontal treatment	10.1	*0.2	*0.1	2.0	12.2	19.3	15.4	28.3
Decayed tooth repair	41.1	16.1	52.7	53.6	49.3	30.1	17.9	32.6
Extractions	4.8	*0.8	*0.4	*0.6	5.8	8.4	9.8	18.1
Fixed bridges and/or partials	16.0	*–	*0.1	5.8	25.3	23.3	8.5	15.7
Denture or bridge repair	2.7	*–	*–	*0.0	1.9	6.7	7.7	3.8
Full denture construction	6.6	*–	*0.0	*0.1	4.2	15.6	24.8	19.9

NOTE: In the first three categories only, sample persons who had an indicated need for all three appear only in the periodontal treatment group. Those with an indicated need for cleaning and gingivitis treatment appear only in the gingivitis group. Those with an indicated need for cleaning only appear only in that group.

SOURCE: Division of Health Examination Statistics, National Center for Health Statistics: Data from the Health and Nutrition Examination Survey.

Persons 1–74 years of age needing dental care, according to age and family income: United States, 1971–74

(Data are based on dental examinations of a sample of the civilian noninstitutionalized population)

Family income	All ages 1–74 years	Age					
		1–5 years	6–11 years	12–17 years	18–44 years	45–64 years	65–74 years
	Percent of population needing dental care						
Total[1]	64.1	16.6	63.5	67.5	72.7	67.5	61.0
Less than $5,000	68.6	21.2	73.8	77.8	77.7	74.4	60.0
$5,000–$9,999	69.4	19.2	71.0	77.5	79.2	72.9	61.4
$10,000–$14,999	62.2	13.6	62.2	61.5	71.3	66.2	65.7
$15,000 or more	53.6	8.4	43.3	54.5	60.6	57.6	58.8

[1] Includes unknown family income.

NOTE: See table 63 for base population.

SOURCE: Division of Health Examination Statistics, National Center for Health Statistics: Data from the Health and Nutrition Examination Survey.

Utilization of Health Resources[a]

Ambulatory Care

While the number of physicians per 10,000 population has increased during the past several years, the overall number of ambulatory physician visits per person per year has been fairly stable at about 5 visits.

The physician visit rate for white people has also remained stable during the 1970's, whereas the rate for people in the all other color group has been increasing. During 1975–76, the overall visit rate for white people was 9 percent higher than the visit rate for all others. However, white people 25–44 years of age reported 9 percent fewer visits per person per year, and those 45–64 years of age reported 6 percent fewer visits per person per year than all others.

Physician visit rates tend to be higher for older people than for younger ones, reflecting the increased frequency, complexity, and chronicity of conditions associated with aging. During 1975–76, children under 18 years of age averaged 4.1 visits per person per year, while people 65 years of age and over averaged 6.7 visits per person per year.

During the 1960's, individuals in families with higher incomes averaged more physician visits per person per year than those in families with lower incomes. However, since 1970, this trend has reversed. During 1975–76, people in low-income families (less than $5,000 per year) reported 6.0 visits per person per year compared with 4.9 visits reported by persons in high-income families ($15,000 or more per year). This higher use of physician services among the poor may reflect a greater need for services because of deficient health resulting from environmen-tal factors, past inequities in receiving health care, and reluctance to obtain medical services because of the expense involved. For example, during 1976, people in low-income families reported 32.5 days of restricted activity per person per year compared with 12.8 days reported by people in high-income families. Medicaid and Medicare have permitted the use of physicians' services by individuals with low incomes to become more nearly consonant with the severity of their health problems.

People who assessed their health to be fair or poor had a physician visit rate almost 3 times the rate for those who assessed their health to be excellent or good, 10.9 visits per person per year compared with 4.2 visits.

Disabling illness, low income, and a lack of private health insurance coverage tend to occur together. Most individuals receiving Social Security disability benefits have their medical care expenses covered under Medicare; and individuals receiving Supplementary Security Income payments have their expenses covered under Medicaid, but many disabled individuals have no third-party coverage for their expenses. Private health insurance for people under 65 years of age is generally obtained through the regular employment of a family member, but many individuals who suffer from disabling conditions are unable to hold steady jobs that would enable them to obtain health insurance. Such individuals are also frequently limited to the relatively low incomes provided by public disability programs.

In 1975, the prevalence of activity limitation was greater among individuals without private health insurance than among those with some coverage. Because of the high prevalence of ill health among the non-insured, they used appreciably more hospital care than those with insurance and, at certain ages, they averaged more visits with physicians.

Health insurance reimbursements for am-

[a] Prepared by Joseph Gfroerer and Cecilia A. Young, Division of Analysis, National Center for Health Statistics.

NOTE: Unless otherwise noted, data are from the ongoing data-collection systems of the National Center for Health Statistics. In many instances the data have been published in the *Vital and Health Statistics* series.

bulatory care are generally paid on a fee-for-service basis. Payments for a particular patient directly reflect the visits and the diagnostic and therapeutic procedures received by that patient. However, a small segment of the population has its care covered under an alternative insurance scheme, a prepaid group practice plan. In 1975, there were only 6 million people under 65 years of age, or 3 percent of the population, with such coverage.

The prepaid group practice provides a wide variety of services for an annual per capita premium. Generally, the out-of-pocket payment a patient can expect to make for care under a fee-for-service arrangement is greater than the out-of-pocket payment under a prepaid group plan since the latter typically provides comprehensive coverage with little or no direct patient payments. Furthermore, incentives for keeping in-hospital care to a minimum are generally stronger for physicians working under the prepaid group plan arrangement than for physicians working on a fee-for-service basis.

Under Health Maintenance Organization legislation, the Federal Government has been actively promoting the growth of membership in prepaid group plans. Therefore, the use of medical services by subscribers to prepaid group plans is of interest, even though there is a relatively small segment of the population with that type of coverage at present.

In 1975, subscribers to prepaid group plans had appreciably more ambulatory physician contacts but fewer days in the hospital than individuals with other forms of coverage. However, prepaid group plan memberships are considerably more concentrated in metropolitan areas and in the West than memberships in other private health insurance plans. Since the use of ambulatory services tends to be above average in metropolitan areas, and the use of hospital services tends to be below average in the West, the distinctive pattern of service use in prepaid group plans may in part reflect these geographic factors. Nevertheless, the national statistics on the use of services are congruent with other research findings indicating that, within a given community, there is a greater tendency for prepaid group plan members to substitute ambulatory care for in-hospital care than for people with other types of coverage. The relative absence of financial barriers for the subscriber to use ambulatory services and the incentives to the physician to employ ambulatory services rather than in-hospital services undoubtedly contribute to the differentials.

Physician visit rates, by place of residence, varied across the United States, with a range from 5.7 visits per person per year in the West to 4.7 visits in the North Central and South in 1975–76. People living outside of metropolitan areas made fewer visits per person per year than those living in metropolitan areas. This may be a reflection of the greater concentration and availability of practicing physicians in metropolitan areas.

Physician visits are made in a number of settings including private offices, hospital outpatient clinics or emergency rooms, and various types of freestanding clinics. Almost 70 percent of the population in 1974 received care in these settings with 63 percent of the population contacting a physician in his or her private office. People in high-income families were more likely to use only the doctor's office than those in low-income families. The reverse was true for all other places of care. Contact with all other settings was more common among people in low-income families. White people were more likely to use the doctor's office only or in combination with the hospital outpatient department than all other people. Conversely, all other people were more likely than white people to use only the hospital outpatient department.

Two socioeconomic factors associated with levels of utilization by place of care are family income and race. People in each age group with low family incomes reported more visits to the hospital outpatient clinic or emergency room than those with high family incomes during 1975–76. Conversely, people with high family incomes generally reported more visits to the doctor's office and more telephone contacts than those with low family incomes. White people also reported more visits to the doctor's office and more telephone contacts than all other people, while all other people reported more visits than white people to the hospital outpatient clinic or emergency room.

The levels of utilization of medical services are sometimes used as a proxy measure of health status. However, the use of health services may only indicate accessibility of services, not actual health status or need for medical care, since improved accessibility to care tends to result in increased use of services.

In addition to the physician visit data collected through the national Health Interview Survey, the National Center for Health Statistics collects detailed data on visits to physicians in their private office practices through the National Ambulatory Medical Care Survey. Both surveys reported about three office visits per person per year during 1975–76. Office visits per person per year generally increased with age. However, the number of visits per person per year was higher for females than for males, for white people than for all others, and for people in metropolitan areas than for those in nonmetropolitan areas.

Overall, physicians reported medical or special exams as the most common principal reason for office visits in 1975–76. Acute upper respiratory infection, except influenza, was the leading principal disease diagnosis for both males and females. This condition was most often diagnosed in children under 15 years of age. For males, heart disease was the next most common disease diagnosis; for females, it was hypertension. For both of these diseases, there was a sharp increase in the number of office visits per person per year between people 25–44 years of age and those 45–64 years of age, and the number of visits per person per year continued to rise for people 65 years of age and over.

Primary care physicians provided the majority of office-based ambulatory care; general and family physicians alone accounted for 2 out of every 5 visits.

Visits to specialists varied by the location of practice. Sixty-two percent of the office visits in nonmetropolitan areas were to general and family practitioners compared with 32 percent in metropolitan areas. The ratios of general and family practitioner visits to internist visits for hypertension and heart disease were 1.5 and 0.9, respectively, in metropolitan areas compared with 6.3 and 3.3, respectively, in nonmetropolitan areas. The ratio of general and family practitioner visits to obstetrician and gynecologist visits for prenatal care was 0.2 in metropolitan areas

compared with 0.9 in nonmetropolitan areas.

The average office-based physician dealt chiefly with patients who had been seen before; new patient visits accounted for only 15 percent of the visits during 1975–76. Similarly, the average office-based physician dealt chiefly with problems for which the patient had already been treated. Slightly more of the visits in metropolitan areas were for "old" problems (63 percent) than in nonmetropolitan areas (59 percent). Many of the "old" problems were chronic conditions such as hypertension, heart disease, diabetes mellitus, hay fever, and malignant neoplasms.

The largest proportion of office visits, about 49 percent in 1975–76, received "not serious" evaluations from physicians, which may reflect the substantial number of visits for preventive care, routine maintenance care, and care for self-limiting conditions such as prenatal care, eye examinations, and treatment for the common cold.

Drug therapy was the most frequent form of therapy provided in office-based practice; about 44 percent of all visits in 1975–76 resulted in a drug being prescribed. In metropolitan areas, 42 percent of all visits resulted in such treatment compared with 48 percent of all visits in nonmetropolitan areas.

The duration of visit is defined as the time spent in face-to-face encounter between physician and patient. In about 73 percent of the office visits, face-to-face contacts lasted 15 minutes or less. By location of practice, 72 percent of the office visits in metropolitan areas lasted 15 minutes or less compared with 78 percent in nonmetropolitan areas. The duration of visit varied by diagnosis. For example, the duration of visit was 5 minutes or less for 40 percent of the visits for prenatal care, whereas the duration of visit was 31 minutes or more for nearly 50 percent of the visits for neuroses and psychotic disorders.

Generally, in office-based practices, some form of followup was scheduled. For about 60 percent of visits in 1975–76, the patient was directed to make a return visit at a specified time—by location of practice, the disposition of 63 percent of the visits in metropolitan areas was to make a return visit at a specified time compared wth 54 percent of the visits in nonmetropolitan areas.

During 1974–75, 0.5 visits per person per year were reported for general checkups, eye exams, and immunizations and 4.2 visits were reported for diagnoses or treatments. Visit rates for general checkups were highest for children under 18 years of age at 0.4 visits per person per year, and visit rates for diagnoses or treatments were highest for people 65 years of age and over at 6 visits per person per year.

Of the nearly 58 million episodes of injuries reported in 1975, almost 43 percent were first medically attended in hospital outpatient clinics or emergency rooms with another 33 percent treated at the doctor's office. For almost 13 percent of the injuries, medical advice was first sought by telephone. Use of the hospital outpatient clinics or emergency rooms generally decreased, while use of the doctor's office generally increased, with increasing age and increasing family income.

The Consumer Product Safety Commission reports on the products associated with injuries treated in hospital emergency rooms. In 1977, the Commission estimated that over 9 million product-related injuries were treated in hospital emergency rooms; more than half of these were to persons under 18 years of age, and more than 60 percent were to males. For all ages and especially for the older age groups, a home structure (including doors, windows, stairs, etc.) was the major cause of injury. In addition, a considerable number of injuries to persons under 45 years of age were related to the use of some type of sports ball or other sports and recreational equipment.

The role of drug abuse in emergency room utilization is investigated by a reporting system of the Drug Enforcement Administration and National Institute on Drug Abuse. In the May 1976–April 1977 report, suicide attempts constituted 39 percent of the drug-abuse reports. With increasing age, psychic effects and dependence were reported less and suicide attempts or gestures were reported more as the motivation for taking the drug. About 48 percent of all drug cases for females involved a suicide attempt, while for males the motivational factors were about evenly distributed among psychic effects, dependence, and suicide. Diazepam (Valium) was reported in 18 percent of the drug abuse cases, and alcohol used in combination with at least one other drug was reported in 16 percent. Diazepam was the most commonly

reported drug in each age group; alcohol in combination with another drug was the second most common, except for people 20–29 years of age who reported heroin and morphine more often.

The use of another major component of ambulatory service, dental care, which is often viewed as an elective form of care, varies widely between different socioeconomic groups. During 1975–76, 1.6 dental visits per person per year were reported. However, only about half of the population in 1976 saw a dentist at all during the year. White people reported nearly twice as many dental visits per person per year as all others, and people in families with high incomes reported more than twice as many dental visits as those in low-income families. Only 34 percent of the low family income population visited the dentist during 1976 compared with 62 percent of the high family income population. The largest differences in the number of dental visits per year by income were for children under 18 years of age and people 65 years of age and over.

Family income was also related to different reasons for visiting a dentist. During 1971–74, people 25–74 years of age who saw a dentist reported that the main reason for the visit was for a checkup or cleaning. However, people with less than $4,000 family income who reported a visit said that the main reason for their visit was to have a tooth pulled or to have other surgery, whereas people in every other family income group reported that the main reason was for a checkup or cleaning. This suggests that the poor with limited resources assign a relatively low priority to dental care until a serious problem occurs and, as a result, they lag behind the rest of the population in their use of dental services.

Differences also existed in the patterns of dental care according to place of residence, with people living in metropolitan areas reporting 43 percent more dental visits than those living outside metropolitan areas. As in the case of physician utilization, this may reflect the greater concentration and availability of licensed dentists practicing in metropolitan areas.

In addition to physician and dental care, other components of ambulatory care include services received from chiropractors, podiatrists, and physical therapists. In 1974, an estimated 7.5 million people or 3.6 percent of the population used the services of a chiropractor; 5.0 million people or 2.4 percent consulted a podiatrist; and 3.2 million people or 1.6 percent used the services of a physical therapist. Contact with each of these practitioners was, with few exceptions, more prevalent among older people and white people than it was among younger people and those in the all other color group.

Care received for mental disorders is another component of ambulatory utilization. The increase in the use of outpatient psychiatric services is associated with reductions in the use of inpatient psychiatric hospital services, increases in the use of new drug therapies, and expansion of insurance benefits for outpatient psychiatric services. In 1975, an estimated 32.0 million people or 15 percent of the population had mental disorders. About 60 percent received care from the outpatient medical sector, such as the doctor's office, the neighborhood health center, or the hospital outpatient department. About 15 percent received care from the outpatient mental health sector, such as the community mental health center or the freestanding multiservice clinic.

Physician visits, according to source or place of care and selected characteristics: United States, average annual 1975–76

(Data are based on household interviews of a sample of the civilian noninstitutionalized population)

Selected characteristic	Source or place of care					
	All sources or places of care [1]	Doctor's office [2]	Hospital outpatient department [3]	Telephone	Company or industry clinic	Home
	Visits per 1,000 population					
Total [4]	4,997.6	3,394.7	649.4	611.7	45.0	54.4
Sex						
Male	4,297.9	2,849.4	647.0	465.4	74.2	42.4
Female	5,649.8	3,903.0	651.5	748.2	17.8	65.6
Color						
White	5,053.6	3,489.1	580.8	659.6	44.0	57.5
All other	4,626.0	2,768.4	1,103.9	293.9	52.0	33.8
Age						
Under 18 years	4,119.6	2,612.3	583.4	696.5	*1.3	25.1
18–24 years	4,701.6	2,994.0	681.7	517.1	64.9	*22.6
25–44 years	4,972.3	3,407.5	627.9	595.7	88.2	14.1
45–64 years	5,680.2	4,004.9	768.6	554.4	65.0	64.4
65 years and over	6,732.1	5,017.1	625.1	623.1	*7.5	262.0
Family income						
Less than $5,000	5,950.7	3,769.1	1,031.3	559.8	*19.7	109.9
$5,000–$9,999	5,035.3	3,357.5	787.3	511.1	37.7	51.3
$10,000–$14,999	4,779.3	3,274.9	619.8	627.9	64.5	22.1
$15,000 or more	4,869.8	3,424.9	442.4	723.5	50.2	52.9
Geographic region						
Northeast	5,142.9	3,271.2	785.8	663.3	60.3	95.0
North Central	4,727.9	3,279.9	547.7	650.4	53.9	34.5
South	4,726.0	3,256.2	604.8	492.7	35.9	48.2
West	5,694.2	3,972.0	703.2	699.5	28.1	42.5
Location of residence [5]						
Within SMSA	5,193.1	3,440.2	716.1	669.8	54.2	57.7
Large SMSA	5,307.0	3,485.6	765.5	671.8	64.5	63.7
Core counties	5,341.8	3,498.3	867.4	588.9	63.0	64.2
Fringe counties	5,233.1	3,458.9	549.6	847.5	67.5	62.6
Medium SMSA	5,150.4	3,439.9	646.0	694.4	46.5	54.9
Other SMSA	4,805.7	3,245.3	672.1	602.3	*28.5	38.5
Outside SMSA	4,459.2	3,269.5	465.6	451.7	19.7	45.5
Adjacent to SMSA	4,607.8	3,321.8	527.0	474.9	25.6	44.7
Not adjacent to SMSA	4,257.5	3,198.4	382.3	420.3	*11.7	46.6
Self-assessment of health						
Excellent or good	4,151.8	2,860.0	494.3	511.1	45.5	37.5
Fair or poor	10,925.7	7,138.9	1,739.5	1,321.2	43.0	170.6

[1] Includes other and unknown sources or places of care.
[2] Includes private doctor's office, doctor's clinic, or group practice.
[3] Includes hospital outpatient clinic or emergency room.
[4] Includes unknown family income.
[5] Grouped according to the April 1973 Office of Management and Budget metropolitan-nonmetropolitan designations.

SOURCE: Division of Health Interview Statistics, National Center for Health Statistics: Data from the Health Interview Survey.

Physician visits, according to source or place of care, age, and color: United States, fiscal years 1964 and 1967 and selected calendar years 1970–76

(Data are based on household interviews of samples of the civilian noninstitutionalized population)

Age, color, and year	Visits per 1,000 population	Source or place of care					
		All sources or places of care[1]	Doctor's office[2]	Hospital outpatient department[3]	Telephone	Company or industry clinic	Home
		Percent distribution					
TOTAL[4]							
Fiscal year 1964	4,544.5	100.0	69.8	11.9	10.6	0.6	5.4
Fiscal year 1967	4,320.4	100.0	71.8	9.3	11.3	0.8	3.3
1970	4,638.3	100.0	69.4	10.6	12.2	1.0	2.0
1973	5,009.8	100.0	69.1	10.7	12.7	0.8	1.4
1974	4,945.1	100.0	68.8	11.9	12.3	0.8	1.1
1975	5,051.5	100.0	68.0	12.9	12.5	0.9	0.8
1976	4,944.0	100.0	67.9	13.1	12.0	0.9	1.4
AGE							
Under 15 years							
Fiscal year 1964	3,754.9	100.0	61.4	13.6	19.1	*	4.6
Fiscal year 1967	3,725.2	100.0	62.8	10.8	20.1	*	2.5
1970	3,985.2	100.0	62.1	12.2	18.5	*	0.7
1973	4,328.3	100.0	61.2	12.0	19.3	*	1.6
1974	4,249.2	100.0	61.6	12.0	19.5	*	0.8
1975	4,414.6	100.0	61.5	14.3	18.6	*	0.5
1976	4,203.6	100.0	64.0	13.1	17.8	*	0.6
15-24 years							
Fiscal year 1964	4,286.1	100.0	71.7	15.2	8.1	*	2.1
Fiscal year 1967	4,001.7	100.0	71.7	10.1	9.6	0.9	1.3
1970	4,238.6	100.0	69.4	11.3	9.6	1.5	*
1973	4,510.6	100.0	66.6	12.4	10.5	1.4	0.8
1974	4,282.3	100.0	64.8	15.7	9.5	0.7	*
1975	4,426.6	100.0	63.8	15.0	11.7	1.2	*
1976	4,082.4	100.0	65.4	15.1	9.5	0.9	0.8
25-44 years							
Fiscal year 1964	4,520.6	100.0	74.6	11.9	8.4	1.0	2.5
Fiscal year 1967	4,362.9	100.0	76.1	9.8	8.3	1.7	1.4
1970	4,585.4	100.0	72.2	9.9	11.2	1.5	1.1
1973	5,143.0	100.0	70.7	10.0	12.3	1.3	0.5
1974	4,975.6	100.0	69.1	12.2	12.0	1.6	0.6
1975	5,056.3	100.0	67.8	13.3	12.2	1.9	*
1976	4,890.4	100.0	69.2	12.0	11.8	1.7	0.4

45-64 years						
Fiscal year 1964	5,038.2	100.0	76.8	10.0	6.1	1.0	4.5
Fiscal year 1967	4,659.3	100.0	77.1	8.4	7.2	1.2	3.4
1970	5,206.0	100.0	72.7	10.7	9.3	1.4	2.0
1973	5,454.5	100.0	73.7	10.1	9.9	0.9	0.8
1974	5,517.6	100.0	74.1	10.7	9.2	1.0	0.9
1975	5,629.9	100.0	72.6	12.1	9.7	0.9	0.7
1976	5,729.9	100.0	68.5	15.0	9.9	1.4	1.5
65 years and over						
Fiscal year 1964	6,657.3	100.0	64.2	8.5	8.2	*	17.3
Fiscal year 1967	6,002.6	100.0	73.8	6.0	7.8	*	10.5
1970	6,269.0	100.0	72.7	7.8	9.6	*	7.9
1973	6,542.4	100.0	75.1	8.4	9.4	*	4.4
1974	6,730.8	100.0	75.6	8.7	9.2	*	4.2
1975	6,607.7	100.0	76.2	9.0	8.5	*	2.9
1976	6,853.8	100.0	72.9	9.5	9.9	*	4.8
COLOR						
White						
Fiscal year 1964	4,706.2	100.0	71.0	10.0	11.2	0.6	5.5
Fiscal year 1967	4,485.7	100.0	72.9	7.7	12.0	0.8	3.4
1970	4,751.7	100.0	70.5	9.2	12.9	1.0	2.1
1973	5,084.4	100.0	70.2	9.0	13.6	0.8	1.5
1974	5,027.7	100.0	69.5	10.6	13.0	0.8	1.2
1975	5,107.3	100.0	69.0	11.7	13.3	0.8	0.8
1976	5,000.2	100.0	69.1	11.3	12.8	0.9	1.4
All other						
Fiscal year 1964	3,329.8	100.0	57.0	31.8	4.1	*	4.4
Fiscal year 1967	3,111.4	100.0	60.3	25.8	4.0	*	2.2
1970	3,836.0	100.0	59.9	23.3	5.4	1.6	1.1
1973	4,493.9	100.0	60.1	23.4	5.9	1.2	0.9
1974	4,384.4	100.0	62.8	22.0	6.3	0.5	0.6
1975	4,678.7	100.0	60.6	22.0	6.9	1.0	0.4
1976	4,574.2	100.0	59.0	25.7	5.8	1.2	1.1

[1] Includes other and unknown sources or places of care.
[2] Includes private doctor's office, doctor's clinic, or group practice.
[3] Includes hospital outpatient clinic or emergency room.
[4] Includes all ages and both color groups.

SOURCE: Division of Health Interview Statistics, National Center for Health Statistics: Data from the Health Interview Survey.

Physician visits, according to source or place of care, age, family income, and color: United States, average annual 1975–76
(Data are based on household interviews of a sample of the civilian noninstitutionalized population)

Age, family income, and color	Visits per 1,000 population	Source or place of care		
		Doctor's office[1]	Hospital outpatient department[2]	Telephone
		Percent of visits		
UNDER 18 YEARS				
Family income				
Less than $5,000	4,324.1	55.8	23.0	11.1
$5,000–$9,999	3,701.9	57.4	20.7	13.3
$10,000–$14,999	4,096.0	65.1	12.5	18.3
$15,000 or more	4,448.8	67.1	9.3	20.0
Color				
White	4,289.1	65.3	11.9	18.2
All other	3,253.5	50.9	29.1	8.5
18–24 YEARS				
Family income				
Less than $5,000	5,151.0	51.3	18.0	9.6
$5,000–$9,999	5,209.0	61.9	18.5	10.6
$10,000–$14,999	4,721.8	70.6	10.2	12.2
$15,000 or more	4,209.5	70.6	10.2	11.9
Color				
White	4,721.2	65.1	12.6	11.6
All other	4,579.9	54.9	26.7	6.9
25–44 YEARS				
Family income				
Less than $5,000	6,304.2	57.9	23.9	9.9
$5,000–$9,999	4,884.1	67.3	15.6	9.3
$10,000–$14,999	4,838.9	69.1	12.9	11.9
$15,000 or more	4,943.4	71.1	8.2	14.2
Color				
White	4,911.1	69.5	11.4	12.8
All other	5,401.5	62.2	20.3	6.7
45–64 YEARS				
Family income				
Less than $5,000	7,550.9	65.5	18.0	8.7
$5,000–$9,999	5,760.6	71.6	14.2	8.7
$10,000–$14,999	5,462.3	68.9	15.7	9.4
$15,000 or more	5,462.7	72.4	10.0	11.5
Color				
White	5,645.2	71.0	12.4	10.4
All other	5,983.6	66.4	22.5	4.3
65 YEARS AND OVER				
Family income				
Less than $5,000	6,805.9	74.9	9.8	8.5
$5,000–$9,999	7,117.2	75.1	9.1	8.7
$10,000–$14,999	6,647.2	75.9	11.1	10.0
$15,000 or more	6,294.0	74.4	6.4	10.5
Color				
White	6,755.6	74.9	8.4	9.9
All other	6,501.4	70.5	18.7	*3.0

[1] Includes private doctor's office, doctor's clinic, or group practice.
[2] Includes hospital outpatient clinic or emergency room.
SOURCE: Division of Health Interview Statistics, National Center for Health Statistics: Data from the Health Interview Survey.

Physician visits, according to source or place of care, age, and location of residence: United States, average annual 1975-76

(Data are based on household interviews of a sample of the civilian noninstitutionalized population)

Age and location of residence	Visits per 1,000 population	Source or place of care			
		Doctor's office[1]	Hospital outpatient department[2]	Telephone	Home
		Percent of visits			
UNDER 18 YEARS					
Location of residence					
Within SMSA	4,354.9	62.2	15.0	17.4	0.5
Large SMSA	4,433.6	61.7	15.6	17.1	0.7
Core counties	4,263.9	60.3	19.4	14.4	*0.6
Fringe counties	4,758.3	64.2	9.2	21.7	*0.8
Medium SMSA	4,310.5	63.1	13.8	18.2	*0.3
Other SMSA	4,142.0	62.4	15.0	16.9	*0.7
Outside SMSA	3,487.1	67.4	11.5	15.2	*0.8
Adjacent to SMSA	3,534.0	68.6	11.5	15.1	*0.6
Not adjacent to SMSA	3,420.9	65.6	11.5	15.5	*1.2
18-24 YEARS					
Location of residence					
Within SMSA	4,790.4	62.0	15.0	11.9	*0.5
Large SMSA	4,909.8	61.8	17.3	11.4	*0.6
Core counties	5,063.6	62.6	17.6	10.5	*0.5
Fringe counties	4,544.7	59.8	16.7	13.5	*0.9
Medium SMSA	4,810.1	62.9	11.1	13.2	*0.3
Other SMSA	4,259.8	60.4	14.9	10.6	*0.8
Outside SMSA	4,448.0	68.9	12.9	8.3	*0.3
Adjacent to SMSA	4,893.5	69.3	14.0	7.9	*0.4
Not adjacent to SMSA	3,850.8	68.2	11.0	8.9	*0.2
25-44 YEARS					
Location of residence					
Within SMSA	5,204.8	67.3	13.2	12.5	0.3
Large SMSA	5,368.2	67.6	12.6	12.4	*0.3
Core counties	5,484.4	68.7	13.7	10.9	*0.2
Fringe counties	5,136.4	65.5	10.5	15.4	*0.5
Medium SMSA	5,086.0	66.2	13.9	12.5	*0.5
Other SMSA	4,746.6	68.1	14.0	13.0	*_
Outside SMSA	4,259.2	73.3	10.6	10.2	*0.1
Adjacent to SMSA	4,358.8	72.0	10.9	10.7	*0.1
Not adjacent to SMSA	4,118.6	75.3	10.2	9.4	*0.2

45-64 YEARS

Location of residence					
Within SMSA	5,848.6	68.4	14.5	10.4	1.2
Large SMSA	5,975.8	67.0	15.6	10.3	1.2
Core counties	6,011.5	66.4	17.3	9.1	1.4
Fringe counties	5,897.9	68.4	11.7	12.9	*0.8
Medium SMSA	5,663.0	70.6	11.8	10.8	1.5
Other SMSA	5,717.4	70.3	16.3	9.8	*0.6
Outside SMSA	5,212.1	77.0	10.4	7.9	*0.9
Adjacent to SMSA	5,447.3	74.7	12.2	7.6	*1.0
Not adjacent to SMSA	4,904.3	80.3	7.7	8.3	*0.7

65 YEARS AND OVER

Location of residence					
Within SMSA	7,003.4	72.2	10.2	10.2	4.2
Large SMSA	6,953.6	70.5	11.0	10.0	4.7
Core counties	6,996.4	69.3	12.8	9.2	4.4
Fringe counties	6,830.1	74.1	5.8	12.3	5.6
Medium SMSA	7,502.8	72.4	10.3	11.0	3.7
Other SMSA	6,047.9	79.8	6.3	8.6	2.9
Outside SMSA	6,141.3	80.2	7.0	7.0	3.2
Adjacent to SMSA	6,356.6	76.0	8.9	8.2	3.3
Not adjacent to SMSA	5,876.6	85.9	4.4	5.3	*3.1

[1] Includes private doctor's office, doctor's clinic, or group practice.
[2] Includes hospital outpatient clinic or emergency room.

NOTE: The locations of counties are grouped according to April 1973 Office of Management and Budget metropolitan-nonmetropolitan designations.

SOURCE: Division of Health Interview Statistics, National Center for Health Statistics: Data from the Health Interview Survey.

Persons utilizing specific places of outpatient medical care during the year prior to interview, according to selected characteristics: United States, 1974

(Data are based on interviews of a sample of the civilian noninstitutionalized population)

Selected characteristic	All persons	Place of care							Persons not utilizing out-patient place of care
		Doctor's office[1] only	Doctor's office in combination with—			Hospital out-patient depart-ment[2] only	Free-stand-ing clinic[3] only	Hospital out-patient depart-ment[2] and free-stand-ing clinic[3]	
			Hospital out-patient depart-ment[2]	Free-stand-ing clinic[3]	Hospital out-patient depart-ment[2] and free-standing clinic[3]				
		Percent distribution							
Total[4]	100.0	45.7	13.2	2.8	1.7	4.2	1.2	0.6	30.6
Sex									
Male	100.0	38.7	13.0	3.1	2.0	4.4	1.5	0.6	36.6
Female	100.0	52.3	13.5	2.5	1.4	4.0	0.8	0.6	25.0
Color									
White	100.0	47.8	13.5	2.7	1.5	3.3	1.0	0.4	29.8
All other	100.0	31.5	11.6	3.6	2.8	10.0	2.2	1.8	36.5
Age									
Under 17 years	100.0	44.9	14.4	2.1	1.2	5.1	1.0	0.7	30.7
17-44 years	100.0	43.2	13.8	3.7	2.7	3.9	1.6	0.8	30.4
45-64 years	100.0	46.9	11.5	3.0	1.2	3.7	1.1	0.3	32.4
65 years and over	100.0	55.8	11.2	0.8	0.5	3.4	*	*	27.8
Family income									
Less than $5,000	100.0	40.0	13.5	3.1	2.1	6.8	1.7	1.4	31.4
$5,000-$9,999	100.0	42.3	13.8	2.8	2.0	5.5	1.5	0.7	31.5
$10,000-$14,999	100.0	47.1	13.4	2.7	1.8	3.5	0.1	0.4	30.1
$15,000 or more	100.0	51.0	13.1	2.9	1.4	2.4	0.9	0.3	28.0
Geographic region									
Northeast	100.0	44.8	14.9	2.6	1.6	4.6	1.2	0.5	29.8
North Central	100.0	47.2	13.6	3.0	1.7	3.0	0.9	0.6	30.1
South	100.0	44.9	12.1	3.0	1.8	4.7	1.3	0.7	31.7
West	100.0	46.3	12.3	2.5	1.6	4.6	1.3	0.6	30.8
Place of residence									
SMSA	100.0	45.0	13.6	3.1	1.8	4.8	1.3	0.7	29.8
Central city	100.0	40.5	13.2	3.4	2.2	6.6	1.7	1.2	31.2
Outside central city	100.0	48.4	13.8	2.8	1.5	3.5	0.9	0.3	28.7
Outside SMSA	100.0	47.4	12.5	2.2	1.4	2.7	1.0	0.4	32.5
Self-assessment of health									
Excellent or good	100.0	45.9	12.2	2.8	1.5	3.9	1.2	0.5	31.9
Fair or poor	100.0	44.8	20.0	2.9	3.1	5.7	0.8	0.9	21.8

[1] Includes persons utilizing a private doctor's office, doctor's clinic, or group practice.
[2] Includes persons utilizing the hospital outpatient clinic or the emergency room.
[3] Includes persons utilizing the company or industry clinic, public health clinic, or the neighborhood health center.
[4] Includes unknown family income.

SOURCE: Division of Health Interview Statistics, National Center for Health Statistics: Data from the Health Interview

Office visits to physicians, according to color, sex, and age of patient: United States, average annual 1975–76

(Data are based on reporting by a sample of office-based physicians)

Age of patient	Color								
	Total			White			All other		
	Both sexes	Male	Female	Both sexes	Male	Female	Both sexes	Male	Female
	Office visits per 1,000 population								
All ages	2,770.7	2,276.4	3,231.5	2,864.6	2,353.2	3,345.2	2,147.7	1,749.8	2,499.2
Under 1 year	5,865.9	5,950.9	5,776.8	6,117.2	6,234.7	5,993.6	4,651.9	4,565.0	4,741.3
1-4 years	2,440.7	2,576.4	2,299.1	2,581.4	2,728.6	2,426.9	1,775.1	1,845.1	1,703.9
5-9 years	1,685.7	1,754.6	1,614.0	1,841.5	1,895.0	1,785.5	899.7	1,033.3	765.1
10-14 years	1,351.9	1,390.1	1,312.2	1,457.3	1,514.9	1,397.1	796.2	720.8	872.3
15-19 years	1,975.1	1,578.4	2,368.7	2,090.6	1,705.5	2,475.4	1,322.5	841.6	1,780.0
20-24 years	2,575.4	1,590.5	3,488.5	2,634.4	1,613.3	3,601.6	2,204.1	1,434.8	2,827.1
25-29 years	2,881.8	1,786.2	3,912.5	2,872.1	1,774.2	3,930.8	2,949.6	1,879.9	3,795.7
30-34 years	2,764.7	1,948.5	3,530.9	2,771.3	1,942.4	3,568.2	2,719.1	1,995.5	3,293.2
35-39 years	2,749.7	2,161.6	3,280.7	2,781.5	2,144.7	3,373.6	2,541.7	2,286.3	2,731.4
40-44 years	2,744.1	2,112.2	3,342.6	2,754.6	2,089.6	3,394.5	2,664.6	2,297.0	2,972.8
45-49 years	3,080.4	2,465.6	3,656.4	3,116.4	2,466.7	3,732.5	2,802.6	2,456.7	3,096.8
50-54 years	3,217.4	2,520.5	3,858.9	3,244.3	2,540.4	3,897.5	2,987.8	2,343.8	3,540.9
55-59 years	3,505.7	3,037.6	3,939.4	3,543.2	3,056.7	3,994.6	3,164.3	2,862.2	3,440.0
60-64 years	3,809.9	3,449.5	4,117.2	3,852.6	3,467.8	4,183.7	3,390.3	3,259.8	3,492.3
65-69 years	4,274.9	3,876.6	4,595.1	4,410.3	3,997.9	4,741.9	3,007.2	2,739.9	3,221.7
70-74 years	4,586.1	4,160.1	4,893.0	4,697.2	4,331.2	4,958.5	3,509.5	2,590.5	4,231.6
75 years and over	4,259.9	4,072.0	4,372.0	4,402.5	4,261.9	4,485.2	2,770.3	2,267.3	3,115.9

NOTE: Rates are based on the average annual civilian noninstitutionalized population, excluding Alaska and Hawaii.

SOURCE: Division of Health Resources Utilization Statistics, National Center for Health Statistics: Data from the National Ambulatory Medical Care Survey.

Office visits to physicians, according to age of patient, sex, most common principal diagnosis, and ICDA code: United States, average annual 1975-76

(Data are based on reporting by a sample of office-based physicians)

Sex, most common principal diagnosis, and ICDA code[1]	All ages	Age of patient				
		Under 15 years	15-24 years	25-44 years	45-64 years	65 years and over
		Office visits per 1,000 population				
Both sexes[2]	2,770.7	1,982.1	2,259.0	2,794.2	3,377.2	4,356.6
Medical or special exams --- Y00	205.2	360.2	196.7	175.5	125.9	71.2
Acute URI[3] except influenza --- 460-465	175.6	326.6	138.0	131.3	121.7	88.9
Medical and surgical aftercare --- Y10	135.1	77.3	99.6	155.4	185.1	191.6
Hypertension --- 400,401,403	110.9	1.9	8.2	54.1	269.9	385.2
Heart disease --- 390-398,402,404,410-414,420-429	103.5	*5.3	*7.2	26.4	188.7	536.9
Ischemic heart disease --- 410-414	75.1	1.0	1.5	13.1	145.3	400.9
Prenatal care --- Y06	101.3	*5.6	270.4	195.0	*1.6	...
Neuroses and nonpsychotic disorders --- 300-309	100.1	24.5	69.6	182.8	124.6	88.4
Arthritis and rheumatism --- 710-718	86.7	5.8	19.6	56.6	169.1	315.5
Infections and inflammations of skin --- 680-698	85.1	91.9	79.0	78.9	85.5	93.9
Diseases of the ear and mastoid process --- 380-389	84.2	169.1	47.4	49.3	61.1	74.3
Bronchitis, emphysema, asthma --- 490-493	76.6	83.9	33.8	51.4	109.4	131.4
Sprains and strains --- 840-848	68.6	17.7	77.2	104.7	89.1	49.0
Eye diseases, except refractive --- 360-369,371-379	68.3	34.0	27.2	35.1	92.7	259.5
Diabetes mellitus --- 250	46.2	*3.9	*6.9	18.8	92.2	196.2
Refractive errors --- 370	41.3	23.1	42.7	42.3	60.2	42.7
Hay fever --- 507	40.8	47.1	36.4	49.9	35.0	22.3
Obesity --- 277	38.0	5.8	37.8	70.6	48.3	17.0
Malignant neoplasms --- 140-209	35.0	*3.3	*5.6	14.4	70.1	146.1
Diseases of sebaceous glands (acne) --- 706	34.3	13.1	96.3	35.6	13.7	*12.6
Fracture --- 800-829	33.9	33.3	31.9	28.0	36.9	47.0
Lacerations --- 870-907	33.9	40.9	41.7	31.7	24.6	25.9
Synovitis, bursitis, tenosynovitis --- 731	28.4	*5.1	13.1	32.3	56.5	47.0
Observation without need for medical care --- 793	26.7	23.3	27.1	34.0	25.2	19.4
Influenza --- 470-474	24.7	17.7	19.0	31.0	31.1	24.1
Cystitis --- 595	23.3	*4.9	25.1	28.0	32.6	35.6
Disorders of menstruation --- 626	18.5	*1.9	32.8	33.4	16.1	*1.9
Menopausal symptoms --- 627	18.3	...	*1.6	14.2	63.6	*12.8
Diseases of central nervous system --- 320-349	16.6	*4.3	12.4	19.6	24.7	31.1
Nervousness, debility --- 790	14.7	*1.3	8.1	20.1	27.0	21.7
Diseases of breast --- 610-611	13.7	*1.5	12.4	25.1	17.6	*10.8
Acute bronchitis, bronchiolitis --- 466	12.8	15.8	*7.6	9.1	15.7	17.6
Ulcer --- 531-534	12.7	*1.2	*7.2	17.4	21.6	21.6
Pneumonia --- 480-486	12.4	18.6	8.3	8.4	12.3	15.1
Male[2]	2,276.4	2,057.5	1,584.0	1,976.5	2,823.7	4,022.0
Acute URI[3] except influenza --- 460-465	166.0	326.5	121.5	112.2	97.0	88.7
Medical or special exams --- Y00	166.0	354.0	134.7	91.5	80.9	73.0
Medical and surgical aftercare --- Y10	127.8	91.5	109.7	125.6	162.1	203.9
Heart disease --- 390-398,402,404,410-414,420-429	109.6	5.0	7.6	30.5	238.4	576.0
Ischemic heart disease --- 410-414	81.9	*0.9	*1.4	17.6	194.5	425.2

Diagnosis	Code						
Hypertension	400,401,403	84.0	1.6	11.4	54.4	223.7	251.4
Diseases of ear and mastoid process	380-389	82.3	174.3	44.5	39.9	54.9	68.9
Infections and inflammations of skin	680-698	78.9	99.0	63.1	67.5	82.0	77.4
Sprains and strains	840-848	77.3	19.1	93.8	123.7	93.2	48.6
Neuroses and other nonpsychotic disorders	300-309	76.8	31.3	55.1	138.0	92.3	49.6
Bronchitis, emphysema, asthma	490-493	75.8	95.8	25.0	39.3	97.6	178.6
Arthritis and rheumatism	710-718	60.6	*6.0	17.1	48.6	128.4	197.3
Eye diseases, except refractive	360-369,371-379	58.8	33.5	26.0	32.8	85.3	220.0
Lacerations	870-907	49.1	56.8	65.7	45.8	35.3	*31.2
Fracture	800-829	40.1	41.4	49.7	39.7	34.0	*31.0
Diabetes mellitus	250	38.3	*3.0	*6.6	18.4	79.7	174.9
Hay fever	507	36.9	55.4	31.9	39.1	21.7	*20.8
Malignant neoplasms	140-209	33.8	*2.8	*3.9	*10.7	61.1	195.1
Refractive errors	370	32.5	20.1	31.3	34.9	47.4	*31.1
Influenza	470-474	27.1	19.0	22.7	32.0	33.9	*31.9
Synovitis, bursitis, tenosynovitis	731	26.9	*7.0	*15.1	33.9	46.3	47.2
Diseases of sebaceous glands (acne)	706	26.4	*9.9	77.6	19.8	*14.0	*14.6
		3,231.5	1,903.7	2,907.4	3,557.3	3,881.5	4,590.8
Female²							
Medical or special exams	Y00	241.7	366.5	256.4	253.9	166.9	69.9
Prenatal care	Y06	195.4	*9.8	530.1	376.9	*3.1	....
Acute URI,³ except influenza	460-465	184.5	326.8	153.9	149.2	144.2	89.1
Medical and surgical aftercare	Y10	142.0	62.5	89.8	183.2	206.1	183.0
Hypertension	400,401,403	136.1	2.2	5.1	53.9	312.0	478.8
Neuroses and nonpsychotic disorders	300-309	121.8	17.4	83.5	224.7	153.9	115.6
Arthritis and rheumatism	710-718	111.1	*5.6	21.9	64.2	206.2	398.1
Heart disease	390-398,402,404,410-414,420-429	97.8	5.7	6.8	22.6	143.4	509.6
Ischemic heart disease	410-414	68.7	*1.2	*1.5	9.0	100.5	383.8
Infections and inflammations of skin	680-698	90.9	84.4	94.2	89.6	88.6	105.5
Diseases of ear and mastoid process	380-389	86.0	163.7	50.3	58.1	66.7	78.0
Bronchitis, emphysema, asthma	490-493	77.3	71.6	42.3	62.8	120.2	98.4
Eye diseases, except refractive	360-369,371-379	77.2	34.5	28.4	37.3	99.5	287.2
Sprains and strains	840-848	60.6	16.2	61.2	87.0	85.3	49.2
Obesity	277	58.6	*6.6	62.2	112.6	71.2	*19.9
Diabetes mellitus	250	53.6	*4.8	*7.2	19.1	103.6	211.1
Refractive errors	370	49.5	26.3	53.7	49.3	71.8	50.9
Hay fever	507	44.4	38.4	40.8	60.1	47.1	*23.3
Diseases of sebaceous glands (acne)	706	41.7	16.4	114.3	50.3	13.5	*11.3
Cystitis	595	37.4	*8.7	44.2	45.2	50.6	44.9
Malignant neoplasms	140-209	36.1	*3.9	*7.2	64.6	78.3	111.8
Disorders of menstruation	626	35.8	*3.9	64.3	30.7	30.7	3.3
Menopausal symptoms	627	35.4	....	*3.2	27.5	121.6	*21.7
Observation without need for further medical care	793	35.3	25.0	37.7	50.7	33.1	*23.2
Synovitis, bursitis, tenosynovitis	731	29.8	*3.2	*11.1	30.8	65.8	46.8
Fracture	800-829	28.1	24.9	*14.8	17.2	39.6	58.3
Diseases of breast	610-611	25.6	*2.2	22.9	48.3	32.6	*16.1

[1] Diagnostic groupings and code number inclusions are based on the *Eighth Revision International Classification of Diseases, Adapted for Use in the United States.*

[2] Both sexes, male, and female include office visits to physicians for the most common and all other principal diagnoses.

[3] Upper respiratory infections.

NOTE: Rates are based on the average annual civilian noninstitutionalized population, excluding Alaska and Hawaii.

SOURCE: Division of Health Resources Utilization Statistics, National Center for Health Statistics: Data from the National Ambulatory Medical Care Survey.

Office visits to physicians, according to physician specialty, age of patient, most common principal diagnosis, and ICDA code: United States, average annual 1975–76

(Data are based on reporting by a sample of office-based physicians)

Age of patient, most common principal diagnosis, and ICDA code[1]		Office visits per 1,000 population	Physician specialty							
			All specialties	General and family practice	Internal medicine	Pediatrics	Obstetrics and gynecology	Other medical	Other surgical	Other
			Percent distribution							
All ages[2]		2,770.7	100.0	39.8	11.3	9.3	8.4	6.1	20.8	4.3
Acute URI,[3] except influenza	460-465	175.6	100.0	57.6	6.9	24.6	1.1	0.9	7.1	1.8
Hypertension	400,401,403	110.9	100.0	58.9	27.7	*0.2	1.6	4.3	5.9	1.4
Heart disease	390-398,402,404,410-414,420-429	103.5	100.0	46.1	36.2	*0.5	*0.2	12.5	2.5	2.0
Ischemic heart disease	410-414	75.1	100.0	47.6	37.4	*0.0	*0.1	10.8	2.3	*1.7
Prenatal care	Y06	101.3	100.0	25.1	*0.3	*0.6	72.9	*0.0	*0.9	*0.3
Neuroses and nonpsychotic disorders	300-309	100.1	100.0	29.7	10.6	2.2	*1.1	*1.4	3.2	51.8
Arthritis and rheumatism	710-718	86.7	100.0	55.6	23.6	*1.0	*0.6	2.2	13.9	3.1
Infections and inflammations of skin	680-698	85.1	100.0	42.9	6.6	12.7	*1.2	26.2	9.7	*0.7
Diseases of ear and mastoid process	380-389	84.2	100.0	34.5	4.3	28.7	*0.5	*1.1	29.8	*1.2
Bronchitis, emphysema, asthma	490-493	76.6	100.0	46.8	14.8	17.8	*0.4	16.0	2.7	*1.5
Sprains and strains	840-848	68.6	100.0	51.7	7.4	*2.0	*0.8	*0.7	30.1	7.3
Eye diseases, except refractive	360-369,371-379	68.3	100.0	8.2	2.1	3.0	*0.2	*1.0	84.6	*1.0
Diabetes mellitus	250	46.2	100.0	59.5	30.2	*1.1	*0.6	*2.9	5.0	*0.9
Refractive errors	370	41.3	100.0	*0.7	*2.5	*0.1	*–	*0.1	96.7	*–
Hay fever	507	40.8	100.0	26.3	9.9	17.8	*0.3	34.3	11.1	*0.3
Obesity	277	38.0	100.0	68.6	12.8	*1.9	4.3	*0.5	7.3	4.6
Malignant neoplasms	140-209	35.0	100.0	18.6	28.3	*0.8	3.6	14.8	33.4	*0.6
Diseases of sebaceous glands (acne)	706	34.3	100.0	15.6	*1.4	*1.9	*0.9	67.9	12.3	*–
Fracture	800-829	33.9	100.0	30.1	*3.3	*4.2	*0.4	*0.4	60.2	*1.3
Lacerations	870-907	33.9	100.0	55.7	*3.8	9.5	*0.7	*0.2	24.2	5.8
Synovitis, bursitis, tenosynovitis	731	28.4	100.0	44.8	11.2	*1.3	*0.3	*2.0	37.5	*2.9
Influenza	470-474	24.7	100.0	78.5	7.3	8.8	*1.0	*1.0	*2.2	*1.4
Cystitis	595	23.3	100.0	55.2	6.5	*1.9	7.1	*0.4	28.3	*0.6
Under 15 years[2]		1,982.1	100.0	31.6	1.7	47.1	1.0	2.9	13.8	2.0
Medical or special exams	Y00	360.2	100.0	23.7	*0.7	70.1	0.7	*0.1	3.5	*1.3
Acute URI,[3] except influenza	460-465	326.6	100.0	42.5	2.0	49.8	0.6	*0.0	3.3	1.8
Diseases of ear and mastoid process	380-389	169.1	100.0	28.5	*0.7	54.8	0.3	*0.6	14.2	*1.0
Infective and parasitic diseases	000-136	151.8	100.0	36.1	*2.3	48.7	0.8	7.3	*3.4	*1.3
Infections and inflammations of skin	680-698	91.9	100.0	39.2	*1.8	43.3	1.4	10.9	*2.8	*0.6
Bronchitis, emphysema, asthma	490-493	83.9	100.0	29.2	*2.2	58.1	0.5	7.7	*1.3	*1.1
Hay fever	507	47.1	100.0	19.5	*4.4	48.8	0.2	21.7	*5.3	*0.2
15-24 years[2]		2,259.0	100.0	42.2	6.0	3.6	18.0	7.8	18.0	4.4
Prenatal care	Y06	270.4	100.0	30.4	*0.4	*0.4	67.3	*0.0	*1.1	*0.4
Medical or special exams	Y00	196.7	100.0	49.0	6.2	7.4	24.2	*0.3	10.9	*2.0
Acute URI,[3] except influenza	460-465	138.0	100.0	73.3	8.3	6.3	*2.0	*1.0	8.1	*0.9

Diagnosis	Code									
Disease of sebaceous glands (acne)	706	96.3	100.0	11.6	*0.5	*1.5	*1.1	81.6	*3.7	*–
Infections and inflammations of skin	680-698	79.0	100.0	47.1	*6.7	*3.4	*0.8	28.1	13.4	*0.5
Sprains and strains	840-848	77.2	100.0	59.2	*4.5	*1.5	*1.0	*0.4	27.5	5.8
Neuroses and nonpsychotic disorders	300-309	69.6	100.0	29.7	*6.1	*3.0	*1.3	*0.3	*2.8	56.9
25–44 years²		2,794.2	100.0	38.4	9.5	0.4	16.8	5.6	21.7	7.5
Prenatal care	Y06	195.0	100.0	19.0	*0.1	*0.1	80.0	*–	*0.6	*0.2
Neuroses and nonpsychotic disorders	300-309	182.8	100.0	21.6	7.5	*0.1	*1.7	*1.3	*2.3	65.6
Medical or special exams	Y00	175.5	100.0	36.1	9.3	*0.6	40.2	*1.4	11.0	*1.4
Acute URI,³ except influenza	460-465	131.3	100.0	71.3	11.1	*0.9	*1.6	*1.4	11.9	*1.7
Sprains and strains	840-848	104.7	100.0	45.8	6.6	*0.7	*0.8	*0.7	37.4	7.9
Infections and inflammations of skin	680-698	78.9	100.0	47.1	7.7	*0.4	*1.7	30.8	11.9	*0.5
Obesity	277	70.6	100.0	68.7	10.8	*0.3	*5.6	*0.3	8.1	*6.2
Arthritis and rheumatism	710-718	56.6	100.0	56.0	23.0	*–	*0.5	*2.5	14.8	*3.2
Hypertension	400,401,403	54.1	100.0	52.8	31.7	*0.2	*3.4	*4.7	*5.7	*1.4
Bronchitis, emphysema, asthma	490-493	51.4	100.0	54.9	16.6	*2.2	*0.6	19.0	*3.5	*3.3
Hay fever	507	49.9	100.0	30.1	*10.4	*4.5	*0.5	40.5	14.1	*–
Diseases of ear and mastoid process	380-389	49.3	100.0	45.6	*6.7	*0.5	*0.7	*0.9	44.7	*0.9
45–64 years²		3,377.2	100.0	43.1	17.1	0.3	3.9	6.9	24.7	4.1
Hypertension	400,401,403	269.9	100.0	57.9	29.1	*0.1	*1.3	4.4	6.0	*1.2
Arthritis and rheumatism	710-718	169.1	100.0	57.2	22.3	*0.7	*0.4	*1.7	15.6	*2.0
Ischemic heart disease	410-414	145.3	100.0	44.0	39.4	*0.1	*0.2	12.4	*3.1	*0.8
Medical or special exams	Y00	125.9	100.0	40.2	16.5	*0.2	24.4	*1.3	16.0	*1.4
Neuroses and nonpsychotic disorders	300-309	124.6	100.0	39.4	14.9	*0.0	*0.3	*2.0	*4.5	38.9
Acute URI,³ except influenza	460-465	121.7	100.0	70.1	12.4	*1.0	*0.9	*2.6	10.0	*3.0
Bronchitis, emphysema, asthma	490-493	109.4	100.0	54.7	21.7	*0.9	*0.3	18.1	*2.9	*1.5
Eye diseases, except refractive	360-369,371-379	92.7	100.0	*6.4	*2.6	*0.2	*–	*1.2	89.2	*0.4
Diabetes mellitus	250	92.2	100.0	57.0	32.9	*0.1	*0.1	*3.4	*5.9	*0.6
Sprains and strains	840-848	89.1	100.0	54.2	9.7	*0.4	*0.7	*1.0	26.0	8.0
Infections and inflammations of skin	680-698	85.5	100.0	38.8	8.8	*0.5	*0.8	38.4	11.2	*1.5
Malignant neoplasms	140-209	70.1	100.0	17.1	31.4	*–	2.9	14.6	33.1	*0.9
Menopausal symptoms	627	63.6	100.0	56.3	11.6	*–	24.1	*0.3	*4.0	*3.7
Diseases of ear and mastoid process	380-389	61.1	100.0	35.9	*9.2	*–	0.6	*3.3	50.8	*0.3
Synovitis, bursitis, tenosynovitis	731	56.5	100.0	45.9	13.2	*–	*0.5	*2.1	36.8	*1.6
65 years and over²		4,356.6	100.0	44.0	20.8	*0.2	1.4	7.2	24.1	2.3
Ischemic heart disease	410-414	400.9	100.0	49.5	36.3	*0.0	*–	10.0	*1.7	*2.4
Hypertension	400,401,403	385.2	100.0	62.6	24.1	*0.3	*1.3	4.1	6.0	*1.6
Arthritis and rheumatism	710-718	315.5	100.0	54.5	25.7	*0.4	*0.4	*2.9	11.6	4.4
Eye diseases, except refractive	360-369,371-379	259.5	100.0	*4.1	*2.0	*–	*0.1	*0.6	92.7	*0.5
Diabetes mellitus	250	196.2	100.0	64.0	26.9	*0.4	*0.4	*2.4	*4.7	*1.3
Malignant neoplasms	140-209	146.1	100.0	20.8	25.4	*–	*1.8	16.3	35.6	*0.0
Bronchitis, emphysema, asthma	490-493	131.4	100.0	52.0	25.2	*0.5	*0.1	18.3	*3.1	*0.8

¹ Diagnostic groupings and code number inclusions are based on the *Eighth Revision International Classification of Diseases, Adapted for Use in the United States.*

² All ages and age groups include office visits to physicians for the most common and all other principal diagnoses.

³ Upper respiratory infections.

NOTE: Rates are based on the average annual civilian noninstitutionalized population, excluding Alaska and Hawaii.

SOURCE: Division of Health Resources Utilization Statistics, National Center for Health Statistics: Data from the National Ambulatory Medical Care Survey.

Office visits to physicians, according to prior visit status, seriousness of problem, age of patient, most common principal diagnosis, and ICDA code: United States, average annual 1975-76

(Data are based on reporting by a sample of office-based physicians)

Age of patient, most common principal diagnosis, and ICDA code[1]	Office visits per 1,000 population	Prior visit status			Seriousness of problem		
		Patient never seen before	Patient seen before		Serious or very serious	Slightly serious	Not serious
			Current problem	Another problem			
		Percent of visits			Percent of visits		
All ages[2]	2,770.7	14.6	62.2	23.2	19.2	32.3	48.5
Acute URI,[3] except influenza — 460-465	175.6	14.2	39.3	46.5	7.9	41.1	51.0
Hypertension — 400,401,403	110.9	4.9	89.3	5.9	22.3	46.3	31.4
Heart disease — 390-398,402,404,410-414,420-429	103.5	5.3	86.4	8.3	50.6	33.4	16.0
Ischemic heart disease — 410-414	75.1	4.9	88.0	7.1	52.2	32.8	14.9
Prenatal care — Y06	101.3	8.2	84.4	7.5	3.7	7.1	89.2
Neuroses and nonpsychotic disorders — 300-309	100.1	10.6	77.3	12.1	41.6	30.6	27.8
Arthritis and rheumatism — 710-718	86.7	10.0	72.5	17.5	21.6	42.3	36.1
Infections and inflammations of skin — 680-698	85.1	19.0	47.1	33.9	11.5	34.3	54.3
Diseases of ear and mastoid process — 380-389	84.2	18.8	48.7	32.5	15.0	45.8	39.3
Bronchitis, emphysema, asthma — 490-493	76.6	9.3	71.3	19.4	26.2	47.8	26.0
Sprains and strains — 840-848	68.6	19.7	52.0	28.3	12.9	44.2	42.9
Eye diseases, except refractive — 360-369,371-379	68.3	21.9	62.8	15.3	29.4	35.4	35.2
Diabetes mellitus — 250	46.2	4.0	88.4	7.5	41.4	34.4	24.3
Refractive errors — 370	41.3	38.8	51.4	9.8	*2.5	9.5	88.0
Hay fever — 507	40.8	8.2	83.3	8.6	6.2	36.8	57.0
Obesity — 277	38.0	17.6	73.1	9.3	9.4	30.0	60.6
Malignant neoplasms — 140-209	35.0	9.3	81.0	9.7	75.4	13.6	11.0
Diseases of sebaceous glands (acne) — 706	34.3	18.2	65.6	16.1	6.7	27.2	66.2
Fracture — 800-829	33.9	16.9	64.9	18.2	28.3	27.0	27.0
Lacerations — 870-907	33.9	26.0	37.1	36.8	17.0	30.8	52.2
Synovitis, bursitis, tenosynovitis — 731	28.4	17.0	49.1	33.9	10.5	41.9	47.6
Influenza — 470-474	24.7	11.4	26.2	62.3	10.2	56.6	33.2
Cystitis — 595	23.3	13.0	52.1	34.9	12.6	55.9	31.5
Under 15 years[2]	1,982.1	14.5	51.4	34.1	11.3	31.6	57.1
Medical or special exams — Y00	360.2	10.9	65.0	24.1	0.8	2.8	96.5
Acute URI,[3] except influenza — 460-465	326.6	12.5	42.0	45.5	8.8	43.8	47.4
Diseases of ear and mastoid process — 380-389	169.1	12.7	53.7	33.6	14.7	52.1	33.2
Infective and parasitic diseases — 000-136	151.8	18.3	30.7	51.1	11.5	39.0	49.4
Infections and inflammations of skin — 680-698	91.9	17.5	41.0	41.5	10.5	31.9	57.6
Bronchitis, emphysema, asthma — 490-493	83.9	6.9	66.3	26.8	16.5	55.0	28.5
Hay fever — 507	47.1	*5.5	*85.6	8.9	*6.8	34.7	58.5
15-24 years[2]	2,259.0	20.9	53.6	25.6	12.2	27.8	59.9
Prenatal care — Y06	270.4	9.6	83.2	7.2	3.7	6.7	89.6
Medical or special exams — Y00	196.7	31.7	39.6	28.7	*1.6	*3.3	95.1
Acute URI,[3] except influenza — 460-465	138.0	20.3	32.5	47.1	6.2	34.4	59.4

Diagnosis	Code							
Diseases of sebaceous glands (acne)	706	96.3	16.9	10.3	72.8	*6.5	28.7	64.8
Infections and inflammations of skin	680-698	79.0	21.5	33.0	45.4	*9.5	29.4	61.1
Sprains and strains	840-848	77.2	22.8	35.2	42.0	*8.9	43.4	47.8
Neuroses and nonpsychotic disorders	300-309	69.6	15.0	13.2	71.8	41.7	35.2	23.1
25-44 years[2]		**2,794.2**	**17.7**	**59.9**	**22.4**	**17.4**	**30.7**	**51.9**
Prenatal care	Y06	195.0	6.6	86.3	7.1	3.5	7.5	89.0
Neuroses and nonpsychotic disorders	300-309	182.8	9.5	81.6	8.9	50.1	28.1	21.7
Medical or special exams	Y00	175.5	23.1	54.2	22.7	1.0	3.9	95.1
Acute URI,[3] except influenza	460-465	131.3	17.5	36.0	46.6	6.0	39.5	54.5
Sprains and strains	840-848	104.7	22.1	56.3	21.6	13.3	47.6	39.1
Infections and inflammations of skin	680-698	78.9	23.4	47.5	29.1	10.0	33.0	57.1
Obesity	277	70.6	19.0	71.1	9.9	9.4	29.2	61.4
Arthritis and rheumatism	710-718	56.6	17.2	59.0	23.8	25.3	35.7	39.0
Hypertension	400,401,403	54.1	*9.9	*82.9	7.2	25.7	44.3	30.0
Bronchitis, emphysema, asthma	490-493	51.4	17.5	61.4	21.1	19.7	51.4	28.9
Hay fever	507	49.9	*9.9	*80.4	9.7	*5.7	40.3	54.0
Diseases of ear and mastoid process	380-389	49.3	30.5	35.9	33.6	16.5	41.3	42.3
45-64 years[2]		**3,377.2**	**11.8**	**68.9**	**19.2**	**24.2**	**35.3**	**40.4**
Hypertension	400,401,403	269.9	4.6	90.3	5.1	21.8	48.3	29.8
Arthritis and rheumatism	710-718	169.1	10.9	71.5	17.6	21.3	44.5	34.2
Ischemic heart disease	410-414	145.3	7.2	87.2	5.6	55.0	29.7	15.3
Medical or special exams	Y00	125.9	14.5	65.1	20.4	*2.2	6.0	91.8
Neuroses and nonpsychotic disorders	300-309	124.6	9.7	75.5	14.7	33.4	31.9	34.7
Acute URI,[3] except influenza	460-465	121.7	10.9	40.3	48.7	9.3	40.7	50.0
Bronchitis, emphysema, asthma	490-493	109.4	9.1	76.5	14.4	31.2	45.0	23.7
Eye diseases, except refractive	360-369,371-379	92.7	17.8	67.1	15.2	33.5	36.3	30.2
Diabetes mellitus	250	92.2	*3.5	*89.0	7.5	45.5	34.4	20.1
Sprains and strains	840-848	89.1	15.0	58.3	26.7	15.3	44.5	40.2
Infections and inflammations of skin	680-698	85.5	16.5	52.6	30.9	15.3	41.7	43.0
Malignant neoplasms	140-209	70.1	*9.2	80.5	10.2	75.4	12.3	12.3
Menopausal symptoms	627	63.6	*6.1	82.4	11.5	*3.3	18.5	78.2
Diseases of ear and mastoid process	380-389	61.1	22.9	48.8	28.3	15.3	39.4	45.3
Synovitis, bursitis, tenosynovitis	731	56.5	18.2	48.6	33.2	*11.8	42.8	45.4
65 years and over[2]		**4,356.6**	**8.0**	**75.9**	**16.1**	**29.5**	**35.2**	**35.3**
Ischemic heart disease	410-414	400.9	*2.4	89.8	7.8	49.2	35.6	15.2
Hypertension	400,401,403	385.2	*3.0	90.7	6.3	21.3	44.8	33.8
Arthritis and rheumatism	710-718	315.5	5.0	82.4	12.6	21.1	43.0	35.9
Eye diseases, except refractive	360-369,371-379	259.5	16.3	72.7	11.0	34.7	31.0	34.3
Diabetes mellitus	250	196.2	*3.0	*90.0	6.9	36.4	34.3	29.3
Malignant neoplasms	140-209	146.1	*6.9	83.3	9.9	77.1	14.8	*8.1
Bronchitis, emphysema, asthma	490-493	131.4	*4.5	*84.9	10.6	42.4	38.2	19.5

[1] Diagnostic groupings and code number inclusions are based on the *Eighth Revision International Classification of Diseases, Adapted for Use in the United States.*

[2] All ages and age groups include office visits to physicians for the most common and all other principal diagnoses.

[3] Upper respiratory infections.

NOTE: Rates are based on the average annual civilian noninstitutionalized population, excluding Alaska and Hawaii.

SOURCE: Division of Health Resources Utilization Statistics, National Center for Health Statistics: Data from the National Ambulatory Medical Care Survey.

Office visits to physicians, according to selected diagnostic and therapeutic service provided, age of patient, most common principal diagnosis, and ICDA code: United States, average annual 1975–76

(Data are based on reporting by a sample of office-based physicians)

Age of patient, most common principal diagnosis, and ICDA code [1]		Office visits per 1,000 population	Selected diagnostic service [2]			Selected therapeutic service [2]		
			General history or exam	Blood pressure check	Clinical lab test	Drug prescribed	Medical counseling	Injection, immunization or desensitization
			Percent of visits					
All ages [3]		2,770.7	16.3	33.2	22.8	43.6	12.9	17.6
Acute URI,[4] except influenza	460–465	175.6	11.5	20.5	19.9	80.4	7.2	28.1
Hypertension	400,401,403	110.9	12.8	79.9	20.6	61.0	14.6	9.7
Heart disease	390–398,402,404,410–414,420–429	103.5	17.3	74.0	25.4	55.2	17.4	12.4
Ischemic heart disease	410–414	75.1	16.2	76.6	25.4	55.6	18.2	11.8
Prenatal care	Y06	101.3	13.7	73.9	59.7	16.5	10.0	1.6
Neuroses and nonpsychotic disorders	300–309	100.1	10.8	25.1	9.4	37.2	15.4	8.3
Arthritis and rheumatism	710–718	86.7	13.5	42.9	18.6	53.2	12.9	28.8
Infections and inflammations of skin	680–698	85.1	8.3	16.0	11.0	63.5	13.1	27.9
Diseases of ear and mastoid process	380–389	84.2	12.0	12.3	7.1	65.9	9.5	13.4
Bronchitis, emphysema, asthma	490–493	76.6	12.2	32.8	11.6	63.4	12.1	40.9
Sprains and strains	840–848	68.6	10.4	20.1	5.9	38.6	16.5	8.9
Eye diseases, except refractive	360–369,371–379	68.3	13.5	5.3	3.7	33.6	7.5	2.3
Diabetes mellitus	250	46.2	16.3	66.7	71.6	45.3	21.3	13.7
Refractive errors	370	41.3	20.7	*1.5	*1.6	*2.5	*2.6	*0.1
Hay fever	507	40.8	6.9	9.2	4.8	31.9	10.3	68.2
Obesity	277	38.0	19.2	67.2	21.2	63.6	31.1	14.8
Malignant neoplasms	140–209	35.0	13.8	31.9	35.3	27.2	12.8	18.7
Diseases of sebaceous glands (acne)	706	34.3	5.3	4.9	*4.1	56.8	15.9	6.2
Fracture	800–829	33.9	5.9	10.2	*1.2	12.9	14.3	*2.3
Lacerations	870–907	33.9	*2.9	7.5	*1.4	19.8	6.4	24.7
Synovitis, bursitis, tenosynovitis	731	28.4	9.3	22.4	8.0	44.0	13.8	38.5
Influenza	470–474	24.7	9.9	26.3	14.0	79.8	7.7	46.1
Cystitis	595	23.3	14.9	32.6	71.4	70.4	10.0	9.2
Under 15 years [3]		1,982.1	22.6	7.8	16.8	41.4	13.1	26.2
Medical or special exams	Y00	360.2	59.8	15.2	23.6	6.1	17.9	51.5
Acute URI,[4] except influenza	460–465	326.6	14.1	4.8	23.6	78.2	7.7	22.2
Diseases of ear and mastoid process	380–389	169.1	13.0	*2.2	6.6	72.3	9.7	14.4
Infective and parasitic diseases	000–136	151.8	17.6	6.8	27.1	54.6	14.0	14.2
Infections and inflammations of skin	680–698	91.9	7.7	*2.6	6.7	60.1	13.1	31.6
Bronchitis, emphysema, asthma	490–493	83.9	11.9	*2.8	8.1	63.0	11.8	45.1
Hay fever	507	47.1	*7.7	*1.2	*4.3	27.5	*10.6	67.8
15–24 years [3]		2,259.0	15.5	31.8	27.1	42.2	12.0	12.5
Prenatal care	Y06	270.4	13.8	74.5	62.1	17.2	10.2	*1.4
Medical or special exams	Y00	196.7	44.3	49.9	52.0	23.1	8.6	8.0
Acute URI,[4] except influenza	460–465	138.0	10.1	27.2	21.3	83.7	5.8	32.3

Diagnosis	Code						
Diseases of sebaceous glands (acne)	706	96.3	4.3	*2.4	66.1	17.2	*5.8
Infections and inflammations of skin	680–698	79.0	*6.9	13.2	61.0	10.9	31.1
Sprains and strains	840–848	77.2	*6.9	15.4	43.1	21.7	*5.9
Neuroses and nonpsychotic disorders	300–309	69.6	*11.0	18.8	35.9	14.3	*3.1
25–44 years[3]		**2,794.2**	**15.8**	**34.3**	**42.0**	**12.8**	**13.0**
Prenatal care	Y06	195.0	12.6	74.0	15.2	9.4	*1.0
Neuroses and nonpsychotic disorders	300–309	182.8	6.8	17.5	29.9	12.3	5.3
Medical or special exams	Y00	175.5	47.4	57.7	21.3	8.8	*2.4
Acute URI[4] except influenza	460–465	131.3	8.9	32.3	84.0	6.5	30.0
Sprains and strains	840–848	104.7	12.4	16.9	40.1	18.1	7.6
Infections and inflammations of skin	680–698	78.9	8.2	17.0	67.4	13.0	22.7
Obesity	277	70.6	17.4	67.4	64.0	32.3	15.5
Arthritis and rheumatism	710–718	56.6	16.6	32.3	52.7	14.8	23.8
Hypertension	400,401,403	54.1	15.0	81.2	56.9	16.8	*8.9
Bronchitis, emphysema, asthma	490–493	51.4	15.2	35.5	62.1	15.0	39.7
Hay fever	507	49.9	*5.0	*10.4	33.4	11.5	69.8
Diseases of ear and mastoid process	380–389	49.3	12.2	19.2	66.4	*9.2	*10.3
45–64 years[3]		**3,377.2**	**15.1**	**41.2**	**45.9**	**13.6**	**18.5**
Hypertension	400,401,403	269.9	13.6	78.8	61.6	15.8	9.2
Arthritis and rheumatism	710–718	169.1	12.0	40.6	54.9	12.5	29.7
Ischemic heart disease	410–414	145.3	18.1	78.6	51.0	18.1	8.2
Medical or special exams	Y00	125.9	52.4	59.8	18.4	9.0	*4.1
Neuroses and nonpsychotic disorders	300–309	124.6	12.8	32.8	46.2	17.2	13.3
Acute URI,[4] except influenza	460–465	121.7	9.6	40.4	80.0	7.2	39.1
Bronchitis, emphysema, asthma	490–493	109.4	11.5	46.1	63.8	11.0	40.2
Eye diseases, except refractive	360–369,371–379	92.7	13.9	8.1	31.8	*7.4	*3.0
Diabetes mellitus	250	92.2	18.1	69.2	50.1	25.1	12.2
Sprains and strains	840–848	89.1	11.0	28.6	36.8	11.3	12.9
Infections and inflammations of skin	680–698	85.5	*7.6	22.9	66.8	15.1	26.6
Malignant neoplasms	140–209	70.1	15.6	30.1	28.1	13.4	22.2
Menopausal symptoms	627	63.6	19.3	50.3	39.7	17.4	58.5
Diseases of ear and mastoid process	380–389	61.1	13.5	26.3	58.9	*9.9	12.2
Synovitis, bursitis, tenosynovitis	731	56.5	*10.9	22.6	46.4	*10.6	42.9
65 years and over[3]		**4,356.6**	**13.0**	**48.5**	**46.2**	**12.8**	**18.4**
Ischemic heart disease	410–414	400.9	14.3	75.1	58.5	17.1	14.6
Hypertension	400,401,403	385.2	10.1	80.8	61.5	11.4	10.5
Arthritis and rheumatism	710–718	315.5	13.4	52.6	52.5	12.7	31.6
Eye diseases, except refractive	360–369,371–379	259.5	14.2	*4.0	25.0	7.4	*1.1
Diabetes mellitus	250	196.2	12.4	66.7	43.5	17.0	16.7
Malignant neoplasms	140–209	146.1	11.9	33.8	28.9	10.2	15.9
Bronchitis, emphysema, asthma	490–493	131.4	11.7	57.5	64.1	14.0	35.5

[1] Diagnostic groupings and code number inclusions are based on the *Eighth Revision International Classification of Diseases, Adapted for Use in the United States.*

[2] More than one service was possible.

[3] All ages and age groups include office visits to physicians for the most common and all other principal diagnoses.

[4] Upper respiratory infections.

NOTE: Rates are based on the average annual civilian noninstitutionalized population, excluding Alaska and Hawaii.

SOURCE: Division of Health Resources Utilization Statistics, National Center for Health Statistics: Data from the National Ambulatory Medical Care Survey.

Office visits to physicians, according to duration of visit, age of patient, most common principal diagnosis, and ICDA code: United States, average annual 1975-76

(Data are based on reporting by a sample of office-based physicians)

Age of patient, most common principal diagnosis, and ICDA code[1]	Office visits per 1,000 population	Duration of visit[2]				
		1–5 minutes	6–10 minutes	11–15 minutes	16–30 minutes	31 minutes or more
		Percent of visits				
All ages[3]	2,770.7	15.1	31.5	26.6	19.5	5.5
Acute URI[4] except influenza ___ 460–465	175.6	21.0	45.4	23.8	8.8	*0.6
Hypertension ___ 400,401,403	110.9	13.8	32.5	30.7	17.0	3.6
Heart disease ___ 390–398,402,404,410–414,420–429	103.5	5.1	25.1	33.5	29.4	6.0
Ischemic heart disease ___ 410–414	75.1	4.9	26.3	34.1	28.3	5.4
Prenatal care ___ Y06	101.3	39.8	33.5	14.9	10.1	1.5
Neuroses and nonpsychotic disorders ___ 300–309	100.1	4.9	14.1	14.2	19.9	46.5
Arthritis and rheumatism ___ 710–718	86.7	8.5	29.9	29.6	25.8	5.0
Infections and inflammations of skin ___ 680–698	85.1	25.1	35.6	22.9	11.7	*1.2
Diseases of ear and mastoid process ___ 380–389	84.2	20.0	41.8	23.3	12.9	*1.6
Bronchitis, emphysema, asthma ___ 490–493	76.6	13.5	38.0	26.6	15.4	4.0
Sprains and strains ___ 840–848	68.6	15.3	31.9	25.3	24.2	2.8
Eye diseases, except refractive ___ 360–369,371–379	68.3	11.5	27.7	29.5	26.1	4.6
Diabetes mellitus ___ 250	46.2	7.1	27.8	33.8	23.7	4.8
Refractive errors ___ 370	41.3	*1.6	9.4	33.9	46.6	7.9
Hay fever ___ 507	40.8	23.4	28.0	16.5	10.4	5.1
Obesity ___ 277	38.0	20.2	32.6	21.1	19.2	4.3
Malignant neoplasms ___ 140–209	35.0	13.8	23.1	29.6	26.8	5.4
Diseases of sebaceous glands (acne) ___ 706	34.3	18.7	42.8	25.2	9.5	2.2
Fracture ___ 800–829	33.9	15.0	31.4	25.8	23.8	*3.0
Lacerations ___ 870–907	33.9	27.3	30.0	21.4	17.5	*1.4
Synovitis, bursitis, tenosynovitis ___ 731	28.4	15.4	29.3	30.5	20.9	*3.4
Influenza ___ 470–474	24.7	10.6	36.9	20.9	29.8	*1.3
Cystitis ___ 595	23.3	16.2	38.1	28.0	14.1	*1.9
Under 15 years[3]	1,982.1	18.2	39.1	26.2	11.9	1.9
Medical or special exams ___ Y00	360.2	8.9	33.6	40.9	14.6	*1.2
Acute URI[4] except influenza ___ 460–465	326.6	19.6	50.3	22.9	6.6	*0.3
Diseases of ear and mastoid process ___ 380–389	169.1	23.9	46.8	21.0	7.1	*0.4
Infective and parasitic diseases ___ 000–136	151.8	17.7	42.0	25.4	11.8	*1.0
Infections and inflammations of skin ___ 680–698	91.9	30.0	37.7	18.7	6.4	*0.5
Bronchitis, emphysema, asthma ___ 490–493	83.9	15.9	43.9	23.1	9.8	2.7
Hay fever ___ 507	47.1	19.9	26.4	17.1	*8.9	*5.2
15–24 years[3]	2,259.0	20.0	34.4	24.1	15.8	4.5
Prenatal care ___ Y06	270.4	41.8	32.1	15.2	9.6	*1.1
Medical or special exams ___ Y00	196.7	12.2	30.4	31.4	21.8	*3.0
Acute URI[4] except influenza ___ 460–465	138.0	24.2	42.3	23.9	8.3	*0.9

Diagnosis	Code						
Diseases of sebaceous glands (acne)	706	96.3	19.6	45.8	24.5	*6.1	*1.4
Infections and inflammations of skin	680–698	79.0	28.9	37.8	20.8	10.2	*0.8
Sprains and strains	840–848	77.2	22.9	34.3	22.8	17.7	*2.0
Neuroses and nonpsychotic disorders	300–309	69.6	*3.4	12.8	13.0	19.1	51.6
25–44 years [3]		2,794.2	15.6	30.1	24.7	19.9	8.2
Prenatal care	Y06	195.0	38.3	35.3	13.9	10.4	*1.9
Neuroses and nonpsychotic disorders	300–309	182.8	3.6	10.9	10.9	15.8	58.5
Medical or special exams	Y00	175.5	4.8	22.2	33.8	30.6	8.5
Acute URI,[4] except influenza	460–465	131.3	21.4	42.6	25.2	10.0	*0.4
Sprains and strains	840–848	104.7	15.3	31.1	25.4	24.6	*3.1
Infections and inflammations of skin	680–698	78.9	26.5	32.3	22.3	14.7	*1.6
Obesity	277	70.6	21.7	34.2	22.3	15.8	*3.7
Arthritis and rheumatism	710–718	56.6	*9.9	25.9	28.4	30.6	*3.5
Hypertension	400,401,403	54.1	15.3	31.7	25.9	19.0	*4.9
Bronchitis, emphysema, asthma	490–493	51.4	12.0	41.7	23.8	15.5	*3.1
Hay fever	507	49.9	23.2	31.4	16.9	*8.6	*4.0
Diseases of ear and mastoid process	380–389	49.3	17.2	43.0	22.9	15.5	*1.4
45–64 years [3]		3,377.2	12.2	28.3	28.0	23.4	6.4
Hypertension	400,401,403	269.9	14.0	30.4	32.5	16.5	4.2
Arthritis and rheumatism	710–718	169.1	9.4	30.3	30.9	23.2	5.1
Ischemic heart disease	410–414	145.3	6.2	25.1	33.6	28.4	5.9
Medical or special exams	Y00	125.9	*4.3	18.8	26.5	34.1	15.2
Neuroses and nonpsychotic disorders	300–309	124.6	7.7	18.5	17.2	22.7	33.5
Acute URI,[4] except influenza	460–465	121.7	22.0	39.4	24.2	12.6	*1.1
Bronchitis, emphysema, asthma	490–493	109.4	10.7	36.3	28.3	18.7	*5.1
Eye diseases, except refractive	360–369,371–379	92.7	11.6	25.6	28.1	28.5	*5.4
Diabetes mellitus	250	92.2	*6.6	27.5	34.1	25.7	*4.4
Sprains and strains	840–848	89.1	10.3	30.2	28.7	26.8	*3.7
Infections and inflammations of skin	680–698	85.5	19.5	36.1	26.5	14.0	*1.6
Malignant neoplasms	140–209	70.1	12.8	26.5	29.3	25.4	*4.5
Menopausal symptoms	627	63.6	17.5	31.9	19.3	22.3	*4.6
Diseases of ear and mastoid process	380–389	61.1	13.6	30.7	28.7	22.4	*4.6
Synovitis, bursitis, tenosynovitis	731	56.5	12.7	29.4	35.0	19.4	*2.9
65 years and over [3]		4,356.6	10.9	27.5	29.9	24.9	4.9
Ischemic heart disease	410–414	400.9	3.9	26.4	35.2	28.4	4.8
Hypertension	400,401,403	385.2	13.3	36.2	29.3	16.7	*2.3
Arthritis and rheumatism	710–718	315.5	6.5	31.2	28.5	27.3	5.6
Eye diseases, except refractive	360–369,371–379	259.5	8.6	23.5	32.5	29.1	5.8
Diabetes mellitus	250	196.2	7.9	28.2	32.4	23.0	*4.7
Malignant neoplasms	140–209	146.1	14.0	19.3	30.1	28.1	*7.4
Bronchitis, emphysema, asthma	490–493	131.4	13.3	27.5	32.5	21.0	*4.9

[1] Diagnostic groupings and code number inclusions are based on the *Eighth Revision International Classification of Diseases, Adapted for Use in the United States.*

[2] Time spent in face-to-face contact between physician and patient.

[3] All ages and age groups include office visits to physicians for the most common and all other principal diagnoses.

[4] Upper respiratory infections.

NOTE: Rates are based on the average annual civilian noninstitutionalized population, excluding Alaska and Hawaii.

SOURCE: Division of Health Resources Utilization Statistics, National Center for Health Statistics: Data from the National Ambulatory Medical Care Survey.

Office visits to physicians, according to selected disposition of visit, age of patient, most common principal diagnosis, and ICDA code: United States, average annual 1975–76

(Data are based on reporting by a sample of office-based physicians)

Age of patient, most common principal diagnosis, and ICDA code[1]	Office visits per 1,000 population	Selected disposition[2]			
		No followup	Return at specified time	Return if needed	Telephone followup
		Percent of visits			
All ages[3]	2,770.7	12.3	60.2	21.9	3.5
Acute URI,[4] except influenza — 460–465	175.6	21.1	25.6	45.9	8.3
Hypertension — 400,401,403	110.9	2.6	86.1	10.2	*1.0
Heart disease — 390–398,402,404,410–414,420–429	103.5	2.5	83.9	8.8	2.0
Ischemic heart disease — 410–414	75.1	*1.8	86.3	8.2	*1.2
Prenatal care — Y06	101.3	*1.4	94.6	3.2	*0.5
Neuroses and nonpsychotic disorders — 300–309	100.1	5.7	70.9	19.8	3.6
Arthritis and rheumatism — 710–718	86.7	6.1	62.3	28.2	2.8
Infections and inflammations of skin — 680–698	85.1	12.7	49.9	32.8	5.3
Diseases of ear and mastoid process — 380–389	8.4	17.7	51.5	25.9	2.5
Bronchitis, emphysema, asthma — 490–493	76.6	8.0	59.6	27.6	5.0
Sprains and strains — 840–848	68.6	12.1	57.5	25.6	2.4
Eye diseases, except refractive — 360–369,371–379	68.3	9.2	64.9	20.3	*1.4
Diabetes mellitus — 250	46.2	*1.8	85.0	10.8	5.8
Refractive errors — 370	41.3	26.1	40.8	32.2	*0.2
Hay fever — 507	40.8	4.7	74.5	19.6	*1.8
Obesity — 277	38.0	*3.0	85.8	11.3	*1.4
Malignant neoplasms — 140–209	35.5	*1.9	82.8	5.9	*1.8
Diseases of sebaceous glands (acne) — 706	34.3	8.0	73.7	15.1	*0.7
Fracture — 800–829	33.9	8.4	72.8	13.4	*1.9
Lacerations — 870–907	33.9	26.1	56.4	14.0	*1.3
Synovitis, bursitis, tenosynovitis — 731	28.4	8.7	50.1	31.3	5.8
Influenza — 470–474	24.7	20.0	21.5	53.0	*5.5
Cystitis — 595	23.3	5.0	67.0	25.3	*4.7
Under 15 years[3]	1,982.1	19.9	47.6	26.0	6.1
Medical or special exams — Y00	360.2	24.6	64.9	11.0	*1.1
Acute URI,[4] except influenza — 460–465	326.6	20.6	26.3	42.9	11.9
Diseases of ear and mastoid process — 380–389	169.1	15.8	54.6	24.6	*2.3
Infective and parasitic diseases — 000–136	151.8	20.5	32.0	33.9	14.3
Infections and inflammations of skin — 680–698	91.9	17.1	43.7	36.5	7.1
Bronchitis, emphysema, asthma — 490–493	83.9	7.7	53.5	33.2	*6.6
Hay fever — 507	47.1	*6.0	77.6	19.0	*2.1
15–24 years[3]	2,259.0	16.4	56.6	21.8	3.0
Prenatal care — Y06	270.4	*1.1	94.8	3.7	*0.5
Medical or special exams — Y00	196.7	52.4	32.2	13.1	*2.6
Acute URI,[4] except influenza — 460–465	138.0	25.1	22.6	46.3	6.3
Diseases of sebaceous glands (acne) — 706	96.3	*7.6	77.1	14.5	*0.1
Infections and inflammations of skin — 680–698	79.0	14.9	43.1	35.1	*3.9
Sprains and strains — 840–848	77.2	14.1	53.2	26.4	*2.4
Neuroses and nonpsychotic disorders — 300–309	69.6	*5.0	69.7	21.1	*5.3

Diagnosis	Code					
25–44 years[3]		2,794.2	11.9	60.1	22.1	2.9
Prenatal care	Y06	195.0	*1.7	94.8	*2.5	*0.5
Neuroses and nonpsychotic disorders	300–309	182.8	5.2	76.6	15.2	*2.6
Medical or special exams	Y00	175.5	36.2	42.8	18.2	*2.7
Acute URI,[4] except influenza	460–465	131.3	23.8	22.0	48.4	5.4
Sprains and strains	840–848	104.7	9.7	64.0	21.7	*2.3
Infections and inflammations of skin	680–698	78.9	12.9	49.3	32.2	*4.9
Obesity	277	70.6	*2.4	89.1	8.4	*1.1
Arthritis and rheumatism	710–718	56.6	*7.1	56.1	33.3	*3.6
Hypertension	400,401,403	54.1	*3.0	86.5	*9.3	*1.9
Bronchitis, emphysema, asthma	490–493	51.4	*10.2	50.7	32.3	*7.9
Hay fever	507	49.9	*3.5	71.0	22.2	*1.6
Diseases of ear and mastoid process	380–389	49.3	19.0	40.9	32.9	*2.8
45–64 years[3]		3,377.2	8.9	64.7	21.3	2.9
Hypertension	400,401,403	269.9	2.6	87.3	9.2	*0.7
Arthritis and rheumatism	710–718	169.1	7.2	60.7	28.4	*3.0
Ischemic heart disease	410–414	145.3	*1.7	86.9	7.0	*1.7
Medical or special exams	Y00	125.9	32.1	45.3	18.6	*2.9
Neuroses and nonpsychotic disorders	300–309	124.6	6.7	65.5	24.5	*3.5
Acute URI,[4] except influenza	460–465	121.7	15.7	27.3	53.4	*4.2
Bronchitis, emphysema, asthma	490–493	109.4	7.1	67.0	23.3	*3.7
Eye diseases, except refractive	360–369,371–379	92.7	8.7	69.5	15.0	*1.0
Diabetes mellitus	250	92.2	*2.3	88.6	9.9	*2.9
Sprains and strains	840–848	89.1	8.9	55.5	30.4	*2.2
Infections and inflammations of skin	680–698	85.5	9.2	59.5	26.2	*5.6
Malignant neoplasms	140–209	70.1	*1.7	84.4	*5.3	*1.7
Menopausal symptoms	627	63.6	*6.5	60.9	30.8	*2.7
Diseases of ear and mastoid process	380–389	61.1	18.6	53.3	24.2	*2.8
Synovitis, bursitis, tenosynovitis	731	56.5	*7.3	48.9	35.5	*6.0
65 years and over[3]		4,356.6	5.9	71.1	18.0	2.7
Ischemic heart disease	410–414	400.9	*1.8	86.9	9.1	*0.8
Hypertension	400,401,403	385.2	*2.4	84.1	12.4	*1.2
Arthritis and rheumatism	710–718	315.5	*3.5	69.0	25.9	*1.4
Eye diseases, except refractive	360–369,371–379	259.5	5.7	72.5	16.9	*1.0
Diabetes mellitus	250	196.2	*1.7	81.5	12.0	8.1
Malignant neoplasms	140–209	146.1	*1.6	82.5	*5.3	*1.7
Bronchitis, emphysema, asthma	490–493	131.4	*6.5	69.4	20.0	*2.4

[1] Diagnostic groupings and code number inclusions are based on the *Eighth Revision International Classification of Diseases, Adapted for Use in the United States*.

[2] More than one disposition was possible.

[3] All ages and age groups include office visits to physicians for the most common and all other principal diagnoses.

[4] Upper respiratory infections.

NOTE: Rates are based on the average annual civilian noninstitutionalized population, excluding Alaska and Hawaii.

SOURCE: Division of Health Resources Utilization Statistics, National Center for Health Statistics: Data from the National Ambulatory Medical Care Survey.

Episodes of persons injured, according to source or place of first medical attention, sex, age, and family income:
United States, 1975

(Data are based on household interviews of a sample of the civilian noninstitutionalized population)

Sex, age, and family income	All medically attended episodes in thousands[1]	Source or place of first medical attention				
		Total	Doctor's office[2]	Hospital outpatient department[3]	Telephone	Other[4]
		Percent distribution				
Total[5] _ _ _ _ _ _ _ _ _	57,855	100.0	32.9	42.8	12.5	11.1
Sex						
Male _ _ _ _ _ _ _ _ _ _ _	31,217	100.0	29.7	48.6	8.6	12.5
Female _ _ _ _ _ _ _ _ _ _	26,639	100.0	36.7	36.0	17.1	9.5
Age						
Under 18 years _ _ _ _ _ _	22,249	100.0	30.7	46.9	15.3	6.8
18–44 years _ _ _ _ _ _ _	23,648	100.0	30.9	41.7	10.0	16.5
45–64 years _ _ _ _ _ _ _	8,207	100.0	40.8	39.4	11.4	8.4
65 years and over _ _ _ _ _	3,751	100.0	41.5	32.8	*14.1	*9.1
Family income						
Less than $5,000 _ _ _ _ _	9,391	100.0	31.1	45.2	9.3	13.8
$5,000–$9,999 _ _ _ _ _ _	12,664	100.0	30.9	46.1	10.5	11.0
$10,000–$14,999 _ _ _ _ _	13,937	100.0	32.5	38.9	14.4	13.4
$15,000 or more _ _ _ _ _	18,341	100.0	36.1	40.2	14.8	8.9

[1] Includes medically attended episodes of persons while inpatients in hospitals.
[2] Includes private doctor's office, doctor's clinic, or group practice.
[3] Includes hospital outpatient clinic or emergency room.
[4] Includes home, company or industry clinic, other, or unknown place of first medical attention.
[5] Includes unknown family income.

SOURCE: Division of Health Interview Statistics, National Center for Health Statistics: Data from the Health Interview Survey.

Persons who received services from selected medical practitioners during the year prior to interview, according to selected characteristics: United States, 1974

(Data are based on interviews of a sample of the civilian noninstitutionalized population)

Selected characteristic	Selected medical practitioner				
	Physician	Dentist	Chiro-practor	Podiatrist	Physical therapist
	Percent of population who received services				
Total[2]	63.4	49.3	3.6	2.4	1.6
Sex					
Male	56.9	47.6	3.8	1.6	1.6
Female	69.6	50.9	3.5	3.1	1.5
Color					
White	65.5	51.6	4.0	2.5	1.6
All other	49.4	33.9	1.0	1.7	1.4
Age					
Under 17 years	62.5	50.1	1.1	1.0	0.6
17–44 years	63.4	55.3	4.2	1.4	1.8
45–64 years	62.5	47.0	6.2	4.1	2.3
65 years and over	68.4	28.1	3.9	7.0	2.2
Family income					
Less than $5,000	58.7	33.5	3.2	2.8	2.0
$5,000–$9,999	60.9	39.6	3.8	2.2	1.8
$10,000–$14,999	65.0	51.8	4.1	1.9	1.3
$15,000 or more	68.4	64.1	3.5	2.7	1.4
Geographic region					
Northeast	63.8	53.2	3.3	3.9	1.4
North Central	65.5	51.2	4.2	2.6	1.7
South	61.8	43.7	2.5	1.3	1.3
West	62.8	51.1	5.0	2.0	1.9
Place of residence					
SMSA	63.4	51.7	3.0	2.8	1.6
Central city	59.4	47.0	2.4	3.1	1.6
Outside central city	66.6	55.4	3.4	2.5	1.5
Outside SMSA	63.5	43.9	5.1	1.5	1.5
Self-assessment of health					
Excellent or good	62.4	51.6	3.5	2.2	1.1
Fair or poor	70.8	35.1	4.4	4.0	4.3

[1] Includes persons receiving care at a private doctor's office, doctor's clinic, or group practice.

[2] Includes unknown family income.

SOURCES: Division of Health Interview Statistics, National Center for Health Statistics: Data from the Health Interview Survey; National Center for Health Statistics: Utilization of selected medical practitioners, United States, 1974, by L. J. Howie. *Advance Data from Vital and Health Statistics,* No. 24. DHEW Pub. No. (PHS) 78–1250. Public Health Service. Hyattsville, Md., March 24, 1978.

Product-related injuries treated in hospital emergency rooms, according to age, sex, and category of consumer product: United States, 1977

(Data are based on reporting by a sample of hospital emergency rooms)

Sex and product category	Estimated number of injuries	Age							
		All ages	Under 6 years	6–11 years	12–17 years	18–24 years	25–44 years	45–64 years	65 years and over
		Percent distribution							
Both sexes[1]	9,390,793	100.0	15.2	15.4	21.2	15.9	20.1	8.4	3.7
Home structures and fixtures, construction materials	2,146,375	100.0	16.2	13.8	14.4	14.7	21.9	12.1	6.8
Stairs, ramps, and landings (indoors or outdoors)	581,894	100.0	14.0	6.7	11.5	15.6	24.9	16.2	11.0
Nails, tacks, and screws	295,900	100.0	9.3	21.5	18.4	14.6	24.3	10.1	1.8
Space heating, cooling, and ventilating appliances	99,474	100.0	31.9	12.8	10.2	10.5	18.7	10.6	5.2
Home furnishings	684,639	100.0	39.9	13.5	7.0	8.5	13.8	9.0	8.1
Home communications and hobby equipment	56,140	100.0	39.4	8.9	9.5	12.8	17.8	7.0	4.6
General household appliances	58,721	100.0	26.4	9.7	9.2	10.0	21.4	14.9	8.3
Kitchen appliances and unpowered housewares	609,887	100.0	8.1	8.3	14.9	22.2	30.8	12.7	2.9
Knives and cutlery	310,380	100.0	3.9	8.5	16.9	22.0	31.8	13.6	3.1
Packaging and containers for household products	221,551	100.0	16.0	16.7	17.9	15.8	23.0	9.2	3.0
Home and family maintenance products	133,062	100.0	37.3	9.3	11.9	13.5	18.6	7.5	1.8
Home workshop apparatus	346,373	100.0	5.1	5.0	11.3	16.5	35.3	19.9	6.8
Yard and garden equipment	217,428	100.0	7.6	9.6	13.9	11.1	31.5	19.5	6.5
Child nursery equipment	44,343	100.0	80.2	5.0	1.8	4.2	4.1	2.7	1.8
Toys (excluding riding or ride-on toys)	100,256	100.0	36.1	26.8	17.4	9.4	8.8	1.4	0.2
Riding or ride-on recreational equipment	773,867	100.0	12.7	36.9	33.7	6.6	7.8	1.9	0.3
Bicycles	493,239	100.0	14.0	41.1	30.1	5.8	6.7	1.8	0.5
Sports ball and related equipment	1,399,871	100.0	0.8	12.0	43.6	23.9	18.4	1.1	0.1
Football	406,484	100.0	0.4	12.7	60.3	19.0	7.1	0.3	0.0
Baseball	400,275	100.0	1.9	15.0	27.8	24.9	28.8	1.4	0.2
Basketball	371,880	100.0	0.2	5.7	45.1	31.8	16.5	0.6	0.1
Winter sports and related equipment	217,699	100.0	1.5	16.6	36.8	22.0	18.2	4.4	0.4
Other sports and recreational equipment	701,428	100.0	14.8	24.6	27.3	12.1	15.1	5.1	1.0
Miscellaneous	776,633	100.0	14.9	18.0	17.7	17.6	20.5	8.1	3.0
Glass (unknown origin)	358,778	100.0	13.7	23.1	18.6	18.6	19.3	5.4	1.0
Products under regulation by other Federal agencies[2]	803,044	100.0	20.6	8.4	13.3	20.2	23.4	10.4	3.6
Male	5,785,661	100.0	14.7	15.8	23.9	17.0	19.4	6.9	2.3
Home structures and fixtures, construction materials	1,172,419	100.0	18.2	15.5	15.9	15.5	21.3	9.5	4.1
Stairs, ramps, and landings (indoors or outdoors)	233,897	100.0	20.8	7.8	12.5	16.4	22.9	11.5	7.9
Nails, tacks, and screws	194,247	100.0	9.4	21.3	20.4	14.7	23.4	9.2	1.6
Space heating, cooling, and ventilating appliances	65,617	100.0	31.9	12.1	10.5	11.5	19.7	10.2	4.1
Home furnishings	342,785	100.0	47.9	16.1	7.4	8.1	10.7	5.5	4.2
Home communications and hobby equipment	30,072	100.0	43.1	9.0	11.2	10.9	16.5	5.7	3.5
General household appliances	25,531	100.0	35.1	10.3	8.0	8.4	15.8	18.9	3.5
Kitchen appliances and unpowered housewares	304,579	100.0	9.5	10.6	18.4	22.4	26.9	10.0	2.2
Knives and cutlery	191,287	100.0	4.0	9.7	20.7	23.4	28.9	10.8	2.4

Product	Number	Total							
Packaging and containers for household products	120,356	100.0	17.7	20.5	19.8	16.5	18.0	6.0	1.4
Home and family maintenance products	83,894	100.0	36.1	10.0	13.6	15.7	16.8	6.0	1.8
Home workshop apparatus	289,102	100.0	3.8	4.2	11.9	17.4	36.5	19.8	6.3
Yard and garden equipment	170,249	100.0	6.7	9.4	14.9	12.2	32.1	19.3	5.0
Child nursery equipment	22,209	100.0	87.1	4.8	2.0	2.2	2.3	1.3	0.3
Toys (excluding riding or ride-on toys)	67,356	100.0	34.5	27.2	20.4	9.5	6.8	1.3	0.2
Riding or ride-on recreational equipment	490,024	100.0	12.2	35.5	37.1	6.7	6.5	1.5	0.4
Bicycles	326,218	100.0	12.7	39.3	34.1	6.0	5.7	1.6	0.5
Sports ball and related equipment	1,127,207	100.0	0.7	11.3	43.2	24.9	18.7	1.1	0.1
Football	387,300	100.0	0.4	12.4	60.7	19.1	7.0	0.3	0.0
Baseball	292,909	100.0	1.5	15.5	26.4	24.7	30.2	1.5	0.1
Basketball	306,107	100.0	0.3	4.6	40.3	35.3	18.9	0.6	0.0
Winter sports and related equipment	144,170	100.0	1.3	16.1	36.0	23.6	18.8	4.0	0.3
Other sports and recreational equipment	436,171	100.0	13.3	22.5	28.3	13.4	16.2	5.2	1.1
Miscellaneous	412,588	100.0	16.1	21.2	19.1	16.1	17.3	7.7	2.4
Glass (unknown origin)	202,087	100.0	14.5	27.1	20.1	18.0	15.6	3.8	0.8
Products under regulation by other Federal agencies²	481,330	100.0	19.4	7.9	14.2	22.3	24.7	9.0	2.4
Female	3,594,677	100.0	16.0	14.9	17.0	14.2	21.1	10.8	5.9
Home structures and fixtures, construction materials	971,196	100.0	13.9	11.7	12.5	13.8	22.7	15.2	10.1
Stairs, ramps, and landings (indoors or outdoors)	347,070	100.0	9.5	5.9	10.8	15.0	26.2	19.4	13.1
Nails, tacks, and screws	101,401	100.0	9.1	22.1	14.4	14.6	25.9	11.7	2.1
Space heating, cooling, and ventilating appliances	33,638	100.0	31.7	14.3	9.9	8.6	16.9	11.4	7.2
Home furnishings	341,247	100.0	31.9	11.0	6.6	8.9	16.9	12.6	12.0
Home communications and hobby equipment	25,934	100.0	35.0	8.8	7.6	15.1	19.3	8.4	5.9
General household appliances	33,190	100.0	19.8	9.3	10.1	11.2	25.8	11.8	12.0
Kitchen appliances and unpowered housewares	304,290	100.0	6.8	5.9	11.3	21.8	34.7	15.5	3.7
Knives and cutlery	118,430	100.0	3.6	6.6	10.9	19.6	36.7	18.3	4.2
Packaging and containers for household products	100,860	100.0	14.1	12.3	12.1	14.7	28.9	13.0	4.9
Home and family maintenance products	49,168	100.0	39.5	8.1	9.1	9.6	21.7	10.0	2.0
Home workshop apparatus	56,905	100.0	11.6	8.9	8.2	12.1	29.1	20.7	9.3
Yard and garden equipment	46,981	100.0	10.8	10.4	10.5	7.1	29.3	20.3	11.6
Child nursery equipment	22,100	100.0	73.4	5.3	1.7	6.3	5.9	4.2	3.3
Toys (excluding riding or ride-on toys)	32,750	100.0	39.6	25.8	11.0	9.1	12.7	1.4	0.4
Riding or ride-on recreational equipment	283,399	100.0	13.6	39.4	27.6	6.5	10.2	2.4	0.2
Bicycles	166,759	100.0	16.6	44.6	22.3	5.5	8.6	2.1	0.3
Sports ball and related equipment	270,580	100.0	1.5	14.8	45.8	19.3	17.4	1.1	0.2
Football	18,877	100.0	1.0	19.2	53.2	18.2	7.8	0.6	—
Baseball	106,416	100.0	3.0	13.5	31.5	25.2	25.3	1.2	0.3
Basketball	65,283	100.0	0.2	10.8	67.5	15.3	5.3	0.7	0.1
Winter sports and related equipment	73,396	100.0	1.9	17.7	38.3	19.1	17.1	5.3	0.5
Other sports and recreational equipment	264,724	100.0	17.3	28.1	25.5	9.9	13.3	5.0	0.8
Miscellaneous	363,037	100.0	13.5	14.4	16.2	19.3	24.2	8.7	3.6
Glass (unknown origin)	156,254	100.0	12.4	18.0	16.8	19.4	24.3	7.4	1.4
Products under regulation by other Federal agencies²	321,272	100.0	22.2	9.0	11.9	17.0	21.6	12.5	5.5

¹ Includes unknown sex.
² Other than the U.S. Consumer Product Safety Commission.

NOTE: Alaska and Hawaii are excluded from the National Electronic Injury Surveillance System.

SOURCE: U.S. Consumer Product Safety Commission: Data from the National Electronic Injury Surveillance System.

Emergency room reports of drug abuse patients, according to motivation for taking substance, age, sex, and race: United States, reporting areas, May 1976–April 1977

(Data are based on reporting by a sample of hospital emergency rooms)

Age, sex, and race	Number of emergency room reports	Motivation for taking substance					
		All motivations	Psychic effects	Dependence	Suicide attempt or gesture	Other	Unknown or non-response
		Percent distribution					
Total	123,164	100.0	20.8	16.1	38.8	2.4	21.9
Age							
Under 10 years	121	100.0	9.9	–	15.7	28.1	46.3
10–19 years	25,418	100.0	28.1	5.8	38.8	2.1	25.2
20–29 years	53,789	100.0	21.7	21.2	34.7	2.1	20.3
30–39 years	23,291	100.0	17.3	18.3	41.8	2.4	20.3
40–49 years	11,190	100.0	14.2	14.2	47.0	2.9	21.6
50 years and over	7,930	100.0	11.7	10.3	48.6	4.7	24.7
Unknown	1,425	100.0	14.0	16.8	29.6	1.5	38.2
Sex							
Male	51,129	100.0	25.4	24.7	25.5	2.3	22.0
Female	71,832	100.0	17.5	9.9	48.3	2.5	21.8
Unknown	203	100.0	24.6	19.7	32.5	1.0	22.2
Race							
White	74,455	100.0	20.9	11.2	44.1	2.4	21.4
Black	28,698	100.0	23.2	31.0	25.5	2.7	17.6
Other races	4,782	100.0	22.6	21.7	36.3	2.0	17.4
Unknown	15,229	100.0	15.3	9.8	38.7	2.2	34.0

NOTES: Includes only medical emergencies related directly or indirectly to drug ingestion. One emergency room episode can involve more than one drug. Each drug included in an episode constitutes a drug report. Data are for 24 standard metropolitan statistical areas.

SOURCE: Drug Enforcement Administration, U.S. Department of Justice, and National Institute on Drug Abuse, U.S. Department of Health, Education, and Welfare: Data from Project DAWN V.

Ranks of leading drugs in drug abuse reports from emergency rooms, according to age of patient and type of drug: United States, reporting areas, May 1976–April 1977

(Data are based on reporting by a sample of hospital emergency rooms)

Type of drug	Age					
	All ages	10–19 years	20–29 years	30–39 years	40–49 years	50 years and over
20 most commonly named drugs	Number of reports	Ranks of leading drugs				
Diazepam	21,800	1	1	1	1	1
Alcohol (in combination)[2]	19,171	2	3	2	2	2
Heroin/Morphine	12,634	6	2	3	4	11
Aspirin	7,093	3	4	4	6	5
Flurazepam	4,594	11	8	5	3	3
D-Propoxyphene	4,357	5	6	7	7	8
Chlordiazepoxide	3,739	13	12	6	5	4
Marijuana or Hashish	3,602	4	9	++	++	++
Methadone	3,355	++	5	9	13	++
Phenobarbital	3,078	10	13	10	9	7
Amitriptyline	2,999	15	14	8	8	6
Secobarbital	2,975	9	10	11	10	9
Secobarbital/Amobarbital	2,910	14	7	12	15	10
Methaqualone	2,214	12	11	17	17	16
Acetaminophen	2,076	8	17	15	16	14
Ethchlorvynol	2,012	++	15	13	11	12
PCP	1,790	7	18	++	++	++
Perphenazine/Amitriptyline	1,527	17	++	14	11	13
Cocaine	1,433	16	16	18	++	++
Clorazepate	1,343	++	++	16	14	15

[1] Includes persons under 10 years of age and persons with unknown age.

[2] Alcohol is included only when involved in a medical emergency along with at least one other drug. Alcohol alone is excluded.

NOTES: The symbol ++ denotes that the drug does not rank in the top 20 drugs. Only medical emergencies related directly or indirectly to drug ingestion are included. One emergency room episode can involve more than one drug. Each drug included in an episode constitutes a drug report. Although there were 152 emergency room reports for children under 10 years of age, the number of episodes by drug of abuse were too small for ranking purposes. Data are for 24 standard metropolitan statistical areas.

SOURCE: Drug Enforcement Administration, U.S. Department of Justice, and National Institute on Drug Abuse, U.S. Department of Health, Education, and Welfare: Data from Project DAWN V.

Dental visits, according to age of patient and selected characteristics: United States, average annual 1975–76

(Data are based on household interviews of a sample of the civilian noninstitutionalized population)

Selected characteristic	Age					
	All ages	Under 18 years	18–24 years	25–44 years	45–64 years	65 years and over
	Dental visits per 1,000 population					
Total[1]	1,612.1	1,563.2	1,726.7	1,664.0	1,758.2	1,200.2
Sex						
Male	1,483.0	1,466.0	1,498.5	1,488.3	1,590.0	1,261.4
Female	1,732.3	1,663.8	1,940.1	1,828.0	1,911.5	1,157.4
Color						
White	1,706.7	1,716.9	1,832.3	1,730.2	1,819.0	1,254.7
All other	984.1	777.8	1,071.7	1,200.3	1,231.0	665.1
Family income						
Less than $5,000	1,063.7	918.5	1,611.7	1,220.1	1,134.5	726.3
$5,000–$9,999	1,293.0	1,030.9	1,617.7	1,288.9	1,433.5	1,362.2
$10,000–$14,999	1,513.0	1,379.1	1,611.1	1,536.1	1,631.3	1,602.8
$15,000 or more	2,148.8	2,225.3	2,023.9	2,054.9	2,244.8	2,005.5
Geographic region						
Northeast	1,859.5	1,747.7	2,080.7	1,984.5	1,969.7	1,408.0
North Central	1,645.4	1,689.1	1,759.7	1,675.4	1,764.1	1,072.7
South	1,290.5	1,202.8	1,324.8	1,364.2	1,442.8	1,044.2
West	1,815.1	1,798.1	1,925.9	1,768.8	2,011.3	1,409.4
Location of residence[2]						
Within SMSA	1,753.2	1,670.0	1,764.8	1,818.6	1,952.0	1,403.0
Large SMSA	1,885.5	1,802.0	1,841.8	1,929.8	2,125.8	1,554.7
Core counties	1,828.2	1,659.6	1,857.6	1,855.2	2,118.8	1,607.6
Fringe counties	2,007.0	2,074.6	1,804.3	2,078.6	2,141.2	1,402.1
Medium SMSA	1,614.3	1,582.4	1,731.2	1,646.7	1,760.2	1,164.1
Other SMSA	1,518.4	1,343.8	1,533.5	1,736.4	1,621.9	1,323.6
Outside SMSA	1,223.4	1,275.9	1,618.0	1,189.8	1,219.7	758.6
Adjacent to SMSA	1,292.1	1,307.0	1,682.2	1,288.3	1,326.6	789.7
Not adjacent to SMSA	1,130.2	1,232.1	1,531.8	1,050.6	1,079.8	720.5

[1] Includes unknown family income.
[2] Grouped according to the April 1973 Office of Management and Budget metropolitan-nonmetropolitan designations.

SOURCE: Division of Health Interview Statistics, National Center for Health Statistics: Data from the Health Interview Survey.

Persons 25-74 years of age who visited a dentist during the year prior to interview, according to reason for visit, age, and family income: United States, 1971-74

(Data are based on interviews of a sample of the civilian noninstitutionalized population)

Age and family income	Percent of population 25-74 years with dental visit	Reason for visit								
		All reasons	Regular checkup or cleaning	Toothache	Teeth filled	Trouble with gums	Tooth pulled or other surgery	Repair of dental plate	New dental plate made	Other
		Percent distribution								
Total[1]	44.3	100.0	49.4	3.2	17.4	2.3	10.4	5.6	3.8	7.9
Age										
25-34 years	47.4	100.0	50.0	3.4	21.7	1.5	11.4	1.7	1.9	8.4
35-44 years	49.9	100.0	53.9	3.6	15.0	2.2	11.2	3.2	3.2	7.6
45-54 years	47.9	100.0	49.1	3.1	17.7	2.7	8.1	7.1	4.6	7.3
55-64 years	37.6	100.0	47.1	1.1	13.3	2.7	9.3	10.1	7.4	9.3
65-74 years	31.6	100.0	41.5	4.7	15.5	2.5	12.0	12.7	4.7	6.0
Family income										
Less than $4,000	24.6	100.0	24.0	4.5	14.2	7.7	25.6	8.1	8.9	6.9
$4,000-$6,999	32.5	100.0	30.2	4.6	20.6	2.2	15.1	13.2	6.5	7.7
$7,000-$9,999	41.2	100.0	49.0	3.9	16.5	1.5	11.2	5.8	4.6	7.5
$10,000-$14,999	45.6	100.0	50.9	3.5	18.6	2.4	10.1	4.6	3.3	6.6
$15,000 or more	61.5	100.0	61.3	1.5	15.6	1.5	5.0	3.7	2.4	8.9

[1] Includes unknown family income.

SOURCE: Division of Health Examination Statistics, National Center for Health Statistics: Data from the Health and Nutrition Examination Survey.

Discharges, days of care, and average length of stay in non-Federal short-stay hospitals, according to sex and age: United States, 1965 and 1975

(Data are based on a sample of hospital records)

Sex and age	Discharges		Days of care		Average of length of stay	
	1965	1975	1965	1975	1965	1975
	Number per 1,000 population				Number of days per discharge	
Both sexes [1,2]	151.7	162.8	1,185.6	1,254.9	7.8	7.7
Under 15 years	71.5	71.5	351.5	328.0	4.9	4.6
15–44 years	177.0	155.4	1,042.9	885.1	5.9	5.7
45–64 years	174.3	194.7	1,713.5	1,748.9	9.8	9.0
65 years and over	263.9	359.3	3,446.7	4,165.9	13.1	11.6
Male [2]	121.3	134.0	1,017.9	1,104.4	8.4	8.2
Under 15 years	79.2	78.6	388.6	364.8	4.9	4.6
15–44 years	97.7	92.8	682.4	633.9	7.0	6.8
45–64 years	169.2	188.3	1,688.0	1,699.9	10.0	9.0
65 years and over	276.3	386.9	3,411.2	4,379.0	12.3	11.3
Female [2]	179.8	189.7	1,338.6	1,395.2	7.4	7.4
Under 15 years	63.4	64.1	311.7	289.7	4.9	4.5
15–44 years	249.2	214.6	1,370.6	1,122.1	5.5	5.2
45–64 years	178.4	200.5	1,822.8	1,793.6	9.7	8.9
65 years and over	252.8	339.9	3,452.4	4,016.4	13.7	11.8

[1] 1965 figures include data for which sex was not stated.
[2] 1965 figures include data for which age was not stated.

NOTE: Excludes newborn infants. Rates are based on the civilian noninstitutionalized population.

SOURCE: National Center for Health Statistics: Utilization of short-stay hospitals, annual summary for the United States, 1975, by A. Ranofsky. *Vital and Health Statistics.* Series 13-No. 31. DHEW Pub. No. (HRA) 77–1782. Health Resources Administration. Washington. U.S. Government Printing Office. Apr. 1977.

Discharges and days of care in non-Federal short-stay hospitals per 1,000 population, according to sex and age: United States, average annual 1975–76

(Data are based on a sample of hospital records)

Age	Discharges				Days of care			
	Both sexes	Male	Female[1]		Both sexes	Male	Female[1]	
			Including deliveries	Excluding deliveries			Including deliveries	Excluding deliveries
	Number per 1,000 population							
All ages	163.0	134.7	189.4	160.6	1,245.3	1,098.9	1,381.8	1,265.4
Under 1 year	204.9	233.9	174.5	174.5	1,266.0	1,433.5	1,090.6	1,090.6
1–4 years	90.0	101.6	77.8	77.8	367.5	410.7	322.5	322.5
5–9 years	60.5	66.5	54.3	54.3	240.2	259.5	220.1	220.1
10–14 years	48.5	50.2	46.6	44.9	219.0	234.8	202.7	194.9
15–19 years	115.2	74.7	155.3	101.2	564.4	436.2	691.6	477.6
20–24 years	171.2	85.4	250.8	138.7	827.3	553.6	1,081.2	656.8
25–29 years	182.3	88.0	271.0	160.8	950.1	576.7	1,301.3	845.3
30–34 years	157.7	97.2	214.4	160.9	917.8	644.0	1,174.8	942.5
35–39 years	149.4	113.0	182.2	163.4	1,000.7	821.5	1,162.5	1,074.2
40–44 years	158.2	125.5	189.2	183.8	1,148.4	941.8	1,344.1	1,320.3
45–49 years	171.1	147.9	192.7	192.2	1,355.7	1,186.6	1,514.2	1,511.0
50–54 years	183.7	172.1	194.4	194.0	1,550.3	1,489.3	1,606.4	1,604.5
55–59 years	201.8	199.4	204.1	204.1	1,850.3	1,789.6	1,906.5	1,906.5
60–64 years	231.9	254.4	212.6	212.6	2,311.1	2,507.2	2,143.9	2,143.9
65–69 years	280.5	311.5	255.5	255.5	2,981.8	3,314.4	2,714.5	2,714.5
70–74 years	323.9	358.0	299.4	299.4	3,708.0	4,011.8	3,489.1	3,489.1
75–79 years	396.5	429.7	375.1	375.1	4,735.3	5,059.7	4,526.6	4,526.6
80–84 years	480.4	516.4	459.5	459.5	5,793.9	6,095.7	5,619.5	5,619.5
85 years and over	665.1	731.9	631.8	631.8	8,288.2	8,959.0	7,953.9	7,953.9

[1] Rates for females are shown both for all females and for all females not having delivery (ICDA codes 650–662) as first-listed diagnosis.

NOTE: Excludes newborn infants. Rates are based on the civilian noninstitutionalized population.

SOURCE: Division of Health Resources Utilization Statistics, National Center for Health Statistics: Data from the Hospital Discharge Survey.

Discharges from non-Federal short-stay hospitals per 1,000 population, according to age, sex, leading diagnostic category, and ICDA code: United States, average annual 1975–76

(Data are based on a sample of hospital records)

First-listed diagnosis and ICDA code[1]	All ages	Age			
		Under 15 years	15-44 years	45-64 years	65 years and over
		Discharges per 1,000 population			
Both sexes					
All diagnoses	163.0	71.4	154.4	195.0	361.3
Diseases of the heart 390–398, 402, 404, 410–414, 420–429	12.8	0.4	2.3	23.7	66.0
Ischemic heart disease 410–414	9.0	*0.1	1.2	17.7	46.3
Malignant neoplasms 140–209	7.6	0.5	2.2	14.5	34.2
Fracture 800–829	5.5	3.6	4.4	5.0	16.2
Delivery 650–662	14.9	0.3	33.8	*0.1	...
Neuroses and nonpsychotic disorders 300–309	5.4	0.8	6.5	8.1	6.1
Cerebrovascular disease 430–438	2.9	*0.1	0.2	3.4	20.5
Pneumonia 480–486	3.5	4.5	1.2	3.1	11.5
Psychoses 290–299	1.7	*0.0	2.1	2.1	2.7
Diabetes mellitus 250	2.6	0.4	1.4	4.5	9.3
Arthritis and rheumatism 710–718	2.4	0.2	1.1	4.9	8.7
Cholelithiasis (gallstones) 574	2.2	*0.0	1.8	4.1	5.4
Diseases of arteries, arterioles, capillaries 440–448	1.5	*0.0	0.3	2.2	8.6
Displacement of intervertebral disc 725	1.8	*0.0	2.0	3.5	1.3
Benign neoplasms 210–228	3.4	0.7	3.9	5.4	3.4
Bronchitis, emphysema, asthma 490–493	2.5	2.5	1.0	3.3	6.6
Diseases of central nervous system 320–349	1.6	1.1	1.3	1.9	3.2
Ulcer 531–534	1.9	*0.1	1.4	3.7	5.1
Sprains and strains 840–848	1.9	*0.2	2.6	2.5	1.9
Eye diseases and conditions 360–379	2.8	1.4	0.8	3.5	13.6
Inguinal hernia 550, 552	2.4	1.9	1.4	3.9	4.9
Hyperplasia of prostate 600	1.1	*0.0	*0.0	1.8	7.4
Congenital anomalies 740–759	1.6	3.2	1.2	1.0	0.9
Disorders of menstruation 626	2.8	*0.1	4.2	4.0	0.8
Intercranial injury 850–854	1.7	2.1	2.0	0.9	1.3
Appendicitis 540–543	1.4	1.8	1.8	0.6	*0.4
Lacerations 870–907	1.6	1.1	2.2	1.2	1.3
Gastritis and duodenitis 535	1.4	0.3	1.4	2.0	2.4
Hypertension 400,401,403	1.2	*0.0	0.8	2.6	2.6
Male					
All diagnoses	134.7	78.5	93.4	189.2	387.9
Diseases of the heart 390–398,402,404,410–414,420–429	14.3	0.5	2.9	31.8	73.8
Ischemic heart disease 410–414	10.5	*0.1	1.8	25.0	52.5

Diagnosis	Code[1]					
Malignant neoplasms	140–209	7.2	0.5	1.5	12.8	43.0
Fracture	800–829	5.9	4.5	6.5	4.9	9.4
Neuroses and nonpsychotic disorders	300–309	5.6	0.7	6.4	9.9	6.7
Cerebrovascular disease	430–438	2.8	*0.1	*0.2	4.1	21.2
Pneumonia	480–486	3.7	5.0	1.2	3.3	13.5
Hyperplasia of prostate	600	2.4	*0.0	*0.0	3.8	18.0
Diseases of arteries, arterioles, capillaries	440–448	1.7	*0.0	0.3	2.9	11.2
Inguinal hernia	550,552	4.4	3.0	2.5	7.7	10.4
Psychoses	290–299	1.4	*0.1	2.1	1.5	2.3
Displacement of intervertebral disc	725	2.0	*0.0	2.5	3.9	*1.1
Ulcer	531–534	2.3	*0.1	1.7	4.5	7.0
Diabetes mellitus	250	2.1	0.4	1.2	3.8	7.9
Bronchitis, emphysema, asthma	490–493	2.5	3.0	0.7	3.1	8.9
Diseases of central nervous system	320–349	1.5	1.2	1.2	2.0	3.6
Arthritis and rheumatism	710–718	1.9	*0.3	1.0	4.1	6.2
Sprains and strains	840–848	2.0	*0.2	3.0	2.6	1.4
Lacerations	870–907	2.4	1.5	3.5	1.7	1.7
Intercranial injury	850–854	2.3	2.7	2.7	1.1	1.4
Cholelithiasis (gallstones)	574	1.1	*0.0	0.6	2.4	4.3
Eye diseases and conditions	360–379	2.5	1.5	0.8	3.4	11.9
Congenital anomalies	740–759	1.7	3.9	0.9	0.9	*1.1
All diagnoses		189.4	63.9	212.1	200.3	342.7
Female						
Diseases of the heart	390–398,402,404,410–414	11.3	*0.4	1.7	16.4	60.6
Ischemic heart disease	410–414	7.5	*0.1	0.7	11.1	42.0
Delivery	650–662	28.8	0.6	65.6	*0.2	....
Malignant neoplasms	140–209	8.0	0.4	3.0	15.9	28.0
Fracture	800–829	5.2	2.7	2.5	5.1	20.9
Neuroses and nonpsychotic disorders	300–309	5.1	0.8	6.7	6.4	5.7
Cerebrovascular disease	430–438	3.1	*0.1	0.3	2.8	20.0
Arthritis and rheumatism	710–718	2.9	*0.2	1.2	5.5	10.5
Psychoses	290–299	1.9	*0.0	2.2	2.8	3.0
Cholelithiasis (gallstones)	574	3.2	*0.0	3.0	5.6	6.2
Diabetes mellitus	250	3.0	0.4	1.5	5.2	10.4
Benign neoplasms	210–228	5.4	0.8	6.8	8.6	4.0
Pneumonia	480–486	3.3	3.9	1.3	3.0	10.0
Disorders of menstruation	626	5.3	*0.2	8.1	7.6	1.4
Displacement of intervertebral disc	725	1.5	*0.0	1.6	3.1	1.5
Bronchitis, emphysema, asthma	490–493	2.4	2.0	1.4	3.5	5.0
Diseases of arteries, arterioles, capillaries	440–448	1.2	*0.0	0.2	1.6	6.8
Diseases of central nervous system	320–349	1.6	1.0	1.4	1.9	2.9
Sprains and strains	840–848	1.8	*0.1	2.3	2.5	2.3
Eye diseases and conditions	360–379	3.1	1.3	0.8	3.7	14.8
Ulcer	531–534	1.5	*0.1	1.1	2.9	3.8
Congenital anomalies	740–759	1.5	2.5	1.5	1.0	*0.7
Hypertension	400,401,403	1.3	*0.0	0.8	2.9	3.2

[1] Diagnostic groupings and code number inclusions are based on the *Eighth Revision International Classification of Diseases, Adapted for Use in the United States.* Codes 760–771, 773, and 779 are not used in the Hospital Discharge Survey.

NOTE: Rankings are based on number of days of care. Rates are based on the average annual civilian noninstitutionalized population.

SOURCE: Division of Health Resources Utilization Statistics, National Center for Health Statistics: Data from the Hospital Discharge Survey.

Table 104   Days of care in non-Federal short-stay hospitals per 1,000 population, according to age, sex, leading diagnostic category, and ICDA code: United States, average annual 1975–76

(Data are based on a sample of hospital records)

First-listed diagnosis and ICDA code[1]	All ages	Age			
		Under 15 years	15-44 years	45-64 years	65 years and over
		Days of care per 1,000 population			
Both sexes					
All diagnoses	1,245.3	322.1	864.7	1,733.3	4,167.2
Diseases of the heart ---- 390–398, 402, 404, 410–414, 420–429	135.1	3.3	19.1	234.9	755.3
Ischemic heart disease ---- 410–414	97.3	*1.2	11.1	178.7	538.5
Malignant neoplasms ---- 140–209	98.2	4.3	21.4	188.4	477.0
Fracture ---- 800–829	61.2	22.4	37.9	54.2	270.5
Delivery ---- 650–662	60.2	*1.4	136.1	*0.7	...
Neuroses and nonpsychotic disorders ---- 300–309	48.4	7.0	56.6	69.4	72.6
Cerebrovascular disease ---- 430–438	38.9	*0.8	2.8	42.5	279.7
Pneumonia ---- 480–486	31.7	26.3	9.4	31.1	141.8
Psychoses ---- 290–299	27.3	*1.4	32.2	36.8	51.2
Diabetes mellitus ---- 250	26.7	*2.7	10.1	48.1	114.2
Arthritis and rheumatism ---- 710–718	26.5	*1.8	9.1	49.2	116.5
Cholelithiasis (gallstones) ---- 574	22.5	*0.2	15.3	40.5	71.5
Diseases of arteries, arterioles, capillaries ---- 440–448	21.1	*0.3	2.7	29.1	135.0
Displacement of intervertebral disc ---- 725	19.9	*0.2	21.9	40.6	18.7
Benign neoplasms ---- 210–228	19.7	*2.5	21.2	34.6	26.1
Bronchitis, emphysema, asthma ---- 490–493	18.2	11.1	6.1	27.8	68.1
Diseases of central nervous system ---- 320–349	17.9	9.7	12.9	22.8	49.2
Ulcer ---- 531–534	17.7	*0.5	9.7	34.5	60.8
Sprains and strains ---- 840–848	14.6	*2.4	18.2	20.2	17.8
Eye diseases and conditions ---- 360–379	13.4	3.6	3.3	17.8	72.1
Inguinal hernia ---- 550, 552	13.1	5.0	6.8	23.5	39.4
Hyperplasia of prostate ---- 600	12.1	*0.1	*0.6	15.4	84.0
Congenital anomalies ---- 740–759	10.4	19.0	6.7	8.6	9.3
Disorders of menstruation ---- 626	10.4	*0.3	15.7	14.9	3.1
Intercranial injury ---- 850–854	9.8	7.3	11.4	8.2	12.5
Appendicitis ---- 540–543	8.6	9.9	9.7	6.3	*4.8
Lacerations ---- 870–907	8.6	4.2	11.1	7.5	10.5
Gastritis and duodenitis ---- 535	8.1	*1.1	7.3	12.4	19.6
Hypertension ---- 400, 401, 403	8.0	*0.4	4.9	18.0	19.9
Male					
All diagnoses	1,098.9	354.7	623.7	1,690.2	4,392.3
Diseases of the heart ---- 390–398, 402, 404, 410–414, 420–429	147.8	*3.0	25.3	315.0	818.9
Ischemic heart disease ---- 410–414	110.8	*0.9	16.9	254.1	587.2

Diagnosis	Code[1]					
Malignant neoplasms	140–209	93.9	*4.9	15.3	169.3	586.8
Fracture	800–829	56.2	28.3	55.5	49.3	161.5
Neuroses and nonpsychotic disorders	300–309	49.3	7.0	53.3	83.5	78.4
Cerebrovascular disease	430–438	36.8	*0.8	*2.3	51.0	287.7
Pneumonia	480–486	32.3	28.9	8.7	32.2	161.8
Hyperplasia of prostate	600	25.0	*0.2	*1.2	32.3	204.0
Diseases of arteries, arterioles, capillaries	440–448	25.0	*0.3	*3.2	37.0	182.6
Inguinal hernia	550, 552	24.3	8.3	12.3	45.9	83.8
Psychoses	290–299	21.4	*1.7	29.0	22.7	39.3
Displacement of intervertebral disc	725	21.3	*0.3	24.8	44.1	*15.2
Ulcer	531–534	21.1	*0.4	11.6	41.7	84.8
Diabetes mellitus	250	21.1	*2.5	9.1	40.4	92.8
Bronchitis, emphysema, asthma	490–493	18.8	13.9	4.5	25.4	90.6
Diseases of central nervous system	320–349	18.6	10.2	14.0	23.6	55.7
Arthritis and rheumatism	710–718	17.9	*2.1	6.7	37.5	77.1
Sprains and strains	840–848	13.5	*0.9	18.8	19.0	*12.2
Lacerations	870–907	12.4	5.8	18.3	8.8	*10.7
Intracranial injury	850–854	12.2	8.0	15.6	9.1	*14.8
Cholelithiasis (gallstones)	574	12.0	*0.0	4.6	24.1	57.5
Eye diseases and conditions	360–379	11.4	*4.3	*3.3	17.0	61.1
Congenital anomalies	740–759	11.4	23.7	5.7	*7.3	*12.2
Female						
All diagnoses		1,381.8	288.2	1,092.5	1,772.7	4,009.6
Diseases of the heart	390–398, 402, 404, 410–414, 420–429	123.2	*3.6	13.3	161.9	710.8
Ischemic heart disease	410–414	84.6	*1.5	5.7	110.1	504.5
Delivery	650–662	116.4	*2.9	264.7	*1.3	400.2
Malignant neoplasms	140–209	102.2	*3.8	27.1	205.8	346.9
Fracture	800–829	65.9	16.2	21.3	58.7	68.6
Neuroses and nonpsychotic disorders	300–309	47.5	7.1	59.8	56.6	274.1
Cerebrovascular disease	430–438	40.8	*0.9	*3.3	34.7	144.1
Arthritis and rheumatism	710–718	34.6	*1.4	11.4	59.8	59.6
Psychoses	290–299	32.9	*1.1	35.2	49.6	81.3
Cholelithiasis (gallstones)	574	32.2	*0.3	25.5	55.5	129.1
Diabetes mellitus	250	32.0	*2.9	10.9	55.1	31.6
Benign neoplasms	210–228	31.8	*3.1	36.1	56.1	127.9
Pneumonia	480–486	31.3	23.7	10.1	30.1	*5.3
Disorders of menstruation	626	20.0	*0.6	30.6	28.4	21.1
Displacement of intervertebral disc	725	18.6	*0.2	19.2	37.3	52.3
Bronchitis, emphysema, asthma	490–493	17.7	8.3	7.7	30.0	101.7
Diseases of arteries, arterioles, capillaries	440–448	17.4	*0.3	*2.1	21.9	44.6
Diseases of central nervous system	320–349	17.2	9.2	11.9	22.0	21.8
Sprains and strains	840–848	15.5	*3.9	17.6	21.2	79.8
Eye diseases and conditions	360–379	15.3	*3.0	*3.2	18.5	43.9
Ulcer	531–534	14.5	*0.6	7.9	27.8	*7.4
Congenital anomalies	740–759	9.6	14.1	7.6	9.8	25.0
Hypertension	400, 401, 403	9.5	*0.5	4.9	20.9	

¹ Diagnostic groupings and code number inclusions are based on the *Eighth Revision International Classification of Diseases, Adapted for Use in the United States.* Codes 760–771, 773, and 779 are not used in the Hospital Discharge Survey.

NOTE: Rankings are based on number of days care. Rates are based on the average annual civilian noninstitutionalized population.

SOURCE: Division of Health Resources Utilization Statistics, National Center for Health Statistics: Data from the Hospital Discharge Survey.

Average length of stay for patients discharged from non-Federal short-stay hospitals, according to age, sex, leading diagnostic category, and ICDA code: United States, average annual 1975–76

(Data are based on a sample of hospital records)

First-listed diagnosis and ICDA code	All ages	Age			
		Under 15 years	15–44 years	45–64 years	65 years and over
		Number of days per discharge			
Both sexes					
All diagnoses	7.6	4.5	5.6	8.9	11.5
Diseases of the heart --- 390–398, 402,404, 410–414, 420–429	10.6	8.0	8.4	9.9	11.4
Ischemic heart disease --- 410–414	10.9	15.8	9.1	10.1	11.6
Malignant neoplasms --- 140–209	12.9	9.3	9.5	13.0	14.0
Fracture --- 800–829	11.1	6.2	8.6	10.9	16.7
Delivery --- 650–662	4.0	4.5	4.0	5.6	...
Neuroses and nonpsychotic disorders --- 300–309	9.0	9.0	8.6	8.6	11.9
Cerebrovascular disease --- 430–438	13.2	10.8	11.4	12.4	13.7
Pneumonia --- 480–486	9.1	5.9	7.6	9.9	12.4
Psychoses --- 290–299	16.4	*29.9	15.1	17.2	19.0
Diabetes mellitus --- 250	10.3	7.0	7.4	10.6	12.2
Arthritis and rheumatism --- 710–718	10.9	7.6	8.5	10.1	13.4
Cholelithiasis (gallstones) --- 574	10.2	*9.4	8.4	10.0	13.2
Diseases of arteries, arterioles, capillaries --- 440–448	14.4	*6.5	9.9	13.2	15.7
Displacement of intervertebral disc --- 725	11.4	*14.2	10.7	11.7	14.2
Benign neoplasms --- 210–228	5.9	3.8	5.4	6.4	7.8
Bronchitis, emphysema, asthma --- 490–493	7.4	4.5	5.9	8.3	10.2
Diseases of central nervous system --- 320–349	11.4	8.7	10.0	11.8	15.4
Ulcer --- 531–534	9.3	6.1	7.1	9.4	11.9
Sprains and strains --- 840–848	7.6	12.9	6.9	8.0	9.3
Eye diseases and conditions --- 360–379	4.7	2.5	4.2	5.0	5.3
Inguinal hernia --- 550, 552	5.5	2.7	5.0	6.0	8.1
Hyperplasia of prostate --- 600	10.5	*10.0	*25.3	8.5	11.3
Congenital anomalies --- 740–759	6.5	6.0	5.6	9.0	10.6
Disorders of menstruation --- 626	3.8	*3.4	3.8	3.7	3.9
Intercranial injury --- 850–854	5.7	3.4	5.7	8.7	9.7
Appendicitis --- 540–543	6.1	5.6	5.5	10.1	11.2
Lacerations --- 870–907	5.3	3.9	5.1	6.3	7.8
Gastritis and duodenitis --- 535	5.9	3.3	5.2	6.3	8.0
Hypertension --- 400,401,403	7.0	*10.1	6.3	7.0	7.7
Male					
All diagnoses	8.2	4.5	6.7	8.9	11.3
Diseases of the heart --- 390–398, 402, 404, 410–414, 420–429	10.3	6.3	8.7	9.9	11.1
Ischemic heart disease --- 410–414	10.5	*11.2	9.2	10.2	11.2

Diagnosis	Code					
Malignant neoplasms	140–209	13.1	9.4	10.3	13.2	13.6
Fracture	800–829	9.6	6.3	8.5	10.1	17.2
Neuroses and nonpsychotic disorders	300–309	8.8	9.6	8.4	8.5	11.7
Cerebrovascular disease	430–438	13.2	*11.5	11.3	12.5	13.6
Pneumonia	480–486	8.7	5.8	7.2	9.7	12.0
Hyperplasia of prostate	600	10.5	*10.0	*25.3	8.5	11.3
Diseases of arteries, arterioles, capillaries	440–448	14.6	*6.2	11.0	12.8	16.3
Inguinal hernia	550, 552	5.6	2.7	5.0	6.0	8.1
Psychoses	290–299	14.9	*34.2	13.9	15.6	17.3
Displacement of intervertebral disc	725	10.6	*20.5	9.9	11.2	13.9
Ulcer	531–534	9.2	*5.0	7.0	9.2	12.1
Diabetes mellitus	250	10.0	6.6	7.4	10.5	11.8
Bronchitis, emphysema, asthma	490–493	7.4	4.7	6.1	8.1	10.1
Diseases of central nervous system	320–349	12.0	8.6	12.1	12.0	15.6
Arthritis and rheumatism	710–718	9.5	7.7	6.9	9.1	12.5
Sprains and strains	840–848	6.7	*4.2	6.4	7.4	9.0
Lacerations	870–907	5.1	4.0	5.3	5.2	6.5
Intercranial injury	850–854	5.4	3.0	5.7	8.4	10.3
Cholelithiasis (gallstones)	574	10.9	*1.5	8.4	10.3	13.2
Eye diseases and conditions	360–379	4.6	2.8	4.1	5.1	5.1
Congenital anomalies	740–759	6.7	6.1	6.3	8.4	11.1
Female						
All diagnoses		7.3	4.5	5.2	8.9	11.7
Diseases of the heart	390–398, 402, 404, 410–414, 420–429	10.9	10.4	8.0	9.9	11.7
Ischemic heart disease	410–414	11.3	*21.4	8.7	9.9	12.0
Delivery	650–662	4.0	4.5	4.0	5.6	...
Malignant neoplasms	140–209	12.8	9.1	9.1	12.9	14.3
Fracture	800–829	12.6	6.1	8.7	11.5	16.6
Neuroses and nonpsychotic disorders	300–309	9.3	8.5	8.9	8.8	12.1
Cerebrovascular disease	430–438	13.3	*10.2	11.4	12.2	13.7
Arthritis and rheumatism	710–718	11.8	7.4	9.8	10.8	13.8
Psychoses	290–299	17.5	*25.0	16.1	18.0	20.0
Cholelithiasis (gallstones)	574	10.0	*10.6	8.4	9.9	13.2
Diabetes mellitus	250	10.6	7.3	7.4	10.7	12.4
Benign neoplasms	210–228	5.9	3.9	5.3	6.5	7.9
Pneumonia	480–486	9.5	6.0	7.9	10.1	12.8
Disorders of menstruation	626	3.8	*3.4	3.8	3.7	3.9
Displacement of intervertebral disc	725	12.3	*9.7	11.8	12.2	14.4
Bronchitis, emphysema, asthma	490–493	7.4	4.2	5.7	8.5	10.4
Diseases of arteries, arterioles, capillaries	440–448	14.0	*6.9	8.7	13.9	14.9
Diseases of central nervous system	320–349	10.7	8.8	8.4	11.7	15.2
Sprains and strains	840–848	8.5	*26.2	7.6	8.6	9.5
Eye diseases and conditions	360–379	4.9	2.3	4.3	5.0	5.4
Ulcer	531–534	9.5	*7.2	7.3	9.7	11.6
Congenital anomalies	740–759	6.3	5.7	5.2	9.6	10.2
Hypertension	400, 401, 403	7.1	*11.5	6.0	7.1	7.8

¹ Diagnostic groupings and code number inclusions are based on the *Eighth Revision International Classification of Diseases, Adapted for Use in the United States.* Codes 760–771, 773, and 779 are not used in the Hospital Discharge Survey.

NOTE: Rankings are based on number of days of care.

SOURCE: Division of Health Resources Utilization Statistics, National Center for Health Statistics: Data from the Hospital Discharge Survey.

Discharges, days of care, and average length of stay in non-Federal short-stay hospitals, according to color, age, and family income: United States, average annual 1975–76

(Data are based on a sample of hospital records and household interviews of a sample of the civilian noninstitutionalized population)

Item and family income	Total					White					All other				
	All ages	Under 15 years	15–44 years	45–64 years	65 years and over	All ages	Under 15 years	15–44 years	45–64 years	65 years and over	All ages	Under 15 years	15–44 years	45–64 years	65 years and over
Discharges	Number per 1,000 population														
All incomes[1]	163	71	154	195	361	164	73	149	195	370	159	61	191	193	271
Less than $5,000	230	96	202	283	382	237	100	182	291	397	210	89	258	260	292
$5,000–$9,999	185	79	187	218	342	192	85	185	221	351	153	59	196	195	214
$10,000–$14,999	155	76	156	190	406	157	79	156	191	405	137	45	162	168	439
$15,000 or more	129	56	125	171	338	130	58	123	172	339	94	30	153	157	*305
Days of care															
All incomes[1]	1,245	322	865	1,733	4,167	1,219	312	808	1,652	4,161	1,418	372	1,232	2,435	4,231
Less than $5,000	2,189	579	1,282	3,191	4,442	2,195	580	1,178	2,901	4,364	2,170	578	1,567	4,084	4,919
$5,000–$9,999	1,419	351	998	2,046	3,888	1,464	378	949	1,994	3,975	1,190	257	1,225	2,407	2,579
$10,000–$14,999	1,064	301	682	1,625	4,658	1,065	309	816	1,633	4,674	1,057	*239	1,122	1,529	*4,364
$15,000 or more	852	210	692	1,304	3,783	842	206	668	1,304	3,725	984	*262	998	1,305	*5,014
Average length of stay	Number of days per discharge														
All incomes[1]	7.6	4.5	5.6	8.9	11.5	7.4	4.3	5.4	8.5	11.2	8.9	6.1	6.5	12.6	15.6
Less than $5,000	9.5	6.0	6.3	11.3	11.6	9.3	5.8	6.5	10.0	11.0	10.3	6.5	6.1	15.7	16.8
$5,000–$9,999	7.7	4.4	5.3	9.4	11.4	7.6	4.4	5.1	9.0	11.3	7.8	4.4	6.3	12.3	12.1
$10,000–$14,999	6.9	4.0	5.4	8.6	11.5	6.8	3.4	5.2	8.5	11.5	7.7	*5.3	6.9	9.1	*9.9
$15,000 or more	6.6	3.8	5.5	7.6	11.2	6.5	3.9	5.4	7.6	11.0	10.5	*8.7	6.5	8.3	*16.4

[1] Includes unknown income.

NOTE: Excludes newborn infants. Rates are based on the civilian noninstitutionalized population.

SOURCES: Division of Health Interview Statistics, National Center for Health Statistics: Data from the Health Interview Survey; Division of Health Resources Utilization Statistics, National Center for Health Statistics: Data from the Hospital Discharge Survey.

Operations per 1,000 population for inpatients discharged from non-Federal short-stay hospitals, according to sex, age group, leading surgical category, and ICDA Seventh and Eighth Revision codes: United States, average annual 1965–66 and 1975–76

(Data are based on a sample of hospital records)

Age group and leading surgical category[1]	ICDA codes[2]		Sex					
			Both sexes		Male		Female	
	Seventh Revision	Eighth Revision	1965–66 average[3]	1975–76 average	1965–66 average	1975–76 average	1965–66 average	1975–76 average
			Operations per 1,000 population					
Under 15 years								
All operations[4]	---	---	41.1	40.7	47.3	46.4	34.5	34.7
Tonsillectomy with or without adenoidectomy	27.1–27.2	21.1–21.2	16.2	8.5	16.3	8.5	16.0	8.6
Myringotomy		17.0	---	3.9	---	4.5	---	3.4
Repair of inguinal hernia	40.0–40.1	38.2–38.3	2.3	2.0	4.0	3.4	0.6	0.6
Closed reduction of fracture without fixation	[5]82.0	[5]82.0	2.2	1.9	2.9	2.4	1.5	1.4
Appendectomy[6]	45.1	41.1	2.3	1.8	2.5	2.0	2.1	1.7
Adenoidectomy without tonsillectomy	27.3	21.3	0.6	1.5	0.7	1.7	0.5	1.4
Resection and recession of eye muscle	11.2–11.3	10.5–10.6	1.1	1.0	1.2	1.0	1.1	1.0
Dilation of urethra	64.5	57.5	0.5	0.9	*0.2	*0.3	0.8	1.5
Excision of lesion of skin and subcutaneous tissue	89.1	92.1–92.2	1.0	0.9	1.0	0.9	1.0	0.8
15–44 years								
All operations[4]	---	---	87.1	100.6	54.8	56.9	116.2	141.8
Biopsy		A1–A2	---	4.1	---	1.7	---	6.3
Tonsillectomy with or without adenoidectomy	27.1–27.2	21.1–21.2	2.8	2.2	2.3	1.4	3.3	2.9
Excision of lesion of skin and subcutaneous tissue	89.1	92.1–92.2	3.5	1.9	3.6	1.7	3.3	2.2
Appendectomy[6]	45.1	41.1	2.6	1.9	2.7	1.9	2.5	1.9
Cholecystectomy	53.5	43.5	1.7	1.8	0.6	0.5	2.7	3.0
Exploratory laparotomy	41.1	39.1	1.2	1.5	0.7	0.7	1.6	2.1
Repair of inguinal hernia	40.0–40.1	38.2–38.3	1.7	1.4	3.2	2.6	0.4	0.3
Rhinoplasty and repair of nose	21.4	19.3	0.6	1.3	0.6	1.2	0.7	1.4
Surgical removal of teeth	24.2	99.4	1.0	1.3	0.7	0.9	1.3	1.6
Excision of semilunar cartilage of knee joint	83.5	86.5	0.7	1.2	1.1	2.0	*0.2	0.6
Partial mastectomy	38.1	65.2	1.6	1.2	*0.1	*0.1	3.0	2.3
Suture of skin or mucous membrane	89.4	92.5	1.8	1.2	2.9	1.8	0.9	0.6
Closed reduction of fracture without fixation	[5]82.0	[5]82.0	1.5	1.1	2.3	1.6	0.8	0.6

45–64 years

Operation	Code	Code						
All operations[4]	---	---	97.9	122.9	82.4	100.8	112.0	143.1
Biopsy		A1–A2	---	9.4	---	6.5	---	12.1
Repair of inguinal hernia	40.0–40.1	38.2–38.3	4.4	4.1	8.5	8.0	0.6	0.6
Cholecystectomy	53.5	43.5	4.0	4.0	2.2	2.4	5.6	5.4
Excision of lesion of skin and subcutaneous tissue	89.1	92.1–92.2	3.8	3.4	3.7	3.2	3.9	3.6
Cardiac catheterization	30.4–30.5	30.2	0.3	2.8	*0.3	4.0	*0.3	1.6
Extraction of lens	[5]17.3–17.5	[5]14.4–14.6	1.2	1.9	1.3	2.0	1.2	1.9
Hemorrhoidectomy	49.3	51.3	3.0	1.9	3.4	2.1	2.6	1.7
Partial mastectomy	38.1	65.2	1.6	1.7	*0.1	*0.1	3.0	3.1
Exploratory laparotomy	41.1	39.1	1.5	1.6	1.4	1.3	1.6	1.9
Excision of intervertebral cartilage	83.4	86.4	0.8	1.6	1.0	1.8	0.7	1.3
Dilation of urethra	64.5	57.5	0.7	1.4	0.8	1.2	0.6	1.6

65 years and over

Operation	Code	Code						
All operations[4]	---	---	107.5	154.9	119.6	178.9	97.7	138.2
Biopsy		A1–A2	---	13.9	---	16.0	---	12.4
Extraction of lens	[5]17.3–17.5	[5]14.4–14.6	5.8	10.9	5.0	9.3	6.4	11.9
Reduction of fracture with fixation	[5]82.2	[5]82.2	5.4	6.8	2.9	3.6	7.4	9.0
Repair of inguinal hernia	40.0–40.1	38.2–38.3	4.7	5.2	9.3	11.2	1.1	1.0
Cholecystectomy	53.5	43.5	4.3	4.7	3.1	4.0	5.3	5.2
Excision of lesion of skin and subcutaneous tissue	89.1	92.1–92.2	3.5	4.0	3.8	4.5	3.2	3.7
Insertion or replacement of electronic heart device		30.4–30.5	---	3.7	---	4.6	---	3.0
Resection of small intestine or colon	46.2–46.5	47.4–47.6	2.3	3.4	1.8	3.5	2.6	3.3
Dilation of urethra	64.5	57.5	1.2	3.2	1.9	4.8	*0.6	2.0
Local excision and destruction of lesion of bladder	63.1	56.1–56.2	2.1	3.1	3.4	5.6	*1.0	1.4
Exploratory laparotomy	41.1	39.1	2.2	2.7	1.9	2.6	2.4	2.8
Closed reduction of fracture without fixation	[5]82.0	[5]82.0	2.9	2.5	1.7	1.2	3.9	3.4

[1] Operations applicable to one sex are not listed in this table. See table 109.

[2] Surgical groupings and code number inclusions are based on the *Seventh Revision and Eighth Revision International Classification of Diseases, Adapted for Use in the United States.*

[3] Includes data for which sex was not stated.

[4] Includes operations not listed in table, including operations applicable to one sex.

[5] These codes are modifications of ICDA codes for use in the Hospital Discharge Survey.

[6] Limited to estimated number of appendectomies, excluding those performed incidental to other abdominal surgery.

NOTE: Excludes newborn infants. Rates are based on the civilian noninstitutionalized population.

SOURCE: Division of Health Resources Utilization Statistics, National Center for Health Statistics: Data from the Hospital Discharge Survey.

Operations applicable to one sex per 1,000 population for inpatients discharged from non-Federal short-stay hospitals, according to age, sex, selected surgical category, and ICDA Seventh and Eighth Revision codes: United States, average annual 1965-66 and 1975-76

(Data are based on a sample of hospital records)

Sex and selected surgical category	ICDA codes[1]		Age									
	Seventh Revision	Eighth Revision	All ages		Under 15 years		15-44 years		45-64 years		65 years and over	
			1965-66 average[2]	1975-76 average	1965-66 average	1975-76 average	1965-66 average	1975-76 average	1965-66 average	1975-76 average	1965-66 average	1975-76 average
Operation applicable to males						Operations per 1,000 males						
Prostatectomy	66.1–66.3	58.1–58.3	2.2	2.6	*0.0	*0.0	*0.1	*0.0	*3.0	3.7	18.5	21.4
Operations applicable to females						Operations per 1,000 females						
Dilation and curettage of uterus	72.8	70.3, 74.7	7.8	9.8	*0.1	*0.1	12.9	15.2	11.3	13.3	3.0	3.6
Hysterectomy	72.3–72.6, [3]72.9	69.1–69.5	5.0	6.5	*—	*0.1	7.5	8.9	8.6	10.6	2.9	3.2
Oophorectomy; salpingo-oophorectomy	70.2–70.5	67.2–67.5	2.9	4.2	*0.0	*0.1	4.5	5.3	4.9	8.0	1.4	2.2
Ligation and division of fallopian tubes, bilateral	71.5	68.5	0.7	3.6	*—	*0.0	1.7	8.2	*0.0	*0.3	*—	*0.0
Cesarean section	78.0–78.4	77	1.7	3.3	*—	*0.1	4.3	7.4	*0.0	*0.0	...	...
Dilation and curettage after delivery or abortion	77.1	78.1	3.1	2.7	*0.0	*0.1	7.6	6.1	*0.1	*0.1	...	...
Repair of obstetrical laceration	77.2–77.3	78.2–78.3	1.9	2.1	*0.0	*0.1	4.8	4.8	*0.0	*0.0	*—	*0.0
Plastic repair of cystocele and/or rectocele	74.4	71.4	1.6	1.7	*—	*0.0	1.6	1.5	3.5	3.7	2.8	2.1
Salpingectomy, bilateral	71.2	68.2	0.4	1.5	*0.0	*0.0	0.9	3.4	*0.2	*0.3	*0.0	*0.0

[1] Surgical groupings and code number inclusions are based on the *Seventh Revision* and *Eighth Revision International Classification of Diseases, Adapted for Use in the United States.*

[2] Includes data for which age was not stated.

[3] The code 72.9 has been added for the Hospital Discharge Survey to include not otherwise specified hysterectomy.

SOURCE: Division of Health Resources Utilization Statistics, National Center for Health Statistics: Data from the Hospital Discharge Survey.

Inpatient Care in Long-Term Facilities

Inpatient long-term care facilities include long-stay psychiatric and other hospitals (i.e., hospitals with an average length of stay of 30 days or more), nursing homes, facilities for the mentally retarded, homes for dependent children, homes or resident schools for the emotionally disturbed, resident facilities for drug abusers or alcoholics, and various other types of institutions. Patients in these facilities need treatment or management of a chronic condition or are too incapacitated to care for themselves.

The Survey of Institutionalized Persons (SIP), conducted by the Census Bureau in 1976, provides data on the utilization of nursing homes and other long-term care institutions, excluding long-stay hospitals and correctional institutions. Although data from this survey are for 1976, the sample for the survey was taken from the 1973 Master Facility Inventory, and facilities newly opened after 1973 were not included. As a result, the SIP estimates are slight undercounts.

Two-thirds of the estimated 1.6 million residents in the institutions surveyed in 1976 were 65 years of age and over. There were more men than women under 65 years of age, but nearly 70 percent of institutionalized people 65 years of age and over were women.

Seventy-nine percent of institutionalized people 65 years of age and over and 68 percent of those 18–64 years of age entered institutions primarily because they needed medical or nursing care. Another 13 percent of people 65 years of age and over and 17 percent of those 18–64 years of age entered because their families were unable to care for them. For residents under 18 years of age, 38 percent entered institutions because they

needed medical or nursing care, and 31 percent were admitted because their families were unable to care for them. Another 14 percent of those under 18 years of age were committed or assigned to the institution.

The services needed and received by people in institutions in 1976 varied by age. The need for medical and nursing care rose sharply with age, as did the proportion of those needing these services who received them at least once a month. Psychiatric care and physical therapy were required more by younger people in institutions than by the elderly. However, the proportions of those needing these services who received them were higher among the elderly. The need for educational training and social workers declined with increasing age.

The nursing home is a relatively new institution in the United States. Prior to the 1930's, few nursing homes existed. With the enactment of the Social Security Act in 1935 and the 1965 amendments to the Social Security Act (i.e., Medicare and Medicaid), Federal funds became available for the health care of the elderly and the poor. Today, nursing homes provide most of the long-term inpatient care in the United States. About two-thirds of the beds in long-term facilities are in nursing homes.

According to preliminary data from the National Nursing Home Survey, there were 1,287,400 residents in nursing homes in 1977. This NCHS survey includes data from all types of nursing homes, including domiciliary care homes and personal care homes without nursing, which were excluded from the 1973–74 National Nursing Home Survey. Eighty-five percent of nursing home residents in 1977 were 65 years of age and over.

Seventy-one percent of all residents were women, while only 59 percent of the U.S. population 65 years of age and over in 1977 were women. Since women, on the average, live longer than men, an elderly woman is

---

NOTE: Unless otherwise noted, data are from the ongoing data-collection systems of the National Center for Health Statistics. In many instances the data have been published in the *Vital and Health Statistics* series.

more likely than an elderly man to be widowed and thus be without the help and companionship a spouse can provide. In 1977, 58 percent of all nursing home residents were widowed. Data on marital status by sex are not available for 1977, but in 1973–74, 73 percent of female residents and 42 percent of male residents were widowed. Another possible reason for the high proportion of women in nursing homes is that elderly women tend to have lower incomes than elderly men and, as a result, they may be less able to pay for better housing, food, and possibly outside help if they remain at home.

In 1976, there were just under a million discharges from nursing homes. Three-fourths of the patients discharged were alive. However, a breakdown by age shows that about 90 percent of the discharges under 65 years of age were alive, while only 65 percent of the discharges 85 years of age and over were alive.

Thirty-seven percent of the residents in nursing homes in 1977 had diseases of the circulatory system as their primary diagnosis at their last examination; about half of these had arteriosclerosis. Another 22 percent of nursing home residents were diagnosed as having mental disorders and senility without psychosis.

More than half of the residents in nursing homes in 1977 had been in another health facility prior to their admission to the nursing home, and more than half of these had been in general or short-stay hospitals. Sixty-four percent of the residents in nursing homes in 1977 had been in the home for at least a year, and 31 percent had been in for 3 years or more. However, of the patients discharged in 1976, 52 percent had been in the home for less than 3 months. Less than 10 percent of patients discharged from nursing homes in 1976 had been in the home for 3 years or more.

The disparity between the length of time spent in the facility by residents and discharged patients suggests that there are two separate groups of persons who use nursing homes—those admitted for relatively long periods of time because there is little chance for improvement in their chronic problems, and those admitted for relatively short periods of time because they need recuperative care.

Most long-stay hospital care is received in long-stay psychiatric hospitals. More than three-fourths of all inpatient days spent in long-stay hospitals in 1976 were spent in psychiatric hospitals.

The National Institute of Mental Health (NIMH) provides data on inpatient and outpatient use of all types of psychiatric facilities, including short-stay and long-stay psychiatric hospitals, psychiatric units of general hospitals, residential treatment centers, federally-funded community mental health centers, freestanding outpatient clinics, and other mental health facilities.

As a result of the development of community-based programs for the diagnosis, treatment, and rehabilitation of persons with mental disorders, the locus of care for persons with such disorders has shifted from the large State mental hospitals to community-based facilities, particularly outpatient psychiatric services and community mental health centers. In 1955, 1.7 million episodes of care were provided by the facilities that report to NIMH. Of these, 49 percent were provided by State and county mental hospitals, 23 percent by outpatient psychiatric services, and 16 percent by non-Federal general hospital inpatient psychiatric units. By 1975, the number of episodes of care provided by all facilities increased to 6.4 million. Of these, only 9 percent were provided by State and county mental hospitals and 9 percent by non-Federal general hospital inpatient psychiatric units. However, 72 percent were provided by outpatient psychiatric service facilities.

More than a hundred million inpatient days of care were spent in mental health facilities in 1975, but this was 50 million less than in 1971. Seventy-eight percent of the inpatient days in 1971 and 67 percent of the days in 1975 were spent in State and county mental hospitals. Less than 8 percent of the inpatient days in all mental health facilities in 1971 were spent in the psychiatric units of general hospitals, but this figure increased to more than 12 percent in 1975.

Although the number of inpatient days in mental health facilities decreased between 1971 and 1975, the number of inpatient additions (new admissions, readmissions, or people who return from leave) increased 19 percent. This reflects the decreasing average length of stay for psychiatric inpatients. Most of the increase in inpatient additions was accounted for by a 211-percent increase in inpatient additions to federally-funded community mental health centers and freestanding outpatient clinics.

Facilities for the mentally retarded had about 163,000 residents in 1976, a decrease of nearly 40,000 from 1971. Although the admission rate has remained relatively stable since 1946, the net release rate of the resident patient population in mental retardation facilities began to rise in the late 1960's and has continued to increase. The introduction of new methods of treatment and management during this period and policies of deinstitutionalization contributed to this trend.

Despite the trend in mental health care away from institutionalization and toward outpatient psychiatric care, increased need for long-term health care can be expected over the next few years as the number of elderly people in the United States increases. Planning for appropriate care and the means to pay for it are of high priority. Providing alternative arrangements for care on a non-institutionalized basis is also of considerable concern.

Nursing home residents for 1977 and nursing home discharges and percent discharged alive for 1976, according to age, sex, color, and marital status: United States

(Data are based on resident records in a sample survey of nursing homes)

Age, sex, color, and marital status	1977 residents		1976 discharges	
	Number	Percent distribution	Number	Percent discharged alive
Total	1,287,400	100.0	973,100	74.2
Age				
Under 65 years	189,500	14.7	135,400	89.9
65–74 years	202,000	15.7	161,200	73.4
75–84 years	470,600	36.6	381,800	75.9
85 years and over	425,300	33.0	294,700	65.3
Sex				
Male	369,400	28.7	349,700	74.8
Female	918,000	71.3	623,400	73.9
Color				
White[1]	1,180,300	91.7	---	---
All other	107,100	8.3	---	---
Marital status[2]				
Married	160,800	12.5	192,100	80.1
Widowed	743,700	57.8	552,300	71.8
Divorced or separated	87,600	6.8	84,700	86.2
Never married	265,900	20.7	106,300	69.4
Unknown	*29,400	*2.3	37,700	*65.8

[1] Excludes Spanish-American (Hispanic).
[2] For resident data, marital status at time of data collection. For discharge data, marital status at time of discharge.

NOTE: Data are provisional.

SOURCE: National Center for Health Statistics: Comparison of nursing home residents and discharges, 1977 National Nursing Home Survey, by E. Hing and A. Zappolo. *Advance Data from Vital and Health Statistics,* No. 29. DHEW Pub. No. (PHS) 78–1250. Public Health Service, Hyattsville, Md., May 1978.

Institutionalized population, according to age, color, and sex: United States, 1976

(Data are based on resident records in a sample survey of institutions)

Color and sex	Institutionalized population							
	All ages[1]	Under 18 years	18–64 years	65 years and over	All ages[1]	Under 18 years	18–64 years	65 years and over
	Number of persons				Persons per 1,000 resident population			
Total[2,3] _____	1,550,100	151,530	334,120	1,027,850	7.2	2.3	2.6	44.8
Male[2]_____	596,820	85,410	182,420	322,530	5.7	2.6	2.9	34.4
Female[2]_____	947,880	64,750	151,250	703,150	8.6	2.0	2.3	51.8
White[3] _____	1,410,020	115,350	292,750	970,070	7.6	2.1	2.6	46.6
Male _____	524,850	63,580	158,210	299,040	5.8	2.3	2.9	35.4
Female _____	885,170	51,760	134,540	671,030	9.3	1.9	2.4	54.2
All other[3] _____	134,670	34,810	40,920	55,610	4.7	3.2	2.6	26.4
Male _____	71,970	21,820	24,210	23,490	5.3	4.0	3.3	25.9
Female _____	62,710	12,990	16,710	32,120	4.2	2.4	2.0	26.8

[1] Includes unknown age.
[2] Includes unknown color.
[3] Includes unknown sex.

NOTE: Excludes persons in long-stay hospitals and penal and/or juvenile detention facilities.

SOURCE: U.S. Bureau of the Census: *Current Population Reports.* Series P-23, No. 69. Washington. U.S. Government Printing Office, June 1978.

Institutionalized population, according to age and primary reason for admission to facility for institutional care: United States, 1976

(Data are based on resident records or reporting by staff in a sample survey of institutions)

Population and primary reason for admission	Age			
	All ages[1]	Under 18 years	18-64 years	65 years and over
	Number of persons			
Institutionalized population[2] _____	1,550,100	151,530	334,120	1,027,850
	Percent distribution			
All admissions[2] _____	100.0	100.0	100.0	100.0
Needed medical or nursing care _____	72.3	37.9	68.5	79.0
No money or resources to keep person at home _____	0.6	1.1	1.0	0.5
Committed or assigned to facility _____	2.6	14.4	4.5	0.3
Family unable to care for person _____	15.5	30.6	16.7	12.7
Education and training _____	1.2	8.4	1.9	0.0
Other reasons _____	6.3	7.0	5.3	6.5

[1] Includes unknown age.
[2] Includes residents for which reason for admission is unknown.

NOTE: Excludes persons in long-stay hospitals and penal and/or juvenile detention facilities.

SOURCE: U.S. Bureau of the Census: *Current Population Reports.* Series P-23, No. 69. Washington. U.S. Government Printing Office, June 1978.

Services needed and received by the institutionalized population, according to age and type of service: United States, 1976

(Data are based on reporting by staff in a sample survey of institutions)

Type of service	All ages[1]		Age					
			Under 18 years		18–64 years		65 years and over	
	Percent of population needing specified services	Percent of those needing services who are receiving them[2]	Percent of population needing specified services	Percent of those needing services who are receiving them[2]	Percent of population needing specified services	Percent of those needing services who are receiving them[2]	Percent of population needing specified services	Percent of those needing services who are receiving them[2]
Medical	75.2	73.9	49.7	57.9	70.6	65.1	80.2	77.6
Nursing	81.0	99.7	44.8	94.7	68.7	98.6	90.6	99.7
Psychiatric	10.4	70.9	32.3	68.9	24.8	66.9	2.5	86.4
Physical/speech therapy	19.6	74.1	30.1	75.4	23.4	61.3	17.1	79.7
Occupational therapy	15.2	82.4	14.1	70.2	18.8	74.0	14.4	87.5
Educational training	12.7	95.0	76.7	98.4	21.6	90.9	0.5	82.0
Social work	40.4	71.7	60.3	80.8	50.1	67.8	34.4	71.0
Other services	37.4	93.5	41.0	94.6	43.7	93.2	35.6	93.6

[1] Includes unknown age.
[2] Receiving services at least once a month.

NOTE: See table 111 for number of institutionalized persons. Excludes persons in long-stay hospitals and penal and/or juvenile detention facilities.

SOURCE: U.S. Bureau of the Census: Current Population Reports. Series P–23, No. 69. Washington. U.S. Government Printing Office, June 1978.

Nursing home residents for 1977 and nursing home discharges for 1976, according to selected characteristics: United States

(Data are based on resident records and information from a caregiver in a sample survey of nursing homes)

Selected characteristic	Number	Percent distribution
RESIDENTS, 1977		
Total	1,287,400	100.0
Primary diagnosis at last examination		
Diseases of the circulatory system	477,400	37.1
Congestive heart failure	57,100	4.4
Arteriosclerosis	235,600	18.3
Hypertension	45,300	3.5
Stroke	102,300	7.9
Mental disorders and senility without psychosis	287,600	22.3
Psychosis, including senile	85,000	6.6
Chronic brain syndrome	91,600	7.1
Mental retardation	59,500	4.6
Other or unknown diagnoses	522,400	40.6
Diabetes	77,200	6.0
Fractures	40,900	3.2
Diseases of the nervous system	60,700	4.7
Arthritis or rheumatism	57,100	4.4
Living arrangement prior to admission		
Private or semiprivate residence	529,100	41.1
With others	325,000	25.2
Another health facility[1]	694,800	54.0
Another nursing home	164,600	12.8
General or short-stay hospital	405,700	31.5
Mental hospital	80,000	6.2
Unknown or other arrangement	63,500	4.9
Length of stay[2]		
Less than 3 months	167,000	13.0
3 to less than 6 months	126,000	9.8
6 to less than 12 months	175,400	13.6
1 to less than 3 years	416,200	32.3
3 years or more	402,800	31.3
DISCHARGES, 1976		
Total	973,100	100.0
Length of stay		
Less than 3 months	504,400	51.8
3 to less than 6 months	116,800	12.0
6 to less than 12 months	110,300	11.3
1 to less than 3 years	148,200	15.2
3 years or more	93,400	9.6

[1] 347,300 of these residents, admitted from another health facility, had gone to that facility from a private or semiprivate residence.

[2] For residents in 1977, time interval between admission date for each resident and survey date.

NOTE: Data are provisional.

SOURCE: National Center for Health Statistics: Comparison of nursing home residents and discharges, 1977 National Nursing Home Survey, by E. Hing and A. Zappolo. *Advance Data from Vital and Health Statistics,* No. 29. DHEW Pub. No. (PHS) 78–1250. Public Health Service, Hyattsville, Md., May 17, 1978.

Nursing homes and beds, according to type of care provided and ownership of home: United States, 1971 and 1976

(Data are based on reporting by facilities)

Type of ownership	1971			1976[2]		
	All homes	Nursing care	Personal care and other[1]	All homes	Nursing care	Personal care and other[2]
Nursing homes			Number			
All ownerships	22,004	12,871	9,133	20,185	13,312	6,873
Government	1,368	872	496	1,369	1,058	311
Federal	67	18	49	85	62	23
State-local	1,301	854	447	1,284	996	288
Proprietary	17,049	9,963	7,086	15,153	9,657	5,496
Nonprofit	3,587	2,036	1,551	3,663	2,597	1,066
Church	912	500	412	986	716	270
Other	2,675	1,536	1,139	2,677	1,881	796
Beds in nursing homes						
All ownerships	1,201,598	917,707	283,891	1,406,778	1,173,519	233,259
Government	122,972	91,708	31,264	154,684	131,057	23,627
Federal	5,764	1,557	4,207	6,385	5,639	746
State-local	117,208	90,151	27,057	148,299	125,418	22,881
Proprietary	803,696	663,031	140,665	952,795	807,856	144,939
Nonprofit	274,930	162,968	111,962	299,299	234,606	64,693
Church	81,336	43,655	37,681	91,400	69,053	22,347
Other	193,594	119,313	74,281	207,899	165,553	42,346

[1] Includes personal care homes with nursing, personal care homes without nursing, and domiciliary care homes.
[2] Provisional data. The change from Federal to State data collection in 16 States may have introduced changes in data collection procedures, coverage, definitions, and concepts between 1973 and 1976.

SOURCES: National Center for Health Statistics: *Health Resources Statistics, Health Manpower and Health Facilities, 1974.* DHEW Pub. No. (HRA) 75–1509. Health Resources Administration. Washington. U.S. Government Printing Office, 1974; *Health Resources Statistics, Health Manpower and Health Facilities, 1976–77.* Public Health Service, DHEW, Hyattsville, Md. To be published.

Beds in nursing homes and beds per 1,000 resident population 65 years of age and over, according to type of home, geographic division, and State: United States, 1976

(Data are based on reporting by facilities)

Geographic division and State	Population 65 years and over in thousands	Number of beds	Type of home		
			Total	Nursing care	Personal care and other[1]
			Beds per 1,000 resident population		
United States	22,934	1,406,778	61.3	51.2	10.2
New England	1,400	102,647	73.3	56.9	16.4
Maine	128	8,644	67.5	50.5	17.0
New Hampshire	91	6,256	68.7	62.3	6.5
Vermont[2]	53	5,130	96.8	55.9	40.9
Massachusetts[2]	682	50,940	74.7	57.0	17.7
Rhode Island[2]	116	7,330	63.2	50.9	12.3
Connecticut	330	24,347	73.9	60.0	13.9
Middle Atlantic	4,259	201,144	47.2	38.3	8.9
New York	2,068	102,591	49.6	37.0	12.6
New Jersey	787	34,463	43.8	36.7	7.1
Pennsylvania[2]	1,404	64,090	45.6	41.3	4.4
East North Central	4,157	306,858	73.8	62.8	11.0
Ohio	1,089	64,096	58.9	53.0	5.8
Indiana	540	35,935	66.5	58.2	8.3
Illinois	1,171	87,805	75.0	63.0	12.0
Michigan[2]	834	66,416	79.6	60.9	18.7
Wisconsin[2]	523	52,606	100.6	90.3	10.3
West North Central	2,066	169,637	82.1	69.6	12.5
Minnesota[2]	445	43,036	96.7	81.9	14.8
Iowa	367	32,856	89.5	71.8	17.7
Missouri[2]	608	33,628	55.3	46.7	8.7
North Dakota	75	6,753	90.0	70.1	19.9
South Dakota	86	7,840	91.2	72.5	18.6
Nebraska[2]	196	23,022	117.5	108.8	8.7
Kansas	289	22,502	77.9	68.4	9.5
South Atlantic	3,707	153,602	41.4	33.6	7.9
Delaware	51	2,228	43.7	37.2	6.5
Maryland	350	18,874	53.9	47.3	6.7
District of Columbia	72	2,872	39.9	31.4	8.5

Virginia²	441	64.6	44.9	19.7
West Virginia	214	26.1	20.5	5.5
North Carolina²	513	47.6	25.7	21.9
South Carolina	240	36.0	33.9	2.1
Georgia	443	66.9	65.9	1.0
Florida	1,383	23.8	21.0	2.7
East South Central	1,473	46.7	39.4	7.3
Kentucky	373	55.1	36.8	18.3
Tennessee²	453	44.3	40.6	3.7
Alabama	388	49.7	45.0	4.7
Mississippi	259	34.5	32.8	1.8
West South Central	2,164	76.4	69.1	7.3
Arkansas	277	67.6	63.7	3.9
Louisiana	355	53.7	51.1	2.6
Oklahoma	339	77.0	73.5	3.5
Texas²	1,193	85.0	74.5	10.5
Mountain	880	56.5	50.0	6.5
Montana	77	68.8	61.0	7.8
Idaho²	81	59.5	49.1	10.4
Wyoming	34	52.7	45.5	7.2
Colorado²	218	104.2	94.1	10.1
New Mexico	94	32.4	25.9	6.4
Arizona²	235	25.2	23.2	2.0
Utah	94	48.6	42.5	6.1
Nevada	47	33.5	29.1	4.4
Pacific	2,830	66.8	52.9	13.9
Washington	374	80.4	70.7	9.7
Oregon	266	59.8	48.2	11.6
California	2,121	65.6	50.5	15.0
Alaska	9	86.9	76.7	10.2
Hawaii	60	52.9	42.1	10.8

¹ Includes personal care homes with nursing, personal care homes without nursing, and domiciliary care homes.

² The change from Federal to State Data collection in these States may have introduced changes in data collection procedures, coverage, definitions, and concepts between 1973 and 1976.

NOTE: Date are provisional.

SOURCE: National Center for Health Statistics: *Health Resources Statistics, Health Manpower and Health Facilities, 1976–77.* Public Health Service, DHEW, Hyattsville, Md. To be published.

Inpatient health facilities other than hospitals and nursing homes, according to selected characteristics and type of facility: United States, 1976

(Data are based on reporting by facilities)

Type of facility	Selected characteristic					
	Number of facilities	Number of beds	Number of inpatient days of care	Number of residents	Occupancy rate[1]	FTE[2] employees per 100 beds
All facilities	6,280	375,805	119,323,686	326,021	86.8	73.9
Mentally retarded	1,875	182,454	59,839,902	163,497	89.6	81.8
Emotionally disturbed	1,543	62,687	19,550,622	53,417	85.2	87.3
Dependent children	867	40,133	12,002,604	32,794	81.7	47.4
Drug abusers or alcoholics	883	28,156	8,208,282	22,427	79.7	41.3
Deaf and/or blind	125	19,041	6,272,508	17,138	90.0	57.3
Unwed mothers	105	3,055	779,946	2,131	69.8	47.5
Physically handicapped	87	4,599	1,343,220	3,670	79.8	126.6
Multipurpose	508	23,860	7,537,404	20,594	86.3	66.7
All others	287	11,820	3,789,198	10,353	87.6	76.8

[1] Percent of beds which are occupied.
[2] Full-time equivalent employees.

SOURCE: Division of Health Manpower and Facilities Statistics, National Center for Health Statistics: Data from the Master Facility Inventory.

Beds per 1,000 population in all hospitals and general hospitals: Selected countries, 1970 and most recent data year available

(Data are based on reporting by government administrations)

Country	1970		Most recent data year		
	All hospitals	General hospitals	Year	All hospitals	General hospitals
	Beds per 1,000 population			Beds per 1,000 population	
Canada	9.8	5.7	1975	9.2	5.7
United States	7.9	4.7	1976	6.7	4.9
Mexico	1.1	0.5	1974	1.2	0.8
Sweden	15.0	7.4	1975	15.1	7.2
England and Wales	9.2	---	1974	8.6	---
Netherlands	9.0	5.5	1976	---	4.8
German Democratic Republic	11.1	---	1976	10.7	8.5
German Federal Republic	11.1	6.5	1975	11.8	7.0
France	---	---	1974	---	8.1
Switzerland	11.2	6.1	1976	11.4	5.8
Italy	10.6	6.6	1974	10.5	7.4
Israel	5.9	3.4	1976	5.7	3.4
Japan	10.2	5.8	1975	10.4	6.4
Australia	12.0	---	1977	---	6.7

NOTE: Countries are grouped by continent. Definitions and inclusions of hospital beds may differ in various countries.

SOURCES: World Health Organization: *World Health Statistics Annual, 1970 and 1977*, Vol. III. Geneva. World Health Organization, 1974 and 1977; World Health Organization: Unpublished data; Bureau of Statistics, Office of the Prime Minister: *Japan Statistical Yearbook 1975 and 1977*. 25th and 27th ed. Tokyo. Printing Bureau, Ministry of Finance, 1975 and 1977.

Age Differences in Expenditures for Health Care

The age distribution of the population has a direct bearing on the amount and distribution of the Nation's health care expenditures. Per capita expenditures for people 65 years of age and over, nearly all of whom are covered by Medicare, are higher than per capita expenditures for those under 65 years of age. The difference between the two age groups generally reflects the more serious nature of illness and greater prevalence of chronic conditions among older people. They are hospitalized more frequently than younger people and they stay longer when they are admitted.

In fiscal year 1976, $120.4 billion were spent for personal health care services (i.e., the health services and supplies received directly by individuals). Personal health care estimates are derived by subtracting from total national health expenditures amounts devoted to research and medical facilities construction, administrative costs of government health programs, private fundraising activities for health, and retained earnings of private health insurers. Of the $120.4 billion spent, 15 percent or $17.9 billion was spent to care for people under 19 years of age, 56 percent or $67.7 billion for people 19–64 years of age, and 29 percent or $34.9 billion for people 65 years of age and over.

The average per capita health care bill during fiscal year 1976 was $1,521 in the oldest age group, $547 in the intermediate group, and $249 in the youngest group. The amount spent per capita for the elderly was 6 times that for the youngest population. Per capita nursing home expenditures for the elderly were 18 times greater than for people 19–64 years of age. Expenses for hospital care, drugs, physicians services, and eyeglasses ranged from 1.9 to 2.6 times greater for the elderly than for persons 19–64 years of age. The health expenses of older people were paid by public sources to a greater extent than those of younger people. During 1976, third-party payments, both private and public, accounted for about 68 percent of all personal health care expenditures. Public payments accounted for about 40 percent of the personal expenditures for all ages. However, the public contribution varied from 68 percent for the elderly to 26 percent for people under 19 years of age.

Personal health care expenditures by age group varied according to the type of expenditure (provider) and source of funds (public or private). In 1976, nearly half of the total spending for personal health care in the two older age groups (19–64 years of age and 65 years of age and over) was for hospital care. Public programs covered a greater proportion of hospital expenses than other expenses for all age groups, paralleling the coverage patterns of private health insurance.

For the oldest age group, public sources (i.e., Medicare, Medicaid, and the Veterans Administration) paid 91 percent of the total bill for hospital services. Public sources, chiefly Medicaid, paid 40 percent of the total hospital services bill for the intermediate age group. Public expenditures for physician services utilized by the elderly and intermediate age groups amounted to about 60 and 16 percent, respectively. For the elderly, Medicare paid more than two-thirds of hospital expenditures and about one-half of the expenses for services of physicians and also for "other professionals" who mainly provide home health care services. Medicare does not cover expenses associated with dental services, outpatient drugs, eyeglasses and appliances, or "other health services." Some portion of the bill for these services may be picked up by Medicaid or other State and local programs.

Public and private third parties have been paying an increasing share of personal health care expenses for all ages, and these payments accounted for two-thirds of personal health care spending in 1976. Medicare covered the largest portion of the health care bill for the elderly. However, about one-third of the health care bill was paid directly by the elderly for noncovered services, for required deductibles and coinsurance for covered services, and for premiums for Medicare supplemental medical insurance (Part B) and private health insurance to cover gaps in

Medicare coverage. For the population under 65 years of age, private health insurance coverage expanded steadily, accompanied by an increase in the share of expenses covered by public programs.

Personal health care expenditures for persons 65 years of age and over and percent distribution, according to source of funds and type of expenditure: United States, fiscal year 1976

(Data are compiled by the Health Care Financing Administration)

Type of expenditure	All sources	Private	Source of funds Public Total	Medicare	Other
			Amount in millions		
Total	$34,853	$11,248	$23,605	$14,953	$8,652
Hospital care	15,775	1,425	14,350	11,179	3,171
Physician services	5,863	2,387	3,476	3,218	258
Dentist services	722	679	43	–	43
Other professional services	534	193	341	265	76
Drugs and drug sundries	2,777	2,385	392	–	392
Eyeglasses and appliances	432	424	8	–	8
Nursing home care	8,032	3,731	4,301	291	4,010
Other health services	717	24	693	–	693
			Percent distribution		
Total	100.0	32.3	67.7	42.9	24.8
Hospital care	100.0	9.0	91.0	70.9	20.1
Physician services	100.0	40.7	59.3	54.9	4.4
Dentist services	100.0	94.1	5.9	–	5.9
Other professional services	100.0	36.1	63.9	49.6	14.3
Drugs and drug sundries	100.0	85.9	14.1	–	14.1
Eyeglasses and appliances	100.0	98.1	1.9	–	1.9
Nursing home care	100.0	46.4	53.6	3.6	50.0
Other health services	100.0	3.4	96.6	–	96.6

SOURCE: Gibson, R. M., Mueller, M. S., and Fisher, C. R.: Age differences in health care spending, fiscal year 1976. *Social Security Bulletin* 40(8): 3–14, Aug. 1977.

Personal health care aggregate and per capita expenditures, according to age, source of funds, and type of expenditure: United States, fiscal year 1976

(Data are compiled by the Health Care Financing Administration)

Aggregate amount in millions

Type of expenditure	All ages			Under 19 years			19–64 years			65 years and over		
	All sources	Private	Public	All sources	Private	Public	All sources	Private	Public	All sources	Private	Public
Total	$120,431	$72,013	$48,417	$17,880	$13,190	$4,690	$67,698	$47,576	$20,122	$34,853	$11,248	$23,605
Hospital care	55,400	25,004	30,396	6,461	3,750	2,711	33,164	19,828	13,336	15,775	1,425	14,350
Physician services	26,350	19,718	6,632	5,539	4,822	717	14,948	12,509	2,439	5,863	2,387	3,476
Dentist services	8,600	8,131	469	2,021	1,813	208	5,857	5,638	218	722	679	43
Other professional services	2,400	1,607	793	504	354	150	1,362	1,060	302	534	193	341
Drugs and drug sundries	11,168	10,144	1,023	2,129	1,986	143	6,262	5,774	488	2,777	2,385	392
Eyeglasses and appliances	1,980	1,866	114	329	310	19	1,219	1,133	86	432	424	8
Nursing home care	10,600	4,744	5,856	159	84	75	2,409	929	1,480	8,032	3,731	4,301
Other health services	3,933	800	3,133	738	71	667	2,478	705	1,773	717	24	693

Per capita amount

Type of expenditure	All ages			Under 19 years			19–64 years			65 years and over		
	All sources	Private	Public	All sources	Private	Public	All sources	Private	Public	All sources	Private	Public
Total	$551.50	$329.78	$221.72	$249.16	$183.80	$65.36	$547.29	$384.62	$162.67	$1,521.36	$490.98	$1,030.38
Hospital care	253.70	114.50	139.20	90.03	52.25	37.78	268.11	160.30	107.81	688.59	62.21	626.38
Physician services	120.67	90.30	30.37	77.18	67.19	9.99	120.85	101.13	19.72	255.92	104.19	151.73
Dentist services	39.38	37.23	2.15	28.16	25.26	2.90	47.35	45.58	1.76	31.53	29.66	1.88
Other professional services	10.99	7.36	3.63	7.03	4.93	2.10	11.01	8.57	2.44	23.31	8.42	14.89
Drugs and drug sundries	51.14	46.45	4.69	29.66	27.67	1.99	50.62	46.68	3.95	121.22	104.09	17.13
Eyeglasses and appliances	9.07	8.55	0.52	4.59	4.32	0.27	9.85	9.16	0.69	18.86	18.49	0.36
Nursing home care	48.54	21.72	26.82	2.22	1.17	1.05	19.47	7.51	11.96	350.61	162.86	187.75
Other health services	18.01	3.66	14.35	10.28	0.99	9.29	20.03	5.70	14.34	31.31	1.05	30.25

NOTE: Data are preliminary estimates.

SOURCE: Gibson, R. M., Mueller, M. S., and Fisher, C. R.: Age differences in health care spending, fiscal year 1976. *Social Security Bulletin* 40(8): 3–14, Aug. 1977.

Estimated personal health care aggregate and per capita expenditures under public programs, according to age, source of public funds, and program: United States, fiscal year 1976

(Data are compiled by the Health Care Financing Administration)

Aggregate amount in millions

Program	All ages			Under 19 years			19-64 years			65 years and over		
	All public sources	Federal	State and local	All public sources	Federal	State and local	All public sources	Federal	State and local	All public sources	Federal	State and local
Total	$48,417	$33,683	$14,735	$4,690	$2,863	$1,828	$20,122	$11,763	$8,359	$23,605	$19,057	$4,548
Health insurance for the aged and disabled—Medicare	16,942	16,942	...	35	35	...	1,955	1,955	...	14,953	14,953	...
Temporary disability insurance	74	...	74	...	...	...	74	...	74	...	...	...
Workmen's compensation (medical benefits)	2,125	66	2,059				2,061	64	1,997	64	2	62
Public assistance—Medicaid	14,593	7,959	6,634	2,511	1,369	1,141	6,493	3,541	2,952	5,589	3,048	2,540
General hospital and medical care	6,902	1,265	5,636	795	361	434	4,089	831	3,258	2,018	73	1,945
Defense Department hospital and medical care (including military dependents)	3,207	3,207	...	806	806	...	2,310	2,310	...	...	...	...
Maternal and child health services	588	301	287	498	255	243	90	46	44	91	91	...
Veterans' hospital and medical care	3,759	3,759	...	...	...	...	2,873	2,873	...	886	886	...
Medical vocational rehabilitation	229	183	46	46	37	9	179	143	36	5	4	1

Per capita amount

Program	All ages			Under 19 years			19-64 years			65 years and over		
	All public sources	Federal	State and local	All public sources	Federal	State and local	All public sources	Federal	State and local	All public sources	Federal	State and local
Total	$221.68	$154.22	$67.47	$65.32	$39.87	$25.45	$162.66	$95.09	$67.57	$1,030.79	$832.18	$198.61
Health insurance for the aged and disabled—Medicare	77.57	77.57	...	0.49	0.49	...	15.80	15.80	...	652.96	652.96	...
Temporary disability insurance	0.34	...	0.34	...	...	...	0.60	...	0.60	...	...	...
Workmen's compensation (medical benefits)	9.73	0.30	9.43				16.66	0.52	16.14	2.79	0.09	2.70
Public assistance—Medicaid	66.82	36.44	30.38	34.97	19.07	15.90	52.49	28.62	23.86	244.06	133.10	110.96
General hospital and medical care	31.60	5.79	25.81	11.07	5.03	6.04	33.06	6.72	26.34	88.12	3.19	84.93
Defense Department hospital and medical care (including military dependents)	14.68	14.68	...	11.23	11.23	...	18.67	18.67	...	...	...	...
Maternal and child health services	2.69	1.38	1.31	6.94	3.55	3.39	0.73	0.37	0.36	3.97	3.97	...
Veterans' hospital and medical care	17.21	17.21	...	...	...	...	23.23	23.23	...	38.69	38.69	...
Medical vocational rehabilitation	1.05	0.84	0.21	0.64	0.52	0.11	1.45	1.16	0.29	0.22	0.17	0.05

NOTE: Data are preliminary estimates.

SOURCE: Mueller, M. S., Gibson, R. M., and Fisher, C. R.: Age differences in health care spending, fiscal year 1976. Social Security Bulletin 40(8):3–14, Aug. 1977.

Personal health care per capita expenditures, according to source of payment and age: United States, fiscal years 1966–76

(Data are compiled by the Health Care Financing Administration)

Age and fiscal year	All personal health care expenditures	Source of payment				
		Direct payment	Third-party payment			
			Total	Private health insurance	Philanthropy and industry	Government
All ages			Per capita amount			
1966	$ 181.96	$ 93.79	$ 88.17	$ 44.90	$3.62	$ 39.65
1967	205.45	93.35	112.10	46.43	3.74	61.92
1968	228.75	93.91	134.84	51.35	3.84	79.66
1969	256.59	102.06	154.53	59.44	4.01	91.09
1970	289.76	117.00	172.76	69.44	4.29	99.03
1971	320.84	125.55	195.29	79.83	4.60	110.86
1972	353.00	132.73	220.27	88.00	4.89	127.37
1973	386.84	142.32	244.53	98.27	5.28	140.98
1974[1]	425.15	153.59	271.56	107.32	5.68	158.56
1975[1]	488.23	164.15	324.08	124.17	6.15	193.76
1976[2]	551.50	179.05	372.46	143.61	7.13	221.72
Under 65 years						
1966	154.96	79.13	75.82	42.25	3.48	30.09
1967	171.55	82.59	88.96	47.98	3.71	37.27
1968	185.39	85.22	100.17	53.11	3.80	43.26
1969	206.36	91.14	115.21	61.54	4.01	49.66
1970	232.50	100.71	131.79	71.98	4.31	55.50
1971	255.09	104.77	150.32	83.11	4.62	62.59
1972	278.23	106.96	171.27	91.81	4.04	74.52
1973	309.45	118.38	191.07	102.67	5.34	83.07
1974[1]	347.87	135.84	212.03	112.33	5.76	93.94
1975[1]	390.79	142.70	248.10	130.21	6.25	111.63
1976[2]	437.83	152.74	285.09	150.89	7.26	126.94
65 years and over						
1966	445.25	236.72	208.52	70.71	4.92	132.89
1967	535.03	198.01	337.03	31.38	4.05	301.59
1968	646.65	177.90	468.75	34.42	3.87	430.45
1969	735.19	206.02	529.17	39.42	4.00	485.75
1970	828.31	270.20	558.11	45.54	4.06	508.50
1971	925.98	316.78	609.20	49.67	4.38	555.15
1972	1,033.51	367.40	666.11	53.33	4.49	608.30
1973	1,081.35	357.16	724.19	58.81	4.70	660.69
1974[1]	1,109.54	310.75	798.78	62.94	5.00	730.85
1975[1]	1,335.72	350.77	984.94	71.65	5.20	908.10
1976[2]	1,521.36	403.53	1,117.83	81.45	6.00	1,030.38

[1] Revised estimates.
[2] Preliminary estimates.

SOURCE: Gibson, R. M., Mueller, M. S., and Fisher, C. R.: Age differences in health care spending, fiscal year 1976. *Social Security Bulletin* 40(8): 3-14, Aug. 1977.

Health care coverage status, according to type of coverage: United States, 1976

(Data are based on household interviews of a sample of the civilian noninstitutionalized population)

Type of coverage	Health care coverage status			
	Number of persons in thousands	Cumulative number of persons in thousands	Percent of population	Cumulative percent of population
Private hospital insurance [1]	159,957	159,957	75.9	75.9
Medicare coverage only [2]	7,756	167,713	3.7	79.6
Medicaid coverage only [3]	12,162	179,875	5.8	85.4
Other programs only [4]	5,084	184,959	2.4	87.8
Private hospital insurance, but kind of coverage unknown	1,624	186,583	0.8	88.6
Unknown if covered	861	187,444	0.4	89.0
No coverage	23,200	210,644	11.0	100.0

[1] Includes all persons with private hospital insurance coverage whether or not they have other coverage (e.g. Medicare) as well.

[2] Includes persons over 65 years of age who have Medicare with no private coverage and persons under 65 years of age who have Medicare with no other public or private coverage.

[3] Includes persons who did not have private insurance or Medicare, and reported either (a) receipt of Medicaid services in the previous year, or (b) eligibility for Medicaid as a reason for not having other coverage, or (c) receipt of benefit payments under Aid to Families with Dependent Children or Supplemental Security Income in the past year.

[4] Includes military (Civilian Health and Medical Program of the Uniformed Services), Veterans Administration, private surgical coverage only, and professional courtesy as reasons for holding no other type of public or private coverage.

NOTE: In order to avoid multiple counting of individuals, these estimates were derived by assigning each individual to one coverage category only. Persons with both private insurance and Medicare, for example, were placed in the private insurance category. As a result, Medicare and Medicaid estimates do not correspond to counts available from those programs.

SOURCE: Division of Health Interview Statistics, National Center for Health Statistics: Unpublished data from the Health Interview Survey.

Health care coverage status, according to type of coverage and selected characteristics: United States, 1976

(Data are based on household interviews of a sample of the civilian noninstitutionalized population)

Selected characteristic	Type of coverage [1]							
	Private insurance or Medicare		Medicaid		Other programs		No insurance	
	Number of persons in thousands	Percent of population	Number of persons in thousands	Percent of population	Number of persons in thousands	Percent of population	Number of persons in thousands	Percent of population
Total [2]	167,713	79.6	12,162	5.8	5,084	2.4	23,200	11.0
Age								
Under 6 years	13,237	70.0	2,373	12.5	631	3.3	2,469	13.0
6–18 years	37,942	75.3	4,550	9.0	1,474	2.9	5,825	11.6
19–54 years	79,283	77.5	4,177	4.2	2,365	2.4	12,550	12.6
55–64 years	16,292	82.1	815	4.1	527	2.7	1,919	9.7
65 years and over	20,958	96.1	247	1.1	87	0.4	437	2.0
Sex								
Male	81,367	80.1	4,923	4.8	2,381	2.3	11,748	11.6
Female	86,346	79.2	7,239	6.6	2,704	2.5	11,452	10.5
Color								
White	150,855	82.5	6,883	3.8	4,369	2.4	18,675	10.2
All other	16,858	60.7	5,279	19.0	716	2.6	4,525	16.3
Family income								
Less than $3,000	6,409	51.0	3,068	24.4	176	1.4	2,740	21.8
$3,000–$4,999	9,097	55.4	3,438	20.9	194	1.2	3,500	21.3
$5,000–6,999	11,534	62.8	2,271	12.4	470	2.6	3,857	21.0
$7,000–9,999	18,327	75.8	1,097	4.5	843	3.5	3,658	15.1
$10,000–14,999	38,619	86.8	715	1.6	1,283	2.9	3,437	7.7
$15,000 or more	69,960	92.3	[3]426	0.6	1,663	2.2	3,104	4.1
Place of residence								
SMSA, central city	46,109	75.1	6,008	9.8	1,409	2.3	7,168	11.7
SMSA, outside central	70,219	84.8	2,983	3.6	1,892	2.3	6,669	8.1
Outside SMSA, nonfarm	46,354	77.4	3,069	5.1	1,676	2.8	8,106	13.5
Outside SMSA, farm	5,031	76.9	102	1.6	107	1.6	1,257	19.2
Geographic region								
Northeast	40,394	83.1	3,449	7.1	468	1.0	3,683	7.6
North Central	47,973	85.3	2,752	4.9	464	0.8	4,458	7.9
South	50,717	75.1	3,471	5.1	2,682	4.0	9,833	14.6
West	28,629	74.9	2,490	6.5	1,470	3.8	5,225	13.7

[1] Excludes 1,624 thousand persons who said they had hospital insurance but did not know the kind of coverage they had and 861 thousand persons who did not know if they were covered by health insurance.

[2] Includes unknown family income.

[3] Persons with high incomes can qualify for Medicaid in at least 2 ways: (1) previous year's income is employed, yet family dissolution or catastrophic illness could have occurred in the survey year causing Medicaid use or eligibility; (2) in certain States, large families with incomes in excess of $15,000 could qualify for Medicaid coverage.

NOTE: The information in the footnotes and general note for table 163 also apply to this table.

SOURCE: Division of Health Interview Statistics, National Center for Health Statistics: Unpublished data from the Health Interview Survey.

Persons 65 years of age and over with supplemental health insurance coverage, according to color, type of coverage, and family income: United States, 1976

(Data are based on household interviews of a sample of the civilian noninstitutionalized population)

Family income	Color									
	White					All other				
	Population 65 years and over	Private hospital insurance only[1]	Medicare only[2]	Private hospital insurance and Medicare[3]	Other[4]	Population 65 years and over	Private hospital insurance only[1]	Medicare only[2]	Private hospital insurance and Medicare[3]	Other[4]
	Number of persons in thousands									
All incomes[5]	19,768	1,833	6,117	11,165	653	2,030	127	1,219	491	193
Less than $3,000	2,658	133	1,372	1,032	121	547	*9	404	78	56
$3,000–$4,999	4,005	236	1,485	2,201	83	566	*29	357	137	43
$5,000–$6,999	3,183	255	892	1,950	86	226	*13	108	95	*10
$7,000–$9,999	2,581	305	537	1,691	48	145	*13	72	37	*23
$10,000–$14,999	2,183	283	458	1,382	60	126	*11	54	47	*14
$15,000 or more	2,509	411	478	1,505	115	131	*22	54	49	*6
	Percent distribution									
All incomes[5]	100.0	9.3	30.9	56.5	3.3	100.0	6.3	60.0	24.2	9.5
Less than $3,000	100.0	5.0	51.6	38.8	4.5	100.0	*1.6	73.9	14.3	10.2
$3,000–$4,999	100.0	5.9	37.1	55.0	2.1	100.0	*5.1	63.1	24.2	7.6
$5,000–$6,999	100.0	8.0	28.0	61.3	2.7	100.0	*5.7	47.8	42.0	*4.4
$7,000–$9,999	100.0	11.8	20.8	65.5	1.9	100.0	*9.0	49.6	25.5	*15.9
$10,000–$14,999	100.0	13.0	21.0	63.3	2.7	100.0	*8.7	42.9	37.3	*11.1
$15,000 or more	100.0	16.4	19.0	60.0	4.6	100.0	*16.8	41.2	37.4	*4.6

[1] Includes persons who have private health insurance and who do not explicitly say they have Medicare.
[2] Includes persons who have Medicare and who do not explicitly say they have private health insurance.
[3] Includes persons who have private hospital insurance and Medicare.
[4] Includes persons who do not fall into previous categories; persons who are not sure of their coverage, persons who do not have any coverage, and persons who have Medicaid coverage only.
[5] Includes unknown income.

SOURCE: Division of Health Interview Statistics, National Center for Health Statistics: Unpublished data from the Health Interview Survey.

Private health insurance coverage status, according to type of plan and selected characteristics:
United States, 1975

(Data are based on household interviews of a sample of the civilian noninstitutionalized population)

Selected characteristic	All persons	Covered—type of plan			Not covered	Unknown
		All types of coverage	Prepaid group practice	Fee for service		
	Number of persons in thousands					
Total	209,065	158,085	6,532	151,552	47,433	3,547
Age						
Under 17 years	61,945	45,090	2,010	43,079	15,647	1,208
17–44 years	82,738	64,224	2,664	61,561	17,155	1,358
45–64 years	43,094	35,481	1,451	34,031	6,989	623
65 years and over	21,287	13,290	408	12,882	7,641	357
64 years and under	187,777	144,795	6,124	138,671	39,792	3,190
Sex						
Male	100,865	77,231	3,234	73,997	21,925	1,709
Female	108,199	80,853	3,298	77,555	25,508	1,838
Color						
White	181,874	143,028	5,310	137,718	36,058	2,788
All other	27,191	15,057	1,222	13,834	11,374	759
Place of residence						
SMSA, central city	61,562	43,646	2,930	40,717	16,710	1,205
SMSA, outside central city	82,093	67,464	3,018	64,446	13,305	1,324
Outside SMSA, nonfarm	58,700	42,201	543	41,659	15,604	895
Outside SMSA, farm	6,710	4,773	42	4,731	1,814	124
Geographic region						
Northeast	49,086	38,790	2,148	36,642	9,442	854
North Central	55,892	46,148	763	45,385	9,030	714
South	66,854	46,650	359	46,291	18,880	1,324
West	37,233	26,497	3,263	23,234	10,081	655
Family income[1]						
Less than $3,000	14,676	5,351	171	5,180	9,014	311
$3,000–$4,999	17,074	7,530	241	7,289	9,197	348
$5,000–$9,999	45,273	30,561	962	29,600	14,014	698
$10,000–$14,999	47,103	40,470	1,689	38,780	5,960	674
$15,000–$24,999	48,872	44,290	2,211	42,080	4,015	567
$25,000 or more	20,996	19,395	978	18,417	1,382	219

[1] Includes unknown family income.

SOURCE: Division of Health Interview Statistics, National Center for Health Statistics: Unpublished data from the Health Interview Survey.

Private health insurance coverage status percent distribution, according to type of plan and selected characteristics: United States, 1975

(Data are based on household interviews of a sample of the civilian noninstitutionalized population)

Selected characteristic	All persons	Covered—type of plan			Not covered	Unknown
		All types of coverage	Prepaid group practice	Fee for service		
		Percent of persons				
Total[1]	100.0	100.0	100.0	100.0	100.0	100.0
Age						
Under 17 years	29.6	28.5	30.8	28.4	33.0	34.1
17–44 years	39.6	40.6	40.8	40.6	36.2	38.3
45–64 years	20.6	22.4	22.2	22.5	14.7	17.6
65 years and over	10.2	8.4	6.2	8.5	16.1	10.1
64 years and under	89.8	91.6	93.8	91.5	83.9	89.9
Sex						
Male	48.2	48.9	49.5	48.8	46.2	48.2
Female	51.8	51.1	50.5	51.2	53.8	51.8
Color						
White	87.0	90.5	81.3	90.9	76.0	78.6
All other	13.0	9.5	18.7	9.1	24.0	21.4
Place of residence						
SMSA, central city	29.4	27.6	44.9	26.9	35.2	34.0
SMSA, outside central city	39.3	42.7	46.2	42.5	28.1	37.3
Outside SMSA, nonfarm	28.1	26.7	8.3	27.5	32.9	25.2
Outside SMSA, farm	3.2	3.0	0.6	3.1	3.8	3.5
Geographic region						
Northeast	23.5	24.5	32.9	24.2	19.9	24.1
North Central	26.7	29.2	11.7	29.9	19.0	20.1
South	32.0	29.5	5.5	30.5	39.8	37.3
West	17.8	16.8	50.0	15.3	21.3	18.5
Family income						
Less than $3,000	7.0	3.4	2.6	3.4	19.0	8.8
$3,000–$4,999	8.2	4.8	3.7	4.8	19.4	9.8
$5,000–$9,999	21.7	19.3	14.7	19.5	29.5	19.7
$10,000–$14,999	22.5	25.6	25.9	25.6	12.6	19.0
$15,000–$24,999	23.4	28.0	33.8	27.8	8.5	16.0
$25,000 or more	10.0	12.3	15.0	12.2	2.9	6.2

[1] Includes unknown family income.

SOURCE: Division of Health Interview Statistics, National Center for Health Statistics: Unpublished data from the Health Interview Survey.

Nursing Homes: Charges for Care and Sources of Payment

Based on surveys of nursing homes conducted by the National Center for Health Statistics in 1964, 1969, and 1973–74, the average monthly charge for nursing home care increased from $185 in 1964 to $479 in 1973–74 or 159 percent. The largest percent increase in average charges occurred between 1964 and 1969 when charges increased 81 percent, or about 13 percent per year.

In contrast, the average charge increased by only 43 percent from 1969 to 1973–74, or about 8 percent per year. The slowing of the rate of increase during the 5-year period after 1969 was in part a consequence of the price and wage controls imposed by the Economic Stabilization Program that were in effect during the latter half of the period. The effects of the controls have apparently continued since the expiration of the program in the spring of 1974. Preliminary data from the 1977 National Nursing Home Survey show the average total monthly charge for nursing home residents during that year was $669, an increase of 40 percent over the 3½ year period between the 1977 and 1973–74 surveys, or 10 percent per year.

Over the course of a nursing home stay, payments for charges may come from several different sources. For example, Medicare may pay fully for the first 20 days of a nursing home stay. However, the next 8 days may involve only partial payment through Medicare supplemented by personal funds to cover the coinsurance payment, about $300 per month in 1973–74. Then Medicaid may be used to pay for some portion of the remainder of the stay. In general, the longer the patient remains in a nursing home the more likely it is that charges will be paid by Medicaid or other public assistance programs.

Data are available regarding the primary source of payment used by patients for the month preceding the 1973–74 survey of nursing home residents. Since the complement of patients residing in a nursing home at any given point in time is disproportion-ately made up of long-stay patients, the information derived from a survey of current patients reflects the sources of nursing home revenue rather than the funding of a typical nursing home admission.

In 1973–74, Medicaid was the most frequent primary source of payment used for charges to residents in nursing homes. Forty-eight percent of all nursing home residents received care financed primarily by Medicaid. The next most frequent primary source of payment was the resident's own income or family support (37 percent), followed by other public assistance or welfare (11 percent). Only a minority of the residents (1 percent) used Medicare for primary payment. Less than 1 percent of all the residents used each of the remaining sources (i.e., church support, Veterans Administration contract, initial payment/life care, no charge for care, and miscellaneous source) as the primary source of payment. Overall, 60 percent of the residents used public funds (i.e., Medicare, Medicaid, other public assistance or welfare) for primary payment.

The average monthly charge for residents receiving care primarily financed by Medicare ($754) was significantly higher than for those whose care was financed by any other source of payment. In comparison, significantly lower average charges were paid by residents using Medicaid ($503) and their own income or family support ($491). The average monthly charge for residents receiving care financed by other public assistance or welfare was $381. The average charge for residents using all other sources was the lowest at $225, probably because of the minimal charges for the life-care and no-charge residents who are included in this category.

The Medicaid program, initiated in 1966, was designed to ease the burden of medical care costs for the poor of all ages. The 1973–74 data show that utilization of Medicaid funds for nursing home care was extensive. Medicaid was the dominant source of payment for most residents in certified facilities.

The proportion of Medicaid residents was 54 percent in facilities certified by both Medicare and Medicaid, 59 percent in Medicaid certified skilled nursing homes, and 53 percent in intermediate care facilities. The proportion of private pay residents (i.e., those relying on their own income or family support for primary payment) was 36 percent in facilities certified by both Medicare and Medicaid, 32 percent in Medicaid-certified skilled nursing homes, and 36 percent in intermediate care facilities.

The utilization of Medicaid benefits was greater in large facilities since these facilities were most likely to be participating in the program. The proportion of Medicaid residents increased from 37 percent in small facilities (less than 50 beds) to 52 percent in large facilities (200 beds or more). In contrast, the residents' use of their own incomes for payment correspondingly decreased as the size of the facility increased.

This pattern may reflect a tendency on the part of private pay residents to utilize lower-cost, noncertified services since charges tend to be lower in small facilities. In contrast to Medicaid, use of Medicare benefits in nursing homes was infrequent. Nationally, only 1 percent of the residents used this source for primary payment during the month preceding the survey. About the same proportion of residents used this source regardless of the type of service or ownership, size, or region classification of their facility. Within facilities certified by both Medicare and Medicaid, Medicare recipients made up only 3 percent of the residents.

Monthly charge for care in nursing homes and percent distribution of residents, according to selected facility and resident characteristics: United States, 1964, 1969, and 1973-74

(Data are based on reporting by a sample of nursing homes)

Selected facility and resident characteristic	Year					
	1964 [1]		1969 [1]		1973-74	
	Average total monthly charge[2]	Percent distribution of residents	Average total monthly charge[2]	Percent distribution of residents	Average total monthly charge[2]	Percent distribution of residents
All facilities	$185	100.0	$335	100.0	$479	100.0
FACILITY CHARACTERISTIC						
Type of service provided						
Nursing care	211	72.0	356	81.4	495	64.8
Personal care with nursing	118	28.0	242	18.6	448	35.2
Ownership						
Proprietary	208	60.2	352	68.0	489	69.8
Nonprofit and government	150	39.8	300	32.0	456	30.2
Size						
Less than 50 beds	---	---	288	27.3	397	15.2
50–99 beds	---	---	345	36.0	448	34.1
100–199 beds	---	---	363	26.2	502	35.6
200 beds or more	---	---	352	10.6	576	15.1
Geographic region						
Northeast	209	28.4	395	22.5	651	22.0
North Central	172	36.5	302	36.0	433	34.6
South	162	18.7	311	27.3	410	26.0
West	198	16.5	370	14.2	454	17.4
All residents	185	100.0	335	100.0	479	100.0
RESIDENT CHARACTERISTIC						
Age						
Under 65 years	162	11.4	288	10.8	434	10.6
65–74 years	186	18.9	332	16.5	473	15.0
75–84 years	188	41.8	343	39.5	488	35.5
85 years and older	190	28.0	343	33.2	485	38.8
Sex						
Male	175	34.6	323	30.4	466	29.1
Female	191	65.4	340	69.6	484	70.9
Level of care received						
Intensive nursing care	221	33.0	374	33.7	510	40.6
Other nursing care[3]	197	30.3	335	43.0	469	42.1
Personal care	162	25.6	293	18.0	435	16.4
No nursing or personal care	97	11.1	230	5.3	315	0.9

[1] Data have been adjusted to exclude residents of personal care homes.

[2] Includes life-care residents and no-charge residents.

[3] Data in 1964 and 1969 for other nursing care correspond to combined data for the limited and routine nursing care categories of 1973–74.

SOURCE: National Center for Health Statistics: Charges for care and sources for payment for residents in nursing homes, United States, National Nursing Home Survey, Aug. 1973-Apr. 1974, by E. Hing. *Vital and Health Statistics.* Series 13–No. 32. DHEW Pub. No. (PHS) 78–1783. Public Health Service. Washington. U.S. Government Printing Office. Nov. 1977.

Monthly charge for care in nursing homes and percent distribution of residents, according to the primary source of payment during the month prior to the survey, certification, type of service provided, ownership, size, and geographic region of the home: United States, August 1973-April 1974

(Data are based on reporting by a sample of nursing homes)

Certification, type of service provided, ownership, size, and geographic region	Primary source of payment										
	Average total monthly charge					Percent distribution of residents					
	Own income or family support	Medicare	Medicaid	Other public assistance or welfare	All other sources[1]	Total	Own income or family support	Medicare	Medicaid	Other public assistance or welfare	All other sources[1]
All homes[2]	$491	$754	$503	$381	$225	100.0	36.7	1.1	47.9	11.4	3.0
Certification											
Both Medicare and Medicaid[3]	613	754	591	480	334	100.0	36.0	2.9	54.0	4.9	2.2
Skilled nursing home only[4]	489	...	489	469	308	100.0	31.8	...	58.6	7.8	1.8
Intermediate care facility only	388	...	375	333	*389	100.0	35.8	...	53.1	9.7	1.4
Not certified	377	...	...	330	*89	100.0	50.6	...	...	39.3	10.2
Type of service provided											
Nursing care	516	803	501	398	296	100.0	35.9	1.2	51.1	9.5	2.3
Personal care with nursing	447	*623	507	361	156	100.0	38.2	0.8	41.9	14.7	4.3
Ownership											
Proprietary	525	754	486	373	406	100.0	34.5	1.2	52.0	11.0	1.4
Nonprofit and government	427	*751	556	397	136	100.0	41.9	0.9	38.4	12.2	6.6
Size											
Less than 50 beds	429	*625	431	296	*128	100.0	41.5	*0.6	37.1	17.5	3.4
50-99 beds	484	*786	449	356	186	100.0	37.8	0.9	47.9	10.9	2.5
100-199 beds	523	787	508	414	256	100.0	36.3	1.3	50.8	8.8	2.8
200 beds or more	506	*689	656	496	307	100.0	30.7	*1.3	51.6	12.3	4.1
Geographic region											
Northeast	637	*957	718	538	131	100.0	30.6	1.4	53.2	10.5	4.5
North Central	449	*738	454	360	252	100.0	44.4	0.8	35.6	16.1	3.0
South	452	*615	408	306	278	100.0	31.0	1.1	55.2	10.3	2.4
West	487	*672	442	323	*314	100.0	37.9	*1.2	54.6	4.6	1.9

[1] Includes church support, Veterans Administration contract, initial payment/life care, no charge for care, and miscellaneous sources.

[2] Includes only those residents who have lived in the nursing home for at least one month.

[3] Includes 20,900 residents in facilities certified by Medicare only.

[4] Includes 122,900 residents in facilities certified by Medicaid as both skilled nursing homes and intermediate care facilities.

SOURCE: National Center for Health Statistics: Charges for care and sources for payment for residents in nursing homes, United States, National Nursing Home Survey, Aug. 1973-Apr. 1974, by E. Hing. Vital and Health Statistics. Series 13—No. 32. DHEW Pub. No. (PHS) 78-1783. Public Health Service. Washington. U.S. Government Printing Office. Nov. 1977.

Monthly charge for care in nursing homes and percent distribution of residents, according to the primary source of payment during the month prior to the survey, age, sex, primary reason for admission, and length of stay since current admission: United States, August 1973-April 1974

(Data are based on reporting by a sample of nursing homes)

Age, sex, primary reason for admission, and length of stay since current admission	Primary source of payment									
	Average total monthly charge					Percent distribution of residents				
	Own income or family support	Medicare	Medicaid	Other public assistance or welfare	All other sources[1]	Own income or family support	Medicare	Mediaid	Other public assistance or welfare	All other sources[1]
All residents[2]	$491	$754	$503	$381	$225	100.0	100.0	100.0	100.0	100.0
Age										
Under 65 years	497	*1,214	457	351	325	5.2	*1.4	12.0	20.9	19.8
65–74 years	470	*778	503	367	*264	12.6	*21.1	16.3	17.6	12.4
75–84 years	790	725	517	385	219	40.2	46.1	33.7	26.9	36.1
85 years and over	498	*760	505	402	152	42.0	31.5	38.0	34.6	31.7
Sex										
Male	471	*812	495	360	341	28.4	23.9	28.3	31.5	43.3
Female	499	735	506	390	*136	71.6	76.1	71.7	68.5	56.7
Primary reason for admission										
Physical	506	764	514	408	281	81.2	96.1	84.2	67.5	59.2
Social	384	*572	452	305	*126	8.6	*0.5	4.0	7.9	20.5
Behavioral	467	*480	436	331	*313	9.6	*2.9	11.3	22.9	9.6
Economic	*420	*558	*484	*302	*22	0.6	*0.5	0.6	*1.7	10.8
Length of stay since current admission										
1 to less than 6 months	549	795	517	412	331	21.7	82.5	17.1	13.2	17.9
6 to less than 12 months	512	*629	516	400	*276	18.3	*6.0	15.1	12.1	8.5
1 to less than 3 years	485	*473	503	392	261	34.5	*7.1	37.6	33.6	25.9
3 to less than 5 years	456	*740	500	367	*197	13.0	*1.9	15.9	17.3	15.5
5 years or more	412	*477	474	348	136	12.6	*2.5	14.3	23.9	32.2

[1] Includes church support, Veterans Administration contract, initial payment/life care, no charge for care, and miscellaneous sources.
[2] Includes only those residents who have lived in the nursing home for at least 1 month.

SOURCE: National Center for Health Statistics: Charges for care and sources for payment for residents in nursing homes, United States, National Nursing Home Survey, Aug. 1973-Apr. 1974, by E. Hing. Vital and Health Statistics. Series 13—No. 32. DHEW Pub. No. (PHS) 78–1783. Public Health Service. Washington. U.S. Government Printing Office. Nov. 1977.

Special Health Problems of Aged Blacks*

Jacquelyne Johnson Jackson**

Aging, Nos. 287-288 (September-October 1978). U.S. Department of Health, Education, and Welfare, Administration on Aging.

The growing numbers of aged blacks, those 65 and over (now approaching 2 million), and their expanding needs for and use of formal health resources are increasing the concerns of aging and health experts about their *special* health problems, even though consensus about the definition of *special* is slim.

Consider hypertension. Is it *special* because it is uniquely black? No. For example, about three-fifths of aged blacks, and two-fifths of aged whites have definite hypertension. Does its greater prevalence among blacks make it *special*? Some think so. Does racial discrimination in the delivery of health services make it *special*? Or does the disproportionately higher incidence of poverty among blacks make it *special*? Some operationalize *special* in this way as well.

Contemporary aged blacks do have some special health problems, but few, if any, of them are racially unique. Those arguing the contrary typically have economically or politically vested interests, best served by unfairly categorizing elderly blacks monolithically, and by ignoring the tremendous social changes in recent years in the delivery and use of health resources by aged blacks.

*The preparation of this article was partially supported by a National Institute on Mental Health Grant (#5 T21 MH 13661-05), through a postdoctoral training program in social epidemiology.

**Jacquelyne Johnson Jackson, who holds a Ph.D. in Sociology from The Ohio State University, is currently an Associate Professor of Medical Sociology, Department of Psychiatry, and Senior Fellow, Center for the Study of Aging and Human Develoment, Duke University Medical Center, Durham, N.C. Editor of BLACK AGING, and former editor of the Journal of Health and Social Behavior (1972-1975), she is also a Fellow of the Gerontological Society. Active in a number of professional organizations, she has written extensively about aging and aged blacks.

This article is intended to begin a much needed discussion of the special health problems of aged blacks, where, as Alice in Wonderland, *special* means whatever I wish it to mean at any given point. It focuses primarily on health perceptions, age changes, prevalent diseases, functional health, and the use of health resources as they relate to aged blacks. Partially due to sparse data and ideological conflicts, it raises far more issues than it resolves. Perhaps its most significant issue is the conditions under which health resources should be color-blind or color-specific for aged blacks.

Health Perceptions

Do aged blacks perceive health as a problem? Not surprisingly, most do. A secondary analysis[1] of the 1974 Harris survey on aging[2] showed that about two-thirds identified poor health as a problem. Over 90 percent regarded their general health as a problem, and reported difficulties in walking or climbing stairs. About 82 percent had visited a physician or health clinic at least once during the past year. Around 75 percent thought they were conveniently located to physicians or health clinics. Most reported familial aid when ill.

With one exception, aged blacks and whites had similar perceptions. The exception: low-income, aged blacks were substantially more likely to consider insufficient medical care as a serious problem. This difference may be real, or a reflection of the gross income categories used for comparison.

In any case, obtaining satisfactory medical care is a very special health problem for poor aged blacks.

Age Changes

Health problems intensify with aging, regardless of race. Two examples are vision and hearing. In 1971, the prevalence rate per 1,000 for visual impairment among aged blacks of 245.7, was more than twice that of 99.6 for blacks, 45-64 years old. The rate for severe visual impairment among aged blacks was 78.1. The hearing impairment rates were 88.7 for blacks, 45-64 years old; 181.4 for those 65-74 years old; and 322.2 for those 75+ years of age. These types of impairments may also be influenced by disease, but, in any case, they are not special, in the sense of uniqueness, to aged blacks.

Yet, many aged blacks do encounter particular difficulties in seeing ophthalmologists and otologists, or in obtaining prescribed aids, such as corrective lenses or hearing aids. Some are victimized by unscrupulous mail-order companies, due partially to insufficient and inadequately enforced consumer protection laws. In addition, many poor aged simply lack money to purchase aids.

Prevalent Diseases

Reliable data regarding diseases among aged blacks are still scant and fragmented. Neither is much known about relationships between various conditions, such as obesity and strokes,[3] nor between their morbidity and mortality. Recent mortality rates, based upon the underlying cause of death, show that diseases of the heart, malignant neoplasms, and cerebrovascular diseases account for about three-fourths of the deaths of all aged blacks. A similar pattern exists for aged whites.

Many persons view hypertension and heart diseases as special medical problems of aged blacks, due to racial differences. Malnutrition, nutritional ignorance, obesity (especially in women), and poverty are typically regarded as the relevant high risk factors. As previously indicated, definite hypertension is more prevalent among aged blacks than whites. For example, between 1971-74, the black/white prevalence ratio for females was 1.72, and, for males, 1.60.[4] In 1973 death rates from hypertension for aged blacks were somewhat higher than those for aged whites, but the latter experienced higher mortality rates from diseases of the heart.

The limited nutritional data available about aged blacks suggest that their mean caloric intake is below standard, regardless of income level, as based upon body weight for age, sex, and height. Below standard, however, does not necessarily imply insufficiencies. Shank concluded that the diets of blacks, 60 or more years of age, were characteristically low in iron, thiamine, and calcium, but they showed no serious deficiencies.[5] Some later data which I examined for blacks, 65-74 years of age, showed black men to be above standard in calcium and iron intake, and both black women and men to be above standard in thiamine intake.[6] No serious dietary deficiencies existed then either.

Ostfeld, whose research subjects have included poor black aged, questioned the traditional assumptions about undernutrition and overnutrition in older persons: the "kind of serious consequences" expected in younger persons did not seem to appear in older persons. Also, some forms of heart or cerebrovascular diseases commonly thought to be affected substantially by obesity may not be so affected among the aged.[7]

Nutritional ignorance may not be so widespread among aged blacks as many persons believe. Their conceptions of their nutritional requirements may differ substantially from those of nutritional experts, but the latter rarely develop individualized requirements. Instead, they try to fit the individual to a group.

Clearly, as suggested above, much more information is needed about the effects of over- or undernutrition, education, and poverty upon hypertension and heart diseases among aged blacks. At this point in time, we can only regard hypertension and heart diseases as special medical problems of aged blacks because of their generally widespread prevalence.

Other diseases or disorders which are prevalent among aged blacks are malignant neoplasms and arthritis. These tend to be more ignored by gerontologists, perhaps because the racial gaps are not as wide here as they are in hypertension, for example. On the other hand, diabetes is frequently mentioned, since it is more prominent among aged blacks, especially among women.

Functional Health

Functional health provides some measure of the ability and capacity for maintaining self-care. A comparison of some 1971 data about the days of restricted activity, bed disability, and, among the currently employed, lost work days per person per year, for nonwhite and white persons, by sex, 65-74 and 75+ years of age,[8] reconfirmed well-established findings of greater dysfunctionality among nonwhites and among lower income persons. Within both racial groups, functional ability decreased with age, and women were somewhat more disabled than men. These kinds of data suggest that special medical problems related to functionality may be more characteristic of nonwhites than whites, and of the poor than the non-poor. However, a more appropriate way of using the data may be to identify more clearly the specific subsets with functional disabilities and their special problems. In other words, mere identification by race, sex, and income is insufficient.

Some 1972 and 1974 data about limitations of activity and mobility, broken out by gross income categories,[9] showed that over one-half of all nonwhite aged with incomes under $5,000 had some type of activity limitation, as did about two-fifths of their higher income counterparts. About one-fourth of the lower income group, and one-fifth of the upper income group had limited mobility. Further, about 7 percent of the lower income group was house-confined. Unfortunately, estimates were not available for the upper income group.

Thus, about one-fourth of all aged blacks are probably affected by serious limitations of their activities or mobility. Such conditions undoubtedly create special problems for them, and, where applicable, for at least some of their relatives and friends. We know much about the kinds of special problems which the afflicted aged may have, such as those related to inadequate physical facilities, dependence on others for personal care, and, on occasion, the need for institutionalization. What we know little about, however, is the kind and range of special problems confronting specific relatives and friends who provide aid to ailing aged blacks.

Many health providers believe that aged blacks almost always reside in households containing extended families. Further, they believe aged blacks are always taken care of by their kin. Thus, too many of them, unfamiliar with the changing realities of black subcultures, base care modalities, following hospital discharge, for example, upon the presence of kin, without prior assurance from family members that they can or wish to provide such care. This is truly a special problem for some aged blacks.

Current data show clearly that well over one-third of all aged blacks now live alone. The proportions living alone are increasing. Even when relatives are present within the same city, residential proximity between aged blacks and their kin seems to be widening. Often, transportation problems complicate visiting.

Another emergent trend also frequently ignored is the rising proportion of younger black women within the labor force. This means, in part, that they are no longer available for "around-the-clock" nursing of ill aged.

Consequently, some of the special health problems of aged blacks too ill to maintain themselves include access to day-care centers or to nursing homes. Frequently, and especially so within smaller geographical areas, such units are located outside the areas where most blacks live. Some bureaucratic problems here include policies related to location of facilities, desegregation of facilities, and a "break-even" use size.

Use of Health Resources

The number of physician visits per person per year has long been used as an index of the use of health resources. For many years, this index showed fewer such visits among aged blacks than aged whites, and positive associations between visitation and income. Such recent factors as desegregated medical facilities, neighborhood clinics, increases in the number of black physicians, expanded health insurance coverage among blacks, and Medicare and Medicaid have all diminished considerably the previously negative effects of race and income upon physician visitation among the aged. By at least 1971, the average number of visits was somewhat higher among aged nonwhites than whites, although the former are still somewhat less likely, even now, to visit office-based physicians in patient care.[10]

Many critics of medical care for blacks emphasize racial disparities between the quantity and location of medical visits, focusing primarily upon fewer visits by blacks of all ages, as compared to whites, and a greater proportion of the former than the latter receiving care from health clinics. That view, undoubtedly valid historically, seems far less appropriate or useful today. However, it is understandable since attitudinal changes tend to lag behind behavioral changes.

In any case, a special health problem of some aged blacks, especially the poor, is that they are subjected to unnecessary multiple visits by physicians and clinics. Much the same may occur when they seek dental care. I know of one instance in which a black dentist, heavily dependent upon Medicaid, cleaned the lower half of a patient's teeth, and had her make a return appointment for the upper half. No condition contraindicated cleaning both the upper and lower halves in the initial visit.

However, as strange as it may seem, profits increase with multiple visits.

The greater average length of hospitalization stays among blacks is frequently attributed to the fact that they are more ill. Yet, this assumption may need questioning. Ruling out accidental cases, including gunshot wounds, I suspect that the greater stay may also be explicable by less swiftness in medical attention, or in completing the required diagnostic tests.

By now, many persons are well aware of escalating hospital costs and the surplus of hospital beds across the nation. Racial differences may *not* exist in unnecessary weekend or holiday hospitalization mandated by physicians to fill beds, but, if such differences are present, this may be another variable accounting for currently longer average stay. Most of us can provide ready examples of this phenomenon. I know of one where a relative was informed that he must check into the hospital on a Saturday before noon. I tried to discourage him since the following Monday was a holiday, but he insisted on following the physician's orders. Age, by then, may have lowered his resistance level. In any case, he first saw his physician on the following Tuesday. Aides failed to carry out the physician's instructions for various diagnostic tests that day, so his length of hospitalization was increased for several additional days.

In situations when postponement of seeking medical attention occurs, blacks are often characterized as being fatalistic, or less likely to define themselves as being ill. Many, of course, experience great difficulties in seeking attention during normal "banking hours" maintained by many physicians and clinics. But, I suspect that an additional factor may be operative. That is, for some conditions, blacks tend to seek medical advice from friends, and few of their friends are physicians or other health providers. Consequently, they delay care. Consider for example, a case where an older black woman may be experiencing abnormal bleeding, and black physicians or physicians who are also friends or at least known are not available to her. What might she do? If reluctant to subject herself to pelvic examination by white physicians, she may do nothing. Bleeding may cease. She may consider herself in satisfactory health. But, in some instances, the avoidance of medical care could be extremely costly. The critical point: health behavior of many blacks, including aged blacks, is influenced heavily by their informal relationships with health providers. For this very important reason, more black physicians more

widely distributed where blacks reside are needed to diminish this kind of very special health problem among some blacks.

Many critics of health care facilities for aged blacks have focused heavily upon inadequate institutionalization. Much of that criticism has been unfounded, principally because they determine that racial discrimination is operative, and detrimentally so to aged blacks, whenever the proportion of institutionalism among aged blacks is less than that among aged whites. Such judgments ignore the differential age distribution of the two populations. The aged white population is older. Thus, greater institutionalization would be expected. Further, those critics assume that the need for institutionalization among aged blacks equals that among aged whites. Such may not be the case. At this point in time, we do not know what proportion of institutionalized aged blacks are improperly institutionalized, nor, for that matter, how many noninstitutionalized aged blacks need institutionalization.

In fact, we have relatively little data about institutionalized aged blacks. Based upon a 1973-1974 survey,[11] we do know that the 49,300 black residents of nursing homes in the United States were 4.6 percent of the total number of residents. Almost one-fourth of them were under 65 years of age, although only 11 percent of all residents were under that age. Slightly over half were in the South, a somewhat smaller proportion than might have been expected by chance alone. This suggests that aged blacks may experience particular difficulties in obtaining institutionalization within the South, or that other factors, such as past memories of exclusion, play a role.

About two-thirds of the blacks were in nursing homes containing between 50 and 200 beds. About four-fifths were in proprietary homes, and about 87 percent were in certified homes.

Due largely to their poor health status, few participated in leisure activities, such as occasional overnight or weekend visits with relatives or friends, or in religious activities. While somewhat less than one-fifth had no visitors, most of them were visited at least monthly. Probably about two-fifths were visited at least weekly. The available data about visitations were not based upon the existence or proximity of relatives or friends. Consequently, the special problems which may exist when institutionalized blacks have relatives or friends who refuse to visit remain unknown. Decreasing visitation does seem to increase with length of hospitalization. In some cases, institutionalized aged may have outlived their friends and relatives.

As a simultaneous step, the National Center on Health Statistics, which has improved considerably its collection of data from aged blacks, needs to be urged to close quickly the many outstanding gaps. That agency should be requested to collect, analyze, and disseminate needed information about all relevant aspects of the health statuses and conditions of aging and aged blacks. This information should include matters pertaining to the delivery and use of health resources, such as factors affecting drug compliance among hypertensive patients. Color-specific legislation, with adequate Congressional appropriations, may be needed here. The research sample, national in scope, should over-sample for specific categories of aged blacks, such as aged black males without spouses in rural areas of the South.

Certainly studies investigating the quality of care received by aged blacks in various health settings, including clinics, is needed to, among other things, resolve the issue of the most appropriate site for their medical care. My belief is that office-based private physicians do not always provide the best care, even when those physicians are black. Some consideration should be given, as well, to relationships between the quantity and quality of care, and, of course, adequate measurements of those phenomena. Also to be considered are health settings where race is or is not a factor, including particular preferences of aged blacks for black health providers.

Clarification of the special medical and related problems of aged blacks is needed, with an understanding that turnover through death and new entrants within that population is relatively rapid. Thus, findings based upon given cohorts may not apply to successive cohorts. This clarification must also be based upon emerging findings showing clearly that the overall health statuses of aged blacks and whites are not substantially different.

Needless to say, abuses or exploitations of aged blacks under Medicare or Medicaid, even when the abusers or exploiters are black, must be identified and halted. Color-blind legislation is appropriate here.

Finally, any consideration of the special health problems of aged blacks cannot ignore those of younger blacks. Reverse age discrimination, becoming more prevalent within our society, as in the case of reduced drug prices for the aged, regardless of income or need, must be con-sidered. Perhaps, those special benefits are unconstitutional. Eligibility might be deter-mined more appropriately by income levels. In any case, the down-the-road effects of increasing reverse age discrimination must be considered, if, for no other reason than to prevent the aged from becoming a minority group.

One special problem which many aged blacks in nursing homes may have is that few of the staff and residents are sufficiently knowledgeable about some of the racial hardships or notable events which they wish to discuss. One simple example is that even many younger black adults remain unaware of voting disenfranchisement of blacks in years past (but not so many years ago!) in the South.

Some black critics of nursing homes, them-selves non-aged and generally ignorant about nursing homes, harp on the lack of "soul food." When pushed to define soul food, however, difficulties abound, due to failures to recognize the considerable heterogeneity in black diets throughout the years. For example, some aged blacks *never* ate chitterlings. Others never cooked collard greens with salt back meat. Therefore, rather than rely heavily upon the advice of uninformed "outsiders" about the special problems which aged blacks may or do encounter in nursing homes, cogent research may be in order.

Data about home care for needy aged blacks are also slim, but it is reasonable to assume that adequate home care is sometimes adversely affected by insufficient physical facilities, and other typically specified variables. Information about the special medical and related problems of aged blacks being cared for within their homes, or the homes of others, is yet needed. For example, many blacks believe strongly (and, perhaps, rightly) that black domestics or home-care attendants work less efficiently for blacks than non-blacks. Is this now true? If so, for whom is it true among aged blacks, and how does it affect those requiring such services?

Implications

By now, you know how I applied the Alician principle. Very seriously, determining precisely the special health problems of aged blacks is presently impossible, given the scant data available about them, and quite importantly, their considerable heterogeneity in health atti-tudes and behaviors, including dietary patterns. Concentration upon hypertensive aged blacks, for example, ignores those burdened with malignant neoplasms or corns and callouses.

Health is a crucial problem for most aged blacks. Needed yesterday are (1) sufficient knowledge, periodically up-dated, about their health patterns, with an intensive focus upon biomedical research and related areas; (2) well-distributed health providers qualified to serve them; and (3) wherever necessary, sufficient societal supports to provide them with tangible and intangible rewards, such as hearing aids, necessary for health maintenance.

As a first step in this direction, highly reliable and experienced gerontologists, health providers, and biomedical researchers who can chart needed research should be convened. It is important to stress that such a conference would concentrate upon the health patterns and conditions of aged blacks, and not those of aged nonwhites. The participants would not be selected on the basis of race, but on the basis of their ability to contribute to the task at hand.

This caution is advisable, since the few Federal attempts to set forth research needs for aged blacks in the past have generally ignored critical participants, including biomedical researchers, epidemiologists, health planners, and health providers experienced in treating aged blacks. For example, the recent set of recommendations about minority aging developed for the Federal Council on Aging is, in my view, repetitive and primitive, and fails to address appropriately the significant health problems of aged blacks.

REFERENCES

[1] Jacquelyne J. Jackson and Bertram E. Walls, "Myths and Realities about Aged Blacks," in *Readings in Gerontology*, Second Edition, edited by M. Brown (St. Louis: C. V. Mosby Company, 1978).

[2] Louis Harris & Associates. *The Myth and Reality of Aging in America* (Washington, D.C. National Council on the Aging, 1975).

[3] See, e.g., Adrian M. Ostfeld, "Nutrition and Aging—Discussant's Perspective," in *Epidemiology of Aging*, edited by Adrian M. Ostfeld and Don C. Gibson (Washington, D.C.: United States Government Printing Office, no date given, DHEW Publication No. (NIH) 75-711, pp. 215-222.

[4] The 1971-74 prevalence rates per 100 for definite hypertension for persons 55-64 years of age were 54.5 for black females, 49.9 for black males, 31.7 for white females, and 31.1 for white males; for persons 65-74 years of age, 58.8 for black females, 50.1 for black males, 42.3 for white females, and 35.3 for white males. Jean Roberts, "Blood Pressure Levels of Persons 6-74 Years, United States, 1971-1974." See *Vital and Health Statistics*, Series 11, No. 203, DHEW Pub. No. (HRA) 78-1648 (Washington, D.C.: U. S. Government Printing Office, 1977).

[5] Robert E. Shank, "Nutrition and Aging," in *Epidemiology of Aging, op. cit.*, pp. 199-213.

[6] The data were obtained from the National Center for Health Statistics, *Dietary Intake Findings United States, 1971-1974*, Vital and Health Statistics, Series 11, #202, DHEW Publication # (HRA) 77-1647 (Washington, D.C.: United States Government Printing Office, 1977).

[7] Ostfeld, *op. cit.*

[8] Specifically, the number of days of restricted activity per person per year for non-white females was 59.9 for those 65-74 years, and 65.2 for those 75 or older. Corresponding data for their male counterparts were 43.5 and 67.8 days. The average number of days of bed disability per person per year for nonwhite females was 24.2 for those 65-74 years, and 35.4 for those 75 or older; for nonwhite males, the average was 16.5 for those 65-74 years, and 32.3 for those 75 or older.

[9] The available data about limitations of activity and mobility were self-reported data, causing us to emphasize that the correlations between self-reports and medical reports are not known for aged blacks. This is especially important since lower income persons may tend to exaggerate their physical conditions or illnesses. Also, we do not know the extent to which such self-reported limitations are affected by physical resources. For example, individuals experiencing arthritis with adequate personal transportation may be far less likely to report serious limitations than those dependent upon poor public transportation.

[10] In 1975, nonwhite aged accounted for only 1.1 percent of all visits to office-based physicians in patient care. Of those who visited, about 11 percent were new patients for the specific physician, 18 percent were old patients with new problems, and the remaining 71 percent were old patients with old problems. The physicians felt that about 31 percent of these patients had serious problems, about 36 percent, slightly serious problems, and the problems of the remaining 33 percent were not serious, according to Hugo K. Koch, "National Ambulatory Medical Care Survey," *Vital and Health Statistics*, Series 13, #33, DHEW Publication (PHS) 78 1784 (Hyattsville, Maryland: National Center for Health Statistics, 1978).

[11] Donald K. Ingram, "Profile of Chronic Illness in Nursing Homes, United States, August 1973-April 1974," *Vital and Health Statistics*, Series 13, #29, DHEW Publication (PHS) 78-1780 (Hyattsville, Maryland, National Center for Health Statistics, 1977).

[12] John Nowlin, "Successful Aging: Health and Social Factors in an Interracial Population," *BLACK AGING*, 2, 1977.

Part four:
Resources

Transitions in Middle-Age and Aging Families: A Bibliography* from 1940 to 1977**

Robert A. Lewis***

The Family Coordinator, Vol. 27, No. 4, October, 1978. Special Issue: Aging in a Family Context, Timothy N. Brubaker and Lawrence E. Sneden, II, Guest Editors. Copyright © 1978 by the National Council on Family Relations, Minneapolis. Reprinted with permission.

One way to view adult development or aging individuals within the context of the family is to focus upon those major turning points (role transitions) in family life which affect and are affected by aging family members. For much too long aging has been considered something which mysteriously happens to men and women at their 65th birthday. It is time to recognize fully that all individuals are aging and that those who are the more aged probably affect family groups at all points in their existence, e.g., grandparents are continuously interacting with younger generations.

In order to acknowledge these facts, the turning point of child-launching was chosen as the starting point in this bibliography, since it is clearly one of those times when an older generation (the parents) is vitally concerned with placing the youngest generation into the society and assisting their children,

albeit somewhat covertly, in choosing mates and setting up their own families of procreation.

Since there has been no major bibliography which has related the areas of adult development/aging and family study, we have spent literally three years in consulting all possible sources of bibliographic information, including every known gerontological and family-related journal, book and thesis which was available to us. The extensive libraries at the Andrus Gerontology Center at the University of Southern California and the Gerontology Center and Institute for the study of Human Development at the Pennsylvania State University were especially helpful in generating some of the lesser known articles and reports not yet published.

References are classified according to the major role transitions in later family life, as follows:

I. **The Transition into Child Launching** . .
   A. *Parents' Efforts in Mate Selection and Placement of Children into Society*. . . . .
   B. *Intergenerational Value Transmission: Continuities and Discontinuities* . . . .
II. **The Transition into Post-parenthood** . .
   A. *Return to the Dyadic Relationship* .
   B. *Love, Marriage and Time: Disengagement and Disenchantment*. . . . .
   C. *Dual-careers and Career Changes* .
III. **The Transition into Grandparenthood** .
IV. **The Transition into Retirement** . . . .
V. **The Transition into Aging** . . . .
   A. *Economic, Social and Housing Needs of Aging Couples* . . . .

*This bibliography was made possible by a grant provided through the Gerontology Center, College of Human Development, The Pennsylvania State University. Special appreciation is given to Gail Berman, Philip Freneau, Carol Kelly, Janice Koester, Adrian Krisbert and Ed Schelb, without whose efforts this contribution would not have been made.

**Since considerable time and effort have gone into the building of this bibliography, it should be quite inclusive of family research on the middle and aging years of the family life cycle through 1977. Therefore, if an article is not found in a topical section where one thinks it should be, it may be located elsewhere in the bibliography under a related section. In other words, we have attempted to minimize the overlap of references in order to keep the bibliography in the shortest form possible.

***Robert Lewis is Director, Center for Family Studies, Arizona State University, Tempe, Arizona 85281.

I. The Transition into Child Launching

A. *Parents' Efforts in Mate Selection and Placement of Children into Society*

Adams, B. N. Structural factors affecting parental aide to married children. *Journal of Marriage and the Family*, 1964, **26**, 327-331.

Allingham, J. D. Class regression: An aspect of the social stratification process. *American Sociological Review*, 1967, **32**, 442-449.

Almquist, E., & Angrist, S. Career salience and atypicality of occupational choice among college women. *Journal of Marriage and the Family*, 1970, **32**, 242-249.

Angrist, S. Variations in women's adult aspirations. *Journal of Marriage and the Family*, 1972, **34**, 465-468.

Astin, H. S., & Bisconti, A. S. *Career plans of college graduates of 1965 and 1970.* C.P.C. Foundation Report No. 2. (Available from the College Placement Council, Inc., P.O. Box 2263, Bethlehem, PA 18001) 1973.

Ayoub, M. R. The family reunion. *Ethnology*, 1966, **5**, 415-433.

Barnett, R. C. Vocational planning of college women: A psycho-social study. *Proceedings: The American Psychological Association.* Washington: The Association, 1967.

Bartz, K., & Nye, F. I. Early Marriage: A propositional formulation. *Journal of Marriage and the Family*, 1970, **32**, 258-268.

Baruch, R. The achievement motive in women: Implications for career development. *Journal of Personality and Social Psychology*, 1967, **5**, 260-267.

Baruch, B. Maternal influences upon college women's attitudes toward women and work. *Developmental Psychology*, 1972, **6**, 32-37.

Bates, A. Parental roles in courtship. *Social Forces*, 1942, **20**, 483-486.

Bell, R. The daughter's role during the "launching stage." *Journal of Marriage and Family Living*, 1962, **24**, 384-388.

Bradley, C. A. *Changes in family structure, family roles, and affective behavior for husbands and wives during the launching stage.* Unpublished master's thesis. Athens, Georgia: The University of Georgia, 1972.

Brewer, J. M. *Marital adjustment in the launching years.* Unpublished Master's thesis. Athens, Georgia: The University of Georgia, 1973.

Brim, O. G., & Foyer, R. A note on the relation of values and social structure to life planning. *Sociometry*, 1956, **19**, 54-60.

Bruce, J. A. The role of mothers in the social placement of daughters: Marriage or work? *Journal of Marriage and the Family*, 1974, **36**, 492-497.

Bruce, J. A. Intergenerational solidarity versus progress for women. *Journal of Marriage and the Family*, 1976, **36**, 492-497.

Caro, G. *Paths toward adulthood, a study of post high school activities.* (Publication 142), (Available from community Studies, Inc., ZWYO, Kansas City, MO 753-6529). 1965.

Childs, D. Some reference groups of university students. *Educational Research*, 1970, **12**, 145-149.

Christensen, H. Lifetime family and occupational role projections of high school students, *Marriage and Family Living*, 1961, **23**, 181-183.

Coleman, J. *How do the young become adults?* Paper presented at the American Educational Research Association, Annual Meeting, 1972.

Coombs, R. H. Reinforcement of values in the parental home as a factor in mate selection. *Marriage and Family Living*, 1962, **24**, 155-157.

Crowne, D. P., Conn, L. K., Marlowe, D., & Edwards, C. N. Some developmental antecedents of level of aspiration. *Journal of Personality*, 1969, **37**, 73-92.

Cutright, P. E. Income and family events: Getting married. *Journal of Marriage and the Family*, 1970, **32**, 628-637.

Davidson, B. Nothing's too good for my daughter. *Saturday Evening Post*, 1966, August 13, 28-35.

de Lissovoy, V. High school marriages: A longitudinal study. *Journal of Marriage and the Family*, 1973, **35**, 245-255.

Dinitz, S., Banks, F., & Pasamanick, B. Mate selection and social class: Changes during the past quarter century. *Marriage and Family Living*, 1960, **22**, 348-351.

Driscoll, R., Davis, K. E., & Lipetz, M. E. Parental interference and romantic love: The Romeo and Juliet effect. *Journal of Personality and Social Psychology*, 1972, **24**, 1-10.

Dynes, R. R., Clark, A. C., & Dinitz, S. Levels of occupational aspiration: Some aspects of family experience as a variable. *American Sociological Review*, 1956, **21**, 212-215.

Duvall, E. M. *In-laws: Pro and con.* New York: Association Press, 1954.

Elder, G. H., Jr. Achievement motivation and intelligence in occupational mobility: A longitudinal analysis. *Sociometry*, 1968, **31**, 327-354.

Elder, G. H., Jr. Occupational level, achievement motivation, and social mobility: A longitudinal analysis. *Journal of Counseling Psychology*, 1968, **15**, 1-7.

Elder, G. H., Jr. Appearance and education in marriage mobility. *American Sociological Review*, 1969, **34**, 519-533.

Ellis, E. Social psychological correlates of upward social mobility among unmarried career women. *American Sociological Review*, 1952, **17**, 558-563.

Feldman, H. *Parents and marriage: Myths and realities.* Paper presented at Merrill Palmer Conference on the Family, 1969.

Goldsen, R. K., Rosenberg, M., Williams, R. M. Jr., & Suchman, E. A. *What college students think.* Princeton, N.J.: Van Nostrand, 1960.

Hartog, J. de. *The fourposter* (Act 3, Scene 1), New York: Random House, 1952.

Haydee, A. R., M. Weekend of living together of parents and sons. *Revista Del Instituto De La Juventud*, 1971, **35**, 9-29.

Heilbrun, A. B., Harrel, S. N., & Gillard, B. J. Achievement motivation and fear of social nonreaction upon achievement motivation. *Child Development*, 1967, 267-281.

Hermand, H. J., Laak, J. J., & Meas, P. C. Achievement motivation and fear of failure in family and school. *Developmental Psychology*, 1972, **6**, 520-528.

Hewitt, L. E. Student perceptions of traits desired in themselves as dating and marriage partners. *Marriage and Family Living*, 1958, **20**, 344-349.

Hill, R. *Family development in three generations.* Cambridge, Mass.: Schenkman, 1970.

Hill, R., & Aldous, J. Socialization for marriage and parenthood. In David A. Goslin (Ed.), *Handbook of socialization.* Chicago: Rand McNally, 1969.

Hiltner, H. J. Changing family tasks of adults. *Marriage and Family Living*, 1953, **15**, 110-113.

Hobart, C. Emancipation from parents and courtship in adolescence. *Pacific Sociological Review*, 1958, **6**, 25-29.

Hudson, J. W., & Henze, L. F. Campus values in mate

selection: A replication. *Journal of Marriage and the Family*, 1969, **31**, 772-775.

Jacobson, G., & Ryder, R. G. Parental loss and some characteristics of the early marriage relationship. *American Journal of Orthopsychiatry*, 1969, **39**, 779-787.

Kahana, B. *Do parents undergo a middle age crisis? Perceptions of young adults*. A paper presented at the meetings of the Gerontological Society. Louisville, October 26-30, 1975.

Lane, R. E. Fathers and sons: Foundations of political belief. *American Sociological Review*, 1959, **24**, 502-511.

Lee, R., & Casebier, M. *The spouse gap: Weathering the marriage crisis during middlescence*. Nashville: Abingdon, 1971.

Leemon, T. A. *The rites of passage in a student culture: A study of the dynamics of transition*. New York: Teachers College Press, 1972.

Lerrigo, M. O., & Southard, H. *Approaching adulthood*. Chicago: American Medical Association, 1970.

Lewis, R. A. Social reaction and the formation of dyads: An interactionist approach to mate selection. *Sociometry*, 1973, **34**, 490-518.

Lewis, R. A. *Papers, peers and pairs: A reformulation for mate selection theory*. A paper presented to the Theory Construction Workshop, National Council on Family Relations, Toronto, October, 1973.

Lewis, R. A. Social influences on marital choice. In S. E. Dragastin & G. E. Elder, Jr. (Eds.), *Adolescence in the life cycle*. Washington, D.C.: Hemisphere, 1975.

Long, B. H., Ziller, R. C., & Henderson, E. H. Developmental changes in the self-concept during adolescence. *The School Review*, 1969, **76**, 210-230.

Lopiccolo, J. Mothers and daughters: Perceived and real difference in sexual values. *Journal of Sex Research*, 1973, **9**, 171-177.

Marquand, J. P. *The late George Apley*. Boston: Little, Brown, 1937.

McGuire, C. Conforming, mobile, and divergent families. *Marriage and Family Living*, 1952, **14**, 113.

Meier, H. C. Mother-centeredness and college youths' attitudes toward social equality for women: Some empirical findings. *Journal of Marriage and the Family*, 1972, **34**, 115-121.

Mueller, C. W., & Pope, H. Marital instability: A study of its transmission between generations. *Journal of Marriage and the Family*, 1977, **39**, 83-93.

Paul, N. L., & Paul, B. B. *A marital puzzle: Transgenerational analysis in marriage*. New York: Norton, 1975.

Riley, M. W., Forer, A., Hess, B., & Toby, M. L. Socialization for the middle and later years. In D. A. Goslin (Ed.), *Handbook of socialization theory and research*. Chicago: Rand McNally, 1969.

Rodgers, R. H. The occupational role of the child: A research frontier in the developmental conceptual framework. *Social Forces*, 1966, **45**, 217-224.

Roe, A. Early determinants of vocational choice. *Journal of Counseling Psychology*, 1957, **4**, 212-217.

Rosen, L., & Bell, R. Mate selection in the upper class. *Sociological Quarterly*, 1966, **7**, 157-166.

Rubin, Z. Do American women marry up? *American Sociological Review*, 1968, **5**, 750-760.

Ryder, R., Kafka, J., & Olson, D. Separating and joining influences in courtship and early marriage. *American Journal of Orthopsychiatry*, 1971, **41**, 450-464.

Schnaiberg, A., & Goldberg, S. Closing the circle: The impact of children on parental status. *Journal of Marriage and the Family*, 1975, **37**, 937-953.

Schulberg, B. *What makes Sammy run?* New York: Bantam, 1945.

Solomon, D. Adolescents' decisions: A comparison of influence from parents with that from other sources. *Marriage and Family Living*, 1961, **23**, 393-395.

Sussman, M. B. Parental participation in mate selection

and its effect upon family continuity. *Social Forces*, 1953, **32**, 76-81.

Sussman, M. B., & Burchinal, L. Kin family network: Unheralded structure in current conceptualizations of family functioning. *Marriage and Family Living*, 1962, **24**, 231-240.

Troll, L., Neugarten, B., & Kraines, R. Similarities in values and other personality characteristics in college students and their parents. *Merrill-Palmer Quarterly*, 1969, **15**, 323-336.

Woelfel, J. Significant others and their role relationships to students in a high school population. *Rural Sociology*, 1972, **37**, 86-97.

B. *Intergenerational Value Transmission: Continuities and Discontinuities*

Aldous, J. The consequences of intergenerational continuity. *Journal of Marriage and the Family*, 1965, **27**, 462-468.

Aldous, J., & Hill, R. Social cohesion, lineage type, and intergenerational transmission. *Social Forces*, 1965, **43**, 471-482.

Baltes, P., & Nesselroade, J. Cultural change and adolescent personality development: An application of longitudinal sequences. *Developmental Psychology*, 1970, **32**, 244-256.

Bath, J., & Lewis, E. Attitudes of young female adults toward some areas of parent-adolescent conflict. *Journal of Genetic Psychology*, 1972, **100**, 241-253.

Bell, R. R., & Buerkle, J. V. Mother and daughter attitudes to premarital sexual behavior. *Marriage and Family Living*, 1961, **23**, 390-392.

Bell, R. R., & Buerkle, J. V. Mother-daughter conflict during the launching stage. *Marriage and Family Living*, 1962, **24**, 384-388.

Bengtson, V. L. *A pilot study of intergenerational relations as perceived by college students: The "generation gap" at University of Southern California*. Unpublished paper, 1968.

Bengtson, V. L. *The "generation gap": Differences by generation and by sex in the perception of parent-child relations*. Unpublished paper presented at Pacific Sociological Association, Seattle, Washington, April 24, 1969.

Bengtson, V. L. The generation gap: A review and typology of social-psychological perspective. *Youth and Society*, 1970, **2**, 7-32.

Bengtson, V. L. Inter-age perceptions and the generation gap. *The Gerontologist*, 1971, **11**, 85-89.

Bengtson, V. L., & Black, K. D. Intergenerational relations and continuities in socialization. In P. Baltes & K. W. Schaie (Eds.), *Life span developmental psychology: Personality and socialization*. New York: Academic Press, 1973.

Bengtson, V. L., & Lovejoy, M. C. Values, personality, and social structure: An intergenerational analysis. *American Behavioral Scientist*, 1973, **16**, 880-912.

Bengtson, V. L., & Kuypers, J. A. Generational difference and the developmental stake. *Aging and Human Development*, 1971, **2**, 249-260.

Birren, J. E., & Bengtson, V. L. The truth about the generation gap. *National Retired Teachers Association Journal*, 1970, **20**, 31-32.

Blood, L., & D-Angelo, R. A progress research report on value issues in conflict between runaways and their parents. *Journal of Marriage and the Family*, 1974, **36**, 486-491.

Borke, H. Continuity and change in the transmission of adaptive patterns over two generations. *Marriage and Family Living*, 1963, **25**, 294-299.

Borke, H. A family over three generations: The transmission of interacting and relating patterns. *Journal of Marriage and the Family*, 1967, **29**, 639-655.

Braungart, R. G. Status politics and student politics: An analysis of left- and right-wing student activists. *Youth and Society*, 1971, **3**, 195-209.

Brim, O., Jr. Socialization after childhood. In O. Brim, Jr. and S. Wheeler (Eds.), *Socialization through the life cycle*. New York: Wiley, 1966.

Brunswick, A. F. What generation gap? A comparison of some generational differences among blacks and whites. *Social Problems*, 1969-70, **17**, 358-370.

Calonico, J. M., & Thomas, D. L. Role taking as a function of value similarity and affect in the nuclear family. *Journal of Marriage and the Family*, 1973, **35**, 655-665.

Clausen, J. A. Perspectives on childhood socialization. In J. A. Clausen (Ed.), *Socialization and society*. Boston: Little, Brown, 1968.

Connell, R. W. Political socialization in the American family: The evidence re-examined. *Public Opinion Quarterly*, 1972, **36**, 321-333.

Davis, K. The sociology of parent-youth conflict. *American Sociological Review*, 1940, **5**, 523-534.

Dinkel, R. M. Parent-child conflict in Minnesota families. *American Sociological Review*, 1943, **8**, 412-419.

Elder, G. H., Jr. *Adolescent socialization and personality development*. Chicago: Rand McNally, 1968.

Ellenwood, J. L. *One generation after another: On the training of children and their parents*. New York: Scribner's Sons, 1953.

Eisenstadt, S. N. *From Generation to Generation*. Glencoe, Ill.: Free Press, 1965.

Fallding, H. A proposal for the empirical study of values. *American Sociological Review*, 1965, **30**, 223-233.

Fengler, A., & Wood, V. The generation gap: An analysis of attitudes on contemporary issues. *The Gerontologist*, 1972, **12**, 124-128.

Feuer, L. S. *The conflict of generations: The character and significance of student movements*. New York: Basic, 1969.

Fisher, S., & Mendell, D. The communication of neurotic patterns over two and three generations. *Psychiatry*, 1956, **10**, 41-46.

Flacks, R. The liberated generation: An exploration of the roots of student protest. *Journal of Social Issues*, 1967, **23**, 52-72.

Foote, N. The old generation and the new. In E. Ginsberg (Ed.), *The nation's children*, Vol. 3. New York: Columbia University Press, 1960.

Foner, A. Age stratification and age conflict in political life. *American Sociological Review*, 1974, **39**, 187-196.

Fortune-Yankelovich Survey. What they believe. *Fortune*, 1969, **79**, 70-71, 179-181.

Friedenberg, E. J. Current patterns of a generational conflict. *Journal of Social Issues*, 1969, **25**, 21-30.

Friedman, L. N., Gold, A. R., & Christie, R. C. Dissecting the generation gap: Intergenerational and intrafamilial similarities and differences. *Public Opinion Quarterly*, 1972, **36**, 334-346.

Furstenberg, F. F., Jr. The transmission of mobility orientation in the family. *Social Forces*, 1971, **49**, 595-603.

Goertzel, T. Generational conflict and social change. *Youth and Society*, 1972, **3**, 327-352.

Goslin, D. A. (Ed.). Introduction. In D. Goslin (Ed.), *Handbook of socialization theory and research*. Chicago: Rand McNally, 1969.

Gravatt, A. E. Family relations in middle and old age: A review. *Journal of Gerontology*, 1953, **8**, 197-201.

Gray, R. M., & Smith, T. C. Effect of employment on sex differences in attitudes toward the parental family. *Marriage and Family Living*, 1960, **22**, 36-38.

Henry, J. Family structure and the transmission of neurotic behavior. *American Journal of Orthopsychiatry*, 1951, **21**, 800-818.

Hill, R., Foote, N., Aldous, J., Carlson, R., & MacDonald, R. *Family development in three generations*. Cambridge: Schenkman, 1970.

Inglehart, R. The silent revolution in Europe: Intergenerational change in post-industrial societies. *American Political Science Review*, 1971, **65**, 991-1017.

Irving, H. Relationships between married couples and their parents. *Social Casework*, 1971, **42**, 91-96.

Jacobsen, R. B., Berry, K. J., & Olson, K. F. An empirical test of the generation gap: A comparative intrafamily study. *Journal of Marriage and the Family*, 1975, **37**, 841-852.

Jennings, M. K., & Niemi, R. The transmission of political values from parent to child. *American Political Science Review*, 1968, **42**, 169-184.

Jennings, M. K., & Niemi, R. *Continuity and change in political orientations: A longitudinal study of two generations*. A paper presented at the annual meeting of the American Political Science Association, New Orleans, Louisiana, September 4-8, 1973.

Kalish, R. A., & Johnson, A. I. Value similarities and differences in three generations of women. *Journal of Marriage and the Family*, 1972, **34**, 49-54.

Kandel, D. Adolescent marijuana use: Role of parents and peers. *Science*, 1973, **181**, 1067-1070.

Kandel, D. Inter- and intra-generational influences on adolescent marijuana use. *Journal of Social Issues*, 1974, **30**, 107-135.

Kandel, D., & Lesser, G. *Youth in two worlds*. San Francisco: Jossey-Bass, 1972.

Kasschau, P., Ransford, E., & Bengtson, V. L. Generational consciousness and youth movement participation: Contrasts in blue-collar and white-collar youth. *Journal of Social Issues*, 1974, **30**, 69-94.

Kavaler, L. Hidden conflicts in marriage. *Parents Magazine*, 1969, **44**, 35-37; 86-90.

Keniston, K. *Young radicals: Notes on committed youth*. New York: Harcourt, 1968.

Kluckhohn, C. Values and value-orientations in the theory of action: An exploration in definition and classification. In T. Parsons & E. Shils (Eds.), *Toward a general theory of action*. Cambridge: Harvard University Press, 1951.

Kohn, M. L. *Class and conformity: A study in values*. Homewood, Illinois: Dorsey, 1969.

Koller, M. Studies in three-generation households. *Marriage and Family Living*, 1964, **16**, 205-206.

Koller, M. R. *Families: A multigenerational approach*. New York: McGraw-Hill, 1974.

Laufer, R. Sources of generational conflict and consciousness. In P. Altbach & R. Laufer (Eds.), *The new pilgrims: Youth protest in transition*. New York: David McKay, 1972.

Laufer, R., & Bengston, V. L. Generations and social stratification in advanced industrial society. *Journal of Social Issues*, 1974, **30**, 181-206.

Lerner, R. M., Schroeder, C., Rewitzer, M., & Weinstock, A. Attitudes of high school students and their parents toward contemporary issues. *Psychological Reports*, 1972, **31**, 255-258.

Lesser, G., & Kandel, D. Parental and peer influences on educational plans of adolescents, *American Sociological Review*, 1969, **34**, 213-223.

Lewis, R. A. Socialization into national violence: Familial correlates of hawkish attitudes toward war. *Journal of Marriage and the Family*, 1971, **33**, 699-708.

Lewis, R. A. The generation gap in sexual beliefs. A comment. *Sexual Behavior*, 1972, **2**, 2.

Lewis, R. A. Parents and peers: Socialization agents in the coital behavior of young adults. *The Journal of Sex Research*, 1973, **9**, 156-170.

Lewis, R. A. The family life of the hawk. In S. Steinmetz & M. Straus (Eds.), *Violence in the family*, New York: Dodd, Mead, 1974.

Lopiccolo, J. Mothers and daughters: Perceived and real difference in sexual values. *Journal of Sex Research*,

1973, **9**, 171-177.

Mannheim, K. The problem of generations. In D. Kecskemeti (Ed.), *Essays on the sociology of knowledge.* London: Routledge and Kegan Paul, 1952.

Mead, M. *Culture and commitment: A study of the generation gap.* New York: Doubleday, 1969.

Neugarten, B. L. Continuities and discontinuities of psychological issues into adult life. *Human Development,* 1968, **12**, 121-130.

Neugarten, B., Moore, J., & Lowe, J. C. Age norms, age constraints and adult socialization. *American Journal of Sociology,* 1964, **70**, 710-717.

Neugarten, B. L., & Datan, N. Sociological perspectives on the life cycle. In P. Baltes & K. W. Schaie, (Eds.), *Lifespan developmental psychology.* New York: Academic Press, 1973.

Olejntk, A. B., & McKinney, J. P. Parental value orientation and generosity in children. *Developmental Psychology,* 1973, **8**, 311.

Payne, S., & Summers, D. V. Value differences across three generations. *Sociometry,* 1973, **36**, 20-30.

Penn, J. R. Intergenerational differences: Scientific fact or scholarly opinion. *Youth and Society,* 1974, **3**, 350-359.

Pope, H., & Knudsen, D. D. Premarital sexual norms, the family, and social change. *Journal of Marriage and the Family,* 1965, **27**, 314-323.

Raymond, B., Damino, J., & Kandel, N. Sex stereotyping in values: A comparison of three generations and two sexes. *Perceptual and Motor Skills,* 1974, **39**, 163-166.

Reich, C. *The greening of America.* New York: Random House, 1970.

Riley, M. W., Fonel, A., Hess, B., & Toby, M. L. Socialization for the middle and later years. In D. A. Goslin (Ed.), *Handbook of socialization theory and research.* Chicago: Rand McNally, 1968.

Rokeach, M. *Beliefs, attitudes and values: A theory of organization and change.* San Francisco: Jossey-Bass, 1968.

Rokeach, M. *The nature of human values.* New York: Free Press, 1973.

Roper, B. S., & Labeff, E. Sex roles and feminism revisited: An intergenerational attitude comparison. *Journal of Marriage and the Family,* 1977, **39**, 113-119.

Rosen, B. C. Family structure and value transmission. *Merrill-Palmer Quarterly,* 1964, **10**, 59-75.

Roszak, T. *The making of a counter culture: Reflections on the technocratic society and its youthful opposition.* London: Faber, 1969.

Slater, P. M. *The pursuit of loneliness,* Boston: Beacon Press, 1970.

Starr, J. M. The peace and love generation: Changing attitudes toward sex and violence among college youth. *Journal of Social Issues,* 1974, **31**, 73-106.

Strommen, M., Brekke, M., Underwager, R., & Johnson, A. *A study of generations.* Minneapolis: Augsburg, 1972.

Sussman, M. B. *Family continuity: Factors which affect relationships between families at generational levels.* An unpublished doctoral dissertation. Yale University, 1951.

Sussman, M. B. Parental participation in mate selection and its effect upon family continuity. *Social Forces,* 1953, **32**, 76-87.

Sussman, M. B. Family continuity: Selective factors which affect relationships between families at generational levels. *Marriage and Family Living,* 1954, **16**, 112-120.

Thomas, E. L. Political attitude congruence between politically active parents and college-aged children. *Journal of Marriage and the Family,* 1971, **33**, 375-386.

Thomas, E. L. Generational discontinuity in beliefs: An exploration of the generation gap. *Journal of Social Issues,* 1974, **30**, 1-22.

Thurnher, M., Spence, D., & Lowenthal, M. Value confluence and behavioral conflict in intergenerational relations. *Journal of Marriage and the Family,* 1974, **36**, 308-319.

Troll, L. E. Issues in the study of generations. *Aging and Human Development,* 1970, **1**, 199-218.

Troll, L. E. Is parent-child conflict what we mean by the generation gap? *The Family Coordinator,* 1972, **21**, 347-349.

Troll, L. E., Neugarten, B., & Kraines, R. Similarities in values and other personality characteristics in college students and their parents. *Merrill-Palmer Quarterly,* 1969, **15**, 323-337.

Weider, D. L., & Zimmerman, D. H. Generational experience and the development of freak culture. *Journal of Social Issues,* 1974, **30**, 137-161.

Williams, R. M. Change and stability in values and value systems. In B. Barber & A. Inkles (Eds.), *Stability and social change.* Boston: Little, Brown, 1971.

Yankelovich, D. *The changing values on campus.* New York: John D. Rockefeller, III, Fund, 1972.

Yost, E. D., & Adamek, R. J. Parent-child interaction and changing family values: A multivariate analysis. *Journal of Marriage and the Family,* 1974, **36**, 115-121.

Youmans, E. G. Age stratification and value orientations. *International Journal of Aging and Human Development,* 1973, **4**, 53-65.

II. The Transition into Post-Parenthood
A. *Return to the Dyadic Relationship*

Axelson, L. J. Personal adjustment in the postparental period. *Marriage and Family Living,* 1960, **22**, 66-68.

Bell, R. R., & Buerkle, J. U. Mother-daughter conflict during the launching stage. *Marriage and Family Living,* 1962, **24**, 384-388.

Benaim, S., & Allen, I. (Eds.), *The middle years,* London, England: T. V. Publications, 1967.

Brayshaw, J. A. Middle-aged marriage: Idealism, realism and the search for meaning. *Marriage and Family Living,* 1962, **24**, 358-364.

Burr, W. R. Satisfaction with various aspects of marriage over the life cycle: A random middle class sample. *Journal of Marriage and the Family,* 1970, **32**, 29-37.

Chilman, C. S. Families in development at mid-stage of the family life cycle. *The Family Coordinator,* 1968, **17**, 297-312.

Cuber, J. F., & Harroff, P. The more total view: Relationships among men and women of the upper middle class. *Marriage and Family Living,* 1963, **25**, 140-145.

Curlee, J. Alcoholism and the empty nest. *Bulletin of the Menninger Clinic,* 1969, **33**, 170-171.

Davidoff, I. F., & Markewich, M. E. The postparental phase in the life cycle of fifty college-educated women. *Digest of Doctoral Theses for Teacher's College.* New York: Columbia University Press, 1961.

Dentler, R. A., & Pineo, P. Sexual adjustment, marital adjustment and personal growth of husbands: A panel analysis. *Marriage and Family Living,* 1960, **22**, 45-48.

Deutscher, I. Socialization for postparental life. In A. Rose (Ed.), *Human behavior and social process.* Boston: Houghton-Mifflin, 1962.

Deutscher, I. The quality of postparental life: Definitions of the situation. *Journal of Marriage and the Family,* 1964, **26**, 52-59.

Deutscher, I. From parental to postparental life. *Sociological Symposium,* 1969, **3**, 47-60.

Duvall, E. New family roles in middle life. In C. Tibbitts & W. Donahue (Eds.), *Aging in the modern world.* Ann Arbor: University of Michigan Press, 1957.

Foote, N. N. Matching of husband and wife in phases of development. *Transactions of Third World Congress of Society,* 1956, **4**, 24-34.

Foote, N. N. New roles for men and women. *Journal of Marriage and the Family,* 1961, **23**, 326-329.

Franzblau, R. N. *The middle generation.* New York: Holt, Rinehart, 1971.

Gingles, R., & Kezar, E. *Crises of the middle years.* A paper given at the annual meetings of the National Council on Family Relations, St. Louis, October 22, 1974.

Glenn, N. D. Psychological well-being in the postparental stage: Some evidence from national surveys. *Journal of Marriage and the Family*, 1975, **37**, 105-110.

Glick, P. C. Updating the life cycle of the family. *Journal of Marriage and the Family*, 1977, **39**, 5-13.

Gravatt, A. E. An exploratory study of marital adjustment in later maturity. *The Family Coordinator*, 1957, **6**, 23-25.

Gross, I. *Potentialities of women in the middle years.* East Lansing: Michigan State University Press, 1956.

Gurin, G., Veroff, J., & Feld, S. *Americans view their mental health: A nationwide interview study.* New York: Basic Books, 1960.

Hagestad, G. O., & Fagan, M. A. *Patterns of fathering in the middle years.* A paper presented at the annual meetings of the National Council on Family Relations, October 23-26, St. Louis, Missouri, 1974.

Harkins, E. B., & House, J. S. *Effects of empty nest transition on self-report of psychological and physical well-being.* Paper presented at the meetings of the Gerontological Society, Louisville, October 26-30, 1975.

Havinghurst, R. J. The leisure activities of the middle aged. *American Journal of Sociology*, 1957, **63**, 152-162.

Havinghurst, R. J. Middle-age—The new prime of life. In C. Tibbits & W. Donahue (Eds.), *Aging in the modern world.* Ann Arbor: University of Michigan Press, 1957.

Hiltner, H. J. Changing family tasks of adults. *Marriage and Family Living*, 1953, **15**, 110-113.

Jackson, D. W. Advanced aged adults' reflections of middle age. *The Gerontologist*, 1974, **14**, 255-257.

Jaques, E. Death and the mid-life crisis. *International Journal of Psycho-Analysis*, 1965, **46**, 502-514.

Johnson, R. E. Some correlates of extramarital coitus. *Journal of Marriage and the Family*, 1970, **32**, 449-455.

Kerckhoff, R. K. Marriage and middle age. *The Family Coordinator*, 1976, **25**, 5-11.

Kitching, J. C. The self-concept of middle aged women. Florida State University, *Home Economics*, 1972, 22-31.

Kling, S. C. Why middle-aged men revolt. *Family Weekly*, 1969, **October 26**, 6-7.

Lee, R., & Casebier, M. *The spouse gap: Weathering the marriage crisis during middlescence.* Nashville: Abingdon, 1971.

Lowrey, L. G. Adjustment over the life span. In George Lawton (Ed.), *New goals for old age.* New York: Columbia University Press, 1943.

Marmor, J. The crisis of middle age. *American Journal of Orthopsychiatry*, 1967, **37**, 336-337.

Morgan, M. I. The middle life and the aging family. *The Family Coordinator*, 1972, **18**, 296-297.

Murray, J. Family structure in the preretirement years. *Social Security Bulletin*, 1973, **36**, 2-44.

Murstein, B. I. The complementary need hypothesis in newlyweds and middle aged married couples. *Journal of Abnormal and Social Psychology*, 1961, **63**, 194-197.

Neugarten, B. *Middle age and aging: A reader in social psychology.* Chicago: University of Chicago Press, 1968.

Neugarten, B., & Gutmann, D. Age-sex roles and personality in middle age: A thematic apperception study. In B. Neugarten (Ed.), *Middle age and aging.* Chicago: University of Chicago Press, 1968.

Peterson, J. A. *Married love in the middle years.* New York: Association Press, 1968.

Pineo, P. C. Disenchantment in the later years of marriage. *Journal of Marriage and the Family*, 1961, **23**, 3-11.

Pineo, P. C. Development patterns in marriage. *The Family Coordinator*, 1969, **18**, 135-139.

Roe, A., & Baruch, R. Occupational changes in the adult years. *Personnel Administration*, 1967, **30**, 26-32.

Rollins, B. C., & Feldman, H. Marital satisfaction over the family life cycle. *Journal of Marriage and the Family*, 1970, **32**, 20-28.

Rollins, B. C., & Cannon, K. L. Marital satisfaction over the family life cycle: A reevaluation. *Journal of Marriage and the Family*, 1974, **36**, 271-282.

Saunders, L. E. Social class and the postparental perspective. *Dissertation Abstracts International*, 1970, **30**, 4578A.

Schorr, A. L. On selfish children and lonely parents. *The Public Interest*, 1966, **4**, 8-12.

Spanier, G. B., Lewis, R. A., & Cole, C. L. Marital adjustment over the family life cycle: The issue of curvilinearity. *Journal of Marriage and the Family*, 1975, **37**, 263-275.

Spence, D., & Lonner, T. The empty nest: A transition within motherhood. *The Family Coordinator*, 1971, **20**, 369-374.

Sussman, M. Activity patterns of post-parental couples and their relationship to family continuity. *Marriage and Family Living*, 1955, **17**, 338-341.

Sussman, M. B. Intergenerational family relationships and social role changes in middle age. *Journal of Gerontology*, 1960, **15**, 71-75.

Troll, L. Approval of spouse in middle age. *Proceedings, American Psychological Association*, 1969.

Vedder, C. B. (Ed.) *Problems of the middle aged.* Springfield, Ill.: Charles C. Thomas, 1965.

Whitman, H. Let go of that dream. In C. B. Vedder (Ed.), *Problems of the middle aged.* Chicago, Illinois: Charles C. Thomas, 1965.

B. Love, Marriage and Time: Disengagement and Disenchantment

Bossard, J. H. S., & Boll, E. S. Marital unhappiness in the life cycle. *Marriage and Family Living*, 1955, **17**, 10-14.

Burr, W. R. Satisfaction with various aspects of marriage over the life cycle: A random middle class sample. *Journal of Marriage and the Family*, 1970, **32**, 29-37.

Dentler, R. A., & Pineo, P. C. Marriage adjustment, sexual adjustment and personal growth of husbands: A panel study. *Marriage and Family Living*, 1960, **22**, 45-48.

Deutscher, I. The quality of post-parental life: Definition of situation. *Journal of Marriage and the Family*, 1964, **26**, 52-59.

Fengler, A. The effects of age and education on marital ideology. *Journal of Marriage and the Family*, 1973, **35**, 264-270.

Flint, A. A., Jr. Crisis in marriage. *American Journal of Orthopsychiatry*, 1967, **37**, 335-336.

Gravatt, A. E. Exploratory study of marital adjustment in later maturity. *The Family Coordinator*, 1957, **6**, 23-25.

Gurin, G., Veroff, J., & Feld, S. *Americans view their mental health: A nationwide interview study.* New York: Basic Books, 1960.

Johnson, R. E. Some correlates of extramarital coitus. *Journal of Marriage and the Family*, 1970, **32**, 449-455.

Kelley, E. L. The reassessment of specific attitudes after twenty years. *Journal of Social Issues*, 1961, **17**, 29-37.

Knox, D. H., Jr. Conceptions of love at three developmental levels. *The Family Coordinator*, 1970, **19**, 151-157.

Luckey, E. B. Number of years married as related to personality perception and marital satisfaction. *Journal of Marriage and the Family*, 1966, **28**, 44-48.

Marmor, J. The crisis of middle age. *American Journal of Orthopsychiatry*, 1967, **37**, 336.

Paris, B. L., & Luckey, E. B. A longitudinal study of marital satisfaction. *Sociology and Social Research*, 1966, **50**, 212-223.

Pineo, P. C. Disenchantment in the later years of marriage. *Marriage and Family Living*, 1961, **23**, 3-11.

Pineo, P. C. Six marriage types. *Canada's Mental Health*, 1963, **49**, 225-233.

Pineo, P. C. Development patterns in marriage. *The Family Coordinator*, 1969, **18**, 135-139.

Pineo, P. C., & Dentler, R. A. Sexual adjustment, marital adjustment and the personal growth of husbands: A panel analysis. *Marriage and Family Living*, 1960, **22**, 45-48.

Rollins, B. C., & Feldman, H. Marital satisfaction over the family life cycle. *Journal of Marriage and the Family*, 1970, **32**, 20-28.

Rollins, B. C., & Cannon, K. L. Marital satisfaction over the family life cycle: A reevaluation. *The Journal of Marriage and the Family*, 1974, **36**, 271-282.

Rose, A. M. Factors associated with the life satisfaction of middle-class, middle-aged persons. *Marriage and Family Living*, 1955, **17**, 15-19.

Siegel, N. *Intimacy and the older marriage*. A paper presented at the annual meetings of the National Council on Family Relations, St. Louis, Missouri, October 24, 1974.

C. Dual Careers and Career Changes

Becker, H. S., & Strauss, A. L. Careers, personality, and adult socialization. *American Journal of Sociology*, 1956, **62**, 253-263.

Belbin, E., & Belbin, R. M. New careers in middle age. In B. L. Neugarten (Ed.), *Middle age and aging*. Chicago: University of Chicago Press, 1968.

Burke, R. J., & Weir, T. Some personality differences between members of one career and two-career families. *Journal of Marriage and the Family*, 1976, **38**, 453-459.

Clopton, W. Personality and career change. *Industrial Gerontology*, 1973, **17**, 9-17.

Epstein, C. Law partners and marital partners. *Human Relations*, 1971, **24**, 549-564.

Heckman, N. A., Bryson, R., & Bryson, J. B. Problems of professional couples: A content analysis. *Journal of Marriage and the Family*, 1977, **39**, 323-330.

Holmstrom, L. L. *The two-career family*. Cambridge, Mass.: Schenkman, 1972.

Leslie, G. R., & Richardson, A. H. Life-cycle, career pattern, and the decision to move. *American Sociological Review*, 1961, **26**, 894-902.

Lopata, H. Z. *Occupation: Housewife*. London: Oxford University Press, 1971.

Martin, T. W., Berry, K. J., & Jacobsen, R. B. The impact of dual-career marriages on female professional careers: An empirical test of a Parsonian hypothesis. *Journal of Marriage and the Family*, 1975, **37**, 734-742.

Rapoport, R., & Rapoport, R. *Dual-career families*. Baltimore, Md.: Pelican/Penguin, 1971.

Rapoport, R., & Rapoport, R. N. Further considerations on the dual career family. *Human Relations*, 1971, **24**, 519-533.

Rapoport, R., & Rapoport, R. N. Early and later experiences as determinants of adult behaviour: Married women's family and career patterns. *British Journal of Sociology*, 1971, **22**, 16-30.

Rapoport, R., & Rapoport, R. N. *Dual-career families reexamined: New integrations of work and family*. New York: Harper, 1976.

Rosen, B., Thomas, H. J., & Prestwich, T. L. Dual-career marital adjustment: Potential effects of discriminatory managerial attitudes. *Journal of Marriage and the Family*, 1975, **37**, 565-572.

Turner, C. Dual work households and marital dissolution. *Human Relations*, 1971, **24**, 535-548.

Veroff, J., & Feld, S. *Marriage and work in America: A study of motives and roles*. New York: Van Nostrand, 1970.

Wilensky, H. L. Orderly careers and social participation: The impact of work history on social integration in the middle mass. *American Sociological Review*, 1961, **26**, 521-539.

III. The Transition into Grandparenthood

Albrecht, R. The parental responsibilities of grandparents. *Marriage and Family Living*, 1954, **16**, 201-204.

Albrecht, R. The role of older people in family rituals. In C. Tibbetts & W. Donahue (Eds.), *Social and psychological aspects of aging: Aging around the world*. New York: Columbia University Press, 1962.

Apple, D. The social structure of grandparenthood. *American Anthropologist*, 1956, **58**, 656-662.

Atchley, R. C. *The social forces in later life: An introduction to social gerontology*. Belmont, Calif.: Wadsworth, 1972.

Boyd, R. R. The valued grandparent: A changing social role. In W. Donahue (Ed.), *Living in the multigeneration family*. Ann Arbor: Institute of Gerontology, 1969.

Brandt, C. Tips from an old pro grandmother. *Home Life*, 1968, **32**, 26-28.

Cavan, R. S. Self and role in adjustment in old age. In A. M. Rose (Ed.), *Human Behavior and Social Process*. Boston: Houghton Mifflin, 1962.

Davis, R. H. Grandparenting: Varying themes in films. *The Gerontologist*, 1977, **17**, 45-47.

Gilford, R., & Black, D. *The grandchild-grandparent dyad: Ritual or relationship?* Paper presented at the 25th Annual Meeting of the Gerontological Society, San Juan, Puerto Rico, December 17-21, 1972.

Hader, M. The importance of grandparents in family life. *Family Process*, 1965, **4**, 228-240.

Hentig, H. V. The sociological function of the grandmother. *Social Forces*, 1946, **24**, 389-392.

Kahana, B., & Kahana, E. Grandparenthood from the perspective of the developing grandchild. *Developmental Psychology*, 1970, **3**, 98-105.

Kalish, R. A. Of children and grandfathers: A speculative essay on dependency. *Gerontologist*, 1967, **7**, 65-69; 79.

Mead, M. What is modern grandparent's role? *Redbook*, June 1966, 28, 30.

Mead, M. How it feels to be a grandmother. *Redbook*, July 1970, 169.

Nahemow, N. *Grandparenthood in transition: A comparison of two societies*. A paper presented at the 27th annual meeting of the Gerontological Society, Portland, Oregon, October 28-November 1, 1974.

Neugarten, B. L., & Weinstein, K. K. The changing American grandparent. *Journal of Marriage and the Family*, 1964, **26**, 199-204.

Nimkoff, M. F. Family relationships of older people. *The Gerontologist*, 1961, **1**, 92-97.

Richardson, F. H. *Grandparents and their families: A guide for three generations*. New York: McKay, 1964.

Robertson, J. F. Grandmother: A study of role conceptions. *Journal of Marriage and the Family*, 1977, **39**, 165-174.

Robertson, J. F. Significance of grandparents: Perceptions of young adult grandchildren. *The Gerontologist*, 1977, **16**, 137-140.

Saltx, R. Evaluation of a foster grandparent program. In A. Kalushin (Ed.), *Child welfare services: A sourcebook*. New York: Macmillan, 1970.

Updegraff, S. G. Changing role of the grandmother. *Journal of Home Economics*, 1968, **60**, 177-180.

IV. The Transition into Retirement

Ash, P. Pre-retirement counseling. *The Gerontologist*, 1966, **6**, 97-102.

Atchley, R. C. *Retired women: A study of self and role*. American University: Department of Sociology, 1968. (Abstract in DA 28:5151A).

Atchley, R. C. Retirement and leisure participation: Continuity or crisis? *The Gerontologist*, 1971, **11**, 13-17.

Atchley, R. C. Retirement and work orientation. *The Gerontologist*, 1971, **11**, 29-32.

Back, K. W. The ambiguity of retirement. In E. W. Busse & E. Pfeiffer (Eds.), *Behavior and adaptation in late life*. Boston: Little, Brown, 1969.

Back, K. W., & Guptill, C. S. Retirement and self-ratings. In I. H. Simpson & J.C. McKinney (Eds.), *Social aspects of aging*. Duke, N.C.: Duke University Press, 1966.

Ballweg, J. A. Resolution of conjugal role adjustment after retirement. *Journal of Marriage and the Family*, 1967, **29**, 277-281.

Bultena, G. L., & Marshall, D. G. Family patterns of migrant and nonmigrant retirees. *Journal of Marriage and the Family*, 1970, **32**, 89-93.

Barfield, R. E. *The automobile worker and retirement: A second look*. Kansas City, Mo.: Institute for Social Research, 1970.

Barfield, R. E., & Morgan, J. N. *The decision and the experience*. Kansas City, Mo.: Institute for Social Research, 1969.

Barron, M. L., Streib, G., & Suchman, E. A. Research on the social disorganization of retirement. *American Sociological Review*, 1952, **17**, 479-482.

Bell, B. D. *A three phase approach to retirement and life satisfaction*. A paper given at the meetings of the Gerontological Society, Louisville, October 26-30, 1975.

Bellino, R. Psychosomatic problems of military retirement. *Psychosomatics*, 1969, **10**, 318-321.

Bengston, V. L. Cultural and occupational differences in level of present role activity in retirement. In R. J. Havighurst, M. Thomae, B. L. Neugarten, & J. K. A. Munnichs (Eds.), *Adjustment to retirement: A cross-national study*. Assen, The Netherlands: Van Gorkum, 1969.

Bengston, V. L., Chirboga, D. C., & Keller, A. C. Occupational differences in retirement: Patterns of role activity and life-outlook among Chicago retired teachers and steelworkers. In R. J. Havighurst, M. Thomae, B. L. Neugarten, & J. K. A. Munnichs (Eds.), *Adjustment to retirement: A cross-national study*. Assen, The Netherlands: Van Gorkum, 1969.

Bice, T. W., & Eichhorn, R. L. When hard workers retire. *Rural Society*, 1968, **33**, 480-483.

Breen, L. Z. Retirement norms, behavior and functional aspects of normative behavior. In R. H. Williams, C. Tibbits, & W. Donahue (Eds.), *Processes of aging*. New York: Atherton, 1969.

Brooks, T. R. Dilemma of retirement. *Dun's Review and Modern Industry*, 1965, **86**, 84.

Buckley, J. C., & Schmidt, H. *The retirement handbook: A complete planning guide to your future* (3rd ed.). New York: Oxford, 1961.

Buhler, C. Meaningful living in the mature years. In R. Kleemeier (Ed.), *Aging and leisure: A research perspective into the meaningful use of time*. New York: Oxford University Press, 1961.

Butler, R. N. The testing of creativity in later life: Studies of creative people and creative process. In S. Levin & R. Kahana (Eds.), *Psychodynamic studies on aging: Creativity, reminiscing and dying*. New York: International Universities Press, 1971.

Bynum, J. E., Jr. *An exploration of successful retirement adjustment: The formulation of hypotheses*. Unpublished doctoral dissertation, Washington State University, 1972.

Carlberg, G. P. *When a husband retires*. Montclair, N.J.: Economic Press, 1958.

Carp, F. M. Retirement crisis. *Science*, 1967, **157**, 102-103.

Carp, F. M. (Ed.), *Retirement*. New York: Behavioral Publications, 1972.

Charles, D. C. Effects of participation in a pre-retirement program. *Gerontology*, 1971, **1**, 24-28.

Chen, R. The emotional problems of retirement. *Journal of the American Gereatrics Society*, 1968, **16**, 290-295.

Crawford, M. P. Retirement and disengagement. *Human Relations*, 1971, **24**, 255-278.

Darnley, F., Jr. Adjustment to retirement: Integrity or despair. *The Family Coordinator*, 1975, **24**, 217-225.

Davidson, W. R., & Kuze, K. R. Psychological, social, and economic meaning of work in modern society: Their effects on the working facing retirement. *The Gerontologist*, 1965, **5**, 129.

Davis, A. C. *Effect of retirement on family relationships*. Unpublished master's thesis, Duke University, 1967.

Dressler, D. Life adjustment of retired couples. *International Journal of Aging and Human Development*, 1973, **4**, 335-349.

Ekerdt, D. J., & Rose, C. L. *Preference for later retirement: A longitudinal analysis*. A paper given at the Gerontological Society meetings, Louisville, October 26-30, 1975.

Ellison, D. L. Work, retirement and the sick role. *The Gerontologist*, 1968, **8**, 189-192.

Epstein, L. A. Early retirement and wo k-life experience. *Social Security Bulletin*, 1966, **29**, 3-10.

Fields, C. L. *Behind the curtain of retirement*. Philadelphia: Dorrance, 1966.

Fillenbaum, G. G. On the relation between attitude to work and attitude to retirement. *Journal of Gerontology*, 1971, **26**, 244-248.

Fillenbaum, G. G. Retirement planning programs—at what age, and for whom? *Gerontology*, 1971, **26**, 33-37.

Fillenbaum, G. G. The working retired. *Journal of Gerontology*, 1971, **26**, 82-89.

Fillenbaum, G. G., & Maddox, G. L. Work after retirement: An investigation into some psychologically relevant variables. *The Gerontologist*, 1974, **14**, 418-424.

George, L. K. *The impact of retirement on morale: A longitudinal study*. A paper presented at the 27th annual meeting of the Gerontological Society, Portland, Oregon, October 28-November 1, 1974.

Giffen, M. B., & McNeil, J.S. Effects of military retirement on dependents. *Archives of General Psychiatry*, 1967, **17**, 717-722.

Gilford, R. *Marital satisfaction in retirement*. A paper presented at the 27th annual meeting of the Gerontological Society, Portland, Oregon, October 28-November 1, 1974.

Gordon, M. S. Work and patterns of retirement. Andrus Gerontology Center Library, University of Southern California, Berkeley, California (no date).

Goudy, W., Jr., & Barb, K. H. *Changes in the relationship between attitudes toward work and attitudes toward retirement: A longitudinal study*. A paper given at the meetings of the Gerontological Society, Louisville, October 26-30, 1975.

Halpern, D. The relationship of work values to satisfaction with retirement and future time perspective. *Dissertation Abstracts*, 1967, **28**, (5B) 2125-2126.

Hansen, G. D. *Home managerial tasks, perceived competence, and related social, psychological, and economic consequences for retired couples*. Unpublished doctoral dissertation, Oregon State University, 1969.

Hart, M. *When your husband retires*. New York: Appleton, 1960.

Haus, M. R., & Sussman, M.B. The second career—variant of a sociological concept. *Journal of Gerontology*, 1978, **22**, 439-444.

Havighurst, R. J. Flexibility and the social roles of the retired. *The American Journal of Sociology*, 1954, **59**, 310-311.

Havighurst, R. J., & DeVories, A. Life styles and free time activities of retired men. *Human Development*, 1969, **12**, 34-54.

Havighurst, R. J., Munnicks, M. A., Joep, T., Neugarten, B. L., & Thomas, M. *Adjustment to retirement: A cross-national study*. Assen, Netherlands: Van Gorkum, 1969.

Havighurst, R. J., Neugarten, B. L., & Bengston, V. L. A cross-sectional study of adjustment to retirement. *The Gerontologist*, 1966, **6**, 137-138.

Heflin, T. L. *The prediction of retirement adjustment.* Unpublished doctoral dissertation, the University of Oregon, 1972.

Heflin, T. L. *Predicting retirement adjustment—a new approach.* A paper presented at the 27th annual meeting of the Gerontological Society, Portland, Oregon, October 28-November 1, 1974.

Heidbreder, E. M. Factors in retirement adjustment: White-collar/blue-collar experience. *Industrial Gerontology,* 1972, **12**, 69-79.

Hersey, J., & Hersey, R. *These rich years: A journal of retirement.* New York: Scribners' Sons, 1969.

Heyman, D. K. Does a wife retire? *The Gerontologist,* 1970, **10**, 54-56.

Heyman, D. K., & Jeffers, F. C. Wives and retirement: A pilot study. *Journal of Gerontology,* 1968, **23**, 488-496.

Hoyt, G. C. The process and problems of retirement. *Journal of Business,* 1954, **27**, 164-178.

Jacobson, D. Willingness to retire in relation to job strain and type of work. *Industrial Gerontology,* 1972, **13**, 65-74.

Jones, C. C. *The opportunities of age: Stimulating interviews with active retired people and some contemplating retirement.* Boston: Christopher Publishing, 1959.

Kerchoff, A. C. Husband-wife expectations and reactions to retirement. *Journal of Gerontology,* 1964, **19**, 510-516.

Kerchoff, A. C. Family and retirement. In I. H. Simpson & J. C. McKinney (Eds.), *Social aspects of aging.* Durham, N.C.: Duke University Press, 1966.

King, C. E., & Howell, W. H. Role characteristics of flexible and inflexible retired persons. *Sociology and Social Research,* 1965, **49**, 153-165.

Lambing, M. L. B. Leisure-time pursuits among retired blacks by social status. *The Gerontologist,* 1972, **12**, 363-367.

Lipman, A. Marital roles of the retired aged. *Merrill-Palmer Quarterly of Behavior and Development,* 1960, **6**, 192-195.

Lipman, A. Role conceptions and morale of couples in retirement. *Journal of Gerontology,* 1961, **16**, 267-271.

Lipman, A. Role conceptions of couples in retirement. In C. Tibbits & W. Donahue (Eds.), *Social and psychological aspects of aging.* New York: Columbia University Press, 1962.

Lloyd, R.G. Social and personal adjustment of retired persons. *Sociology and Social Research,* 1955, **39**, 312-316.

Maddox, G. L. Adaptation to retirement. *The Gerontologist,* 1970, **10**, 14-19.

Martin, J., & Doran, A. Evidence concerning the relationship between health and retirement. *Sociological Review,* 1966, **14**, 329-343.

McKain, W. C. *Retirement marriage.* Storrs, Conn.: Storrs Agricultural Experiment Station, University of Connecticut, 1969.

Monk, A. Factors in preparation for retirement by middle-aged adults. *The Gerontologist,* 1971, **11**, 348-351.

Morse, N. C., & Weiss, R. S. The function and meaning of work and the job. *American Sociological Review,* 1955, **20**, 191-198.

Neugarten, B., & Havighurst, R. J. *Adjustment to retirement: A cross national study.* Assen: Van Gorkum, 1969.

Ontario (Province) Ministry of Community and Social Services. *Retirement and preparation for retirement: A selected bibliography and source-book.* Toronto, Homes for the Aged—Office in Aging Branch, Ontario Ministry of Community and Social Services, 31 pp. (Over 200 articles, books, and journals on aging, retirement.)

Orbach, H. L. Social values and the institutionalization of retirement. In R. H. Williams, C. Tibbits, & W. Donahue (Eds.), *Processes of aging.* New York: Atherton, 1963.

Palmore, E. B. Why do people retire? *Aging and human development,* 1971, **2**, 269-283.

Palmore, E. B. Differences in the retirement patterns of men and women. *The Gerontologist,* 1965, **5**, 4-8.

Payne, S. L. The Cleveland survey of retired men. *Personnel Psychology,* 1953, **6**, 81-110.

Peppers, L. G. Patterns of leisure and adjustment to retirement. *The Gerontologist,* 1976, **16**, 441-446.

Plonk, M. A., & Pulley, M. A. Financial management practices of retired couples. *The Gerontologist,* 1977, **17**, 256-261.

Pollak, O. *Positive experiences in retirement.* Wharton School of Finance and Commerce. Philadelphia: University of Pennsylvania, 1957.

Pollard, L. L. *Retirement—black and white.* New York: Exposition Press, 1974.

Pollman, W. A. Early retirement: Relationship to variation in life satisfaction. *Gerontology,* 1971, **1**, 45-49.

Preston, C. E. Subjectively perceived agedness and retirement. *Journal of Gerontology,* 1968, **23**, 201-203.

Rose, C. L. *Preferred age of retirement: A causal analysis.* A paper presented at the 27th annual meeting of the Gerontological Society, Portland, Oregon, October 28-November 1, 1974.

Rose, C. L., & Mogey, J. M. Aging and preference for later retirement. *International Journal of Aging and Human Development,* 1972, **3**, 45-62.

Rosenberg, G. *The worker grows old.* San Francisco: Jossey-Bass, 1970.

Saleh, S. D., & Grygier, T. G. Self-perception of productivity before retirement. *Personnel Administration,* 1966, **29**, 35-39.

Schmitz-Scherzer, R., & Strodel, I. Age dependency of leisure time activity. *Human Development,* 1971, **14**, 47-49.

Shanas, E. Health and adjustment in retirement. *The Gerontologist,* 19--, **10**,

Sherman, S. R. Assets on the threshold of retirement. *Social Security Bulletin,* 1973, **36**, 37-45.

Sherman, S. R. Leisure activities in retirement housing. *Journal of Gerontology,* 1974, **29**, 324-335.

Sheppard, H. L. Employment and retirement: Roles and activities. *The Gerontologist,* 1972, **12**, 29-35.

Slavick, F., & McConnell, J. W. *Flexible versus compulsory retirement policies.* Excerpts from a paper delivered at the IRRA meetings in Pittsburgh, Pennsylvania, December, 1962.

Smedley, L. T. The patterns of early retirement. *AFL-CIO American Federationist,* 1974, **81**, 1-5.

Smith, R. A. When your husband reaches retirement. *Changing Times,* 1968, **22**, 39-40.

Soileau, R. R. *The implications of early and career socialization for social and leisure patterns among the elderly.* Unpublished doctoral dissertation, Louisiana State University, 1972.

Streib, G. F. Morale of the retired. *Social Problems,* 1956, **3**, 270-276.

Streib, G. F. Family patterns in retirement. *Journal of Social Issues,* 1968, **14**, 44-60.

Streib, G. F. Does retirement ruin health? *Harvest Years,* 1972, **9**, 33-35.

Streib, G. F. Retirement: Crises or continuities? *Proceedings.* Gainesville, Fla.: University of Florida Press, 1975.

Streib, G. F., Thompson, W. E., & Suchman, E. A. The Cornell study of occupational retirement. *Journal of Social Issues,* 1958, **14**, 3-17.

Streib, G. F., & Schneider, C. J. Jr. *Retirement in American society.* Ithaca, N.Y.: Cornell University Press, 1971.

Thompson, G. B. Work versus leisure roles: An investigation of morale among employed and retired men. *Journal of Gerontology,* 1973, **28**, 339-344.

Thompson, W. E. Pre-retirement anticipation and adjustment in retirement. *Journal of Social Issues,* 1958, **14**, 35-45.

Thompson, W. E., & Streib, G. Meaningful activity in a family context. In F.W. Kleemeir (Ed.), *Aging and leisure: A research perspective into the meaningful use of time.* New York: Oxford University Press, 1961.

Thompson, W. E., Streib, G. F., & Kosa, J. The effect of retirement on personal adjustment: A panel analysis. *Journal of Gerontology,* 1960, **15,** 165-169.

Thurnher, M. Goals, values, and life evaluations at the preretirement stage. *Journal of Gerontology,* 1974, **29,** 85-96.

Walker, J., & Price, K. *Retirement choice and retirement satisfaction.* A paper given at the meetings of the Gerontological Society, Louisville, October 26-30, 1975.

V. The Transition into Aging

Back, K. W. Transition to aging and the self-image. *Aging and Human Development,* 1971, **2,** 296-304.

Black, D. The older person and the family. In H. Davis (Ed.), *Aging: Prospects and issues.* Los Angeles: Ethel Percy Andrus Gerontology Center, University Southern California, 1974.

Brody, E. M. The aging family. *The Gerontologist,* 1966, **6,** 201-206.

Brody, S. J., & Brody, E. M. The aged, their families and the law.

Brotman, H. B. *Marriages of older persons in 1968.* U.S. Administration on Aging (Statistical Memo #22, May 15, 1973). Washington, D.C.: U.S. Government Printing Office, 1973.

Buhler, C., Brind, A., & Horner, A. Old age as a phase of human life. *Human Development,* 1968, **11,** 53-63.

Busse, E. W., & Pfeiffer, E. *Behavior and adaptation in late life.* Boston: Little, Brown, 1969.

Butler, R. N. Crises and contributions in later life. *American Journal of Orthopsychiatry,* 1967, **37,** 337-338.

Carter, L., Montgomery, J., & Stinnett, N. Older persons' perceptions of their marriages. *Journal of Marriage and the Family,* 1972, **34,** 665-670.

Cavan, R. S. Self and role in adjustment during old age. *Marriage and Family Living,* 1967, **20,** 278-288.

Chen, R., & Thompson, F. W. Old dogs, new tricks—adjustment problems of the aged. *Journal of the Kansas Medical Society,* 1965, **6,**

Chown, S. M. Age and the rigidities. *Journal of Gerontology,* 1961, **16,** 353-362.

Cumming, E., & Henry, W. *Growing old.* New York: Basic Books, 1961.

Dowd, J. J. *Aging as exchange: A preface to theory.* A paper presented at the 27th annual meeting of the Gerontological Society, Portland, Oregon, October 28-November 1, 1974.

Fritz, D. B. *Growing old is a family affair.* Richmond, Va.: John Knox, 1972.

Goldfarb, A. I. The intimate relations of older people. In S. M. Farber, et al. (Eds.), *Man and civilization: The family's search for survival.* New York: McGraw-Hill, 1965.

Havighurst, R. J. Successful aging. *Sociology and Social Research,* 1972, **56,** 289-300.

Hyuck, M. H. *Growing older.* Englewood Cliffs, N.J.: Prentice-Hall, 1974.

Jackson, J. J. The blacklands of gerontology. *Aging and Human Development,* 1971, **2,** 156-171.

Jackson, J. J. Marital life among aging blacks. *The Family Coordinator,* 1972, **21,** 21-27.

Kaplan, H. B., & Pokorny, A. D. Aging and self attitude: A conditional relationship. *Aging and Human Development,* 1970, **1,** 241-249.

Kent, D. P. The elderly in minority groups: Variant patterns of aging. *The Gerontologist,* 1971, **11,** 26-29.

Kent, D. P. The Negro aged. *The Gerontologist,* 1971, **11,** 48-52.

Kutner, B., Fanshel, D., Togo, A. M., & Langner, T. S. Factors related to adjustment in old age. In R. G. Kuhlen, & G. G. Thompson (Eds.), *Psychological studies of human development.* New York: Appleton-Century-Crofts, 1970.

L'Engle, M. *The summer of the great-grandmother.* New York: Farrar, Straus, and Giroux, 1974.

Linch, A. Normal "crises" in adult life. *American Journal of Orthopsychiatry,* 1967, **37,** 335-339.

Lipman, A. Marital roles of the retired aged. *Merrill-Palmer Quarterly of Behavior and Development,* 1960, **6,** 192-195.

Lowenthal, M. F., & Haven, C. Interaction and adaptation: Intimacy as a critical variable. *American Sociological Review,* 1968, **33,** 20-30.

Maas, H. O., & Kuypers, J.A.*From thirty to seventy: A forty-year longitudinal study of adult life styles and personality.* San Francisco: Jossey-Bass, 1974.

McKain, W. C. A new look at older marriages. *The Family Coordinator,* 1972, **21,** 61-69.

McKarracher, D. G. The impact of aging in the family. In S. Liebman (Ed.), *Emotional forces in the family.* Philadelphia: Lippincott, 1959.

Morgan, M. I. The middle life and the aging family. *The Family Coordinator,* 1972, **18,** 296-297.

Morton, R. K. *Problems in the later years of married life.* Presented at the 1970 annual meeting of the Society for the Study of Social Problems. *Sociological Abstracts,* 1970, **18,** 971 (Supplement 2).

National Council on the Aging, Inc. *The myth and reality of aging in America.* Washington: NCOA, 1975.

Neugarten, B. L. *Middle age and aging.* Chicago: University of Chicago Press, 1968.

Neugarten, B. L., & Moore, J. The changing age status system. In B. L. Neugarten (Ed.), *Middle age and aging.* Chicago: University of Chicago Press, 1968.

Neugarten, B. L., & Peterson, W. A study of the American age-grade system. Vol. III in *Fourth Congress of the International Association of Gerontology.* Firenze, Italy: Tito Mattioli, 1957.

Pacaud, S., & Pacaud, L. Attitudes, behavior and opinions of elderly persons in the setting of modern family. *Psychological Abstracts,* Monographies Francaises de Psychologie, 1969, **16,** 146-

Parsons, T. Old age as a comsummatory phase. *The Gerontologist,* 1963, **3,** 53-54.

Peterson, J. A. *A developmental view of the aging family.* Unpublished paper. USC, Andrus Gerontological Library, 1968.

Peterson, J. A. Marital and family therapy involving the aged. *The Gerontologist,* 1973, **13,** 27-31.

Phillips, B. S. A role theory approach to adjustment in old age. *American Sociological Review,* 1957, **22,** 212-217.

Pincus, A. Toward a developmental view of aging for social work. *Social Work,* 1967, **12,** 33-41.

Poe, W. D. *The old person in your home.* New York: Scribner, 1969.

Poorkaj, H. Social-psychological factors and successful aging. *Sociology and Social Research,* 1972, **56,** 289-300.

Porter, B. R., & Christensen, T. Exploring the golden years of marriage. *Family Perspective,* 1966, **1,** 3-10.

Riley, M., & Foner, A. *Aging and society: An inventory of research findings* (Vol. 1). New York: Russell Sage Foundation, 1968.

Riley, M. W. *Aging and society* (Vol. 2). New York: Russell Sage Foundation, 1972.

Riley, M.W., Johnson, M., & Foner, A. *Aging and society: A sociology of age stratification* (Vol. 3). New York: Russell Sage Foundation, 1972.

Rosow, I. Adjustment of the normal aged. In R. H. Williams (Ed.), *Process of Aging II.* New York: Atherton, 1963.

Rosow, I. *Social integration of the aged.* New York: Free Press, 1967.

Rosow, I. *Socialization to old age.* Berkeley: University of California Press, 1973.

Schonfield, D. Geronting: Reflections on successful aging. *The Gerontologist,* 1967, **7,** 270-273.

Schonfield, D. Family life education study: The later adult

years. *The Gerontologist*, 1960, **10**, 115-118.

Schonfield, D., & Hooper, A. Future commitments and successful aging. II. Special groups. *Journal of Gerontology*, 1973, **28**, 197-201.

Shanas, E. *Old people in three industrial societies*. New York: Atherton, 1968.

Shanas, E. The family and the aged in western societies. *Sociological Symposium*, 1968, **2**, 147-152.

Shanas, E., Townsend, P., Wedderburn, D., Friis, H., Milhoj, P., & Stehouwer, J. *Old people in three industrial societies*. New York: Atherton, 1968.

Smith, W. M., Jr. Retirement: Family life cycle. *Marriage and Family Living*, 1954, **6**, 36-40.

Smith, W. M., Jr. Family plans for later years. *Marriage and Family Living*, 1955, **7**, 15-19.

Spark, G., Spark, M., & Brody, E. The aged are family members. *Family Process*, 1970, **9**, 195-210.

Spence, D. L. The role of futurity in aging adaptation. *The Gerontologist*, 1968, **3**, 180-183.

Stinnet, N., & Montgomery, J. E. Youths' perceptions of marriages of older persons. *Journal of Marriage and the Family*, 1968, **30**, 392-396.

Stinnett, N., Collins, J., & Montgomery, J. E. Marital need satisfaction of older husbands and wives. *Journal of Marriage and the Family*, 1970, **32**, 428-434.

Stinnett, N., Carter, L. M., & Montgomery, J. E. Older persons' perceptions of their marriages. *Journal of Marriage and the Family*, 1972, **34**, 665-670.

Streib, G. F. Old age and the family: Facts and forecasts. *American Behavioral Scientist*, 1970, **14**, 25-39.

Streib, G. F. Older families and their troubles: Familial and social responses. *The Family Coordinator*, 1972, **21**, 5-18.

Streib, G. F., & Thompson, W. The older person in a family context. In C. Tibbetts (Ed.), *Handbook of social gerontology*. Chicago: University of Chicago Press, 1960.

Tibbitts, C. *Middle-aged and older people in American society*. Washington, D.C.: U.S. Government Printing Office, 1965.

Townsend, P. *The family life of old people: An inquiry in East London*. London: Routledge and Kegan Paul, 1957.

Troll, L. E. The family of later life: A decade review. *Journal of Marriage and the Family*, 1971, **33**, 263-290.

Weg, R. B. Aging and the aged in contemporary society. *Journal of Physical Therapy*, 1973, **53**, 749-756.

Williams, R., & Wirths, C. *Lives through the years*. New York: Atherton, 1965.

A. Economic, Social and Housing Needs of Aging Couples

Albrecht, R. Social roles in the prevention of senility. *Journal of Gerontology*, 1951, **4**, 380-386.

Aldrich, C. K., & Mendkoff, E. Relocation of the aged and disabled: A mortality study. *Journal of the American Geriatrics Society*, 1963, **3**, 185-194.

Anderson, N. N. Approaches to improving the quality of long-term care for older persons. *The Gerontologist*, 1974, **14**, 519-524.

Bell, T. The relationship between social involvement and feeling old among residents in homes for the aged. *Journal of Gerontology*, 1967, **22**, 17-22.

Bennett, R. The meaning of institutional life. *The Gerontologist*, 1963, **3**, 117-125.

Bennett, R., Nahemow, L., & Zubin, J. The effects on residents of homes for the aged on social adjustment. USPHS Grant No. 0029. Mimeographed progress report, 1964.

Bernstein, H., Miller, M., & Sharkey, H. *The missing parent: Institutional rediscovery*. A paper presented at the Gerontological Society meetings, Louisville, October 26-30, 1975.

Bersford, J. C., & Rivlin, A. N. Privacy, poverty and old age. *Demography*, 1966, **3**, 247-258.

Blau, Z. S. Structural constraints of friendships in old age. *American Sociological Review*, 1961, **26**, 429-439.

Bloom, M. Measurement of the socio-economic status of the aged: New thoughts on an old subject. *The Gerontologist*, 1972, **12**, 375-378.

Brady, D. S. Influences of age on saving and spending patterns. *Monthly Labor Review*, 1955, **28**, 1240-1244.

Britton, J. H., Mather, W. G., & Lansing, A. K. Expectations for older persons in a rural community: Living arrangements and family relationships. *Journal of Gerontology*, 1961, **16**, 156-162.

Britton, J. H., Mather, W. G., & Lansing, A.K. Expectations for older persons in a rural community: Community participation. *Rural Sociology*, 1962, **27**, 387-395.

Brokington, F., & Lempert, S. M. *Social needs of over-80's: The Stockport Survey*. Manchester: Manchester University Press, 1966.

Brody, E. M., & Brody, S. J. A ninety-minute inquiry: The expressed needs of the elderly. *The Gerontologist*, 1970, **10**, 99-106.

Brody, E. M., & Spark, G. M. Institutionalization of the aged: A family crisis. *Family Process*, 1966, **5**, 76-90.

Brown, A. S. Satisfying relationships for the elderly and their patterns of disengagement. *The Gerontologist*, 1974, **14**, 258-262.

Brudno, J. J. Group programs with adult offspring of newly admitted residents in a geriatrics setting. *Journal of the American Geriatrics Society*, 1964, **12**, 385-394.

Bultena, G. L. Age-grading in the social interaction of an elderly male population. *Journal of Gerontology*, 1968, **23**, 539-543.

Bultena, G., & Wood, V. The American retirement community: Bane or blessing. *Journal of Gerontology*, 1969, **24**, 209-217.

Butler, R. N. How to grow old and poor in an affluent society. *International Journal of Aging and Human Development*, 1973, **4**, 277-279.

Carp, F. M. Effects of improved housing on the lives of older people. In B. L. Neugarten (Ed.), *Middle Age and Aging*. Chicago: University of Chicago Press, 1969.

Carp, F. M. The mobility of older slum-dwellers. *The Gerontologist*, 1972, **12**, 57-65.

Carp, F. M. Impact of improved housing on morale and life satisfaction. *The Gerontologist*, 1975, **15**, 511-515.

Carp, F. M. Impact of improved living environment on health and life expectancy. *The Gerontologist*, 1977, **17**, 242-249.

Cutler, S. J. The availability of personal transportation, residential location, and life satisfaction among the aged. *Journal of Gerontology*, 1972, **27**, 383-389.

Cutler, S. J. Voluntary association participation and life satisfaction: A cautionary research note. *Journal of Gerontology*, 1973, **29**, 416-422.

Dick, H. R. Residential patterns of aged persons prior to institutionalization. *Journal of Marriage and the Family*, 1964, **26**, 96-98.

Dodds, S., Mangum, W. P., Sherman, S. R., Walkey, R. P., & Wilner, D. M. Psychological effects of retirement housing. *The Gerontologist*, 1968, **8**, 170-175.

Downing, J. Factors afflicting the selective use of a social club for the aged. *Journal of Gerontology*, 1957, **12**, 81-84.

Goldfarb, A. I. Institutional case of the aged. In E. W. Busse & E. Pfeiffer (Eds.), *Behavior and adaptation in late life*. Boston: Little, Brown, 1969.

Goldschnieder, C. Differential residential mobility of the older populations. *Journal of Gerontology*, 1966, **21**, 103-108.

Gottesman, L., & Hutchinson, E. *Characteristics of the institutionalized elderly*. Unpublished paper. Andras Gerontology Center Library, University of Southern California, 1972.

Graney, M. Happiness and social participation in old age. *The Gerontologist*, 1973, **13**, 66.

Hamovitch, M., & Peterson, J. E. Housing needs and satisfactions of the elderly. *The Gerontologist*, 1969, **9**, 30-32.

Hamovitch, M. B., Peterson, J. A., & Larson, A. E. *Housing needs and satisfactions of the elderly*. Gerontology Center, University of Southern California, no date.

Habenstein, R. W., & Biddle, E. H. *Decisions to relocate the residence of aged persons* (Technical Report #89). Columbia, Missouri: Center for Research in Social Behavior, 1974.

Hansen, G. D. *Home managerial tasks, perceived competence, and related social, psychological, and economic consequences for retired couples*. Unpublished doctoral dissertation. Corvallis, Oregon: Oregon State University.

Harger, E. *Considerations in regard to retirement communities*. State of New Jersey, Dept. of Community Affairs, Division on Aging, Trenton, N.J., no date, 18625.

Harootyan, R. A. *Housing and racial differences in residential mobility desires of older people*. A paper given at the meetings of the Gerontological Society, Louisville, October 26-30, 1975.

Hoyt, G. C. The life of the retired in a trailer park. *American Journal of Sociology*, 1954, **59**, 361-370.

Jabus, R. One way street—an indepth view of adjustment to a home for the aged. *The Gerontologist*, 1969, **9**, 268-275.

Jackson, J. J. Comparative life styles and family and friend relationships among older black women. *The Family Coordinator*, 1972, **21**, 477-485.

Jones, D. C. Spatial proximity, interpersonal conflict, and friendship formation in the intermediate-care facility. *The Gerontologist*, 1975, **15**, 150-154, 169.

Kahana, E., & Coe, R. Self and staff conceptions of institutionalized aged. *The Gerontologist*, 1968, **9**, 264-267.

Kahana, B., & Kahana, E. Changes in mental status of elderly patients in age-integrated and age-segregated hospital milieus. *Journal of Abnormal Psychology*, 1970, **75**, 177-181.

Knox, W. E. Solidarity, interaction and activities of older parents and children in an urban industrial context. From *Proceedings of the 7th Intergenerational Congress of Gerontology*, 1966, **6**, 281-286.

Krasner, J. D. The reaction of the adult child to the institutionalization of the aged parent. In W. Donahue (Ed.), *Living in the multigenerational family*. Ann Arbor: Institute of Gerontology, 1969.

Kreps, J. M. Economics of retirement. In E. W. Busse & E. Pfieffer (Eds.), *Behavior and adaptation in late life*. Boston: Little, Brown, 1969.

Kreps, J. M. Economics of aging: Work and income through the lifespan. *American Behavioral Scientist*, 1970, **14**, 81-90.

Kuypers, J. A., & Bengtson, V. L. Competence and social breakdown: A social-psychological view of aging. *Human Development*, 1973, **16**, 37-49.

Lago, D. J., & Hoffman, S. *Increasing nursing home residents' interaction: An application of structured group interaction techniques*. A paper presented at the 82nd annual convention of the American Psychological Association, New Orleans, La., August 3, 1974.

Lawton, M. P., & Simon, B. The ecology of social relationships in housing for the elderly. *The Gerontologist*, 1968, **8**, 108-115.

Linn, M. W., & Gurel, L. Family attitude in nursing home placement. *The Gerontologist*, 1972, **12**, 220-224.

Lipman, A. B., & Slater, R. Homes for old people: Toward a positive environment. *The Gerontologist*, 1977, **17**, 146-156.

Looft, W.R., & Charles, D. C. Egocentrism and social interaction in young and old adults. *Aging and Human Development*, 1971, **2**, 21-28.

Lowenthal, M. F., & Haven, C. Interaction and adaptation: Intimacy as a critical variable. *American Sociological Review*, 1968, **33**, 20-30.

Maddox, G. L. Persistence of life style among the elderly: A longitudinal study of patterns of social activity in relation to life satisfaction. In B. Neugarten (Ed.), *Middle age and aging*. Chicago: University of Chicago Press, 1968.

Marcoen, A. Role patterns of the institutionalized aged. *Psychological Belgica*, 1970, **10**, 201-224.

Martin, W. C. Activity and disengagement: Life satisfaction of inmovers into a retirement community. *The Gerontologist*, 1973, **13**, 224-227.

McCuan, E. R. Geriatric day care: A family perspective. *The Gerontologist*, 1976, **16**, 517-521.

Miller, M. B., & Harris, A. P. Family cognizance of disability in the aged on nursing home placement. *Social Casework*, 1964, **45**, 150-154.

Miller, M. B., & Harris, A. P. Social factors and family conflicts in a nursing home population. *Journal of the American Geriatrics Society*, 1965, **13**, 845-851.

Miller, S. J. The social dilemma of the aging leisure participant. In A. M. Rose & W. A. Peterson (Eds.), *Older people and their social world*. Philadelphia: Davis, 1965.

Mitchell, D. L., & Goldfarb, A. I. Psychological needs of aged patients at home. *American Journal of Public Health*, 1966, **56**, 1716-1721.

Morris, J. N. Changes in morale experienced by elderly institutional applicants along the institutional path. *The Gerontologist*, 1975, **15**, 345-349.

Mumford, L. For older people—not segregation but integration. *Architectural Record*, 1956, **119**, 191-194.

Nelson, L. M., & Winter, M. Life disruption, independence, satisfaction, and consideration of moving. *The Gerontologist*, 1975, **15**, 160-164.

Palmore, E. B. The effects of aging on activities and attitudes. *The Gerontologist*, 1968, **8**, 259-263.

Peterson, D. A. Financial adequacy in retirement: Perceptions of older Americans. *The Gerontologist*, 1972, **12**, 379-383.

Peterson, J. A., & Larson, A. E. *Socio-psychological factors in selecting retirement housing*. Revised version of paper read at the Research Conference on Patterns of Living and Housing of Middle-aged and Older People. Washington, D.C., March, 1965.

Pollak, O. Social adjustment in old age: A research planning report. (Bulletin 59) New York: Social Science Research Council, 1948.

Rautman, A. L. Role reversal in geriatrics. *Mental Hygiene*, 1962, **46**, 116-120.

Rohner, E. J. A study of residents of six four-season retirement communities in New Jersey. New York University, Graduate School of Business Administration, 1972.

Rose, A. M., & Peterson, W. A. *Older people and their social world: The sub-culture of the aging*. Philadelphia, Pa.: Davis, 1965.

Rosenthal, S. Medical costs are getting out of hand. *Forbes*, March 15, 1968, 101-124.

Rosow, I. Housing and local ties of the aged. In B. L. Neugarten (Ed.), *Middle age and aging*. Chicago: University of Chicago Press, 1965.

Rosow, I. *Social integration of the aged*. New York: Free Press, 1967.

Rosow, I. The social context of the aging self. *The Gerontologist*, 1973, **13**, 82-87.

Rubenstein, D. *The survey of the social participation of the elderly in congregate care facilities as a means for the development of public social policy*. Gerontology Society, 26th annual meeting, Nov. 8, 1973.

Saul, S. R. Study of family factors relating to application to a home for the aged. *Dissertation Abstract* (29), (7a) 2375, obtainable from university microfilms as No. 69-674. Columbia University, New York, N.Y., 1969.

Schooler, K. K. The relationship between social interaction and morale of the elderly as a function of environmental characteristics. *The Gerontologist*, 1969, **9**, 25-29.

Schonfield, D. Future commitments and successful aging: I. The random sample. *Journal of Gerontology*, 1973, **28**, 189-196.

Schonfield, D., & Hooper, A. Future commitments and successful aging: II. Special groups. *Journal of Gerontology*, 1973, **28**, 197-201.

Sears, D. W. Elderly housing: A need determination technique. *The Gerontologist*, 1974, **14**, 182-187.

Sequin, M. M. Opportunity for peer socialization in a retirement community. *The Gerontologist,* 1973, **3**, 208-213.

Shanas, E. Living arrangements of older people in the U.S. *The Gerontologist*, 1961, **1**, 27-29.

Shanas, E. Living arrangements and housing of old people. In E. W. Busse & E. Pfeiffer (Eds.), *Behavior and adaptation in late life.* Boston: Little, Brown, 1969.

Sherman, S. R., Mangum, W. P., Dodds, S., Walkley, R. P., & Wilner, D. M. Psychological effects of retirement housing. *The Gerontologist*, 1968, **8**, 170-175.

Siegel, R. L. The pros and cons of retirement cities. *House Beautiful*, 1964, **106**, 218-222.

Soldo, B. J., & Myers, G. C. *The changing profile of living arrangements among the elderly, 1960-1970.* A paper given at the meetings of the Gerontological Society, Louisville, October 26-30, 1975.

Solomon, B. Social functioning of economically dependent aged. *The Gerontologist*, 1967, **7**, 213-217.

Stone, C. L. Living arrangements and social adjustment of the aged. *The Family Coordinator*, 1957, **6**, 12-14.

Thomson, W. O. The pattern of life of the elderly who live alone. *Social and Industrial Medicine,* Public Health, 1958.

Thompson, R. W., & Chen, R. Experiences with older psychiatric patients and spouses together in a residential treatment setting. *Bulletin Menninger Clinic*, 1966, **80**, 1.

Thompson, W. E., & Streib, G. F. Situational determinants: Health and economic deprivation in retirement. *Journal of Social Issues*, 1958, **14**, 18-34.

Tissue, T. Old age and the perception of poverty. *Sociology and Social Research*, 1972, **56**, 331-343.

Tissue, T., & Wells, L. Antecedent lifestyles and old age. *Psychological Reports*, 1971, **29**, 1100.

Townsend, P. The effects of family structure on the likelihood of admission to an institution in old age: The application of a general theory. In E. Shanas & G. Streib (Eds.), *Social structure and the family generational relations.* Englewood Cliffs, New Jersey: Prentice-Hall, 1965.

Webber, I. L. The organized social life of the retired in two Florida communities. *American Journal of Sociology*, 1954, **59**, 340-346.

Weiss, L., & Lowenthal, M. F. Perceptions and complexities of friendship in four stages of the adult life cycle. *Proceedings of the 81st Annual Convention of the American Psychological Association,* Montreal, Canada, 1973, **8**, 773-774.

Wilkinson, A. *An analysis of the process of change prior to institutionalization.* A paper presented at the 27th annual meeting of the Gerontological Society, Portland, Oregon, October 28-November 1, 1974.

Williams, R. H., & Loeb, M. B. The adult's social life space and successful aging: Some suggestions for a conceptual framework. In B. L. Neugarten (Ed.), *Middle age and aging.* Chicago: University of Chicago Press, 1968.

Wilner, D. M., Sherman, S. R., Walkley, R. P., Dodds, S., & Mangum, W. Demographic characteristics of planned retirement housing sites. *The Gerontologist*, 1968, **8**, 164-169.

Woodward, H., Gingles, R., & Woodward, J. C. Loneliness and the elderly as related to housing. *The Gerontologist*, 1974, **14**, 349-351.

Zborowski, M., & Eyde, L. D. Aging and social participation. *Journal of Gerontology*, 1962, **17**, 424-430.

B. *Life Satisfaction among Aging Couples*

Alston, J. P., & Dudley, C. J. Age, occupation, and life satisfaction. *The Gerontologist*, 1973, **13**, 58-61.

Bell, B. D. Cognitive dissonance and the life satisfaction of older adults. *Journal of Gerontology*, 1974, **29**, 564-571.

Bloom, M. Discontent with contentment scales. *The Gerontologist*, 1975, **15**, 99.

Brown, A. S. Satisfying relationships for the elderly and their patterns of disengagement. *The Gerontologist,* 1974, **14**, 258-262.

Bultena, G. L. Life continuity and morale in old age. *The Gerontologist*, 1969, **9**, 251-253.

Clemente, F., & Sauer, W. J. Race and morale of the urban aged. *The Gerontologist*, 1974, **14**, 342-344.

Edwards, J. N., & Klemmack, D. L. Correlates of life satisfaction: A re-examination. *Journal of Gerontology*, 1973, **28**, 497-502.

Freeman, G. T. *Self-fulfillment and aging: A vocational psychology in the management of a tri-powered life.* Watkins Glen, N.Y.: The American Life Foundation and Study Institute, 1973.

Gerber, K. E. *Life satisfaction, locus of control and demographic variables in a diverse group of the retired.* A paper given at the meetings of the Gerontological Society, Louisville, October 26-30, 1975.

Glenn, N. D. The contribution of marriage to the psychological well-being of males and females. *Journal of Marriage and the Family*, 1975, **37**, 594-600.

Kurtz, J. J., & Wolk, S. Continued growth and life satisfaction. *The Gerontologist*, 1975, **15**, 129-131.

Lester, B. J. *Quality of life as defined by older persons.* A paper given at the meetings of the Gerontological Society, Louisville, October 26-30, 1975.

Maddox, G. L. Persistence of life style among the elderly: A longitudinal study of patterns of social activity in relation to life satisfaction. In B. L. Neugarten (Ed.), *Middle age and aging: A reader in social psychology.* Chicago, III.: University of Chicago Press, 1968.

Nehrke, M. F., Hulicka, I. M., & Morganti, J. B. *The relationship of age to life satisfaction, locus of control and self concept in elderly domiciliary residents.* A paper given at the meetings of the Gerontological Society, Louisville, October 26-30, 1975.

Neugarten, B. L., Havighurst, R. J., & Tobin, S. S. The measurement of life satisfaction. *Journal of Gerontology*, 1961, **16**, 134-143.

Rose, A. M. Factors associated with the life satisfaction of middle class, middle-aged persons. *Marriage and Family Living*, 1955, **17**, 15-19.

Schonfield, D. Future commitments and successful aging: I. The random sample. *Journal of Gerontology*, 1973, **28**, 189-196.

Spreitzer, E., & Snyder, E. E. Correlates of life satisfaction among the aged. *Journal of Gerontology*, 1974, **29**, 454-458.

Tobin, S. S., & Neugarten, B. L. Life satisfaction and social interaction in the aging. *Journal of Gerontology*, 1961, **29**, 454-458.

Wilker, L. *Toward a convergence in the measurement of psychological well-being.* A paper given at the meetings of the Gerontological Society, Louisville, October 26-30, 1975.

Wilson, R. W. *Life change and psychological well-being: A longitudinal study.* A paper given at the meetings of the Gerontological Society, Louisville, October 26-30, 1975.

Wolk, S., & Kurtz, J. Positive adjustment and involvement during aging and expectancy for internal control. *Journal of Consulting and Clinical Psychology*, 1975, **43**, 173-178.

C. *Physical and Mental Health*

Battistella, R. M. Social bases of medical care behavior

among aged and middle-aged persons. *Dissertation Abstracts*, 1966, **27**, 536-537.

Bellin, S. S., & Hardt, R. H. Marital status and mental disorders among the aged. *American Sociological Review*, 1958, **23**, 155-162.

Bultena, G. L. Life continuity and morale in old age. *The Gerontologist*, 1969, **9**, 251-253.

Burnside, I. M. Accoutrements of aging. *Nursing Clinics of North America*, 1972, **7**, 291-301.

Busse, E. W., & Pfeiffer, E. Functional psychiatric disorders in old age. In E. W. Busse & E. Pfeiffer (Eds.), *Behavior and adaptation in late life.* Boston: Little, Brown, 1969.

Butler, R. N. Directions in psychiatric treatment of the elderly: Role of perspective of the life cycle. *The Gerontologist*, 1969, **9**, 134-138.

Butler, R. N., & Lewis, M. I. *Aging and mental health.* St. Louis: C. V. Mosby, 1973.

Campe, W. P. Planning for care and treatment of the mentally impaired aged. In *Mental impairment in the aged.* Proceedings of the Institute of Mentally Impaired Aged held at the Philadelphia Geriatric Center, (April 6-8), Philadelphia: Maurice Jacobs Press, 1965.

Christopherson, V. A. Family reactions to illness. In W. Donahue (Ed.), *Living in the multigeneration family.* Ann Arbor: Institute of Gerontology. The University of Michigan-Wayne State University, 1969.

Coakley, M. S. *When parents grow old.* Pulaski, Wisconsin: Franciscan Publishers, 1967.

Dawson, A. M., & Baller, W. R. Relationship between creative activity and health in elderly people. *Journal of Psychology*, 1972, **82**, 49-58.

Dicicco, L., & Apple, D. Health needs and opinions of older adults. Public Health Reports, Public Health Service, U.S. Dept. of HEW, 1958, **73**, 479-487.

Estes, E. H., Jr. Health experience in the elderly. In E. W. Busse & E. Pfeiffer (Eds.), *Behavior and adaptation in late life.* Boston: Little, Brown, 1969.

Goldfarb, A. I. Masked depression of the old. *American Journal of Psychotherapy*, 1967, **21**, 791-796.

Gubrium, J. F. Environmental effects of morale in old age and the resources of health and solvency. *The Gerontologist*, 1970, **10**, 294-296.

Gubrium, J. F. Apprehensions of coping incompetence and responses of fear in old age. *International Journal of Aging and Human Development*, 1973, **4**, 111-125.

Hoenig, J., & Hamilton, M. W. Elderly psychiatric patients and the burden on the household. *Psychiatria Et Nuerologia*, 1966, **152**, 281-293.

Jaeger, D. *The aged ill.* New York: Appleton-Century-Crofts, 1970.

Kaplan, H., & Pokorny, A. D. Aging and self-attitude: A conditional relationship. *Aging and Human Development*, 1972, **2**, 241-249.

Kaplan, O. (Ed.). *Mental disorders in later life* (2nd ed.). Stanford: Stanford University Press, 1956.

Lawton, M. P., & Brody, E. M. Assessment of older people: Self-maintaining and instrumental activities of daily living. *The Gerontologist*, 1969, **9**, 179-186.

Lipman, A. *Health insecurity of the aged.* Paper presented at the 14th Annual Scientific Meeting of the Gerontological Society, Inc., November 10, 1961, Pittsburgh, Pa.

Lowenthal, M. F. Social isolation and mental illness in old age. *American Sociological Review*, 1964, **29**, 54-70.

Lowenthal, M. F., Berkmann, P. L., & Associates. *Aging and mental disorder in San Francisco: A social psychiatric study.* San Francisco: Jossey-Bass, 1967.

Marden, P. G., & Burnight, R. G. Social consequences of physical impairment in aging population. *The Gerontologist*, 1969, **9**, 39-46.

Miller, M. B., & Harris, A. P. The chronically ill aged: Paradoxical patient-family behavior. *Journal of the American Geriatrics Society*, 1965, **14**, 580-595.

Peterson, J. A. Marital and family therapy involving the aged. *The Gerontologist*, 1973, **13**, 27-31.

Pollman, W. A. Early retirement: A comparison of poor health to other retirement factors. *Journal of Gerontology*, 1971, **26**, 41-45.

Rynerson, B. Need for self-esteem in the aged: A literature review. *Journal of Psychiatric Nursing and Mental Health Services*, 1972, **10**, 22-26.

Ryser, C., & Sheldon, A. Retirement and health. *Journal of the American Geriatrics Society*, 1969, **17**, 180-190.

Savitsky, E., Sharkey, H., & Sulesky, F., et al. Clinical services to the aged with special reference to family study. *American Journal of Orthodopsychist*, 1969, **39**, 498-503.

Selye, H. Stress and aging. *Journal of American Geriatric Society*, 1970, **18**, 669-680.

Shanas, E. *The health of older people: A social survey.* Cambridge, Mass.: Harvard University Press, 1962.

Spence, D. L., Cohen, S., & Kowalski, C. *Resocialization of the mentally ill elderly.* A paper presented at the 27th annual meeting of the Gerontological Society, Portland, Oregon, October 28-November 1, 1974.

Thompson, W. E., & Streib, G. F. Situational determinants: Health and economic deprivation in retirement. *Journal of Social Issues*, 1958, **14**, 18-34.

Trela, J. E., & Simmons, L. Health and other factors affecting membership and attrition in a senior center. *Journal of Gerontology*, 1971, **26**, 46-51.

Urban, H. G., & Lagox, D. Life history and antecedents in psychiatric disorders of the aging. *The Gerontologist*, 1973, **13**, 502-508.

U.S. Department of Health, Education and Welfare. Persons 55 years and over receiving care at home, July 1967-June 1968. From *Monthly Vital Statistics Report*, 1968, **19**, 1-4.

Wynne, R. D. Drug overuse among the elderly: A growing problem. *Perspectives on Aging*, 1973, **2**, 15-18.

Youmans, E. G. Age group, health, and attitudes. *The Gerontologist*, 1974, **14**, 249-254.

Zimberg, S. The elderly alcoholic. *The Gerontologist*, 1974, **14**, 221-224.

D. Sex and Aging

Adamopoulos, D. A., Loraine, J. A., & Dove, G. A. Endocrinological studies in women approaching the menopause. *The Journal of Obstetrics and Gynecology of the British Commonwealth*, 1971, **78**, 62-79.

Allen, C. The aging homosexual. In I. Ruben (Ed.), *The third sex.* New York: New Book, 1961.

Amulree, L. Sex and the elderly. *Practitioner*, 1954, 172, 431-435.

Anderson, H., & Cote, P. *Sexuality and the socially active aged.* A paper presented at the meetings of the Gerontological Society, Louisville, October 26-30, 1975.

Baker, M. G. Psychiatric illness after hysterectomy. *British Medical Journal*, 1968, **2**, 91-95.

Bellamy, D. Hormonal effects in relation to aging in mammals. *Symposia Society Experimental Biology*, 1967, **21**, 427.

Berezin, M. S. *Sex and old age: A review of the literature.* A paper presented at the Seventh Annual Scientific Meeting of the Boston Society for Gerontologic Psychiatry, September 23, 1967.

Berezin, M. S. *Sex and old age: A review of the literature.* The Journal of Geriatric Psychiatry, 1969, **2**, 131-149.

Botwinick, J. Drives, expectancies, and emotions. In J. E. Birren (Ed.), *Handbook of aging and the individual.* Chicago: University of Chicago Press, 1959.

Bowers, L. M., Cross, R. N., Jr., & Lloyd, F. A. Sexual function and urologic disease in the elderly male. *Journal of the American Geriatrics Society*, 1963, **11**, 647-652.

Bowman, K. M. The sex life of the aging individual. *Geriatrics*, 1954, **9**, 83-84.

Bowman, K. M. The sex life of the aging individual. In M. F. DeMartino (Ed.), *Sexual behavior and personality characteristics*. New York: Citadel Press, 1963.

Brecker, E., & Brecker, R. *An analysis of human sexual response*. Boston: Little, Brown, 1966.

Burnside, I. Sexuality and aging. *Medical Arts and Sciences*, 1973, **27**, 13-27.

Calleja, M. A. Homosexual behavior in older men. *Sexology*, 1967, **42**, 46-48.

Cameron, P. Masculinity-feminity in the aged. *Journal of Gerontology*, 1968, **23**, 63-65.

Cameron, P., & Biber, H. Sexual thought throughout the life-span. *The Gerontologist*, 1973, **13**, 144-147.

Christenson, C. V., & Gagnon, J. H. Sexual behavior in a group of older women. *Journal of Gerontology*, 1965, **20**, 351-357.

Christenson, C. V., & Johnson, A. R. Sexual patterns in a group of older never married women. *Journal of Geriatric Psychiatry*, 1973, **6**, 80-98.

Claman, A. D. Introduction to panel discussion: Sexual difficulties after 50. *Canadian Medical Association Journal*, 1966, **91**, 94-207.

Cleveland, M. Sex in marriage: At 40 and beyond. *The Family Coordinator*, 1976, **25**, 233-240.

Crawford, M. P., & Hooper, D. Menopause, aging and family. *Social Science and Medicine*, 1973, **7**, 469-482.

Davis, M. A., Strandford, N. M., & Lanzl, L. H. Estrogens and the aging process. *Journal of the American Medical Assocation*, 1966, **196**, 129-134.

Dean, S. R. Sin and senior citizens. *Journal of the American Geriatrics Society*, 1966, **14**, 935-938.

Denicola, P., & Peruzza, M. Sex in the aged. *Journal of the American Geriatrics*, 1974, **22**, 380-382.

Dentler, R. A., & Pineo, P. Sexual adjustment, marital adjustment and personal growth of husbands: A panel analysis. *Journal of Marriage and the Family*, 1960, **22**, 45-48.

Ellis, W. J., & Grayhack, J. T. Sexual function in aging males after orchiectomy and estrogen therapy. *Journal of Urology*, 1963, **89**, 895-899.

Epstein, L. J., Mills, C., & Simon, A. Antisocial behavior of the elderly. *Comprehensive Psychiatry*, 1970, **11**, 36-42.

Ervin, C. V. Psychologic adjustment to mastectomy. *Human Sexuality*, 1973, **7**, 2.

Feigenbaum, E. M., Lowenthal, M.F., & Trier, M. L. *Sexual attitudes in the elderly*. Paper presented at the Gerontological Society, New York, 1966.

Feigenbaum, E. Sexual attitudes in the elderly. *Geriatrics*, 1967, **22**, 42-59.

Fisher, C. Dreaming and sexuality. In R. M. Lowenstein, L. M. Newman, M. Schur, & A. J.Solnit (Eds.), *Psychoanalysis—a general psychology*. New York: International Universities Press, 1961.

Fisher, C., Gross, J., & Zuch, J. Cycle of penile erection synchronous with dreaming (REM) sleep. *Archives of General Psychiatry*, 1965, **12**, 29-45.

Finkle, A. L., et al. Sexual function in aging males: Frequency of coitus among clinic patients. *Journal of the American Medical Association*, 1959, **170**, 1391-1393.

Finkel, A. L. Sex problems in later years. *Medical Times*, 1967, **95**, 416-419.

Finkle, A. L. Sexual function during advancing age. In I. Rossman (Ed.), *Clinical geriatrics*. Philadelphia: Lippincott, 1971.

Finkle, A. L. Emotional quality and physical quantity of sexual activity in aging males. *Journal of Geriatric Psychiatry*, 1973, **6**, 70-79.

Finkle, A. L., & Prain, D. V. Sexual potency in elderly men before and after prostectomy. *Journal of the American Medical Association*, 1966, **196**, 139-143.

Finkle, A. L., Tobenkin, J. I., & Karg, S. J. Sexual potency in aging males: I. Frequency of coitus among clinic patients. *Journal of the American Medical Association*, 1959, **170**, 113-115.

Finkle, A. L., & Moyers, T. G. Sexual potency in aging males: IV. Status of private patients before and after prostatectomey. *Journal of Urology*, 1960, **84**, 152-157.

Formmer, D. J. Changing age of the menopause. *British Medical Journal*, 1964, **2**, 349-351.

Frank, L. R. *The conduct of sex*. New York: Morrow, 1961.

Freeman, J. T. Sexual capacities in the aging male. *Geriatrics*, 1961, **16**, 37-43.

Freeman, J. T. Sexual aspects. In E. V. Cowdry (Ed.), *The care of the geriatric patient*. St. Louis: Mosby, 1963.

Gosppert, H. The sexual problem of aging. *Jahrbuch Fusr Psychologie, Psychotherapie Und Medizinische Anthropologie*, 1966, **14**, 261-267.

Greenblatt, R. B., & Scarpa-Smith, C. J. Nymphomania in postmenopausal women. *Journal of American Geriatrics Society*, 1959, **7**, 339-342.

Hader, M. Homosexuality as part of our aging process. *Psychiatric Quarterly*, 1966, **40**, 515-524.

Hamilton, G. V. Changes in personality and psychosexual phenomena with age. In E. V. Cowdry (Ed.), *Problems of aging*. Baltimore: Williams and Wilkins, 1939.

Hirt, N. B. The psychiatrist's view. Panel discussion: Sexual difficulties after 50. *Canadian Medical Association Journal*, 1966, **94**, 213-214.

Hsu, C. J., & Chen, P. H. Sexual activities in older male. *Journal of the American Medical Association*, 1965, **64**, 129.

Jackson, D. D. Forbidden ground: Book review of *Human Sexual Response. Medical Opinion and Review*, 1966, **2**, 32-33.

Jones, K. L., Shainberg, L. W., & Byer, C. O. *Sex*. New York: Harper and Row, 1969.

Kassell, V. Polygyny after 60. *Geriatrics*, 1966, **21**, 214-218.

Kassell, V. RX: Sex for senior citizens. *Psychology Today*, June, 1974, 18-20.

Kelly, J. J. *Brothers and brothers: The gay man's adaptation to aging*. Florence Heller School of Social Welfare, Brandeis University, Waltham, Massachusetts, 1974.

Kinsey, A. C., Pomeroy, W. B., & Martin, C. I. *Sexual behavior in the human male*. Philadelphia: Saunders, 1948.

Kinsey, A. C., Pomeroy, W. B., Martin, C. I., & Gebhard, P. H. *Sexual behavior in the human female*. Philadelphia: Saunders, 1953.

Kleegman, S. J. Frigidity in women. *Quarterly Review of Surgical Obstetrics and Gynecology*, 1959, **16**, 243-248.

Kleemeier, R. W. Some psychosocial implications of amputations in the geriatric patient. In *The geriatric amputee*. Washington, D.C.: National Academy of Sciences—National Research Council.

Kosberg, J. J. The nursing home: A social work paradox. *Social Work*, 1973, **18**, 104-109.

Kretzschmar, W. A., & Stoddard, F. J. Psychological changes in the aging female. *Clinical Obstetrics and Gynecology*, 1964, **7**, 451-463.

Krippene, A. Today's facts about senior sex. *Harvest Years*, June 1973, 6-10.

Kupperman, H. S., Wetchler, B. B., & Blatt, M. H. G. Contemporary therapy of the menopausal syndrome. *American Medical Association Journal*, 1959, **171**, 1627-1642.

Levin, S. Some comments on the distribution of narcissistic and object libido in the aged. *International Journal of Psycho-Analysis,* 1965, **46**, 200-208.

Leviton, D. The significance of sexuality as a deterrent to suicide among the aged. *Omega*, 1973, **4**, 163-175.

Le Witter, M., & Abarbanel, A. Aging and sex. In A. Ellis & A. Abarbanel (Eds.), *The encyclopedia of sexual behavior* (Vol. 1). New York: Hawthorn, 1961.

Lobsenz, N. M. Leisure and sexual behavior. In E. Palmore (Ed.), *Normal aging* (Vol. II). Durham, N.C.: Duke University Press, 1974.

Lobsenz, N. M. Sex and the senior citizen. *The New York Times Magazine,* January 20, 1974, 8, 9, 28, 30, 32, 34.

Loeb, M. B., & Wasow, M. *Sexuality and the aged in nursing homes.* A paper presented at the 27th annual meeting of the Gerontological Society, Portland, Oregon, October 28-November 1, 1974.

Masters, W. H., & Ballew, J. W. The third sex. *Geriatrics,* 1955, **10,** 1-4.

Masters, W. H., & Johnson, V. E. *Human sexual response.* Boston: Little, Brown, 1966.

Masters, W. H., & Johnson, V. E. Human sexual response: The aging female and aging male (abridged from Human Sexual Response). Boston: Little, Brown, 1966.

Masters, W. H., & Johnson, V. E. The aging male and aging female. In B. Neugarten (Ed.), *Middle age and aging.* Chicago: University of Chicago Press, 1968.

McCary, J. L. *Human sexuality.* Princeton, N.J.: Von Nostrand, 1973.

Meema, H. E., et al. Loss of compact bone due to menopause. *Obstetrics and Gynecology,* 1965, **26,** 333.

Neubeck, G. (Ed.), *Extramarital relations.* Englewood Cliffs, New Jersey: Prentice-Hall, 1969.

Neugarten, B. L., & Kraines, R. J. Menopausal symptoms in women of various ages. *Psychosomatic Medicine,* 1965, **27,** 266-273.

Neugarten, B., Wood, V., Kraines, R., & Loomis, B. Women's attitudes toward the menopause. *Vita Humana,* 1963, **6,** 110-151.

Newman, G., & Nichols, C. R. Sexual activities and attitudes in older persons. *Journal of the American Medical Association,* 1960, **173,** 33-35.

Nichols, W. The older homosexual. *One Magazine,* June-July, 1957, 5-8.

Pease, R. R. Female professional students and sexuality in the aging male. *The Gerontologist,* 1974, **14,** 153-157.

Pfeiffer, E. Sexual behavior in old age. In E. W. Busse & E. Pfeiffer (Eds.), *Behavior and adaptation in late life.* Boston: Little, Brown, 1969.

Pfeiffer, E. Romance and the aged. *Time,* June 4, 1973, 48.

Pfeiffer, E. Sexual attitudes and behavior in the elderly. *Geriatric Focus,* 1973, **12,** 6-7.

Pfeiffer, E., & Davis, G. C. Determinants of sexual behavior in middle and old age. *Journal of the American Geriatrics Society,* 1972, **20,** 151-158.

Pfeiffer, E., Verwoerdt, A., & Davis, G. C. Sexual behavior in middle life. *American Journal of Psychiatry,* 1972, **128,** 82-87.

Pfeiffer, E., Verwoerdt, A., & Davis, G. C. Sexual behavior in aged men and women. I. Observations on 254 community volunteers. *Archives of General Psychiatry,* 1968, **19,** 753-758.

Pfeiffer, E., Verwoerdt, A., & Wang, H. S. The natural history of sexual behavior in a biologically advantaged group of aged individuals. *Journal of Gerontology,* 1969, **24,** 193-198.

Pineo, P. C., & Dentler, R. A. Sexual adjustment, marital adjustment and the personal growth of husbands: A panel analysis. *Marriage and Family Living,* 1960, **22,** 45-48.

Reuben, D. *Everything you always wanted to know about sex.* New York: Basic, 1969.

Rubin, I. *Sexual life after sixty.* New York: Basic, 1965.

Rubin, I. The "sexless older years"—A socially harmful stereotype. *Annals of the American Academy of Social Sciences,* 1968, **376,** 86-95.

Schaffer, R. S. Will you still need me when I'm 64? In K. Jay & A. Young (Eds.), *Out of the closets: Voices of gay liberation.* New York: Douglas, 1972.

Scheingold, L. D., & Wagner, N. N. *Sound sex and the aging heart.* New York: Human Science Press, 1974.

Spiegel, R. Depressions and the feminine situation. *Revista De Psicoanalisis, Psiquiatria Y Psicologia,* 1969, **11,** 47-58.

Stokes, W. R. Sexual function in the aging male. *Geriatrics,* 1951, **5,** 304-308.

Stokes, W. R. Sexual pleasure in the late years. *Professional Psychology,* 1971, **2,** 361-362.

Verwoerdt, A., Pfeiffer, E., & Wang, H. S. Sexual behavior in senescence: I. Changes in sexual activity and interest of aging men and women. *Journal of Geriatric Psychiatry,* 1969, **2,** 163-180.

Verwoerdt, A., Pfeiffer, E., & Wang, H. S. Sexual behavior in senescence: II. Patterns of sexual activity and interest. *Geriatrics,* 1969, **24,** 137-154.

Vincent, C. E. (Ed.). *Human sexuality in medical practice.* Springfield, III.: Thomas, 1968.

Weinberg, J. Sexual expression in late life. *American Journal of Psychiatry,* 1969, **126,** 713-716.

Weinberg, M. S. The male homosexual: Age-related variations in social and psychological characteristics. *Social Problems,* 1970, **17,** 527-537.

Whiskin, F. E. The geriatric sex offender. *Geriatrics,* 1967, **22,** 168-172.

Wilson, J. G. Signs of sexual aberration in old men. *Journal of the American Geriatrics Society,* 1956, **4,** 1105-1107.

VI. **The Transition into Singleness: Death and Bereavement**
   A. *Widows, Widowers and Isolation*

Abrahams, R. B. Mutual help for the widowed. *Social Work,* 1972, **17,** 54-61.

Adams, D. L., & Pihlblad, C. T. Widowhood, social participation, and life satisfaction. *Aging and Human Development,* 1972, **3,** 323-328.

Arling, G. The elderly widow and her family, neighbors and friends. *Journal of Marriage and the Family,* 1976, **38,** 757-768.

Atchley, R. C. Dimensions of widowhood in later life. *The Gerontologist,* 1975, **15,** 176-178.

Bahr, H. M., & Harvey, C. D. Widowhood, morale and affiliation. *Journal of Marriage and the Family,* 1974, **36,** 97-106.

Bellin, S. S., & Hardt, R. H. Marital status and mental disorders among the aged. *American Sociological Review,* 1958, **23,** 155-162.

Berardo, F. M. *Social adaptation to widowhood among a rural-urban population.* Washington State University, College of Agriculture: Agricultural Experiment Station Bulletin 689.

Berardo, F. M. Widowhood status in the United States: Perspective on a neglected aspect of the family life cycle. *The Family Coordinator,* 1968, **17,** 191-201.

Berardo, F. M. Survivorship and social isolation: The case of the aged widower. *The Family Coordinator,* 1970, **19,** 11-25.

Bock, E. W. Aging and suicide: The significance of marital, kinship and alternative relations. *The Family Coordinator,* 1972, **21,** 71-79.

Bock, E. W., & Webber, I. L. *Marriage and suicide: Reinforcing and alternative relationships for elderly males.* Paper presented at the annual meeting of the National Council on Family Relations, October, 1970.

Bock, E. W., & Webber, I. L. Suicide among the elderly: Isolating widowhood and mitigating alternatives. *Journal of Marriage and the Family,* 1972, **34,** 24-31.

Bornstein, P. E., & Clayton, P. J. The anniversary reaction. *Diseases of the Nervous System,* 1972, **33,** 470-472.

Buhler, C. Loneliness in maturity. *Journal of Humanistic Psychology,* 1969, **9.**

Chevan, A., & Korson, H. J. The widowed who live alone: An examination of social and demographic factors. *Journal of Social Forces,* 1972, **51,** 45-53.

Clayton, P., Desmarais, L., & Winokur, G. A study of normal bereavement. *American Journal of Psychiatry,* 1968, **125,** 168-178.

Clayton, P. J., Halikes, J. A., Maurice, W. L., & Robins, E. The bereavement of the widowed. *Diseases of the Ner-*

vous System, 1971, **32**, 597-604.

Clayton, P. J., Halikas, J. A., & Maurice, W. L. The depression of widowhood. *The British Journal of Psychiatry*, 1972, **120**, 71-78.

Clayton, P. J., Halikas, J. A., Maurice, W. L., & Robins, E. Anticipatory grief and widowhood. *British Journal of Psychiatry*, 1973, **122**, 47-51.

Cosneck, B. J. *A study of the social problems of aged widowed persons in an urban area.* University of Florida. Family Sociology. Abstract in *DA* (Dissertation Abstracts), 1966, **27**, 3525A.

Cumming, E. The multigenerational family and the crisis of widowhood. In W. Donahue et al., (Eds.), *Living in the multigeneration family* (No. 3). Ann Arbor: Institute of Gerontology. The University of Michigan—Wayne State University, 1969.

Cutter, F. *Coming to terms with death: How to face the inevitable with wisdom and dignity.* Chicago: Nelson-Hall, 1974.

Dubourg, G. O., & Mandelboote, B. M. Mentally ill widows. *International Journal of Social Psychiatry*, 1966, **12**, 63-65.

Feifel, H. Older persons look at death. *Geriatrics*, 1956, **11**, 127-130.

Feurey, B. Making widowhood work. *Retirement years.* New York: Harvest Years, 1973.

Flesch, R. The condolence call. In A. H. Kutscher (Ed.), *Death and bereavement.* Springfield, Ill.: Thomas, 1969.

Fromm-Reichmann, F. Loneliness. In W. G. Bennis et al., (Eds.), *Interpersonal dynamics.* Homewood, Ill.: Dorsey, 1968.

Glick, I. O., Weiss, R. S., & Parkes, C. M. *The first year of bereavement.* New York: Wiley, 1974.

Gorer, G. *Death, grief and mourning.* Garden City, N.Y.: Doubleday, 1967.

Gubruim, J. F. Marital desolation and the evaluation of everyday life in old age. *Journal of Marriage and the Family*, 1974, **36**, 107.

Handel, P. J. The relationship between subjective life expectations, death anxiety and general anxiety. *Journal of Clinical Psychology*, 1969, **25**, 39-42.

Harlan, W. H. *Isolation and conduct in later life: A study of four hundred and sixty-four Chicagoans of ages sixty to ninety-six.* Unpublished doctoral dissertation, University of Chicago, 1951.

Harvey, C. D., & Bahr, H. M. Widowhood, morale, and affiliation. *Journal of Marriage and the Family*, 1974, **36**, 97-106.

Heyman, D. K., & Gianturco, D. Long term adaptation by the elderly to bereavement. *Journal of Gerontology*, 1973, **28**, 349-362.

Hiltz, S. R. Helping widows: Group discussions as a therapeutic technique. *The Family Coordinator*, 1975, **24**, 331-336.

Jackson, E. N. Attitudes toward death in our culture. In A. H. Kitscher (Ed.), *Death and bereavement.* Springfield, Ill.: Thomas, 1969.

Jeffers, F. C., Nichols, C. R., & Eisdorfer, C. Attitudes of older persons toward death: A preliminary study. *Social and Psychological Aspects of Aging.* New York: Columbia University Press, 1962.

Jeffers, F. C., & Verwoerdt, A. How the old face death. In E. W. Busse & E. Pfeiffer (Eds.), *Behavior and adaptation in late life.* Boston: Little, Brown, 1969.

Jensen, G. D., & Wallace, J. G. Family mourning process. *Family Process*, 1967, **6**, 56-66.

Kalish, R. A. *Death and bereavement: An annotated social science bibliography through 1965.* Unpublished paper, 1965.

Kalish, R. A. Death and dying: A briefly annotated bibliography. In Brim, O. G. et al., (Eds.), *The dying patient.* New York: Russell Sage Foundation, 19

Kavanaugh, R. E. *Facing death.* Los Angeles: Nash, 1972.

Kraus, A. S., & Lilienfeld, A. M. Some epidermiological aspects of the high mortality in the young widowed group. *Journal of Chronic Diseases*, 1959, **10**, 207.

Kreis, B., & Pattie, A. *Up from grief.* New York: Seabury Press, 1969.

Krieger, G. W., & Bascue, L. O. Terminal illness: Counseling with a family perspective. *The Family Coordinator*, 1975, **24**, 351-355.

Krupp, G. Maladaptive reactions to the death of a family member. *Social Casework*, 1972, **53**, 425-434.

Langer, M. *Learning to live as a widow.* New York: Julian Messner, 1957.

Liberman, M. A. Psychological correlates of impending death: Some preliminary observations. *Journal of Gerontology*, 1965, **20**, 181-190.

Liberman, M. A. Observations on death and dying. *The Gerontologist*, 1966, **2**, 70-72, 125.

Lindemann, E. Symtomotology and management of acute grief. *American Journal of Psychiatry*, 1944, **101**, 141-148.

Lindemann, E. Acute grief: Symptoms and management. *Child and Family*, 1965, **4**, 73-85.

Lopata, H. Z. Loneliness: Forms and components. *Social Problems*, 1969, **17**, 248-261.

Lopata, H. Z. Role changes in widowhood: A work perspective. In D. Cowgill & L. Holmes (Eds.), *Aging in different societies.* New York: Appleton-Century-Crofts, 1970.

Lopata, H. Z. The social involvement of American widows. *American Behavioral Scientist*, 1970, **14**, 41-57.

Lopata, H. Z. Social relations of widows in urbanizing societies. *Sociological Quarterly*, Spring, 1972, 259-271.

Lopata, H. Z. *Widowhood in an American city.* Cambridge, Mass.: Schemnkman, 1972.

Lopata, H. Z. Social relations of black and widowed women in a northern metropolis. *American Journal of Sociology*, 1973, **78**, 241-248.

Lopata, H. Z. Self-identity in marriage and widowhood. *The Sociological Quarterly*, 1973, **14**, 407-418.

Lopata, H. Z. Living through widowhood. *Psychology Today*, July, 1973, 87-92.

Lowenthal, M. Antecedents of isolation and mental illness in old age. *Archives of General Psychology*, 1965, **12**, 245-254.

Maddison, D. The relevance of conjugal bereavement for preventive psychiatry. *British Journal of Psychiatry*, 1968, **41**, 223-233.

Maddison, D., & Viola, A. The health of widows in the year following bereavement. *Journal of Psychosomatic Research*, 1968, **12**, 297-306.

Maddison, D., & Walker, W. L. Factors affecting the outcome of conjugal bereavement. *British Journal of Psychiatry*, 1967, **113**, 1057-1067.

Marris, P. *Widows and their families.* London: Routledge & Kegan Paul, 1958.

Metropolitan Life Insurance Company. The American widow. *Statistical Bulletin*, 1962, XLII.

Moriarty, D. M. (Ed.). *The loss of loved ones: The effects of a death in the family on personality development.* Springfield, Ill.: Thomas, 1967.

Morison, R. S. Death "process or event." *Science*, 1971, . **173**, 694-702.

Parkes, C. M. Recent bereavement as a cause of mental illness. *British Journal of Psychiatry*, 1964, **110**, 198.

Parkes, C. M. Effects of bereavement on physical and mental health: A study of the medical records of widows. *British Medical Journal*, 1964, **2**, 274-279.

Parkes, C. M. Bereavement and mental illness: I. A clinical study, *British Journal of Medical Psychology*, (Part 1), 38:1-12; (Part 2), 38: 13-26.

Parkes, C. M. The first year of bereavement: A longitudinal study of the reaction of London widows to the death of their husbands. *Psychiatry*, 1970, **33**, 444-467.

Parkes, C. M. *Bereavement: Studies of grief in adult life.*

New York: International Universities Press, 1972.

Parkes, C. M., Benjamin, B., & Fitzgerald, R. G. Broken heart: A statistical study of increased mortality among widowers. *British Medical Journal*, 1969, **1** (5646): 740-743.

Parkes, C. M. Bereavement and mental illness: II. A classification of bereavement reactions. *British Journal of Medical Psychology*, 1965, **38**, 13-26.

Paul, N. L., & Grosser, G. H. Operational mourning and its role in conjoint family therapy. *Community Mental Health Journal*, 1965, **1**, 339-345.

Peniston, D. H. The importance of death education in family life. *Family Life Coordinator*, 1962, **11**, 15-18.

Petrowsky, M. Marital status, sex and the social networks of the elderly. *Journal of Marriage and the Family*, 1976, **39**, 749-756.

Pihlblad, C. T., & Adams, D. L. Widowhood, social participation and life satisfaction. *Aging and Human Development*, 1972, **3**, 323-330.

Pincus, L. *Death and the family*. New York: Pantheon, 1974.

Powers, E. A., & Bultena, G. L. Sex differences in intimate friendships of old age. *Journal of Marriage and the Family*, 1976, **32**, 739-747.

Silvermann, P. R. The widow-to-widow program. *Mental Hygiene* (National Association for Mental Health, New York), 1978, **53**, 333-337.

Silvermann, P. R. Widowhood and preventive intervention. *The Family Coordinator*, 1972, **21**, 95-102.

Somerville, R. M. Death education as part of family life education: Using imaginative literature. *The Family Coordinator*, 1971, **20**, 209-224.

Strugnell, C. *Adjustment to widowhood and some related problems: A selective and annotative bibliography*. New York: Health Sciences Publishing Corp., 1974.

Townsend, P. Isolation, desolation and loneliness. In E. Shanas, D. Wedderburn, H. Friis, P. Mithoj, & J. Stehoumer (Eds.), *Old people in three industrial societies*. New York: Wiley, 1968.

Tunstall, J. *Old and alone: A sociological study of old people*. London: Routledge, 1966.

Vernon, G. M. *Sociology of death: An analysis of death-related behavior*. New York: Ronald Press, 1970.

Volkhart, E. H., & Michael, S. T. Bereavement and mental health. In R. Fulton (Ed.), *Death and identity*. New York: Wiley, 1965.

Walker, W. L., & Maddison, D. Factors affecting the outcome of conjugal bereavement. *British Journal of Psychiatry*, 1967, **113**, 1057-1067.

Webber, I. Suicide among the elderly. *Journal of Marriage and the Family*, 1972, **34**, 24-32.

Wolff, K. The problem of death and dying in the geriatric patient. *Journal of The American Geriatrics Society*, 1970, **18**, 953-991.

Young, M., Benjamin, B., & Wallis, C. The mortality of widowers. *The Lancet*, 1963, **2**, 454-456.

Zalk, R. L. *Successful widow*. New York: Fleet Publishing, 1957.

B. Love and Remarriage for Aging Singles

Bernard, J. Widowhood, divorce, and remarriage. *Marriage and Family Interaction*, 1970, **32**, 501-504.

Cavan, R. S. Speculations on innovations to conventional marriage in old age. *The Gerontologist*, 1973, **13**, 409-411.

Dean, S. R. Sin and senior citizens. *Journal of the American Geriatrics Society*, 1966, **14**, 935-938.

Gilmore, A. Attitudes of the elderly to marriage. *Gerontologia Clinica*, 1973, **15**, 124-132.

Gubrium, J. J. Marital desolation and the evaluation of everyday life in old age. *Journal of Marriage and the Family*, 1974, **36**, 107-113.

Martin, J. R. *Divorce and remarriage*. Herald Press, 1974.

McKain, W. C. A new look at older marriages. *The Family Coordinator*, 1972. **21**, 61-69.

Peterson, J. A., & Payne, B. *Love in the later years*. Association Press, 1975.

Roberts, W. L., & Roberts, A. E. *Factors in life style of couples married over fifty years*. A paper presented at the meetings of the Gerontological Society, Louisville, October 26-30, 1975.

Stephens, J. Romance in the SRO: Relationships of elderly men and women in a slum hotel. *The Gerontologist*, 1974, **14**, 279-282.

Treas, J., & Van Hilst, A. Marriage and remarriage rates among older Americans. *The Gerontologist*, 1976, **16**, 132-136.

A Directory of State and Area Agencies on Aging

The Emerging Aging Network, 1978, Select Committee on Aging,
U.S. House of Representatives, Washington, D.C.

ALABAMA

(Federal Region IV)

STATE AGENCY ON AGING

Mr. Emmett Eaton, Director,
Commission on Aging,
740 Madison Ave.,
Montgomery, Ala. 36104,
(205) 832–6640

AREA AGENCIES

PSA	Area agency address	Director and telephone number
1	Northwest Alabama Council of Governments, P.O. Box 2603, Muscle Shoals, Ala. 35660.	Mr. Elliott Conway, Sr (105) 383–3861.
2	West Alabama Planning and Development Commission, P.O. Box 28, Tuscaloosa, Ala. 35401.	Ms. Carole Hill, (205) 345–5545
3	Birmingham Regional Planning Commission, 2112 11th Ave., south suite 220, Birmingham, Ala. 35203.	Mr. Thomas B. Holmes, (205) 251–8139.
3	Office of Senior Citizens Activities, 309 North 23d St., Birmingham Ala. 35222.	Ms. Barbara Bonfield, (205) 251–7868.
4	East Alabama Regional Planning and Development Commission, 1001 Leighton, P.O. Box 2186, Anniston, Ala. 36201.	Mr. Porter Benefield, (205) 237 8623.
5	South Central Alabama Development Commission, 2815 East South Blvd., Montgomery, Ala. 36116.	Ms. Sylvia Alexander, (205) 281–2196.
6	Alabama-Tombigee Rivers Regional Planning and Development Commission, Clifton St., P.O. Box 269, Camden, Ala. 36726.	Mr. C. Emmett McConnell, Jr., (205) 682–4234.
7	Southeast Alabama Regional Planning and Development Commission, P.O. Box 1406, Dothan, Ala. 36301.	Mr. William Cathell, (205) 794 4092.
8	South Alabama Regional Planning Commission. International Trade Center, 250 North Water St., P.O. Box 1665, Mobile, Ala. 36601.	Ms. Joan B. McMillan, (205) 433–7417.
9	Central Alabama Aging Consortium, 808 South Lawrence St., Montgomery, Ala. 36104.	Ms. Brenda Kirk, (205) 262–7316
10	Lee County Council of Governments, P.O. Box 1072, Auburn, Ala. 36830.	Ms. Linda Conway Adams, (205) 821–7845.
11	North Central Alabama Area Agency on Aging, City Hall Tower, 5th floor, 402 Lee St., P.O. Box 1069, Decatur, Ala. 35601.	Ms. Viki Gonia, (205) 355–4515
12	Top of Alabama Regional Council of Governments, Central Bank Bldg., suite 350, Huntsville, Ala. 35801.	Mr. Bob Gonia, (205) 533–3335

ALASKA*
(Federal Region X)

STATE AGENCY ON AGING

Mr. M. D. Plotnick, Coordinator,
Alaska Office on Aging,
Pouch H–OIC,
Juneau, Alaska 99811,
(907) 465–4903

*The State of Alaska serves as a single planning and service area.

ARIZONA
(Federal Region IX)

STATE AGENCY ON AGING

Mr. John B. Fooks, Chief
Bureau on Aging,
Department of Economic Security,
P.O. Box 6123,
Phoenix, Ariz. 85005,
(602) 271–4446

AREA AGENCIES

PSA	Area agency address	Director and telephone number
1	Area Agency on Aging Region I, 1802 East Thomas Rd. suite 8, Phoenix, Ariz. 85016.	Dr. Alice Drought, (602) 264–2255.
2	Pima County Council on Aging, 100 East Alameda, suite 406, Tucson, Ariz. 85701.	Mrs. Marion Lupu, (602) 624–4419.
3	Northern Arizona Council of Government's, P.O. Box 57, Flagstaff, Ariz. 86002.	Ms. Jackie Sweet, (602) 774–1895.
4	District IV Council of Government's, 377 South Main St., No. 202, Yuma, Ariz. 85364.	Ms. Irene Six, (602) 782–1886
5	No area agency on aging	
6	Southeastern Arizona Governments Organization, P.O. Box 204, Bisbee, Ariz. 85603.	Mr. Tim Welsh, (602) 432–2237

ARKANSAS
(Federal Region VI)

STATE AGENCY ON AGING

Mrs. Delores Martin, Acting Director,
Office on Aging,
Department of Human Services,
1200 Westpark Dr.,
Little Rock, Ark. 72204,
(501) 371–2441

AREA AGENCIES

PSA	Area agency address	Director and telephone number
1	Northwest Arkansas Area Agency on Aging, P.O. Box 190, Harrison, Ark. 72601.	Mr. Lloyd Kennedy, (501) 741–5404.

2	White River Area Agency on Aging, P.O. Box 2396, White River Regional Services Center, Highway 25 North, Batesville, Ark. 72501.	Mr. Jon Looney, (501) 793–5270
3	East Arkansas Area Agency on Aging, P.O. Box 5035, Jonesboro, Ark. 72401.	Mr. Herb Sanderson, (501) 972–5980.
4	Southeast Arkansas Area Agency on Aging, P.O. Box 6806, 1108 Popular, Pine Bluff, Ark. 71601.	Mr. John White, (501) 536–1971
5	Central Arkansas Area Agency on Aging, 1700 West 13th, Little Rock, Ark. 72202.	Mrs. Dixie Matthews, (501) 372–5566/5497/5498.
6	West Central Arkansas Area Agency on Aging, P.O. Box 1558, 2814 Malvern, Hot Springs, Ark. 71901.	Mr. Darrell Smith, (501) 321–2214.
7	Southwest Arkansas Area Agency on Aging, P.O. Box 767, Municipal Bldg., Magnolia, Ark. 71753.	Mr. David Sneed, (501) 234–4030.
8	Western Arkansas Area Agency on Aging, P.O. Box 2067, 523 Garrison Ave., Fort Smith, Ark. 72902.	Mr. Jim Medley, (501) 785–2651

CALIFORNIA

(Federal Region IX)

STATE AGENCY ON AGING

Mrs. Janet J. Levy, Director,
Department of Aging,
918 J. St.,
Sacramento, Calif. 95814,
(916) 322–3887/5290

AREA AGENCIES

PSA	Area agency address	Director and telephone number
1	No area agency on aging	
2	Do	
3	Do	
4	Area 4 Agency on Aging, 1832 Tribute Rd., upstairs, Sacramento, Calif. 95815.	Deanna Lea, (916) 929–6802
5A	North Bay Senior Planning Council, 1302 Holm Rd., Petaluma, Calif. 94952.	Henry Mattimore, (707) 763–2295.
5B	Marin County Area Agency on Aging, Marin City Civic Center, Room 279, San Rafael, Calif. 94930.	Mr. Michael Bradney, (415) 479–1100, extension 3011.
6	San Francisco City and County Commission on Aging, 1095 Market St. No. 700, San Francisco, Calif. 94103.	Glenn B. McRibbin, (415) 558–2126.
7	Area 7 Area Agency on Aging, 2450 Stanwell Dr., suite 220, Concord, Calif. 94520.	Jane McClelland, (415) 671–4233.
8	San Mateo County Area Agency on Aging, 617 Hamilton St., Redwood City, Calif. 94063.	Mr. Thomas J. Jordan, (415) 364–5600, extension 4511.
9	Alameda County Department on Aging, 1755 Broadway, 5th floor, Oakland, Calif. 94612.	Mr. Eddie J. James, (415) 874–7233/5741.
10	Council on Aging of Santa Clara County, Inc., 277 West Hedding St., San Jose, Calif. 95110.	Mr. Richard Fisher, (408) 287–7111.
11A	Area Agency on Aging-Area 11–A, 1100 Kansas Ave., suite E, Modesto, Calif. 95350.	Ms. Beverly Carr, (209) 521–7066.
11B	San Joaquin County Area Agency on Aging, 222 East Weber, room 144, Stockton, Calif. 95202.	Ms. Charlotte Humphrey, (209) 944–2504/2420.
12	No area agency on aging	
13	Do	
14	Do	
15	Do	
16	Do	
17	Tri-County Area Agency on Aging, 1270–A Coast Village Circle, Montecito, Calif. 93108.	Ms. Joan Tadeo, (805) 969–5080

PSA	Area agency address	Director and telephone number
18	No area agency on aging	
19	Los Angeles County Department of Senior Citizens Affairs, 601 South Kingsley Dr., Los Angeles, Calif. 90005.	Mr. Leon Harper, (213) 385–4221.
20	Office on Aging, San Bernardino County, 602 South Tippecanoe, room 1320, Building No. 3, San Bernardino, Calif. 92415.	Mr. Phil Nathanson, (714) 383–3673
21	County of Riverside Office on Aging, 3601 University Ave., suite 201, Riverside, Calif. 92501.	Mr. Fred Hubbard, (714) 787–6557.
22	Senior Citizens Program Office, 801–C North Broadway, Santa Ana, Calif. 92701.	Mr. Walter Scales, (714) 834–6017.
23	San Diego County Office of Senior Citizens Affairs, 1955 4th Ave., San Diego, Calif. 92101.	Ms. Lola Hobbs, (714) 236–3269
24	No area agency on aging	
25	Aging Division Community Development Department City Hall, suite 2100, 200 North Spring St., Los Angeles, Calif. 90012.	Mr. Jerry C. Cimmarusti, (213) 485–4402.

COLORADO

(Federal Region VIII)

STATE AGENCY ON AGING

Ms. Dorothy Anders, Director,
Division of Services for the Aging,
Department of Social Services,
1575 Sherman St.,
Denver, Colo. 80203
(303) 839–2651

AREA AGENCIES

PSA	Area agency address	Director and telephone number
1	Northeastern Colorado Area Agency on Aging, P.O. Box 1782, Sterling, Colo. 80851.	Vacant, (303) 522–0040
2	Larimer-Weld Area Agency on Aging, 201 East 4th St., room 201, Loveland, Colo. 80537.	Mr. Gary Houser, (303) 667–3288.
3	Region III Office on Aging, 2480 West 26th Ave., Denver, Colo. 80211.	Mrs. Wendy Snow, (303) 758–5166.
4	Pikes Peak Area Agency on Aging, 27 East Vermijo, Colorado Springs, Colo. 80904.	Ms. Jeremy Huffman, (303) 471–7080.
5	East Central Council of Governments, P.O. Box 28, Stratton, Colo. 80836.	Ms. Shelley Hornung, (303) 348–5562
6	Lower Arkansas Valley Area Agency on Aging, Bent County Courthouse, Las Animas, Colo. 81054.	Mr. Jerry Garcia, (303) 456–0061.
7	District 7 Area Agency on Aging, 1 City Hall Pl., 3d floor, Pueblo, Colo. 81003.	Mr. Manuel Esquibel, (303) 544–4307.
8	Department of Aging, Box 28, Adams State College, Alamosa, Colo. 81101.	Modesto Salazar, (303) 589–7927
9	San Juan Basin Area Agency on Aging, 1911 North Main St., Durango, Colo. 81301.	Mr. Lawrence Marsh, (303) 259–1967.
10 11 12	Rocky Mountain Area Agency on Aging, P.O. Box 351, Rifle, Colo. 81650.	Mr. Dave Norman, (303) 243–9322.
13	Upper Arkansas Area Agency on Aging, 1310 East Rainbow Blvd., No. 17, Salida, Colo. 81201.	Ms. Betty Cook, (303) 275–3342

CONNECTICUT

(Federal Region I)

STATE AGENCY ON AGING

Mrs. Marin Shealy, Director,
Department on Aging,
90 Washington St., room 312,
Hartford, Conn.   06115,
(203) 566–2480

AREA AGENCIES

PSA	Area agency address	Director and telephone number
1	Northwestern Connecticut Agency on Aging, Inc., 20 East Main St., room 344, Waterbury, Conn. 06702.	Ms. Barbara Grant, (203) 753–2145.
2	Community Council of the Capitol Region, North Central Connecticut Agency on Aging, 999 Asylum Ave., Hartford, Conn. 06115	Mr. James Gaito, (203) 278–2044.
3	Eastern Connecticut Agency on Aging, 317 Main St., Norwich, Conn. 06360.	Ms. Linda Eckert, (203) 887–3561.
4	Southwestern Connecticut Area Agency on Aging, 328 Park Ave., Bridgeport, Conn. 06604.	Mr. Clifford Laube, (203) 333–9288.
5	South Central Connecticut Agency on Aging, 15 June St., Woodbridge, Conn. 06525.	Mr. Daro Quiring, (203) 389–9541/9543.

DELAWARE *

(Federal Region III)

STATE AGENCY ON AGING

Ms. Eleanor L. Cain, Director,
Division of Aging,
Department of Health and Social Services,
1901 North Dupont Highway,
New Castle, Del.   19720,
(302) 421–6791

*Serves as single planning and service area for State of Delaware.

FLORIDA

(Federal Region IV)

STATE AGENCY ON AGING

Mr. E. Bentley Lipscomb, Director,
Program Office of Aging and Adult Services,
Department of Health and Rehabilitative Services,
1323 Winewood Blvd.,
Tallahassee, Fla.   32301,
(904) 488–2650

AREA AGENCIES

PSA	Area agency address	Director and telephone number
1	No area agency on aging	
2	Area Agency on Aging of North Florida 2639 North Monroe St., suite 145–B/Box 12, Tallahassee, Fla.	Mrs. Margaret Lynn Duggar, 32303. (904) 385–2133.

3	Area Agency on Aging, 3008 Northwest 13th St., Gainesville, Fla. 32601.	Mrs. Virgie H. Cone, (904) 378–6716/6749.
4	Northeast Florida Area Agency on Aging, 1045 Riverside Ave., suite 250, Jacksonville, Fla. 32204.	Mr. David Adkins, (904) 355–3777.
5	Tampa Bay Regional Planning Council, 3151 3d Ave. North, 5th floor, 300 Center West, St. Petersburg, Fla. 33713.	Ms. Julia Greene, (813) 821–2811.
6	Area Agency on Aging, W. T. Edwards Hospital, 4000 West Buffalo Ave., Tampa, Fla. 33614.	Mrs. Grace Ganley, (813) 877–3053.
7	East Central Florida Regional Planning Council, 1011 Wymore Rd., suite 105, Winter Park, Fla. 32789.	Dr. James Mowbray, (305) 645–3339.
8	South Central Florida Area Agency on Aging, P.O. Box 2258, 3049 Cleveland Ave., Fort Myers, Fla. 33901.	Ms. Maeve Foster, (813) 332–2211.
9	Gulfstream Areawide Agency on Aging, Indian River Community College, 3209 Virginia Ave., Fort Pierce, Fla. 33450.	Mr. George Tsismanakis, (305) 464–2000, extension 363.
10	Area Agency on Aging of Broward County, Inc., 5950 Park Dr., Margate, Fla. 33063.	Dr. Nan Hutchison, (305) 973–1350/51.
11	United Way of Dade County, 955 Southwest 2d Ave., Miami, Fla. 33130.	Mr. Carl Dahl, (305) 854–8311

GEORGIA

(Federal Region IV)

STATE AGENCY ON AGING

Mr. Troy Bledsoe, Director,
Aging Section,
Department of Human Resources,
618 Ponce De Leon Ave. N.E,
Atlanta, Ga. 30308,
(404) 894–5333

AREA AGENCIES

PSA	Area agency address	Director and telephone number
1	No area agency on aging	
2	Atlanta Regional Commission, 230 Peachtree St., suite 200, Atlanta, Ga. 30303.	Mrs. Cheryll Schramm, (404) 656–7767.
3	Central Savannah River Area Planning and Development Commission, P.O. Box 2800, 2123 Wrightsboro Rd., Augusta, Ga. 30904.	Sister Elizabeth Ann Ney, (404) 828–2356.
4	No area agency on aging	
5	Coastal Area Planning and Development, P.O. Box 1316, Brunswick, Ga. 31520.	Ms. Christine Long, (912) 264–7363.
6	Coastal Plains Area Planning and Development Commission, P.O. Box 1223, Valdosta, Ga. 31601.	Ms. Pauline Carter, (912) 247–3454/3459.
7	Coosa Valley Area Planning and Development Commission, P.O. Drawer "H", Rome, Ga. 30161.	Mr. Ralph Peters, (404) 295–6485.
8	Georgia Mountains Area Planning and Development Commission Aging Program, P.O. Box 1720, Gainesville, Ga. 30501.	Mrs. Pat Viles, (404) 536–3431
9	No area agency on aging	
10	Do	
11	Do	
12	Do	
13	Middle Georgia Area Planning and Development Commission, 711 Grand Bldg., Macon, Ga. 31201.	Mrs. Nancy Thompson, (912) 744–6160.

14	North Georgia Area Planning and Development Commission, 212 North Pentz St., Dalton, Ga. 30720.	Mr. Lawrence Besel, (404) 226–1670.
15	Northeast Georgia Planning and Development Commission, 305 Research Rd., Athens, Ga. 30601.	Ms. Claire Hamilton, (404) 548–3141.
16	No area agency on aging	
17	Do	
18	Southwest Georgia Area Planning and Development Commission, P.O. Box 346, Camilla, Ga. 31730.	Mr. Ted Heiland, (912) 439–4315.

HAWAII

(Federal Region IX)

STATE AGENCY ON AGING

Mr. Renji Goto, Director,
Executive Office on Aging,
1149 Bethel St., room 307,
Honolulu, Hawaii 96813,
(808) 548–2593

AREA AGENCIES

PSA	Area agency address	Director and telephone number
1	Kauai County Office of Elderly Affairs, 4396 Rice St., Lihue, Hawaii 96766.	Mrs. Eleanor J. Lloyd, (808) 245–4737.
2	Honolulu Area Agency on Aging, 51 Merchant St., Honolulu, Hawaii 96813.	Mr. Horace E. Maclaren, (808) 523–4361.
3	Maui County Committee on Aging, 200 South High St., Wailuku, Hawaii 96793.	Mr. Robert Yokoyama, (808) 244–7837.
4	Hawaii County Office of Aging, 34 Rainbow Dr., Hilo, Hawaii 96720.	Mr. William Takaba, (808) 961–3794.

IDAHO

(Federal Region X)

STATE AGENCY ON AGING

Mr. Kenneth Wilkes, Acting Director,
Idaho Office on Aging,
State House,
Boise, Idaho 83720,
(208) 384–3833

AREA AGENCIES

PSA	Area agency address	Director and telephone number
1	Panhandle Area Council, P.O. Box 880, Coeur d'Alene, Idaho 83814	Ms. Katie Salo, (208) 667–1556
2	Community Action Agency, Inc., 1032 Bryden Ave., Lewiston, Idaho 83501	Ms. Bessie Lotze, (208) 746–3351
3	Idaho-Oregon Regional Planning and Development Association, P.O. Box 311, Weiser, Idaho 83672.	Mr. Elwin Grout, (208) 549–2411
4	College of Southern Idaho, P.O. Box 1238, Twin Falls, Idaho 83301.	Mr. Phil Sampson, (208) 733–9554, extension 204.
5	Southeast Idaho Council of Governments, P.O. Box 4169, 436 North Main, P.O. Box 4169, Pocatello, Idaho 83201.	Sister Anthony Marie, (208) 233–4032.
6	Eastern Idaho Special Services Agency, P.O. Box 1098, Idaho Falls, Idaho 83401.	Mr. Mike Kormanik, (208) 522–5391.

ILLINOIS

(Federal Region V)

STATE AGENCY ON AGING
David Munson, Acting Director,
Department on Aging,
Monadnock Bldg., room 731,
53 West Jackson Blvd.
Chicago, Ill. 60604,
(217) 785-3340

AREA AGENCIES

PSA	Area agency address	Director and telephone number
1	Northwest Illinois Area Agency on Aging, Eastmoor Bldg., 4223 East State St., Rockford, Ill. 61108.	Mrs. Janet B. Ellis, (815) 226-4901.
2	Region Two Area Agency on Aging, P.O. Box 809, River Rd., Kankakee, Ill. 60901.	Mr. Charles Johnson, (815) 939-0727.
3	Western Illinois Area Agency on Aging, 2201-11th St., Rock Island, Ill. 61201.	Mr. Sid L. Granet, (309) 797-4319.
4	Central Illinois Area Agency on Aging, 300 East War Memorial Dr., room 300, Peoria, Ill. 61614.	Mr. Frank G. Blumb, (309) 676-4312.
5	East Central Illinois Area Agency on Aging, 2714 McGraw Dr., Bloomington, Ill. 61701.	Mrs. Phyllis H. Pinkerton, (309) 662-9393.
6	West Central Illinois Area Agency on Aging, 112 North 7th St., P.O. Box 428, Quincy, Ill. 62301.	Miss Lynn Niewohner, (217) 223-7904.
7	Project LIFE Area Agency on Aging, 1029 South 4th, Springfield, Ill. 62704.	Ms. Dorothy Kimball, (217) 522-8954.
8	Southwestern Illinois Area Agency, on Aging, 8787 State St., Edgemont Bldg., suite 107, East St. Louis, Ill.	Ms. Nancy C. Silvers, (618) 397-4118.
9	Midland Area Agency on Aging, 140 South Locust St., room 413, Centralia, Ill. 62801.	Mr. David P. Seibert, (618) 532-1853.
10	Southeastern Illinois Area Agency, Inc., 425 Market St., Mount Carmel, Ill. 62863.	Ms. Barbara Poshard, (618) 262-8001.
11	Egyptian Area Agency on Aging, Inc., John A. Logan College, Carterville, Ill. 62918.	Mr. William F. Price, (618) 985-4011.
12	Mayor's Office for Senior Citizens and Handicapped, 180 North LaSalle St., suite 500, Chicago, Ill. 60601.	Mr. Robert J. Ahrens, (312) 744-4016.
13	Suburban Cook County Area Agency on Aging, 223 West Jackson Blvd., suite 1200, Chicago, Ill. 60606.	Lynne Brenne, acting, (312) 341-1400.

INDIANA

(Federal Region V)

STATE AGENCY ON AGING
Mr. Maurice E. Endwright, Director,
Commission on Aging and Aged,
Graphic Arts Bldg.,
215 North Senate Ave.,
Indianapolis, Ind. 46202,
(317) 633-5984

AREA AGENCIES

PSA	Area agency address	Director and telephone number
1	Area I Agency on Aging, 5518 Calumet Ave., Hammond, Ind. 46320.	Mr. Jerry Long, (219) 937-3500

PSA	Area agency address	Director and telephone number
2	Area 2 Agency on Aging, REAL Services of St. Joseph County, Inc., P.O. Box 1835, 622 North Michigan, South Bend, Ind. 46634.	Mr. Jim Oleksak, (219) 233–8205 (800–552–2916).
3	Northeast Area III Council on Aging, Foellinger Center, 227 East Washington Blvd., Fort Wayne, Ind. 46802.	Ms. L. Joyce Smith, (219) 423–7491 (800–552–3662).
4	Area IV Council on Aging, 1001 South St., Lafayette, Ind. 47901.	Ms. Fay B. Ebrite, (317) 742–0061 (800–382–7666).
5	Area V Council on Aging, Inc., 912 E. Market, Logansport, Ind. 46947.	Mr. Terrence R. McGovern, (219) 722–4801 and 753–4311.
6	Area VI Council on Aging, 1968 West Main St., Muncie, Ind. 47303.	Ms. Karen Gardner DeHart, (317) 289–1121, (800–382–8683).
7	Area VII Agency on Aging, West Central Indiana Economic Development District, P.O. Box 627, 700 Wabash Ave., Terre Haute, Ind. 47808.	Ms. Jean Cox, (812) 238–1561, (800–742–0804).
8	Central Indiana Council on Aging, Inc., 146 East Washington St., 2d floor, Indianapolis, Ind. 46204.	Mr. John Riggle, (317) 633–6191
9	Area 9 Agency on Aging, Indiana University East, 2325 Chester Blvd., Richmond, Ind. 47374.	Ms. L. Jane Rice, (317) 966–1795.
10	Area 10 Agency on Aging, 2295 Bloomfield Rd., Bloomington, Ind. 47401.	Mr. A. Louis Bridgewaters, (812) 334–3383.
11	Area 11 Agency on Aging, P.O. Box 904, 2756 25th St., Columbus, Ind. 47201.	Mr. Thomas A. Ross, (812) 372–9989.
12	Area 12 Agency on Aging, P.O. Box 177, Dillsboro Manor, Lenover St., Dillsboro, Ind. 47018.	Ms. Sally Dobson, (812) 432–5000.
13A	Area 13A Agency on Aging, P.O. Box 336, Community Service Center, 2d and Indianapolis Sts., Vincennes, Ind. 47591.	Mr. Gerald Wibert, (812) 882–6370.
13B	Area 13B Agency on Aging, Southwestern Indiana Regional Council on Aging, Inc., 528 Main St., Evansville, Ind. 47708.	Mr. Robert Patrow, (812) 425–6128.
14	Area 14 Agency on Aging, South Central Indiana Council for the Aging and Aged, Inc., 317 East 5th St., New Albany, Ind. 47150.	Ms. Thelma Bertrand, (812) 948–9161.
15	Area 15 Council on Aging, P.O. Box 128, Orleans Airport, Orleans, Ind. 47452.	Mr. Gene Purlee, (812) 865–3033.

IOWA

(Federal Region VII)

STATE AGENCY ON AGING

Mr. Glenn R. Bowles, Director,
Commission on Aging,
415 West 10th St.,
Jewett Bldg.,
Des Moines, Iowa 50319,
(515) 281–5187

AREA AGENCIES

PSA	Area agency address	Director and telephone number
1	Area I Agency on Aging, Area One Voc-Tec. School, Calmar, Iowa 52132.	Mr. George Pfister, (319) 562–3263.
2	North Central Iowa Area Agency on Aging II, V, XII, 500 College Dr., Mason City, Iowa 50401.	Mr. Donald Ryerkerk, (515) 421–4339.

3	Area IV Agency on Aging, SIMPCO, P.O. Box 447, 626 Insurance Exchange Bldg., Sioux City, Iowa 51102.	Mr. Rick Motz, (712) 279–6220.
4	Hawkeye Valley Area Agency on Aging VI, VII, 210 East 5th St., Box 2576, Waterloo, Iowa 50706.	Mr. Chris Harshbarger, (319) 233–5214.
5	Great River Bend Area Agency on Aging, IX, Bi-State Metropolitan Planning Commission, 1504 3d Ave., Rock Island, Ill. 61201.	Ms. Dottie Seyfried, (309) 788–6338.
6	Heritage Area Agency on Aging X, Kirkwood Community College, 6301 Kirkwood Blvd, SE., Cedar Rapids, Iowa 52406.	Mr. Russ Proffitt, (319) 398–5559.
7	Area XI Area Agency on Aging, Central Iowa Regional Association of Local Governments, 104½ East Locust, Des Moines, Iowa 50309.	Ms. Carolyn Bayreder, (515) 244–3257.
8	Area XIV Agency on Aging, 201 West Mills St., Creston, Iowa 50801.	Ms. Lois Houston, (515) 782–4040.
9	Area XV Area Agency on Aging, SIEDA, Bldg. No. 17, Ottumwa Industrial Airport, Ottumwa, Iowa 52501.	Ms. Shirley Baird, (515) 682–8741.
10	Iowa Western Area XIII Agency on Aging, Iowa Western Community College, 2700 College Rd., Kanesville Center, room 203, Council Bluffs, Iowa 51501.	Mr. Frank Kowal, (712) 328–2540.
11	Iowa Lakes Area Agency on Aging III, P.O. Box 1533, 2328 Highway Blvd., Spencer, Iowa 51301.	Mr. Richard Ambrosius, (712) 262–1775.
12	Southeast Iowa Area Agency on Aging XVI, Memorial Auditorium, 3d floor, Front and Jefferson, Burlington, Iowa 51601.	Mr. William F. Holvoet, (319) 753–2191.
13	Area VIII Agency on Aging, 469 Emmett St., Dubuque, Iowa 52001.	Ms. Marguerite Carter, (319) 583–3547.

KANSAS
(Federal Region VII)
STATE AGENCY ON AGING
Max M. Mills, Secretary,
Kansas Department on Aging,
610 West 10th St.,
Topeka, Kans. 66612,
(913) 296–4986
AREA AGENCIES

PSA	Area agency address	Director and telephone number
1	Wyandotte-Leavenworth Area Agency on Aging, 5th floor, City Hall, 701 North 7th St., Kansas City, Kans. 66101.	Ms. Anita Favors, (913) 371–3142.
2	Central Plains Area Agency on Aging, 455 North Main, Wichita, Kans. 67202.	Ms. Irene Hart, (316) 268–4661
3	Northwest Kansas Area Agency on Aging, 208 East 7th St., Hays, Kans. 67601.	Mr. Merlin Sizlove, (913) 628–8204.
4	Jayhawk Area Agency on Aging, 444 Southeast Quincy, Suite 170, Topeka, Kans. 66603.	Ms. Donna Kidd, (913) 235–1367.
5	Southeast Kansas Area Agency on Aging, Box 269, Chanute, Kans. 66720.	Mr. Jerry D. Williams, (316) 431–2980.
6	Southwest Kansas Area Agency on Aging, 1107 6th Ave., Dodge City, Kans. 67801.	Ms. Mary Stuecker, (316) 225–0510.
7	Mid-America Council on Aging, 132 South Main, Ottawa, Kans. 66067.	Ms. Shirley Higdon, (913) 782–1900.
8	North Central/Flint Hills Area Agency on Aging, 217 South Seth Childs Rd., Manhattan, Kans. 66502.	Mr. John Churchill, (913) 776–9294.
9	Northeast Kansas Area Agency on Aging, 107 Oregon West, P. O. Box 56, Hiawatha, Kans. 66434.	Ms. Anna Mae Shaffer, (913) 742–7324.
10	South Central Area Agency on Aging, P.O. Box 1122, Arkansas City, Kans. 67005.	Ms. Betty Londeen, (316) 442–0268.

KENTUCKY

(Federal Region IV)

STATE AGENCY ON AGING

Mr. Thomas S. Cathell, Director,
Aging Program Unit,
Department for Human Resources,
275 East Main St.,
5th floor west,
Frankfort, Ky. 40601,
(502) 564-6930

AREA AGENCIES

PSA	Area agency address	Director and telephone number
1	Purchase Area Development District, P.O. Box 588, Mayfield, Ky. 42066.	Ms. Rebecca Blaine, (502) 247-7171.
2	Pennyrile Area Development District, 609 Hammond Plaza, Fort Campbell Blvd., Hopkinsville, Ky. 42240.	Ms. Agnes Davis, (502) 886-9484
3	Green River Area Development District, P.O. Box 628, Owensboro, Ky. 42301.	Ms. Nelda Barnett, (502) 926-4433.
4	Barren River Area Development District, P.O. Box 2120, Bowling Green, Ky. 42101.	Mr. Bill Guthrie, (502) 781-2381
5	Lincoln Trail Area Development District, 305 First Federal Bldg., Elizabethtown, Ky. 42701.	Ms. Becky McMahan, (502) 769-2393/2002.
6	Kentuckiana Regional Planning and Development Agency, 505 West Ormsby St., Louisville, Ky. 40203.	Ms. Betty Rulander, (502) 587-3804.
7	Northern Kentucky Area Development District, 7505 Sussex Dr., Florence, Ky. 41042.	Ms. Deanna Skees, (606) 283-1885.
8	Buffalo Trace Area Development District, State National Bank Bldg., Maysville, Ky. 41056.	Ms. Beth Hillemmeyer, (606) 564-6894.
9	Gateway Area Development District, P.O. Box 107, Owingsville, Ky. 40360.	Mr. Jim Templeton, (606) 674-6355.
10	Fivco Area Development District, P.O. Box 636, Catlettsburg, Ky. 41129.	Mr. Bob Haight, (606) 739-5191
11	Big Sandy Area Development District, 552 Southlake Dr., Prestonsburg, Ky. 41653.	Ms. Phyllis Stanley, (606) 886-6869/6897.
12	Kentucky River Area Development District, P.O. Box 986, Hazard, Ky. 41701.	Mr. Kenneth Blair, (606) 436-3158.
13	Cumberland Valley Area Development District, Route 2, Box 4A, London, Ky. 40741.	Mr. Phillip Martin, (606) 864-7391.
14	Lake Cumberland Area Development District, P.O. Box 377, Jamestown, Ky. 42629.	Mr. Bob Bowe, (502) 343-3154
15	Bluegrass Area Development District, 120 East Reynolds Rd., Lexington, Ky. 40503.	Ms. Peggy Chadwick, (606) 272-6656.

LOUISIANA

(Federal Region VI)

STATE AGENCY ON AGING

Mr. O. B. Butler, Director,
Bureau of Aging Services,
Office of Human Development,
Department of Health and Human Resources,
P.O. Box 44282, Capitol Station,
Baton Rouge, La. 70804,
(504) 342-2744

AREA AGENCIES

PSA	Area agency address	Director and telephone number
1	Area Agency on Aging, District 1, 4915 Magazine St., New Orleans, La. 70115.	Mrs. Margaret Roman, (504) 899-9376.
2	Capital Area Agency on Aging, District II, P.O. Box 66638, Baton Rouge, La. 70806.	Mrs. Sandra Adams, (504) 343-9278.
3	Area Agency on Aging, District III, 402 West 5th St., Lafourche Parish Agricultural Bldg., Thibodaux, La. 70301.	Mr. Irwin Joubert, (504) 446-3714.
4	Area Agency on Aging, District IV, Acadiana Humanitarian Health Planning Council, P.O. Box 52223, Lafayette, La. 70501.	Mr. Al Edwin Thierry, (504) 234-4558.
5	Area Agency on Aging, District V, P.O. Box 6505, Pioneer Bldg., Lake Charles, La. 70606.	Mrs. Orriene Fender, (318) 439-6113.
6	Area Agency on Aging, District VI, Kisatchie-Delta Regional Planning and Development District, 1220 MacArthur Dr., Alexandria, La. 71301.	Mrs. Kristin Duke, (318) 448-5454.
7	Area Agency on Aging, District VII, 425 Milam St., Ricou-Brewster Bldg., suite 427, Shreveport, La. 71101.	Mrs. Olivia Whitehurst, (318) 425-1559.
8	Area Agency on Aging, District VIII, North Delta Regional Planning and Development District, Inc., 2115 Justice St., Monroe, La. 71201.	Mrs. Jeanne Williams, (318) 387-2572.

MAINE

(Federal Region I)

STATE AGENCY ON AGING

Ms. Patricia Riley, Director,
Bureau of Maine's Elderly,
State House,
Augusta, Maine 04333,
(207) 289-2561

AREA AGENCIES

PSA	Area agency address	Director and telephone number
1	Arrostook Regional Task Force of Older Citizens, 457 Main St., P.O. Box 1288, Presque Isle, Maine 04769.	Mr. Stephen Farnham, (207) 764-3396.
2	Eastern Task Force on Aging, 153 Illinois Ave., Bangor, Maine 04401.	Mr. Willis Spaulding, (207) 947-0561.
3	Central Maine Senior Citizens Association, P.O. Box 484, Augusta, Maine 04330.	Mr. William Inlow, (207) 622-9344.
4	Western Maine Older Citizens Council, 65 Central Ave., Lewiston, Maine 04240.	Mr. Robert Armstrong, (207) 784-8797.
5	Cumberland York Senior Citizens Council, 142 High St., Suite 401, Portland, Maine 04101.	Mr. Donald Sharland, (207) 775-6503.

MARYLAND
(Federal Region III)

STATE AGENCY ON AGING

Matthew Tayback, Sc. D., Director,
Office on Aging,
State Office Bldg.,
301 West Preston St.,
Baltimore, Md. 21201,
(301) 383–5064

AREA AGENCIES

PSA	Area agency address	Director and telephone number
1	Western Maryland Area Agency, Algonquin Motor Lodge, room 510, Cumberland, Md. 21502.	Mr. Joel Shoap, (301) 777–2167.
2	MAC, Inc., 1504 Riverside Dr., Salisbury, Md. 21801.	Mr. Joseph Eberly, (301) 742–0505.
3	Baltimore City Area Agency, Waxter Center, 861 Park Ave., Baltimore, Md. 21201.	Mr. Eugene Bartell, (301) 396–4932.
4	No area agency	
5	Central Maryland Area Agency on Aging, Johnsville School, 5745 Bartholow Rd., Eldersburg, Md. 21784.	Mrs. Carolyn Del Giudice, (301) 795–8606.
5A	Baltimore County Aging Programs and Services, 32 West Susquehanna Ave., Towson, Md. 21204.	Mr. Tim Fagan, (301) 494–2594
6	No area agency	
7A	Montgomery County Area Agency on Aging, 14 Maryland Ave., Rockville, Md. 20850.	Mr. Donald Wassmann, (301) 279–1480.
7B	Prince Georges County Area Agency on Aging, Division of Programs for the Elderly, 9171 Central Ave., Capitol Heights, Md. 20027.	Mr. Magan Pathik, (301) 350–6666.

MASSACHUSETTS
(Federal Region I)

STATE AGENCY ON AGING

Mr. Stephen G. Guptill, Director
Department of Elder Affairs
110 Tremont St., 5th Floor
Boston, Mass. 02108
(617) 727–7751/7752

AREA AGENCIES

PSA	Area agency address	Director and telephone number
1A	Berkshire Home Care Corp., 246 North St., Pittsfield, Mass. 01201.	Mr. Frederick H. Whitham, (413) 499–1353.
1B	Franklin County Home Care Corp., Central St., Turners Falls, Mass. 01376.	Ms. Margaret O. Keane, (413) 774–2994.
1C	Highland Valley Elder Service Center, Inc., 42 Gothic St., Northampton, Mass. 01060.	Mr. Robert V. Gallant, (413) 586–3130.
1D	Holyoke/Chicopee Regional Senior Services, Inc., 198 High St., Holyoke, Mass. 01040.	Ms. Priscilla Chalmers, (413) 538–9020.

PSA	Area agency address	Director and telephone number
1E	Home Care Corp. of Springfield, Inc., 1414 State St., Springfield, Mass. 01109.	Mr. James Piscioneri, (413) 781–8800.
2	Region II Area Agency on Aging, Inc., 697 Main St., Holden, Mass. 01520.	Mr. James McNamera, (617) 829–5364.
3A	Senior Home Care Services, Inc., 94 Main St., Gloucester, Mass. 01903.	Mr. Guntis Licis, (617) 281–1750.
3B	Northshore Elder Services, Inc., Northshore Shopping Center, Peabody, Mass. 01960.	Mr. William Carney, (617) 532–0330.
3C	Greater Lynn Senior Services, Inc., 25 Exchange St., Lynn, Mass. 01902.	Ms. Janet McAveeney, (617) 599–0110.
3D	Chelsea/Revere/Winthrop Home Care Center, Inc., 385 Broadway, P.O. Box 189, Revere, Mass. 02151.	Mr. James Cunningham, (617) 284–8375.
3E	Mystic Valley Elder Home Care, Inc., 341A Forest St., Malden, Mass. 02148.	Ms. Elyse Salend, (617) 324–7705.
3F	Somerville/Cambridge Home Care Corp., 249 Elm St., Somerville, Mass. 02144.	Mr. Lewis Levenson, (617) 628–2601/2602.
3G	Minuteman Home Care Corp., 365 Waltham St., Lexington, Mass. 02173.	Mr. Jon Pynoos, (617) 862–6200.
3H	West Suburban Elder Services, Inc., 51 Spring St., Watertown, Mass. 02172.	Ms. Grace Newman, (617) 926–3311.
3I	No area agency on aging	
3J	Baypath Senior Citizens Services, Inc., 5 Edgell Rd., Framingham, Mass. 01701.	Mr. Bruce Hausch, (617) 620–0840.
3K	No area agency on aging	
3L	South Shore Home Care Services, c/o Hersey House, 229 North St., Hingham, Mass. 02043.	Ms. Eileen Kirby, (617) 749–6832.
4A	No area agency on aging	
4B	Bristol County Home Care, 178 Pine St., Fall River, Mass. 02720.	Ms. Elizabeth Bielawski, (617) 675–2101.
4C	Coastline Elderly Services, Inc., 13 Welby Rd., New Bedford, Mass. 02745.	Mr. David Alves, (617) 998–3016.
4D	Elder Services of Cape Cod and the Islands, Inc., 146 Main St., Hyannis, Mass. 02601.	Dr. James Peace, (617) 771–4248.
5	Elder Services of the Merrimack Valley, 420 Common St., Lawrence, Mass. 01840.	Mr. George Moran, (617) 683–7747.
6A	Commission on Affairs of the Elderly, 1 City Hall Sq., room 271, Boston, Mass. 02201.	Ms. Ina Resnikoff, (617) 725–4366, extension 125.
6B	No area agency on aging	

MICHIGAN

(Federal Region V)

STATE AGENCY ON AGING

Ms. Elizabeth J. Ferguson, Director,
Office of Services to the Aging,
300 East Michigan,
P.O. Box 30026,
Lansing, Mich. 48909,
(517) 373–8230

AREA AGENCIES

PSA	Area agency address	Director and telephone number
1A	Detroit-Wayne County Area Agency on Aging, 3110 Book Bldg., 1249 Washington Blvd., Detroit, Mich. 48226.	Mr. Fred C. Ferris, (313) 224–0960.
1B	Area Agency on Aging 1–B, 29508 Southfield Rd., Suite 100, Southfield, Mich. 48076.	Ms. Sandra K. Reminga, (313) 569–0333.
2	Region II Commission on Aging, 611 South Center., Adrian, Mich. 49221.	Mr. Charles L. Anson, (517) 265–7881.
3	Southcentral Michigan Commission on Aging, room 127, Connor's Hall, Nazareth College, Nazareth, Mich. 49074.	Ms. Sarah Renstrom, (616) 343–4996.
4	Region IV Area Agency on Aging, Peoples State Bank Bldg., room 8, 517 Ship St., St. Joseph, Mich. 49085.	Mr. Robert L. Dolsen, (616) 983–0177.
5	Valley Area Agency on Aging, 708 Root St., room 110, Old Sears Bldg., Flint, Mich. 48503.	Ms. Valaria Conerly, (313) 239–7671.
6	Tri-County Office on Aging, 500 West Washtenaw, Lansing, Mich. 48933	Ms. Roxanna O'Connor, (517) 487–1066.
7	Region VII Area Agency on Aging, 971 Midland Rd., Saginaw, Mich. 48603.	Mr. Richard Catalino, (517) 793–1416.
8	Area Agency on Aging of Western Michigan, Inc., room 1108, Peoples Bldg., 60 Monroe N.W., Grand Rapids, Mich. 49503.	Mr. Lawrence L. Murray, Jr., (616) 456–5664.
9	Northeast Michigan Community Services Agency, Inc., 275 Bagley St., Alpena, Mich. 49707.	Ms. Christine Baumgardner, (517) 356–3474.
10	Northwest Michigan Planning and Development Services, Inc., 2334 Aero Park Ct., Traverse City, Mich. 49684.	Mr. Ronald W. Crummel, (616) 947–8920.
11	Region 11 Area Agency on Aging, UPCAP Services, Inc., 118 North 22d St., Escanaba, Mich. 49829.	Ms. Kathryn Kumkoski, (906) 786–4701.
14	Region 14 Council on Aging, 1111 4th St., Muskegon, Mich. 49441.	Mr. James Peliotes, (616) 722–7811.

MINNESOTA

(Federal Region V)

STATE AGENCY ON AGING

Mr. Gerald A. Bloedow, Director,
Minnesota Board on Aging,
Suite 204, Metro Square Bldg.,
7th and Robert St., St. Paul, Minn. 55101
(612) 296–2544

AREA AGENCIES

PSA	Area agency address	Director and telephone number
1	Region I Area Agency on Aging, 425 Woodland Ave., Crookston, Minn. 56716.	Mr. Gerald Berglin, (218) 281–1396.

2	Headwaters-Northwest Area Agency on Aging, Headwaters Regional Development Commission, Box 584, Bemidji, Minn. 56601.	Ms. Marcia Nottingham, (218) 751–3108.
3	Region 3 Area Agency on Aging, Arrowhead Regional Development Commission, 200 Arrowhead Pl., Duluth, Minn. 55802.	Mr. Steven Krasner, (218) 722–5545.
4	Region 4 Area Agency on Aging, West-Central Regional Development Commission, Administration Bldg., Fergus Falls Community College, Fergus Falls, Minn. 56537.	Ms. Laurel Sorlie, (218) 739–3356.
5 7E 7W	Tri-Regional Area Agency on Aging, Region 5 Regional Development Commission, 102 6th St., North Staples, Minn. 56479.	Mr. John Fellerer, (218) 894–3233.
6E 6W 8	Southwestern Area Agency on Aging, Southwest Regional Development Commission, 2711 Broadway, Slayton, Minn. 56172.	Mr. Fred DeJong, (507) 836–8549.
9	Region 9 Area Agency on Aging, Region 9 Development Commission, 120 South Broad, Mankato, Minn. 56001.	Ms. Connie Noterman, (507) 387–5643.
10	Region 10 Area Agency on Aging, Southeastern Regional Development Commission, 301 Marquette Bank Bldg., South Broadway at 2d St. S.E., Rochester, Minn. 55901.	Mr. Gil Wilkins, (507) 285–2585/2550.
11	Region 11 Area Agency on Aging, Metropolitan Council, 300 Metro Square, 7th and Robert Sts., St. Paul, Minn. 55101.	Dr. Jane Whiteside, (612) 291–6305.

MISSISSIPPI

(Federal Region IV)

STATE AGENCY ON AGING

Mr. Norman Harris, Director,
Mississippi Council on Aging,
P.O. Box 5136,
Fondren Station, 510 George St.,
Jackson, Miss. 39216,
(601) 354–6590

AREA AGENCIES

PSA	Area agency address	Director and telephone number
1	North Delta Area Agency on Aging, P.O. Box 1244, Clarksdale, Miss. 38614.	Ms. Gloria Dear, (601) 627–3401
2	South Delta Area Agency on Aging, Route 1, Box AB 52, Greenville, Miss. 38701.	Mrs. Sylvia Jackson, (601) 378–3831.
3	North Central Area Agency on Aging, P.O. Box 668, Winona, Miss. 38967.	Mr. Carl Cooper, (601) 283–2675.
4	Golden Triangle Area Agency on Aging, P.O. Drawer DN, Mississippi State, Miss. 39762.	Mr. Bobby Gann (coordinator), (601) 325–3855.
5	Trace Regional Area Agency on Aging, P.O. Box 7, Belden, Miss. 38826.	Ms. Jane Mapp, (601) 844–4081.
6	Northeast Mississippi Area Agency on Aging, P.O. Drawer 6D, Booneville, Miss. 38829.	Mr. Billy Moore, (601) 728–6248.
7	Central Mississippi Area Agency on Aging, 2675 River Ridge Rd., Jackson, Miss. 39216.	Mr. Joe S. Patterson, (601) 981–1511.
8	East Central Mississippi Area Agency on Aging, 410 Decatur St., Newton, Miss. 39345.	Ms. Jenifer Buford, (601) 683–2401.
9	Southern Mississippi Area Agency on Aging, 1020 32d Ave., Gulfport, Miss. 39501.	Mrs. Jane Kennedy, (601) 868–2311.
10	Southwest Mississippi Area Agency on Aging, P.O. Box 429, Meadville, Miss. 39653.	Dr. John W. Waid, (601) 384–5881.

MISSOURI

(Federal Region VII)

STATE AGENCY ON AGING

Mr. E. C. Walker, Director,
Office of Aging,
Division of Special Services,
Department of Social Services,
Broadway State Office Bldg.,
P.O. Box 570,
Jefferson City, Mo. 65101,
(314) 751–2075

AREA AGENCIES

PSA	Area agency address	Director and telephone number
1	Southwest Missouri Office on Aging, 317 St. Louis, St., Springfield, Mo. 65804.	Mr. Winston W. Bledsoe, (417) 862–0762.
2	Southeast Missouri Area Agency on Aging, 1915 North Kings Highway, Cape Girardeau, Mo. 63701.	Mr. Vearl Caid, (314) 335–3331
3	District III Area Agency on Aging, P.O. Box 556, 604 North McGuire, Warransburg, Mo. 64093.	Mr. Leonard W. Westphal, (816) 747–3107.
4	Northwest Missouri Area Agency on Aging, Box 207, County Courthouse, Albany, Mo. 64402.	Mr. Ronald Rauch, (816) 726–3800.
5	Northeast Missouri Area Agency on Aging, P.O. Box 1067, 400 North Baltimore, Kirksville, Mo. 63501.	Mr. Earl Welty, (816) 665–4682
6	Central Missouri Area Agency on Aging, room 209, Professional Bldg., 909 University Ave., Columbia, Mo. 65201.	Mr. Alan DeBerry, (314) 443–5823.
7	Mid-America Regional Council, Aging Program, 20 West 9th St., Kansas City, Mo. 64105.	Ms. Jean Bacon, (816) 474–4240
8	Mid-East Missouri Area Agency on Aging, Kimberly Bldg., suite 212, 2510 South Brentwood Blvd., Brentwood, Mo. 63144.	Mr. Floyd D. Richards, (314) 889–3050.
9	Mayor's Office for Senior Citizens, 560 Delmar Blvd., St. Louis, Mo. 63101.	Lucius F. Cervantes, S.J., Ph.D. Commissioner, (314) 621–5600.

MONTANA

(Federal Region VIII)

STATE AGENCY ON AGING

Mr. Holly Luck, Acting Director,
Aging Services Bureau,
Department of Social and Rehabilitation Services,
P.O. Box 4210,
Helena, Mont. 59601,
(406) 449–5650

AREA AGENCIES

PSA	Area agency address	Director and telephone number
1	Area Agency I on Aging, 306 North Kendrick, Glendive, Mont. 59330.	Mr. Earl Hubley, (406) 365–3364.
2	Area II Agency on Aging, 202½ Main St., Roundup, Mont. 59072.	Ms. Betty Stockert, (406) 323–1320.
3	Area Agency III on Aging, 9 4th Ave. S.W., Conrad, Mont. 59425.	Ms. Earline Zoeller, (406) 278–5662.

4 Area Agency on Aging IV, P.O. Box 721, Helena, Mont. 59601. — Vacant, (406) 442–1552

5 Area V Agency on Aging, 115 East PA St., Anaconda, Mont. 59711. — Ms. Jane Anderson, (406) 563–3310.

6 Western Montana Agency on Aging, 723 5th Ave. East, Kalispell, Mont. 59901. — Ms. Polly Nikolaisen, (406) 755–5300, extension 336.

7 Tribal Elders Program, R.R. 1, Box 58, Harlem, Mont. 59526. — Cynthia LaCounte, (406) 323–2205.

NEBRASKA

(Federal Region VII)

STATE AGENCY ON AGING

Mr. David Howard, Director,
Commission on Aging,
P.O. Box 95044,
301 Centennial Mall, South,
Lincoln, Nebr. 68509,
(402) 471–2307

AREA AGENCIES

PSA	Area agency address	Director and telephone number
A	Eastern Nebraska Office on Aging, 885 South 72d St., Omaha, Nebr. 68114.	Mr. J. Kenton Fancolly, (402) 444–6540.
B	Lincoln Area Agency on Aging, 100 North 9th St., Lincoln, Nebr. 68508.	Mr. James E. Zietlow, (402) 475–7640.
C	Northeast Nebraska Agea Agency on Aging, North Stone Bldg. at Regional Center, P.O. Box 1447, Norfolk, Nebr.- 68701.	Tim Austin, assistant, (402) 371–7454.
F	South Central Nebraska Area Agency on Aging, 2000 Central Ave., Kearney, Nebr. 68847.	Dennis Loose, (308) 234–1851___
G	Midland Area Agency on Aging, P.O. Box 905, Hastings, Nebr. 68901.	Mr. Jerry Ryan, (402) 463–4565_
H	Blue Rivers Area Agency on Aging, Beatrice National Bank Bldg., room 23, 109½ South 6th St., Beatrice, Nebr. 68310.	Mr. Fred Holtz, (402) 223–3124_
J	West Central Nebraska Area Agency on Aging, Craft State Office Bldg., 200 South Silber, North Platte, Nebr. 69101.	Mr. James E. Lowe, (308) 534–6780.
L	Western Nebraska Area Agency on Aging, P.O. Box 54, Scottsbluff, Nebr. 69361.	Mrs. Rena Mackrill, (308) 635–0851.

NEVADA*

(Federal Region IX)

STATE AGENCY ON AGING

Mr. John B. McSweeney, Director,
Department of Human Resources,
Division of Aging,
505 East King St.,
Kinkead Bldg., room 101,
Carson City, Nev. 89710,
(702) 885–4210

*The State of Nevada serves as a single planning and service area.

NEW HAMPSHIRE*

(Federal Region I)

STATE AGENCY ON AGING

Mrs. Claira P. Monier, Director,
Council on Aging,
P.O. Box 786,
14 Depot St.,
Concord, N.H. 03301,
(603) 271–2751

---

*The State of New Hampshire serves as a single planning and service area.

NEW JERSEY

(Federal Region II)

STATE AGENCY ON AGING

Mr. James J. Pennestri, Director,
Division on Aging,
Department of Community Affairs,
P.O. Box 1768,
363 West State St.,
Trenton, N.J. 08625,
(609) 292–4833

AREA AGENCIES

PSA	Area agency address	Director and telephone number
1	Atlantic County Office on Aging, Atlantic City Social Service Bldg., 1601 Atlantic Ave., 6th floor, Atlantic City, N.J. 08410.	Mr. Stephen J. Bruner, (609) 348–4361.
2	Bergen County Office on Aging, 355 Main St., Hackensack, N.J. 07601.	Mrs. Mildren Krasnow, (201) 646–2625.
3	Burlington County Office on Aging, Lumberton Rd., County Office Bldg., 49 Rancocas Rd., Mount Holly, N.J. 08060.	Ms. Linda Coffey, (609) 267–0610.
4	Camden County Office on Aging, 129 White House Pike, Audubon, N.J. 08106.	Mr. Edward L. Donohue, (609) 546–0044 and 784–7744.
5	Cape May Office on Aging, Social Service Bldg., Box 222, Rio Grande, N.J. 08242.	Mrs. Ann Zahora, (609) 886–2784/2785.
6	Cumberland County Office on Aging, 29 Fayette St., Bridgeton, N.J. 08302.	Dale Finch, (609) 451-8000 extension 357.
7	Essex County Office on Aging, 520 Belleville Ave., Belleville, N.J. 07109.	Mr. Bernard J. Gallagher, (201) 751–6050.
8	Gloucester County Office on Aging, 44 Delaware St., Woodbury, N.J. 08096.	Mrs. Margaret Mendoze, (609) 845–1600, extension 270.
9	Hudson County Office on Aging, Murdock Hall, 114 Clifton Pl., Jersey City, N.J. 07340.	Mr. Michael F. Reilly, (201) 434–6900.
10	Hunterdon County Office on Aging, Community Bldg., Flemington, Route 31 North, Box 49A, RD 6, Flemington, N.J. 08822.	Mrs. Mary Housel, (201) 782–4300, extension 362/363.
11	Mercer County Office on Aging, 640 South Broad St., Trenton, N.J. 08611.	Mr. Carl West, (609) 989–6661
12	Middlesex County Office on Aging, Middlesex County Office Annex, 841 Georges Rd., North Brunswick, N.J. 08902.	Mr. Thomas E. Hamilton, (201) 246–6293/6295.
13	Monmouth County Office on Aging, 10 Lafayette Pl., Freehold, N.J. 07728.	Mrs. Gloria Filippone, (201) 431–7450.

PSA	Area agency address	Director and telephone number
14	Morris County Office on Aging, Court House, Morristown, N.J. 07960.	Mr. Norman Van Houten, (201) 285–6393.
15	Ocean County Office on Aging, Court House, Toms River, N.J. 08753.	Mr. Philip Rubenstein, (201) 244–2121, extension 403/404.
16	Passiac County Office on Aging, Rea House, 675 Goffle Rd., Hawthorne, N.J. 07506.	Mr. Rayomnd Fink, (201) 525–5000, extension 456/469.
17	Salem County Office on Aging, 94 Market St., Salem, N.J. 08079.	Miss Constance Undy, (609) 935–7510.
18	Somerset County Office on Aging, 36 Grove St., Somerville, N.J. 08876.	Mrs. Jean Siiberg, (201) 725–4700, extension 212/213.
19	Sussex County Office on Aging, 46 Trinity St., Newton, N.J. 07860.	Robert Callahan, (201) 383–5098.
20	Union County Office on Aging, 208 Commerce Pl., Elizabeth, N.J. 07201.	Mr. Peter M. Shields, (201) 353–5000, extension 515.
21	Warren County Office on Aging, Court House Annex, Oxford St. and Hardwick, Belvidere, N.J. 07823.	Mrs. Anne B. Schneider, (201) 475–5361.

NEW MEXICO

(Federal Region VI)

STATE AGENCY ON AGING

Mr. Willie Vigil, Director,
Commission on Aging,
Pera Bldg., room 515,
Santa Fe, N. Mex. 87501,
(505) 827–2802

AREA AGENCIES

PSA	Area agency address	Director and telephone number
1	District 1 Area Agency on Aging, 309 South 3d, Gallup, N. Mex. 87301.	Ms. Peggy Folk, (505) 722–4327.
2	North Central New Mexico Area Agency on Aging, P.O. Box 4248, Santa Fe, N. Mex. 87501.	Mr. Gene Varela, (505) 827–2014
3	Middle Rio Grande Area Agency on Aging, 505 Marquette Ave., NW., suite 1320, Albuquerque, N. Mex. 87102.	Ms. Gloria Bruno, (505) 766–7836.
4	Eastern Plains Area Agency on Aging, Curry County Courthouse, Clovis, N. Mex. 88101.	Ms. Ruby Goforth, (505) 762–7714.
5	Southwestern New Mexico Area Agency on Aging, 109 East Pine St., Deming, N. Mex. 88030.	Mr. Mark Rogers, (505) 546–8816.
6	Southeastern New Mexico Area Agency on Aging, P.O. Box 6639 RIAC, Roswell, N. Mex. 88201.	Mr. Lupe Mendez, (505) 347–5425.
7	Southern Rio Grande Area Agency on Aging, P.O. Box 216, Socorro, N. Mex. 87801.	Mr. J. Lester Rigby, (505) 835–2475.

NEW YORK

(Federal Region II)

STATE AGENCY ON AGING

Mrs. Lou Glasse, Director,
Office for the Aging,
New York State Executive Department,
Empire State Plaza,
Agency Building No. 2,
Albany, N.Y. 12223,
(518) 474–5731

AREA AGENCIES

PSA	Area agency address	Director and telephone number
1	Albany County Department for Aging, 600 Broadway, Albany, N.Y. 12207.	Mr. Richard Healy, (518) 445–7511.
2	Allegany County Office of the Aging, 17 Court St., Belmont, N.Y. 14813.	Ms. Diane Bollman, (716) 593–5460.
3	Broome County Office for the Aging, County Office Bldg., Government Plaza, Binghamton, N.Y. 13902	Mr. Kevin Tobin, (607) 772–2821.
4	Cattaraugs County Department of the Aging, 116 South Union St., Olean, N.Y. 14760	Ms. Kathleen Horner, (716) 372–0303.
5	Cayuga County Office for the Aging, County Office Building, 160 Genesee St., Auburn, N.Y. 13021.	Mrs. Joan Gallo, (315) 253–1226.
6	Chautauqua County Office for the Aging, County Office Bldg., Room 341, Mayville, N.Y. 14757.	Mr. Sven Hammar, (716) 753–4417.
7	Chemung County Office for the Aging, 214 West Grey St., Elmira, N.Y. 14901.	Sister Juliana O'Hara, (607) 737–2914.
8	Chenango County Office for the Aging, 12 Henry St., Norwich, N.Y. 13815.	Mr. William J. Fiorello, (607) 335–4624.
9	Clinton County Office for the Aging, 137 Margaret Street, Plattsburgh, N.Y. 12901.	Vacant, (518) 561–8800, extension 273.
10	Columbia County Office for the Aging, 70 North 3d St., Hudson, N.Y. 12534.	Miss Helen Montag, (518) 828–4258.
11	Cortland County Office for the Aging, Court House, Cortland, N.Y. 13045.	Mrs. Helen Anderson, (607) 756–5691.
12	Delaware County Office for the Aging, 6 Court St., Delhi, N.Y. 13753.	Mr. Neal E. Lane, (607) 746–6333.
13	Dutchess County Office for the Aging, 236 Main St., Poughkeepsie, N.Y. 12601.	Mrs. Patricia Pine, (914) 485–9920.
14	Erie County Office for the Aging, Rath Bldg., Room 1329, Buffalo, N.Y. 14202.	Mr. Clifford Whitman, (716) 846–8522.
15	Essex County Office for the Aging, Maple St., Elizabethtown, N.Y. 12932.	Vacant, (518) 873–6301, extension 75.
16	Franklin County Office for the Aging, County Courthouse, 63 West Main St., Malone, N.Y. 12953.	Mr. William O'Reilly, (518) 483–1610.
17	Fulton County Office for the Aging, County Office, Johnston, N.Y. 12095.	Vacant, (no phone)
18	Genesee County Office for the Aging, Batavia-Genesee Senior Center, 2 Bank St., Batavia, N.Y. 14020.	Mr. Roger Tiede, (716) 343–1611.
19	Greene County Department for the Aging, 153 Jefferson Heights, Catskill, N.Y. 12414.	Mr. Philip Schlenker, (518) 943–5332.
21	Herkimer County Office for the Aging, County Office Bldg.—Mary St., Herkimer, N.Y. 13350.	Mr. Daglas Brewer, (315) 866–4010.
22	Jefferson County Office for the Aging, 175 Arsenal St., Watertown, N.Y. 13601.	Mr. Douglas C. Gleason, (315) 785–3191.
23	Lewis County Office for the Aging, Lewis County Courthouse, Lowville, N.Y. 13367.	Mr. Randy Streeter, (315) 376–7753.
24	Livingston County Office for the Aging, Livingston County Campus, Bldg. 2, Mt. Morris, N.Y. 14510.	Ms. Gloria Harrington, (716) 658–2881, extensions 47, 48.

PSA	Area agency address	Director and telephone number
25	Madison County Office for the Aging, 20 Eaton St., Morrisville, N.Y. 13408.	Ms. Margaret Williams, (315) 684-9424.
26	Monroe County Office for the Aging, 375 Westfall Rd., Rochester, N.Y. 14620.	Mr. Gary Merritt, (716) 442-6350.
27	Montgomery Countywide Office for the Aging, 23 New St., Amsterdam, N.Y. 12010.	Miss Carmela Simiele, (518) 843-2300.
28	Nassau County Department of Senior Citizen Affairs, One Old Country Rd., Carle Pl., N.Y. 11514.	Ms. Adelaide Attard, (516) 535-4414.
29	Niagara County Office for the Aging, Civil Defense Bldg., Lockport, N.Y. 14094.	Mr. Victor Cooke, (716) 433-2614.
30	Oneida County Office for the Aging, County Office Bldg., 800 Park Ave., Utica, N.Y. 13501.	Mr. Anthony Montoya, (315) 798-5771.
31	Metropolitan Commission on Aging (Onondaga County), Civic Center—10th Floor, 421 Montgomery St., Syracuse, N.Y. 13202.	Mrs. Roslyn Bilford, (315) 425-2362.
32	Ontario County Office for the Aging, 120 North Main St., Canadaigua, N.Y. 14424.	Ms. Rita Condon, (716) 394-7070.
33	Orange County Office for the Aging, 60 Erie St., 3d Floor, Goshen, N.Y. 10924.	Mrs. Anne Cortese (914) 294-5151, extension 283/286.
34	Orleans County Office for the Aging, 151 Platt St., Albion, N.Y. 14411.	Ms. Carole Blake, (716) 589-7743.
35	Oswego County Office for the Aging, River Front Office Bldg., East 1st St., Oswego, N.Y. 13126.	Ms Mary King, (315) 349-3231
36	Otsego County Office for the Aging, County Office Bldg., Cooperstown, N.Y. 13326.	Mrs. Patricia Leonard, (607) 547-4233.
37	Putnam County Office for the Aging, County Office Bldg., Carmel, N.Y. 10512.	Mrs. Marion Hayes, (914) 225-6441.
38	Rensselaer County Department for the Aging, 8 Winter St., Troy, N.Y. 12180.	Mr. Paul Tazbir, (518) 270-5343.
39	Rockland County Office for the Aging, Building B, Health and Social Services Complex, Pomona, N.Y. 10970.	Mrs. Virginia Weil, (914) 354-0200.
40	St. Lawrence County Office for the Aging, County Office Bldg., Canton, N.Y. 13617.	Mr. Joseph Sears, (315) 379-2204.
41	Saratoga County Office for the Aging, 40 Church Ave., Ballston Spa, N.Y. 12020.	Ms. Susan Baird, (518) 885-9761.
42	Schenectady County Office for the Aging, 101 Nott Terrace, Schenectady, N.Y. 12308.	Mrs. Virginia H. Pigott, (518) 382-3258.
43	Schoharie County Office for the Aging, 1 Lark St., Cobleskill, N.Y. 12043.	Mrs. Ethel Benninger, (518) 234-4219.
44	No area agency on aging	
45	Seneca County Office for the Aging, P.O. Box 480, Seneca Falls, N.Y. 13148.	Mr. Robert L. Lindner, (315) 539-9285.
46	Steuben County Area Agency on Aging, Senior Center, Hornell, N.Y. 14843	Judy Herman, (607) 324-4891
47	Suffolk County Office for the Aging, County Center-North Complex, 65 Jetson Lane, Hauppauge, N.Y. 11787.	Mrs. Elizabeth Taibbi, (516) 234-2622.
48	Sullivan County Office for the Aging, New County Government Center, Monticello, N.Y. 12701.	Mr. James J. Galligan, (914) 794-1404.
49	Tioga County Office for the Aging, 231 Main St., Owego, N.Y. 13827.	Ms. Jean Hefft, (607) 687-4120
50	Tompkins County Office for the Aging, 225 South Fulton St., Ithaca, N.Y. 14850.	Vacant, (607) 274-5427
51	Ulster County Office for the Aging, 17 Pearl St., Kingston, N.Y. 12401.	Mrs. Antoinette Tennant, (914) 331-9300, extension 403.
52	Warren/Hamilton Counties Office for the Aging, Warren County Municipal Center, Lake George, N.Y. 12845.	Mr. Louis Spelman, Jr., (518) 792-9951, extension 325.

PSA	Area agency address	Director and telephone number
53	Washington County Office for the Aging, P.O. Box 56, Whitehall, N.Y. 12887.	Mr. Kenneth Ducharme, (518) 499–2468.
54	Wayne County Office for the Aging, County Office Bldg., Lyons, N.Y. 14489.	Mr. John C. Perry, (315) 946–4163.
55	Westchester County Office for the Aging, County Office Bldg., White Plains, N.Y. 10601.	Mr. Joseph A. Tortelli, (914) 682–2669.
56	Wyoming County Office for the Aging, 76 North Main St., Warsaw, N.Y. 14569.	Mrs. Mary Lou Felton, (716) 786–3144.
57	Yates County Area Agency for the Aging, 218 Liberty St., Penn Yan, N.Y. 14527.	Mr. Foster Van Dusen, (315) 536–2368.
60	New York City Department for the Aging, 250 Broadway, New York, N.Y. 10007.	Ms. Janet Sainer, (212) 577–0848.
61	Akwesasne Office for the Aging, St. Regis-Mohawk Indian Reservation, Hogansburg, N.Y. 13655.	Vacant, (518) 358–2272, extention 42/43.

NORTH CAROLINA

(Federal Region IV)

STATE AGENCY ON AGING

Mr. Nathan H. Yelton, Director
North Carolina Division of Aging,
Department of Human Resources,
708 Hillsborough St., Suite 200,
Raleigh, N.C. 27603
(919) 733–3983

AREA AGENCIES

PSA	Area agency address	Director and telephone number
1A	No area agency on aging	
2B	Land of Sky Regional Council—B, P.O. Box 2175, Asheville, N.C. 28802.	Mrs. Joan B. Tuttle, (704) 254–8131.
3C	Isothermal Planning and Economic Division, P.O. Box 841, Rutherfordton, N.C. 28139.	Ms. Myra Lynch, (704) 287–2281.
4D	Region D COG, Executive Arts Bldg., Furman Rd., Boone, N.C. 28607.	Ms. Kim Dawkins, (704) 264–5558.
5E	Western Piedmont Council of Governments, 30 3d St. NW., Old City Hall Bldg., Hickory, N.C. 28601.	Mr. R. Douglas Taylor, (704) 322–9191.
6F	Centralina Council of Governments—F, P.O. Box 4168, Charlotte, N.C. 28204.	Mr. Charles Page, (704) 372–2416
7G	Piedmont Triad Council of Governments—6, 2120 Pinecroft Rd.—Four Seasons Offices, Greensboro, N.C. 27407.	Mr. Roger Bell, (919) 294–4907
8H	Pee Dee Council of Governments, P.O. Box 728, Troy, N.C. 27371.	Mrs. Judith Crawford, (919) 576–6261.
9J	Triangle J Council of Governments, P.O. Box 12276, Research Triangle Park, N.C.	Mr. Dave Moser, (919) 549–0551
10K	Region K Council of Governments, P.O. Box 709, Henderson, N.C. 27536.	Mr. Steven Norwood, (919) 492–8561.
11L	Region L Council of Governments, P.O. Drawer 2748, Rocky Mount, N.C. 27801.	Mrs. Sandra R. Ray, (919) 446–0411.
12M	Region M Senior Services, Inc., P.O. Box 53305, Fayetteville, N.C. 28305.	Mr. Cliff LeCornu, (919) 485–7111.
13N	Lumber River Council of Governments—N, P.O. Drawer 1528, Lumberton, N.C. 28358.	Mrs. Betty Rising, (919) 738–8104.
14	No area agency on aging	

15P	Neuse River Council of Governments—P, P.O. Box 1717, New Bern, N.C. 28560.	Mrs. Gayle Thames, (919) 638-3185.
16Q	Mid-East Economic Development Commission—Q, P.O. Box 1218, Washington, N.C. 27889.	Mrs. Mary Long Tankard, (919) 946-8043.
17R	Albemarle Regional Planning Commission—R, P.O. Box 646, Hertford, N.C. 27944.	Ms. Annette Fairless, (919) 426-5756.

NORTH DAKOTA*

(Federal Region VIII)

STATE AGENCY ON AGING

Mr. Gerald D. Shaw, Administrator
Aging Services Unit,
Community Services Division,
Social Services Board of North Dakota,
State Capitol Bldg.,
Bismarck, N. Dak. 58505
(701) 224-2577

*The State of North Dakota serves as a single planning and service area.

OHIO

(Federal Region V)

STATE AGENCY ON AGING
Mr. Martin Janis, Director,
Ohio Commission on Aging,
50 West Broad St., 9th Floor,
Columbus, Ohio 43215,
(614) 466-5500/5501

AREA AGENCIES

PSA	Area agency address	Director and telephone number
1	Council on Aging of the Cicinnati Area, 601 Provident Bank Bldg., 7th and Vine, Cincinnati, Ohio 45202.	Mr. William Bogart, (513) 721-1025.
2	Area Agency on Aging, Miami Valley Council on Aging, 184 Salem Ave., Dayton, Ohio 45406.	Mr. Donald Trummel, (513) 225-3046.
3	Area Agency on Aging PSA 3, 311 East Market St., 311 Bldg., Suite 201, Lima, Ohio 45801.	Mr. Roger J. Stauffer, (419) 227-7506.
4	Area Agency on Aging, 506 Madison, Suite 106, Toledo, Ohio 43604.	Mr. Billie Sewell, (419) 248-4234.
5	District 5 Area Agency on Aging, 50 Blymer Ave., P.O. Box 966, Mansfield, Ohio 44901.	Ms. Caroline Ford, (419) 524-4178.
6	Central Ohio Area Agency on Aging, 272 South Gift St., Columbus, Ohio 43215.	Ardath Lynch, (614) 222-7250
7	Area Agency on Aging District 7, Rio Grande College, Box 978, Rio Grande, Ohio 45674.	Mr. John Allen, (614) 245-5353. extension 216.
8	Buckeye Hills-Hocking Valley Development District, Suite 410, St. Clair Bldg., 216 Putnam St., Marietta, Ohio 45750.	Ms. Molly Varner, (614) 374-9436.
9	Area Agency on Aging Region 9, Box 429, 127 South 10th St., Cambridge, Ohio 43725.	Mr. Boyer Simcox, (614) 439-4478.
10A	Western Reserve Area Agency on Aging, 1276 West 3d St., Marion Bldg., room 512, Cleveland, Ohio 44113.	Mr. Paul Alandt, (216) 623-7560
10B	Area Office on Aging, P.O. Box F-351, Akron, Ohio 44308.	Ms. Barbara Love, (216) 376-9172.
11	District 11 Area Agency on Aging, 112 West Commerce Plaza, Suite 303, Youngstown, Ohio 44503.	Ms. Martha Murphy, (216) 2938.

OKLAHOMA

(Federal Region VI)

STATE AGENCY ON AGING

Mr. Roy R. Keen, Director
Special Unit on Aging,
Department of Institutions,
Social and Rehabilitative Services,
P.O. Box 25352,
Oklahoma City, Okla. 73125
(405) 521–2281

AREA AGENCIES

PSA	Area agency address	Director and telephone number
1	NECO Area Agency on Aging, P.O. Drawer E, Vinita, Okla. 74301.	Mr. Fred Gates, (918) 256–6478
2	EODD Area Agency on Aging, P.O. Box 1367, Muskogee, Okla. 74401.	Mr. Scott Moxom, (918) 682–7891
3	KEDDO Area Agency on Aging, P.O. Box 638, Wilburton, Okla. 74578.	Mr. Larry Duke, (918) 465–2367
4	SODA Area Agency on Aging Association, P.O. Box 848, 16 E St. SW., Ardmore, Okla. 73401.	Mr. Kenneth Hollingsworth, (405) 226–2250.
5	COEDD Area Agency on Aging, 16 East 9th St., Shawnee, Okla. 74801.	Ms. Jan George Womack, 521–3609/3944.
6	Tulsa Area Agency on Aging, Room 214, 200 Civic Center, Tulsa, Okla. 74103.	Mr. Boyd Talley, (918) 518–5430/5439.
7	NODA Area Agency on Aging, 1800 South Van Buren, Enid, Okla. 73701.	Ms. Marcia Miller, (405) 237–4810.
8	Areawide Aging Agency, Inc., P.O. Box 1474, 125 NW. 5th St., Oklahoma City, Okla. 73102.	Ms. Charlotte Heard, (405) 236–2426.
9	ASCOG Area Agency on Aging, 802 Main St., P.O. Box 1647, Duncan, Okla. 73533.	Mr. Gene Werner, (405) 252–0595.
10	SWODA Area Agency on Aging, P.O. Box 569, Burns Flat, Okla. 73624.	Mr. Dwayne King, (405) 562–4886.

OREGON

(Federal Region X)

STATE AGENCY ON AGING

Marvin M. Janzen, Administrator
Office of Elderly Affairs,
Department of Human Resources,
772 Commercial St., SE.,
Salem, Oreg. 97310
(503) 378–4728

AREA AGENCIES

PSA	Area agency address	Director and telephone number
1	District 1 Area Agency on Aging, Box 488, Cannon Beach, Oreg. 97110.	Mr. Victor L. Stamm, (503) 436–1156.
2A1	Clackamas County Area Agency on Aging, P.O. Box 32, Marylhurst, Oreg. 97036.	Mr. Lyle Remington, (503) 655–8465.
2A2	No area agency on aging	
2A3	County Aging Programs, Washington County, room 405, Administration Bldg., 150 North 1st Ave., Hillsboro, Oreg. 97123.	Mr. Robert J. Tepper, (503) 640–3489. 640–3489.

PSA	Area agency address	Director and telephone number
2B	Bureau of Human Resources, Aging Services Division, 522 SW. 5th—8th floor, Portland, Oreg. 97204.	Mr. Robert Holdridge, (503) 248–4752.
3	District 3 Area Agency on Aging, Mid Willamette Valley Council of Governments, 4th Floor, Senator Bldg., 220 High St. NE., Salem, Oreg. 97301.	Mr. Ed Sage, (503) 588–6177
4	Tri County Area Agency on Aging, No. 7 Wellsher Bldg., 460 SW. Madison, Corvallis, Oreg. 97330.	Mrs. Betty Johnson, (503) 757–6851.
5	District 5 Area Agency on Aging, Lane Council of Governments, Lane County Public Service Bldg., North Plaza Level, 125 8th Ave., Eugene, Oreg. 97401.	Vacant, (503) 687–4283
6	Douglas County Program on Aging, Douglas County Courthouse, room 309, 1034 SE. Douglas, Roseburg, Oreg. 97470.	Mr. John De Groot, (503) 672–3311 extension 386.
7	Coos-Curry Council of Governments, P.O. Box 647, North Bend, Oreg. 97459.	Mark Bean, (503) 756–2563
8	District 8 Area Agency on Aging, 33 North Central, room 211, Medford, Oreg. 97501.	Mr. Don Bruland, (503) 779–9134.
9	Mid Columbia Area Agency on Aging, Wasco County Courthouse, annex B, 502 East 5th St., The Dalles, Oreg. 97058.	Mr. Keith Sutton, (503) 296–2266.
10	No area agency on aging	
11	No area agency on aging	
12	Eastern Central Oregon Association of Counties, P.O. Box 339, Pendleton, Oreg. 97801.	Mr. Rollin Reynolds, (503) 276–6732.
13	No area agency on aging	
14A	____do____	
14B	____do____	

PENNSYLVANIA

(Federal Region III)

State Agency on Aging

Mr. Robert T. Huber, Acting Commissioner
Office for the Aging, Department of Public Welfare,
Health and Welfare Bldg.,
Room 511, P.O. Box 2675,
7th and Forster St.,
Harrisburg, Pa. 17120
(717) 787–5350

AREA AGENCIES

PSA	Area agency address	Director and telephone number
1	Erie County Area Agency on Aging, Greater Erie Community Action Commission, 18 West 9th St., Erie, Pa. 16501.	Mr. Richard Browdie, (814) 454–4581.
2	Crawford County Office of Aging, 915 Liberty St., Meadville, Pa. 16335.	Ms. Pauline Mooney, (814) 336–1580.
3	North Central Pennsylvania Office of Human Services, 208 Main St., Ridgway, Pa. 15853.	Mrs. Yolanda Jeselnick, (814) 776–2191.
4	Beaver/Butler Area Agency on Aging, 224 Beaver St., (Fallston), Pa. 15066.	Mr. R. Brandon James, (412) 728–2242.

PSA	Area agency address	Director and telephone number
5	Indian County Area Agency on Aging, Indian Springs Rd., Heatherbrae Sq., Indiana, Pa. 15701.	Mrs. Carole Ling, (412) 329–4500.
6	Allegheny County Area Agency on Aging, 1706 Allegheny Bldg., 429 Forbes Ave., Pittsburgh, Pa. 15219.	Mrs. Nancy Van Vuuren, (412) 355–4349.
7	Westmoreland County Office of Aging, 524 East Pittsburgh St., Greensburg, Pa. 15601.	Mr. William Zalot, (412) 836–1111.
8	Mon Valley Health & Welfare Council, Mon Valley Community Health Center, Eastgate 8, Monessen, Pa. 15062.	Mr. Bob Willison, (412) 684–9000.
9	Somerset County Office for the Aging, 147 East Union St., P.O. Box 30, Somerset, Pa. 15501.	Mrs. Martha Garman, (814) 443–2681.
10	Cambria County Area Agency on Aging, R.D. 3, Box 429A, Ebensburg, Pa. 15931.	Mr. John W. Waterstream, (814) 472–5580.
11	Blair County Office of Services for the Aging, 1512 12th Ave., Altoona, Pa. 16601.	Mr. Daniel Ainscough, (814) 946–1237.
12	Bedford/Fulton/Huntingdon Area Agency on Aging, 231 Juliana St., Bedford, Pa. 15522.	Ms. Jean McClure, (814) 623–8149.
13	Centre County Area Agency on Aging, Centre Community Hospital, 2d Floor, Willow Bank Unit, Bellefonte, Pa. 16823.	Mrs. Cynthia Edvar, (814) 355–7861.
14	Lycoming/Clinton Bi-County Office of Aging, P.O. Box 770, 352 East Water St., Lock Haven, Pa. 17745.	Mrs. Virginia Crosby, (717) 748–8665.
15	Columbia/Montour Area Agency on Aging, 243 West Main St., Bloomsburg, Pa. 17815.	Mr. Robert LeVan, (717) 784–9272.
16	Northumberland County Area Agency on Aging, 235 West Spruce St., Shamokin, Pa. 17872.	Mr. Michael Johnson (acting), (717) 648–6828.
17	Union/Snyder County Office of Aging, 404 East Main St., Middleburg, Pa. 17842.	Miss Farida Zaid, (717) 837–0675.
18	Mifflin/Juniata Area Agency on Aging, Buena Vista Circle, Lewistown, Pa. 17044.	Ms. Carlene Hack, (717) 242–0315.
19	Franklin County Office for the Aging, Franklin Farm Lane, Chambersburg, Pa. 17201.	Mr. Robert Keith, (717) 263–2153.
20	Adams County Area Agency on Aging, 26 North Washington St., Gettysburg, Pa. 17325.	Ms. Susan Yenchko, (717) 334–9577.
21	Cumberland County Office on Aging, 35 East High St., Carlisle, Pa. 17013.	Ms. Jacqueline Nowak, (717) 243–8442.
22	Perry County Office for the Aging, Court House Annex, South Carlisle St., New Bloomfield, Pa. 17068.	Mr. Herbert Stewart, (717) 582–2131, ext. 220.
23	Dauphin County Area Agency on Aging, 17 South Second St., Harrisburg, Pa. 17101.	Mr. Lewis L. Crippen, (717) 255–2877.
24	Lebanon County Area Agency on Aging, 710 Maple St., Room 209—Senior Centers, Lebanon, Pa. 17042.	Mr. Michael Kristovensky, (717) 273–9262.
25	York County Area Agency on Aging, 125 East Market St., York, Pa. 17401.	Mrs. Kathleen Boas, (717) 846–4884.
26	Lancaster County Office of Aging, 50 North Duke St., Lancaster, Pa. 17602.	Mr. Peter Dys, (717) 299–7979
27	Chester County Services for Senior Citizens, 14 East Biddle St., West Chester, Pa. 19380.	Mr. Wayne Stevenson, (215) 431–6350.
28	Office on Older Adults, Montgomery County Court House, One Montgomery Plaza, 4th Floor, Norristown, Pa. 19401.	Mr. Edward Keenan, (215) 275–5000, ext. 533/534.
29	Bucks County Adult Services, Neshaminy Manor Center, Doylestown, Pa. 18901.	Mrs. Margaret O'Neill, (215) 343–2800.
30	Delaware County Services for the Aging, 322 West State St., P.O. Box 166, Media, Pa. 19063.	Mr. John Bauer, (215) 565–427

PSA	Area agency address	Director and telephone number
31	Philadelphia Corporation of Aging, 1317 Filbert St., Room 420, Philadelphia, Pa. 19107.	Mr. Rodney Williams, (215) 241-8200.
32	Berks County Area Agency on Aging, 124 South 5th St., Reading, Pa. 19602.	Mr. Peter Archey, (215) 378-1635/1856.
33	Lehigh County Area Agency on Aging, Court House Annex, 523 Hamilton St., Allentown, Pa. 18101.	Mr. Peter Johnstone, (215) 434-9471.
34	Northamption County Area Agency on Aging, 204 Northampton St., Easton, Pa. 18042.	Ms. Beverly Corkhill, (215) 253-9321.
35	Wayne/Pike/Area Agency on Aging, 314 10th St., Honesdale, Pa. 18431.	Mrs. Margaret Nuttycombe, (717) 253-5535.
36	Area Agency on Aging, Northern Tier Regional Planning and Development Commission, 507 Main St., Towanda, Pa. 18848.	Mrs. Carole McLellan, (717) 265-9103.
37	Luzerne/Wyoming Counties Office for Aging, 85 East Union St., Wilkes-Barre, Pa. 18701.	Mr. Charles Adams, (717) 822-1158.
38	Lackawanna County Area Agency on Aging, Lackawanna County Office Bldg., 200 Adams Ave., Scranton, Pa. 18503.	Mr. Michael Rodgers, (717) 961-6707.
39	Carbon County Area Agency on Aging, P.O. Box 251, Jim Thorpe, Pa. 18229.	Mr. Leonard Marzen, (717) 325-2726.
40	Schuylkill County Area Agency on Aging, 2d and Norwegian Sts., Pottsville, Pa. 17901.	Mrs. Carol Stabinski, (717) 622-3103.
41	Clearfield County Office of Aging, P.O. Box 906, 121 South 2d St., Clearfield, Pa. 16830.	Jack Frisch, Ph. D. (814) 765-2696.
42	Jefferson County Office of Aging, R.D. No. 1 (Old Jefferson Manor), Brookville, Pa. 15825.	Ms. Shirley Sharp, (814) 849-3096.
43	Area Agency on Aging (Forest and Warren Counties), Experience, Inc., 900 4th Ave., P.O. Box 886, Warren, Pa. 16365.	Mr. W. Robert Walsh, (814) 726-1700.
44	Clarion/Venango Area Agency on Aging, Venango County Bureau of Human Services, P.O. Box 231, Franklin, Pa. 16323.	Ms. Lois Daley (acting), (814) 437-6821.
45	Armstrong County Area Agency on Aging, 200 Oak Ave., Kittanning, Pa. 16201.	Mr. Wendell Davis, (412) 548-8205.
46	Lawrence County Office on Aging, 20 South Mercer St., New Castle, Pa. 10101.	Ms. Myra Wolcott, (412) 658-5661.
47	Mercer County Area Agency on Aging, Mercer County Court House, Mercer, Pa. 16137.	Ms. Ann Marie Spiardi, (412) 662-3800, extension 75/83.
48	Monroe County Area Agency on Aging, 154 Washington St., East Stroudsburg, Pa. 18301.	Ms. Dorothy Kaufman, (717) 424-5290.

RHODE ISLAND*

(Federal Region I)

STATE AGENCY ON AGING

Ms. Anna M. Tucker, Director
Rhode Island,
Department of Elderly Affairs,
79 Washington St., Providence, R.I. 02903
(401) 277-2858

*Rhode Island serves as a single planning and service area.

SOUTH CAROLINA

(Federal Region IV)

STATE AGENCY ON AGING

Mr. Harry Bryan, Director
Commission on Aging,
915 Main St.,
Columbia, S.C.   29201
(803) 758–2576

AREA AGENCIES

PSA	Area agency address	Director and telephone number
1	South Carolina Appalachian Council of Governments, 211 Century Dr., P.O. Drawer 6668, Greenville, S.C. 29606.	Mrs. Yvonne Simpson, (803) 242–9733.
2	Upper Savannah Council of Governments, P.O. Box 1366, Greenwood, S.C. 29646.	Mrs. Miriam Patterson, (803) 229–6627.
3	Catawba Regional Aging Program, SCN Center Suite 300, 100 Dave Lyle Blvd., Rock Hill, S.C. 29730.	Ms. Sandra Howie (803) 327–9041.
4	Central Midlands Regional Planning, Council Aging Program, Suite 155, Dutch Plaza, 800 Dutch Square Blvd., Columbia, S.C. 29210.	Mr. George Dick, (803) 798–1243.
5	Lower Savannah Council of Governments, P.O. Box 850, Highway 215, Aiken, S.C. 29801.	Ms. Connie L. Heider, (803) 649–7981.
6	Santee-Lynches Council for Governments, 36 East Calhoun St., P.O. Box 1837, Sumter, S.C. 29150.	Mr. James A. Crawford, (803) 775–7382.
7	Pee Dee Regional Planning and Development Program for the Aging, P.O. Box 5719, Darlington Highway, Florence, S.C. 29502.	Mr. Hampton MacIntyre, (803) 669–3138.
8	Waccamaw Regional Planning and Development Council, P.O. Drawer 419, 1001 Front St., Georgetown, S.C. 29440.	Ms. Linda Coker, (803) 546–8502.
9	Trident Area Program for the Aging, P.O. Box 2696, 106 King St., Charleston, S.C. 29403.	Ms. Leslie Jamison, (803) 723–1676.
10	Lowcountry Council of Governments, P.O. Box 98, Point South, Yemassee, S.C. 29945.	Dr. Sue Scally, (803) 726–5536/ 5538.

SOUTH DAKOTA*

(Federal Region VIII)

STATE AGENCY ON AGING

Ms. Sylvia Base, Administrator
Office of Adult Services and Aging,
Department of Social Services,
Richard F. Kneip Bldg.—Illinois St.,
Pierre, S. Dak.   57501
(605) 773–3656

*The State of South Dakota serves as a single planning and service area.

TENNESSEE

(Federal Region IV)

STATE AGENCY ON AGING

Mr. Tom Henry, Director
Commission on Aging
Room 102, S&P Building
306 Gay St.
Nashville, Tenn. 37201
(615) 741-2056

AREA AGENCIES

PSA	Area agency address	Director and telephone number
1	First Tennessee-Virginia Development District, 207 North Boone St., Johnson City, Tenn. 37601.	Mr. Tom Reece, (615) 928-0224.
2	East Tennessee Human Resource Agency, 4711 Old Kingston Pike, Knoxville, Tenn. 37919.	Mrs. Ann Elliott, (615) 584-0244.
3	Southeast Tennessee Development District, 413 James Bldg., 735 Broad St., Chattanooga, Tenn. 37402.	Mr. Viston Taylor, (615) 266-5781.
4	Upper Cumberland Development District, 300 Brugess Falls Rd., Cookeville, Tenn. 38501.	Mrs. Nancy Peace, (615) 432-4111.
5	Mid-Cumberland Development District, 501 Union Bldg., 6th Floor, 5th Ave. and Union St., Nashville, Tenn. 37219.	Mr. Rick Fowlkes, (615) 244-1212.
6	South Central Tennessee Development District, 805 Nashville Highway, Columbia, Tenn. 38401.	Mr. Lowell Crawford, (615) 381-2040.
7	Northwest Tennessee Development District, P.O. Box 63, Martin, Tenn. 38237.	Mr. David Frizzell, (901) 587-4213.
8	Southwest Tennessee Development District, P.O. Box 2385, Jackson, Tenn. 38301.	Ms. Anne Lewis, (901) 668-1142
9	Memphis Delta Development District, 1192 Vollintiae, Memphis, Tenn. 38107.	Mrs. Mary O. Coats, (901) 528-2600/2609.

TEXAS

(Federal Region VI)

STATE AGENCY ON AGING

Mr. Vernon McDaniel, Director
The Governor's Committee on Aging,
Office of the Governor,
P.O. Box 12786,
Capitol Station,
Austin, Tex. 78711
(512) 475-2717

AREA AGENCIES

PSA	Area agency address	Director and telephone number
1	Panhandle Area Agency on Aging, P.O. Box 9257, Amarillo, Tex. 79104.	Mr. Mike McQueen, (806) 372-3381.
2	South Plains Area Agency on Aging, 1611 Avenue M, Lubbock, Tex. 79401.	Ms. Betty J. Shannon, (806) 762-8721.
3	North Texas Area Agency on Aging, 2101 Kemp Blvd., Wichita Falls, Tex. 76309.	Ms. Yvonne Null, (817) 322-5281.
4	North Central Texas Area Agency on Aging, P.O. Drawer COG, Arlington, Tex. 76011.	Mr. John Bruni, (817) 640-3300.

PSA	Area agency address	Director and telephone number
4B	Dallas County Area Agency on Aging, 212 North St. Paul, 1725 Corrigan Tower, Dallas, Tex., 75201.	Mr. Norman Moorehead, (214) 741–5851.
4C	Tarrant County Area Agency on Aging, 210 East 9th St., Fort Worth, Tex. 76102.	Mr. Wilton G. Jewell, (817) 335–3473.
5	Arkansas-Texas Area Agency on Aging, P.O. Box 5307, Texarkana, Tex. 75501.	Ms. Beverly Cherney, (214) 794–3481.
6	East Texas Area Agency on Aging, 5th Floor, Citizens Bank Bldg., Kilgore, Tex. 75662.	Mr. Claude Andrews, (214) 984–8641.
7	West Central Texas Area Agency on Aging, P.O. Box 3195, 3349 North 12th St., Abilene, Tex. 79604.	Mr. Chris Kyker, (915) 672–8544.
8	West Texas Area Agency on Aging, The Mills Bldg., Suite 700, 303 North Oregon St., El Paso, Tex. 79901.	Mr. Mario Griffin, (915) 532–2910.
9	Permian Basin Area Agency on Aging, P.O. Box 6391, Midland, Tex. 79701.	Mr. W. E. Smith, (915) 563–1061.
10	Concho Valley Area Agency on Aging, 17 South Chadbourne, Suite 200, San Angelo, Tex. 76903.	Ms. Odene Crawford, (915) 653–1214.
11	Heart of Texas Area Agency on Aging, 110 South 12th St., Waco, Tex. 76701.	Ms. Cathy Terrell, (817) 756–6631.
12	Capital Area Agency on Aging, 611 South Congress, Suite 400, Austin, Tex. 78704.	Mr. Conley Kemper, (512) 443–7653.
13	Brazos Valley Area Agency on Aging, P.O. Drawer 4128, 3006 East 29th St., Bryan, Tex. 77801.	Ms. Roberta Lindquist, (713) 822–7421.
14	Deep East Texas Area Agency on Aging, 272 East Lamar St., Jasper, Tex. 75951.	Ms. Martha Jones, (713) 384–5704.
15	South East Texas Area Agency on Aging, P.O. Drawer 1387, Nederland, Tex. 77627.	Mr. James H. Robb, (713) 727–2384.
16A	Houston-Galveston Area Agency on Aging, P.O. Box 22777, Houston, Tex. 77027.	Mr. Paul Ulrich, (713) 627–3200
16B	Harris County Area Agency on Aging, 1010 Louisiana, Suite 910, Houston, Tex. 77002.	Mr. Raul De Los Santos, (713) 222–4445.
17	Golden Crescent Area Agency on Aging, P.O. Box 2028, Victoria, Tex. 77901.	Ms. Betty Beck, (512) 578–1587
18A	Alamo Area Council of Governments, Three Americas Bldg., Suite 400, San Antonio, Tex. 78205.	Mr. Frank Adamo, (512) 225–5201.
18B	Bexar County Area Agency on Aging, Three Americas Bldg., Suite 400, San Antonio, Tex. 78205.	Ms. Minnie Williams, (512) 225–5201.
19	South Texas Area Agency on Aging, P.O. Box 2187, 600 South Sandman, Laredo International Airport, Laredo, Tex. 78041.	Ms. Lupita Rubio, (512) 722–3995.
20	Coastal Bend Area Agency on Aging, P.O. Box 9909, Corpus Christi, Tex. 78408.	Mr. Bill Moore, (512) 883–5743
21	Lower Rio Grande Valley Area Agency on Aging, First National Bank Bldg., Suite 301/303, McAllen, Tex. 78501.	Ms. Gloria Saca, (512) 682–3481
22	Texoma Area Agency on Aging, 10000 Grayson Drive, Denison, Tex. 75020.	Ms. Janis Gray, (214) 786–2955
23	Central Texas Area Agency on Aging, P.O. Box 729, Belton, Tex. 76513.	Mr. Dan Mizell, (817) 939–1801
24	Middle Rio Grande Area Agency on Aging, P.O. Box 1461, Del Rio, Tex. 78840.	Ms. Josefina Rowe, (512) 775–1581.

UTAH

(Federal Regional VIII)

STATE AGENCY ON AGING

Mr. Leon Povey, Director,
Division on Aging,
Department of Social Services,
150 West North Temple, Room 315,
Box 2500,
Salt Lake City, Utah 84102
(801) 533–6422

AREA AGENCIES

PSA	Area agency address	Director and telephone number
1	Bear River Area Agency on Aging, Cache County Aging Program, 236 North 100 E., Logan, Utah 84321.	Mr. Robert Green, (801) 752–9456.
2A	Weber County Department on Aging, Human Service Bldg., 350 Healy, Ogden, Utah. 84401.	Mr. Ken Bradshaw, (801) 399–8318.
2B	Davis County Area Agency on Aging, Davis County Courthouse, Farmington, Utah 84025.	Ms. Alice Johnson, (801) 295–2394.
2E	Salt Lake-Tooele Area Agency on Aging, Bldg. No. 1 Basement, 2033 South State, Salt Lake City, Utah 84115.	Ms. Shauna O'Neill, (801) 487–1344.
3	Mountainland Area Agency on Aging, 160 East Center St., Provo, Utah 84601.	Pat Bersie, (801) 377–2262
4	Center Utah Aging Programs, Courthouse, Junction, Utah 84740.	Dr. Robert Teichart, (801) 577–2834.
5	District V Area Agency on Aging, P.O. Box O, St. George, Utah 84770.	Ms. Gayla Foster, (801) 673–3548.
6A	Uintah Basin Area Agency on Aging, P.O. Box 1449, Roosevelt, Utah 84066.	Vacant, (801) 722–4518
6B	Ute-Ouray Area Agency on Aging, P.O. Box 67, Fort Duchesne, Utah 84026.	Mr. Robert Holmes, (801) 772–5141.
7A	Southeastern Utah Area Agency on Aging, P.O. Drawer A–1, Price, Utah 84501.	Mr. William Howell, (801) 637–4268.

VERMONT

(Federal Region I)

STATE AGENCY ON AGING

Mrs. Pearl Somaini-Dayer, Director,
Office on Aging,
Agency of Human Services
Waterbury Office Complex
State Office Bldg.
Montpelier, Vt. 05602
(802) 241–2400

AREA AGENCIES

PSA	Area agency address	Director and telephone number
1	Southeastern Vermont Area Agency on Aging, 139 Main St., Brattleboro, Vt. 05301.	Mr. Geoffrey Gaddis, (802) 257–0569.
2	Area Agency on Aging for Northeastern Vermont, 44 Main St., Box 640, St. Johnsbury, Vt. 05819.	Ms. Merry Brewer, (802) 748–5182.

3 Champlain Valley Area Agency on Aging, 179 South Winooski Ave., Burlington, Vt. 05401.
Ms. Mary Ellen Spencer, (802) 862–3734.

4 Bennington-Rutland Area Agency on Aging, 135 North Main St., Rutland, Vt. 05701.
Mr. Charles Sherman, (802) 775–0486.

5 Central Vermont Area Agency on Aging, 295 North Main St., Barre, Vt. 05641.
Mr. Craig Hammond, (802) 479–0531.

VIRGINIA

(Federal Region III)

STATE AGENCY ON AGING

Mr. Edwin L. Wood, Director,
Office on Aging,
830 East Main St., Suite 950,
Richmond, Va. 23219
(804) 786–7894

AREA AGENCIES

PSA	Area agency address	Director and telephone number
1	Mountain Empire Older Citizens, 330 Norton, P.O. Box 1097, Wise, Va. 24293.	Ms. Marilyn Pace, (703) 328–2302.
2	Appalachian Agency for Senior Citizens, Box S.V.C.C., Richlands, Va. 24641.	Roger Sword, (703) 964–4915
3	District 3 Governmental Cooperative, Senior Citizens Services Division, 110 Strother St., Marion, Va. 24354.	Mr. George Tulli, Jr., (703) 783–8158.
4	New River Valley Agency on Aging, 143 3d St. N.W., Pulaski, Va. 24301.	Mrs. Mary Elyn Lauth, (703) 980–8888.
5	League of Older Americans, 401 West Campbell Ave., Roanoke, Va. 24016.	Mr. Richard Young, (703) 345–0451.
6	Valley Program for Aging Services, Inc., P.O. Box 817, Waynesboro, Va. 22980.	Mrs. Ruth Perry, (703) 942–7141.
7	Shenandoah Area Agency on Aging, Inc., Route 1, Box 329 A, Winchester, Va. 22601.	Mr. Michael Toht, (703) 869–4100.
8a	Alexandria Area Agency on Aging, 115 North Patrick St., Alexandria, Va. 22314.	Ms. Susan Parry, (703) 750–6609.
8b	Arlington Area Agency on Aging, Arlington Court House, Room 204, Arlington, Va. 22201.	Ms. Karen Evans, (703) 338–2401.
8c	Fairfax County Area Agency on Aging, 4100 Chain Bridge Rd., Fairfax, Va. 22030.	Ms. Donna Foster, (703) 691–3384.
8d	Coordinator of Senior Services, 18 North King St., Leesburg, Va. 22075.	Kathleen Bocek, (703) 777–0257
8e	Coordinator of Senior Citizen Services, Office of Personnel, Prince William County, 9300 Peabody St., Manassas, Va. 22110.	Ms. Stephanie R. Egly, (703) 368–9171.
8f	City Hall, 300 Park Ave., Falls Church, Va. 22046__	Ms. Charlene Costello, (703) 241–5100.
9	Rappahannock-Rapidan Area Agency on Aging, 401 South Main St., Culpeper, Va. 22701.	Ms. Sallie Stemple, (703) 825–6494.
10	Jefferson Area Board for Aging, 415 8th St., N.E., Charlottesville, Va. 22901.	Mr. Jim Elmore, (804) 977–3444
11	Central Virginia Commission on Aging, Forest Hill Center, Linkhorne Dr., Lynchburg, Va. 24503.	Mr. Wallace Clair, (804) 384–0372.
12	Piedmont Seniors of Virginia, Inc., 29 Broad St., Martinsville, Va. 24112.	Mrs. June Gay, (703) 632–6442
13	Southside Office on Aging, Inc., Brunswick County Courthouse Bldg., P.O. Box 726, Lawrenceville, Va. 23868.	Mr. T. H. E. Jones, (804) 848–4433.

PSA	Area agency address	Director and telephone number
14	Piedmont Senior Resources, Inc., P.O. Box 398, Burkeville, Va. 23922.	Mr. Ronald Dunn, (804) 767–5588.
15	Capital Area Agency on Aging, 6 North 6th St., Richmond, Va. 23219.	Mr. Louis Barretta, (804) 648–8381.
16	Rappahannock Area Agency on Aging, Inc., 601 Caroline St., 3d Floor, Fredericksburg, Va. 22401.	Mr. Frank Beddow, (703) 371–3375.
17 18	Northern Neck-Middle Peninsula Area Agency on Aging, Inc., P.O. Box 387, Saluda, Va. 23149.	Mr. Allyn Gemerek, (804) 758–2386.
19	Crater District Area Agency on Aging, P.O. Box 1808, Petersburg, Va. 23803.	Mr. Richard Bull, (804) 732–7020.
20	SEVAMP, 16 Koger Executive Center, Suite 145, Norfolk, Va. 23502.	Ms. Kathleen Donoghue, (804) 461–9481.
21	Peninsula Agency on Aging, Inc., 944 Denbigh Blvd., Newport News, Va. 23602.	Mrs. Betty Reams, (804) 874–2495.
22	Eastern Shore Community Development Group, Inc., P.O. Box 316, Accomac, Va. 23301.	Mr. William Davies, (804) 787–3532.

WASHINGTON

(Federal Region X)

STATE AGENCY ON AGING

Mr. Charles Reed, Director,
Bureau of Aging,
Department of Social and Health Services,
OB–43G,
Olympia, Wash. 98504
(206) 753–2502

AREA AGENCIES

PSA	Area agency address	Director and telephone number
1	Olympic Area Agency on Aging, P.O. Box 31, Montesano, Wash. 98563.	Mr. Terry Loughran, (206) 249–5736, SCAN 234–2632.
2	Northwest Washington Area Agency on Aging, Northwest Regional Council Forest Street, Annex of the Whatcom County Courthouse, 1000 Forest St., Bellingham, Wash. 98225.	Mr. Dewey Desler, (206) 676–6749, SCAN 644–6749.
3	Snohomish County Area Agency on Aging, Grants Administration Office, 4th floor, County Administration Bldg., Everett, Wash. 98201.	Ms. Liz Roberts, (206) 259–9521, SCAN 649–9521.
4	King County Area Agency on Aging, 400 Yesler Bldg., Seattle, Wash. 98104.	Mr. Mark Stensager, (206) 625–4711, SCAN 861–4711.
5	Area Agency on Aging No. 5, 2401 South 35th St., Pierce County Annex No. 15, Tacoma, Wash. 98409	Ms. Bonnie McMahon, (206) 593–4828, SCAN 462–2494.
6	Lewis/Mason/Thurston Area Agency on Aging, P.O. Box 1304, Chehelis, Wash. 98532.	Ms. Christine Spaulding, (206) 748–9121 extension 250, toll-free 1–800–562–6130.
7	Southwest Washington Area Agency on Aging, P.O. Box 425, Vancouver, Wash. 98666.	Dr. Patricia Anderson, (206) 694–6577.
8	North Central Washington Area Agency on Aging, 1300 5th St., Wenatchee, Wash. 98801.	Mr. Jack Charlton, (509) 662–1651 extension 276, SCAN 241–2640.
9	Yakima-Southeast Washington Area Agency on Aging, 708 N. 16th Ave., Yakima, Wash. 98901.	Ms. Becky Martelli, (509) 575–4226/4331, SCAN 665–4226.

10	Yakima Indian Nation Area Agency on Aging, P.O. Box 311, Toppenish, Wash. 98948.	Ms. Arlene Olney, (509) 865–4443.
11	Spokane Co. Area Agency on Aging, West 1101 College Ave., suite 160, Public Health Bldg., Spokane, Wash. 99201.	Mr. Ted Stevens, (509) 327–3341.
12	Colville Indian Area Agency on Aging, P.O. Box 150, Nespelem, Wash. 99155.	Ms. Margaret Rochelle, (509) 634–4203.

WEST VIRGINIA

(Federal Region III)

STATE AGENCY ON AGING

Louise B. Gerrard, Ph. D., Director,
West Virginia Commission on Aging,
State Capitol,
Charleston, W. Va. 25305
(304) 348–3317

AREA AGENCIES

PSA	Area agency address	Director and telephone number
1	Region 1 Area Agency on Aging, Region 1 Planning and Development Council, P.O. Box 1442, Princeton, W. Va. 24740.	Mrs. Sharon Hondos, (304) 425–9508.
2	Southwestern Area Agency on Aging, Southwestern Community Action Council, Inc., 540 5th Ave., Huntington, W. Va. 25701.	Mr. Charles Karschnik, (304) 525–5151.
3	Region 3 Area Agency on Aging, Community Council of Kanawha Valley, Inc., 702½ Lee St., Charleston, W. Va. 25301.	Ms. Gail Dreyer, (304) 342–5107
4	Eastern Highlands Area Agency on Aging, Nicholas County Community Action Association, 909 Broad St., Summerville, W. Va. 26651.	Mr. Tim Bailes, (304) 872–1162
5	Region 5 Area Agency on Aging, Mid-Ohio Valley Regional Council, 217 4th St., Parkersburg, W. Va. 26101.	Ms. Peggy Rash, acting, (304) 422–0522, 485–3801.
6	Region 6 Area Agency on Aging, Region 6 Planning and Development Council, 201 Deveny Bldg., Fairmont, W. Va. 26554.	Mr. Donald Spencer, (304) 366–5693.
7	Region 7 Area Agency on Aging, Region 7 Planning and Development Council, 64 West Main St., Buckhannon, W. Va. 26201.	Ms. Betty Burgess Betler, (304) 472–0395.
8/9	Regions 8/9 Area Agency on Aging, Region 8 Planning and Development Council, P.O. Box 305, Petersburg, W. Va. 26847.	Mr. Chris Franklin, (304) 257–4166.
10/11	Northern Panhandle Area Agency on Aging, Bel-O-Mar Regional Council, 2177 National Rd., Wheeling, W. Va. 26003.	Mr. A. Paul Holdren, (304) 242–1800.

WISCONSIN

(Federal Region V)

STATE AGENCY ON AGING

Mr. Douglas W. Nelson, Director,
Bureau of Aging,
Department of Health and Social Services,
One West Wilson Street, Room 700,
Madison, Wis. 53702
(608) 266–2536

AREA AGENCIES

PSA	Area agency address	Director and telephone number
1	Area Agency on Aging, District 1, 1245 East Washington Ave., Madison, Wis. 53703.	Mr. Arthur Hendrick, (608) 256–4460.
2A	Area Agency on Aging, District 2A, 1442 North Farwell Ave., Milwaukee, Wis. 53202.	Mr. Fred Lindner, (414) 278–4283.
2B	Area Agency on Aging, District 2B, 500 Riverview Ave., Room 204, Waukesha, Wis. 53186.	Mr. Charles F. Parthum, Jr., (414) 547–1573.
3	Area Agency on Aging, District 3, 314 West Wisconsin Ave., Suite 8–9, Appleton, Wis. 54911.	Mr. Harry Collins, (414) 739–9531.
4	Area Agency on Aging, District 4, 1221 Bellevue Ave., Green Bay, Wis. 54302.	James Kellerman, (414) 465–1662.
5	Area Agency on Aging, District 5, Grandview Bldg., 1707 Main, La Crosse, Wis. 54601.	Mr. Larry White, (608) 784–4360.
6	Area Agency on Aging, District 6, 318 Eau Claire St., Eau Claire, Wis. 54701.	Ms. Rosemary Howard, (715) 836–4105.
7	North Central Area Agency on Aging, City Hall, 1004 East 1st St., Merrill, Wis. 54452.	Ms. Barbara White, (715) 536–8323.
8	Area Agency on Aging, District 8, Hayward Lakes Realty Bldg., 301 West 1st St., P.O. Box 526, Hayward, Wis. 54843.	Mr. James Gratehouse, (715) 634–2464.

WYOMING

(Federal Region VIII)

STATE AGENCY ON AGING

Mr. Stan Torvik, Director,
Aging Services,
Department of Health and Social Services,
Division of Public Assistance and Social Services,
Hathaway Bldg., Room 372,
Cheyenne, Wyo. 82002
(307) 777–7561

AREA AGENCIES

PSA	Area agency address	Director and telephone number
1	Eastern Wyoming Area Agency on Aging, 2125 Cy Ave., Casper, Wyo. 82601.	Mrs. Carol Smith, (307) 265–1365.
2	Western Wyoming Area Agency on Aging, 205 Masonic Temple Bldg., Riverton, Wyo. 82501.	Mrs. Marjorie Woods, (307) 856–6378.

AMERICAN SAMOA*

(Federal Region IX)

STATE AGENCY ON AGING

Mr. Tali Maae, Director,
Territorial Aging Program,
Government of American Samoa,
Office of the Governor,
Pago Pago, American Samoa   96920
(Oakland overseas operator—Samoa 3–1254 or 3–4116)

*Serves as a single planning and service area.

DISTRICT OF COLUMBIA*

(Federal Region III)

STATE AGENCY ON AGING

Mr. D. Richard Artis, Director,
District of Columbia Office on Aging,
1012 14th St. N.W., Suite 1106,
Washington, D.C.   20005
(202) 724–5622

* The District of Columbia serves as a single planning and service area.

GUAM*

(Federal Region IX)

STATE AGENCY ON AGING

Mr. Joaquin Camucho, Director,
Office of Aging,
Department of Public Health
and Social Service,
P.O. Box 2816,
Agana, Guam   96910
749–9901, ext. 324

*Guam serves as a single planning and service area.

PUERTO RICO

(Federal Region II)

STATE AGENCY ON AGING

Miss Alicia Ramirez Suarez, Director,
Gericulture Commission,
Department of Social Services,
Box 11398,
Santurce, P.R. 00910
(809) 722–2429, or 724–7400 ext. 2213

AREA AGENCIES

PSA	Area agency address	Director and telephone number
1	Area Agency on Aging, Box 3997, Aguadilla, P.R. 00603.	Mr. Edgardo J. Rosa, (809) 891–1095.
2	Area Agency on Aging, 67 Cristobal Colon, Arecibo, P.R. 00612.	Miss Olga Rodriguez, (809) 878–4095.

3	Area Agency on Aging, Building C, Ruiz Soler Hospital, Road No. 2, Km. 8.6, Bayamon 00619.	Mr. Gilbert Broco, Jr., (809) 781–5861—4200.
4	Area Agency on Aging, Box 6351, Caguas, P.R. 00625.	Mrs. Fe Sotomayor, (809) 743–6867.
5	Area Agency on Aging, 100 East, Ignacio Arzuago St., Carolina, P.R. 00630.	Miss Maria D. Carrasquillo, (809) 752–4275 (veterans).
6	Area Agency on Aging, Box 585, Arroyo, P.R. 00615	Mrs. Edna Rodriguez, (809) 839–3010.
7	Area Agency on Aging, Box 178, Humacao, P.R. 00661.	Vacant
8	Area Agency on Aging, Box 447, Mayaguez, P.R. 00708.	Mr. Rogelio Casasus, (809) 833–4536.
9	Area Agency on Aging, Box 5173, Ponce, P.R. 00731__	Mr. Luis A. Rolon, (809) 844–3195.
10	Human Resources Department, Box 3632, Old San Juan Station, San Juan, P.R. 00904.	Mrs. Eva Freyre, (809) 723–0077, 723–1129

TRUST TERRITORY OF THE PACIFIC*

(Federal Region IX)

STATE AGENCY ON AGING

Ms. Leona Peterson, Director,
Office of Aging,
Community Development Division,
Government of the Trust Territory of the Pacific Islands,
Saipan, Mariana Islands, 96950
(overseas operator–2134)

* The Trust Territory of the Pacific Islands serves as a single planning and service area.

VIRGIN ISLANDS*

(Federal Region II)

STATE AGENCY ON AGING

Mrs. Gloria M. King, Director,
Commission on Aging,
P.O. Box 539,
Charlotte Amalie,
St. Thomas, V.I. 00801
(809) 774–5884

*The Virgin Islands serves as single planning and service area.

Organizations

ACADEMY FOR EDUCATIONAL
DEVELOPMENT
680 Fifth Avenue
New York, NY 10019

ACTION FOR INDEPENDENT MATURITY
1909 K Street, NW
Washington, D.C. 20049

ADMINISTRATION ON AGING
Office of Human Development
330 Independence Avenue, SW
Washington, D.C. 20201

ADULT EDUCATION ASSOCIATION OF THE
UNITED STATES OF AMERICA
810 18th Street, NW
Washington, D.C. 20006

ADVISORY COUNCIL ON PENSION AND
WELFARE BENEFIT PROGRAMS
3rd St. and Constitution Avenue, NW
Washington, D.C. 20210
(202) 523-8753

AGING RESEARCH INSTITUTE
342 Madison Ave.
New York, NY 10017

AMERICAN AGING ASSOCIATION
c/o Denham Harman, M.D., Executive Director
University of Nebraska College of Medicine
Omaha, NE 68105

AMERICAN ASSOCIATION OF COMMUNITY &
JUNIOR COLLEGES
Older Americans Programs
One Dupont Circle, NW
Washington, D.C. 20036

AMERICAN ASSOCIATION OF EMERITI
P.O. Box 24451
Los Angeles, CA 90024

AMERICAN ASSOCIATION OF HOMES FOR
THE AGING
1050 17th St., NW
Washington, D.C. 20036

AMERICAN ASSOCIATION OF RETIRED
PERSONS
1909 K Street, NW
Washington, D.C. 20049

AMERICAN ASSOCIATION OF RETIRED
PERSONS (LONG BEACH)
215 Long Beach Blvd.
Long Beach, CA 90802

AMERICAN GERIATRICS SOCIETY, INC.
10 Columbus Circle
New York, NY 10019

AMERICAN SOCIETY FOR GERIATRIC
DENTISTRY
Two North Riverside Plaza, Suite 1741
Chicago, IL 60606

AMERICAN SOCIETY OF MATURE CATHOLICS
110 W. Wells St.
Milwaukee, WI 53233

AMERICAN SOCIETY OF PENSION ACTUARIES
1028 Connecticut Avenue, NW
Washington, D.C. 20006

ASSOCIACION NACIONAL PRO PERSONAS
MAYORES
3875 Wilshire Blvd. Suite 401
Los Angeles, CA 90005

ASSOCIATION FOR GERONTOLOGY IN
  HIGHER EDUCATION
1835 K Street, NW, Suite 305
Washington, D.C. 20006

ASSOCIATION FOR THE ADVANCEMENT OF
  AGING RESEARCH
c/o Dr. Bernard Strehler, Executive Chairman
Molecular Biology Department
ACBR, Room 126
Los Angeles, CA 90007

ASSOCIATION OF PRIVATE PENSION AND
  WELFARE PLANS
1028 Connecticut Avenue, NW
Washington, D.C. 20036

BOSTON SOCIETY OF GERONTOLOGICAL
  PSYCHIATRY, INC.
International Universities Press, Inc.
315 Fifth Ave.
New York, NY 10003

BROOKDALE CENTER ON AGING
Hunter College
129 East 79th Street
New York, NY 10021

CENTER ON ARTS AND THE AGING
National Council on the Aging
1828 L Street, NW
Washington, D.C. 20036

CENTRAL BUREAU FOR THE JEWISH AGED
225 Park Ave. South
New York, NY 10009

CHURCH OF THE BRETHREN HOMES AND
  HOSPITALS ASSOCIATION
The Cedars
1111 E. Kansas St.
McPherson, KS 67460

CITIZENS FOR BETTER CARE IN NURSING
  HOMES, HOMES FOR THE AGED AND
  OTHER AFTER-CARE FACILITIES
960 E. Jefferson Avenue
Detroit, MI 48207

CLEARINGHOUSE ON EMPLOYMENT FOR THE
  AGING
80 Reid Avenue
Port Washington, NY 11050

CLUB FOR PHILATELY IN GERONTOLOGY
2525 Centerville Road
Dallas, TX 75228

COALITION FOR TERMINAL CARE
1101 University Avenue, SE
Minneapolis, MN 55414

COLLEGE RETIREMENT EQUITIES FUND
730 Third Avenue
New York, NY 10017

COLORADO GERONTOLOGICAL CONSORTIUM
1020 15th Street, Room 25-M
Denver, CO 80202

COMMISSION OF PROFESSORS OF ADULT
  EDUCATION
Ritter Addition 217
College of Education
Temple University
Philadelphia, PA 19122

COMMUNITY SERVICES ADMINISTRATION
Office of Program Development
1200 19th Street, NW
Washington, D.C. 20506
(202) 632-6694

CONCERNED SENIORS FOR BETTER
  GOVERNMENT
1346 Connecticut Avenue, NW, Room 1213
Washington, D.C. 20036

CONTINUING EDUCATION COUNCIL
Six North Sixth Street
Richmond, VA 23219

COORDINATION COUNCIL FOR SENIOR
  CITIZENS
c/o Senior Citizen's Memorial Center
519 E. Main St.
Durham, NC 27701

DIPLOMATIC AND CONSULAR OFFICERS,
  RETIRED
1718 H Street, NW
Washington, D.C. 20006

EDUCATION NETWORK FOR OLDER ADULTS
36 South Wabash, Suite 714
Chicago, IL 60603

ELDER CRAFTSMEN, INC.
850 Lexington Ave.
New York, NY 10021

FLYING SENIOR CITIZENS OF U.S.A.
96 Tamarack Street
Buffalo, NY 14220

GERONTOLOGICAL SOCIETY
One DuPont Circle
Washington, D.C. 20036

GOLDEN RING COUNCIL OF SENIOR CITIZENS
   CLUBS
22 W. 38th St.
New York, NY 10018

INSTITUTE FOR RETIRED PROFESSIONALS
New School for Social Research
66 W. 12th Street
New York, NY 10011

INSTITUTE FOR RETIREMENT STUDIES
7040 Crawford Hall
Case Western Reserve University
Cleveland, OH 44106

INSTITUTE FOR THE ENRICHMENT OF LATER
   LIFE
1600 South Minnesota Avenue
Sioux Falls, SD 57105

INSTITUTE OF INDUSTRIAL GERONTOLOGY
c/o National Council on Aging
1828 L St., NW
Washington, D.C. 20036

INSTITUTE OF LIFETIME LEARNING
1909 K Street, NW
Washington, D.C. 20049

INTERNATIONAL FEDERATION ON AGEING
1909 K Street, NW
Washington, D.C. 20049

INTERNATIONAL SENIOR CITIZENS
   ASSOCIATION, INC.
11753 Wilshire Blvd.
Los Angeles, CA 90025

INTERNATIONAL SOCIAL SECURITY
   ASSOCIATION
Case Postale No. 1
CH–1211 Geneva 22
Switzerland

JEWISH ASSOCIATION FOR SERVICES FOR
   THE AGED
222 Park Avenue South
New York, NY 10003

JOBS FOR OLDER WOMEN ACTION PROJECT
3102 Telegraph Avenue
Berkeley, CA 94705

LABOR DEPARTMENT
Office of Pension Welfare Benefit Programs
3rd St. and Constitution Avenue, NW
Washington, D.C. 20210

LEGAL SERVICES FOR THE ELDERLY
2095 Broadway
New York, NY 10023

LEGISLATIVE COUNCIL FOR OLDER
   AMERICANS, INC.
110 Arlington St.
Boston, MA 02116

NATIONAL ALLIANCE OF SENIOR CITIZENS
Box 40031
Washington, D.C. 20016

NATIONAL ASSOCIATION FOR HUMAN
   DEVELOPMENT
1750 Pennsylvania, NW
Washington, D.C. 20006

NATIONAL ASSOCIATION FOR PUBLIC
   CONTINUING AND ADULT EDUCATION
1201 16th Street, NW
Washington, D.C. 20036

NATIONAL ASSOCIATION OF AREA AGENCIES
   ON AGING, INC.
1828 L Street, NW
Washington, D.C. 20036

NATIONAL ASSOCIATION OF COUNTIES
   RESEARCH FOUNDATION AGING PROGRAM
1735 New York Avenue, NW
Washington, D.C. 20006

NATIONAL ASSOCIATION OF HUMANISTIC
   GERONTOLOGY
41 Tunnel Road
Berkeley, CA 94705

NATIONAL ASSOCIATION OF JEWISH HOMES
FOR THE AGED
2525 Centerville Road
Dallas, TX 75228

NATIONAL ASSOCIATION OF MATURE
PEOPLE
Box 26792
Oklahoma City, OK 73118

NATIONAL ASSOCIATION OF OLDER
AMERICANS
12 Electric Street
West Alexandria, OH 45381

NATIONAL ASSOCIATION OF RETIRED AND
VETERAN RAILROAD EMPLOYEES
c/o Joseph J. Bredestage
1007 Regina
Cincinnati, OH 45205

NATIONAL ASSOCIATION OF RETIRED
FEDERAL EMPLOYEES
1533 New Hampshire Avenue, NW
Washington, D.C. 20036

NATIONAL ASSOCIATION OF STATE
RETIREMENT ADMINISTRATORS
302 Public Safety Building
Montgomery, AL 36130

NATIONAL ASSOCIATION OF STATE UNITS ON
AGING
West Virginia Commission on Aging
State Capitol
Charleston, W VA 25305

NATIONAL CAUCUS ON THE BLACK AGED
1424 K Street, NW
Washington, D.C. 20005

NATIONAL CENTER FOR VOLUNTARY ACTION
National Information Center on Volunteerism
P.O. Box 1807
Boulder, CO 80306

NATIONAL CENTER ON THE BLACK AGED
1424 K Street, NW
Washington, D.C. 20005

NATIONAL CLEARINGHOUSE ON AGING
Administration on Aging
DHEW Building, Room 4146
330 Independence Avenue, SW
Washington, D.C. 20201

NATIONAL COMMITTEE ON ART EDUCATION
FOR THE ELDERLY
Culver Stockton College
Canton, MO 63435

NATIONAL CONFERENCE OF STATE SOCIAL
SECURITY ADMINISTRATORS
Public Employees Social Security Bureau
Department of Employee Trust Funds
P.O. Box 7931
Madison, WI 53707

NATIONAL CONFERENCE ON PUBLIC
EMPLOYEE RETIREMENT SYSTEMS
275 E. Broad
Columbus, OH 43215

NATIONAL COUNCIL OF SENIOR CITIZENS
1511 K Street, NW
Washington, D.C. 20005

NATIONAL COUNCIL ON BLACK AGING
Box 8522
Durham, NC 27707

NATIONAL COUNCIL ON TEACHER
RETIREMENT
275 E. Broad Street
Columbus, OH 43215

NATIONAL COUNCIL ON THE AGING
1828 L Street, NW
Washington, D.C. 20036

NATIONAL FORUM FOR OLDER WOMEN
Center on Aging
University of Maryland
College Park, MD 20742

NATIONAL GERIATRICS SOCIETY
212 W. Wisconsin Avenue, Third Floor
Milwaukee, WI 53203

NATIONAL HEALTH AND WELFARE
RETIREMENT ASSOCIATION
666 Fifth Avenue
New York, NY 10019

NATIONAL INSTITUTE OF SENIOR CENTERS
c/o National Council on Aging
1828 L Street, NW
Washington, D.C. 20036

NATIONAL INSTITUTE ON AGING
National Institute of Health
Bethesda, MD 20014

NATIONAL RETIRED TEACHERS ASSOCIATION
1909 K Street, NW
Washington, D.C. 20049

NATIONAL RETIREMENT COUNCIL
527 Madison Ave.
New York, NY 10022

NATIONAL VOLUNTARY ORGANIZATION FOR
INDEPENDENT LIVING OF THE AGED
c/o National Council on Aging
1828 L Street, NW
Washington, D.C. 20036

NOW TASK FORCE ON OLDER WOMEN
6412 Telegraph Avenue
Oakland, CA 94609

PENSION BENEFIT GUARANTY CORPORATION
2020 K Street, NW
Washington, D.C. 20006

PENSION RIGHTS CENTER
1346 Connecticut Avenue, NW
Washington, D.C. 20036

PRESIDENT'S COMMISSION ON PENSION
POLICY
736 Jackson Place, NW
Washington, D.C. 20006

RESOURCE CENTER FOR PLANNED CHANGE
One Dupont Circle
Washington, D.C. 20036

RETIRED AND PIONEER RURAL CARRIERS OF
U.S.
c/o George Rosebrooks
Gore Road
Webster, MA 01570

RETIRED BANKERS ASSOCIATION
c/o Lucy Easterwood
6303 Prospect B
Dallas, Texas 75214

THE RETIRED OFFICERS ASSOCIATION
201 N. Washington Street
Alexandria, VA 22314

THE RETIRED PROFESSIONALS
1025 15th Street, NW
Washington, D.C. 20005

RETIREMENT HOUSING FOUNDATION
555 E. Ocean Blvd.
Long Beach, CA 90802

SALVATION ARMY
503 E Street, NW
Washington, D.C. 20001

SENIOR EMPLOYMENT OPPORTUNITIES
c/o National Council of Jewish Women
15 E. 26th St.
New York, NY 10010

SENIORS FOR ADEQUATE SOCIAL SECURITY
136 W. 91st Street
New York, NY 11024

SERVICE CORPS OF RETIRED EXECUTIVES
1441 L Street, NW, Room 100
Washington, D.C. 20416

URBAN ELDERLY COALITION
1828 L Street, NW, Suite 505
Washington, D.C. 20036

VACATIONS FOR THE AGING AND SENIOR
CENTERS ASSOCIATION
225 Park Avenue, South
New York, NY 10003
(212) 777-5000

VIRGINIA CENTER ON AGING
1617 Monument Avenue
Richmond, VA 23220

WESTERN GERONTOLOGICAL SOCIETY
785 Market Street
San Francisco, CA 94103

Periodicals

AAHA Washington Report, bi-m.
American Association of Homes for
   the Aging
1050 17th Street, NW
Washington, D.C. 20036

AARP News Bulletin, bi-m.
American Association of Retired Persons
215 Long Beach Blvd.
Long Beach, CA 90820

Added Years Newsletter, m.
New Jersey Division on Aging
Department of Community Affairs
P.O. Box 2768
Trenton, NJ 08625

Adult Education, q.
Adult Education Association
810 18th Street, NW
Washington, D.C. 20006

AFICS Bulletin, m.
Association of Former International Civil Servants
Palais des Nations
Geneva, Switzerland

Age, q.
The American Aging Association
42nd and Dewey Avenue
Omaha, NE 68105

Age and Ageing, q.
British Geriatric Society and the
   British Society for Research in Ageing
Bailliere, Tindall and Cassell Ltd.
7 & 8 Henrietta Street
London WC2,
England

Age Concern Information Circular, m.
Age Concern England
Bernard Sunley House
60 Pitcairn Road
Mitcham, Surrey CR4 3LL,
England

Age in Action, bi-m.
West Virginia Commission on Aging
State Capitol
Charleston, WV 25305

Age of Achievement, m.
Age of Achievement
337 Securities Building
Seattle, WA 98101

Aged Care and Services Review, bi-m.
The Haworth Press
149 5th Avenue
New York, NY 10010

Ageing International, q.
International Federation on Ageing
1909 K Street, NW
Washington, D.C. 20049

Ageing Times, 3-yr.
British Society of Social & Behavioral
   Gerontology
c/o London Hospital Medical College
57, Turner Street
London, E1 2AD,
England

AGHE Newsletter, q.
Association for Gerontology in Higher Education
One Dupont Circle, NW
Washington, D.C. 20036

Aging, bi-m.
Administration on Aging
U.S. Department of Health,
    Education and Welfare
Superintendent of Documents
Washington, D.C. 20402

Aging and Leisure Living, m.
Medical Life Systems
212 West Wisconsin Avenue
Milwaukee, WI 53203

Aging Education News, m.
Center for Aging Education
Lansing Community College
419 N. Capitol
P.O. Box 40010
Lansing, MI 48901

Aging in the News, q.
Division on Aging
Department of Health and Social Services
1 West Wilson Street
Room 686
Madison, WI 53702

Aging News/Research and Training, m.
Care Reports, Inc.
1230 National Press Building
Washington, D.C. 20045

Aging in Pennsylvania, bi-m.
Office for the Aging
Department of Public Welfare
P.O. Box 2675
Harrisburg, PA 17120

Aging Research and Training News, m.
Care Reports, Inc.
6529 Elgin Lane
Washington, D.C. 20034

Aging Services News
Care Reports, Inc.
1230 National Press Building
Washington, D.C. 20045

Aging Update, m.
Institute for the Study of Aging
University of Miami
P.O. Box 24816
Coral Gables, FL 33124

Aging and Work, q.
National Council on the Aging

1828 L Street, NW
Washington, D.C. 20036

AHCA Journal, bi-m.
American Health Care Association
1200 15th Street, NW
Washington, D.C. 20005

AHCA Weekly Notes, 41-y.
American Health Care Association
1200 15th Street, NW
Washington, D.C. 20005

AIM (Aging in Michigan), bi-m.
Office of Services to the Aging
300 E. Michigan Avenue
P.O. Box 30026
Lansing, MI 48909

American Geriatrics Society Newsletter, m.
American Geriatrics Society, Inc.
10 Columbus Circle
New York, NY 10019

American Health Care Association Journal, m.
Modern Healthcare
P.O. Box 665
Hightstown, NJ 08520

AOA Fact Sheet, m.
U.S. Administration on Aging
Superintendent of Documents
Government Printing Office
Washington, D.C. 20204

Aspects of Aging, bi-m.
Central Bureau for the Jewish Aging
225 Park Avenue South
New York, NY 10003

BARP Newsletter, q.
British Association of Retired Persons
14 Frederick Street
Edinburgh, EH2 2HB,
Scotland

Best Years, q.
National Association of Mature People
Box 26792
Oklahoma City, OK 73125

Black Aging, q.
Post Office Box 8522
Durham, NC 27707

British Journal of Geriatrics and Psychogeriatrics, q.
Stuart Phillips Publications
30 Ringstead Rd.
Sutton, Surrey
England

Bulletin On Aging, bi-ann.
Social Development Branch
Dept. of Economic and Social Affair
United Nations
New York, NY 10017

The California Senior Citizen News, m.
McAnally and Associates
P.O. Box 765
La Canada, CA 92101

Canadian Association on Gerontology Newsletter, q.
Minister of Community and Social Services
801 Bay Street
Toronto, Ontario
Canada

CARCH News, m.
California Association of Residential
 Care Homes
2530 J Street
Suite 302
Sacramento, CA 95816

Catching Up On Aging, bi-m.
CASE Center for Gerontological Studies
The Graduate School and University Center
The City University of New York
33 West 42nd Street
New York, NY 10036

Center News, m.
Center for Studies in Aging
P.O. Box 13438
North Texas State University
Denton, TX 76203

The Center Report, q.
The Center for the Study of Aging
 and Human Development
Box 3003
Duke University Medical Center
Durham, NC 27710

Challenger, q.
Virginia Office on Aging
Suite 95
830 E. Main Street
Richmond, VA 23219

Chapter News, bi-m.
American Association of Retired Persons
215 Long Beach Blvd.
Long Beach, CA 90820

Choice, m.
Retirement Choice Magazine Company
100 Riverview Center
Middletown, CT 06457

Concern for Dying, q.
Concern for Dying
250 West 57th Street
New York, NY 10019

Concord, bi-m.
British Association for Service to
 the Elderly (BASE)
Bernard Sunley House
60 Pitcairn Road
Mitcham, Surrey CR4 3LL
England

Contact for Aging, bi-m.
Office on Aging
State of South Dakota
Department of Social Services
Illinois Street
Pierre, SD 57501

Current Literature on Aging, q.
National Council on the Aging
1828 L Street, NW
Washington, D.C. 20036

Dialogue, m.
AARP-NRTA
1909 K Street, NW
Washington, D.C. 20049

Dynamic Maturity, bi-m.
Action for Independent Maturity
American Association of Retired Persons
1909 K Street, NW
Washington, D.C. 20049

Dynamic Years, bi-m.
AIM (Action for Independent Maturity)
American Association of Retired Persons
Washington, D.C. 20006

Ebenezer, q.
Ebenezer Society
2523 Portland Avenue South
Minneapolis, MN 55404

Education for Aging News, bi-m.
Brookdale Center on Aging
Hunter College
129 E. 79th Street
New York, NY 10021

Educational Gerontology, q.
Hemisphere Publishing Corporation
1025 Vermont Avenue, NW
Washington, D.C. 20005

The Elder, m.
The Elder
P.O. Box 984
New Haven, CT 06504

The Elder Statesman, m.
Federated Legislative Council of
  Elderly Citizens Associations of
  British Columbia
946 West 7th Avenue
Vancouver 9, British Columbia
Canada

Emeritus College Newsletter, m.
Emeritus College of Marin
Kentfield CA 94904

Employment Fellowship Review, q.
Employment Fellowship
Allens Green
Sawbridgeworth, Herts.
England

ERA, m.
California Office on Aging
455 Capitol Mall
Sacramento, CA 95814

Especially for Seniors, q.
Ontario Advisory Council on Senior
  Citizens
3rd Floor, 901 Bay Street
Toronto M5S 1Z1
Canada

Essence: Issues in the Study of Aging,
  Dying and Death
Department of Psychology
Atkinson College
York University
4700 Keele Street
Downsview, Ontario M3J 2R7
Canada

Experimental Aging Research, bi-m.
EAR Inc.
P.O. Box 29
Mt. Desert, ME 04609

Experimental Gerontology, q.
Pergamon House, Inc.
Maxwell House
Fairview Park,
Elmsford, NY 10523

Family Therapy, 3/yr.
Family Therapy Institute of Marin
1353 Lincoln Avenue
San Rafael, CA 94901

50 Plus
150 East 58th Street
New York, NY 10022

Generations, q.
The Western Gerontological Society
785 Market Street
Suite 1114
San Francisco, CA 94103

Geriascope, q.
Canadian Geriatrics Research Society
c/o Geriatric Study Center
350 Christie Street
Toronto, Ontario M6G 3CE
Canada

Geriatopics, q.
Canadian Geriatrics Research Society
c/o Geriatric Study Center
350 Christie Street
Toronto, Ontario M6G 3CE
Canada

Geriatric and Residential Care, m.
HRS Geriatric Publishing Corp.
342 Pipe Stave Hollow Road
Mount Sinai, NY 11766

Geriatrics, m.
Lancet Publications
4015 W. 65th Street
Minneapolis, MN 55435

Gerontologia, bi-m.
S. Karger AG
Arnold Bocklin Strasse 25
4011 Basel
Switzerland

Gerontologia Clinica, bi-m.
S. Karger AG
Arnold Bocklin Strasse 25
4011 Basel
Switzerland

Gerontological Abstracts, 11-y.
University Information Services
P.O. Box 1048
Ann Arbor, MI 48103

The Gerontologist, bi-m.
Gerontological Society
One Dupont Circle, Suite 520
Washington, D.C. 20036

Gerontophiles, bi-m.
Center for Gerontological Studies and Programs
221 Motherly Hall
University of Florida
Gainesville, FL 32611

GeronTopics
A Forum for the Aging Network
15 Garrison Avenue
Durham, NH 03824

The Golden Page, bi-m.
The National Center on the Black Aged,
  Inc.
1424 K Street, NW, Suite 500
Washington, D.C. 20005

Gray Panther Network, irr.
Gray Panthers
3700 Chestnut Street
Philadelphia, PA 19104

The Heartline/NAOA Newsletter, m.
National Association of Older Americans
12 Electric Street
West Alexandria, OH 45381

Higher Education in Retirement, bi-m.
Institute for Retired Professionals
The New School for Social Research
66 W. 12th Street
New York, NY 10011

Home Health Care Services Quarterly, q.
The Haworth Press
149 5th Avenue
New York, NY 10010

Horizon, q.
United Methodist Homes of New Jersey
71 Clark Avenue
Ocean Grove, NJ 07756

Human Values and Aging, bi-ann.
Newsletter
David A. Van Tassel
History Department
Case Western Reserve University
Cleveland, OH 44106

Humanities Exchange, irr.
National Council on Aging
1821 L Street, NW
Washington, D.C. 20036

Industrial Gerontology, q.
National Council on the Aging
1828 L Street, NW, Room 504
Washington, D.C. 20036

*International Journal of Aging and Human
  Development,* q.
National Council on the Aging
1828 L Street, NW
Washington, D.C. 20036

International Senior Citizens News, q.
International Senior Citizens Assoc., Inc.,
11753 Wilshire Boulevard
Los Angeles, CA 90024

International Social Security Review, q.
International Social Security Association
Case Postale 1
CH-1211 Geneva 22,
Switzerland

IRP Review, ann.
Institute for Retired Professionals
New School for Social Research
66 West 12th Street
New York, NY 10021

Items, m.
Social Science Research Council
605 Third Avenue
New York, NY 10009

Journal of Geriatric Psychiatry, s-a.
Boston Society of Gerontological Psychiatry
90 Forest Avenue, NW
Boston, MA 01021

Journal of Gerontological Nursing, bi.m.
C.B. Slack, Inc.
6900 Grove Road
Thorofare, NJ 08086

Journal of Gerontology, bi-m.
Gerontological Society
One Dupont Circle, NW
Washington, D.C. 20036

Journal of Housing, 11/yr.
National Association of Housing and Redevelopment
  Officials
Watergate Building, Suite 404
2600 Virginia Avenue, NW
Washington, D.C. 20037

Journal of Long-Term Care Administration, q.
American College of Nursing Home Administrators
4650 East-West Highway
Washington, D.C. 20014

Journal of the American Geriatrics Society, m.
American Geriatrics Society, Inc.
10 Columbus Circle
New York, NY 10019

Keeping Informed About Senior Services, m.
Louisiana Health & Social & Rehabilitation
  Services Dept.
Suite 402, State Office Building
150 Riverside Mall
Baton Rouge, LA 70801

Legislative Update, q.
Urban Elderly Coalition
1828 L Street, NW, Suite 505
Washington, D.C. 20036

Lifelong Learning: The Adult Years, m.
Adult Education Association
810 18th Street, NW
Washington, D.C. 20006

Life With Dignity, bi-m.
Florida Division of Aging
1317 Winewood Blvd.
Tallahassee, FL 32301

Locke Report, bi-m.
Edward M. Cooney
67 Pleasant Street
Marion, MA 02738

Long-Term Care Administrator, s-m.
American College of Nursing Home Administrators
4650 East-West Highway
Washington, D.C. 20014

Management Assistance Newsletter
Service Corps of Retired Executives
1441 L Street, NW, Room 100
Washington, D.C. 20416

Mature Catholic, bi-m.
American Society of Mature Catholics
1100 W. Wells Street
Milwaukee, WI 53233

Mature Living, bi-m.
Indiana State Commission on the Aging and the Aged
215 North Senate Avenue
Indianapolis, IN 46202

Mature Years, q.
United Methodist Church
201 8th Avenue, South
Nashville, TN 37202

Maturitas, q.
Elsevier/North-Holland
52 Vanderbilt Avenue
New York, NY 10017

Mechanisms of Ageing and Development, bi.m.
Elsevier Sequoia S.A.
Box 851
1001 Lausanne
Switzerland

Medicare Report, s-m.
National Feature Syndicate, Inc.
1066 National Press Building
Washington, D.C. 20045

Metropolitan Pensioner, m.
Metropolitan Pensioners' Welfare Assoc.
Box 2929
Vancouver 3, British Columbia
Canada

Minnesota Senior Spotlight, bi-m.
Governor's Citizens Council on Aging
204 Metro Square
7th and Robert
St. Paul, MN 55101

Modern Geriatrics, bi-m.
Empire House

414 High Road
Chiswick, London W4,
England

Modern Maturity, bi-m.
American Association of Retired Persons
215 Long Beach Blvd.
Long Beach, CA 90820

NARFE Newsletter, irr.
National Association of Retired Federal Employees
1533 New Hampshire Avenue, NW
Washington, D.C. 20036

National News, q.
National Pensioners and Senior Citizens
  Federation
105 - 4th Street, 2nd Floor
Toronto, Ontario MBV 2Y4
Canada

New Age, q.
Age Concern England
Bernard Sunley House
60 Pitcairn Road
Mitcham Surrey
England

News, irr.
Alabama Commission on Aging
740 Madison Avenue
Montgomery, AL 36104

News, m.
Alberta Council on Ageing
8923 - 117th Street
Edmonton, Alberta,
Canada

News, irr.
Illinois Department on Aging
2401 West Jefferson
Springfield, IL 62706

News, bi-m.
New York State Office for the Aging
855 Central Avenue
Albany, NY 12206

Newsletter, m.
American College of Nursing Home Administrators
8641 Colesville Road, Suite 409
Silver Springs, MD 20910

Newsletter
American Council on Consumer Interests
162 Stanley Hall
University of Missouri
Columbia, MO 65201

Newsletter, 9/yr.
American Geriatrics Society
American Council on Consumer Interests
162 Stanley Hall
University of Missouri
Columbia, MO 65201

Newsletter, m.
Canadian Institute of Religion and
  Gerontology
296 Lawrence Ave., East
Toronto, Ontario M4N 1T7
Canada

Newsletter, m.
Department of Elder Affairs
Office of the Secretary
120 Boylston Street
Boston, MA 02116

Newsletter, s-m.
Flying Senior Citizens of U.S.A.
96 Tamarack Street
Buffalo, NY 14220

Newsletter, irr.
Institute of Law and Aging
National Law Center
2000 H Street NW
The George Washington University
Washington, D.C. 20052

Newsletter, q.
International Senior Citizens Association
11753 Wilshire Boulevard
Los Angeles, CA 90025

Newsletter, q.
National Association of Humanistic Gerontology
41 Tunnel Road
Berkeley, CA 94705

Newsletter, q.
Ontario Psychogeriatric Association
114 Starwood Road
Ottawa, Ontario K2G 3N5
Canada

Newsletter, m.
Senior Citizens of Canada
17 Ross Avenue
Agincourt, Ontario
Canada

News 'n' Views, m.
Center for Senior Citizens
National Council of Jewish Women
One W. 47th Street
New York, NY 10036

NHWRA Report, m.
National Health and Welfare Retirement Association
666 Fifth Avenue
New York, NY 10019

Nodak New Day, bi-m.
Social Service Board of North Dakota
Aging Service
State Capitol Building
Bismarck, ND 58505

Normative Aging Study Newsletter
Boston Vertans Administration Outpatient Clinic
John F. Kennedy Federal Building
Boston, MA 02203

NRTA-AARP Legislative Report, bi-m.
NRTA-AARP
1909 K Street, NW
Washington, D.C. 20049

NRTA Journal, bi-m.
National Retired Teachers Association
701 N Montgomery Street
Ojai, CA 93123

NRTA News Bulletin, bi-m.
National Retired Teachers Association
701 N. Montgomery Street
Ojai, CA 93123

Nursing Homes, bi-m.
Nursing Homes
4000 Albermarle Street, NW
Washington, D.C. 20016

Nursing Research, bi-m.
American Nurses Association
National League for Nursing
10 Columbus Circle
New York, NY 10019

Ohio's Heritage, bi-m.
Ohio Commission on Aging
50 W. Broad Street 9th S.E.
Columbus, OH 43215

The Older Nebraskan's Voice, bi-m.
State of Nebraska Commission on Aging
Box 94784 - State Capitol
Lincoln, NE 68509

The Older Rhode Islander, q.
Rhode Island Department of Community
   Affairs, Division on Aging
150 Washington Street
Providence, RI 02903

The Older Texan, bi-m.
Governor's Committee on Aging
Box 12786
Capitol Station
Austin, TX 78711

Omega, q.
Journal of Death and Dying
Baywood Publishing Company, Inc.
43 Central Drive
Farmindale, NY 11735

Options, m.
New York Office for the Aging
250 Broadway, 30th Floor
New York, NY 10007

Oregon Pioneer, q.
Oregon State Program on Aging
722 Commercial Street, SE
Salem, OR 97310

The Outlook, m.
Maryland Office on Aging
1004 State Office Building
301 West Preston Street
Baltimore, MD 21201

Pension & Financial Planning News, q.
Institute of Life Insurance
277 Park Avenue
New York, NY 10017

Pension and Welfare News, m.
Communication Channels, Inc.
461 8th Avenue
New York, NY 10001

Pension World, m.
Pension World
461 Eighth Avenue
New York, NY 10001

Pensioners' Voice, bi-m.
The National Federation of Old Age
   Pensions Associations
91 Preston New Road
Blackburn
England

Perspective on Aging, bi-m.
National Council on the Aging
1828 L Street, NW
Washington, D.C. 20036

Perspectives, q.
Nursing Association
Taylor Place
Senior Adult Centre
1 Overland Drive
Don Mills, Ontario
Canada

Prime Time, m.
Prime Time
420 West 46th Street
New York, NY 10036

Progress Report, q.
National Association of Jewish Homes for the Aged
2525 Centerville Road
Dallas, TX 75228

Public Welfare, q.
American Public Welfare Association
1155 16th Street, NW
Washington, D.C. 20036

Report, bi.m.
Mayor's Office For Senior Citizens
   and Handicapped
180 North LaSalle Street
Chicago, IL 60601

Research on Aging, q.
Quarterly on Social Gerontology
Sage Publications
Beverly Hills, CA 90212

The Retired Officer, m.
The Retired Officers Association
201 N. Washington Street
Alexandria, VA 22314

Retirement Letter, m.
Phillips Publishing, Inc.
8401 Connecticut Avenue, NW
Washington, D.C. 20015

Retirement Life, m.
National Association of Retired Federal Employees
1533 New Hampshire Avenue, NW
Washington, D.C. 20036

Retirement Living, m.
Harvest Years Publishing Co., Inc.
99 Garden Street
Marion, OH 43302

Second Spring, bi-m.
Second Spring Magazine
121 Golden Gate Avenue
San Francisco, CA 94102

Senior Bulletin, q.
Senior Services Inc. Foundation
Box 189
Toms River, NJ 08753

Senior Center Report, m.
National Institute of Senior Centers
c/o National Council on Aging
1828 L Street, NW
Washington, D.C. 20036

Senior Citizens, m.
Andrus Gerontology Center
University of Southern California
Los Angeles, CA 90007

Senior Citizens News, m.
Senior Citizens News
10175 S.W. Barbur Blvd.
Room 109B
Portland, OR 97219

Senior Citizens News, m.
National Council of Senior Citizens
1511 K Street, NW
Washington, D.C. 20005

Senior Citizens' Post, m.
The Senior Citizen's Post
807 S. Duke Street
Durham, NC 27707

Senior Citizens Today, m.
California Assoc. of Residential Care
   Homes

2530 J Street
Suite 302
Sacramento, CA 95816

Senior Focus, irr.
Arkansas Office on Aging Newsletter
Dept. of Human Services
1200 Westpark Bldg.
Little Rock, AR 72204

Senior Guardian, m.
National Alliance of Senior Citizens
777 14th Street, NW
Washington, D.C. 20005

Senior Newsletter, m.
Department of Social and Health Services
MS 433
Olympia, WA 98504

Senior Oklahomans, bi-m.
Department of Institutions
Social & Rehabilitative Services
Oklahoma City, OK 73125

Senior Power, bi-m.
Senior Power Publishing Co.
P.O. Box 62
500 N. Murray Road
Lee's Summit, MO 64063

Senior World, m.
Senior World
4640 Jewell Street
San Diego, CA 92109

Seniority, m.
Social Devices Department
Amalgamated Clothing & Textile
  Workers Union, AFL-CIO
15 Union Square
New York, NY 10003

Social Security Bulletin, m.
Social Security Administration
U.S. Department of Health, Education
  and Welfare
U.S. Government Printing Office
Washington, D.C. 20402

State Council of Older People SCOOP, m.
State Council of Older People
P.O. Box 2507
Augusta, ME 04330

Statistical Notes, irr.
Administration on Aging
U.S. Department of Health, Education and Welfare
Superintendent of Documents
Washington, D.C. 20402

Supportive Services, bi-w.
Care Reports, Inc.
1230 National Press Building
Washington, D.C. 20045

Switchboard, irr.
National Committee on Art Education for the Elderly
Culver Stockton College
Canton, MO 63435

Synagogue Aging, irr.
Synagogue Council of America
432 Park Avenue South
New York, NY 10016

Technical Information Exchange, bi-m.
Urban Elderly Coalition
1828 L Street, NW, Suite 505
Washington, D.C. 20036

The Tennessenior, m.
Tennessee Commission on Aging
306 Gay Street
Nashville, TN 37201

Update, m.
Center for Aging
University of Alabama
Birmingham, AL 35294

Vintage, bi-m.
South Carolina Commission on Aging
915 Main Street
Columbia, SC 29201

Voice of United Senior Citizens of Ontario, m.
United Senior Citizens of Ontario
105 4th Street
Toronto, Ontario M8V 2Y4,
Canada

Volunteer News, m.
Andrus Gerontology Center
University of Southern California
Los Angeles, CA 90007

Washington Report, bi-w.
American Association of Homes for the Aging
1050 17th Street, NW
Washington, D.C. 20036

Washington Report on Long-Term Care, w.
Washington Report on Long-Term Care
475 National Press Building
Washington, D.C. 20045

Weekly Review, bi-w.
Weekly Review
721 N. LaSalle Street
Chicago, IL 60610

Word From Washington, irr.
National Conference on Public Employees Retirement
  System
1390 Logan
Denver, CO 80203

Zantia, q.
Zantia
P.O. Box 149
Annapolis, MD 21404

Part five:
Indexes

Subject index

Organization index

Geographic index